WITHDRAWN FROM STOCK

THE LIBRARY

University of Ulster at Magee

Due Back (subject to recall)

23 MAY 2007		
25 MAY 2007		
10 JAN 2014		
9 - JAN 2015		

Fines will apply to items returned after due date

1323U0009/2270/2/2007

D1437176

EC LAW IN JUDICIAL REVIEW

EC LAW IN JUDICIAL REVIEW

Richard Gordon QC

Visiting Professor in the Faculty of Laws, University College London

OXFORD

UNIVERSITY PRESS

100510979
KM
36.
G67

OXFORD

UNIVERSITY PRESS

Great Clarendon Street, Oxford OX2 6DP

Oxford University Press is a department of the University of Oxford.
It furthers the University's objective of excellence in research, scholarship,
and education by publishing worldwide in

Oxford New York

Auckland Cape Town Dar es Salaam Hong Kong Karachi
Kuala Lumpur Madrid Melbourne Mexico City Nairobi
New Delhi Shanghai Taipei Toronto

With offices in

Argentina Austria Brazil Chile Czech Republic France Greece
Guatemala Hungary Italy Japan Poland Portugal Singapore
South Korea Switzerland Thailand Turkey Ukraine Vietnam

Oxford is a registered trade mark of Oxford University Press
in the UK and in certain other countries

Published in the United States
by Oxford University Press Inc., New York

© Richard Gordon 2007

The moral rights of the author have been asserted
Database right Oxford University Press (maker)

Crown copyright material is reproduced under Class Licence
Number C01P0000148 with the permission of OPSI
and the Queen's Printer for Scotland

First published 2007

All rights reserved. No part of this publication may be reproduced,
stored in a retrieval system, or transmitted, in any form or by any means,
without the prior permission in writing of Oxford University Press,
or as expressly permitted by law, or under terms agreed with the appropriate
reprographics rights organization. Enquiries concerning reproduction
outside the scope of the above should be sent to the Rights Department,
Oxford University Press, at the address above

You must not circulate this book in any other binding or cover
and you must impose the same condition on any acquirer

British Library Cataloguing in Publication Data

Data available

Library of Congress Cataloging in Publication Data

Data available

Typeset by Cepha Imaging Private Ltd, Bangalore, India
Printed in Great Britain
on acid-free paper by
Biddles Ltd, King's Lynn

ISBN 978-0-19-926663-0

1 3 5 7 9 10 8 6 4 2

For Jane and Oonagh

FOREWORD

By Sir Konrad Schiemann
Judge of the Court of Justice of the European Communities

This is an outstanding book unlike any other that I have read. I would have welcomed it in earlier incarnations as a practitioner and as a judge in the Administrative Court and the Court of Appeal. I shall certainly have use for it at the ECJ.

The light in which a lawyer views a set of facts and the way he formulates the legal problem is very much conditioned by the legal system which he is applying. In this country the courts are now often in a position where they can apply one or more of four legal systems which are interacting—public international law, the law of the European Union, the law of the European Convention on Human Rights and the common law as modified by Equity and statute.

Problems can appear in different contexts and can often be seen through the spectacles of more than one of those systems. The analytical tools which have been developed by the courts as an aid to their solution have not always been the same. Even when the same word is used in more than one system to describe an analytical tool the meaning of that word can vary depending on context.

A great virtue of this book is that problems confronting society in general and lawyers in particular are analysed from the different perspectives of more than one of these legal systems. This stimulates thought and should in due course result in more principled and more elegant expositions by practitioners and the courts. Since the English rules on standing are so much more generous than those prevailing in the ECJ and in many European countries we are already seeing preliminary references from England in proceedings which might more naturally have been commenced elsewhere. All this and the generally first-class quality of British advocacy provides great opportunities for the legal profession here to suggest elegant structures which the ECJ and indeed our national courts may adopt for their future judgments. This book should be of use to them.

The analysis is detailed and careful. The footnotes and further references show breadth of reading but the author refrains from gratuitous exhibitionism and tendentious didacticism. The intellectual enthusiasm of the academic has been disciplined by the needs of the practitioner.

This is a book having a clear intellectual framework, a book which one can either read with profit from cover to cover or used as a treasure trove in which quickly to access new lines of thought when confronted by seemingly insoluble conundrums. It is to be welcomed.

Konrad Schiemann
Luxembourg
June 2006

PREFACE

There are many works on EC law. My reason for adding to the pile is that EC law is rarely seen for what it is—an increasingly necessary and hugely important part of a public lawyer's armoury.

Those practising in the area of judicial review have had to become aware of the growing deluge of human rights law as a result of the fanfare that accompanied the passing of the Human Rights Act 1998 on 2 October 2000. The Act was delayed because judges and practitioners had to be trained, and the anticipated resource implications of a new system of law had to be carefully thought through.

EC law has had no such sound effects (or training). It came in with barely a whisper more than 30 years ago. But at that stage there was no developed system of public law in this country. It is the growth of judicial review in the mid-1980s, augmented by its junior human rights partner, which should give EC law a new and distinctive voice in the administrative law arena.

Much has been made, for example, of the subtle and nuanced differences between traditional public doctrines ('good old *Wednesbury*') and the more sophisticated notion of proportionality relevant to the infringement of Convention rights. Little, however, has been made of the differences between proportionality under the European Convention on Human Rights and EC proportionality. An EC law-based judicial review challenge may sound similar to other grounds of review but there are significant differences both in terms of the grounds but also in terms of the available remedy. For EC law judicial review cases, at least, we have a truly Constitutional Court in the Administrative Court because, like the US Supreme Court, judges have the power to disapply Acts of Parliament. That is true of no other domestic public law jurisdiction.

The aim, especially in Parts I and II of the book, has been to focus on EC law in judicial review but also to attempt some integration and comparison between our three public law jurisdictions. The relationship between the Luxembourg and Strasbourg Courts and between those courts and the Administrative Court is of fundamental importance to English public law and is stressed in these pages. Of equal significance is the rapid expansion of EC general principles of law. It is through such principles that EC law now recognizes fundamental rights that go beyond those in the European Convention on Human Rights.

But, although the 'big picture' is critical, it is in the practice areas that public lawyers—not versed in EC law—can come unstuck. Part III of this book focuses on key areas that play a large part in judicial review. This has not been an easy task because the law changes at a frantic pace and there have been very recent developments in the EC procurement regime (a raft of new implementing regulations effective in 2006) as well as (see the Citizens' Directive) in the law on free movement. My objective here has been to make those areas comprehensible in terms of relevant principle and to illustrate the EC principles, where possible, with domestic case analyses. There are practical and important lessons to be learned from the way in which our courts interpret and apply EC law in different contexts and I have tried to draw attention to these where appropriate.

In preparing the manuscript I have a number of debts. I thank Roxanne Selby and Sarah McGrath at OUP who have had the patience of saints and given deferred gratification a new name. A number of fellow members of Brick Court Chambers have assisted with practical answers to queries that have saved me much time. I thank, in particular, Jemima Stratford and Martin Chamberlain who read some of the chapters in transition. Thanks are also due to James Flynn QC and Kelyn Bacon. Colleagues at UCL have also helped and, of those, specific thanks are due to Professor Richard Macrory who alerted me to some important features of EC Environmental Law. Last but not least, I thank my wife Jane and children Edmund and Adam who have given invaluable support.

Needless to say any errors in law or exposition are entirely mine. I have endeavoured to state the law as at 23 June 2006.

Richard Gordon QC
Brick Court Chambers
London
June 2006

CONTENTS—SUMMARY

CONTENTS

I EC LAW IN JUDICIAL REVIEW: PROCEDURE, GROUNDS, AND REMEDIES

II UNDERLYING GENERAL PRINCIPLES IN EC LAW JUDICIAL REVIEW CHALLENGES

III EC LAW AND JUDICIAL REVIEW IN PRACTICE

13. State Aid and Competition

14. Environmental Challenges

TABLE OF CASES

EUROPEAN COURT OF JUSTICE

UNITED KINGDOM

1

TABLE OF LEGISLATION

EUROPEAN LEGISLATION

TREATIES AND CONVENTIONS

LIST OF ABBREVIATIONS

CA	Competition Act 1998
CAT	Competition Appeal Tribunal
CC	Competition Commission
CCA	Consumer Credit Act 1984
CFI	Court of First Instance
CPR	Civil Procedure Rules
DGFT	Director General of Fair Trading
EA	Enterprise Act 2002
ECB	European Central Bank
ECHR	European Convention on Human Rights
ECJ	European Court of Justice
ECSC	European Steel and Coal Community
EC Treaty	Treaty establishing the European Community
EDT	Equal Treatment Directive
EEL	European Environmental Law
EIA	Environmental Impact Assessment
EOC	Equal Opportunities Commission
GATT	General Agreement on Tariffs and Trade
HRA	Human Rights Act 1998
ICCPR	International Covenant on Civil and Political Rights
IPPC	Integrated Pollution Prevention and Control
Ofcom	Office of Communications
OFT	Office of Fair Trading
PCT	Primary Care Trust
SCA	Supreme Court Act 1981
SEA	Single European Act 1986
TEU	Treaty on European Union
WTO	World Trade Organization

PART I

EC LAW IN JUDICIAL REVIEW: PROCEDURE, GROUNDS, AND REMEDIES

1

EC LAW IN JUDICIAL REVIEW— AN OVERVIEW

A. Scheme of Book

The subject of this book is EC law as applied in the national courts by way of judicial **1.01** review. It is not a work concerned with the overall substantive content of EC law[1] or, indeed, with the working of the EC institutions.[2] Nor is it directed to the enforcement of

---

[1] Save and insofar as substantive EC law has, in particular areas, a relationship with national public law. Part III addresses particular areas of EC law which have given rise to domestic public law issues.

[2] That is, the European Parliament, the European Council, and the European Commission. It is though concerned with the case law of the ECJ.

EC law in English courts generally. Its focus is EC law in the context of domestic public law and, in particular, in the context of judicial review proceedings in the Administrative Court and appellate courts. It focuses on the ways in which EC and domestic public law principles overlap but are also to be distinguished from each other.

1.02 This chapter provides a short introduction to the development of EC law in that context. It outlines how and why EC law fits into domestic public law and now plays such an important role. It also explains the basis for using EC law in domestic public law cases.

1.03 The remainder of Part I is concerned with introducing a number of EC law doctrines and showing the relationship between those concepts and domestic public law. Part II is devoted entirely to the general principles of EC law which are now of crucial importance both to interpreting domestic (as well as EC) legislation and in determining the legality of administrative decision-making in public law cases. Part III picks up a number of domestic public law practice areas where EC law is of great significance. Those areas, important in themselves, also illustrate how the national courts increasingly use EC law concepts, often alongside traditional administrative law or human rights grounds to resolve issues in judicial review and other proceedings where public law challenges are raised.

B. Why EC Law Is an Important Part of Domestic Public Law

1.04 In general terms, domestic public law (especially judicial review) is concerned with reviewing the decisions and other public functions of public bodies. It is not, at least for most purposes, directed to substantive factual merit but, rather, to legality of process. In the context of EC law the legality of domestic acts and measures (including, uniquely, primary legislation) will fall to be tested in judicial review by reference to whether the act or measure in question is itself compliant with EC law. A breach of EC law is, therefore, an additional—and potentially very powerful—basis in an increasing number of cases for seeking relief in domestic judicial review proceedings. Where available, it affords a particular basis of challenge. It may arise as a discrete ground of challenge on its own or (more usually) it may arise as a head of complaint in tandem with other grounds based on purely domestic public law principles and/or the newly emerging case law under the Human Rights Act 1998 (HRA). However, the specific principles pertaining to EC law themselves fashion the way in which an EC public law case may be argued or relief obtained in (especially) the Administrative Court.

1.05 It is a central theme of this work that domestic public law cannot, properly, be understood without a knowledge of EC public law principles developed by the European Court of Justice (ECJ) in Luxembourg and of principles developed in relation to fundamental rights under the European Convention on Human Rights (ECHR) developed by the European Court of Human Rights in Strasbourg.[3]

---

[3] Since the late 1980s there has been 'explosive growth' in the practice of, first, EC law and later HRA law in the United Kingdom. See, generally, D Anderson QC, 'The Law Lords and the European Courts' in *Building the UK's New Supreme Court* A le Sueur (ed) (2004).

This is because both systems of law have been incorporated into UK national law and have **1.06** in their turn, inevitably, greatly affected domestic public law.

There are at least two reasons for the considerable impact that EC law has had on domestic **1.07** public law. First, the constitutional impact of incorporation itself has been profound. For the first time the national courts have been required to apply EC and ECHR jurisprudence in cases with an EC/ECHR element and in respect of those elements.[4] In EC, and to a lesser extent ECHR, law the rulings of the ECJ and Strasbourg courts have a binding (or in the case of ECHR jurisprudence quasi-binding)[5] effect mandated by statute.

The unique constitutional nature of particular statutes such as those incorporating EC and **1.08** ECHR rights has only recently been expressly endorsed in domestic law. In his landmark ruling in the *Metric Martyrs* case, Laws LJ put it thus:

> We should recognise a hierarchy of Acts of Parliament: as it were 'ordinary' statutes and 'constitutional' statutes. The two categories must be distinguished on a principled basis. In my opinion a constitutional statute is one which (a) conditions the relationship between the citizen and state in some general, over-arching manner, or (b) enlarges or diminishes the scope of what we would now regard as fundamental constitutional rights—(a) and (b) are of necessity closely related ... The special status of constitutional statutes follows the special status of constitutional rights. Examples are ... the Human Rights Act 1998 ... The [European Communities Act 1972] clearly belongs in this family. It incorporated the whole corpus of substantive Community rights and obligations, and gave overriding domestic effect to the judicial and administrative machinery of Community law. It may be there has never been a statute having such profound effects on so many dimensions of our daily lives. The [1972 Act] is, by the force of the common law, a constitutional statute.[6]

Secondly, and unsurprisingly, there has been an enrichment and expansion of traditional **1.09** administrative law principles to encompass many of the principles contained in these relatively new and sometimes divergent systems of law *even where EC law (or ECHR law) is not engaged.*[7] As Lord Woolf said in *M v Home Office*:[8]

> It would be most regrettable if an approach which is inconsistent with that which exists in Community law should be allowed to persist if this is not strictly necessary.

The enrichment and expansion of domestic public law from incorporation of EC law is **1.10** also exemplified by the wide range of sources taken into account by the ECJ when interpreting and clarifying EC law.[9] These sources include international treaties that have not

---

⁴ Further, to the extent that application of separate domestic public law principles would adversely affect the enforcement of EC rights, EC law would prevail (see paras 1.37–1.46).
⁵ See the Human Rights Act 1998 (HRA), s 2.
⁶ *Thoburn v Sunderland City Council* [2002] EWHC 195, [2003] QB 151, para 62.
⁷ See, eg *R v Goldstein* [1983] 1 WLR 151, 155B, per Lord Diplock (referring to the EC concept of proportionality).
⁸ [1994] 1 AC 377, 422.
⁹ The same point may be made as to the wide range of sources deployed by the European Court of Human Rights in Strasbourg which include international treaties which have not been incorporated into domestic law but which become part of the corpus of domestic public law indirectly through the court having to take Strasbourg Court judgments into account under HRA, s 2. Further, important questions may arise as to the extent to which Community secondary legislation must comply with the requirements of public international law. See the recent reference by the Administrative Court in *R (International Association of Independent Tanker Owners) v Secretary of State for Transport* [2006] EWHC 1577.

been incorporated into national law but which the national courts must take account of and follow if and to the extent that they are encompassed as part of the ECJ ruling because of the binding nature of ECJ judgments on the national courts (see below).

1.11   As Lord Hoffmann put it in *R v Hertfordshire County Council, ex p Green Environmental Industries Ltd*:[10]

> [S]ince the [Environmental Protection Act 1990] gives effect to a Directive it must be interpreted according to principles of Community law, including its doctrines of fundamental rights. For this purpose Community law looks to analogous principles in national laws of member states and the international conventions and covenants to which they are parties . . .

C. The Development of Public Law in London, Luxembourg, and Strasbourg

1.12   Despite this increasing convergence between the relevant public law principles in the respective European legal regimes as between each other and as between those regimes and traditional domestic public law, there remain significant differences. This is explained, to some extent, by the fact that the rationale for each of these regimes was different at least in origin.

1.13   At bottom, EC public law rests on a series of economic imperatives. The underlying purpose of the EC Treaties was one of economic integration. That integration was to be established by a common market free of internal restrictions on trade. Central tenets of the Treaties as, for example, the four freedoms (freedom of movement of workers, the right to establish a trade or profession and to provide services, freedom of movement of goods and capital) progressive approximation of economic policies and creation of a common customs tariff reflect this fundamental economic purpose.

1.14   There is, though, a tension between economics as a regulating principle of law and the wider constitutional concerns that underpin the protection of fundamental rights. In the words of one commentator:

> The language of economics and the utilitarian philosophy which underpins it have displaced an older political language in which questions about controlling public power, ensuring accountability and political participation were central.[11]

1.15   The rationale for the European Convention on Human Rights is, as might therefore be expected, very different from that in EC law. As is well known, the Convention was negotiated in order to guarantee rights of a type that were jeopardized in the holocaust. It was intended to cement the moral foundations of any new European order that might emerge after the Second World War. It is a moral as opposed to an economic foundation that is required to provide continuing and effective protection for fundamental rights.

---

[10]   [2000] 2 AC 412, 422.
[11]   L Siedentop, *Democracy in Europe* (2000) 33.

However, both the EC and ECHR regimes share one characteristic which is that they are **1.16** largely indifferent to the tradition of parliamentary sovereignty which underpins domestic public law. In order to guarantee effective protection of EC rights and ECHR rights, parliamentary sovereignty cannot be allowed to operate as a barrier to enforcement of those rights. In that sense, EC and ECHR laws have always been, essentially, supra-national in character.

The justification for domestic administrative law is rather different and acknowledges **1.17** parliamentary sovereignty. As Wade and Forsyth observe:

> A first approximation to a definition of administrative law is to say that it is the law relating to the control of governmental power. This, at any rate, is the heart of the subject, as viewed by most lawyers. The governmental power in question is not that of Parliament: Parliament as the legislature is sovereign and, subject to one exception, is beyond legal control.[12]

Tellingly, the exception noted by Wade and Forsyth is EC law.[13] In an important sense, par- **1.18** liamentary sovereignty is the bedrock of English domestic administrative law because it is the touchstone for the ultra vires principle. In traditional domestic judicial review the presumed intention of Parliament is what circumscribes the limits of governmental power.

If public law principles under the three legal regimes had remained rooted to the respective **1.19** justifications for their existence it is unlikely that EC and ECHR law would have been incorporated (certainly successfully incorporated) into national law so as to become part of domestic public law. In the event, however, each of the regimes has had to recognize the existence of the other.

As will be seen in this work, so far as domestic public law is concerned, it is managing with **1.20** relative success to accommodate both of the European public law traditions as well as many of its own doctrines that pre-dated incorporation. But the process is a continuing one and is, at least in part, dependent on EC and ECHR law being able to live together in harmony since, with the passing of the HRA into national law on 2 October 2000, it is necessary to reconcile two potentially opposing systems of law as part of UK public law. In reality what has happened over the years is that EC, ECHR and domestic administrative law have moved closer together.

Historically, the ECJ was resistant to the idea that fundamental rights were either intrinsic **1.21** to the Treaty or part of the general principles of EC law.[14] This position reflected the tension, as between domestic law and EC law, inherent in the then developing concept of EC

---

[12] W Wade and C Forsyth, *Administrative Law* (9th edn, 2004) 4.

[13] Although, ECHR law under the HRA may, perhaps, be regarded as a quasi-exception since under HRA, s 4 the court has power to make a declaration of incompatibility in respect of domestic statutes where the statute in question is, in the view of the court, incompatible with the ECHR. The difference is, however, that even if a declaration of incompatibility is made the offending statutory provision continues to have full force and legal effect unless and until repealed (see HRA, s 4(6)).

[14] See, eg, Case 1/58 *Stork v High Authority* [1959] ECR 17; Joined Cases 36–38 and 40/59 *Geitling v High Authority* [1960] ECR 423.

law supremacy. If a Member State were free to depart from uniform provisions of EC law then, axiomatically, EC law could not be supreme. As the ECJ held in *Costa v ENEL*:[15]

> The transfer by the States from their domestic legal system to the Community legal system of the rights and obligations arising under the Treaty carries with it a permanent limitation on their sovereign rights, against which a subsequent unilateral act incompatible with the concept of Community law cannot prevail.

1.22 But such an extreme assertion of *Community* sovereignty may ignore the true content of what was actually transferred by the Member States when acceding to the Treaty.[16] There are two relevant points. First, it is hardly conceivable that 'the national parliaments would have ratified a Treaty which was capable of violating the fundamental tenets of their own constitutions'.[17] Secondly, applying the standards of public international law, it is at least arguable that peremptory norms consented to by the United Kingdom include the protection of fundamental human rights so that no international obligations could be separately incurred which were capable of violating those rights.[18]

1.23 Thus, if a direct conflict were to emerge between EC law and the protection of fundamental rights in domestic law (including under the HRA) parliamentary sovereignty might hold the key to its resolution. The national courts would, arguably, have to engage in a process of determining the parliamentary intent when entering into the Treaty.[19]

1.24 In fact, any prospect of direct conflict has receded considerably as a result of the more flexible attitude taken by the ECJ when confronted with objections by the constitutional courts of certain Member States (most notably Germany and Italy) that provisions of EC law could not survive with incompatible domestic law provisions.[20]

1.25 In a series of cases, culminating in the ECJ's Opinion 2/94, the ECJ has now authoritatively stated that:

> It is well settled that fundamental rights form an integral part of the general principles of law whose observance the court ensures. For that purpose, the court draws inspiration from the constitutional traditions common to the Member States and from the guidelines supplied by international treaties for the protection of human rights on which the Member States have collaborated or of which they are signatories. In that regard, the court has stated that the [European] Convention [on Human Rights] has special significance.

---

15 Case 6/64 [1964] ECR 585, 593.

16 A point not lost on Laddie J in Case C–206/01 *Arsenal Football Club v Reed* [2003] Ch 454 who refused to apply the ECJ's preliminary ruling under Art 234 (ex 177) EC on the basis that the ECJ had exceeded its interpretative jurisdiction! The Court of Appeal reversed this decision holding that the ECJ had not exceeded its interpretative jurisdiction.

17 F Mancini and D Keeling, 'Democracy and the European Court of Justice' (1994) 57 MLR 175, 187.

18 As to peremptory norms in public international law, see A Cassesse, *International Law* (2001).

19 However, that proposition is not without controversy. Importantly, the issue of *Kompetenz Kompetenz* (the competence to decide on competences) may require the determination of what is within the scope of EC law to be decided by the ECJ rather than by the national court—see Arts 230 and 234 EC and note, generally, M Claes, *The National Courts' Mandate in the European Constitution* (2006) especially 606 et seq. and ch 24. For an exploration of some of the potential for conflict, see A O'Neill QC, 'Fundamental Rights and the Constitutional Supremacy of Community Law in the United Kingdom after Devolution and the Human Rights Act' [2002] PL 724.

20 For a helpful survey, see A Clapham, *Human Rights and the European Community: A Critical Overview* (1991).

For its part, domestic public law has evolved to the point where it now appears to recognize **1.26** constitutional rights which bear strong affinity to fundamental rights under the ECHR (as incorporated by the HRA into domestic law) as recognized, in practice, in EC law.

Such recognition is crystallized in the principle of legality. The best summary of this prin- **1.27** ciple is that of Lord Browne-Wilkinson in *R v Secretary of State for the Home Department, ex p Pierson*.[21] He said this:

> A power conferred by Parliament in general terms is not to be taken to authorise the doing of acts by the donee of the power which adversely affect the legal rights of the citizen or the basic principles on which the law of the United Kingdom is based unless the statute conferring the power makes it clear that such was the intention of Parliament.

In essence, the 'basic principles' referred to by Lord Browne-Wilkinson constitute a set of **1.28** assumptions (or presumptions) that Parliament will legislate in a certain manner even though there can, as a matter of implicitly assumed constitutional theory, be no 'brake' on its sovereign power.

Lord Steyn, in *Pierson*,[22] put it thus: **1.29**

> The presumption that in the event of ambiguity legislation is presumed not to invade common law rights is inapplicable. A broader principle applies. Parliament does not legislate in a vacuum. Parliament legislates for a European liberal democracy founded on the principles and traditions of the common law. And the courts may approach legislation on this initial assumption.

Lord Steyn cites, with approval, a passage from Cross on *Statutory Interpretation*.[23] One sees **1.30** from the extract the kind of assumptions that are sometimes taken to be common sense but which are, as Cross observes, underlying 'constitutional principles'. These include (but are not limited to) the presumption that discretionary powers must be exercised reasonably and fairly. The principles operate:

> . . . at a higher level as expressions of fundamental principles governing both civil liberties and the relations between Parliament, the executive and the courts. They operate here as consti- tutional principles which are not easily displaced by a statutory text.[24]

The central difference between domestic public law and EC public law is that fundamen- **1.31** tal rights once endorsed by the ECJ are enforceable as EC rights *whatever the terms of the domestic statute*. In a purely domestic case the national court is constrained to determine the true parliamentary intent.

This is exemplified by two cases. In *R v Lord Chancellor, ex p Witham*[25] Laws J, giving the **1.32** main judgment of a Divisional Court, observed as follows:

> In the unwritten legal order of the British state, at a time when the common law continues to accord a legislative supremacy to Parliament, the notion of a constitutional right can in my

---

[21] [1998] AC 539, 575. The principle had, perhaps, been foreshadowed (albeit not expressly articulated) by Laws J at first instance in *Ex p Fewings* [1995] 1 All ER 513, 523 and endorsed, in the same case, by the Court of Appeal at [1995] 1 WLR 1037, 1042.

[22] [1998] AC 539, 587. The full analysis is at 587–590. See also per Lord Steyn in *R v Secretary of State for the Home Department, ex p Simms* [2000] AC 115, 130.

[23] 1st edn (1976), (3rd edn, 1995) 142–3.

[24] [1998] AC 539, 588.

[25] [1998] QB 575, 581.

judgment inhere only in this proposition, that the right in question cannot be abrogated by the state save by specific provision in an Act of Parliament, or by regulations whose vires in main legislation specifically confers the power to abrogate. General words will not suffice. And any such rights will be creatures of the common law, since their existence would not be the consequence of the democratic political process but would be logically prior to it . . .

1.33 In *R v Lord Chancellor, ex p Lightfoot*[26] Simon Brown LJ took, as his premise, that Parliament could abrogate constitutional rights by the use of clear words and considered that it could even do so by necessary implication:

> . . . if, as Lord Reid stated in the *Westminster Bank* case [1971] AC 508, 529, rights (however fundamental) can be abrogated 'by irresistible inference from the statute read as a whole,' then it would seem to me logically to follow first that a process of construction of provisions which are in themselves unclear must necessarily be embarked upon . . . Clearly the more fundamental the right affected by the regulation, the less likely it is that Parliament will have authorised its impairment and the greater will be the court's need to be satisfied that such indeed was Parliament's true intention. An irresistible inference will not readily be drawn. But there will be circumstances in which to deny it would be to fly in the face of reason. That in my judgment is the case here.

D. Resolving Conflicts between the Domestic Public Law Jurisdictions

1.34 Differences between EC, ECHR and domestic public law principles will arise in two broad situations:

(1) Where, on the facts of a particular case, there is no overlap between the three systems because (for example) only domestic public law is engaged. Here, because different principles have been developed it is perfectly possible that in a domestic public law case the Administrative Court would either not be able to use particular EC or ECHR principles (as, for example, proportionality which is still not recognized as a discrete domestic public law principle) or that the relevant principle—if capable of being applied separately—might differ in its application (as, for example, the concept of legitimate expectation).[27]

(2) Where there is an overlap between one or more of the three systems. Here, a conflict may arise between the relevant principles to be employed or between decisions of different courts which the Administrative Court or other national court will have to resolve.

1.35 This book considers both types of situation. However, it should be noted that the space between EC, ECHR and domestic public law is, *in areas where they overlap and conflict* probably more apparent than real and that even where such conflict occurs legislative priority is, almost always, accorded to decisions of the ECJ.

---

[26] [2000] QB 597.
[27] See paras 8.74–8.79.

To the extent (where both are engaged) that Convention rights afford less protection in a particular case than domestic constitutional rights, the intention of Parliament is contained in HRA, s 11. This provides that:

> A person's reliance on a Convention right does not restrict—
> (a) any other right or freedom conferred on him by or under any law having effect in any part of the United Kingdom; or
> (b) his right to make any claim or bring any proceedings which he could make or bring apart from sections 7 to 9.

1.36

More difficult is the potential conflict between constitutional and Convention rights on the one hand and EC law on the other. Assuming that each system of law is engaged, cases have arisen where the ECJ has reached a different view of the extent of a right deriving from the ECHR than the Strasbourg Court.[28]

1.37

How is the domestic court to resolve the contradiction? The answer may lie in determining, and applying, Parliament's respective intent in passing the European Communities Act 1972 and the HRA.

1.38

HRA, s 2 permits judges to give a different interpretation to the ECHR than that given by the European Court of Human Rights. This is because the Strasbourg case law has only to be taken into account by the national court but may be departed from. However, in cases engaging fundamental rights within the scope of EC law, s 3(1) of the 1972 Act requires the national court to determine the question in accordance with EC rulings.

1.39

So, where the national court is seeking to decide whether a breach of fundamental rights in EC law has occurred, s 3(1) of the 1972 Act ought to prevail and the ECJ's case law should trump any inconsistent Strasbourg ruling. Section 2 of the 1972 Act which confers supremacy of EC law over (even) inconsistent primary legislation would, in such a case, prevent the HRA from operating to contrary effect *within the sphere of EC law*.[29]

1.40

E. Recognizing the EC Dimension in Domestic Public Law

Public law issues usually arise in judicial review proceedings in the Administrative Court using the procedure in CPR Pt 54, although such issues can arise by way of collateral

1.41

---

[28] cf, eg, Case C–159/90 *SPUC v Grogan* [1991] ECR I–4685 (Advocate General Van Gerven considered that a prohibition against dissemination of information in Ireland would not be in breach of Art 10 ECHR) with *Open Door Counselling and Dublin Well Women v Ireland* (1993) 15 EHRR 97 (on materially identical facts, the Strasbourg Court came to the opposite conclusion).

[29] This is not accepted by all commentators. See, eg, O'Neill (n 19, above) 741–2. In any event, of course, neither the Administrative Court nor any other national court has jurisdiction as a public authority to act incompatibly with the ECHR (see HRA, s 6). Thus, if compliance with EC law triggered a breach of the ECHR there would be an irreconcilable contradiction as between EC law and HRA law *as a matter of domestic law*. Plainly, the Administrative Court would, in such unusual circumstances, be likely to refer the case to the ECJ for a preliminary ruling under Article 234 (ex 177) EC. However, given the supremacy of EC law over domestic law (which, logically, includes the HRA) it is not easy to see how the Administrative Court could ever give primacy to ECHR Convention rights, as defined by the European Court of Human Rights, in Strasbourg over an ECJ formulation of the content of those rights in a Community law context.

challenge in proceedings before other national courts.[30] This is as true of EC public law as it is of ECHR and domestic administrative public law issues. It is, therefore, important not merely to identify the EC element of a case but also to decide whether that element requires the issue to be raised by way of judicial review.

1.42　The underlying criterion in whether an EC case is suitable for judicial review in the Administrative Court is not merely whether there is an element of EC law. What is also required is that the decision-maker is exercising a 'public function'.[31] Nonetheless, the presence of a relevant EC element may be crucial to whether judicial review proceedings may be instituted at all, how the case is argued, and the relief that may be granted.

1.43　As modern judicial review has developed it has had to take account of the three distinct but, in practice, often overlapping systems of law referred to above, namely:

(1) The principles of domestic judicial review.
(2) Fundamental human rights under the European Convention on Human Rights as incorporated into domestic judicial review through the medium of the HRA which came into force on 2 October 2000.
(3) The principles of EC law.

1.44　These regimes overlap both because the principles and remedies governing each are frequently similar and because, in order to rely on any of the three systems of law, a claimant in judicial review proceedings must be able to establish the presence of a necessary 'public function' on the part of a proposed defendant.[32] It is sometimes said that to bring a claim in judicial review a claimant must establish a 'vertical' relationship between himself and the State so as to distinguish judicial review from the 'horizontal' relationship subsisting between private individuals.[33]

1.45　Importantly, however, the three regimes differ in often crucial respects. Remedially, for example, the doctrine of parliamentary sovereignty has required judges in domestic judicial review challenges to give effect to statutes even, on occasion, where particular statutory provisions offend against established common law principle. Ordinarily, judges may not strike down Acts of Parliament. This is so even where a statute is incompatible with a fundamental right under the European Convention on Human Rights.[34]

1.46　But the position in EC law is different because of the supremacy of EC law effected by the European Communities Act 1972, s 2. This important doctrine is examined in Chapter 2.[35]

---

[30] See paras 1.120–1.123.

[31] *R v Panel on Take-overs and Mergers, ex p Datafin Plc* [1987] QB 815.

[32] But the necessary 'public' element may differ according to whether the proceedings are being brought under conventional domestic public law, under the HRA, or in EC law. See paras 2.17–2.29.

[33] There are circumstances in which public law issues can be litigated outside judicial review (see paras 1.120–1.123). There may also be circumstances in which EC issues (and Convention issues under HRA s 3) are litigated 'horizontally' between private individuals but where there is a relationship with public law remedies (see paras 5.28–5.32).

[34] The court may only grant a declaration of incompatibility under HRA, s 4.

[35] See, especially, paras 2.60–2.89.

Essentially, however, it stipulates that EC law binds both nationals of Member States and the Member States themselves and that provisions of national law that may conflict with EC law must be set aside by the domestic courts.[36] Thus, where a statutory provision offends against an enforceable EC law right, the judges are required to disapply the offending provision.[37] Another difference between the regimes is that damages for infringement of rights are awarded on a somewhat different basis in EC law cases to that prevailing in either domestic law or under the HRA.[38]

The three systems also differ in terms of substantive principle. Proportionality, for example, is—at least generally—not applicable in domestic judicial review.[39] However, proportionality is intrinsic to the application of Convention rights under the HRA.[40] It is also an important general principle of EC law which, in a possibly more stringent form, must be applied by the Administrative Court where appropriate.[41] **1.47**

Further, although fundamental rights are protected by each of the three systems, they are protected in different ways both procedurally and substantively. The content of fundamental rights in EC law is neither confined to the European Convention on Human Rights nor limited to the interpretation placed upon those rights by the European Court of Human Rights in Strasbourg.[42] **1.48**

Standing is also different according to whether a judicial review challenge is brought under ordinary domestic principles, under the HRA, or by way of an EC challenge. The test for standing in a purely domestic case is very broad. Under the HRA, however, a claimant must generally be a 'victim' within the meaning of Article 34 of the Convention.[43] This term is fairly narrowly defined and more restrictive than standing would be to litigate a fundamental rights issue in EC law.[44] **1.49**

So, identifying an EC case (or a relevant EC element) suitable for judicial review is of great importance because the EC element: **1.50**

(1) may be relevant to issues of standing;
(2) is likely to affect the remedy granted by the Administrative Court;
(3) will often dictate the substantive principles that the Administrative Court must apply.

---

[36] See, most appositely, Case 6/64 *Costa v ENEL* [1964] ECR 585, 593; Case 106/77 *Amministrazione delle Finanze dello Stato v Simmenthal Spa* [1978] ECR 629 especially para 21.

[37] Case C–213/89 *R v Secretary of State for Transport, ex p Factortame* [1990] ECR 1–2433 para 21. See paras 2.66–2.67.

[38] See paras 5.85–5.189.

[39] *R v Secretary of State for the Home Department, ex p Brind* [1991] 1 AC 696. See, especially, 751 per Lord Templeman, 759 per Lord Ackner, 762 and 766–767 per Lord Lowry.

[40] See, eg, *R (Daly) v Secretary of State for the Home Department* [2001] UKHL 26, [2001] 2 AC 532.

[41] See, eg, *Thomas v Chief Adjudication Officer* [1991] 2 QB 164. The extent to which EC proportionality differs from the proportionality exercise under the HRA and analogous domestic law principles is discussed at paras 11.78–11.92.

[42] See paras 12.11–12.18.

[43] Though this is not necessarily the case when seeking a declaration of incompatibility under HRA, s 4; *Rushbridger v Attorney General* [2003] UKHL 38, [2004] 1 AC 357. cf *Taylor v Lancashire CC* [2005] EWCA Civ 284, [2005] HRLR 17.

[44] See paras 3.61–3.66.

1.51 When considering judicial review proceedings, and confronted with a potential EC case, practitioners should consider the following questions:

(1) Is the EC element of the case sufficient to enable the Administrative Court to apply substantive principles of EC law?

(2) If so, is the case one that *can* be brought by way of judicial review?

(3) If so, is the case one that *must* be brought by way of judicial review?

1.52 Some of these questions raise quite complex issues some of which are explored in more depth in subsequent chapters.

F. Identifying the Requisite EC Public Law Element

Sources of EC law

1.53 As outlined above, identifying the presence of an EC law dimension in a particular case is not determinative of whether a case must be brought by way of judicial review or even whether judicial review proceedings are, in fact, appropriate. Nevertheless, the existence of a relevant EC public law element is likely to have a significant effect on the nature of the proceedings, who can bring the claim, the legal argument, and the remedies obtainable. It may also sometimes be decisive of whether particular proceedings should be commenced by way of judicial review given the need, in many instances, for the existence of the State or emanation of the State for a relevant Community public law obligation to be created.[45]

1.54 The content of EC law is, essentially, derived from:

(1) The Treaty (EC),[46] including the changes made to EC law by the Treaty on European Union (TEU/Maastricht)[47] and Treaty of Amsterdam[48] together with the secondary legislation and administrative acts as adopted by the institutions of the Community in the form of regulations, directives, decisions, recommendations, and opinions.[49]

---

[45] This is predominantly the case where one is concerned with the doctrine of direct effect and directives/decisions outlined at paras 1.67–1.80.

[46] Henceforth, references to 'the Treaty' are to the EC Treaty as amended where appropriate by the later TEU and Treaty of Amsterdam. The Nice Treaty (in force from 1 February 2003) does not make significant legal changes to the existing Treaties. The EU Constitution is of potential significance especially, so far as fundamental rights are concerned, in the EU Charter. Although the Charter is separately considered (see paras 12.19–12.37) its provisions are not yet in force and may not be passed into law.

[47] The most important change to the Treaty effected by the TEU (in force from 1 November 1993) was the creation in Title II of EU citizenship rights under (then) Art 8. These provisions (as later amended) are considered in Chapter 16. The TEU created three pillars of the EU (the citizenship provisions being in the first pillar). Title V (foreign and security policies) contained the second pillar. Title VI contained the third pillar (justice and home affairs).

[48] The Treaty of Amsterdam (in force from 1 May 1999) amended both the EC Treaty and the TEU. In particular, it included the third pillar of Maastricht (above) in the Treaty bringing matters such as immigration and asylum within the competence of the EC institutions. Note, though, that the ECJ has considerably reduced jurisdiction in matters covered by the third pillar. See below.

[49] The Treaty, by Art 300(7), also makes provision for international treaties concluded by the Community to be binding on the Community institutions and the Member States. Article 307 preserves the validity of international agreements concluded by Member States prior to the coming into force of the Treaty but imposes an obligation on Member States to seek to eliminate incompatibility between such pre-existing

(2) The case law of the European Court of Justice (ECJ) and the Court of First Instance (CFI) including the general principles of EC law which will, in appropriate cases, encompass standards commonly accepted by the Member States by reference to public international law[50] and to fundamental rights.[51]

In examining whether the requisite EC public law element is present in order to seek to apply substantive principles of EC law in domestic public law it is necessary to consider a number of different situations. These include the following: **1.55**

(1) National legislative measures or omissions based on national legislation the legality of which is dependent upon a relevant EC obligation that derives from the Treaty or Community secondary legislation.
(2) Acts or omissions of a domestic public body by reason of a Treaty or Community secondary legislative provision.
(3) National legislative measures/omissions and administrative acts or omissions that do not obviously fall into either of the above categories but which are, nonetheless, alleged to contravene general principles of EC law.

National measures or administrative measures based on national legislation that are contrary to an EC obligation

Member States must act in accordance with, and so as to give effect to, obligations imposed by the EC Treaty or Community secondary legislation. For the most part such obligations are required to be 'directly effective' for individuals to be able to rely on them although (see below) this is not always the case. The meaning of the term 'directly effective' is discussed below but the concept is linked to judicial review because, where direct effect is relied on against the State or an emanation of the State, the proceedings will be more likely to sound in public rather than private law.[52] **1.56**

National legislation passed so as to implement EC obligations is susceptible to challenge by judicial review where it is contended that the legislation fails to implement the EC obligation correctly or where legislation mandated by a directive to transpose EC obligations into national law has simply not been passed.[53] It is the EC obligation that is relevant so that, exceptionally, if domestic legislation is dependent for its validity on underlying EC secondary legislation[54] that is itself contended to be unlawful, a challenge to domestic legislation **1.57**

---

treaties and the Treaty. For present purposes the relevance of international treaties is that—whether concluded by the Community or the Member State—their legal status as a matter of EC law is regulated by the Treaty and not by the ECJ or CFI. For the position in respect of direct effect and international agreements, see paras 1.81–1.84 post.

[50] Including unincorporated as well as incorporated treaties which will, in turn, become a source of law at least to the extent that they are relied on by the ECJ. Of the increasing number of cases see, eg, Case C–148/02 *Carlo Garcia Avello v Belgian State* [2003] ECR I–11613 (UN Convention on the Rights of the Child referred to by Advocate General Jacobs). See, generally, S Fatima, *Using International Law in Domestic Courts* (2006).
[51] See Chapter 12.
[52] See, though, the discussion at paras 1.110–1.128.
[53] *R v Customs and Excise, ex p Eurotunnel* [1995] CLC 392. See also para 1.60 below.
[54] A Treaty provision cannot, by definition, be incompatible with EC law.

will also involve an indirect challenge to the contingent EC secondary legislation.[55] In those circumstances the domestic court cannot itself declare EC legislation to be invalid but will be likely to refer the case to the ECJ under Article 234 (ex 177) EC for a preliminary ruling.[56] Administrative acts or omissions founded on domestic EC legislation will also be amenable to judicial review where the administrative act in question deviates impermissibly from EC compliant domestic legislation.

1.58 National measures or administrative acts or omissions founded on national legislation may also be challenged in judicial review proceedings where, although the acts or omissions are derived from domestic law, the domestic legislation (or absence of any legislation) is contrary to an obligation imposed by the EC Treaty or Community secondary legislation.[57]

1.59 Finally, it is well established that whenever a relevant EC obligation is correctly transposed into national law its effects reach individuals through the relevant national measures. In such cases a claimant to judicial review should challenge the particular administrative act or omission said to contravene the EC obligation by reference to the national provisions.[58]

Directly effective provisions of the Treaty and/or Community secondary legislation

1.60 Individuals may also rely on EC obligations that are directly effective, that is obligations *enforceable by an individual* that are directly created in domestic law by certain provisions of the Treaty or by Community secondary legislation (usually a directive) even where there is no transposing national legislation. This includes the situation where there ought to have been transposing legislation in respect of the particular obligation but none has been passed.[59]

1.61 Statutory recognition of this is accorded by s 2(1) of the European Communities Act 1972 which provides as follows:

> All such rights, powers, liabilities, obligations and restrictions from time to time created or arising by or under the Treaties, and all such remedies and procedures from time to time provided for by or under the Treaties, as in accordance with the Treaties are without further enactment to be given legal effect or used in the United Kingdom shall be recognised and available in law, and be enforced, allowed and followed accordingly; and the expression 'enforceable Community right' and similar expressions shall be read as referring to one to which this subsection applies.

---

[55] See, eg *R (ABNA Ltd) v Secretary of State for Health and Food Standards Agency* [2004] Eu LR 88.
[56] See paras 4.92–4.98.
[57] Joined Cases C–92/92 and C–326/92 *Phil Collins* [1993] ECR 1–5145; *R v MAFF, ex p First City Trading* [1997] 1 CMLR 250, para 39.
[58] See, eg, Case 270/81 *Felicitas Rickmers-Linie KG & Co v Finanzamt fur Verkehrsteuern* [1982] ECR 2771, para 24; *Marks & Spencer plc v Commissioners of Customs & Excise* [1999] 1 CMLR 1152, 1160, per Moses J and in the Court of Appeal [2000] 1 CMLR 256, 257.
[59] For a case in point see *R v North Yorkshire County Council, ex p Brown* [1998] Env LR 385. There, the relevant obligation in the Environment Impact Assessment (EIA) Directive had not been transposed into domestic law by the relevant regulations. The case proceeded on the basis that the claimants could challenge the legality of the administrative decision not to require EIA which was found to be in breach of the directly effective rights created by the EIA Directive. This case is further referred to at para 14.47.

This appears to encompass the doctrine of direct effect.[60] Not all EC provisions have direct **1.62** effect. Some provisions are enforceable by Member States alone. Other provisions, are not directly effective because of their vagueness or contingent nature. As will be seen, certain measures—principally directives—only create direct effect against the State or an emanation of the State[61] and cannot be relied on as against private parties. This has obvious significance for judicial review since, at least in general, such claims against the State will be brought in public and not in private law and usually by way of judicial review.

In many instances the cases have clarified whether a particular provision is directly effective **1.63** or not. Where, however, the position has not been clarified it will be necessary to construe the provision in question so as to determine whether or not it is directly effective.

Certain tests have been developed for determining whether or not a particular provision is or is **1.64** not directly effective. In essence the relevant criteria are that the identified provision must be:[62]

(1) sufficiently clear and precise;[63]
(2) unconditional;[64] and
(3) one that leaves no scope for discretion as to its implementation.

Treaty provisions and direct effect

That Treaty provisions themselves are at least capable of creating direct effect was clarified **1.65** by the ECJ in *Van Gend en Loos v Netherlands*.[65] It is now clear that a great many provisions of the Treaty are directly effective[66] and that these even include provisions such as Article 90 EC which contain a time limit for the Member State to adopt implementing measures— the relevant Treaty provision becomes directly effective once the time limit has expired and the Member State has failed to enact the requisite national legislative measures.[67]

Regulations and direct effect

EC regulations will, almost invariably, be directly effective.[68] Article 249 EC categorizes a **1.66** regulation as being of 'general application . . . binding in its entirety and directly applicable

---

[60] Importantly, the fact that EC legislation has direct effect does not necessarily mean that EC secondary legislation complies with the Treaty. Secondary EC legislation may itself be unlawful and may, as explained earlier, be indirectly challenged in domestic judicial review proceedings where the domestic measure complained of depends for its validity upon the underlying validity of EC secondary legislation. The domestic court is likely to refer an indirect challenge to EC secondary legislation to the ECJ for a preliminary ruling under Article 234 (ex 177) EC since only the ECJ may declare EC secondary legislation to be invalid. See para 1.57 and paras 4.92–4.98.

[61] The relevant case law is discussed at paras 1.75–1.76 and at paras 5.66–5.84.

[62] See, generally, Case 9/70 *Grad v Finanzamt Traunstein* [1970] ECR 825.

[63] This does not, necessarily, mean unambiguous since many 'ambiguous' legislative provisions do create individual rights the scope of which the court has to resolve: see, eg, *R v Secretary of State for Home Affairs, ex p Santillo* [1980] ECR 1585, 1611.

[64] In essence this has the consequence that the relevant provision does not require—for the obligation to be imposed—any further measures to be taken.

[65] Case 26/62 [1963] ECR 1.

[66] For further consideration of direct effect in relation to judicial review, see paras 2.155–2.160.

[67] Case 57/65 *Alfons Lutticke GmbH v Hauptzollamt Saarlouis* (judgment 16 June 1966).

[68] For an example in domestic law see, eg, *In Re G (Children) (Foreign Contact Order: Enforcement)* [2003] EWCA Civ 1607, [2004] 1 WLR 521.

in all Member States'. The phrase 'directly applicable' is not, though, synonymous with 'directly effective' because it simply means that regulations will have legal effect in the Member States without the need for implementing legislation. It does not necessarily connote that the regulation in question will be sufficiently precise for it to contain legal rights that may be relied upon by individuals.

Directives and direct effect

1.67 Article 249(3) EC provides that a directive is:

> . . . binding, as to the result to be achieved, upon each Member State to which it is addressed, but shall leave to the national authorities the choice of form and methods.

1.68 Although a directive is binding in substance on Member States it is not directly applicable. This does not, however, mean that it is incapable of producing direct effect. This was finally clarified by the ECJ in *Van Duyn v Home Office*.[69] There, a Dutch national was, on public policy grounds, refused leave to enter the United Kingdom in order to take up employment as a secretary with the Church of Scientology. She sought to rely on a Council directive which restricted grounds of refusal to matters relating to personal conduct. The ECJ held that Mrs Van Duyn was entitled to rely on the directive by reason of the doctrine of direct effect. It is, as explained, entirely possible for certain provisions of a directive to be directly effective but for others not to be.[70]

1.69 The criteria for determining whether a provision is directly effective, referred to above, are equally as applicable to directives as they are to Treaty provisions or regulations. But, because of the nature of directives, they are more elaborate and there are additional factors to be borne in mind.

1.70 The requirements that a particular provision be sufficiently precise and unconditional mean, ordinarily, that for the directly effective obligation to be imposed the obligation must be clearly expressed and no further measures need to be taken whether by the Community institutions or by the Member State. Directives, however (see Article 249 above), stipulate that the Member State has discretion as to the form and methods of implementation although not as to the result to be achieved. In the case of directives it is, therefore, the result that constitutes the relevant obligation so that the result must be expressed in unequivocal terms.[71] As Advocate General Fennelly warned in *Garage Molenhide BVBA v Belgium*[72] to deny direct effect merely because of the alternatives (however various) in transposition is to confuse direct effect with discretion in the manner of transposing the directly effective obligation.[73]

---

[69] Case 41/74 [1974] ECR 1337, paras 9–15. It had, though, been foreshadowed in Case 9/70 *Grad v Finanzamt Traunstein* [1970] ECR 825.

[70] See, eg, Case 8/81 *Becker v Finanzamt Munster-Innenstadt* [1982] ECR 53, paras 29–30.

[71] See, eg, Case C–389/95 *Klattner v Greece* [1997] ECR 1–2719, para 33.

[72] Joined Cases C–286/94, C–340, and 401/95, and C–47/96 [1997] ECR 1–7821, 7299–7300.

[73] Note, too, that the fact that a directive permits derogations does not preclude the creation of direct effect since the legality of the derogations may be reviewed: see Joined Cases C–358/93 and C–416/93 *Bordessa* [1995] ECR 1–361, paras 17–18 and 32–35.

However, a directive does not, ordinarily, create directly effective rights unless and until the **1.71** implementation date has passed.[74] Such rights may be created even later if the directive provides for a later date than the implementation date for its application.[75] It is, nonetheless, at least arguable that where national legislation is introduced prior to the implementation date purporting to implement the directive the directive may be relied upon as having direct effect at that stage.[76]

It has sometimes been suggested that there is a separate definitional criterion for directives **1.72** in the context of 'direct effect'. This is that the relevant provision is intended to create rights for individuals.[77]

However, in *Becker v Finanzamt Munster-Innenstadt*[78] the ECJ said: **1.73**

> ... wherever the provisions of a directive appear, as far as their subject-matter is concerned, to be unconditional and sufficiently precise, those provisions may, in the absence of implementing measures adopted within the prescribed period, be relied upon as against any national provision which is incompatible with the directive or in so far as the provisions define rights which individuals are able to assert against the State.

This formulation, although potentially ambiguous,[79] appears to suggest that it is not **1.74** always necessary to the creation of direct effect for a directive to be intended to create, or have the effect of creating, rights for individuals but that the latter requirement is necessary where the Member State is not seeking to apply a national law against an individual but the individual is relying upon the State's failure to comply with a positive obligation imposed by the directive. So, for example, a pressure group with sufficient standing to seek judicial review[80] might be able to rely upon the provisions of a directive so as to challenge allegedly incompatible national legislation by way of judicial review and would not (further) have to establish that the directive was intended to create individual rights.

Directives and horizontal direct effect

There is another important potential restriction, flowing from the doctrine of direct effect, **1.75** on utilizing directives in judicial review proceedings. The restriction does not apply to either Treaty provisions or to regulations. This is the often cited rule that directives do not

---

[74] See, eg, Case 148/78 *Pubblico Ministero v Ratti* [1979] ECR 1629, especially para 24.

[75] Case C–316/93 *Vannetveld v Le Foyer SA* [1994] ECR 1–763, para 19.

[76] cf Case 80/86 *Officier van Justitie v Kolpinghuis Nijmegen BV* [1987] ECR 3969 and Case 129/96 *Inter-Environment Wallonie ASBL v Region Wallonie* [1998] 1 CMLR 1057 (*effet utile* operates to prevent Member States within the implementation period from seriously compromising the intended result of the directive) with Case C–156/91 *Hansa Fleisch v Landrat des Kreises Schlewig-Flensburg* [1992] ECR 1–5567 where Advocate General Jacobs doubted whether direct effect could be created at all during the implementation period.

[77] See, eg, *Twyford Parish Council v Secretary of State for the Environment* [1992] 1 CMLR 276, per McCullough J. cf *R v Secretary of State for Employment, ex p Equal Opportunities Commission* [1995] 1 AC 1.

[78] Case 8/81 [1982] ECR 53, para 25.

[79] *Twyford Parish Council v Secretary of State for the Environment* [1992] 1 CMLR 276 rejected this interpretation. But see, now, the *EOC* case (at n 77).

[80] See paras 3.53–3.60.

have 'horizontal direct effect'. What it means is that individuals cannot rely on directives as against other individuals in private actions.

1.76 It might be thought that a restriction of this kind, though significant, could have little relevance to judicial review which, by definition, sounds in public rather than private law. In fact, however, the prohibition against directives having horizontal direct effect can be highly relevant to judicial review for the following reasons:

(1) It requires careful selection of an appropriate defendant to the proceedings since only the State or an emanation of the State may be proceeded against by reference to a directive that is said to be directly effective. This is not necessarily the same as identifying a public body that is susceptible to judicial review.[81]

(2) In some cases there are consequences for private individuals in a claimant in judicial review proceedings relying on a directive against the State or State emanation. The question then becomes whether such consequences are permissible or not. If they are not permissible then the judicial review proceedings will fail because the effect of the proceedings will have been to create, under the guise of a public law claim, direct horizontal effect. But in many, if not most, instances the presence of a public law claim is likely to prevail over incidental consequences to a private third party, especially where the third party is not in any legal relationship with the judicial review claimant.[82]

Decisions, recommendations, opinions and direct effect

1.77 Under Article 249 EC a decision is 'binding in its entirety upon those to whom it is addressed'. It is capable of having direct effect.[83]

1.78 So, where a decision is addressed to a Member State it may be relied on in judicial review proceedings where the State fails to comply with the obligation contained in the decision. However, as with directives, some decisions may not be capable of creating rights for individuals.[84]

1.79 Neither recommendations nor opinions are binding. It follows that they are not capable of being directly effective.

1.80 However, even non-binding measures such as these are still able to produce legal effects in the national proceedings of Member States. In *Grimaldi v Fonds des Maladies Professionnelles*[85] the ECJ observed that national courts were:

> bound to take Community recommendations into consideration in deciding disputes submitted to them, in particular where they clarify the interpretation of national provisions adopted in order to implement them or where they are designed to supplement binding EEC measures.

---

81 See paras 2.17–2.29 below.
82 See *R v Durham County Council, ex p Huddleston* [2000] 1 WLR 148. See, also, paras 5.80–5.84 below.
83 Case 9/70 *Grad v Finanzamt Traunstein* [1970] ECR 825, paras 3–5.
84 See, eg, Case 174/84 *Bulk Oil (Zug) v Sun International* [1986] ECR 559, paras 61–62.
85 Case C–322/88 [1989] ECR 4407, paras 16–19.

International agreements and direct effect

International agreements concluded between the EU and one or more third countries take **1.81** a variety of forms. They may, for example, be agreements:

(1) concluded between the Community and third countries under the treaty-making powers of the EC;
(2) such as WTO agreements, where the subject matter overlaps with the EC law; or,
(3) agreements concluded prior to the EC Treaty coming into force.

In some cases, international agreements are specifically given direct effect by secondary EC **1.82** legislation.[86]

By contrast, where the agreement provides that one or more of its provisions is not intended **1.83** to be directly effective, that is conclusive.

But where the agreement is silent the question becomes, as with other sources of **1.84** Community obligations, outlined above, one of construction. Consistently with the rationale underlying the principle of direct effect, the ECJ has held that particular provisions of international agreements will be directly effective where the provision in question is clear and precise and does not depend on the adoption of any subsequent measure.[87] It follows that failure by the contracting State or States to incorporate an international obligation of this kind would not operate to prevent such agreement from being directly effective.[88]

Excluding the operation of the direct effect principle

There are many sources of EC jurisdiction from which direct effect has now been expressly **1.85** excluded or from which ECJ jurisdiction has been removed. These include matters relating to decisions in respect of political and judicial co-operation in criminal matters taken under Title VI TEU[89] and areas within the third pillar of the TEU relating to judicial co-operation in civil matters insofar as such matters relate 'to the maintenance of law and order and the safeguarding of internal security'.[90]

The principle of indirect effect

The concept of *indirect* effect was first developed in the important ECJ ruling in *Von* **1.86** *Colson*.[91] The claim was, in part, brought in private law. It concerned the meaning to be given to a provision of a directive for the purpose of arguing that the amount of compensation in German law in cases of discrimination was too small and contravened Article 6 of the Equal Treatment Directive.[92]

---

86 As, eg, the Dublin Convention to determine the Member State responsible for examining an application for asylum is made directly effective by Regulation (EC) 343/2003.
87 See, eg, Case C–277/94 *Taflan-Met* [1996] ECR 1–4085, para 24; Case C–37/98 *R (Abdulnasir Savas) v Secretary of State for the Home Department* [2000] ECR I–2927.
88 Case 104/81 *Hauptzollamt Mainz v Kupferberg* [1982] ECR 3641, para 17.
89 Article 34(2) TEU.
90 Article 64(1) EC.
91 Case 14/83 *Von Colson and Kamann v Land Nordrhein-Westfalen* [1984] ECR 1891.
92 Directive (EEC) 76/207. For further background on the Equal Treatment Directive, see paras 18.29 et seq.

1.87   The ECJ rejected the claim in terms of the direct effect doctrine. But it went on to hold that national courts had an obligation to interpret national law so as to conform to the terms of the Directive. This obligation was derived from the terms of the then Article 5 EC (now Article 10) which requires Member States to 'take all appropriate measures' to ensure fulfilment of their EC obligations.

1.88   Building on its decision in *Von Colson* the ECJ held in the private law contractual claim in *Marleasing*[93] that a directive could not, of itself, create binding obligations on individuals. However, it also held that Member States and the authorities acting on behalf of the State were obliged to give effect to the results prescribed by a particular directive. That obligation was binding on the national court and extended to the interpretation of domestic legislation whether coming into force before or after the directive. This interpretative obligation, similar to that contained in HRA, s 3,[94] required the national court to interpret national law in every way possible so as to be in conformity with the directive.

1.89   So, although a particular Community provision may not be directly effective it may still be capable of creating *indirect* legal effect by virtue of the interpretative duty placed upon the national courts. Indirect legal effect may thus be an important doctrine in domestic EC public law proceedings and have an effect on the way in which the court decides the EC compliance of primary and secondary legislation and/or the legality of public law administrative acts and omissions even where a claimant cannot claim the benefit of a directly effective EC right.

1.90   Its wider significance lies in the fact that the national court may be required to interpret a provision of national law so as to accord with EC obligations even in proceedings between purely private parties. In this fashion it has, for example, become possible to give effect to directives and regulations in private litigation thereby overcoming some of the obstacles caused by impermissible horizontal effect. This development in EC law is paralleled in HRA cases by the increasing use of HRA, s 3 which requires the court to interpret legislative provisions so far as possible compatibly with the ECHR. This, too, has led to a degree of horizontal application of the HRA in that even in disputes between private parties statutes are now required to be interpreted by reference to ECHR considerations.

State liability and damages

1.91   Article 10 (ex 5) EC which requires Member States to 'take all appropriate measures' to ensure fulfilment of their EU obligations also underpins the notion of State liability which is another means by which, in certain circumstances, the State (or emanation of the State) may be held to be liable in damages for violations of EC law even in circumstances where directly effective rights have not been conferred.

1.92   The law on EC damages is now fairly extensive and is separately considered.[95] If, and to the extent that, damages are claimed, judicial review rather than an ordinary action will often be the appropriate procedure because of the fact that the rationale for damages is the

---

[93] Case C–106/89 *Marleasing SA v La Comercial Internacional De Alimentacion SA* [1990] ECR 4135.
[94] See paras 2.140–2.141.
[95] See paras 5.85–5.183.

violation by the State of an EC obligation and because of the frequently close connection between a claim founded on damages and one relying on the creation of directly effective rights against the State under a directive. However, this may not always be so. The various considerations in selection of procedure are considered below.[96]

National and administrative measures in breach of general principles of EC law

There has been held to be an important difference, so far as the application of domestic law is concerned, between EC obligations arising, ultimately, under the Treaty and obligations said to derive from EC general principles of law. EC general principles of law (such as proportionality, equal treatment, and fundamental rights) are of great importance in the way in which both EC domestic and the EC Treaty and EC secondary legislation is interpreted and enforced. For this reason, Part II of this book is devoted to general principles of EC law and the relationship between such principles and domestic public law. However, the fact that State activity takes place in an EC context is not necessarily the same as State activity being undertaken pursuant to a Treaty obligation and, hence, subject to application of the general principles of EC law. **1.93**

This difficult issue was considered in *R v MAFF, ex p First City Trading Ltd*[97] where the Administrative Court was concerned with the legality of the Beef Stocks Transfer Scheme. The claimant company submitted that the legality of a national measure is subject to the general principles of EC law, as articulated by the European courts, in circumstances where that measure affects Community trade in goods or services. **1.94**

Laws J rejected the submission. He distinguished between the respective sources of EC law and held that general principles have a narrower effect than Treaty provisions. **1.95**

He observed:[98] **1.96**

> These fundamental principles ... are not provided for on the face of the Treaty of Rome. They have been developed by the Court of Justice ... out of the Administrative law of the Member States. They are part of what may perhaps be called the common law of the Community. That being so, it is to my mind by no means self-evident that their contextual scope must be the same as that of Treaty provisions relating to discrimination or equal treatment which are statute law taking effect according to their express terms ...

> Like any statute law containing orders or prohibitions, the Treaty is dirigiste; it is ... to be sharply distinguished from law which is made by a court of limited jurisdiction, such as the Court of Justice.

> The power of the Court of Justice ... to apply ... principles of public law which it had itself evolved cannot be deployed in a case where the measure in question, taken by a Member State, is not a function of Community law at all ... Where action is taken, albeit under domestic law, which falls within the scope of the Treaty's application, then of course the Court has the power and duty to require that the Treaty be adhered to. But no more: precisely because the fundamental principles elaborated by the Court of Justice are not vouchsafed by the Treaty, there is no legal space for their application to any measure or decision taken otherwise than in pursuance of Treaty rights or obligations.

---

[96] See also paras 1.100–1.130.
[97] [1997] 1 CMLR 250.
[98] ibid, paras 39–42.

1.97 Laws J's reasoning is, however, open to question. In *R v MAFF, ex p British Pig Industry Support Group* [99] Richards J expressed 'real doubts' about its correctness. This issue is complex and is separately analysed. [100] If, however, Laws J is right it means that great care must be taken in identifying the basis of a contended EC element. If the case is dependent solely on general principles developed by the ECJ/CFI that are not anchored to a clear and enforceable Treaty obligation, then there may be no basis for the application of EC law at all in domestic public law proceedings.

Identifying an EC public law element—the questions to ask

1.98 When considering whether a case has the requisite EC element for the application of substantive EC public law principles the following questions are relevant:

(1) What is the nature of the EC obligation said to arise?

(2) Does the obligation derive from a Treaty provision or under Community secondary legislation? If the latter, what is the nature of the secondary legislation?

(3) Is the obligation directly effective?

(4) Alternatively, is the obligation indirectly effective or otherwise enforceable and against whom is it enforceable?

(5) Even if otherwise satisfying the criteria for enforceability, is there (in the case of a directive) any impermissible horizontal direct effect?

(6) Is any relevant EC obligation against a private body or individual as opposed to an emanation of the State?

(7) Are damages being claimed against the State or against an emanation of the State?

(8) What is the intended object of the proceedings—is it primarily to challenge a provision of EC domestic legislation or an administrative act or omission directly through the medium of EC law or is it to bring a claim against a private body and/or by means of a private law mechanism such as contract or tort?

(9) Is there any bar against invoking general principles of EC law: in particular, is the claim solely dependent on general principles of EC law without a discrete EC obligation arising?

1.99 The answers to these questions ought, in principle, to suggest whether there is a substantive EC claim at all and, if there is, whether it should be brought in public law by way of judicial review or in private law. But, as suggested below, theory does not always equate with practice. There will be instances where, despite there being an EC public law issue, that issue may be ventilated as well, or even better, in a private as opposed to a public law forum.

G. Can/Must an EC Public Law Case Be Brought by Way of Judicial Review?

Procedural classification of EC enforcement a matter for national rules

1.100 The enforcement of EC rights in a domestic legal system is entirely a matter for national rules. EC law is indifferent to a distinction between public and private law subject, always,

---

[99] [1999] EWHC Admin 826.
[100] See paras 12.62–12.80.

to two essential principles that the national rules must: (1) be equally favourable to similar claims brought under national law and that (2) national rules must not make it impossible, in practice, for EC rights to be exercised.[101]

In theory at least, the general rule as a matter of domestic law is one of procedural exclusivity. Public law claims must be brought by way of judicial review and not in private law proceedings. Although judicial review has, as a procedure, changed over the years the rationale for requiring general resort to judicial review is that it contains important procedural safeguards for public authorities. In *O'Reilly v Mackman*[102] Lord Diplock observed that as a 'general rule' it would be contrary to public policy and an abuse of process to allow a claimant to ventilate public law claims in an ordinary action and, thereby, to 'evade' the safeguards (still) contained in the judicial review procedure to protect public authorities from vexatious or protracted litigation. The most notable of these safeguards is the restricted limitation period for bringing a claim in judicial review. This limitation is, at least generally, applicable to EC claims.[103] **1.101**

The so-called procedural exclusivity rule has, however, been greatly relaxed in the years following *O'Reilly v Mackman*.[104] Nonetheless, taking procedural exclusivity as a starting point is a useful guide as to the situations in which—provided that the case has the necessary EC public law element and that the claimant has sufficient standing to bring the claim[105]—proceedings ought to be commenced in judicial review rather than in private law and even if a claim started in private law proceedings when it should have been brought by way of judicial review is allowed to proceed, the safeguards applicable to judicial review will still be applied.[106] **1.102**

Three possible situations

There are three scenarios which need to be considered:

(1) The case is not one within the scope of EC law although the general context is one with which EC law is concerned. From an EC perspective (though there may be other domestic or HRA reasons why judicial review is a possible option) there is no basis for seeking judicial review on an EC public law ground. **1.103**

---

[101] For consideration of the principles of equivalence and effectiveness in EC law so far as they affect procedural rules in domestic courts, see paras 3.04–3.31.

[102] [1983] 2 AC 237.

[103] See paras 3.87–3.92.

[104] See, especially, *Clark v University of Lincolnshire and Humberside* [2000] 1 WLR 1988.

[105] See paras 3.49–3.80.

[106] In *Clark v University of Lincolnshire and Humberside* [2000]1 WLR 1988, paras 35–39 the Court of Appeal gave examples of how although strict procedural exclusivity will not be applied in the sense that the court will not be over concerned as to the *form* of the proceedings, the court will take steps to ensure that there is no abuse of process in starting public law proceedings other than by judicial review (as eg by refusing discretionary remedies such as declaratory or injunctive relief outside the time period permitted for judicial review even if the claim is begun as a private law action).

(2) The case has a relevant EC element but its features sound only in private law because there is no relevant EC public law element.[107] Again, subject to the case possessing public law elements, under either domestic law or HRA, there is no sensible point in instituting proceedings for judicial review.

(3) The case has the requisite EC public law element. Here, judicial review is appropriate although there are instances where the EC public law element can be raised by way of collateral chall enge in either private law proceedings or as a defence to a criminal prosecution.

Where judicial review cannot be brought

1.104 From the earlier analysis it can be seen that there are a number of situations in which the requisite EC element is likely to be absent altogether. Although there may sometimes be arguments as to why the court should entertain the claim[108] the following situations, in the present state of the law, appear to exclude EC law being used in any proceedings (ie whether brought in public or private law), namely where:

(1) No relevant EC obligation can be identified. This may be so, following the decision in *First City Trading,* even where there is an EC context but where there is no EC obligation deriving from the Treaties or from Community secondary legislation.

(2) There is a Community directive which has impermissible horizontal direct effect. However, care needs to be taken in this situation in case there are arguments suggesting that the measure in question may have indirect effect or that State EC liability in damages may be involved.[109]

1.105 Other cases will arise where, although there is an EC element, the claim can only be one in private law and where, therefore, judicial review is not an available option. This will obviously be so where the purpose of the claim is to enforce a right against a private party rather than an emanation of the State.

Where judicial review may be brought

1.106 The class of case where judicial review can certainly be used and (see below) in many instances must be used involves the assertion by the claimant of a violation by the State or an emanation of the State of an EC public law obligation. The foundation for judicial review is established because such violation plainly involves the exercise of public functions by a public body amenable to review.

1.107 Violations of this kind may take many forms. They will (for example) include the following:

(1) National legislation that fails lawfully to transpose a directly effective EC obligation.

---

[107] As, eg, where there is no State emanation involved and where the EC element of the case affects private parties. The doctrine of indirect effect discussed at paras 1.86–1.90 would be relevant to such a case.

[108] As, eg, the argument that contrary to the decision of the High Court in *First City Trading* general principles of EC law should be used to resolve at least certain disputes having an EC context: see paras 1.93–1.97 and paras 12.62–12.80.

[109] See paras 2.161–2.171 and 5.85–5.183.

(2) A failure to legislate at all where a directly effective EC obligation is required to be transposed into domestic law.

(3) An administrative act or omission that is founded on defective national legislation.

(4) An administrative act or omission where there is no transposing national legislation but the legality of which falls to be tested by reference to a directly effective EC obligation.

(5) Legislative or administrative acts or omissions that violate EC obligations which, although not directly effective, are enforceable under either the principle of indirect effect or the principle of State liability in damages.

Importantly, it is no longer crucial for there to be a particular decision before judicial review **1.108** proceedings can be commenced. It is sufficient for there to be a justiciable issue of law (such as the compatibility of legislation or an existing state of affairs with EC obligations). This was clarified by the House of Lords in Lord Browne-Wilkinson's speech in *R v Secretary of State for Employment, ex p Equal Opportunities Commission*.[110] He said:[111]

> Under Order 53 any declaration as to public rights which could formerly be obtained in civil proceedings in the High Court can now also be obtained in judicial review proceedings. If this were not so ... the purely procedural decision in *O'Reilly v. Mackman,* requiring all public law cases to be brought by way of judicial review, would have had the effect of thenceforward preventing a plaintiff who previously had *locus standi* to bring civil proceedings for a declaration as to public rights (even though there was no decision which could be the subject of a prerogative order) from bringing any proceedings for such a declaration.

Although—in the absence of a specific decision—it is not possible to obtain a quashing **1.109** order in judicial review proceedings, this does not matter given the wide ambit of the declaration. Judicial review is a discretionary remedy and there may be particular reasons why relief will not be granted where there is no decision. For example, the claim may be considered to be academic or hypothetical. However, the court's discretionary power to refuse relief in judicial review proceedings may require modification in an EC context.[112] Nonetheless, provided that there are relevant issues to be decided, the compatibility of EC obligations may be ventilated by way of judicial review without there being any identifiable decision.

There are three areas where, as the case law has developed since *O'Reilly v Mackman*, the **1.110** courts will allow proceedings to be commenced other than by judicial review albeit that the issues could have been litigated in such proceedings. These are where:

(1) the case is inherently unsuitable for judicial review; and/or,

(2) the public law issues arise collaterally in other proceedings; and/or

(3) the borderline between public and private law is unclear.

Inherent unsuitability for judicial review

There are cases where, although it is possible—at least in principle—to institute judicial **1.111** review proceedings, the Administrative Court is not the most suitable forum. In such

---

[110] [1995] 1 AC 1.
[111] ibid 36.
[112] For examples of the difficulties, see paras 14.76–14.80.

instances there are dicta to the effect that the proceedings were appropriately brought despite their not having been brought by way of judicial review.

1.112   Care should, however, be taken in relating these dicta to the particular issues involved in an EC context where fact finding is often more necessary than in other public law arenas. There is, for example, a difference between the general proposition that judicial review is unsuitable for resolving issues of fact because factual error rarely affords a basis for relief and the separate proposition that, where it does, the judicial review procedure may have to accommodate itself to investigating questions of fact.

1.113   Nonetheless, in large measure where resolution of the public law issues depends upon disputed issues of fact, the Administrative Court can resolve the issues on the witness statements alone. So, in *R v Commissioners of Customs and Excise, ex p Lunn Poly Ltd*,[113] an EC judicial review concerning state aid,[114] Lord Woolf MR, in the Court of Appeal, said:[115]

> Where the issue is one of precedent fact, then sometimes it is necessary for there to be oral evidence and cross-examination ... In this case there was sensibly no application for cross-examination. While the task may be difficult, the Divisional Court, and this court on appeal, is usually well able to decide the relevant facts without the need for cross-examination of the evidence which was given by affidavit.

1.114   It was on this basis, for example, that Forbes J granted judicial review against the Ministry of Agriculture, Fisheries, and Food in respect of its designation of authorized places of entry for import of dairy goods both on the domestic law footing of irrationality and also (on precedent fact) as being in breach of (the then) Articles 30 and 36 EC.[116]

1.115   But there will be some cases where, even though judicial review is technically available and relevant as a process to determine the factual issues, the process of investigation is too protracted to merit such proceedings.

1.116   Thus, in *R v Derbyshire County Council, ex p Noble*[117] Woolf LJ observed as follows:[118]

> [T]he present application is one which is unsuitable for disposal on an application for judicial review—unsuitable because it clearly involves a conflict of fact and a conflict of evidence which would require [disclosure] and cross-examination. Cross-examination and [disclosure] can take place on applications for judicial review, but in the ordinary way judicial review is designed to deal with matters which can be resolved without resorting to these procedures.

1.117   And in *Roy v Kensington & Chelsea & Westminster Family Practitioner Committee*[119] Lord Lowry, referring to Woolf LJ's observation in *Ex p Noble*, stated that it:

> reminds us that oral evidence and [disclosure], although catered for by the rules, are not part of the ordinary stock-in-trade of the prerogative jurisdiction.[120]

---

[113]   The substantive public law relating to state aid is examined in Chapter 13.
[114]   [1999] Eu LR 653.
[115]   [1999] Eu LR 653, 662.
[116]   *R v MAFF, ex p Bell Lines Ltd* [1984] 2 CMLR 502.
[117]   [1990] ICR 808.
[118]   ibid 813.
[119]   [1992] 1 AC 624.
[120]   ibid 647. See, also, (eg) *R v IRC, ex p Rossminster* [1980] AC 952, per Lord Scarman.

In an EC context there may be some large damages claims against the State where the tak- **1.118**
ing of oral evidence would be too unwieldy for judicial review proceedings. So, too, the
detail of determining whether a public body has breached EC competition rules may raise
similar difficulties.

There may also, in particular EC cases, be reasons other than disputed issues of fact why the **1.119**
Administrative Court is an inappropriate forum. For example, in *Woolwich Equitable*
Building Society v Inland Revenue Commissioners[121] the fact that a restitutionary remedy was
sought was considered to render the case unsuitable for judicial review.[122] Similarly, in *R v*
Secretary of State for Employment, ex p Equal Opportunities Commission[123] the House of
Lords observed that a claim for redundancy pay the refusal of which was argued to contravene what is now Article 141 EC should proceed in the industrial tribunal. Again, though,
these cases need to be examined in their particular context. There may, for example, be EC
cases where a declaration is claimed as to the State's liability to make reparation in a number of alternative forms for an alleged violation of EC public law. On its face a declaration
of this kind would not have the effect that the proceedings should be commenced in a private as opposed to a public law forum.

Collateral challenges

Since the House of Lords' decision in *O'Reilly v Mackman* (above) the rigour of procedural **1.120**
exclusivity has been relaxed in a number of decisions. It is now well established that, in a
great many instances, public law issues may be ventilated outside judicial review. Raising
public issues in this way is known as the 'collateral challenge' exception to procedural
exclusivity.

The position may be summarized as follows:

(1) Claimants in private law proceedings may litigate public law issues where the issue **1.121**
    arises as a collateral issue in a claim for infringement of a right of the claimant arising
    under private law.[124] EC law is no exception to this.[125]
(2) A defendant in private law civil proceedings may raise a defence on the merits even if
    such defence involves issues of public law.[126]

---

[121] [1993] AC 70.

[122] ibid especially 200, per Lord Slynn.

[123] [1995] 1 AC 1.

[124] See per Lord Diplock in *O'Reilly v Mackman* [1983] 2 AC 237, 285. Lord Diplock's formulation
referred to challenging the invalidity of a 'decision' where it arises collaterally but this needs to be amended
slightly so as to encompass the *ratio* of the *EOC* case: see at para 1.119 above. Note, too, that in *Roy v*
Kensington & Chelsea & Westminster Family Practitioner Committee [1992] 1 AC 624 the House of Lords gave
a strong hint that it would take a generous or 'broad' approach to the collateral challenge exception under this
head: see, especially, per Lord Lowry, 653E–H.

[125] See paras 19.01–19.06.

[126] *Wandsworth London Borough Council v Winder* [1985] AC 461 especially n 509D, n per Lord Fraser:
the 'arguments for protecting public authorities against unmeritorious or dilatory challenges to their decisions have to be set against the arguments for preserving the ordinary rights of private citizens to defend themselves against unfounded claims'.

(3) Whether a defendant in criminal proceedings may challenge the validity of an act done under statutory authority by way of collateral challenge will depend upon the true construction of the statute in question. As Lord Hoffmann observed in *R v Wicks*:[127]

> The question must depend entirely upon the construction of the statute under which the prosecution is brought. The statute may require the prosecution to prove that the act in question is not open to challenge on any ground available in public law, or it may be a defence to show that it is. In such a case, the justices will have to rule upon the validity of the act. On the other hand, the statute may upon its true construction merely require an act which appears formally valid and has not been quashed by judicial review. In such an act nothing but the formal validity of the act will be relevant to an issue before the justices.

1.122 In EC law cases there will be considerable scope for application of collateral public law challenges. Defences to environmental and other prosecutions brought to secure compliance with EC obligations, damages claims and defences,[128] and—in such proceedings—the compatibility of legislative or administrative acts or omissions with relevant EC obligations may all raise important public law issues capable, in this fashion, of being litigated outside judicial review.

1.123 Collateral challenge is addressed in more detail in Chapter 19.[129]

Unclear borderline between public and private law

1.124 The courts are now also unlikely to insist on proceedings being commenced by judicial review where there is overlap or lack of clarity so as to make it obvious that the case should be commenced in the Administrative Court.

1.125 In *Mercury Ltd v Director General of Telecommunications*[130] the House of Lords approved the bringing of proceedings by originating summons seeking a declaration in private law proceedings, rather than judicial review, as to whether the Director General of Fair Trading had acted lawfully in the matters that he took into account when resolving a pricing issue between two parties to a contract who had, under the contract, made a reference to the Director.

1.126 Lord Slynn of Hadley observed that it was:[131]

> of particular importance to retain some flexibility, as the precise limits of what is called 'public law' and what is called 'private law' are by no means worked out . . . It has to be borne in mind that the overriding question is whether the proceedings constitute an abuse of process.

1.127 This flexibility has been emphasized in subsequent cases where, as explained above, the emphasis has been directed towards the consequences as opposed to the formalism of having commenced proceedings in the wrong forum.[132]

---

[127] [1998] AC 92, 112.

[128] For a case in point see *An Bord Bainne Cooperative Ltd (Irish Dairy Board) v Milk Marketing Board* [1984] 2 CMLR 584.

[129] See paras 19.01–19.06.

[130] [1996] 1 WLR 48.

[131] ibid at 57.

[132] See n 106 above. See, also, *Trustees of the Dennis Rye Pension Fund v Sheffield City Council* [1997] 4 All ER 747 which confirms that, if necessary, it seems that the private law court will apply public law safeguards if proceedings are unnecessarily commenced in the wrong forum.

In the EC context this may be especially apposite. For example, in *Bourgoin v MAFF*[133] **1.128**
Oliver LJ observed that the question of whether a directly effective provision created rights
in public or in private law bordered on the 'metaphysical'.[134]

Where judicial review proceedings must be brought

It is, nonetheless, important to recognize that most cases that are brought to establish that **1.129**
the State or an emanation of the State has violated EC law should be brought by way of
judicial review. Although the court is unlikely to penalize a claimant for the wrong choice
of procedure alone,[135] it will be astute to ensure that no procedural advantage has been
obtained by proceeding outside judicial review.

The close connection between many grounds for quashing a decision in EC law, under the **1.130**
HRA, and in domestic public law[136] make it all the more important that they are resolved
by specialist judges and in the most appropriate forum. This will usually be the Administrative
Court.

---

[133] [1986] 1 QB 716.
[134] ibid, 767.
[135] See para 1.102.
[136] See para 2.30.

2

THE EC LAW DIMENSION

A. EC Law Judicial Review Challenges—Their Underlying Basis

As explained in Chapter 1, there are distinctive features of EC law requiring careful consid- **2.01**
eration before a case can be identified as one in respect of which EC domestic public law
challenges (most usually in Administrative Court proceedings) are appropriate.

This chapter refers back to a number of concepts outlined in Chapter 1, and introduces **2.02**
others, so as to examine the general relationship between EC law on the one hand and
domestic law (including the HRA) on the other in domestic public law cases.

The most basic principle is that an EC domestic public law challenge—whether brought **2.03**
in its own right or as part of a challenge overlapping with domestic or HRA grounds of

review—must, in some fashion, derive from Treaty obligations. As Laws J observed in *R v MAFF, exp First City Trading Ltd*:[1]

> Where action is taken, albeit under domestic law, which falls within the scope of the Treaty's application, then of course the Court has the power and the duty to require that the Treaty be adhered to.

2.04 There are two important points of clarification that need to be made to the above statement. First, the fact that the Treaty contains an obligation on a Member State or State emanation[2] is a necessary but not sufficient condition of there being an effective EC ground of challenge. For the Treaty obligation to be capable of constituting a ground of challenge there must be some further EC principle (most often that of direct effect)[3] that enables individuals to bring a public law challenge.

2.05 Secondly, the expression 'scope of the Treaty's application' is still a matter of some controversy.[4] In general terms, EC grounds for seeking judicial review will certainly exist in a case within the scope of EC law and the scope of EC law undoubtedly includes matters covered directly by Treaty obligations. Judicial interpretation by the ECJ as to the meaning and scope of an EC Treaty provision is subject to a number of important EC general principles of law that are discussed in detail in Chapters 6–12.

2.06 The validity of a Treaty provision cannot be challenged by way of judicial review or, indeed, at all. But the true extent of a Treaty obligation may arise in domestic proceedings for judicial review. That obligation will condition the nature and extent of other measures (whether domestic or EC) that are within the scope of the Treaty's application. Most notably these measures include:

(1) EC legislation—necessarily derived from the Treaty—in the form (at least primarily as far as judicial review is concerned) of regulations and directives. This legislation is also subject to judicial interpretation in accordance with EC general principles of law and particular principles of interpretation. The validity of EC legislation in terms of its conformity with the Treaty provision from which it is derived and/or with general principles of EC law may be challenged at least indirectly in domestic judicial review proceedings (or where public law issues are raised by way of collateral challenge) provided that national measures are premised on the underlying legality of that EC legislation. However, as will be seen, it is most unusual for EC legislation to be challenged directly by way of domestic judicial review (but see para 2.23 below). Challenges are usually brought obliquely to the legality of EC legislation by way of domestic public law challenge where there is a national measure or decision of a national body the legality of which is argued to depend on the legality of particular EC legislation. As framed in a judicial review Claim Form and Grounds, the challenge will then be to the legality of the national measure, but by reference to the underlying allegedly defective EC legislation.

---

[1] [1997] 1 Eu LR 195.

[2] The scope of this expression is considered at paras 2.17 et seq.

[3] However, as explained in Chapter 1, direct effect may not be a necessary condition of seeking relief in judicial review or other public law proceedings given the principle of indirect effect: see paras 1.86–1.90.

[4] For further discussion see paras 6.31 et seq.

(2) National legislative measures purporting to transpose/implement EC law into domestic law or, as the case may be, to derogate from EC obligations on a lawful basis. Here, the meaning of domestic law is a matter for the national court but, as will be seen, that court must deploy special principles of interpretation and other doctrines derived from EC law in order to ascertain the true meaning of domestic law in its EC context and whether or not the measure (decision) under challenge has fully implemented the EC obligation. As mentioned in (1) above, some national measures may be unlawful because of an illegality of underlying EC legislation. Whilst domestic judicial review will lie to challenge the national measure on this basis there are important limitations on the jurisdiction of the Administrative Court which are outlined below. In practice, where the ground for challenging the legality of a national measure is the asserted illegality of EC legislation then the Administrative Court will be likely, provided that the ground has substance, to refer the case to the ECJ for a preliminary ruling under Article 234 (ex 177) EC.

(3) Domestic administrative acts or omissions[5] purporting to act directly in conformity with EC law or a national legislative measure derived from EC law. Here, similar principles apply and similar issues arise as in the case of national legislative measures.

So, in all domestic judicial review cases said to raise specific EC grounds of challenge with distinctive potential EC remedies, it is ultimately necessary to establish—as the underlying basis of entitlement to raise such challenges and to seek such remedies—that the national measure or administrative action in question is contrary to a Treaty obligation of some kind. **2.07**

B. Jurisdictional Limits of the Court in EC Law Judicial Review Cases

It is now well established that a national court does not have jurisdiction to declare acts of the EC authorities to be *invalid*.[6] **2.08**

The rationale for this limitation on domestic jurisdiction was explained by the ECJ in *Woodspring District Council v Bakers of Nailsea Ltd*.[7] The court said this: **2.09**

> Divergences between courts in Member States as to the validity of Community acts would be liable to place in jeopardy the very unity of the Community legal order and detract from the fundamental principle of legal certainty.[8]

---

⁵ Such acts and omissions include derogations from EC law.
⁶ See, especially, Case 314/85 *Foto-Frost v Hauptzollamt Lubeck-Ost* [1987] ECR 4199, paras 14–15. There is a qualified exception to this in that (see para 19 of *Foto-Frost*) '. . . the rule that national courts may not themselves declare Community acts invalid may have to be qualified in certain circumstances in the case of proceedings relating to an application for interim measures'. As to the jurisdiction of the Administrative Court to grant interim relief in such cases in the course of judicial review proceedings, see paras 3.137 et seq.
⁷ Case C–27/95 [1997] ECR I–19847.
⁸ ibid para 20.

2.10 This restriction does not, however, prevent a claimant from bringing judicial review proceedings directed to the validity of a Community act provided that there is a national measure to challenge. This is so for two reasons:

(1) Although the Administrative Court[9] (and any appellate court) may not pronounce acts of the EC authorities to be invalid, it may refer the case to the ECJ for a preliminary ruling under Article 234 (ex 177) EC since the ECJ is always competent to make such declaration.

(2) By contrast, the Administrative Court does possess jurisdiction to declare underlying EC acts to be *valid*. In that way, if the Administrative Court holds a Community act to be valid, a dissatisfied claimant may seek permission to appeal to the Court of Appeal coupled with an application for a preliminary ruling at that stage. As the ECJ observed in the *Woodspring* case:[10]

> ... national courts may consider the validity of a Community act and, if they consider that the grounds put forward before them by the parties in support of invalidity are unfounded, they may reject them, concluding that the measure is completely valid. In so doing, they are not calling into question the existence of the Community measure.

2.11 In view of the currently strict *locus standi* rules under Article 230 (ex 173) EC attaching to direct actions to the ECJ, it has been suggested that the inability of the national courts to declare a Community act to be invalid may create considerable injustice to claimants aggrieved by such act but unable to link the Community act with any national measure. For example, Mancini and Keeling argue as follows:

> A Regulation may, as a matter of substance, be patently and outrageously unlawful; it may breach the principles of non-discrimination and proportionality, violate fundamental rights and inflict huge financial loss on large numbers of persons; but unless one of those persons can show that he is somehow singled out by the Regulation and injured more severely than the category to which he belongs, he will be unable to challenge it directly before the European Court. All he can do is to defy the Regulation and wait till an attempt is made to enforce it against him in the national courts, where he may of course contest the validity of the Regulation and succeed in having the issue referred to the European Court under Article [234].[11]

2.12 However, the jurisdictional limitations on national courts to declare EC measures to be invalid ought not to result in practical difficulty. Since *R v Secretary of State for Employment, ex p Equal Opportunities Commission*,[12] it is clear that declaratory relief may lie to challenge matters that could not be the subject of quashing, prohibitory, or mandatory orders and that do not constitute a 'decision'. In *EOC* itself, for example, the challenge was to the contents of a letter expressing a view as to the compatibility of the Employment Protection (Consolidation) Act 1978 with EC law.

2.13 In the light of *EOC* there does not always have to be some national measure affecting the claimant before domestic judicial review proceedings may be commenced. Indeed, it is

---

[9] References to domestic judicial review proceedings include, where appropriate, public law issues raised by way of collateral challenges. See paras 1.120 et seq.

[10] See Case C–27/95 [1997] ECR I–19847, para 19.

[11] F Mancini and D Keeling, 'Democracy and the European Court of Justice' (1994) 57 MLR 175, 188.

[12] [1995] 1 AC 1.

now settled law that a national court has at least jurisdiction to make a reference to the ECJ relating to the validity of a directive in advance of the adoption of domestic implementing measures and where it considers the arguments relating to invalidity are well founded it *must* stay the proceedings and make a reference under Article 234.[13] In *R v Secretary of State for Health ex p Imperial Tobacco Ltd*,[14] for example, the Administrative Court requested a preliminary ruling under Article 234 (ex 177) EC as to the validity of a directive even though there was no national implementing legislation in force.

Care must be taken to distinguish between: (1) absence of jurisdiction and (2) the discretionary doctrine of prematurity whereby the Administrative Court may decline to grant relief in its discretion because an application for judicial review is made too early. **2.14**

In *Imperial Tobacco* (above) it was, arguably, not premature for judicial review proceedings to be issued to challenge the introduction of national measures to implement the provisions of a directive imposing the obligation on Member States to restrict tobacco advertising. This was because there was no power in the Member State not to implement the directive. Subsequently, in *Imperial Tobacco*,[15] and following the making of the reference, the claimants successfully sought an injunction to prevent the laying of domestic regulations to implement the directive. Turner J observed that the court might have reached a different conclusion if only a discrete part of the directive (as opposed to the directive in its entirety) had been the subject of legal challenge. **2.15**

In other cases, however, it may be premature to seek to challenge implementing domestic legislation even on the ground of an alleged underlying invalidity in prior EC legislation. This will especially be so where the Member State has discretion as to implementation and where the domestic measure, as passed, may not conflict with EC law at all.[16] **2.16**

C. Defendants to EC Law Judicial Review Challenges

From the perspective of EC law there is a distinction between 'public' and 'private' bodies which mirrors, though is not identical to, the dichotomy in domestic public law between public bodies amenable to judicial review (or on an analogous basis subject to liability under the HRA) and bodies exercising purely private functions that are outside the scope of judicial review altogether. **2.17**

However, the public/private distinction serves a different purpose in EC law. In EC law, unlike domestic public law, some enforceable obligations may undoubtedly lie against private individuals as well as against public bodies.[17] The principle rationale for an EC public/private **2.18**

---

[13] See Case C–344/04 *R (IATA and ELFAA) v Department of Transport* (nyr, 12 January 2006); *R (International Association of Independent Tanker Owners) v Secretary of State for Transport* [2006] EWHC 1577.

[14] [1999] Eu LR 582.

[15] [1999] COD 138, 140.

[16] For an instance of permission to apply for judicial review being refused on the ground of prematurity see Gravells, 'Disapplying an Act of Parliament pending a Preliminary Ruling: Constitutional Enormity or Community Law Right?' [1989] PL 568, n 25.

[17] Note, eg, the terms of Article 249 (ex 189) EC providing for the 'general application' of regulations.

divide is, rather, that in general terms it operates as a boundary to prevent *directives* from having so-called *horizontal effect*, that is consequences on third party private persons,

2.19 It is now well established under the doctrine of horizontal effect that directives may only be enforced against 'emanations of the State' and that they may not be applied in litigation between private individuals. The ambit of horizontal effect and possible exceptions to it is addressed in more detail below.[18] Its origin appears to lie in the fact that the Treaty source of authority for directives (Article 249 (ex 189) EC) makes directives binding only as to 'the result to be achieved'. Thus, there is a measure of subjective judgment on the part of the Member State in implementing directives. By contrast, private individuals have no power to legislate. So, whereas there would be unfairness in permitting a Member State to benefit from its illegality in relation to implementing a directive, no parallel unfairness lies in respect of individuals.[19]

2.20 There is though, undoubtedly, a similarity between the concept of an emanation of the State in EC law and that of: (1) public bodies amenable to domestic judicial review, and (2) 'public authorities' under the HRA.

2.21 For example, in *Foster v British Gas plc*[20] the ECJ held as follows:

> . . . a body, whatever its legal form, which has been made responsible pursuant to a measure adopted by the State, for providing a public service under the control of the State and has for that purpose special powers beyond those which result from the normal rules applicable in relations between individuals is included in any event among the bodies against which the provisions of a Directive capable of having direct effect may be relied upon.

2.22 Although this statement of general principle is made by reference to the enforceability of directives, it can readily be seen that the constituent elements of an emanation of the State are very similar to those needed to confer domestic judicial review jurisdiction on the Administrative Court and to engage liability under the HRA.

2.23 As appears from *Foster*, in order to constitute a State emanation for EC law purposes, the entity in question must: (1) act pursuant to responsibility under a State measure, (2) provide a public service, (3) do so under the control of the State, and (4) possess special powers over and above those pertaining to relations between individuals.

2.24 The test for amenability to domestic judicial review has become broader over the years. However, there must be an exercise of what may, loosely, be termed 'governmental' functions. So, whilst it is no longer necessary for there to be a statutory source of authority the functions being undertaken must, it has been observed, at least be 'woven into [a] system of governmental control'.[21] Such a requirement appears to connote many, if not all, of the elements required to establish an emanation of the State in EC law.

---

[18] See paras 2.161 et seq.

[19] See A Ward, *Judicial Review and the Rights of Private Parties in EC Law* (2000), 160–161.

[20] Case C–188/89 [1990] ECR 3313, para 20.

[21] *R v Disciplinary Committee of the Jockey Club, ex p Aga Khan* [1993] 1 WLR 909, per Sir Thomas Bingham MR.

Similarly, in order to be subject to obligations under the HRA there must be a 'public **2.25** authority' within the meaning of HRA, s 6. The meaning of this expression is not without difficulty.[22] In substance, however, there is a clear affinity between the type of entity amenable to domestic (non-HRA) judicial review and the notion of a 'public authority' under HRA, s 6 and the courts have been reluctant to give any broader meaning to those bodies susceptible to judicial review under the HRA than under ordinary domestic principles of amenability to review.[23]

For these reasons it is sometimes assumed that the expression 'emanation of the State' is, **2.26** at least for practical purposes, the same as the touchstone for susceptibility to domestic judicial review or subjection to the HRA.

Certainly, domestic court decisions on the bodies qualifying as State emanations in EC law **2.27** and limitations placed by the national courts upon that concept exemplify the close relationship between the notion of an emanation of the State and the domestic judicial review jurisdiction of the Administrative Court. In *Foster*, applying the above-mentioned principles enunciated by the ECJ, the House of Lords held that British Gas, prior to privatization, was an emanation of the State. By contrast, Rolls Royce (before privatization) was not.[24] In other borderline cases, the national courts have often come down on the side of an entity being an emanation of the State. Thus, for example, both a voluntary-aided school[25] and a recently privatized water company[26] have been held to be State emanations.

However, care is needed before simply transposing the criteria for potential amenability to **2.28** a particular form of liability in EC law (enforceability of directives) to the amenability, more generally, of these challenges or other forms of EC challenge to domestic judicial review. Nor, in any event, are State emanations for the purpose of the enforcement of directives co-extensive with all forms of EC bodies that are amenable to judicial review under CPR Pt 54. The following points should, in particular, be noted:

(1) Given that the purpose of fashioning a principle of State emanation is in order to ensure that EC directives are enforced fairly against the body responsible for implementation, the relationship between the State and any surrogate body might be thought to be very close.

---

[22] See, eg, D Oliver, 'Functions of a Public Nature under the Human Rights Act' [2004] PL 329.

[23] See, eg, for the narrower approach, *Poplar Housing and Regeneration Community Association v Donoghue* [2002] QB 48, 65, per Lord Woolf. See also *R (Heather) v Leonard Cheshire Foundation* [2002] EWCA Civ 336, [2002] 2 All ER 936. cf *Aston Cantlow and Wilmcote v Wallbank* [2003] UKHL 37, [2004] 1 AC 46. It should, however, be noted that a number of recent decisions of the European Court of Human Rights have addressed circumstances in which the acts of non-governmental organizations can engage the responsibility of the State. Such bodies would not be amenable to judicial review but would nonetheless, in all probability, render the body in question a public authority under the HRA: see, eg, *Wos v Poland* (judgment 1 March 2005); *Sychev v Ukraine* (judgment 11 October 2005). Notwithstanding these cases, in *R (Johnson) v Havering LBC* [2006] EWHC 1714 Forbes J held that the principles established in *R (Heather) v Leonard Cheshire Foundation* (above) were binding and that (for the purposes of the HRA) a private care home making arrangements for persons in need of care and accommodation was not exercising public functions under the HRA.

[24] *Doughty v Rolls Royce* [1992] ICR 358.

[25] *National Union of Teachers v Governing Body of St Mary's Church of England (Aided) Junior School* [1997] ICR 334.

[26] *Griffin v South West Water Services Ltd* [1994] IRLR 15.

However, the concept of a State emanation has been extremely broadly applied in the case law and, arguably, outside the parameters of domestic judicial review. The same imperatives that apply to the enforcement of directives in EC law do not necessarily apply to the bodies amenable to the domestic judicial review jurisdiction (including HRA cases). As one commentator has observed in relation to EC law:

> . . . under the broad conception of the term 'public authority' as applied in Community law, the range of actors required to comply with directly effective directives has included entities that lie at the very cusp of government authority. Indeed, it could be said that bodies that might have been more comfortably viewed as falling within the private sector have been obliged to observe Articles 10 and 249 duties pertaining to directives.[27]

(2) Under the HRA, the test for whether a 'public authority' has functions that are 'public' in nature (the test for amenability to judicial review)[28] will depend upon whether the authority is a standard or a 'hybrid' authority. In the latter case only 'public' functions of the authority give rise to liability to obligations under the HRA. Such obligations are, by definition, primarily enforceable by way of judicial review. But if the authority is a standard authority, such as a local authority, then it is subject to the 'reach' of the HRA in respect of the exercise of *all* of its functions.[29] However, it is at least questionable whether *all* the functions of a standard authority are, in principle, reviewable under CPR Pt 54 by the Administrative Court. In the same way, an emanation of the State has obligations in EC law that may go well beyond a traditional classification of its functions as 'public' in nature. Only its 'public' functions would appear to be enforceable by way of domestic judicial review.

(3) Outside the important area of the enforceability of directives there may be entities that are judicially reviewable in an EC context even if such bodies do not fulfil the criteria necessary to constitute an emanation of the State. Provided that a case is within the scope of EC law[30] then EC general principles of law will apply. One of those principles—the principle of effectiveness—requires effective remedies to be available in national courts for breaches of EC rights.[31] So, if the absence of a remedy in judicial review meant that no remedy was otherwise available in national law, it is likely in an EC context that the Administrative Court would, in order to comply with the principle of effectiveness, be required to assume jurisdiction over an ostensibly 'private' body.[32]

2.29 In short, it cannot simply be assumed the concept of State emanation is co-extensive with domestic judicial review jurisdiction (including HRA jurisdiction). It is very important on

---

[27] See Ward (n 19 above), 162.

[28] Materially, CPR r 54.2 defines judicial review as a claim to review the lawfulness of 'the exercise of a public function'.

[29] Note the discussion in Oliver (n 22 above) 347–348. See, also, Case 152/84 *Marshall v Southampton and South-West Hampshire Area Health Authority (Teaching)* [1986] QB 401; Case 222/84 *Johnston v Chief Constable of the Royal Ulster Constabulary* [1986] ECR 1651.

[30] For analysis of this concept see paras 6.31 et seq.

[31] See, further, for application of the principle of effectiveness to remedies, paras 5.13–5.22.

[32] The same considerations do not necessarily apply to the HRA analogue since the requirement of providing an effective remedy for breaches of fundamental rights under the ECHR (Art 13 ECHR) has not been incorporated into domestic law under the HRA.

a practical level for practitioners in judicial review to understand the general approach of the ECJ and domestic courts to the question of whether a body is or is not a State emanation. Resolution of that question may well affect obtainable remedies including, significantly, that of damages.[33]

D. Relationship between EC Law and Other Grounds of Challenge in Judicial Review Cases

General

In considering, so far as the Administrative Court is concerned, the relationship in an EC case between: (1) available grounds of review in domestic judicial review and/or under the HRA and (2) available grounds of review in EC law, the following points should be borne in mind: **2.30**

(1) The traditional tripartite classification of the available grounds for seeking domestic judicial review is that adumbrated by Lord Diplock in *Council of Civil Service Unions v Minister for the Civil Service*.[34] That formulation recognises three principal grounds of review, namely: (1) illegality, (2) irrationality, and (3) procedural impropriety. One or more of these grounds may, at least in name, be deployed in an EC judicial review challenge as they may in a case involving a complaint of a breach under the HRA. For example, a breach of an EC regulation will afford an illegality ground for judicial review of national measures that conflict with the EC regulation.

(2) However, the principles to be applied in determining—in an EC context—whether a national measure is unlawful or unfair are those to be derived from the Treaty, the relevant case law of the ECJ and general principles of EC law developed by that court. Further, the operation and availability of administrative law principles in EC-based applications for judicial review will often depend upon other distinct doctrines of EC law such as those of direct effect, supremacy of EC law, and special principles of interpretation.[35] What this means is that, amongst other things, a concept familiar to English administrative lawyers such as procedural impropriety or legitimate expectation may have to be applied differently in an EC context from an HRA or purely domestic context.[36]

(3) Even well-established principles of statutory interpretation may have to be applied differently in an EC judicial review challenge. It has, for example, been held that an Act of Parliament enacted subsequently to the European Communities Act 1972 cannot have the effect of *impliedly* repealing the 1972 Act—itself a 'constitutional statute'.[37] Thus, in *Thoburn v Sunderland City Council*[38] (the Metric Martyrs case) a Divisional Court held that subordinate legislation adopted in 1994 under s 2(2) of the 1972 Act repealed the

---

[33] See, generally, Chapter 5.
[34] [1985] AC 374.
[35] See paras 2.58 et seq.
[36] See, generally, Chapters 6–12.
[37] *Thorburn v Sunderland City Council* [2002] 3 WLR 247, paras 61 and 68–70.
[38] [2002] 3 WLR 247.

Weights and Measures Act 1985 rather than the 1985 Act having the effect of impliedly repealing the 1972 Act by permitting subordinate legislation contrary to EC law.

(4) Despite this, domestic administrative law principles may have an independent, and sometimes important, part to play in a challenge primarily founded on EC law. Whilst, given the supremacy of EC law,[39] principles of domestic law cannot 'trump' those of EC law, there may be particular domestic law reasons why a national measure is unlawful.

(5) Certainly, where an EC challenge succeeds on EC grounds the scope of relief will be wider than if it succeeds on purely domestic grounds. On purely domestic judicial review grounds there can—because of the doctrine of parliamentary sovereignty—be no assault on the validity of primary legislation. In a challenge under the HRA, the same doctrine also prevents a direct challenge to the validity of primary legislation although a declaration of incompatibility may be obtained on the footing that the statutory provision in question is incompatible with the ECHR. However, in effect, directly effective rights derived from EC law may be used as a ground of review to challenge even the validity of primary legislation. This is because of the principle of the supremacy of EC law examined below.[40] Although—since it is *Parliament* that is required to implement an international Treaty—there are constitutional difficulties in granting a declaration that the Government is in breach of EC obligations in respect of particular primary legislation[41] the same effect can be achieved by means of a declaration of incompatibility. Where EC law differs from the position under the HRA is that under EC law the courts must give effect to rules of EC law even where this involves suspending or disapplying the provisions of primary legislation.[42]

European Communities Act 1972, s 2

2.31 Difficult constitutional issues can arise involving the application of the domestic public law ultra vires doctrine in cases with an EC element. Such cases exemplify the point made above that there may be cases where domestic public law rather than an EC ground of challenge is the proper and sole basis for a national measure being unlawful.

2.32 Section 2(2)[43] of the European Communities Act 1972 provides (materially) as follows:

(2) Subject to Schedule 2 to this Act, at any time after its passing Her Majesty may by Order in Council, and any designated Minister or department may by regulations, make provision:

(a) for the purpose of implementing any Community obligation of the United Kingdom, or enabling any such obligation to be implemented, or of enabling any rights enjoyed or to be enjoyed by the United Kingdom under or by virtue of the Treaties to be exercised; or

(b) for the purpose of dealing with matters arising out of or related to any such obligation or rights or the coming into force, or the operation from time to time, of subsection (1) above;

---

[39] See paras 2.60 et seq.
[40] See paras 2.60 et seq.
[41] *R v Secretary of State for Employment, ex p Equal Opportunities Commission* [1995] 1 AC 1, 27.
[42] Case C–213/89 *R v Secretary of State for Transport, ex p Factortame Ltd (No 2)* [1991] 1 AC 603.
[43] For further analysis of s 2 of the 1972 Act (s 2(1) and (4)), see paras 2.68 et seq.

and in the exercise of any statutory power or duty, including any power to give directions or to legislate by means of orders, rules, regulations or other subordinate instrument, the person entrusted with the power or duty may have regard to the objects of the Communities and to any such obligations or rights as aforesaid . . .

Plainly, subordinate legislation that is itself contrary to EC law or that derives from invalid   **2.33**
Community legislation will, necessarily, be ultra vires (1972 Act, s 2(2)(a)). As Henry J put it in *R v MAFF, ex p FEDESA*:[44]

> If the directive is invalid, it is incapable of creating a Community obligation. Without a Community obligation, a statutory instrument purporting to give effect to a Community obligation is void.

To that extent, an ultra vires challenge would be founded on analysis of the true content of   **2.34**
the EC obligation. Domestic ultra vires would add little to the argument.

However, there may also be circumstances in which *as a matter of domestic law* subordinate   **2.35**
legislation that is passed under s 2 of the 1972 Act may be ultra vires even where the underlying EC legislation is valid and has been complied with.

Here, the question will be the scope of s 2(2)(a)–(b) of the 1972 Act. To what extent does   **2.36**
s 2 enable subordinate legislation to be made that is not directly implementing any EC obligation at all.

The issue had been the subject of conflicting decisions in earlier cases but was directly   **2.37**
addressed by the Court of Appeal in *Oakley Inc v Animal Ltd and the Secretary of State for Trade and Industry*.[45]

There, the Secretary of State (as intervener) appealed against a first instance ruling that the   **2.38**
Registered Designs Regulations 2001, reg 12, was ultra vires. Member States were required under Directive (EC) 98/71 to approximate their laws in respect of registered designs. But Article 11.8 provided an option enabling Member States to derogate and retain in force existing legislation for designs registered under that legislation (old designs). The Secretary of State issued the 2001 Regulations which (pursuant to Article 11.8) retained in force the old designs.

At first instance, the Deputy High Court Judge considered that a policy choice permitted   **2.39**
by the directive had to be enacted by primary legislation and went beyond the power permitted by either s 2(2)(a) or (b) of the 1972 Act because it was not an obligation to which s 2 referred. He adopted what he suggested was a narrow approach to s 2 because it operated as a Henry VIII clause allowing, in effect, primary legislation to be passed by subordinate legislation.

This literal and narrow approach to the reach of s 2 was rejected by the Court of Appeal.   **2.40**
In allowing the appeal, the Court of Appeal held that s 2(2) was not a Henry VIII clause and that it was *sui generis*. By s 2(2)(a) of the 1972 Act Parliament had provided a machinery for

---

[44] [1988] 3 CMLR 661, para 5.
[45] [2005] EWCA Civ 1191, [2006] 2 WLR 294.

implementing results which, under Article 249 EC, it was bound to achieve. Waller LJ observed (para 20) that:

> In so far as the United Kingdom uses secondary legislation under Section 2(2)(a) to bring into force directives it does not seem to me to be meaningful to talk in terms of narrow construction or otherwise; the regulations are bringing into force that directive and obligations flowing from that directive, and the correct approach is to construe the regulations by reference to the directive which is being introduced.

2.41 The court considered that 'a line by line approach to the Directive' was not envisaged by s 2(2)(a) and that it was illogical to infer that in enacting s 2(2)(a) Parliament could possibly have intended to require further primary legislation in order to keep existing primary legislation in force.

2.42 In relation to s 2(2)(b) the Court of Appeal did not pronounce definitively on its scope. Somewhat imprecisely, Waller LJ said (para 39):

> It seems to me that Section 2(2)(b) from its position in Section 2, from the fact that it adds something to both subsection (1) and (2), and from its very wording is a subsection to enable further measures to be taken which naturally arise from or closely relate to the primary purpose being achieved. I accept that I will be accused of adding the words 'naturally' and 'closely', but I believe that describes the context which provides the meaning of the words.

2.43 May LJ reasoned (para 47) as follows:

> There is a distinction between providing something which, although it is a choice, is a choice which the implementation of the Directive requires you to make, and one which is not so required, but which has the effect of tidying things up or making closely related original choices which the Directive does not necessarily require. Section 2(2)(b) is confined by its words and context.

2.44 Jacob LJ observed (para 79) as follows:

> My own view, provisional though it must be in the absence of any specific context relevant to this case, is this: that s 2(2)(a) covers all forms of implementation— whether by way of choice of explicit option or by way of supply of detail . . . s 2(2)(a) . . . adds more . . . How much more must depend on the particular circumstances of the case . . . Whether a particular statutory instrument falls within [the phrase 'matters arising out of or related to'] must depend on what it purports to do and the overall context.

2.45 The Court of Appeal was careful not to rule on whether Otton LJ had been correct in giving s 2(2)(b) a wide scope in dicta expressed in *R v Secretary of State for Trade and Industry, ex p Unison*.[46]

2.46 The result arrived at so far as s 2(2)(a) of the 1972 Act is concerned is, plainly, sensible. In *Department of the Environment, Food and Rural Affairs v Asda Ltd*[47] a similar broad approach (albeit without reference to s 2) to interpretation of the vires of domestic regulations

---

[46] [1996] ICR 1003. cf, per Lord Johnston in *Addison v Denholm Ship Management (UK) Ltd* [1997] ICR 770 who queried the broad scope accorded to s 2(2)(b) in *Unison*. In *Betts v Brintel Helicopters Ltd* [1997] 2 All ER 840, 853–4, the Court of Appeal noted the discrepancy between *Unison* and *Addison* but did not find it necessary to decide the point. In *Oakley* the Court of Appeal was generally critical of Lord Johnston's restrictive approach to s 2(2)(b).

[47] [2003] UKHL 71, [2004] 1 WLR 105.

was taken by the House of Lords. It was there held that subordinate legislation may implement not merely existing EC obligations but also future amendments to those obligations.

Nonetheless, there may be more complex cases where, if the concept of an EC obligation is **2.47** made over-broad, the passing of subordinate national legislation under s 2 of the 1972 Act would entail onerous burdens on the Member State including the national court. This may follow from the fact that even where a directive or regulation contains no penalties or monitoring procedure, Article 10 (5) EC 'requires the Member States to take all measures necessary to guarantee the application and effectiveness of Community law'.[48] For this reason, care must be given by the national court when scrutinizing the legality of statutory instruments issued under s 2(2)(a) or (b) of the 1972 Act. This is a potentially fertile area for domestic public law challenges (or defences by way of collateral challenge) and, as *Oakley* appears to suggest, there is some scope for argument on a case-by-case basis.

E. Overlapping Grounds

As mentioned above, even though a claim said to be based on EC law fails, there may—on **2.48** the same facts—be a distinctive claim founded on purely domestic principles of administrative law or applying the separate principles of interpretation under the HRA (including judgments of the European Court of Human Rights in Strasbourg).

This may occur, most obviously, in three situations: **2.49**

(1) When properly analysed, the claim—though initially based on EC law arguments—is not a case within the scope of EC law[49] at all.
(2) The challenge may be able to be atomized with part of the case being capable of being determined by recourse to EC law and part by reference to domestic principles (including HRA principles) of law.
(3) EC law principles do not enable the claim to succeed but, taken in isolation, domestic or HRA principles would do.

In the first scenario, there is no difficulty. If the case does not fall within the province of EC law **2.50** it follows that principles of EC law cannot be applied. The challenge may only be determined by recourse to the relevant system or systems of law appropriate to the case. There is, thus, no conflict between EC law and the application of domestic (including HRA) principles.

Similarly, in the second model, there is no conflict between EC and domestic law in applying **2.51** each system of law as appropriate to the challenge. Examples have been given above in the context of the operation of s 2(2) of the European Communities Act 1972. It may be, for example, that on the same set of facts a judicial review challenge is made to domestic subordinate legislation purporting to implement an EC obligation. There may be an EC challenge to the validity of the underlying EC legislation. That challenge will be determined by reference to EC principles. However, there could be a separate challenge to the vires of the same measure

---

[48] Case 177/95 *Ebony Maritime and Loten Navigation Co Ltd v Preffetto della Provincia di Brindisi* (judgment 27 February 1997) para 95.
[49] For analysis of what this means, see paras 6.31 et seq.

under s 2(2) independent of the legality of the underlying EC legislation. In such a case the legality of the subordinate legislation might be determined solely by reference to domestic law principles such as the true 'reach' of s 2(2) or there may be mixed EC and domestic law issues such as the nature of the EC obligation in question and the true scope of s 2(2).

2.52   However, it is the third possibility that can give rise to problems. In a case falling within the scope of EC law, where the EC arguments have failed, the application of discrete domestic and/or HRA arguments may sometimes, if they would produce a different result, be inconsistent with EC law. For example, as is separately explained,[50] the ECJ has not always applied the ECHR in the same way as has the European Court of Human Rights. This is so because the ECHR is not, of itself, a source of EC law but is, rather, an indicator of common values in the Member States. Further, of necessity, the ECJ analyses fundamental rights so as to give effect to the particular imperatives of EC law. This may not always produce the same result as an interpretation under the HRA.

2.53   It seems probable that, at least in most cases, the fact that a different outcome is reached by application of (for example) HRA principles to that arrived at applying EC principles does not make it impermissible for the Administrative Court to apply the HRA. Indeed, subject to overriding requirements of EC law, it would appear to be unlawful for the Administrative Court not to apply the HRA since—as a public authority under HRA, s 6—the court must act compatibly with the ECHR.

2.54   A good example of this is afforded by the facts of *R (International Transport Roth GmbH) v Secretary of State for the Home Department*.[51] There, the legislative regime imposing immigration penalties on truckers in whose lorries clandestine entrants arrived was challenged by way of judicial review. There were mixed grounds of challenge under both the HRA (Article 6 and Article 1 of Protocol 1) and under EC law where it was contended that there was an unlawful interference with EC Treaty rights as to freedom of movement of goods and/or freedom to provide services.

2.55   At first instance, the claimants succeeded on both grounds. But, on appeal, the Court of Appeal whilst upholding (by a majority) the HRA arguments, allowed the Government's appeal in part and held unanimously that there was no unlawful interference with Treaty rights. Although a different outcome was, therefore, reached by application of HRA rather than EC principles there was no conflict between HRA and EC law.[52]

---

[50] See Chapter 12, especially at para 12.100.

[51] [2002] EWCA Civ 158, [2003] QB 728. This case is the subject of more detailed examination in a case analysis in Chapter 17.

[52] Of course, the outcome may—from the claimant's point of view—be successful from application of EC law as opposed to HRA or other domestic grounds of challenge. For an example at first instance see *R (Watts) v Bedford Primary Care Trust* [2004] EWCA Civ 166, [2004] 2 CMLR 55. Although the Court of Appeal made a reference under Art 234 (ex 177) EC as to whether the government is required to fund medical treatment abroad by reason of NHS delays, Munby J at first instance held in the claimant's favour on the EC issues but ruled against her on the HRA submissions. The ECJ has now delivered judgment in the claimant's favour— see further Chapter 19 where the case is the subject of a detailed case analysis. Note, too, *R v Chief Constable of Sussex, ex p International Trader's Ferry Ltd* [1999] 2 AC 418 where at first instance a Divisional Court ruled in favour of the claimants applying EC proportionality but against the claimants on *Wednesbury* irrationality grounds. However, both the Court of Appeal and the House of Lords ruled against the claimants on both grounds holding that the same outcome was produced whichever of the two tests was applied.

However, to the extent that an outcome produced by applying HRA principles would pro- **2.56**
duce an *incompatibility* with EC law it seems clear that the national court could not apply
the HRA without contravening its duties to follow rulings of the ECJ. This is not least
because the national court is itself an emanation of the State under Article 10 (ex 5) EC and
may not act incompatibly with EC law. Although there is a parallel provision in HRA, s 6,
the doctrine of the supremacy of EC law[53] over domestic law (including, it must be
supposed, the HRA) means that EC law ought to prevail over any contrary outcome.

A situation in which potential conflict could, at least in theory, occur is where a successful **2.57**
outcome under the HRA was itself contrary to EC law as being in tension with a competing EC Treaty right. In particular, there have been instances where there is a divergence
between rulings of the ECJ and the European Court of Human Rights as to the meaning
and scope of a relevant Convention right.[54] In such cases, so far as the EC dimension of the
case is concerned, the English court would appear to be bound to follow the ECJ ruling.[55]

F. Special Features of EC Law Judicial Review Challenges

Four distinctive principles

There are at least four distinctive principles that must be confronted when arguing EC **2.58**
cases before the Administrative Court. They are:

(1) The principle of the supremacy of EC law over domestic law.
(2) Distinct principles of interpretation.
(3) General principles of EC law.
(4) Direct effect and the horizontal and vertical effect of directives.

The supremacy principle and the nature of horizontal and direct effect are necessary fea- **2.59**
tures that flow from the imposition of EC law on national legal systems with effects on individuals and undertakings. By contrast, general principles of EC law and special principles
of interpretation are principles that are also intrinsic to establishing the proper content of
EC law. The various principles set out above are often applied in combination and should
not, necessarily, always be regarded as separate in character. Thus, for example, the general
principle of effectiveness of EC law would, as part of the general principles of EC law, be
compromised if—on the facts of a particular case—EC law were not accorded supremacy
over national law. Similarly, interpretation of legislative measures requires statutes to be
interpreted insofar as is possible consistently with the general principles of EC law. So, the
interpretation of Acts of Parliament must, in an EC context, involve the application of general principles of EC law. It is, indeed, via the EC principles of interpretation that general
principles of EC law are applied by the national courts.

---

[53] See paras 2.60 et seq.
[54] See paras 12.100 et seq.
[55] See paras 12.128 et seq.

Supremacy of EC law

The issue

2.60 Supremacy of EC law is an extremely important doctrine in terms of domestic judicial review. As a principle it is unequivocal and unyielding. In the words of one commentator, it connotes that 'the most minor piece of technical Community legislation ranks above the most cherished constitutional norm'.[56] It also means that not only the national courts but also public bodies susceptible to judicial review must, equally, give effect to EC law and not apply inconsistent provisions (even statutory provisions) of national law.[57] It is by no means clear, though, how far this latter obligation extends and the exact application to public bodies of EC doctrines that are applicable to the Administrative Court such as legal certainty (the operation of precedent) and the autonomy of national procedural rules.[58]

2.61 In determining the nature and degree of primacy of EC law over domestic law it is necessary, in a domestic judicial review context, to address the problem from the perspective of:

(1) Pronouncements of the ECJ.

(2) Domestic legislation and the approach of the national courts.

(3) Limitations to the principle of supremacy.

ECJ jurisprudence

2.62 So far as the ECJ is concerned, the position—at least in respect of directly effective provisions of EC law—is clear. The ECJ has consistently ruled that provisions of EC law have legal supremacy and must prevail over inconsistent provisions of domestic law.

2.63 The basis for the doctrine was first hinted at in *Van Gend en Loos*.[59] Although the case was largely concerned with the principle of direct effect, the ECJ pointed out that:

> . . . the Community constitutes a new legal order in international law, for whose benefit the States have limited their sovereign rights, albeit within limited fields.

2.64 In *Costa v ENEL*[60] the ECJ went further, observing that:

> The reception, within the laws of each Member State, of provisions having a Community source, and more particularly of the terms and of the spirit of the Treaty, has as a corollary the impossibility, for the Member State, to give preference to a unilateral and subsequent measure against a legal order accepted by them on a basis of reciprocity.

2.65 In *Simmenthal*,[61] the ECJ was even more specific. It stated in the clearest terms not only that EC law prevailed over domestic legislation even if the latter was adopted

---

[56] S Weatherill, *Law and Integration in the European Union* (1995), 106. See, also, *A v Chief Constable of West Yorkshire* [2005] 1 AC 51, para 9, per Lord Bingham: '[i]t is, of course, well established that the law of the Community prevails over any provision of domestic law inconsistent with it'.

[57] Case 103/88 *Fratelli Constanzo SpA v Commune di Milano* [1989] ECR 1839.

[58] For further discussion of the extent of the *Constanzo* ruling, see M Claes, *The National Courts' Mandate in the European Constitution* (2006) ch 10.

[59] Case 26/62 *Van Gend en Loos v Nederlandse Administratie der Belastingen* [1963] ECR 1, 3.

[60] Case 6/64 [1964] ECR 585.

[61] Case 106/77 *Amministrazione delle Finanze dello Stato v Simmenthal SpA* [1978] ECR 629, para 21.

after the Treaty but also that the national offending provision must be set aside
It said this:

> ... every national court must, in a case within its jurisdiction, apply Community law in its
> entirety and protect rights which the latter confers on individuals and must accordingly set
> aside any provision of national law which may conflict with it, whether prior or subsequent
> to the Community rule.

The statement in *Simmenthal* was restated by the ECJ in *R v Secretary of State for Transport,*   **2.66**
ex p Factortame Ltd (No 2).[62] There, the ECJ held that English domestic legal rules preventing the grant of interim injunctive relief against the Crown were incompatible with EC law
as impairing its effectiveness in terms of the protection of asserted EC Treaty rights.

Applying *Simmenthal,* the ECJ ruled that interim relief must be available, and the domes-   **2.67**
tic prohibition set aside, even where—according to the logic of the court's judgment—that
involved suspending the operation of an Act of Parliament. As the Court stated:

> The full effectiveness of Community law would be ... impaired if a rule of national law could
> prevent a court seized of a dispute governed by Community law from granting interim relief in
> order to ensure the full effectiveness of the judgment to be given on the existence of the rights
> claimed under Community law. It follows that a court which in those circumstances would
> grant interim relief, if it were not for a rule of national law, is obliged to set aside that rule.[63]

Supremacy in terms of domestic legislation and the general approach of the English courts

So far as EC law is concerned, the legislative position in domestic law is regulated by the   **2.68**
European Communities Act 1972. Whatever the ambit of that Act (see below) there is no
doubt that EC law takes priority over, to say the least, the overwhelming majority of national
measures. It extends, of course, not merely to legislative provisions and to proceedings before
national courts but also to the exercise of an administrative discretion which must be exercised
in conformity with EC law.[64] It may also be used as a defence to a criminal charge founded on
incompatible national legislation.[65]

Section 2(1) of the 1972 Act stipulates:

> All such rights, powers, liabilities, obligations and restrictions from time to time created or   **2.69**
> arising by or under the Treaties, and all such remedies and procedures from time to time pro-
> vided for by or under the Treaties, as in accordance with the Treaties are without further
> enactment to be given legal effect or used in the United Kingdom shall be recognised and
> available in law, and be enforced, allowed and followed accordingly; and the expression
> 'enforceable Community right' and similar expressions shall be read as referring to one to
> which this subsection applies.

---

[62] Case C–213/89 [1991] AC 603.

[63] ibid para 21. The obligation to set aside incompatible national rules may even extend to national provi-
sions that—albeit incompatible—are not in practice applied: see Case 167/73 *Commission v France* [1974]
ECR 359. Incompatibility may sometimes be indirect as well as direct: see, eg, Case 83/78 *Pigs Marketing
Board v Redmond* [1978] ECR 2347, para 56.

[64] See, eg, *R v Secretary of State for the Home Department, ex p the Mayor and Burgess of the London Borough
of Harrow* [1996] 2 CMLR 524.

[65] Case 269/80 *R v Tymen* [1981] ECR 3079.

2.70   As explained at para 2.32 above, s 2(2) of the 1972 Act confers power for the further implementation of EC obligations through subordinate legislation.[66] Section 2(4) then provides
(materially) thus:

> . . . any such provision . . . as might be made by Act of Parliament, and any enactment passed
> or to be passed . . . shall be construed and have effect subject to the foregoing provisions of
> this section.

2.71   It is not immediately obvious whether the combined effect of s 2(1) and (4) is to operate as
a statutory reflection of the principle of supremacy of EC law on a *Simmenthal* basis or
whether it has a lesser effect, namely that of representing merely an obligation–albeit an
important one—of interpretation.

2.72   There would appear to be little constitutional difficulty, so far as the effect of the 1972 Act
is concerned, in relation to the interpretation and legal effect of both primary and subordinate legislation passed *before* that Act came into force. To the extent that it is inconsistent
with EC law such legislation is impliedly repealed by the passing of the 1972 Act.[67]
Similarly, post-1972 EC-incompatible subordinate legislation relying for its validity upon
enabling pre-1972 Act statutory authority is unlawful because its source of authority has
also been impliedly repealed.

2.73   Difficulty arises in relation to EC-incompatible primary legislation passed after 1972, and
in relation to post-1972 subordinate legislation that is inconsistent with EC law and which
derives its authority from a post-1972 statute.

2.74   These issues have arisen in the case law but have not, thus far, all been decisively resolved.
Different views have been expressed at different times. For example, in *HP Bulmer Ltd
v J Bollinger SA*[68] and in *Garland v British Rail Engineering*[69] *obiter* views were expressed by
(respectively) Lord Denning MR in the Court of Appeal and by Lord Diplock in the House
of Lords to the effect that an expressly worded statute passed after 1972 would have to be
followed by the English courts *even if it were inconsistent with EC law.*

2.75   However, since those early cases, specific situations have arisen in which the problems of
post-1972 domestic legislation conflicting with EC law have had to be examined more
closely by the English courts.

2.76   The various *Factortame* cases[70] have had to consider the *Simmenthal* principle in the context of a complaint by Spanish shipowners relating to the exclusion of their fleets from UK
territorial waters. The complaint involved the contention that certain provisions of the

---

[66]   This power is expressed to be subject to Sch 2 to the Act. Schedule 2 specifies a number of exceptions to
the power as, eg, the power to increase taxation, the power to introduce retrospective legislation, or the power
to create new criminal offences.

[67]   See, eg, Case 121/85 *Conegate v HM Customs and Excise* [1987] QB 254.

[68]   [1974] Ch 401.

[69]   [1983] 2 AC 751.

[70]   *R v Secretary of State for Transport, ex p Factortame Ltd* [1990] 2 AC 85; *(No 2)* [1991] 1 AC 603;
(No 3) [1992] QB 680; *(No 4)* [1996] QB 404; *(No 5)* [1999] 3 WLR 1062.

Merchant Shipping Act 1988 and dependent subordinate legislation were contrary to EC laws on freedom of establishment and discrimination.[71]

Initially, the approach of the House of Lords, in the first *Factortame* case, following an application in the course of judicial review proceedings that the 1988 Act be disapplied as an interim measure, was to hold that there was no power to disapply an Act of Parliament *ad interim* even if it was incompatible with EC law. Nor, in any event, could interim injunctive relief be granted against the Crown (a rule of national law). However, the House referred the question of whether the absence of interim relief violated EC law under the then Article 177 (now 234) EC to the ECJ for a preliminary ruling. **2.77**

Following the ECJ's ruling that *Simmenthal* must be applied[72] the case came back before the House of Lords. The dicta of Lord Bridge are significant. He said this:[73] **2.78**

> Some public comments on the decision of the Court of Justice, affirming the jurisdiction of the courts of the member states to override national legislation if necessary to enable interim relief to be granted in protection of rights under Community law, have suggested that this was a novel and dangerous invasion by a Community institution of the sovereignty of the United Kingdom Parliament. But such comments are based on a misconception. If the supremacy within the European Community of Community law over the national law of member states was not always inherent in the EEC Treaty it was certainly well established in the jurisprudence of the Court of Justice long before the United Kingdom joined the Community. Thus, whatever limitation of its sovereignty Parliament accepted when it enacted the European Communities Act 1972 was entirely voluntary. Under the terms of the 1972 Act it has always been clear that it was the duty of a United Kingdom court, when delivering final judgment, to override any rule of national law found to be in conflict with any directly enforceable rule of Community law. Similarly, when decisions of the Court of Justice have exposed areas of United Kingdom statute law which failed to implement Council directives, Parliament has always loyally accepted the obligation to make appropriate and prompt amendments. Thus there is nothing in any way novel in according supremacy to rules of Community law in areas to which they apply and to insist that, in the protection of rights under Community law, national courts must not be prohibited by rules of national law from granting interim relief in appropriate cases is no more than a logical recognition of that supremacy.

Whilst these dicta have direct resonance in the context of interim relief in judicial review proceedings,[74] they represent an approach to sovereignty in the context of EC law that strongly suggests that s 2(1) and s 2(4) of the 1972 Act are substantive rather than merely interpretative obligations. In particular, they suggest that the exercise of parliamentary sovereignty lay in contracting to join the EC on terms that included the primacy of EC law over national law. **2.79**

However, in the event of Parliament expressly legislating not to follow EC law in a discrete area it is by no means clear that the English courts would be able to hold that Parliament **2.80**

---

[71] In the event, the claims were successful.
[72] See paras 2.66–2.67.
[73] *R v Secretary of State for Transport, ex p Factortame Ltd (No 2)* [1991] AC 603, 658–9.
[74] See paras 3.132 et seq.

University of Ulster LIBRARY

had limited its own sovereignty in passing the 1972 Act so that it could not so legislate. Lord Bridge's observations were *obiter* and do not form part of the leading speech of Lord Goff.

2.81　True it is that in *Thoburn v Sunderland City Council*[75] a Divisional Court held that the doctrine of *implied* repeal did not extend to a 'constitutional' statute such as the European Communities Act 1972 so that a subsequent statute – *in casu* the Weights and Measures Act 1985—did not impliedly repeal inconsistent EC law. This important decision also marks a break with the *obiter* judgments in some of the earlier cases.

2.82　However, in a very significant passage in his judgment in *Thoburn*, Laws LJ observed (para 59):

> ... there is nothing in the [European Communities Act] which allows the [European Court], or any other institution of the EU, to touch or qualify the conditions of Parliament's legislative supremacy in the United Kingdom. Not because the legislature chose not to allow it; because by our law it could not allow it. That being so, the legislative and judicial institutions of the EU cannot intrude upon those conditions. The British Parliament has not the authority to authorise any such thing. Being sovereign, it cannot abandon its sovereignty. Accordingly there are no circumstances in which the jurisprudence of the [European Court] can elevate Community law to a status within the corpus of English domestic law to which it could not aspire by any route of English law itself. This is, of course, the traditional doctrine of sovereignty. If it is to be modified, it certainly cannot be done by the incorporation of external texts. The conditions of Parliament's legislative supremacy in the United Kingdom necessarily remain in the United Kingdom's hands.

2.83　The implications of this (albeit *obiter*) reasoning suggest a distinction between the legal effect of the European Communities Act 1972 and Parliament's continued unqualified sovereignty even in an EC context. Whilst the 1972 Act has a distinctive legal effect and operates to reflect EC law supremacy, nothing in the 1972 Act, according to this reasoning, qualifies Parliament's continued legislative sovereignty.

2.84　However, the respective views of Lord Bridge and Laws LJ are at least potentially reconcilable. On Laws LJ's reasoning in *Thoburn* it follows that the relationship between Acts passed subsequent to the 1972 Act and the 1972 Act itself reflects the supremacy of EC law *as a direct consequence of parliamentary sovereignty* in enacting the European Communities Act 1972 (Lord Bridge's analysis in *Factortame*). This may mean that statutes passed subsequent to the European Communities Act 1972 may not conflict with EC law for to do so would be for a legislature that had willingly signed up to the EC to select which EC obligations it intended to follow.[76] But continued legislative sovereignty makes it possible for Parliament to withdraw from the EC altogether, thereby freeing itself from the necessity of continued compliance with EC law.[77]

2.85　As Lloyd LJ observed in *R v Secretary of State for Foreign and Commonwealth Affairs, ex p Rees-Mogg*[78] it is, after all, possible for the Government to 'denounce the Treaty'.

---

[75] [2002] 3 WLR 247, see n 37 and text above.

[76] Note, too, that by s 3(1) of the European Communities Act 1972 any question as to the effect of the Treaties or of Community legislation must be decided 'in accordance with the principles of any relevant decision of the European Court'. The supremacy of EC law is, thus, itself a principle adumbrated by the ECJ.

[77] For further analysis see, eg, Sir William Wade, 'Sovereignty—Revolution or Evolution?' (1996) 112 LQR 568; TRS Allan, 'Parliamentary Sovereignty: Law, Politics and Revolution' (1997) 113 LQR 443.

[78] [1994] QB 552.

Limitations to the principle of supremacy of EC law

There are two principal qualifications[79] to the principle of supremacy of EC law that, at **2.86** least potentially, may qualify its scope and that are, in any event, likely to surface as a response to many judicial review challenges.

First, the ECJ has held that it respects national autonomy in the procedural rules govern- **2.87** ing proceedings in the domestic courts subject, always, to EC general principles, especially those of effectiveness and equivalence. Respect for national autonomous procedural rules in the context of these principles is examined separately.[80] Essentially, however, it has been said that in such areas EC law only interferes in exceptional cases[81] as where such procedural rules make the effective implementation of EC rights impossible in practice. Most notably, so far as domestic judicial review is concerned arguments may arise as to the validity of a national limitation rule or questions of *locus standi*.

There is possible tension between, on the one hand, the ECJ's pronouncements on respect **2.88** for procedural autonomy and, on the other, the supremacy principle. The two principles may, indeed, sometimes be confused or possibly one of them applied to the exclusion of the other. For example, in *Factortame (No 1)* the question of interim relief was approached from the perspective of the principle of supremacy. Whether it could have been approached differently, by reference to considerations of national procedural autonomy, is perhaps open to question. Nonetheless, the ECJ did not in its ruling in that case seek to reconcile the various principles. Nor has it done so in other cases.

A second possible limitation to the supremacy principle is that it may be limited to rights **2.89** that are directly effective—that is (see below) it may be limited to rights that are capable of being enforced by individuals in the English courts. However, this limitation is, in practice, more apparent than real because of the duty of sympathetic interpretation of the law in EC cases that the courts have come to accept applies even in respect of non-directly effective EC law.[82]

Distinct principles of interpretation

Approaching interpretation in EC domestic public law cases

EC law contains distinct principles of interpretation that have been laid down by the ECJ **2.90** and that must be applied by the national courts. In many respects, the principles are similar to those engaged by HRA, s 3. However, it would be a mistake to view EC interpretative principles and obligations as identical to those under the HRA. Nor, for reasons

---

[79] These limitations are not exhaustive. For example, it has been suggested that EC law may not be treated as superior to domestic law where fraud or abuse is involved. See, eg, Case C–23/93 *TV10 v Commissariaat voor de Media* [1994] ECR I–4795, paras 20–21. Similarly, specific provisions of EC law (as, eg, Art 307 (ex 234) EC relating to the primacy of international obligations concluded prior to the Treaty) may operate to limit the supremacy of EC law in particular contexts.

[80] See paras 3.05 et seq.

[81] See Joined Cases C–427, C–429 and C–436/93 *Bristol Myers Squibb v Paranova AS* [1996] ECR I–3457, 3500, per Advocate General Jacobs.

[82] Nonetheless (see paras 2.130 et seq.) the duty of sympathetic interpretation is, ultimately, subordinate to the true content of domestic law.

developed below, do the national courts always adopt wholesale the interpretative techniques deployed by the ECJ.

2.91 From the perspective of domestic public law it is necessary to examine EC interpretation by reference to the following areas:

(1) The relationship between the English court and the ECJ in relation to EC interpretation questions.

(2) General principles of interpretation in EC cases.

(3) Aids to EC interpretation.

(4) The nature of the EC interpretative obligation on the national court.

Relationship between the English court and the ECJ in the context of interpretation

2.92 Section 3(1) of the European Communities Act 1972 (as amended)[83] provides as follows:

> For the purposes of all legal proceedings any question as to the meaning or effect of any of the Treaties, or as to the validity, meaning or effect of any Community instrument, shall be treated as a question of law and if not referred to the European Court, be for determination as such in accordance with the principles laid down by any relevant decision of the European Court or any court attached thereto.

2.93 For practical purposes,[84] this means that in determining issues of EC law the English courts 'must follow the same principles as the [ECJ]'[85] and must apply any relevant rulings of the EC courts.[86] Interpretation of EC law involves, therefore, applying a distinctive set of principles that—because they emanate from the ECJ—do not simply replicate domestic principles of interpretation. In that fashion, relevant decisions of the ECJ bind the national courts as a matter of statutory obligation.[87]

2.94 The position is, however, slightly more complicated than this statement might suggest. First, the principles adumbrated by the ECJ have to be applied by national courts in a way that, as will be seen, cannot always mirror precisely the principles laid down by that court. Despite this, however, in terms of precedent, the Administrative Court appears not to be constrained by the manner in which a higher court such as the Court of Appeal has interpreted the relevant principles espoused by the ECJ.[88]

2.95 Secondly, it is important to bear in mind that national courts are interpreting not merely the meaning of Community legislation but, at least as commonly, the meaning or effect of national legislation in the light of Community legislation or general principles of EC law.

---

[83] By s 2 of the European Communities (Amendment) Act 1986.

[84] There is an academic debate as to whether preliminary rulings of the ECJ under Art 234 (ex 177) EC are binding on non-parties to the reference: see D Anderson and M Demetriou, *References to the European Court* (2nd edn, 2002) paras 14–032 et seq. However, this debate may be of little practical significance in the UK given the terms of s 3(1) of the European Communities Act 1972.

[85] *HP Bulmer v J Bollinger SA* [1974] Ch 401, 425, per Lord Denning MR.

[86] Thus, the term 'ECJ' includes, in this context, relevant decisions of the CFI.

[87] See, eg, *Lister v Forth Dry Dock* [1990] 1 AC 546, 554 per Lord Keith.

[88] Despite earlier views expressed by Hidden J in *Feehan v Commissioners of Customs & Excise* [1995] 1 CMLR 193, 198–9, in *Kay v Lambeth; Leeds CC v Price* [2006] UKHL 10 the House of Lords accepted that although the doctrine of precedent applies in an HRA case, s 3(1) of the European Communities Act 1972 had a different effect: see per Lord Bingham of Cornhill at para 28. In any event, in EC law, a reference under Art 234 (ex 177) EC may be made applying the same discretionary principles as if there were no national precedent. See *Feehan*, 199. For the relevant criteria as to whether to seek a preliminary ruling see Chapter 4.

In this respect, the content of national law may curtail the way in which ECJ principles can **2.96** be applied by the national court *at least as a matter of interpretation of national law*. In part, this stems from the inherent nature of the interpretative obligation (discussed below)[89] which remains one of interpretation and which does not require national law to be interpreted by national courts in a way that is not possible having regard to the wording of the national provision in question even where the interpretation of national law will render it incompatible with EC law. As explained below, the national court may then have to disapply national law or grant other relief in order effectively to apply EC law principles including those principles laid down by the ECJ.

In part, too, the difficulty of giving precise effect to ECJ rulings in all cases before the **2.97** national courts is to be derived from the need to apply EC general principles of law to the national legislation in question. For example, even if a person or undertaking acts in breach of a directive, no criminal liability will be incurred (or, as the case may be, aggravated) in the absence of specific national legislation providing for such liability.[90] In other words, application of particular general principles of EC law may require specific application in the context of particular domestic legislation.

Finally, there is (at least in theory) an issue as to whether—given the horizontal effect of **2.98** directives—EC interpretative principles can be deployed at all in circumstances where there are no directly effective rights in play. This issue appears now, however, to have been resolved. It is addressed below.

General principles of interpretation in EC cases[91]

Adopting the most general formulation, there are three broad principles of EC interpreta- **2.99** tion that have been enunciated over the years by the ECJ and that are required to be applied by the national courts both in respect of the meaning of provisions of both EC law and domestic law in an EC context.

These principles may be summarized as: **2.100**

(1) The principle of uniform interpretation.
(2) The purposive principle.
(3) The derogation principle.

The principle of uniform interpretation   As an interpretative principle this requires **2.101** EC law to be interpreted uniformly throughout the Community. The principle has particular relevance to the manner in which the national courts should treat different language versions of Community measures. Consistent with the principle of uniform interpretation, each language version is considered to be equally authentic.[92]

---

[89] See paras 2.130 et seq.

[90] See, eg, Joined Cases C–74 and C–129/95 *Criminal Proceedings against X* [1996] ECR I–6609. This is an application, in the EC context, of Art 7 ECHR (no punishment without law).

[91] Reference to general principles of interpretation should not be confused with general principles of EC law which, as will be seen, themselves affect the general principles of interpretation in EC cases. See paras 2.146–2.150.

[92] See, eg, Case C–149/97 *Institute of the Motor Industry v Commissioners of Customs & Excise* [1998] ECR I–7053, para 16.

2.102   There is, thus, sometimes a need to compare different language versions in order to determine the uniform meaning of EC legislation. On the other hand, it is impractical to expect a national court to conduct a comprehensive analysis of all the different language versions of Community legislation in the same way as the ECJ.

2.103   In *R v Commissioners of Customs & Excise, ex p EMU Tabac sarl* [93] the Court of Appeal gave guidance as to the approach that the national court should adopt where different language versions of a Community instrument are considered to be material by one or more parties. It said:

> ... any party which proposes to rely on a version in a foreign tongue [should] alert the other side to this fact and ... seek to agree a translation of that version. If there is agreement it is improbable that the court will wish to disagree. Certainly, if it does then it should indicate its views so that the parties can comment on them. If there is no agreement between the parties then the appropriate course is for the parties' legal advisers first to consider whether it is really likely to be productive in the national court to pursue submissions based on disputed translations of text expressed in foreign languages. That will seldom be the case. If, however, the conclusion of one or more parties is that it is likely to be productive then evidence by translators should be filed on each side. That will usually suffice for the judge to be prepared to come to a decision on the point. Cross-examination is an option, but not one which we would generally wish to encourage. In a case where the difference in meaning attributed to the authentic versions is crucial to the decision and the point is irresolvable on the affidavits then the appropriate course may well be to refer the matter to the ECJ which is linguistically better placed than any national court to resolve the matter.

2.104   Of course, the principle of uniform interpretation is not the only interpretative principle relevant to disputes over linguistic meaning. Other principles of, or aids to, interpretation may be necessary to elucidate the true meaning of EC law or the true meaning of national law through the prism of EC law. These are considered below.

2.105   **The purposive principle**   It is generally important to apply a purposive approach to the interpretation of EC law and national law in an EC context. This exercise is logically prior to that of requiring Member States to interpret national legislation insofar as possible to be compatible with EC law (see below) because it defines the content of the EC law that national law is intended to reflect.

2.106   The ECJ has consistently emphasized the purposive principle in the context of interpretation. But the principle is not absolute. First, it may have to give way to a literal reading of the text where no other reading is possible and where the literal meaning yields a sensible result.[94] As was observed by Advocate General Mayras in *Fellinger*:[95]

> ... when the meaning of the legislation is clear it has to be applied with that meaning, even if the solution prescribed may be thought to be unsatisfactory ... [However] [i]f such a construction were to lead to a nonsensical result in regard to a situation which the Court believed

---

[93] [1997] Eu LR 153, 160.

[94] Where more than one meaning is possible the interpretation that renders the measure most consistent with the Treaty should—so far as the purposive principle is concerned—be adopted: Case 220/83 *Commission v France* [1986] ECR 3363, para 15.

[95] Case 67/79 *Fellinger v Bundesanstalt für Arbeit* [1980] ECR 535, 550.

the provision was intended to cover, certain doubts might properly be entertained in regard to it. In other words, the clear meaning and the literal meaning are not synonymous.

Secondly, the purposive principle has to be applied in the context of the Community legal **2.107** order as a whole. In looking to overall purpose it should be noted, as outlined earlier, that the provisions of the Treaty form the apex of the Community legal order. Below them is Community legislation and, below that, national measures. Underlying each of these are the general principles of EC law.

Thus, a purposive approach requires as much consistency as possible between the various **2.108** levels of this EC legal hierarchy. In *Regeling* [96] Advocate General Cosmas suggested that it followed from the hierarchy implicit in the Community legal order that 'the rules at each level must be in conformity with the rules not only at the next level but at all the higher levels so as to ensure the coherence and effectiveness of the system'. Since the Treaty is interpreted in the light of EC general principles of law it necessarily also follows that Community legislation and national measures must be interpreted so far as is possible in accordance with EC general principles of law. [97] Many instances of such interpretation are given in the extensive coverage of EC general principles of law at Chapters 6–12 below.

Thirdly, however, in the event of a conflict between two or more different purposes the **2.109** court may have to interpret the measure in question in the light of the most dominant of the various purposes. Which of the respective purposes is the most dominant will, of course, depend upon the context. To take one example, consumer protection has in the context of Council Directive (EEC) 89/646 been treated by the ECJ as trumping freedom of movement of goods. [98]

The over-arching relationship between the different arms of the Community legal order **2.110** and the national courts requiring utilization of the purposive principle in a great many cases is now well recognized in domestic law. [99] As Laws LJ has pointed out: [100]

> The common injunction to construe Community measures purposively sometimes amounts not merely to an optional approach which however ought to be preferred, but to a practical necessity; without it, it is not possible to make sense of the legislation at all.

The derogation principle   A third, well-established, principle of interpretation is that **2.111** purported derogations from EC Treaty rights are to be construed restrictively. [101] Further, the burden of establishing that a particular derogation is lawful lies on the party seeking to rely on it. [102]

---

[96] Case C–125/97 *Regeling v Bestuur van de Bedrijfsvereniging voor de Metaalnijverheid* [1998] ECR I–4493, fn 8 to the Advocate General's Opinion.

[97] See, eg, Case C–181/96 *Wilkens v Landwirtschaftskammer Hannover* [1999] ECR I–399, para 19. It is also the case that the Community legal order has a relationship with the international legal order so that EC provisions should, so far as possible, be interpreted consistently with international agreements concluded by the Community: see, eg, C–61/94 *Commission v Germany* [1996] ECR I–3989, para 52.

[98] Case C–366/97 *Criminal Proceedings against Romanelli* [1999] ECR I–855.

[99] See, eg, *Litster v Forth Dry Dock* [1990] 1 AC 546, 558, per Lord Templeman.

[100] *Optident Ltd v Secretary of State for Trade and Industry* [1999] 1 CMLR 782, 810.

[101] Of the many cases see, eg, *Thomas v Adjudication Officer* [1991] 2 QB 164, 180, per Slade LJ.

[102] See, eg, Case C–57/94 *Commission v Italy* [1995] ECR I–1249, para 23.

Aids to EC interpretation

2.112   In order to give effect to the general principles of EC interpretation, it is sometimes permissible to employ certain aids to interpretation. Such aids are not in themselves principles but may be useful, in particular cases, in applying the general principles of interpretation.

2.113   **Opinions of the Advocates General**   Unlike ECJ judgments, the Opinion of the Advocate General is not in any way binding on the national court. However, in certain instances, it may be persuasive provided, always, that the ECJ has itself adopted the Opinion by implication.

2.114   Difficulties arise where, as is often the case, the judgment of the ECJ, whilst agreeing with the Advocate General's conclusion, does not incorporate all the reasoning of the Advocate General. A warning has been given of the danger of reading into the court's judgment everything said by the Advocate General.[103]

2.115   However, that is not to deny all interpretative force to the reasoning of the Advocates General. There are at least some occasions where it appears to be permissible for the national court to read the judgment of the ECJ together with the Opinion of the Advocate General so as to understand the basis of the court's judgment.[104]

2.116   **Judgments of courts of other Member States**   It is also permissible for the national court to have regard to the judgments of courts of other Member States on interpretation of the point of law in issue.

2.117   However, as with the Opinions of Advocates General (see above) there can be dangers in doing so. The position has been succinctly set out by Laddie J in *Wagamama Ltd v City Centre Restaurants plc*[105]

> ... it is right that British courts should pay regard to decisions in the courts of other Member States on equivalent provisions in their law. However ... [i]t would not be right for an English court to follow the route adopted by the courts of another Member State if it is firmly of a different view simply because the other court expressed a view first. The scope of European legislation is too important to be decided on a first-past-the-post basis.

2.118   **Preambles and explanatory notes**   Preambles to Community measures may be of considerable assistance in interpreting the purpose and ambit of the measure in question. However, where the measure is clear then recourse to the preamble is unnecessary. In the event of conflict between the preamble and the measure, the latter prevails.[106]

2.119   The preamble usually consists of a series of recitals. Where the overall purpose of a measure is being sought, the recitals should not be examined in isolation. All relevant recitals should then be considered.[107]

---

[103] *R v MAFF, ex p British Agro-Chemicals Association Ltd* [2000] 1 CMLR 826, 828, per Richards J.
[104] See, eg, *Trafalgar Tours Ltd v Commissioners of Customs & Excise* [1990] 3 CMLR 934.
[105] [1997] Eu LR 313, 325.
[106] Joined Cases 154/83 and 155/83 *Hoche v BALM* [1985] ECR 1215, para 13.
[107] See, eg, *Three Rivers DC v Governor of the Bank of England* [2000] 2 WLR 1220, 1247–8.

Similarly, explanatory notes that are annexed to a community measure and form part of it **2.120** may be looked at for the purpose of interpretation.[108]

Preparatory measures and legislative proposals Preparatory measures in general may be **2.121** referred to as an aid to interpretation.[109] However, it has been observed that they are not of decisive importance in interpreting the relevant legislative intention which is, primarily, to be derived from the meaning of the words, the function of the measure in question and the system of which it is part.[110]

More common is the particular use made of legislative proposals and similar materials. **2.122** These are often referred to, as an aid to interpretation, especially in the context of Commission documents. Recourse has, for example, been made by the House of Lords to a Green Paper of the Commission,[111] and by the Court of Appeal to the Commission's Explanatory Memorandum that had been submitted to the Council accompanying a legislative proposal.[112] This follows similar use by the ECJ of such materials.[113]

In the context of interpreting domestic statutes in an EC context it has been suggested at **2.123** first instance that the rules relating to the introduction of parliamentary materials in accordance with the House of Lords' decision in *Pepper v Hart*[114] may be applied somewhat more flexibly.[115] However, whether those observations continue to apply remains to be seen in the light of the more restrictive approach to parliamentary materials subsequently adopted by the House of Lords (albeit in a purely domestic context) in *R v Secretary of State for the Environment, Transport and the Regions, ex p Spath Holme*.[116]

Declarations in Council minutes In general, minuted declarations of the Council when **2.124** preparing or adopting a measure cannot be relied on as an aid to interpretation.[117] The position is, however, different where the declaration is incorporated by reference into the measure itself.[118]

As a qualification to the general rule, it seems that reference may be made to declarations in **2.125** Council minutes where the declaration clarifies a general concept.[119] In the light of such declarations now being available for public inspection,[120] it is possible that more use may be made of them.

---

[108] Case 143/86 *East v Cuddy* [1988] ECR 625, para 11. Explanatory notes that are provided to accompany a measure—rather than forming part of the measure itself—have less utility for the purposes of interpretation but may be used to confirm an interpretation reached by the court by a separate route.

[109] Case 130/87 *Retter v Caisse de pension des employes prives* [1989] ECR 865, para 16.

[110] See Advocate General Tesauro in Case C–300/89 *Commission v Council* [1991] ECR I–2867, 2895.

[111] *R v London Boroughs Transport Committee, ex p Freight Transport Association Ltd* [1999] 1 WLR 828.

[112] *Re Smith Kline & French Laboratories Ltd* [1988] 3 WLR 896.

[113] See, eg Case C–449/93 *Rockfon AS v Specialarbejderforbundet I Danmark* [1995] ECR I–4291 where the ECJ compared the Commission's initial legislative proposal with the final measure.

[114] [1993] AC 593.

[115] See *Miss U v Mr W and Attorney General (No 1)* [1997] Eu LR 342, 349, per Wilson J endorsing the observations of Clarke J in *Three Rivers District Council v Bank of England (No 2)* [1996] 2 All ER 363, 366.

[116] [2001] 2 AC 349.

[117] See, eg, Case C–292/89 *R v Immigration Appeal Tribunal, ex p Antonissen* [1991] ECR I–745, paras 17–18.

[118] See, eg, Case 329/95 *VAG Sverige* [1997] ECR I–2675, para 23.

[119] Case C–368/96 *R v Licensing Authority, ex p Generics (UK) Ltd* [1998] ECR I–7967, para 27.

[120] See new Art 207(3) EC.

2.126 **Other materials** From time to time, other materials may afford permissible aids to interpretation of EC measures. Sometimes, for example, the national courts have been prepared to have recourse to statements of the Commission especially in relation to threatened infringement action by the Commission or to a stated lack of intention to take infringement action.[121]

2.127 Occasionally, too, courts (largely Advocates General) have looked to particular materials for the purpose of drawing an analogy. They have, for example, looked to the case law of other jurisdictions for comparative assistance, [122]to discrete EC legislation in a comparable area,[123] and even to international agreements.[124] In each such case there must, though, be a true comparison to be made for interpretation to be an appropriate exercise.

The nature of the EC interpretative obligation on the national court

2.128 **Two jurisdictional issues in respect of EC interpretation by the domestic courts** Two jurisdictional questions arise in the context of interpretation. First, as foreshadowed earlier, the fact that a case falls within the scope of EC law[125] does not, of itself, mean that the national court *must*—or even *may*—interpret domestic law consistently with EC law if, properly interpreted, domestic law is simply incompatible with EC law. There may well be remedies available to the party affected by national law being in breach of EC law but that is a separate question from how the offending national measure may be interpreted by the national court. The precise scope of the interpretative obligation on the national court as a matter of EC obligation is, therefore, of importance.

2.129 Secondly, it does not necessarily follow from the fact that a case is one falling within the scope of EC law that the same EC interpretative obligation (or any discrete EC interpretative obligation) that arises in the case of directly effective obligations also arises in relation to EC law that is not directly effective.

2.130 *What is the nature and scope of the EC interpretative obligation on the national court?* The interpretative obligation on the national court in an EC context is one stemming, at least initially, from EC law. As the ECJ observed in *Von Colson and Kamann*:[126]

> in applying the national law and in particular the provisions of a national law specifically introduced to implement [a directive], national courts are required to interpret their national law in the light of the wording and the purpose of the directive in order to achieve the result referred to in the third paragraph of Article 189.

---

[121] See, eg, *Meat and Livestock Commission v Manchester Wholesale Meat and Poultry Market Ltd* [1997] 2 CMLR 361, 377, per Moses J.

[122] As, eg, Advocate General Jacobs in Case C–316/95 *Generics BV v Smith Kline & French Laboratories Ltd* [1997] ECR I–3929, 3942.

[123] See, eg, Case 349/96 *Card Protection Plan Ltd v Commissioners of Customs & Excise* [1999] ECR 973, para 18.

[124] See, eg, Joined Cases C–320, C–328–329, C–337–339/94 *RTI v Ministero delle Poste e Telecomunicazioni* [1996] ECR I–6471, 6484, per Advocate General Jacobs. EC secondary legislation should, if possible, be interpreted consistently with international agreements concluded by the EC itself: see, eg, Case C–61/94 *Commission v Germany* [1996] ECR I–3989, para 52.

[125] For the considerations affecting whether a case is within the scope of EC law, see paras 6.24 et seq.

[126] Case 14/83 *Von Colson and Kamann v Land Nordrhein-Westfalen* [1984] ECR 1891, para 26.

Interpretation is, however, to be distinguished from remedy and the ECJ has made it clear that **2.131** the obligation to interpret national law compatibly with EC law (principally in the context of directives) is not absolute in nature. The obligation is, rather, one of *sympathetic* interpretation.

In *Marleasing*[127] the ECJ said this: **2.132**

> ... in applying national law, whether the provisions in question were adopted before or after the directive, the national court called upon to interpret it is required to do so, as far as possible, in the light of the wording and purpose of the directive in order to achieve the result pursued by the latter.

It is, therefore, clear from *Marleasing*—as it had not, perhaps, been from *Von Colson*—that **2.133** the interpretative obligation applies not merely to legislation implementing a directive but to national law more generally.[128]

In determining the parameters of the sympathetic interpretation obligation it appears from **2.134** the *Marleasing* formulation ('as far as possible') that the ECJ envisaged that the national court would be entitled to take into account its domestic rules of interpretation.[129] Were the position otherwise the ECJ would, in effect, be able to rule on the interpretation by a national court of provisions of national law.

That is the approach adopted post *Marleasing* by the national courts. In *Webb v EMO Air* **2.135** *Cargo (UK) Ltd*,[130] Lord Keith observed as follows:

> ... it is for a United Kingdom court to construe domestic legislation in any field covered by a Community Directive so as to accord with the interpretation of the Directive as laid down by the European Court of Justice, if that can be done without distorting the meaning of the domestic legislation ...

That means (per Lord Keith) that: **2.136**

> ... a national court must construe a domestic law to accord with the terms of a Directive in the same field only if it is possible to do so. That means that the domestic law must be open to an interpretation consistent with the Directive whether or not it is also open to an interpretation inconsistent with it.[131]

However, as with the interpretative obligation under HRA, s 3, care is needed in elucidating **2.137** with accuracy the meaning of the qualifying phrase in *Marleasing* 'as far as possible'.

Judicial pronouncements, both before and after *Marleasing*,[132] have—it is submitted **2.138** rightly—emphasized the importance, even in an EC context, of reaching an interpretation

---

[127] Case C–106/89 *Marleasing SA v La Comercial Internacional de Alimentacion SA* [1990] ECR I–4135, para 8. For subsequent restatement of the principle see, eg, Joined Cases C–74 and C–129/95 *Criminal Proceedings v X* [1996] ECR I–6609, para 24.

[128] For instances of *Marleasing* as applied by the Administrative Court and Court of Appeal see, eg, *R (Friends of the Earth) v Environment Agency* [2003] EWHC 3193, [2004] Env LR 31; *R (Jones) v Mansfield District Council* [2003] EWCA Civ 1408, 2004 Env LR 21.

[129] A view reinforced by the Opinion of the Advocate General in *Marleasing* (n 125 above) point 8.

[130] [1993] 1 WLR 49, 59. To similar effect, see *Bhudi v IMI Refiners Ltd* [1994] 2 CMLR 296, 305, per Mummery J; *R v Secretary of State for the Environment, ex p Greenpeace* [1994] 3 CMLR 737, 751 per Potts J.

[131] [1993] 1 WLR 49, 60.

[132] See, especially, pre-*Marleasing* per Lord Templeman in *Duke v GEC Reliance Ltd* [1988] 1 AC 618, 639.

that is in conformity with the intention of Parliament. Little clear guidance has, though, been given by the national courts as to when it may be possible to interpret national law in a manner inconsistent with EC law.

2.139 Although it is difficult to define, with precision, the limits of departing from the ostensible meaning of a statute, it seems clear that linguistic meaning is only one aspect of the interpretative exercise. As Lord Clyde observed in *Cutter v Eagle Star Insurance Co Ltd; Clarke v Kato*:[133]

> The adoption of a construction which departs boldly from the ordinary meaning of the language of the statute is, however, particularly appropriate where the validity of legislation has to be tested against the provisions of European law. In that context it is proper to strain to give effect to the design and purpose behind the legislation, and to give weight to the spirit rather than the letter. In this way the court may implement the requirement formulated by the European Court of Justice in Marleasing . . .

2.140 In the context of fundamental rights under the ECHR, there is a similar interpretative obligation on the national court under HRA, s 3 to interpret legislation 'so far as it is possible to do so' so as to be Convention compatible. The HRA, s 3[134] cases appear to provide a useful point of comparison for the proper content of interpretation under *Marleasing*. In *Ghaidan v Godin Mendoza*,[135] an ECHR case involving consideration of the scope of Article 14 ECHR, Lord Steyn[136] referred to the strong interpretative obligation required by *Marleasing* and suggested that it was a significant guide to the ambit of HRA, s 3. Similarly, the Court of Appeal has used HRA, s 3(1) to assist in deciding that *Marleasing* enabled that court to read the words 'your total charge to your customers' as extending to cover a charge that was *not* made to the customer.[137] In a similar fashion to the courts' approach to HRA, s 3, and perhaps foreshadowing that approach, it has been held that *Marleasing* interpretation 'must be achieved, if at all, by proper processes of construction, not so far as the court is concerned by the equivalent of legislation'.[138]

2.141 If HRA, s 3 provides a useful template for examination of the scope of the *Marleasing* interpretative obligation in EC cases, then it may (for example) be permissible (and consistent with *Marleasing*) to read down the statutory language as well as implying provisions into the statute.[139] But, just as '[s]ection 3(1) is not available where the suggested interpretation is contrary to express statutory words or is by implication necessarily contradicted by the statute'[140]

---

[133] [1998] 1 WLR 1647.

[134] HRA, s 3(1) provides that '[s]o far as it is possible to do so, primary legislation and subordinate legislation must be read and given effect in a way which is compatible with the Convention rights'.

[135] [2004] 2 AC 557.

[136] ibid para 45. See, also, per Lord Rodger, para 118.

[137] *Customs and Excise Commissioners v First Choice Holidays plc* [2004] STC 1407.

[138] *Re Hartlebury Printers Ltd* [1994] 2 CMLR 704, 712, per Morritt J. The same distinction between interpretation and legislation is also drawn in the HRA, s 3 cases. See, eg, per Lord Woolf in *Poplar Housing and Regeneration Community Association Ltd v Donoghue* [2002] QB 48.

[139] See, eg, per Lord Steyn in *R v A (No 2)* [2002] 1 AC 45. Contrast, though, *Bhudi v IMI Refiners Ltd* [1994] 2 CMLR 296, per Mummery J.

[140] *R (Anderson) v Secretary of State for the Home Department* [2003] 1 AC 837, para 59, per Lord Steyn.

so, too, in an EC context 'the test cannot be the number of words [to be implied] . . . It must be the amount of violence that the change does to the natural meaning of the text.'[141]

Finally, it is emphasized that there are certain jurisdictional limits on the operation of the **2.142** EC interpretative obligation on national courts laid down by *Marleasing*. Thus:

(1) If national legislation purporting to implement a directive is introduced prior to the expiry of the period for implementation laid down by the directive, it seems that national law is still subject to *Marleasing* interpretative principles.[142] However, other national measures (that is, those *not* purporting to implement directives) are not subject to that interpretative obligation until after the time for implementing the directive has passed.[143]

(2) In *Arcaro*[144] the ECJ observed that the interpretative obligation in *Marleasing* 'reaches a limit where such an obligation leads to the imposition on an individual of an obligation laid down by a directive which has not been transposed'. However, as Advocate General Jacobs has observed,[145] this ruling appears to be confined to *criminal* liability.

(3) The interpretation of directives and other Community legislation is always itself subject to the operation of the EC general principles of law (see below). That is why the national court's interpretative obligation is not confined to determining the extent to which national measures are compatible with directives or other community legislation. A national measure may, exceptionally, be unlawful despite compatibility between the national measure and Community legislation because the Community legislation itself violates a general principle of EC law. In such cases, whilst the national court may not declare the Community legislation to be invalid,[146] it may (and, in some cases, *must*)[147] refer the proceedings to the ECJ under Article 234 (ex 177) EC.

Is the EC interpretative obligation relevant to EC law that is not directly effective? It seems **2.143** clear that *Marleasing* principles apply not merely to directly effective provisions of a directive but also to provisions of a directive that are not directly effective. This is because, in order to be directly effective, the relevant provisions of a directive must be unconditional and sufficiently precise.[148] Yet, the ECJ has held that, even in the case of provisions that are

---

[141] *Adams v Lancashire CC* [1996] All ER (EC) 473, 489, per Robert Walker J.

[142] See Case C–156/91 *Hansa Fleisch v Landrat des Kreises Schleswig-Flensburg* [1992] ECR I–5567, per Advocate General Jacobs at paras 23–27 of his Opinion. See, also, per Advocate General Jacobs in Joined Cases C–427, C–429 and C–436/93 *Bristol-Myers Squibb v Paranova AS* [1996] ECR I–3457, 3487.

[143] Such obligation cannot, it is submitted, be derived from pre-*Marleasing* reasoning (see Case 80/86 *Criminal Proceedings against Kolpenghuis Nijmegen BV* [1987] ECR 3969) since, as explained above, the wider ambit of *Marleasing* to non-implementing legislation had not then been clarified. However, once there is national implementing legislation then other national measures would, it is submitted, fall to be interpreted in the light of *Marleasing* whether or not the date for implementation of the directive has passed.

[144] Case C–168/95 *Criminal Proceedings against Arcaro* [1996] ECR I–4705, para 42.

[145] See Case C–456/98 *Centrosteel Srl v Adipol GmbH* [2000] 3 CMLR 711, para 34. It is certainly well established that a directive that has not been implemented by national law cannot affect the criminal liability of persons acting in breach of it. See, eg, Case 80/86 *Kolpinghuis Nijmegen* [1987] ECR 3969, paras 11–14.

[146] See, eg, para 4.92.

[147] See paras 4.92–4.98.

[148] See para 1.64.

not sufficiently precise to create directly effective rights,[149] the national court must interpret national law (so far as possible) in order to achieve the result (there, adequate compensation) prescribed by the directive.

2.144 The significance of this distinction is that there may be cases before the national courts in both judicial review and other proceedings[150] in which a provision of national law falls to be interpreted by the court in accordance with EC principles even though the national measure does not itself give effect to a directly effective EC right stemming from an EC directive. In practical terms, this reduces the necessity of establishing that a provision of a directive is directly effective before being able to rely upon a *Marleasing* interpretation of a transposing national measure. Provided that a claimant in an application for judicial review possesses the requisite standing the question of whether the directive creates directly effective rights may not be decisive as to whether relief is granted.

2.145 In the words of Advocate General Darmon in *Dekker*:[151]

> . . . my approach leads . . . to a distinction which has not often been stressed, between the possibility of relying on a directive, in cases where there are no national rules giving effect to its aims, so as to have its provisions applied directly . . . and reliance on a directive for the sole purpose of the interpretation of national law . . . Whereas the former is confined to those provisions in directives which are sufficiently precise and conditional, and cannot, according to the case-law, govern relations between individuals, the latter is very broad in scope, regardless of whether or not the directive has direct effect and regardless of the parties involved.

General principles of EC law

2.146 The importance of general principles of EC law to the national courts' approach to cases falling within the scope of EC law[152] cannot be over emphasized. This is so for at least three reasons.

2.147 First, as explained elsewhere, the application of such general principles affects the *interpretation* of both Community and national legislation.[153]

2.148 Secondly, compliance with such general principles affects not only interpretation but also legality. For example, a national measure may be unlawful not because it violates particular Community legislation but, rather, because the Community measure in question is itself unlawful as breaching one or more general principles of EC law.

2.149 Finally, as a doctrine, general principles of EC law *may* in an EC context themselves determine, or at least substantially determine, whether or not a case will be treated as falling within the

---

149 Case 14/83 *Von Colson and Kamann v Land Nordrhein-Westfalen* [1984] ECR 1891, especially para 27.

150 Including private law proceedings where national law falls to be interpreted in a dispute between private parties.

151 Case 177/88 *Dekker v VJV-Centrum* [1990] ECR I–3941, para 15 of the Advocate General's Opinion. In this respect, there is a parallel with HRA, s 3 since the court appears to be prepared to interpret statutes by reference to ECHR principles even in litigation between private parties. See, eg, *Wilson v First County Trust Ltd* [2004] 1 AC 816.

152 The expression 'cases falling within the scope of EC law' requires careful consideration and is considered at some length elsewhere. See, especially, paras 6.31 et seq.

153 See, generally, Chapter 6.

scope of EC law. However, this remains somewhat controversial and the relevance of general principles in this respect is separately examined.[154]

Because of their special importance in domestic consideration of EC cases, general principles of EC law are analysed in some detail in Part II of this book. **2.150**

Direct effect and the horizontal and vertical effect of directives

Summary

The doctrine of direct effect and the impermissibility of directives having 'horizontal effect' **2.151**
were addressed, in outline, in Chapter 1.[155] This section revisits these principles in the light of the other doctrines discussed in the present chapter so as to show that care must be taken not to apply the respective principles too rigidly.

The importance of the doctrine of direct effect, which allows individuals to enforce EC **2.152**
rights directly in the national courts, is that it engages: (1) individuals (who may enforce the rights), (2) public bodies (who must comply with the directly effective obligations) and (3) national courts (who must enforce those obligations).

However, the impact of direct effect has, in one sense, been weakened in that it is no longer **2.153**
the sole basis for the enforcement of EC public law. In particular, it cannot be assumed that because an EC provision is not directly effective there is no basis for an application for judicial review.[156]

Similarly, it cannot be assumed that because a judicial review challenge to a national **2.154**
measure founded on an EC directive will have adverse effects on third parties this is, inevitably, to breach the prohibition on directives having horizontal effect.

Direct effect and judicial review

The principle of direct effect, where it applies, means (at least generally) that a relevant **2.155**
Treaty provision or relevant Community legislation is capable of being invoked by individuals in the national courts. The conditions under which direct effect applies have already been outlined.[157]

Where direct effect applies it is, therefore, easy to see how a provision of national law or **2.156**
domestic administrative action, purporting—but failing—to reflect a directly effective right, can be challenged in judicial review. Direct effect will cover the situation where the national implementing measure fails correctly to transpose the directly effective provision of EC law. It will also cover the situation where either there is no national implementing measure because the State has failed to transpose the provision at all or where the supposed implementing measure entirely fails to implement the directly effective provision.[158]

---

[154] See paras 6.34 et seq.
[155] See paras 1.62 et seq.
[156] To many, direct effect is no longer a useful doctrine: see, eg, S Prechel, 'Does Direct Effect Still Matter?' (2000) 37 CML Rev 1047, 1067–68.
[157] See paras 1.62 et seq.
[158] See, eg, Case 103/88 *Fratelli Costanzo SpA v Commune di Milano* [1989] ECR 1839, especially para 29.

Here, the underlying point is that the EC right is enforced directly from the EC legislative provision rather than from national law.

2.157 Conversely, where (most appositely) a directive is implemented correctly by means of domestic implementing measures there is no obvious place for direct effect.[159]

2.158 Importantly, however, judicial review should still in principle be possible if an administrative decision or other action thereafter fails, in its turn, correctly to reflect the hypothetically lawful national legislation. Such decision or action would, in that event, be ultra vires the legislation itself.

2.159 There is a further, and significant, distinction to be made between transposition of a Community directive into national law and the separate duty of implementation of existing EC obligations at all relevant stages. As the Court of Appeal observed in one of the *Three Rivers* cases:[160]

> there may be a category of directives in relation to which a Member State's obligation of proper implementation is not restricted to a once-and-for all legislative process, but also requires a continuing administrative process.[161]

2.160 It is, nonetheless, by no means clear how often in practice judicial review challenges may successfully be made on the ground of defective implementation to administrative measures following lawful transposition of EC directly effective provisions. In particular, a directive (albeit lawfully transposed) may well give the Member State extensive discretion as to administrative enforcement which may make it difficult to challenge administrative decisions.

Horizontal and vertical effect of directives in judicial review proceedings

2.161 In general terms at least, as explained in Chapter 1,[162] there is a prohibition against directives having horizontal effect so as to enable them to be invoked by one individual person against another. This is because directives are enforceable against the State rather than against individuals.

2.162 But the bar against directives having horizontal effect does not necessarily mean that a directive cannot be relied on in judicial review proceedings merely because the provision in question may have adverse consequences for individual third parties.

2.163 This issue has arisen in a few judicial review cases before the Administrative Court relating to the EC requirement, where certain criteria apply, of undertaking an environmental impact assessment prior to the granting of '*development consent*'. In *Huddleston*[163] the question was

---

[159] Case 270/81 *Felicitas Rickmers-Linie KG & Co v Finanzamt für Verkehrsteuern* [1982] ECR 2771, especially para 24.

[160] *Three Rivers District Council v Governor and Company of the Bank of England* [2000] 2 WLR 15.

[161] ibid 80. The House of Lords (reported at [2000] 2 WLR 1220) treated the question as academic in the circumstances of the particular case. To similar effect to the CA in *Three Rivers*, see *Marks & Spencer plc v Commissioners of Customs & Excise* [2000] 1 CMLR 256, 269, per Schiemann LJ.

[162] See paras 1.75 et seq.

[163] *R v Durham County Council, ex p Huddleston* [2000] 1 WLR 1484.

whether a deemed mineral planning permission under the Planning and Compensation Act 1991[164] was invalid under the relevant directive in the absence of an environmental impact assessment. The Court of Appeal, overruling the first instance decision of Richards J, held that it was but that this ruling did not mean giving the directive horizontal effect even though the result of a successful challenge was that the third-party quarry owner would—despite having obtained the statutory benefit of planning permission—now be compelled to await an environmental assessment before being allowed to proceed with the development.

The reasons for the Court of Appeal's decision were twofold. First, the court held that giving effect to the directive did not affect the legal relationship between two private persons. What was engaged was the (vertical) relationship between citizen and State. As the court observed: **2.164**

> there is a fundamental difference between imposing legal obligations on an individual which limit his freedom of action vis-á-vis other individuals and placing conditions on that individual's entitlement to secure a benefit from the State.[165]

Secondly, the court said: **2.165**

> enforcement of a directive by an individual against the State is not rendered inadmissible solely by its consequential effects on other individuals.[166]

Similar questions arose, in the same context, in *Wells*[167] which began as a judicial review challenge in the Administrative Court and was referred by that court to the ECJ for a preliminary ruling under Article 234 (ex 177) EC.   **2.166**

Wells was concerned with decisions under s 22 of the Planning and Compensation Act 1991 whose effect (by the imposition of new planning conditions) was to permit the resumption of mining operations that had previously been subject to virtually unregulated planning consent. The ECJ ruled that such decisions constituted 'development consent' within the meaning of Article 1(2) of Directive (EEC) 85/237. That being so, an environmental impact assessment ought (in the circumstances of the case) to have been required before approving new planning conditions.   **2.167**

In that case it was argued, as it had been in respect of the slightly different statutory provisions in *Huddleston*, that a judicial review challenge to such decisions was prohibited under the principle of impermissible horizontal effect of directives. It constituted, so the argument proceeded, 'inverse direct effect' to oblige the Member State at the request of an individual such as Mrs Wells (the claimant) to deprive another individual or individuals such as the owners of the land—said to be subject to the requirements of environmental impact assessments—of their rights acquired under statute. Such a result was also, so it was contended, contrary to the principle of legal certainty.   **2.168**

---

[164] Sch 2, para 2(6).
[165] [2000] 1 WLR 1484, 1492.
[166] ibid 1494.
[167] Case C–201/02 *R (Wells) v Secretary of State for Transport, Local Government and the Regions* [2004] ECR I–723.

2.169   The ECJ rejected these arguments. It accepted that the principle of legal certainty prevented directives from directly creating obligations for individuals. For them, the provisions of a directive could only create *rights*.[168] Thus, an individual could not rely on a directive against the Member State where it was a matter of a State obligation directly linked to the performance of another obligation falling, pursuant to that directive, on a third party.[169]

2.170   However, the ECJ also observed (echoing *Huddleston*) that:

> ... mere adverse repercussions on the rights of third parties, even if the repercussions are certain, do not justify preventing an individual from invoking the provisions of a directive against the Member State concerned.[170]

2.171   Applying these principles to the environmental impact assessment context of the reference in *Wells*, the ECJ said this:

> In the main proceedings, the obligation on the Member State concerned to ensure that the competent authorities carry out an assessment of the environmental effects of the working of the quarry is not directly linked to the performance of any obligation which would fall, pursuant to Directive 85/337, on the quarry owners. The fact that mining operations must be halted to await the results of the assessment is admittedly the consequence of the belated performance of that State's obligations. Such a consequence cannot, however, as the United Kingdom claims, be described as inverse direct effect of the provisions of that directive in relation to the quarry owners.

G. Types of EC Law Judicial Review Challenge

2.172   There are a variety of domestic challenges by way of judicial review in the Administrative Court that are likely to require determination by reference to the EC principles referred to in this chapter.

2.173   In summary, the principal types of domestic EC challenges will involve one or more of the following:

> (1) *Challenging the manner of performance by national bodies of directly effective Treaty provisions or Community secondary legislation.* *Wells* (above) was an example of such a challenge. There, the national legislative provisions, properly interpreted, constituted a 'development consent' in EC law (by reference to the definition in Directive (EEC) 85/237). Therefore, by failing to require an environmental impact assessment before the imposition of new planning conditions, the local planning authority had acted ultra vires the domestic statute and in breach of directly effective rights in EC law.

---

[168] See, eg, Case 152/84 *Marshall* [1986] ECR 723, para 48.
[169] See n 166 above para 56 of the ECJ's judgment. See, also: Case C–97/96 *Daihatsu Deutschland* [1997] ECR I–6843, paras 24 and 26; Case C–221/88 *Busseni* [1990] ECR I–495, paras 23–26.
[170] See n 166 para 57 of the ECJ's judgment. See, also: Case 103/88 *Fratelli Costanzo* [1989] ECR 1839, paras 28–33; Case C–194/94 *CIA Security International* [1996] ECR I–2201, paras 40–55; Case C–201/94 *Smith & Nephew and Primecrown* [1996] ECR I–5819, paras 33–39; Case C–443/98 *Unilever* [2000] ECR I–7535, paras 45–52.

(2) *Challenging the transposition into domestic law of obligations in EC law: non-implementation and defective implementation.* Here, the domestic challenge will lie to the national body responsible for the original failure to implement and/or the national body reflecting that failure in an administrative decision or other act or omission. It is important to distinguish between the duty of implementation at different stages. There may be a direct challenge to domestic legislation that is contended not properly to transpose Community obligations.[171] Sometimes, however, the obligation to implement, although fulfilled at the stage of passing of national legislation, is not a once-and-for-all obligation so that it continues to affect subsequent administrative decisions and other measures. Administrative decisions are, in general, less susceptible to successful challenge by judicial review on the footing of their failure lawfully to implement the EC obligation following lawful transposition of that obligation in a national legislative measure than they are to challenge on the basis of:

(a) their dependence on defective national legislation, and/or

(b) their dependence on defective EC legislation, and/or

(c) their incompatibility with lawful national or EC measures.

(3) *Challenging derogations.* In these cases, the challenge to a national legislative measure or administrative decision is based on the ground of unlawful derogation from a Community obligation. Whilst limited derogation from EC obligations is sometimes permitted the circumstances are usually highly restricted and derogation in a legislative measure is narrowly construed. Those defending the legality of the measure or administrative decision in question may seek to justify it on the ground of a specific derogation permitted by the Treaty or EC legislation.[172] There, the question will usually be whether or not the derogation is proportionate. Alternatively, the fact of derogation may be denied altogether.[173] In the latter class of case, therefore, there will be two stages of analysis, namely:

(a) whether there is derogation from an existing EC obligation, and

(b) whether any derogation is justified by EC law as being both permitted and proportionate.

(4) *Challenging other measures and administrative decisions argued to be within the scope of Community law.* An increasingly important area that has come under recent judicial scrutiny is the scope of EC law itself. Although challenges may only be made, on an EC basis, to violations that derive from EC law, it is not always obvious whether a particular set of facts raises EC obligations. The problem usually arises where there is an EC context

---

[171] The long-lasting *Factortame* litigation is the paradigm example of such a challenge.

[172] See, eg, *R v MAFF, ex p Bell Lines Ltd* [1984] 2 CMLR 502; *R v Same, ex p Roberts* [1991] 1 CMLR 555. These cases involved what the Administrative Court held, in the event, to be unlawful restrictions on imports under Art 30 (now Art 28) EC even though the Treaty provision permitted restrictions on certain limited grounds.

[173] For example, as explained above, in *R (International Transport Roth GmbH) v Secretary of State for the Home Department* [2002] EWCA Civ 158, [2003] QB 728 the judicial review challenge was to the legislative regime imposing immigration penalties on hauliers in whose lorries clandestine entrants were transported into the United Kingdom. At first instance Sullivan J held that the legislation was contrary not only to the HRA but also because it unlawfully derogated from EC Treaty rights as to the free movement of goods and services. However, in the CA it was held that there was no interference with such rights. The challenge succeeded on the HRA arguments alone.

and it is argued that general principles of EC law apply. For example, in *R v MAFF, ex p First City Trading*[174] the beef stocks transfer scheme was established in response to an EC Commission decision. However, it was not devised in order to implement specific powers or duties obviously deriving from EC law. Laws J held that the EC general principles (most appositely of equal treatment) did not apply because the case was not one falling within the scope of EC law. This is a potentially fertile field of challenge because the precise boundaries of EC law are not set in stone. It also raises constitutional issues since the greater the scope of EC law, the less scope there may be for legislative autonomy on the part of the Member States (including the national courts). Nor is this area free from controversy. The scope of EC law and the applicable principles are examined in more detail in other sections.[175]

(5) *Underlying challenges to the validity of EC legislation.* In an EC setting, national legislative measures and/or administrative decisions are usually dependent for their legality on the supervening legality of prior EC legislation.[176] There cannot, with a reference under Article 234, be a direct challenge by way of judicial review to the validity of EC legislation because the national court lacks jurisdiction to declare EC legislative measures to be unlawful.[177] However, as explained above, that does not necessarily mean that judicial review is inappropriate. It will be appropriate in circumstances where, although the underlying challenge is to EC legislation, there is a need to seek relief in the Administrative Court that is directed towards a national measure[178] (actual or proposed) or administrative decision that is itself dependent on the legality of EC legislation.[179] In that event, although the Administrative Court may not grant relief directly in respect of the EC legislation it may refer the proceedings to the ECJ under Article 234 (ex 177) EC. If the ECJ holds the EC legislation to be unlawful it will inevitably follow that the national measure or administrative decision that is the subject of challenge in the domestic judicial review proceedings will be unlawful. The Administrative Court will then grant direct relief in relation to the offending domestic measure or decision under challenge.[180]

2.174 Some of the above grounds of challenge will overlap as, for example, where judicial review proceedings are instituted on the alternative basis of national legislation said, of itself, to violate EC obligations and on the further or alternative basis of that legislation violating EC obligations because of incompatible EC legislation. In all cases it is important to consider framing the challenge on the widest possible basis.

---

[174] [1997] Eu LR 195.
[175] See, eg, paras 6.24 et seq.
[176] The most obvious exception to this will be where the national measure stems from a Treaty provision rather than from any intervening EC legislation since a Treaty provision is necessarily legally valid.
[177] See paras 4.92 et seq.
[178] Or even, at least in certain instances, *proposed* domestic legislation: see, eg, para 3.141.
[179] See, eg *R (ABNA Ltd) v Secretary of State for Health and Food Standards Agency* [2004] Eu LR 88.
[180] See, further, at paras 3.137 et seq.

3

BRINGING AN EC LAW JUDICIAL REVIEW CHALLENGE IN THE ADMINISTRATIVE COURT

A. Introduction

Much, perhaps the majority of, EC law imposes individually enforceable obligations on the **3.01** State and, as emanations of the State, on its public authorities. As such, and as Chapters 1 and 2 have been designed to show, EC law now plays an increasingly important role in domestic public law and, in particular, judicial review.

3.02 Domestic judicial review has, itself, undergone profound transformation over the past 30 years or so.[1] But the enormous growth of both EC law and, latterly, fundamental rights protection under the HRA has changed and extended its substantive scope and reach in distinctive ways. This growth is also reflected, at least potentially, in the application of the procedural rules to domestic judicial review challenges with an EC dimension.

3.03 This chapter addresses the relevant judicial review procedure in the Administrative Court from the perspective of EC law requirements (including where relevant for comparative purposes the HRA). Central, however, to an understanding of possible modifications to domestic judicial review procedure in an EC context is an appreciation of the principles that make them necessary. These are, therefore, considered first.

B. Principles of EC Law Relevant to Judicial Review Procedure

Overview

3.04 There are three principles of EC law that are especially relevant to domestic judicial review procedure.[2] These are the principles of:

(1) effectiveness;
(2) equivalence; and,
(3) non-discrimination.[3]

3.05 In the context of national procedural rules, the ECJ first formulated these principles in *Rewe-Zentralfinanz v Landwirtschaftskammer Saarland*:[4]

> In the absence of Community rules, it is for the domestic system of each member state to designate the courts having jurisdiction and the procedural conditions governing actions at law intended to ensure the protection of the rights which subjects derive from the direct effects of Community law; it being understood that such conditions cannot be less favourable than those relating to similar actions of a domestic nature . . .
>
> . . . The position would be different only if these rules made it impossible in practice to exercise rights which the national courts have a duty to protect.

3.06 Although this formulation was initially expressed in terms of directly effective rights, the ECJ has clarified that it applies equally to 'all rights which persons enjoy under Community law'[5] potentially encompassing, therefore, those rights arising by virtue of indirect effect leading to State liability in damages.[6]

---

[1] See, eg, R Gordon, *Judicial Review and Crown Office Practice* (1999) paras 3–003 to 3–114.

[2] Equivalence and effectiveness are also analysed in other sections with specific reference to the equal treatment principle, see paras 7.13–7.41.

[3] Including, as in EC law generally, both direct and indirect discrimination.

[4] Case 33/76 [1976] ECR 1989. To similar effect, see: Case 45/76 *Comet BV v Produktschap voor Siergewassen* [1976] ECR 2043; Case C–13/01 *Safalero Srl v Prefetto di Genova* [2003] ECR I–8679. The EC principle of national autonomy in the framing of procedural rules is also reflected in domestic decisions. See, eg, *Autologic plc v Inland Revenue Commissioners* [2005] UKHL 54, [2005] 3 WLR 339.

[5] Cases 6 and 9/90 *Francovich and Bonifaci v Italy* [1991] ECR I–5357.

[6] See paras 5.103 et seq.

It follows from this recognition of national autonomy in the framing of procedural rules that, **3.07** subject to application of these EC general principles, domestic procedure will apply to EC challenges and will ordinarily require—in common with other domestic and HRA cases— public law challenges to be commenced in the Administrative Court by way of judicial review.[7] However, it also follows that the position will be different where, for example, the normal rules make it 'impossible in practice' to protect EC rights. If that occurred, the Administrative Court would be required, as a matter of EC law obligation, to devise new (and, if necessary, preferential) procedural rules so as to enable the relevant EC right to be realized.

There are several procedural areas in judicial review that are, at least potentially, affected by **3.08** the operation of these principles including (most notably) standing, delay, and interim relief. The practical 'reach' of the principles themselves in an EC judicial review challenge is, therefore, of obvious significance.

The effectiveness principle

The principle of effectiveness reflects the Treaty obligation in Article 10 (ex 5) EC which **3.09** requires Member States 'to take all appropriate measures ... to ensure fulfilment of the obligations arising out of this Treaty or resulting from action taken by the institutions of the Community'. Compliance with the principle means that whatever procedural rules are established, such procedures must be effective so as to ensure that EC obligations are adequately fulfilled.

However, nothing in this or the other principles referred to above requires a specific procedure **3.10** to be adopted for that purpose. Subject, always, to those principles being complied with, in the absence of particular Community provisions it is for the Member State to determine which court possesses jurisdiction.[8] It is, subject to the same proviso, for the Member State to decide matters of procedure, evidence, remedy, and substantive law. Judicial review and its attendant procedures are, in this sense at least, discretionary.

There have been many statements—from the ECJ and national courts—of the principle of **3.11** effectiveness as it affects, and potentially limits, domestic procedures generally. These statements have sometimes differed subtly. As noted above, in *Rewe*[9] procedural effectiveness was expressed in terms of the procedural rules adopted not making it 'impossible in practice' to exercise the Community right in question.

In other instances, however, the formulation has been modified. Thus, in *Express Dairy* **3.12** *Foods v Intervention Board for Agricultural Produce*[10] national procedural rules were said to be excluded if they made it 'virtually impossible' or 'excessively difficult' to exercise

---

[7] Subject, always, to public law issues being able to be taken by way of collateral challenge. See paras 1.120 et seq.

[8] See, eg, Case 179/84 *Bozettti v Invernizzi* [1985] ECR 2301, para 17.

[9] Case 33/76 [1976] ECR 1989. See, also, *Preston v Wolverhampton Healthcare NHS Trust (No 2)* [2001] UKHL 5, [2001] AC 455, paras 3–4, per Lord Slynn.

[10] Case 130/79 [1980] ECR 1887. See, to similar effect, Case 199/82 *Amministrazione delle Finanze v San Giorgio* [1983] ECR 3595, para 14. For a statement adopting this formulation in domestic law, see *Autologic Holdings plc v IRC* [2004] EWCA Civ 680, [2005] 1 WLR 52, para 25, per Peter Gibson LJ ('practically impossible or excessively difficult').

the right. In *Denkavit International*[11] Advocate General Jacobs suggested that the correct test was whether or not the rule made it 'unduly difficult' to do so.

3.13 In *Von Colson v Land Nordhrein-Westfalen*[12] the emphasis of the ECJ, in terms of the effectiveness principle, was even more liberal in that the principle was there expressed positively rather than negatively and as being not only necessary to protect individual Community rights but also to be a means of deterring breaches of EC law. Interpreting Article 6 of the Equal Treatment Directive (Directive (EEC) 76/207), the ECJ held that the Community obligation engaged required all Member States:

> to adopt measures which are sufficiently effective to achieve the objective of the Directive. Although the Directive does not require any specific form of sanction for unlawful discrimination it does entail that that sanction be such as to guarantee real and effective judicial protection. It must also have a real deterrent effect on the employer.

3.14 And, in similar vein, in a domestic judicial review case Lord Bingham CJ observed (in positive terms) thus:[13]

> It is a cardinal principle of Community law that the laws of Member States should provide adequate and effective redress for violations of Community law by Member States where these result in infringement of specific individual rights conferred by the law of the Community.

3.15 Importantly, as in other areas, context is highly significant. As the ECJ has stated:[14]

> ... each case which raises the question whether a national procedural provision renders application of Community law impossible or excessively difficult must be analysed by reference to the role of that provision in the procedure, its progress and its special features, viewed as a whole, before the various national instances. In the light of that analysis the basic principles of the domestic judicial system, such as protection of the rights of the defence, the principle of legal certainty and the proper conduct of procedure, must, where appropriate, be taken into consideration.

3.16 When taken together, it is submitted that the various formulations make it clear that the essential concern to which the principle of effectiveness is directed is to ensure that the objective of the relevant Community obligation, the context in which the procedural rule is set and the need to deter breaches of Community law are fully taken into account when determining the legitimacy and/or application of the procedural rule (or absence of a procedural rule) under consideration.

3.17 The ambit of the principle of effectiveness, taken in conjunction with the other relevant principles, is analysed below with specific reference to Administrative Court procedure. Examples of its application to procedural rules in general include the prohibition on

---

[11] Case C–2/94 [1996] ECR I–2827.

[12] Case 14/83 [1984] ECR 1891.

[13] *R v Secretary of State for the Home Department, ex p Gallagher* [1996] 2 CMLR 951, para 10.

[14] Joined Cases C–430/93 and C–431/93 *Van Schijndel v SPF* [1995] ECR 1–4705, para 19; Case C–312/93 *Peterbroeck v Belgium* [1994] ECR 1–4599, para 14. It is, possibly, because the conformity of national procedural rules with the effectiveness principle is context-specific that the ECJ has, thus far, not required harmonization of such rules within the Community. There have, nonetheless, been references in certain of the cases to the problems posed by non-harmonization: see *Rewe/Comet* (n 4 above) and *Express Dairy Foods* (n 10 above).

national provisions that are specifically designed to frustrate the enforcement of directly effective Community rules,[15] the obligation on Member States to give reasons with respect to national decisions which curtail rights afforded by Community law,[16] and the declared illegitimacy of the 'excusable error' doctrine whereby illegality committed over a long period of time became jurisdictionally immune from challenge.[17] The latter is to be distinguished from reasonable limitation periods which, as will be seen,[18] may be justified even where their effect is ultimately to preclude enforcement of a Community right.

Equivalence

In *Levez v TH Jennings (Harlow Pools) Ltd*[19] the ECJ held that: **3.18**

> ... [the] principle of equivalence requires that the rule at issue [is] to be applied without distinction, whether the infringement alleged is of Community law or national law, where the purpose and cause of action are similar.

Whilst the ECJ has consistently ruled that the application of equivalence is, like the   **3.19** principle of effectiveness, a matter for national courts[20] it has also laid down guidelines for the assistance of those courts.

So far as domestic judicial review procedural rules are concerned, there is an important   **3.20** limitation to equivalence. In *Levez* the ECJ reiterated the point that Member States were not required to extend their most favourable rules to protect individual Community rights.[21] It repeated, in relation to equivalence, the principles first enunciated (and earlier cited in respect of *effectiveness)* in *van Schijndel*[22] that 'the national court must take into account the role played by that provision in the procedure as a whole, as well as the operation of any special features of that procedure before the different national courts'.[23]

Thus, in estimating whether the purpose and cause of action of a putative comparator   **3.21** are 'similar' to the procedural rule relevant to the claimed Community right it is material to examine whether the comparator action involves a public authority or is, rather, one affecting private parties only.

This distinction is shown to practical effect in *EDIS v Ministero delle Finanze*.[24] That case   **3.22** concerned a barrier under Italian law preventing the applicants from reclaiming company registration charges imposed by the State in breach of Directive (EEC) 69/335. The applicants contended, by reference to the equivalence principle that it was unlawful for the Italian Government to rely on a three-year limitation period for bringing the claim given the existence of a 10-year limitation period in Italy for repayment claims involving private individuals.

---

[15] See Case 240/87 *Deville v Administration des impots* [1988] ECR 3513.
[16] Case 222/86 *Heylens v UNECTEF* [1987] ECR 4097.
[17] Case C–188/95 *Fantask v Industriministeriet (Erhverv-Sministeriet)* [1997] ECR 6783.
[18] See paras 3.81 et seq.
[19] Case 326/96 [1998] ECR I–7835, para 41.
[20] See, eg, *Levez* (n 19 above) paras 39 and 43; Case C–261/95 *Palmisani v INPS* [1997] ECR I–4025, para 39.
[21] *Levez* (n 19 above) para 42. See, also, eg, Case C–228/96 *Aprile, in liquidation v Amministrazione delle Finanze* [1998] ECR I–7141.
[22] [1995] ECR I–4705.
[23] *Levez* (n 19 above) para 44.
[24] Case C–231/96 [1998] ECR I–4951.

3.23   The ECJ rejected the argument. It held, materially, as follows:[25]

> Community law does not in principle preclude the legislation of a Member State from laying down, alongside a limitation period applicable under the ordinary law to actions between individuals for the recovery of sums paid but not due, special detailed rules governing claims and legal proceedings to challenge the imposition of charges and other levies. The position would only be different if those detailed rules applied solely to actions based on community law for the repayment of such charges and levies.

3.24   In judicial review proceedings, which—in the EC context at least—will involve the State or an emanation of the State,[26] the true comparator for the purpose of applying the principle of equivalence is, therefore, likely to lie in comparable public rather than private law proceedings.

3.25   Further, the determination of whether there is a proper comparison to be made leaves the national court with a measure of judgment as to the object and purpose of the alleged comparator albeit within certain limits.

3.26   In *Rosalba Palmisani v Istituto Nazionale della Previdenza Sociale (INPS)*,[27] for example, the applicants claimed damages for the delayed transposition of Directive (EEC) 80/987. This directive was concerned with protecting employees in the event of their employers' insolvency. INPS was the State agency set up, in conformity with the directive, to manage the fund guaranteeing arrears of wages.

3.27   It was claimed that a limitation period of one year from the date of the national legislative decree implementing the directive was too short, rendering the Community right created by the directive unlawful as required by the principles of effectiveness and equivalence.

3.28   The ECJ rejected the challenge based on effectiveness. So far as equivalence was concerned, the argument was that the one-year limitation period was not equivalent to the five-year limitation period under Article 2043 of the Italian Civil Code for reparation in general claims for non-contractual liability. As to that, the court said this:

> Community law does not in principle preclude the legislation of a Member State from laying down, alongside a limitation period applicable under the ordinary law to actions between individuals for the recovery of sums paid but not due, special detailed rules governing claims and legal proceedings to challenge the imposition of charges and other levies. The position would only be different if those detailed rules applied solely to actions based on community law for the repayment of such charges and levies.

3.29   On proper analysis, then, application of the principle of equivalence requires the Administrative Court to determine the purpose and cause of action of the alleged comparator and determine—on the basis of the information before it—whether it is similar to the purpose and cause of action before it. Generally, comparison as between public and private law causes of action will not provide a true comparison. Even as between causes of action in public law care may be needed. For example, in *Palmisani*[28] the ECJ rejected, as suitable

---

[25]   ibid para 37.
[26]   See para 2.17 et seq. for fuller consideration of a State emanation.
[27]   Case C–261/95 [1997] ECR I–4025.
[28]   ibid paras 36–37.

comparators, applications made under national law to enforce directives generally or actions under national law to obtain social security benefits. The ECJ held that the objectives of such proceedings differed in nature from attempts to activate the compensation scheme under the relevant directive.

Similarly, even where the purpose and causes of action are 'similar' the Administrative Court is, for the purpose of equivalence, conducting a *comparative* exercise as opposed to one that is intended to produce exact results. Factors other than a search for identical features once similarity is established must be considered. Thus in *Levez*,[29] the ECJ observed that particular factors *in that case* that the national court would need to consider if similarity was established included whether the similar procedural rules involved additional cost and/or delay. **3.30**

The advantage of invoking equivalence to challenge a procedural rule in a domestic EC judicial review case is that it obviates the need to establish the 'virtual impossibility' of exercising the Community right in question under that rule which would be required by the principle of effectiveness. On the other hand, it is not an easy principle to deploy, at least so far as time limits are concerned, in public law cases where there is a generally uniform time limit (albeit subject to the case-specific requirement of promptness)[30] for all such challenges. A possible exception, where equivalence might usefully be employed in the sphere of limitation, is in the field of fundamental rights where the HRA lays down differential time limits and where there is an ostensible overlap with EC law (see below). **3.31**

The principle of non-discrimination

It is doubtful whether the principle of non-discrimination adds greatly to the equivalence principle. It is, however, relevant to note that Article 12 EC prohibits discrimination on the grounds of nationality. **3.32**

This prohibition covers both direct and indirect discrimination. So, a procedural rule requiring the giving of security for costs by a non-national in circumstances where nationals are not subject to any such requirement would constitute unlawful direct discrimination in a challenge founded on a Community right.[31] So, too, the discretion formerly conferred by RSC Ord 23 whereby security for costs could be required of a plaintiff who was ordinarily resident out of the jurisdiction exemplifies indirect discrimination given that most plaintiffs so resident would be foreign nationals.[32] **3.33**

Other EC general principles of law relevant to domestic procedural issues

The (now) extensive case law of the ECJ recognizes a number of other general principles of law drawn from the legal systems of the Member States. These include the proportionality principle, principles of legitimate expectation and legal certainty (embracing non-retroactivity) equal treatment and fundamental rights. **3.34**

---

[29] Case 326/96 [1998] ECR I–7835.
[30] See paras 3.81 et seq.
[31] Case C–20/90 *Hubbard v Hamburger* [1993] ECR I–3777.
[32] *Fitzgerald v Williams* [1996] 2 QB 657.

3.35 Many, though not all, of these principles are recognized substantively in domestic judicial review cases and/or under the ECHR as incorporated into domestic law by the HRA. However, even where they are recognized as relevant substantive grounds for review their application may differ according to whether the challenge is founded in 'ordinary' domestic judicial review and/or under the HRA and/or in EC law. The similarities and differences of application of these other general EC principles can be significant and may sometimes affect both the grounds for, and remedies in, the challenge. They are examined in more detail elsewhere.[33]

3.36 However, these EC general principles of law (including fundamental rights) are also sometimes as potentially relevant to the legitimacy of *procedural* rules (or their absence) in EC challenges as the principles of equivalence and effectiveness outlined above.

3.37 In general, so far as *procedural* validity is concerned, these other EC law general principles and those principles to be found in domestic law and in the ECHR jurisprudence are, broadly, similar. However, EC law—like its ECHR counterpart in this respect—stresses more than has, hitherto, been the case in domestic law the need for court decisions to be accompanied by reasons and the requirement of equality of arms (see below). So, too, both EC and ECHR case law give full effect to the proportionality principle which is, as yet, not recognized as a matter of domestic judicial review. The procedural rules in judicial review must in an EC challenge, therefore, also sometimes be set against the standard of additional general EC principles.

Different approach by the Administrative Court to interpretation of procedural rules in EC cases

3.38 Importantly, too, procedural rules are to be *interpreted* more generously in an EC/ECHR context than in a purely domestic context so as to enable the rule in question to accord with EC rights (or, as the case may be, Convention rights) *if such a construction is possible.*[34] This EC interpretative principle has been addressed in some detail in Chapter 2[35] and it applies as much to the interpretation of procedural rules in EC challenges as it does to substantive law.

3.39 If the procedural provision in question cannot be given an EC compliant meaning then it must, at least, be disapplied whether or not it is contained in, or is the compelled or authorized result of, primary legislation.

3.40 So far as procedural provisions deriving from primary legislation are concerned,[36] a different result may obtain in a judicial review challenge founded on the ECHR since the HRA does not

---

[33] See (respectively) Chapter 2 (grounds for judicial review), Chapter 5 (available remedies).

[34] See Case C–106/89 *Marleasing SA v La Comercial Internacional de Alimentacion SA* [1990] ECR I–4135 (for EC law), HRA, s 3 (ECHR cases). The relevant principles of interpretation are examined in Chapter 2 and are, *mutatis mutandis*, equally apposite to construing procedural rules as they are to remedial provisions or substantive law.

[35] See paras 2.130 et seq.

[36] Including rules in subordinate legislation that are compelled or authorized by the primary legislation: see HRA, ss 3(2)(c) and 6(2)(b).

permit disapplication of primary legislation but only a declaration of incompatibility. In a purely domestic challenge, the procedural rule would have to be followed in any event unless such rule was derived solely from subordinate legislation and was itself susceptible to challenge on conventional judicial review grounds.

C. An Outline of Judicial Review Procedure in the Administrative Court

Introduction

A detailed examination of Administrative Court practice is outside the scope of this book.[37] **3.41** What follows is a general outline of the most directly relevant procedural aspects that engage an EC (and, sometimes, an overlapping ECHR) dimension. Those features which may differ, or be more pronounced, in EC challenges are then analysed separately by reference to the principles outlined above.

Changes to the judicial review procedure were introduced following the Bowman **3.42** Report, which was published in March 2000. The modern procedure for judicial review is now contained in Pts 54 and 8[38] of the Civil Procedure Rules (CPR) read in conjunction with s 31 of the Supreme Court Act 1981 (SCA). The Pt 54 Practice Direction (hereafter 'Practice Direction') should also be referred to.

There are three essential stages to an application for judicial review. These are: (1) the **3.43** preliminary stage up to and including the grant of permission to apply for judicial review,[39] (2) the interlocutory stage up to the full hearing and (3) the full hearing.

Stage 1—the preliminary stage (to permission)

In order to embark on the preliminary stage at all there must be a relevant claimant.[40] **3.44** By virtue of SCA, s 31(3) this means any person with a *sufficient interest* in the matter to which the judicial review application relates. This requirement of standing is generally phrased and is, plainly, apt to include those persons seeking to enforce asserted rights under EC law. However, the enforcement of EC rights gives rise to particular problems in which the general case law as it has developed over the years in domestic cases (and, now, somewhat differently in ECHR cases under the HRA) needs to be separately considered. There are also occasions where standing may require more restrictive application where the challenge is founded on EC law. These matters are discussed below.

---

[37] For a helpful guide to the procedure governing those cases that must proceed through the Administrative Court, see M Supperstone and L Knapman, *Administrative Court Practice* (2002). The principles stated here are, however, equally relevant to challenging relevant aspects of procedure in a private law forum where public law issues are raised.

[38] CPR Pt 54 contains the primary provisions governing judicial review procedure (in place of CPR r 8.4) but the procedural rules in Pt 54 must be read in conjunction with CPR Pt 8 which makes general provision for claims.

[39] Permission is a threshold requirement: see CPR r 54.4.

[40] There must, of course, also be a properly joined defendant. In the context of EC law this means the State or an emanation of the State. The meaning of this term has engendered case law which is discussed more fully in Chapter 2.

3.45 The essential steps in the preliminary stage are these:

(1) The claimant must follow the pre-action protocol. This requires the sending of a letter before action to the defendant and any other interested parties[41] containing the date and details (fact and law) of the alleged public law breach. Ordinarily, 14 days should be given to reply although a different limit may, sometimes, be appropriate.

(2) Although the claim should not, usually, be lodged before the defendant's time for reply has expired, the time limits for bringing claims for judicial review are strict. Claimants must act 'promptly' and, in any event, within three months from the date when grounds for the claim first arose.[42] Time cannot be extended by agreement. Importantly, the test is 'promptness' so that it cannot be assumed that a claim is brought timeously merely because it is commenced within three months. The domestic case law on delay is not entirely consistent and questions remain (see below) as to whether the promptness requirement, and other aspects of the delay rules, are compatible (or, at least, *always* compatible) with EC law and/or under the HRA.

(3) In the absence of a satisfactory response, proceedings in judicial review are begun by lodging a claim form (Form N461)[43] including detailed grounds in the Administrative Court Office. Where a claimant wishes to rely on a right under the HRA full details of the claim and remedies sought must be given. There is no separate requirement for claims founded on EC law. However, many EC challenges will raise issues of fundamental rights which overlap with HRA issues. Also, the potential remedies available in EC law are at least as constitutionally significant as those under the HRA. It is suggested, therefore, that practitioners raising EC issues should plead these as fully as any HRA claims.[44]

(4) Subject to contrary direction from the Administrative Court (in practice in non-urgent cases) the defendant (and any interested party)[45] has 21 days from service of the claim form to file an acknowledgement of service.[46] This includes the defendant's summary grounds of opposition to the claim for judicial review. Any person served with a claim form who wishes to take part in the proceedings should file such acknowledgement and summary.[47] If no such acknowledgement is served the defendant may not participate in the permission stage without specific consent from the court.[48] But, whether or not an acknowledgement of service is lodged, the defendant may participate in the

---

[41] This means persons directly affected by the alleged default (see below).

[42] CPR r 54.5.

[43] For the current form see the Court Service website: http://www.courtservice.gov.uk. Written evidence and documents should also be lodged. All this should be accompanied by relevant statutory material (including material from the EC Treaty, EC regulations and/or directives) and a list of essential reading.

[44] Special rules apply, though, to claims under the HRA (see, eg, CPR r 54.5(3)) which do not ostensibly apply to EC claims even where fundamental rights are engaged (unless separately engaged under the HRA).

[45] Referred to here, collectively, as 'the defendant'. An 'interested party' means a person who is 'directly affected' by the claim (see CPR r 54.1(2)(f)) and has been narrowly construed in the case law: see *R v Rent Office Service, ex p Muldoon* [1996] 1 WLR 1103.

[46] CPR r 54.8(2)(a).

[47] CPR r 54.8(1).

[48] CPR r 54.9(1).

full hearing though failure so to lodge may be taken into account by the court when considering costs.[49]

(5) Special provision is made for urgent applications, though in a Practice Statement from the Administrative Court rather than the CPR.[50] Where interim relief is sought the claimant must, in addition to completing a request for urgent consideration,[51] (which should set out the grounds for interim relief) also complete a draft order. In most domestic judicial review challenges the claimant must be prepared to give an undertaking in damages when claiming interim relief. There are, however, arguments (considered below) why, at least in EC challenges, this requirement (one, in any event, of practice rather than jurisdiction) should be dispensed with.[52]

(6) The test for whether permission to apply for judicial review should be granted is, essentially, whether the claimant's case is arguable. This test may be required to be applied more liberally in a challenge founded on EC law because, if permission is refused, the Administrative Court has deprived itself of any opportunity of referring the matter to the ECJ. As a matter of discretion the Administrative Court may refuse to entertain the application where there is an alternative remedy available. EC law is not immune from this potential discretionary bar.[53] By way of contrast, however, the scope for the exercise of discretion *to refuse relief* in an EC case if—following the grant of permission—a case is otherwise made out is small.[54] Permission is first considered on the papers. If refused,[55] there is provision in the CPR for renewal for oral hearing[56] and, if appropriate, by way of appeal to the Court of Appeal.[57] Exceptionally, the House of Lords has jurisdiction to hear an appeal from the Court of Appeal from a refusal of permission by that court in circumstances where a full appeal has been heard by the Court of Appeal and that court's decision is not merely one refusing permission to appeal from the order of the Administrative Court.[58]

Stage 2—the interlocutory stage (from permission to full hearing)

Although interim relief is sometimes granted prior to permission being granted the more usual course is for it to be considered together with the question of permission or thereafter. For this reason it is convenient to treat it as part of the interlocutory stage.   **3.46**

---

[49] CPR r 54.9(2).

[50] *Practice Statement (Administrative Court: Listing and Urgent Cases)* [2002] 1 WLR 810.

[51] This form, also on the Court Service Website (n 43 above), is set out at Annex B to the Practice Statement above.

[52] Similar, above albeit not identical arguments, may be advanced in an HRA challenge (see below).

[53] See, eg, *R v Secretary of State for Employment, ex p Equal Opportunities Commission* [1995] 1 AC 1 where it was held that a claim for redundancy payment founded on allegations of indirect discrimination should have been brought in an employment tribunal rather than in judicial review.

[54] See, especially, *Berkeley v Secretary of State for the Environment* [2001] 2 AC 603.

[55] There is also provision for cases to be transferred and continued as if not commenced under CPR Pt 54: see CPR r 54.20. For guidance on the approach to costs in the event of an unsuccessful permission application see *R (Mount Cook Land Ltd) v Westminster City Council* (2003) 43 EG 137 (CS) (save, exceptionally, only the costs of lodging an acknowledgement of service will be awarded against an unsuccessful claimant at the permission stage).

[56] CPR r 54.11–12. For the necessary action see Practice Statement (n 50 above) at p. 812E.

[57] See CPR r 52.15(1). In practice permission of the Administrative Court to appeal to the Court of Appeal should be sought but may also (or alternatively) be sought from the Court of Appeal: see *R v Secretary of State for Trade and Industry, ex p Eastaway* [2000] 1 WLR 2222, 2225.

[58] *R (Burkett) v London Borough of Hammersmith and Fulham* [2002] 1 WLR 1593 distinguishing, in this respect, its approach in *Eastaway* above.

3.47   On that footing, the steps at the interlocutory stage will usually include the following:

(1) Claimants may apply for interim relief. Jurisdiction to grant interim relief derives from SCA, s 31 and includes interim injunctions and declarations. The procedure is set out in CPR Pts 54 and 25 (the latter being those elements of CPR Pt 8 in respect of interim relief applying to CPR Pt 25 that are unmodified by CPR Pt 54). The principles governing the grant of interim injunctions and declarations are likely to be similar. Similarly, interim relief in the form of a stay of proceedings, under CPR r 54.10, is also obtainable on very similar principles to those that affect the grant of interim injunctions. Special considerations apply to the grant of interim relief in EC cases (see below).

(2) Other interim applications may also be made so as to regulate the procedure at the full hearing. Most notably, these include applications for disclosure, cross-examination, pre-emptive costs, and (sometimes) joinder of parties. Such applications should comply with the procedural requirements of CPR Pt 23 (including, especially, service of an application notice that sets out the order sought and evidence in support). Applications for disclosure and cross-examination are, generally, treated more restrictively than in ordinary actions. It is, however, possible that in EC challenges different and more liberal principles apply (see below). The newly developing jurisdiction to make a protective costs order may also be particularly important in EC challenges (see below).

(3) If permission is granted, then following the grant of permission, the defendant (normally, but subject to any order for abridgement or extension of time) has 35 days to file detailed grounds on which the claim is opposed or supported and any written evidence in support.[59] Although there is no express requirement in the CPR for evidence in response, a claimant may apply for permission to file further evidence under CPR r 54.16. In practice, further evidence (provided that it is relevant, not objected to, and served well in advance of the hearing) will be allowed by the Administrative Court at the hearing without further application.

(4) The Practice Direction requires certain further steps to be taken in preparation for the hearing. The claimant must file and serve a skeleton argument not less than 21 working days prior to the hearing.[60] The defendant must file and serve a skeleton argument in response not less than 14 working days before the hearing.[61] A paginated and indexed bundle must also be filed and served by the claimant.[62]

Stage 3—full hearing

3.48   The remedies that may be granted on a full hearing are important and distinctive so far as EC challenges are concerned. This is, especially, so with regard to damages which are separately considered.[63]

---

[59] CPR r 54.13. The 35-day requirement is actual days rather than 35 working days: see CPR r 2.8.
[60] Practice Direction, para 15.1.
[61] Practice Direction, para 15.2.
[62] Practice Direction, paras 16.1–16.2.
[63] See Chapter 5.

D. Standing and EC Challenges

Standing in domestic law

Questions of standing can present difficulties in EC challenges. This is not because the **3.49** standing rules prevailing in domestic law are restrictive in themselves but, rather, because they may sometimes have to be applied more restrictively in EC cases. Both EC law and HRA law have standing rules which are not necessarily co-extensive either with each other or with purely domestic—and essentially liberal—principles of standing.

By virtue of SCA, s 31(3) a claim for judicial review may be begun by any person with **3.50** a sufficient interest in the matter to which the application relates. So far as domestic judicial review challenges are concerned this general requirement is qualified only by the case law.

As the domestic (ie non-EC/HRA) case law on standing has developed, there are three **3.51** features which should be noted:

(1) There is a two-stage test for determining whether a claimant possesses the requisite standing.[64] At the permission stage the Administrative Court should essentially be concerned to filter out hopeless cases where the claimant is, in truth, interfering in matters which do not concern him. However, at the full hearing there is, potentially at least, fuller scrutiny of standing.

(2) At the substantive hearing, according to the House of Lords in *R v IRC, ex p National Federation of Self-Employed and Small Businesses*,[65] (the Fleet Street Casuals case) standing is often elided with the full legal and factual background. Thus, it will be:

> necessary to consider the powers and duties in law of those against whom relief is asked, the position of the applicant in relation to those powers and duties, and to the breach said to have been committed. . .[66]

And:

> It is a mixed question of fact and law; a question of fact and degree and the relationship between the applicant and the matter to which the application relates, having regard to all the circumstances of the case.[67]

(3) In practice, standing has been applied liberally in domestic cases with social action groups having recognized expertise, such as Greenpeace, being held to enjoy the necessary standing to pursue judicial review claims involving public interest matters. In *R v Secretary of State for Foreign and Commonwealth Affairs, ex p World Development Movement*[68] (the Pergau Dam case) a Divisional Court held that factors relevant to standing in such cases include:
(a) the merits of the challenge,
(b) the importance of vindicating the rule of law,
(c) the importance of the issue raised,
(d) the likely absence of any other person who would bring the challenge,
(e) the nature of the illegality in question, and
(f) the role played by the body in question.

---

[64] *R v IRC, ex p National Federation of Self-Employed and Small Businesses Ltd* [1982] AC 617.
[65] ibid.
[66] ibid 630, per Lord Wilberforce.
[67] ibid 659, per Lord Roskill.
[68] [1995] 1 WLR 386, 395.

3.52 The relevant standing principles applicable to non-EC/HRA judicial review challenges give rise to the following potential difficulties so far as EC challenges are concerned. These are:

(1) Uncertainty.

(2) Difficulties in reconciling those principles with the more limited standing requirements in HRA challenges insofar as such challenges overlap with EC law.

(3) Inconsistency with standing rules before the ECJ.

Uncertainty and the effectiveness/legal certainty principles

3.53 The fusion between law and merits, in the domestic case law on standing, appears to make standing discretionary as opposed to a jurisdictional entitlement. In EC cases there could be a breach of the principles of effectiveness/legal certainty, outlined above,[69] if this were, in practice, to result in an uncertain discretion being exercised so as to make the enforcement of Community rights unduly difficult.

3.54 It seems clear that in most cases there should be no breach of these principles so far as standing requirements for individual EC rights-based challenges are concerned. Where an individual seeks to challenge a domestic measure for asserted breach of an EC right the assertion of the right itself should, in principle, constitute (subject to arguability) a 'sufficient interest'. It is submitted that this should be so even if the right is inchoate or unclear since that, alone, is likely to confer a discretion (and, ultimately, impose a duty) on the court to refer the case to the ECJ at the full hearing.[70] For the Administrative Court in a case that was less than clear to deny standing would be to deprive the claimant of his right (at least ultimately) to have the legal merits of his case adjudicated upon by the ECJ. It would, in other words, be to breach the principle of effectiveness. If, by contrast, the merits of the case are clearly against the claimant then standing is no longer relevant.

3.55 In practice, the Administrative Court has not denied standing to individual claimants asserting rights under EC law. This is exemplified by cases such as *R v Attorney General, ex p ICI*,[71] where Woolf J (and, subsequently, the Court of Appeal) accorded standing to ICI in seeking to challenge, by judicial review, the grant of state aid to one of its commercial rivals.[72]

3.56 Whether EC standing goes further is questionable. As the Pergau Dam case (above) suggests it seems, as a matter of domestic law, to be permissible for groups to bring challenges in the public interest even where such challenges do not involve the assertion of public law entitlement for the claimant directly.

3.57 In *R v Secretary of State for Employment, ex p Equal Opportunities Commission*,[73] a challenge founded on the EC prohibition of sex discrimination, Lord Keith observed as follows:

> In my opinion it would be a very retrograde step now to hold that the EOC has no *locus standi* to agitate in judicial review proceedings questions related to sex discrimination which are of public importance and affect a large section of the population.

---

[69] In this context legal certainty is, perhaps, but an aspect of the principle of effectiveness.

[70] That is, under the *acte clair* doctrine. For the reference procedure and relevant considerations, see Chapter 4.

[71] [1987] 1 CMLR 72.

[72] See Chapter 13 where state aid challenges in judicial review are more fully considered.

[73] [1995] 1 AC 1, 26.

Thus, Mr Rees-Mogg had the requisite standing to challenge the UK's ratification of the   **3.58**
Maastricht Treaty.[74] In *R v Her Majesty's Treasury, ex p Smedley*[75] a taxpayer sought to establish
that a government undertaking to pay a contribution to the European Community, laid
before Parliament in the form of a draft Order in Council, was ultra vires. Although the
challenge failed on its merits, Slade LJ dealt with the argument that the claimant lacked
standing by observing that:

> I do not feel much doubt that Mr. Smedley, if only in his capacity as a taxpayer, has sufficient
> *locus standi* to raise this question by way of an application for judicial review. On the present
> state of the authorities, I cannot think that any such right of challenge belongs to the
> Attorney-General alone.

But the question, so far as the EC principle of effectiveness is concerned, is not whether   **3.59**
the Attorney General has (since the introduction of judicial review in its modern form)
an exclusive right to litigate matters in the public interest but, rather, whether there is
a right to ventilate EC points by way of judicial review in circumstances where the claimant
is not asserting any EC right for himself.

Drawing a parallel with the rationale for the expansion of standing in domestic public law there   **3.60**
may be a basis for permitting standing in at least some of these cases. To deny on a discretionary
basis (say) a social action group from pursuing such a case on the ground of lack of standing may,
in practice, make the enforcement of particular EC rights unduly difficult or may fail sufficiently
to deter violations of EC law and, hence, at least arguably breach the principle of effectiveness.
It has been suggested, for example, that domestic standing rules may fall short of ensuring
effective judicial protection for breaches of directly effective EC environmental law measures.[76]

Overlap between EC and ECHR challenges

With the entry into force of the HRA into domestic law on 2 October 2000 it is important   **3.61**
to understand that domestic standing rules have been restricted so far as HRA judicial
review challenges are concerned. The effect of this particular restriction requires careful
consideration in respect of standing in respect of overlapping challenges in EC law where
identical fundamental rights issues may be being raised. Is there to be standing in one instance
(EC) but not in the other (HRA)? And, if so, by reference to what governing principle?

Where proceedings are brought against a 'public authority' under HRA, s 7(1)(a) for   **3.62**
alleged violation of Convention rights (as defined under the HRA) then standing for such
a challenge is limited by a combination of s 7(3) and (7).[77] By HRA, s 7(3):

> If the proceedings are brought on an application for judicial review, the applicant is to
> be taken to have a sufficient interest in relation to the unlawful act only if he is, or would be,
> a victim of that act.

---

[74] *R v Secretary of State for Foreign and Commonwealth Affairs, ex p Rees-Mogg* [1993] 3 CMLR 101. Similar
observations were made by Lord Diplock in the Fleet Street Casuals case (n 64 above) 644E. In that case,
though, the claimants were denied standing on (presumably) discretionary grounds.
[75] [1985] 1 QB 657.
[76] A Geddes, 'Locus Standi and EEC Environmental Measures' (1992) 4 JEL 29.
[77] The position appears to be broader in HRA claims outside the ambit of s 7: see *Alan Rushbridger v
Attorney General* [2004] 1 AC 357.

3.63 Clearly, many—if not most—proceedings commenced under HRA, s 7 will be claims in judicial review. So, in an HRA context, a person who is not a 'victim' does not possess sufficient standing to bring judicial review proceedings notwithstanding the generality of SCA s 31(3) (above). And a 'victim' has the same meaning as that employed in Article 34 ECHR and is to be applied in HRA cases in the same manner as it is applied by the European Court of Human Rights in Strasbourg.[78]

3.64 The 'victim' test, as applied under Article 34 ECHR, is somewhat more restricted than the domestic principles outlined above. For example:

(1) A 'victim' must—whether a natural or legal person—be 'directly affected' by the alleged violation. This does not only refer to persons who have actually suffered an alleged Convention violation but includes persons who may be affected by a measure in the future.[79] It has been observed that it may not, though, include such potential 'victims' unless there is 'reasonable and convincing evidence of the probability of the occurrence of a violation concerning' the claimant.[80]

(2) Although claims may be brought by a representative on behalf of a victim lacking legal capacity[81] purely public interest challenges may not be mounted by pressure groups purporting to represent others who are 'victims'.[82]

3.65 Although it may be anomalous for HRA challenges to be limited in this way it is submitted that challenges within the scope of EC law cannot be, and are not, so limited. This is so for several reasons.

3.66 First, if the 'victim' test were to be applied to EC challenges raising fundamental rights issues there might, for the reasons advanced above, be a breach of the principle of effectiveness. Secondly, EC challenges—even where raising issues overlapping with HRA proceedings— are not brought under the HRA and are not, therefore, statutorily qualified by HRA, s 7 prohibition. As HRA, s 11 makes clear, a person's right to bring proceedings in which reliance is placed on a Convention right does not restrict any other right or freedom conferred by any law having effect in the United Kingdom or his right to bring any claim which could be brought outside HRA, s 7. So, standing in an EC case is still, so far as domestic law is concerned, regulated by SCA, s 31(3). Thirdly, as will be seen,[83] the ECHR is not itself a source of law in EC cases but forms part of the general principles recognized by Member States to which respect is accorded.

---

[78] HRA, s 7(7).

[79] See, eg, *Bowman v United Kingdom* (1998) 26 EHRR 1.

[80] *R (Hunter) v Ashworth Hospital Authority* [2001] EWHC 872, para 74. However, the Strasbourg cases do not always coincide with this observation: see, eg, *Norris v Ireland* (1988) 13 EHRR 186, para 33 (small risk of law being applied to claimant still gave him 'victim' status).

[81] See, eg, *Campbell and Cosans v United Kingdom* (1982) 4 EHRR 293.

[82] This is strongly at variance with the domestic case law on standing. cf *Greenpeace Schweiz v Switzerland* (1997) 23 EHRR CD 116 (Article 34 test) with *R v Secretary of State for the Environment, ex p Greenpeace* [1994] 4 All ER 352 (domestic test of standing).

[83] See Chapter 12.

Inconsistency with standing rules before the ECJ

There is a disparity between the generally liberal domestic standing rules and the more restrictive standing rules under Article 230 EC which becomes significant where the validity of certain Community measures, most notably directives, are sought to be challenged indirectly in domestic judicial review proceedings. This aspect of standing is also addressed elsewhere.[84] **3.67**

Importantly, only the ECJ may pronounce on the invalidity of Community measures.[85] This means that the sole avenues open to a potential claimant who needs to challenge the validity of a measure upon which a national legislative provision or administrative act or decision depends are (in theory at least) by direct action under Article 230 EC or (indirectly) by judicial review before the Administrative Court which may then make a reference to the ECJ under Article 234 EC. **3.68**

The difficulty is that whereas the domestic rules would, ordinarily, accord standing to a claimant (or interest group) on at least a broad public interest basis consistently with the principles outlined above, the ECJ case law on the scope and ambit of Article 230 EC is much more restrictive. This, in turn, poses problems for the Administrative Court given the restrictive approach of the ECJ itself by whose decisions it is bound. **3.69**

Article 230 EC (as amended) enables Member States and other Community institutions to bring actions before the ECJ to review the legality of acts of the institutions on one or more of certain specified grounds which approximate to the grounds for domestic judicial review.[86] So far as individual claimants are concerned, Article 230 enables any 'natural or legal person' to institute—on the same basis—proceedings against a decision addressed to that person or against 'a decision which, although in the form of a regulation or a decision addressed to another person, is of direct and individual concern' to him. **3.70**

In practice, although not mentioned in Article 230, the ECJ appears to have accepted that directives fall within the potential ambit of Article 230[87] and to have adopted a traditional approach to the notion of 'natural or legal person'. **3.71**

But the ECJ has taken a relatively narrow view of the notion of 'direct and individual concern'. *Direct concern* means that the measure must directly affect the legal situation of the individual concerned and leave no discretion by third parties as to its implementation by intermediate rules.[88] Where the manner of exercise of discretion is certain it seems that a person may be directly affected.[89] However, actions under Article 230 must (generally) be **3.72**

---

[84] See paras 4.34 et seq.

[85] See, eg, Case 314/85 *Foto-Frost v Hauptzollamt Lubeck-Ost* [1987] ECR 4199; *R v MAFF, ex p FEDESA* [1988] 3 CMLR 207, 212, per Henry J; *R v Secretary of State for Trade and Industry, ex p Imperial Tobacco* [2000] 2 WLR 834, 843, per Lord Woolf MR.

[86] Specifically, they are: (1) lack of competence, (2) infringement of an essential procedural requirement, (3) infringement of the Treaty or any rule of law relating to its application, and (4) misuse of powers.

[87] See, eg, Joined Cases T–172 and T–175–177/98 *Salamander v European Parliament and Council* [2000] ECR II. See, also, the discussion in R Brent, *Directives: Rights and Remedies in English and Community Law* (2001) 62–4.

[88] See *Salamander* above, para 52. Of course, the unlawful exercise of discretion may be challenged directly in domestic judicial review proceedings.

[89] Case C–298/89 *Gibraltar v Council* [1993] ECR I–3605, 3634, per Advocate General Lenz.

brought within two months of publication of the measure.[90] Prior to a directive being transposed into domestic law (which will usually be longer than this) it is likely to be difficult for an individual claimant to establish 'direct concern' in any but the clearest case prior to transposition by which time it may well be too late.

3.73 *Individual concern* connotes that the affected individual must be affected in a way that distinguishes him individually as if he were the addressee.[91] This has been interpreted very restrictively. The most important case on this aspect of standing is *Plaumann & Co v Commission.*[92]

3.74 In *Plaumann* the ECJ observed that:

> Persons other than those to whom a decision is addressed may only claim to be individually concerned if that decision affects them by reason of certain attributes which are peculiar to them or by reason of circumstances in which they are differentiated from all other persons and by virtue of these factors distinguishes them individually just as in the case of the person addressed.[93]

3.75 In practice, the test has proved extremely difficult to surmount. In *Plaumann* itself the applicants were large-scale importers of clementines who sought to annul a Commission decision addressed to the German Government refusing consent to reduce customs duties on clementines imported from outside the EC. Even though the applicants' business interests were clearly affected the ECJ held that there was no relevant individual concern. Nor does it appear to give rise to individual concern that particular applicants are affected in a different way to, or more seriously than, other traders,[94] or that an applicant's identity is known to, or ascertainable by, a Community institution at the time that the challenged measure is passed, or even that an individual has participated in the preparation of the measure.[95]

3.76 The problem is even more pronounced in the case of public interest groups who would have standing in a conventional domestic judicial review. Thus, in *Stichting Greenpeace*[96] a number of environmental interest groups and private citizens sought annulment before the ECJ, under Article 230, of a Commission decision releasing funds to support the construction of two power stations in the Canary Islands without an environmental impact assessment. Their application was refused. The ECJ held that the individual applicants had no individual concern since their interests under the Environmental Impact Assessment Directive (Directive (EEC) 85/337) were only indirectly affected by the Commission decision in question. So far as the environmental interest groups were concerned, it was held that they could have no greater standing than affected individuals.

---

[90] Under Art 230(3) EC the period is two months from publication or notification to the claimant or, in the absence thereof, from the day on which it came to the knowledge of the claimant as the case may be.

[91] Case 138/88 *Flourez v Council* [1988] ECR 6393, para 12.

[92] Case 25/62 [1963] ECR 95. *Plaumann* has been applied consistently over the years. See below and, most recently, C–50/00 *Union de Pequenos v Council* [2002] ECR I–6677.

[93] Case 25/62 [1963] ECR 95, 107.

[94] See, eg, Cases 10 and 18/68 *Societa 'Eridania' Zuccherifici Nazionali v Commission* [1969] ECR 459.

[95] Case T–135/96 *UEAPME v Council* [1998] ECR II–2335.

[96] Case C–321/95 P *Stichting Greenpeace Council v Commission* [1998] ECR I–1651.

In judicial review proceedings before the Administrative Court there is, therefore, a significant **3.77** question as to the relevant standing test in circumstances where the claimant would not have standing to challenge a Community measure directly under Article 230 or would have had the requisite standing but did not bring the challenge within the two-month period.[97] In the latter case, should the national court deny standing on the basis that to grant it would be to circumvent the relevant standing rules under Article 230 or should standing be granted so that the ECJ can consider the matter on a reference under Article 234?

In a case where the claimant would *not* have had standing to bring a direct action before the **3.78** ECJ under Article 230 the position appears to be that the Administrative Court may accord standing on a wider basis so as to permit challenge to be made to a national measure the legality of which is contingent on the validity of the underlying Community measure. Although the Administrative Court cannot itself pronounce on the validity of the Community measure in question it may make a reference under Article 234 and the ECJ will not decline to consider it.

So, in *Eurotunnel SA v SeaFrance*[98] the court having found that the applicant was not **3.79** 'directly concerned' by the provisions of the directive that it sought to challenge and could not, therefore, proceed under Article 230 EC held, nonetheless, that the legality of the directive could be challenged indirectly in the national courts and made the subject of a reference which the ECJ would then consider.

But the position is different, at least in some cases, where a claimant had standing to **3.80** challenge the Community measure in time under Article 230 EC but failed to do so. Here, the question is not so much one of standing as of legal certainty. In many instances the ECJ will refuse to consider the matter by way of an Article 234 reference so that, in practice, there is no point in the Administrative Court making a reference. Analytically, the objection to such claimant being able to proceed in judicial review proceedings is as much one of delay as of standing. It is, therefore, further considered below.

E. Delay and EC Challenges

Domestic delay rules

Under CPR r 54.5 claims for judicial review must be brought promptly and, in any event, **3.81** within three months of the date that grounds for the claim first arose.[99] An extension of time may be granted under CPR r 3.4 but there must be an explanation or other reason shown as to why time should be extended. In particular, claims are not necessarily brought in time because they are instituted within three months of the relevant public law default.[100]

---

[97] The circumstances in which this two-month period may be extended are exceptional: see, eg, Case C–195/91 *Bayer AG v Commission* [1994] ECR I–5619, para 26.

[98] Case C–408/95 [1997] ECR I–6315.

[99] In *R (Burkett) v Hammersmith and Fulham London Borough Council* [2002] UKHL 23, [2002] 1 WLR 1593 this requirement was held to require a clear and straightforward interpretation that would yield a readily ascertainable starting point (in context in a planning case the date of the grant of planning permission and not the date of a resolution to grant planning permission).

[100] See, eg, *R v Independent Television Commission, ex p TV NI Ltd*, The Times, 30 December 1991.

3.82   It can readily be seen, therefore, that the promptness requirement lacks a degree of certainty.[101] Whether an extension of time will be granted is discretionary. So if, for example, through no fault of his own a litigant is unable to obtain legal aid to commence judicial review proceedings this may excuse delay but there would remain the need to obtain an extension of time for bringing the proceedings.[102] In the context of EC law the promptness requirement is usually enforced strictly in relation to challenges to administrative decisions and subordinate legislation.[103]

3.83   Even where the Administrative Court grants permission to apply for judicial review there remains, in objective terms, undue delay in the bringing of the proceedings. This means that there is discretion to refuse relief to the claimant at the full hearing if, under SCA, s 31(6), granting relief would cause substantial hardship or substantial prejudice or be detrimental to the rights of any person or to good administration.[104]

3.84   The circumstances in which such discretion may be exercised against a claimant include the length of the delay, the extent and effect of quashing the decision under challenge and the impact if the decision were to be reopened.[105]

3.85   Importantly, there are also circumstances in which the Administrative Court has exercised discretion to refuse relief on similar grounds even where a claimant has issued proceedings promptly.[106]

3.86   In terms of EC judicial review challenges, the time limits in CPR r 54.5 require consideration of the following issues:

   (1) The legality of the three-month time limit (including the promptness requirement and use of discretion).
   (2) Issues arising out of claims for damages against the State including the overlap between damages claims in EC and ECHR fundamental rights cases.
   (3) Special time issues arising in EC judicial review challenges.
   (4) Inconsistency with delay rules before the ECJ.

Legality of the three-month time limit (including promptness and discretion)

3.87   It is extremely unlikely that, of itself, an outer limit of three months for judicial review proceedings to be commenced, subject to discretion to extend time, would ever violate

---

[101] There are even limited circumstances in which a finding of promptness made at the permission stage may be revisited at the full hearing: see *R (Lichfield Securities Ltd) v Lichfield District Council* [2001] 3 PLR 33 qualifying, in that respect, *R v Criminal Injuries Compensation Board, ex p A* [1999] 2 AC 330. According to the decision in *Lichfield* these are where: (1) the judge at the permission stage has so indicated, (2) new and relevant material is introduced at the substantive hearing, (3) exceptionally, the issues at the full hearing place a different aspect on the question of promptness, or (4) the first judge had plainly overlooked something relevant or reached a decision *per incuriam*.

[102] *R v Stratford-upon-Avon District Council, ex p Jackson* [1985] 1 WLR 1319.

[103] See, eg, *R v Hammersmith and Fulham London Borough Council, ex p Council for the Protection of Rural England* [2001] 81 P & CR 73.

[104] *Caswell v Dairy Produce Quota Tribunal for England and Wales* [1990] 2 AC 738.

[105] ibid.

[106] Consider, eg, *R v London Borough of Brent, ex p O'Malley* (1997) 10 Admin LR 265 (risk of collapse of scheme if relief granted with consequent waste of millions of pounds).

EC law. Given that the same time limit applies to all claimants there is no question of any breach of the principle of equivalence. So far as the principle of effectiveness is concerned it is, as has been seen above, because of the principle of legal certainty, compatible with EC law for reasonable limitation periods to be established by the Member States. The reasonableness of the limitation period under consideration must, of course, be viewed in context but there is no reason to suppose that any of the various EC doctrines applicable to the legitimacy of national procedural rules would not endorse the rationale for reasonably stringent time limits for domestic public law challenges with an EC content.

3.88 In the context of judicial review it has been suggested that the three-month period for bringing judicial review proceedings in Ireland is, at least in principle, reasonable but that if the requirement of promptness meant that the period was reduced to less than two months that might be regarded as unreasonable.[107] It may be that the suggestion was made in the light of the fact that Article 230 lays down a (in practice) strict requirement of two months for bringing direct actions against the legality of Community measures.

3.89 However, if that suggestion is well founded the promptness requirement (and, certainly, the residual discretion to refuse relief even where proceedings have been brought promptly) are at risk of being in breach of the principle of effectiveness *at least in individual cases*.

3.90 In *R (Burkett) v Hammersmith and Fulham London Borough Council*[108] the House of Lords left open the question of whether the promptness test, because of its uncertainty, satisfied the requirements of EC law and/or was compliant with Article 6 ECHR. However, in a Strasbourg decision—not cited in *Burkett*—the European Court of Human Rights has held that the promptness requirement is not in breach of Article 6(1) ECHR.[109]

3.91 By virtue of HRA, s 2 decisions of the Strasbourg Court must be taken into account by the Administrative Court though they do not have to be followed. As will be seen,[110] decisions of the ECJ have been in conflict with Strasbourg Court decisions on very similar and sometimes identical questions relating to fundamental rights issues. Whether or not the promptness/discretion aspects of judicial review procedure infringe the EC principle of effectiveness is, in any event, not necessarily to be resolved in the same way as the separate question of whether there is a breach of Article 6 ECHR.

3.92 Therefore, although the three-month time limit is likely to comply with EC law the same cannot, necessarily, be said of the promptness requirement and the discretion to refuse relief even where the claimant has moved for judicial review timeously. In individual cases founded on asserted EC rights, adverse application of time limits to claimants under

---

[107] Case C–208/90 *Emmott v Minister for Social Welfare* [1991] ECR I–4269, 4288, per Advocate General Mischo.

[108] [2002] UKHL 23, [2002] 1WLR 1593.

[109] *LAM v United Kingdom*, Application 41671/98 (unreported, 5 July 2001). See, most recently, *Hardy v Pembrokeshire County Council and Pembrokeshire Coast National Park Authority* [2006] EWCA Civ 240 where this point was noted by the Court of Appeal. This case, which addresses the limitation requirements in domestic judicial review from an ECHR perspective, does not consider the effect of EC general principles of law on delay under CPR Pt 54. See also paras 14.92–14.93.

[110] See para 12.100.

the promptness test (or other exercise of discretion) may be capable of being challenged as breaching the effectiveness principle.

Time limits in EC damages claims

3.93 The relevant limitation period for EC damages claims against the State (including an emanation of the State) will, generally, be the time limit for claims for breach of statutory duty, namely six years from the date of breach.[111] This is because violations of EC law giving rise to damages actions are, ultimately, derived from Treaty provisions which have the same effect in the United Kingdom as statutes.[112]

3.94 Confusion has sometimes arisen because of the fact that it is frequently necessary to establish a public law breach as a necessary part of proving entitlement to damages. For example, public law issues will be raised by the contention that an administrative authority, as an emanation of the State, has unlawfully refused to grant a licence pursuant to the terms of a directive. There may also be an EC claim for damages arising out of the same illegality. The damages claim will reflect a private law right of action against the authority founded in EC law.

3.95 This does not, however, mean either that the damages claim loses its character as a claim in private law or that it is subject to the more draconian time limits appertaining to judicial review (see above). It is, in this context, important to isolate the true time issues in an EC damages claim against the State. Such a claim may often be included in judicial review proceedings but may also be brought in private law with any public law issues being ventilated as a collateral issue in the private law proceedings.[113]

3.96 In terms of remedy, a claim for damages has never been recognized as being derived from public law illegality. It is for this reason that applications for judicial review may include claims for damages but may not seek damages alone.[114] Provision for the claiming of damages in judicial review proceedings is, thus, a concession to convenience allowing for one set of proceedings to be brought (where other relevant and related public law defaults can be raised) and where, if necessary, the damages claim can proceed should the application for judicial review be unsuccessful.[115]

---

[111] Limitation Act 1980, s 2. Issues of causation may, however, arise where appropriate interim relief is not claimed timeously: see para 3.123. The issue of State liability in damages is discussed separately at paras 5.85 et seq.

[112] *Garden Cottage Foods Ltd v Milk Marketing Board* [1982] 3 WLR 514, 516B–G, per Lord Diplock.

[113] See paras 1.120 et seq.

[114] CPR r 54.3(2). It is also why SCA, s 31(4)(b) requires the court to be satisfied before granting damages in judicial review proceedings that if the claim had been made in a private law action begun by the claimant at the time of making his claim for judicial review he would have been awarded damages. So, in ordinary domestic private law actions unrelated to EC law the courts have observed that damages for negligence caused by the exercise of particular statutory powers should not be classified as public law claims: see, eg, *X (Minors) v Bedfordshire CC* [1995] 2 AC 633, 736 per Lord Browne-Wilkinson, cf, though, in Joined Cases C–46/93 and C–48/93 *Brasserie du Pecheur and Factortame* [1996] ECR 1–029, para 101, per Advocate General Tesauro.

[115] Claims for restitution are, like damages, private law claims with a public law element but there is no procedural provision for including such claims in applications for judicial review. It has been said that judicial review adds nothing to such claims and that an order for repayment is more appropriate than declaratory or quashing order relief: see *Woolwich Equitable Building Society v IRC* [1993] AC 70, 200, per Lord Slynn). However, it may be questioned whether the exclusion of such relief from judicial review is really justified given the similarity of such relief with a damages remedy.

If the position were otherwise there would be an inconsistency between the limitation **3.97** period of five years applicable for actions for damages under Article 288(2) EC against institutions of the Community on the one hand and, on the other, an outer time limit of only three months for instituting judicial review proceedings. This would, in turn, raise even more complications in respect of the already uncertain scope of the exhaustion of local remedies rule[116] whereby those persons claiming to be adversely affected by unlawful Community measures must first seek a remedy against domestic national bodies before seeking damages under Article 288(2). That is not to say, however, that pursuing a claim for damages against the State for alleged violation of EC law can be used to bypass the potentially stringent judicial review time requirements where the essence of the complaint sounds in public as opposed to private law. In such circumstances an action for damages brought well outside the time limits for judicial review would be liable to be struck out as an abuse of process of the court.[117]

Special time issues arising in EC judicial review challenges

Reference has been made above, in relation to the effectiveness, equivalence, and non- **3.98** discrimination principles, to the importance of placing a national measure in context when determining whether or not one or more of those principles have been violated by that measure.

Time limits are no exception to application of these principles. However, the case law of **3.99** the ECJ has not always been consistent in elucidating the precise point at which national time rules may legitimately commence. This has a particular relevance for judicial review where, as has been seen, the definition of a starting point—the arising of grounds for the application—is not always specific either.

Prior to the ECJ decision in *Emmott v Minister for Social Welfare and Attorney General*[118] **3.100** it was thought that domestic periods of limitation would, in accordance with cases such as *Rewe* considered above,[119] start to run from the date of breach of the relevant Community instrument.

However, in *Emmott* the ECJ held that until a directive has been fully transposed into **3.101** national law, the State cannot seek to rely on delay in bringing proceedings in order to defeat the rights conferred by the directive. This ruling, if unqualified, suggests also that defective national measures could be challenged by judicial review at any time up until the directive had been fully implemented.

In fact, *Emmott* has now been severely limited in its effect by a number of subsequent decisions **3.102** of the ECJ. In that case, Mrs Emmott had been refused an award of disability benefit by the Irish authorities. At the time of the refusal she was unaware that she possessed directly effective rights under Directive (EEC) 79/7 on equal treatment for men and women in social

---

[116] This doctrine is outside the scope of this work but is well outlined in A Ward, *Judicial Review and the Rights of Private Parties in EC Law* (2000) 294 et seq.
[117] See para 1.102.
[118] Case C–208/90 [1991] ECRI–4269.
[119] See paras 3.05 et seq.

security matters. She became aware of this following a later ruling of the ECJ in a similar case. She asked the Minister to review her case. When, eventually, she was given leave to bring proceedings she was out of time under the prevailing limitation rules. The domestic court referred the case to the ECJ on the question of whether it contravened EC law for the State to rely on limitation rules in defending claims founded on EC directives.

3.103 The ECJ considered that until a directive has been fully implemented into national law an individual could not determine the full extent of his or her rights. It rejected the argument that the doctrine of direct effect could be subject to limitation stipulations that required a challenge to be made to a public body within a reasonable time.

3.104 Importantly, however, in *Emmott*, the Irish authorities themselves had erred in that they had wrongly indicated that Mrs Emmott's claim would be addressed once litigation before the Irish High Court concerning the same directive had been determined. It was this feature that enabled the ECJ to distinguish its decision there from later cases.

3.105 One of the then unforeseen consequences of *Emmott* was that it would, if unqualified in its effect, allow applicants to claim benefits from directives retroactively from their stipulated enforcement date. This was addressed in *Steenhorst*[120] and *Johnson II*[121] where the ECJ held that national limitation rules could validly limit the retroactive effect of such claims.

3.106 Later decisions have emasculated the effect of *Emmott* still further. The ECJ has, in practice, now accepted in a number of rulings that its reasoning in *Emmott* was founded on the particular circumstances of that case. In *Fantask*,[122] for example, the court—distinguishing *Emmott*—observed that the applicant in *Emmott* was deprived, by virtue of a national limitation period, of *any* opportunity to rely on individual rights laid down in an unimplemented directive.

3.107 And in *Edis*[123] the ECJ said:

> Moreover, having regard to the documents before the Court and the arguments presented at the hearing, it does not appear that the conduct of the Italian authorities, in conjunction with the existence of the contested time-limit, had the effect, in this case as it did in *Emmott*, of depriving the plaintiff company of any opportunity of enforcing its rights before the national courts.

3.108 Both prior to cases such as *Fantask* and thereafter, the approach of the national courts has also been to limit the scope and reach of *Emmott*. Thus, in *Biggs v Somerset CC*[124] *Emmott* was said to be restricted to situations involving the non-transposition of directives. In *Preston*[125] Schiemann LJ, in the Court of Appeal, observed that whilst *Emmott* 'has not been overruled by the ECJ, [it] has been consistently confined to the facts'.[126] He also

---

120 Case C–338/91 *Steenhorst-Neerings v Bestuur van de Bedrijfsvereniging voor Detailhandel, Ambachten en Huisvrouwen* [1993] ECR I–5475 paras 16 and 21.
121 Case C–410/92, *Johnson v Chief Adjudication Officer* [1994] ECR I–5483, paras 35–36.
122 Case C–188/95 *Fantask A/S e.a. v Industriministeriet* [1997] ECR I–6783, para 51.
123 Case C–231/96 *Edis v Ministero della Finanze* [1998] ECR I–4951, para 48.
124 [1996] 2 CMLR 292, 305, per Neil LJ.
125 *Preston v Wolverhampton Healthcare Trust* [1997] 2 CMLR 754.
126 ibid 769.

endorsed the approach of Advocate General Jacobs in *Denkavit*[127] who had suggested that *Emmott* is only applicable to the case where the State, itself in default in implementation of a directive, has by its own conduct caused the applicant's delay.[128]

So, in most cases—at least where the State has not contributed to the delay by its own conduct—the time when grounds for an application for judicial review first arise is the effective date of breach. In *R v Customs and Excise, ex p Eurotunnel*,[129] for example, this was held to be the date of the relevant orders transposing a directive into national law. The claimants were out of time because they only sought judicial review some 18 months later.   **3.109**

Similarly, in *R v Secretary of State for Trade and Industry, ex p Greenpeace*[130] Laws J held that the effective date of breach in respect of the Government's alleged unlawful failure to carry out an environmental impact assessment was the date at which damage caused by the directive (argued to have been unlawfully implemented) was imminent. In that case the judge observed that proceedings brought by public interest bodies, such as Greenpeace, had to be brought especially promptly. However, this reasoning was criticized, and not followed, by Kay J in *R v Secretary of State for Trade and Industry, ex p Greenpeace*.[131]   **3.110**

It has also been held that the duty under Article 10 [ex 5] EC to take all appropriate measures to ensure the enforcement of Community rights does not mean that the national authority must (or must even address a discretion to) revoke an earlier decision because of a prior breach of Community law.[132]   **3.111**

It has been suggested that different considerations attach to the starting point for challenging primary legislation contended to be incompatible with EC law.[133] Clearly, where such legislation affects the individual case the date when grounds for the application first arise will be the date of the breach in relation to the claimant.   **3.112**

However, this does not necessarily mean that in all cases a public interest challenge may be made to primary legislation many years after the event. True it is that Member States are under an obligation on the international level to remove incompatible legislation but, analytically, there is no difference in principle so far as individual enforcement is concerned between a decision, subordinate legislation, or primary legislation that offends against EC law. In *R v Secretary of State for Employment, ex p Equal Opportunities Commission*[134] the House of Lords permitted a challenge to primary legislation some 15 years after it was made but in that case the question of delay was neither considered nor argued. It seems probable   **3.113**

---

[127] Case C–2/94 *Denkavit International v Kamer van Koophandel en Fabriken voor Midden-Gelderland* [1996] ECR I–2827, 2851.

[128] [1997] 2 CMLR 754, 770.

[129] [1995] CLC 392. See, also, *R v Hammersmith and Fulham London Borough Council, ex p Council for the Protection of Rural England* [2001] 81 P & CR 73 (*held*: the real date for challenge to failure to carry out an environmental impact assessment was not the date of approval of reserved matters but, rather, the date of the grant of outline planning permission).

[130] [1988] Env LR 415.

[131] [2000] 2 CMLR 94, 132–3.

[132] *R v Hammersmith and Fulham London Borough Council, ex p Council for the Protection of Rural England* [2001] 81 P & CR 73. See, also, *R (Noble Organisation Ltd) v Thanet DC* [2005] EWCA Civ 782.

[133] See C Lewis, 'Judicial Review and EU Law' (2002) JR 272.

[134] [1995] 1 AC 1.

that if the issue were litigated directly the Administrative Court would hold that EC principles of legal certainty militated, at least generally, against such late challenges succeeding.

Inconsistency with delay rules before the ECJ

3.114 As has been seen, particular time issues may arise in some circumstances where a national measure, the legality of which is dependent upon the validity of a Community measure, is sought to be challenged.

3.115 Where the claimant has no standing to bring an action for annulment of the Community measure under Article 230 EC there is no difficulty. But where an individual claimant could have brought proceedings under Article 230 within the strict time limit required by that Treaty provision (almost invariably two months from publication of the measure) and has failed to do so, the ECJ has held that any subsequent action to the national court against the national measure is time-barred.

3.116 This occurred in *TWD Deggendorf.*[135] That was a state aid case in which it was held that TWD Deggendorf, as the beneficiary of the state aid in question, had the right to bring annulment proceedings to challenge the validity of a decision addressed to the Federal Republic of Germany declaring the aid in question to be an unlawful aid and requiring the Government to recover the moneys paid to Deggendorf.

3.117 Although Deggendorf was informed as to the existence of the decision and of its right to bring a challenge under Article 230 (ex 173) EC it chose not to do so but, rather, to challenge its recovery in domestic proceedings before the national court. This, the ECJ ruled, was too late. It refused to entertain a reference by the German court under Article 234 holding that to allow the reference to proceed would be to circumvent the strict time limits laid down by Article 230.

3.118 This has potentially significant implications for the outer three-month time limit in judicial review proceedings before the Administrative Court. For claimants without standing under Article 230 the three-month period will usually start from the date of passing of the national measure in question. However, where claimants clearly possess standing under Article 230 to challenge the relevant Community measure a challenge to an administrative measure implementing the Community measure will, at least in many instances, be too late.

3.119 There will be little point, in identified circumstances, in the Administrative Court exercising its discretion to extend time for the making of the application because, if in an appropriately similar case the approach in *TWD Deggendorf* is followed by the ECJ, any reference under Article 234 will inevitably fail. This is, therefore, a rare instance of a case where domestic time limits are effectively controlled by the ECJ.

3.120 Care is, however, needed in determining the true extent of the ruling in *TWD Deggendorf.* There, the ECJ distinguished *Universitat Hamburg v Hauptzollamt Hamburg-Kehrwieder*[136] where failure to bring proceedings under Article 230 had been held not to prevent a reference by the national court under Article 234 in subsequent domestic proceedings challenging

---

[135] Case C–188/92 *TWD Textilwerke Deggendorf v Germany* [1994] ECR I–833.
[136] Case 216/82 [1983] ECR 2771.

a national measure implementing a Community customs measure. In *TWD Deggendorf* [137] the ECJ observed that in *Hamburg* the national measure that was sought to be challenged:

> was the only measure directly addressed to the person concerned of which it had necessarily been informed in good time and which it could challenge in the courts without encountering any difficulty in demonstrating its interests in bringing proceedings.

So it may be that Deggendorf is confined to the factual situation where the claimants **3.121** in domestic judicial review proceedings had direct knowledge of the Community measure in question and there is no doubt of their standing under Article 230.[138] Although Deggendorf has been applied subsequently,[139] the ECJ has recognized the difficulties caused by the uncertainty of the standing rules under Article 230 EC (see above). In *R v Intervention Board for Agricultural Produce, ex p Accrington Beef Co Ltd*,[140] for example, the ECJ held that the question of the validity of a regulation could be referred by the national court under Article 234 despite the claimant's failure to bring proceedings for annulment given the lack of clarity over whether there was standing under Article 230 (ex 173) EC.

In many, if not most, cases where this issue arises it is likely that there will be a lack of clarity **3.122** over standing under Article 230. For these reasons it is submitted that the Administrative Court should be slow either to refuse an extension of time for bringing judicial review proceedings or, as the case may be, not to accept that the proceedings have been commenced in time given the lack of certainty surrounding the claimant's Article 230 standing.

F. Interim Relief and EC Challenges

General

The principles of effectiveness and equivalence, discussed above, require the Administrative **3.123** Court to have jurisdiction to grant interim relief where necessary. Indeed, failure to claim interim relief in time or at all in a damages claim may result in the chain of causation being broken by contributory negligence on the part of the claimant.[141]

The relevant principles involved in claiming interim relief in an EU judicial review case **3.124** in the Administrative Court will differ according to the particular nature of the challenge. It is, therefore, necessary to examine the principles governing the grant of relief in challenges:

(1) to administrative decisions generally.
(2) where the claim for interim relief requires the suspension of domestic legislation whether primary or subordinate;

---

[137] Case C–188/92 [1994] ECR I–833, para 23.

[138] See, eg, D Wyatt, 'The Relationship between Actions for Annulment and References on Validity after TWG Deggendorf' in J Lonbay and A Biondi (eds), *Remedies for Breach of EC Law* (1996) 55.

[139] Case C–178/95 *Wiljo NV v Belgian State* [1997] ECR I–585 (decision addressed to individual claimant).

[140] Case C–241/95 [1996] ECR I–6699.

[141] Joined Cases C–46/93 and C–48/93 *Brasserie du Pecheur and Factortame* [1996] ECR I–1029 para 84. Note, also, the Opinion of Advocate General Tesauro, para 100.

(3) where the relevant administrative decision or measure is founded on the alleged invalidity of an EC directive or other secondary Community measure;

(4) where the relevant national legislation is founded on a directive but the date for implementation of the directive has not yet passed.

3.125 In addition, the question of undertakings in damages—the traditional quid pro quo for the grant of interim relief—may require special application in an EC context.

Interim relief in EC challenges to administrative decisions generally

3.126 Many EC judicial review challenges will be directed to administrative decisions that are founded on entirely lawful domestic and EC legislative measures. In such cases the ground for challenge (albeit from an EC perspective) will be that the decision-maker has acted unlawfully, disproportionately, or unfairly.[142] The interim relief involved will usually be an interlocutory injunction (or stay) seeking to restrain the decision-maker from implementing the decision in question. It will certainly not involve granting relief in respect of any legislation whether domestic or EC in nature.

3.127 These cases involve the application of the conventional test for interim relief in private law disputes in *American Cyanamid Co v Ethicon Ltd*[143] in a public law context.

3.128 The *Cyanamid* test requires the claimant to establish that there is a serious question to be tried. Whether or not interim relief should be granted depends upon the court's assessment as to where the balance of convenience lies. This requires the court to consider whether damages would be an adequate remedy for either party if unsuccessful at the interlocutory hearing but successful at trial. If an injunction is granted then, almost invariably, a cross-undertaking as to damages is required.[144]

3.129 As can be seen, the *Cyanamid* formulation cannot readily be transposed into public law cases without modification. This is because there is no general right to damages for unlawful administrative action[145] and a public body, by definition acting in the public interest, will ordinarily not have suffered any recoverable loss.[146]

3.130 Further, assessment by the Administrative Court of the balance of convenience will be more difficult to make out because it depends upon consideration of the wider public interest

---

142 These terms, however, have an extended meaning in EC cases in that they are required to be applied in accordance with the general principles of law recognized by the ECJ. As to these, see Chapters 6–12.

143 [1975] AC 396.

144 See *Hoffman-La Roche (F) & Co AG v Secretary of State for Trade and Industry* [1975] AC 295, 361.

145 It is questionable whether EC claims for damages constitute a relevant exception for interim relief purposes since—even in a case directed to the legality of a purely administrative decision and not concerned with contingent legislation—the extent of the breach must be 'sufficiently serious' to merit an award of damages: see paras 5.95 et seq. So, first, an award of damages cannot be presumed merely by virtue of an established breach of EC law. Secondly, the breach may well be so serious if damages can be claimed that they will not constitute an adequate remedy. Thirdly (see para 3.96), damages are merely a convenience in judicial review and do not (at least analytically) constitute a remedy for the public law default alleged.

146 *R v Secretary of State for Transport, ex p Factortame (No 2)* [1991] 1 AC 603, 673A–B, per Lord Goff.

where it is likely to be particularly difficult to balance that interest against the individual financial or other interest of the claimant.[147]

However, where the court is concerned solely with a challenge to the legality of an administra- **3.131** tive decision founded on legislation which is not itself subject to challenge then interim relief is far more likely to be granted.[148]

Interim relief requiring the suspension of domestic legislation

It is undoubtedly true that the grant of interim relief to suspend domestic legislation is **3.132** exceptional. In *R v Secretary of State for Transport, ex p Factortame (No 2)*[149] Lord Goff observed as follows:

> [T]he court should not restrain a public authority by interim injunction from enforcing an apparently authentic law unless it is satisfied, having regard to all the circumstances, that the challenge to the validity of the law is, prima facie, so firmly based as to justify so exceptional a course being taken.

Whether the challenge is sufficiently firmly based may usually be a threshold condition **3.133** of suspending domestic legislation but it is neither always determinative nor easily capable of general application. In *R v HM Treasury, ex p British Telecommunications*[150] the Court of Appeal observed that although the apparent strength of the claimant's case and the undesirability of dis- turbing enacted law were 'almost bound to fall for consideration' the weight and consideration to be given even to these criteria would vary in accordance with the circumstances.[151] As Lord Bingham MR pointed out, the novelty of the point raised might make the strength of the challenge less important. The legislation under attack might be primary legislation raising a higher burden on the claimant in terms of the grant of interim relief or it might be a minor piece of subordinate legislation affecting only a small group in which case the burden would be less.

Other factors may also be relevant. The effect on the claimant of having to comply with the **3.134** legislation is, clearly, material. It may also be that the nature of the EC right in question has a bearing and, in particular, whether the domestic legislation is implementing an EC right that would, otherwise, be directly effective.

In fact, the ECJ has commented that: **3.135**

> the interim legal protection which Community law ensures for individuals must remain the same, irrespective of whether they contest the compatibility of national legal provisions with Community law or the validity of secondary Community law.[152]

This statement of principle may require injection of the 'Community interest' as an important **3.136** factor affecting whether interim relief should be granted to suspend domestic legislation alleged to be contrary to (valid) EC law since it is one of the criteria relevant to determining

---

[147] See, eg, *Sierbein v Westminster City Council* (1987) 86 LGR 431; *Smith v Inner London Education Authority* [1978] 1 All ER 411.
[148] *R v HM Treasury, ex p British Telecommunications* [1994] 1 CMLR 621, 647, para 41.
[149] [1991] 1 AC 603, 673C.
[150] [1994] 1 CMLR 621.
[151] ibid 647–9.
[152] Joined Cases C–143/88 and C–92/89 *Zuckerfabrik Suderdithmarschen AG v Hauptzollamt Itzehoe* [1991] ECR I–415, para 20.

whether interim relief should be granted in respect of domestic decisions or measures founded on allegedly defective secondary Community law (see immediately below).

Interim relief in challenges founded on allegedly invalid EC secondary measures[153]

3.137   As has been seen[154] the Administrative Court may not itself declare a Community measure to be invalid. In *Atlanta*[155] the ECJ held that when determining whether or not to suspend a national measure founded on an allegedly invalid Community rule, national judges must apply the conditions required by the ECJ in claims under Articles 242 and 243 EC. In summary these are that (in context) the Administrative Court is—before granting interim relief in such a case—required to:

(1)   entertain 'serious doubts' as to the validity of the Community measure and refer relevant questions to the ECJ unless the contested measure is already before that court;

(2)   respect relevant decisions of the ECJ or the CFI as to the legality of the measure or any successful interim relief application brought before those courts;

(3)   decide whether the claimant has established 'urgency' and a threat of 'serious and irreparable damage';

(4)   take due account of the 'Community interest' before granting interim relief.

3.138   Although this four-fold test bears some similarity with the test laid down in *Factortame (No 2)* and *British Telecommunications* above, for determining whether interim relief should be granted in EC judicial review challenges concerning the alleged incompatibility of domestic measures with EC law, there is no mention in those cases of the 'Community interest'. It may be that this concept makes it easier to obtain interim relief and it would, therefore, be surprising if the notion of 'Community interest' were not also an important and relevant factor in deciding questions of interim relief in such cases.

3.139   The difficulty of obtaining interim relief where the validity of EC secondary legislation is challenged by way of judicial review has, nonetheless, been overcome on occasion. In *ABNA*[156] the Administrative Court granted interim relief to suspend the operation of domestic legislation implementing a directive requiring manufacturers of certain compound feeds to indicate the percentage of the constituent ingredients by weight. The validity of the directive was challenged in judicial review proceedings on the ground of lack of proportionality and that issue was referred to the ECJ by the Administrative Court under Article 234 (ex 177) EC. The Administrative Court granted interim relief because it considered that serious and irreparable harm would be caused to the affected businesses.

---

[153] It seems probable that there may be a direct challenge in judicial review to allegedly invalid EC secondary legislation without reference to national transposing legislation where such legislation is directly effective: see, eg, *R v Secretary of State for Transport, ex p Omega Air Ltd* (unreported November 25 1999). See, also, *R v Secretary of State for Health, ex p Imperial Tobacco Ltd* [1999] Eu LR 582 discussed at paras 3.140–3.142.

[154] See, in the present context, para 4.92 et seq.

[155] Case C–465/93 *Atlanta Fruchthandelsgesellschaft mbH v Bundesamt für Ernahrung und Forstwirtschaft* [1995] ECR I–3761, paras 39 and 46. See, also, *Zuckerfabrik* (n 152 above).

[156] *R (ABNA) v Food Standards Agency and Secretary of State for Health* [2004] Eu LR 88.

Interim relief in challenges to domestic legislation prior to required implementation

If there is a difference in content between (1) the current 'domestic' test for interim relief **3.140** in EC judicial review challenges where there is alleged incompatibility between domestic measures/legislation and EC law and (2) that when the legality of Community measures is indirectly in issue, the question arises as to whether the relevant test should be a uniform one and, in particular, whether the relevant principles are those of EC law or of national law. This question was confronted, but not resolved, in the recent tobacco litigation which involved a challenge to domestic legislation made prior to the implementation date for a directive.

Council Directive (EC) 98/43 prohibited the advertising and sponsorship of tobacco **3.141** products. The Government's intention was to implement this directive before the required implementation date. The tobacco companies claimed interim relief to prevent this from happening prior to the ECJ determining the validity of the directive in separate judicial review proceedings where a reference for a preliminary ruling had already been made by the Administrative Court.[157]

In the interim relief proceedings the question arose as to whether the relevant principles **3.142** should be governed by EC or domestic law. The Court of Appeal, by a majority, refused interim relief and held that the principles to be applied were those laid down in *Atlanta* (ie EC law principles).[158] It was unnecessary to decide the point in the House of Lords because by the time that the case came before it an Opinion of the Advocate General had been published determining that the directive was invalid. However, the House of Lords would have referred the issue to the ECJ. Three of the Law Lords considered that it was arguable that the principles to be applied sounded in EC law. However, the remaining two Law Lords believed it to be *acte clair* that domestic law governed the matter.[159]

Undertakings as to damages in EC interim relief cases[160]

Ordinarily, and certainly where a claim for interim relief in judicial review proceedings **3.143** prevents a private individual from proceeding to act upon the decision of a public body, the claimant is required to give a cross-undertaking in damages.[161]

The conventional requirement of a cross-undertaking is frequently, in practice, to render **3.144** the claim for interim relief impossible because the claimant will not be able to discharge the undertaking to the defendant or third party if the substantive claim is unsuccessful.

---

[157] The reference was made in Case C–74/99 *R v Secretary of State for Health, ex p Imperial Tobacco* [2000] All ER (EC) 769. The same point came before the ECJ by way of a direct action in Case C–376/98 *Germany v EU Council and EU Parliament* [2000] All ER (EC) 769.

[158] *R v Secretary of State for Health, ex p Imperial Tobacco Ltd* [2002] QB 161.

[159] *R v Secretary of State for Health, ex p Imperial Tobacco* [2001] 1 WLR 127.

[160] The analysis here is founded on the reasoning of Michael Fordham in 'Interim Relief and the Cross-Undertaking' [1997] JR 136.

[161] See *R v Inspectorate of Pollution, ex p Greenpeace* [1994] 1 WLR 570.

3.145   This is, perhaps, especially so in EC challenges where the loss sustained particularly by corporate third parties such as developers or pharmaceutical companies may be substantial and the damages involved well beyond the means of the individual claimant seeking to enforce alleged Community rights of a directly effective nature.

3.146   It was, however, in an EC challenge to the legality of a decision to exclude Lappel Bank from a special protection area that the Pyrrhic victory created by the requirement of cross-under-takings came into sharp relief.[162] The claimant RSPB was refused an 'interim declaration'—a remedy that the House of Lords was prepared to accept for the purpose of argument then existed[163]—and the result was that the development alleged (and subsequently found[164]) to be unlawful as contravening the EC Birds Directive (Directive (EEC) 79/409 on the conservation of wild birds) was able to proceed pending the full hearing. Lord Jauncey said this:[165]

> [Counsel] conceded that his objective in seeking a declaration was to hold up further development of Lappel Bank pending a ruling by the ECJ. Any such hold up could result in a very large commercial loss to the Port of Sheerness and possibly to Swale Borough Council as planning authority. Had they sought an interim injunction against the port authority or other developer proceeding further they would undoubtedly have been required to give such an undertaking as a condition of being granted relief. Instead, they are seeking to achieve the same result without the risk of incurring very substantial expenditure and thereby asking this House to adopt a most unusual course.

3.147   This observation was made in the context of the statement of principle that a claimant cannot, sensibly, expect to achieve more by claiming an interim declaration as opposed to an interim injunction. However, the House of Lords has, in *Factortame (No 2)*[166] itself provided the answer as to why a cross-undertaking as to damages need not be required in every case. As Lord Goff there observed:

> As far as the plaintiff is concerned, the availability of [a damages] remedy will normally preclude the grant to him of an interim injunction. If that is not so, then the court should consider whether, if an injunction is granted against the defendant, there will be an adequate remedy in damages available to him under the plaintiff's undertaking in damages; if so, there will be no reason on this ground to refuse to grant the plaintiff an interim injunction. At this stage of the court's consideration of the case (which I will for convenience call the first stage) many applications for interim injunctions can well be decided. But if there is doubt as to the adequacy of either or both of the respective remedies in damages, then the court proceeds to what is usually called the balance of convenience, and for that purpose will consider all the circumstances of the case.

3.148   So, on this analysis, if the Administrative Court decides not to require a cross-undertaking in damages from the claimant it simply moves to the balance of convenience. The effect of refusing the grant of an interlocutory injunction unless a cross-undertaking in damages is given by the claimant is to deny the claimant—if he cannot afford to give such a

---

[162] *R v Secretary of State for the Environment, ex p Royal Society for the Protection of Birds* (1995) 7 Admin LR 434.

[163] Interim declarations have, since that case, been recognized in the CPR: see para 3.47.

[164] [1997] 2 WLR 123.

[165] (1995) 7 Admin LR 434, 443.

[166] [1991] 1 AC 603, 672, per Lord Goff.

cross-undertaking—the opportunity of having the overall balance of convenience determined by the Administrative Court. At least in the EC context it is strongly arguable that such an approach violates the principle of effectiveness described above and is, accordingly, unlawful.

G. Applications for Disclosure and Cross-examination

Though intrinsic to private law proceedings, neither disclosure nor cross-examination have **3.149** played much part in domestic judicial review. This is because, at least in general, judicial review is concerned neither with factual disputes nor with error of fact. Different considerations will, however, apply in EC challenges where the resolution of factual issues may require disclosure or cross-examination in many cases.

As to disclosure, the conventional disclosure obligations do not apply in judicial review. **3.150** This is clarified, perhaps unusually, by the Pt 54 Practice Direction. Paragraph 12.1 provides that: 'Disclosure is not required unless the court orders otherwise.'

The Administrative Court, therefore, has discretion to order disclosure in respect of specific **3.151** documents or classes of documents. The basis on which this discretion will be exercised is whether disclosure is necessary fairly to dispose of the issues before the court.[167]

Much of the disclosure case law that has built up in domestic judicial review has been **3.152** premised on the limited scope of the Administrative Court's factual role in such proceedings. It is, for example, well established that a claimant will ordinarily not be entitled to disclosure in order to go behind written evidence to ascertain whether the statements contained in it are true unless there is some extrinsic material to suggest that it is inaccurate, misleading, or incomplete.[168]

Similar limitations apply to cross-examination in proceedings for judicial review. CPR r **3.153** 54.16 disapplies applications to cross-examine the maker of a statement under CPR r 8.6. But the court has power to order cross-examination in the exercise of its inherent jurisdiction.

As with disclosure, the circumstances in which cross-examination is ordered in purely **3.154** domestic judicial review cases are restricted. Although the overriding principle is that such an order will be made in the interests of justice,[169] the reality is that the nature of judicial review makes it generally unnecessary for cross-examination to be ordered. There have, in fact, been a number of cases in which it has been observed that it is only on rare occasions that the interests of justice will require that permission for cross-examination be ordered.[170]

---

[167] See, eg, *R v IRC, ex p Rothschild Holdings plc* [1987] STC 163; *R v Secretary of State, ex p Herbage (No 2)* [1987] QB 1077; *R v IRC, ex p Taylor* [1989] 1 All ER 906.

[168] *R v Secretary of State for the Environment, ex p London Borough of Islington* [1992] COD 67.

[169] *O'Reilly v Mackman* [1983] 2 AC 237, 282–3, per Lord Diplock. The CPR overriding objectives compel—albeit by different words—application of the same principle.

[170] See, eg, *George v Secretary of State for the Environment* (1979) 77 LGR 689, per Lord Denning MR; *R v IRC, ex p Rossminster Ltd* [1980] AC 952, 1027.

3.155 There is, however, nothing intrinsically objectionable in granting either disclosure or cross-examination where disposal of the issues requires it. For example, in *R (Wilkinson) v Broadmoor Special Hospital*[171] the Court of Appeal allowed an application for cross-examination on the basis that it was necessary in order to resolve a particular claim arising under the HRA. Without the national court being able in certain HRA challenges[172] to adopt a more liberal approach to disclosure and cross-examination it is clear that the process itself would be susceptible to criticism for breaching obligations under the European Convention on Human Rights.[173]

3.156 The same is true of EC challenges. If, and to the extent that, particular challenges require the Administrative Court to carry out a detailed factual investigation of the merits, then disclosure and cross-examination are likely to be important and should, in principle, be more readily obtainable.

3.157 The relevant EC approach in cases of proportionality (where a merits investigation is most likely to be required) is examined in more detail in Chapter 11. In essence, however, there are—in the present context—two categories of EC case likely to come before the court on judicial review:

(1) Cases where, as a matter of EC law, judicial review is not required to be any more extensive, so far as fact finding is concerned, than in its purely domestic form.

(2) Cases where, unless the Administrative Court undertakes a full factual inquiry, the process of judicial review is in violation of the EC principle of access to the court as part of the principle of effectiveness.

3.158 In the first class of case the court may be able to make necessary relevant findings of fact without the need for extensive inquiry involving cross-examination or widespread disclosure. As Lord Woolf MR put it in *R v Commissioners of Customs and Excise, ex p Lunn Poly Ltd*,[174] an EC state aid challenge:

> Where the issue is one of precedent fact, then sometimes it is necessary for there to be oral evidence and cross-examination ... In this case there was sensibly no application for cross-examination. While the task may be difficult, the Divisional Court, and this court on appeal, is usually well able to decide the relevant facts without the need for cross-examination of the evidence which was given by affidavit.

3.159 However, in the second class of case, cross-examination and disclosure are likely to be required for the national court to be able to discharge its own obligations to the claimant under EC law.

3.160 The task is one of identification rather than principle. The principle of effectiveness requires effective judicial protection which, in turn, connotes the right of access to the court.[175] It is the extent of the principle in determining the appropriate scope of judicial review in any given case that can raise problems.

---

[171] [2002] 1 WLR 419.

[172] This will usually only be so where it is necessary for the Administrative Court to undertake a detailed fact-finding inquiry in order to be Art 6 ECHR compliant.

[173] See, eg, *Peck v United Kingdom* [2003] 36 EHRR 41.

[174] [1999] Eu LR 653, 662.

[175] Case C–222/84 *Johnston v Chief Constable RUC* [1986] ECR 1631, especially para 19.

A case in which a full merits review was not required by the Administrative Court occurred **3.161** in *Upjohn Ltd v Licensing Authority*.[176] There, the ECJ held that Member States were not required to establish a system of judicial review of decisions by a national authority revoking market authorizations for proprietary medicinal products which empowered courts to substitute their assessment of the facts for that of the national authority.

It should be noted that the EC provisions in question, Articles 11 and 21 of Directive **3.162** (EEC) 65/65, conferred directly effective rights. However, the ECJ observed that designation of courts and procedural rules for the enforcement of those rights were matters for the Member State provided that such designation complied with the principles of effectiveness and non-discrimination. So far as these principles were concerned the ECJ considered that a procedure of judicial review whereby the court was empowered to substitute its own view of the facts for that of the national authority was not the only means of ensuring compliance with those principles[177] and of enabling the Community rights conferred by the directive capable of practical enforcement.

In *Upjohn*, national legislation in the form of the Medicines Act 1968 laid down a series of **3.163** hearings before national authorities whereby detailed scientific evidence could be considered and evaluated by the authorities in question. This may have influenced the ECJ. Thus, Article 12 of the directive which required Member States to ensure that decisions suspending or revoking marketing authorizations were open to challenge in legal proceedings could be satisfied by the scope of traditional review.

By contrast, in *Shingara and Radiom*[178] the context was somewhat different. There, the **3.164** claimants had been refused entry into the United Kingdom on the ground of national security. In his Opinion, Advocate General Colomer suggested that the principle of effectiveness required that, amongst other things, 'there must be no restriction on the court's examination of the case'. He elaborated upon this by suggesting that the court's examination must extend 'to the merits of the dispute' by being able to determine 'whether or not the decision was in harmony with the principle of proportionality and other legal rules'. Unless this were so the principle of effectiveness would be breached.[179]

These cases are not necessarily in conflict. What they show is that, in practice, the **3.165** Administrative Court should look at the context of the challenge and the procedures by which facts are determined by the national authority before determining what is required by EC law in terms of the scope of review. The process is not dissimilar from that which the courts have had to engage in to decide whether, in judicial review proceedings under the HRA, the scope of review is sufficient to ensure that, in the instant case, the Administrative Court possesses 'sufficient jurisdiction' to cure any violation of Article 6 ECHR by the national authority making findings of primary fact.

---

[176] Case 120/97 [1999] ECR I–223.
[177] ibid para 33.
[178] Joined Cases C–65 and C–111/95 *R v Secretary of State for the Home Department, ex p Shingara and Radiom* [1997] ECR I–3343.
[179] ibid 3364–3365. To similar effect see *Hodgson v Commissioners of Customs & Excise* [1997] Eu LR 117.

H. Protective Costs Applications

3.166 A protective costs order is an order that either no order or else a limited order for costs be made against the claimant whatever the outcome of the case. The fact that a challenge is founded on EC law does not, at least currently, mean that an order of this nature should be made. In *R v Hammersmith and Fulham London Borough Council, ex p Council for Protection of Rural England, London Branch (No 2)*[180] for example, the Administrative Court, on a challenge to a planning decision argued to be in breach of Council Directive (EC) 85/337, declined to grant protective costs limiting the amount of costs to be awarded against the claimant if unsuccessful.

3.167 The usual conditions for a protective costs award in public law cases were first laid down by Dyson J in *R v Lord Chancellor, ex p Child Poverty Action Group*.[181] These were that:

(1) The application must constitute a 'public interest challenge'. It must contain two elements, namely that (a) the issues raised must be of general importance, and (b) the applicant must have no private interest in the outcome.
(2) In any event, the discretion to make a protective costs order should be exercised only in the most exceptional circumstances. The court should have regard to the financial resources of the parties and the amount of costs likely to be in issue. It would be more likely to make an order where the defendant clearly has a superior capacity to bear the costs of the proceedings than the claimant and where it is satisfied that unless the order is made the defendant would probably discontinue the proceedings and would be acting reasonably in so doing.
(3) It would not often become clear that an issue was of sufficient importance and/or legal merit to displace the normal costs principle that costs follow the event until the hearing of the substantive application.

3.168 This formulation was, essentially, approved with slight modification by the Court of Appeal in *R (Corner House Research) v Secretary of State for Trade and Industry*[182] though the Court of Appeal considered that Dyson J had set the prospects of success necessary to justify the making of such an order too high. There, it was reiterated that a protective costs order would only be made in exceptional circumstances. The Court of Appeal added that the merits of an application for a protective costs order would be enhanced if those acting for the claimant were acting pro bono.

3.169 The essential governing principles, as laid down in *Corner House*, are that a protective costs order may be made where:

(1) the issues raised are of general importance,
(2) the public interest requires that those issues should be resolved,
(3) the applicant has no private interest in the outcome,
(4) it is fair and just to make the order having regard to the respective financial resources of the parties,
(5) if the order is not made the applicant would probably discontinue and would be acting reasonably in so doing.

---

[180] [2000] Env LR 544.
[181] [1999] 1 WLR 347.
[182] [2005] 1 WLR 2600. For further analysis, see B Jaffey, 'Protective Costs Orders in Judicial Review' [2006] JR 171; R Clayton QC, 'Public Interest Litigation, Costs and the Role of Legal Aid' [2006] PL 429.

Costs principles generally (including the making of protective costs orders) may require **3.170**
modification in an EC context having regard to the general principle in EC law of effectiveness
referred to above.

In particular, the criteria laid down in *Child Poverty Action Group* and *Corner House* may be **3.171**
too high in an EC challenge. In judicial review proceedings founded on EC law the
claimant will usually be seeking to enforce a directly effective Community right. It is plain,
therefore, that he will have an interest in the outcome. Further, although the case may be
significant to the claimant it does not follow that it is of sufficient public interest to fall into
the category of case envisaged by Dyson J or the Court of Appeal. For these reasons it is not
immediately easy to see how the requirement of a claimant being required not to have a
private interest in the outcome is compatible with the EC general principle of effectiveness.

In *Wilkinson and Kitzinger*[183] (a non-EC case in the Family Division) Sir Mark Potter said **3.172**
this of the private interest threshold test (para 54):

> ... I find the requirement that the applicant should have 'no private interest in the outcome'
> a somewhat elusive concept to apply in any case in which the applicant, either in private or
> public law proceedings, is pursuing a personal remedy, albeit his or her purpose is essentially
> representative of a number of persons with a similar interest. In such a case, it is difficult to
> see why, if a PCO is otherwise appropriate, the existence of the applicant's private or personal
> interest should disqualify him or her from the benefit of such an order. I consider that the
> nature and extent of the 'private interest' and its weight or importance in the overall context
> should be treated as a flexible element in the Court's consideration of the question whether
> it is fair and just to make the order ...

The protective costs order conditions are intended to be, and are, highly restrictive. They were, **3.173**
however, not applied as strictly in *R (Campaign for Nuclear Disarmament) v Prime Minister*.[184]
In that case, a challenge seeking an advisory declaration, in the context of preparations for
a possible war against Iraq, that UN Security Council Resolution 1441 does not authorize
the use of force in the event of there being a breach, the court made an award of pre-emptive
costs limiting the award of costs against the claimants if unsuccessful to the sum of £25,000.

The Divisional Court was influenced by the exceptional nature of the case. It regarded the **3.174**
following factors of particular importance:

(1) The claimant was a private company limited by guarantee. It possessed only modest
    resources and if an adverse costs order were made it would be at risk of going into
    liquidation or having to curtail its activities severely.
(2) Without the security of a protective costs award it would be unable to proceed with the
    challenge.
(3) The time frame for the challenge was so short that it afforded it no opportunity to seek
    to raise funds elsewhere.
(4) The case was of obvious public importance.
(5) The limit claimed by way of pre-emptive costs was likely, in any event, to meet the
    defendant's entitlement to costs.

---

[183] *Wilkinson and Kitzinger v Attorney General* [2006] EWHC 835 (Fam).
[184] Unreported, 5 December 2002.

3.175 Nonetheless, it is strongly arguable that the EC general principle of effectiveness requires the claimant not to be put in a position where—provided that his case has legal merit—he is unable to pursue the challenge at all.[185] In *Campaign for Nuclear Disarmament* Simon Brown LJ considered that he should:

> . . . seek to give effect to the overriding objective and should have particular regard to the need, so far as practicable, to ensure that the parties are on an equal footing and that the case is dealt with in a way which is proportionate to the financial position of each party.

3.176 It is probable that this, rather than the more restrictive, principles in *Child Poverty Action Group* and *Corner House* should be applied to protective costs applications by the Administrative Court in EC challenges brought by way of judicial review and, perhaps, to costs awards more generally.[186]

---

[185] Note, too, that special considerations may apply in an EC environmental challenge because of the provisions of the Aarhus Convention. See paras 14.88–14.89.

[186] However, the argument in support of a protective costs order that, in an EC case, no party ought to be required to pay more than 10 per cent of its annual turnover by way of a costs award was rejected in *R v Hammersmith and Fulham London Borough Council, ex p Council for Protection of Rural England, London Branch (No 2)* [2000] Env LR 544. The principle of proportionality in costs awards in EC law mandating such an order by the national court was argued to be derived from the ECJ ruling in Case C–72/95 *Kraajveld* [1997] Env LR 265.

4

REFERENCES TO THE ECJ

A. Nature and Purpose of the Preliminary Ruling Process

Article 234 (ex 177) EC provides as follows: **4.01**

The Court of Justice shall have jurisdiction to give preliminary rulings concerning:

(a) the interpretation of this Treaty;

(b) the validity and interpretation of acts of the institutions of the Community and of the ECB;

(c) the interpretation of the statutes of bodies established by an act of the Council, where those statutes so provide.

Where such a question is raised before any court or tribunal of a Member State,[1] that court or tribunal may, if it considers that a decision on the question is necessary to enable it to give judgment, request the Court of Justice to give a ruling thereon.

Where any such question is raised in a case pending before a court or tribunal of a Member State against whose decisions there is no judicial remedy under national law, that court or tribunal shall bring the matter before the Court of Justice.

4.02 Thus, Article 234 affords a method whereby the national court may refer relevant questions of law for decision by the ECJ.[2] It is known as the preliminary ruling or reference procedure. As can be seen from the terminology of the second paragraph, the national court generally has discretion rather than a duty to refer though at the highest appellate level there is a duty to refer.[3] In exercising that discretion, however, the national court must take into account the essential purposes of the preliminary ruling procedure and the body of case law that has developed as to how that discretion should be exercised.

4.03 Any reference made by the Administrative Court in judicial review proceedings (or in proceedings before other courts raising a public law collateral challenge)[4] will be made at some point during the course of those proceedings. As will be seen, the point at which a reference can, or should, be made may depend upon a number of factors. The most important of these will be the state of the evidence because until sufficient facts have been found the legal and factual context in which the question of law arises will be unclear and the court will not be in a position to determine whether a decision by the ECJ is necessary to enable it to give judgment or even to state the questions of law with the requisite precision.[5]

4.04 For these reasons in domestic judicial review challenges it will be only rarely that it is appropriate for a reference to be made at, or prior to,[6] the permission stage of an application for judicial review. Such cases will arise, primarily, where there is an underlying challenge to the validity of secondary Community legislation and where, for that reason, the specific facts are often less important.[7]

---

[1] The expression 'court or tribunal' is widely construed and ought not, in practice, to cause difficulty. It includes, eg, immigration adjudicators (Case C–416/96 *El-Yassini* [1999] ECR I–1209). The essential requirements of a national court or tribunal for the purposes of Art 234 are: (1) whether the body is established by law, (2) whether it is permanent, (3) whether its jurisdiction is compulsory, (4) whether its procedure is *inter partes* and (5) whether it is independent: see Case C–54/96 *Dorsch Consult* [1997] ECR I–4961.

[2] Under the Nice Treaty the Council can transfer jurisdiction over some categories of preliminary reference to the CFI. See Art 225(3) EC (as amended by the Nice Treaty).

[3] In cases before the House of Lords and, on occasion, other courts (see the third paragraph of Article 234 and paras 4.134 et seq.) there is a *duty* to refer where a decision on the question of law is necessary to enable that court to give judgment. In limited instances other reference procedures are applicable For example, under Art 68 EC (introduced by the Treaty of Amsterdam) Art 234 is modified in its application so that the power of making a reference in respect of certain decisions (as, eg, visa decisions) is confined to national courts against whose decisions there is no judicial remedy in national law. See also, Article 35 TEU (preliminary rulings in respect of the validity and interpretation of certain framework decisions and related measures).

[4] Throughout this chapter mention of the Administrative Court should be taken to include any national court hearing a public law collateral challenge.

[5] See, eg, *South Pembrokeshire District Council v Wendy Fair Markets Ltd* [1994] 1 CMLR 213, 223–4.

[6] Nothing in Art 234 dictates the time at which the relevant question of law can be raised. In any event, there are even 'proceedings' before the court prior to the grant of permission: see, eg, *R v Islington LBC, ex p Ewing* [1992] 1 WLR 388.

[7] For cases where an Art 234 reference was made at the permission stage for precisely that reason see *R (ABNA Ltd) v Secretary of State for Health and Food Standards Agency* [2004] Eu LR 88; *R v Secretary of State for Health, ex p Imperial Tobacco Ltd* [1999] COD 137.

There are two purposes to a preliminary ruling. First, the supremacy of EC law requires **4.05** that it be applied uniformly as between the Member States. It is, therefore, important that a body of domestic case law is built up that is not in conflict with that in other Member States.[8]

The second purpose of a reference to Luxembourg is to allow parties without standing for **4.06** a direct action under Article 230 EC or to the validity of secondary Community legislation before the CFI to bring the case before the ECJ by challenging the measure either directly or indirectly in the national court and then obtaining an Article 234 reference, thereby enabling the ECJ to declare the measure to be invalid.[9]

In deciding whether it can or should make a reference under Article 234 the Administrative **4.07** Court is required to consider two threshold questions. These are:

(1) whether it is permissible (or realistic[10]) to refer identified questions to the ECJ at all because such a reference is neither impermissible nor inadmissible; if so,
(2) whether the reference should be made in the exercise of the court's discretion in the light of the relevant principles developed in the case law.

B. Impermissible References

The threshold questions

Article 234 EC renders a reference *impermissible* (because the ECJ is, under that provision, **4.08** not accorded jurisdiction to hear it) in four clearly identified circumstances. In judicial review proceedings[11] the Administrative Court must, first, consider whether a reference would be impermissible by reason of one or more of these circumstances applying.

These arise where: **4.09**

(1) the case concerns provisions of Community law falling outside the scope of Article 234;
(2) the question or questions of law raised are not questions relating to the interpretation or (where so prescribed by Article 234) validity of otherwise relevant provisions of Community law;

---

[8] See, eg, Case 6/64 *Costa v ENEL* [1964] ECR 585, 594; Case C–337/95 *Parfums Christian Dior SA v Evora BV* [1997] ECR I–6013, para 25.

[9] This somewhat circuitous route is necessitated by the fact, that the national court, including the Administrative Court, has no jurisdiction to declare Community legislation to be unlawful: see paras 5.57 et seq. Questions of standing under Art 230 are notoriously difficult but a clear finding that a claimant has standing will deprive such claimant of the Art 234 route if the application for judicial review has not been brought within the time limits laid down by Art 230: see paras 3.67–3.80.

[10] There is a difference between: (1) an impermissible reference (excluded under Article 234 itself), (2) an inadmissible reference (where the ECJ may, as a matter of discretion, decline to hear a reference) and (3) the discretion of the national court not to make a reference. The analysis that follows assumes that the national court would refuse to make an inadmissible reference not as a matter of discretion but for practical purposes as a matter of jurisdiction.

[11] Judicial review proceedings include, for present purposes, all domestic proceedings in which public law issues are raised.

(3) the questions have not been 'raised' before the national court;

(4) a decision on the questions is not necessary to enable the court to give judgment.

Absence of jurisdiction in the ECJ outlined

4.10   The jurisdiction of the ECJ to grant preliminary rulings is necessarily limited by the terms of Article 234 itself to questions of: (1) interpretation of the Treaty and (2) interpretation and validity of acts of the Community institutions. This latter expression embraces not merely secondary EC legislation and other relevant 'acts' but also (see Article 234(c)) the legislation of bodies established by acts of the Council. However (see below) the ECJ possesses only a limited jurisdiction in respect of the Treaty on European Union (TEU).

4.11   From this strict separation of powers as between the ECJ and the national court there are a number of essential restrictions on the jurisdiction of the ECJ and on what may, legitimately, be referred to it for preliminary ruling. In outline:

(1) The jurisdiction of the ECJ is, necessarily, limited to questions of the interpretation and validity of Community law as provided for in the Treaty, so that questions of law that fall outside the scope of the matters defined in Article 234(a)–(c) EC or that go beyond determining relevant matters of interpretation or validity cannot be the subject of a preliminary ruling.

(2) The ECJ should not generally adjudicate as to the facts. It is for the national court to make all necessary findings of fact and then to apply Community law to those facts, in accordance with the preliminary ruling.[12] However, there are certain issues, most notably proportionality, where the distinction between law and fact can become blurred and where the ECJ has, on occasion, been prepared to make findings that particular measures were or were not proportionate.[13]

(3) Nor may the ECJ determine the validity of domestic law although it may, by virtue of its ruling under Article 234, give the national court an interpretation of Community law that will enable that court to decide whether the domestic law in question is valid or invalid as contravening EC law.[14]

(4) The ECJ may not, on a preliminary ruling, review the grounds on which the national court has decided the case.[15]

(5) It is (see also below) now clear that the ECJ will decline jurisdiction to entertain a reference under Article 234 by the national court in circumstances in which a claimant

---

[12]   Case 13/68 *Salgoil SpA v Italian Ministry for Foreign Trade* [1968] ECR 453. See, also, *Practice Direction (ECJ references: procedure) (Guidance of the Court of Justice of the European Communities on References by National Courts for Preliminary Rulings)* [1999] 1 WLR 260, 261, para 3.

[13]   See, eg, Case C–169/91 *Stoke-on-Trent v B&Q* [1992] ECR I–6635 (Sunday trading restrictions were proportional); Case C–285/98 *Kreil* [2000] ECR I–69 (exclusion of women from the military violated the proportionality principle).

[14]   See, eg, Joined Cases C–304, C–330, C–342/94 and C–224/95 *Criminal Proceedings against Tombesi* [1997] ECR I–3561, para 36.

[15]   Joined Cases C–197 and C–252/94 *Societe Bautiaa v Directeur des Services Fiscaux des Landes* [1996] ECR I–505, 516, per Advocate General Cosmas.

had standing to bring proceedings for annulment under Article 230 within the strict two-month time limit laid down thereunder but failed to do so.[16] It seems that, for these purposes, the standing must be obvious.[17] Plainly, however, the addressee of a decision would fall into this category.[18]

Threshold question (1)—are relevant provisions of Community law engaged?

By Article 234 EC the provisions of Community relevant to the jurisdiction of the ECJ to give preliminary rulings are: **4.12**

(1) *interpretation*[19] of the Treaty;
(2) interpretation and validity of acts of the institutions of the Community and of the European Central Bank (ECB);
(3) interpretation of the statutes of bodies established by an act of the Council where those statutes so provide.

The ECJ has jurisdiction to interpret not merely the EC Treaty but also all treaties amend-   **4.13** ing or even supplementing it. Further, by virtue of Article 239 EC the term 'treaty' includes annexes and protocols which are integral to it.

In summary, the principal Treaties (together with relevant annexes and protocols) so sub-   **4.14** ject to the ECJ's preliminary ruling jurisdiction are:

(1) the EC Treaty itself;[20]
(2) the Accession Treaties by which States become members of the Community which invariably confer jurisdiction on the ECJ;
(3) the Single European Act 1986 (SEA)[21] which extended the jurisdiction of the ECJ in respect both of amendments to the founding Treaties introduced by that Act and also in relation to the machinery by which the amendments were made;[22]
(4) certain parts of the TEU which—like SEA—extend Article 234 beyond the specific amendments made to the EC Treaty to include the amending machinery[23] and the Final Provisions which have not been incorporated into the founding Treaties.[24]

---

[16] Case C–188/192 *TWD Textilwerke Deggendorf GmbH v Germany* [1994] ECR I–833. Advocate General Jacobs observed at para 20 of his Opinion that: '... damage to the coherence of the system of remedies would be done if the undertaking were allowed to challenge indirectly, under Article [234], a decision against which the appropriate remedy is clearly a direct action under Article [230]'. It would have the incidental effect of enabling such cases to bypass the CFI where they are currently determined. For further discussion, see paras 3.67–3.80.

[17] Case C–241/95 *R v Intervention Board for Agricultural Produce, ex p Accrington Beef* [1996] ECR I–6699, paras 15–16; Case C–408/95 *Eurotunnel v Seafrance* [1997] ECR I–6315, paras 28–29.

[18] Case C–178/95 *Wiljo* [1997] ECR I–585.

[19] But not, of course, validity.

[20] Also effectively included by reference in the Art 234 jurisdiction are: (1) the Euratom Treaty under Art 150(1)(a) of that Treaty and (2) the ECSC Treaty under Art 41 of that Treaty (the ECSC Treaty expired on 23 July 2002).

[21] It was signed on 17 February 1986 and came into force on 1 July 1987.

[22] SEA, Art 31–32 and Table II.

[23] ie Titles II, III, IV and parts of Title VI.

[24] See TEU Arts 46–53.

4.15 Although not expressly referred to in Article 234 EC, Conventions between Member States negotiated within the framework of Article 293 EC,[25] and even Conventions between Member States negotiated outside that framework,[26] will fall—where they so provide—within the preliminary ruling jurisdiction of the ECJ.

4.16 The second class of EC law provisions that engage jurisdiction under Article 234 EC are acts of the Community institutions including acts of the ECB. Article 234 extends, at least in general, to preliminary rulings concerning both the interpretation and validity of such 'acts'.

4.17 The expression 'acts of the institutions' embraces binding acts in the form of regulations, directives, and decisions. It also covers non-binding acts in the form of recommendations and opinions since such acts may be material to interpreting domestic law. On that footing there may, as was demonstrated in *Mazzolai*,[27] be relevant 'acts' even where the measure in question has no direct effect. However, this is likely to depend upon whether the provision in question is, in some fashion, relevant to the determination of a question arising in the domestic public law proceedings.

4.18 Overall, the ECJ has adopted a broad view of what constitutes a relevant 'act' for the purpose of Article 234 jurisdiction. In particular, there is no exhaustive list that can be referred to.[28] International treaties concluded by the Community fall within the scope of the preliminary ruling procedure[29] as do international agreements where the Community has taken over the obligations of Member States such as the GATT Agreement.[30] However, treaties entered into by Member States prior to their accession to the Community may not, even where their subject matter is Community law, be the subject of a reference.[31] And treaties concluded by Member States that are outside the framework of Community law are also outside the scope of Article 234.[32] Nor is there jurisdiction under Article 234 to give a preliminary ruling on the question of whether an institution has *failed* to act.[33] Any such claim would have to be brought in a direct action under Article 232.

4.19 The 'institutions' whose 'acts' are envisaged by Article 234 include, primarily, those defined in Article 7(1) EC, namely the European Parliament, the Council, the Commission, the

---

[25] In this respect note the Convention on the Mutual Recognition of Companies and Corporate Bodies (*Bulletin of the European Communities*, Supplement 2/69) and the Convention on the Enforcement of Judgments in Civil and Commercial Matters ('Brussels Convention') ([1983] OJ C97/2).

[26] As, eg, the Rome Convention on the Law Applicable to Contractual Obligations [1989] OJ L48.

[27] Case 111/75 *Impresa Costruzioni Comm Quirino Mazzalai v Ferrovia del Renon* [1976] ECR 657.

[28] See, generally, D Anderson and M Demetriou. *References to the European Court* (2nd edn, 2002) paras 3–016 et seq. It is possible that, eg, 'acts' such as internal instructions or international agreements which are susceptible to review under Art 230 EC may fall within the preliminary ruling jurisdiction of the ECJ: see Anderson and Demetriou above, para 3–025.

[29] See, eg, Case 181/73 *Haegeman v Belgium* [1974] ECR 449.

[30] See, eg, Joined Cases 267 to 269/81 *Amministrazione delle Finanze v SPI and SAMI* [1983] ECR 801, paras 12–20.

[31] Case C–13/93 *ONEM v Minne* [1994] ECR I–371, paras 17–18.

[32] This is so even where the Treaty may be linked to the Community and the functioning of its institutions. See, eg, Case 44/84 *Hurd v Jones* [1986] ECR 29, para 20 where the headmaster of a European School was held unable to invoke a Treaty against HM Tax Inspectorate.

[33] Case C–68/95 *T Port GmbH & Co KG v Bundesanstalt fur Landwirtschaft und Ernahrung* [1996] ECR I–6065, para 53.

Court of Justice and the Court of Auditors. In addition, the ECB is expressly included. It is also possible that other institutions falling outside Article 7(1) could fall within the reach of Article 234.[34] Certainly, measures taken by bodies established pursuant to international treaties entered into by the Community may be the subject of a preliminary ruling.[35]

Special considerations attach to 'acts' of the ECJ. Although, in general, the *validity* of 'acts' **4.20** of Community institutions may be the subject of a preliminary ruling under Article 234 EC this does not extend to preliminary rulings of the ECJ itself.[36] This would, however, not seem to prevent the national court from referring a case to the ECJ for the purposes of *interpreting* a previous preliminary ruling of that court. Similar principles may operate in the case of applying Article 234 EC to previous ECJ (or CFI) judgments in direct actions.

Finally, Article 234(c) EC confers jurisdiction on the ECJ to give preliminary rulings as to **4.21** the interpretation of the statutes of bodies established by an act of the Council where those statutes so provide. This jurisdiction has never been invoked.

In the performance of (amongst other things) its task of interpretation and (where relevant) **4.22** determination of validity under Article 234 the ECJ has introduced the concept of general principles of EC law into Community law. These principles are now extremely important and are considered in detail elsewhere in this book.[37]

General principles of EC law do not represent separate provisions of Community law **4.23** under Article 234 but are, rather, aids to interpretation of those aspects of Community law that are within the preliminary rulings jurisdiction. These principles are, for the most part, derived from the laws of the Member States. They include, most notably, fundamental rights, legitimate expectation, the principle of legal certainty, equal treatment, non-retroactivity, and proportionality. Most recently, it has been recognized that these principles include the principle of democracy.[38] In the event, therefore, the ECJ will also give preliminary rulings, where appropriate, on the interpretation of these general principles.[39]

As a matter of principle, relevant provisions of Community law are not engaged so as to **4.24** confer Article 234 jurisdiction on the ECJ where the question of interpretation is one of *domestic* law.[40] However, sometimes, domestic law refers to EC law or incorporates it by reference and, in that way, raises—indirectly at least—questions of interpretation of EC law.

The ECJ has not always been consistent in its approach to such questions. In cases such as **4.25** the two *Foglia v Novello* cases[41] and *Kleinwort Benson Ltd v Glasgow District Council*[42] the

---

[34] See Anderson and Demetriou (n 28 above) para 3–027 referring to H Smit and P Herzog, *Law of the European Economic Community* (1976) para 177.08(b).

[35] See, eg, Case C–192/89 *Sevince v Staatssecretaris van Justitie* [1990] ECR 1–3461, paras 8–11.

[36] Case 69/85 *Wunsche Handelsgesellschaft GmbH & Co v Germany* [1986] ECR 947, 953.

[37] See Chapters 6–12.

[38] Case T–135/96 *UEAPME v Council* [1998] ECR II–2335.

[39] As, eg, in Case 316/86 *Hauptzollamt Hamburg-Jonas v Krucken* [1988] ECR 2213.

[40] See, eg, Case 24/64 *Dingemans v Bestuur der Sociale Verzekeringsbank* [1964] ECR 647, 652.

[41] Case 104/79 *Foglia v Novello (No 1)* [1980] ECR 745, Case 244/80 *Foglia v Novello (No 2)* [1981] ECR 3045.

[42] Case C–346/93 [1995] ECR I–615.

ECJ has declined jurisdiction to give a preliminary ruling on the basis that the questions raised were purely internal in nature.

4.26 In *Kleinwort Benson*, for example, the Court of Appeal had requested a preliminary ruling on certain aspects of the Brussels Convention on the question of whether English or Scottish courts had jurisdiction. Jurisdiction was governed by a domestic statute—the Civil Jurisdiction and Judgments Act 1982—which was, in turn, affected in large measure by the jurisdiction rules established by the Brussels Convention. The ECJ held that it did not possess jurisdiction under Article 234 both because the provisions of the 1982 Act did not entirely replicate the Brussels Convention and also because under the 1982 Act the domestic court was not bound—as it would ordinarily be in the case of a preliminary ruling—to apply ECJ judgments relating to the Brussels Convention when dealing with disputes under domestic jurisdiction.

4.27 Despite these cases the ECJ has usually adopted a more pragmatic approach where such questions are referred to it by national courts. Where possible it will simply reformulate the question so as to identify directly relevant provisions of Community law.[43] In other cases it has either ignored the problem[44] or followed its reasoning in cases such as *Dzodzi v Belgium*.[45] There, the court gave a preliminary ruling on the interpretation of certain provisions of EC social security law in order to clarify provisions of Belgian law sought to be invoked by a Togolese national. The ECJ observed that it was:

> exclusively for national courts which were dealing with a case to assess, with regard to the specific features of each case, both the need for a preliminary ruling in order to enable it to give judgment, and the relevance of the question.

Threshold question (2)—are the questions ones of relevant interpretation/validity?

4.28 There is an important distinction between interpretation and application of Community law. In particular, the ECJ does not have jurisdiction to rule on the application of EC law by the national court.[46]

4.29 But that analytic divide may be more apparent than real. As the ECJ observed in *Durighello v INPS*:[47]

> . . . whereas it is not for the Court, in the context of Article [234] of the Treaty, to rule on the compatibility of a national law with Community law, it does have the jurisdiction to provide the national court with all the elements of interpretation under Community law to enable it to assess that compatibility for the purpose of deciding the case before it.

---

[43] See, eg, Case C–105/96 *Codiesel* [1997] ECR I–3465, paras 12–13. See, also, Case C–62/00 *Marks & Spencer v Customs and Excise Commissioners* [2003] QB 866 where the ECJ observed that '[i]n the procedure laid down by [Article 234] for co-operation between national courts and the [ECJ] it is for the latter to provide the referring court with an answer which will be of use to it and enable it to determine the case before it. To that end, the Court may have to reformulate the questions referred to it.'

[44] See, eg, Case C–275/97 *DE + ES Bauunternehmung* [1999] ECR I–5331.

[45] Joined Cases C–297/88 and C–107/89 [1990] ECR I–1373. See, also, Case C–28/95 *Leur-Bloom v Inspecteur der Belastingdienst/Ondernemingen Amsterdam 2* [1997] ECR I–4161; Case C–267/99 *Adam* [2000] ECR I–7467.

[46] See, eg, Case 59/75 *Pubblico Ministero v Manghera* [1976] ECR 91, para 18.

[47] Case C–186/90 [1991] ECR I–5773, para 10.

So, in practice, the ECJ will—as part of the process of interpretation—often give full, and **4.30** sometimes unequivocal, guidance in its Article 234 ruling as to the proper application of EC law.[48]

So far as questions of *validity* are concerned these are primarily confined to 'acts' of the **4.31** institutions and do not, in any event, extend to Treaty provisions (see above). In practice, the grounds of validity are those listed in Article 230 EC as supplemented (as also in the task of interpretation: see above) by recourse to the general principles of law and (as part of those general principles) fundamental rights.[49]

Under Article 230 the validity of Community measures may be challenged directly on **4.32** grounds of lack of competence, infringement of an essential procedural requirement, infringement of the Treaty or any rule of law relating to its application, or misuse of powers.

These grounds are deployed in a broad fashion by the ECJ. They are rarely isolated or iden- **4.33** tified in the court's judgment and, from the perspective of the national court when consid- ering whether or not the ECJ is likely to accept jurisdiction, it seems probable that almost all cases of conceivable illegality are included in Article 234 validity review.[50]

There is a further relationship between Article 234 and Article 230 that may sometimes be **4.34** of importance in domestic judicial review or other public law proceedings. The ECJ's juris- diction to give a preliminary ruling as to validity is not subject to the restrictive standing rules that apply under Article 230 in a direct action. Nor is there, under Article 234, an effectively rigid two-month time limit for seeking a preliminary ruling as there is under Article 230.

In general terms, domestic standing and limitation rules under CPR Pt 54—where **4.35** satisfied—probably enable the Administrative Court to seek a preliminary ruling from the ECJ.[51]

However, where a claimant possesses standing under the more restrictive rules in Article 230 **4.36** but has failed to make an application in time under that provision the ECJ will decline jurisdiction to give a preliminary ruling under Article 234 on the footing that to do so would be to subvert the strict regime under Article 230.[52]

This has significant implications for the way in which the Administrative Court may **4.37** deal with a domestic judicial review challenge to the validity of secondary Community legislation. It is now well established that the Administrative Court (or any other national court) has no jurisdiction to pronounce on the *invalidity* of Community legislation except indirectly by suspending the operation of such legislation *ad interim* and then under strict criteria laid down by the ECJ.[53] Essentially, there must be urgency and a threat

---

[48] See, eg, Case C–169/91 *Stoke-on-Trent City Council v B&Q plc* [1993] 2 CMLR 509.
[49] See, generally, Chapters 6–12.
[50] See Anderson and Demetriou (n 28 above) para 3–078.
[51] See, though, the discussion at paras 3.53 et seq.
[52] For further discussion, see paras 3.67 et seq.
[53] See, eg, Case 314/85 *Foto-Frost v Hauptzollamt Lubeck-Ost* [1987] ECR 4199.

of serious and irreparable damage to the claimant and due account must be taken of the Community interest.[54]

4.38 So, where it is clear that a claimant in judicial review proceedings had standing to bring a direct action under Article 230 but failed to do so in time the Administrative Court should not seek a preliminary ruling from the ECJ because that court will decline jurisdiction to give such a ruling. In such circumstances a claimant would be regarded by the ECJ as simply engineering a case in the Administrative Court in order to seek an impermissible reference. However, as discussed elsewhere,[55] whether a claimant possesses standing under Article 230 is a complex question and the Administrative Court should be slow to refuse a preliminary ruling unless the position as to Article 230 standing is plain.

4.39 Questions both of interpretation and validity—especially where issues of proportionality arise—may involve determinations of fact. In principle it is for the national court to ascertain the relevant facts.[56] There is limited provision for the ECJ to take account of further information for the purpose of clarification or to complete factual matters that may not have been fully addressed in the reference.[57] However, the national court should not rely on this residual (and very much default) jurisdiction when deciding whether or not the reference is permissible as raising a relevant question of interpretation or validity.

Threshold question (3)—has the question been 'raised' in the proceedings?

4.40 The question or questions of interpretation or validity must have been 'raised' before the national court for Article 234 to be engaged. Unlike the earlier threshold questions of identification of the issue as being one relevant to Community law and as involving interpretation or validity, it is pre-eminently a matter for the national court to determine whether the question has been 'raised' in proceedings before it.

4.41 In practice the issue will be raised by one or both of the parties though the court may raise it of its own motion. There is no restriction on the temporal point at which the issue may be raised. It may, for example, be raised at the permission stage of an application for judicial review. This will, however, not usually be considered appropriate because both parties should be able to put in evidence so that—other considerations aside—the court may fully examine the fourth threshold question, namely whether a reference is necessary in order to enable it to give judgment (see below).

4.42 But if both parties are agreed as to the relevant facts and the necessity of a preliminary ruling there is no reason why a reference cannot be made at the permission stage of an application for judicial review.[58] Indeed, such a course may be desirable in circumstances where the challenge is dependent on a question as to the validity of Community law. As explained

---

[54] See, eg, Case C–465/93 *Atlanta* [1995] ECR I–3761. On interim relief generally, see paras 3.123 et seq.

[55] See paras 3.114–3.122.

[56] See, eg, Case C–30/93 *AC-ATEL Electronics Vertriebs v Hauptzollamt München-Mitte* [1994] ECR I–2305, para 17.

[57] See, eg, Case 47/82 *Vismans v Inspecteur de Invoerrechten en Accijnzen* [1982] ECR 3983, para 8.

[58] *R v Minister of Agriculture, Fisheries and Food, ex p FEDESA* [1988] 3 CMLR 207.

earlier,[59] the Administrative Court cannot pronounce on the invalidity of Community legislation, so that a preliminary ruling is likely to be necessary at some stage if the challenge has potential merit.[60]

Threshold question (4)—is a decision on the question necessary for judgment?

Similarly, a determination of whether a decision on the question is necessary for the court **4.43** to give judgment is a matter for the national court. So if, for example, a claim is founded on both domestic and Community law but can be decided on domestic law alone then Community law issues *may* become redundant and there would, in that event, be no jurisdiction under Article 234 to refer.

Initially, the English courts imposed a strict standard—that of the Community law point **4.44** being 'conclusive'—of when a decision was 'necessary' for judgment.[61] However, subsequent cases have relaxed the criteria somewhat. In a judicial review challenge Lord Bingham MR observed that the reference should be 'critical to the court's final decision'.[62] In *An Bord Bainne Co-operative Ltd v Milk Marketing Board*[63] it was suggested that the test 'should not be interpreted too narrowly'.

So, too, the ECJ's approach to what a domestic court may find necessary to refer is practical. **4.45** It has stated that: '[a] request for a preliminary ruling from a national court may be rejected only if it is quite obvious that the interpretation of Community law sought by that court bears no relation to the actual nature of the case or the subject-matter of the main action'.[64] In *CILFIT Srl v Ministro della Sanita*[65] the ECJ considered that it would not be 'necessary' to refer if the question of law was irrelevant, or the provision had already been interpreted by the ECJ[66] or the correct application was so obvious as to leave no scope for reasonable doubt.

A generous approach is also taken to the nature of the 'decision' necessary for judgment to **4.46** be given. This means a decision on the question itself whether given by the ECJ or the national court.[67] As Chadwick LJ observed in *Trent Tavern Ltd v Sykes*:[68]

> the requirement in Article [234] is that a decision on the question is necessary in order to enable this Court to give judgment; not that a ruling from the Court of Justice is necessary to enable this Court to reach a decision on the question.

---

[59] See para 4.37.

[60] See, eg, *R v Secretary of State for Health, ex p Imperial Tobacco Ltd* [1999] COD 138. Note that if, at any particular stage, the challenge is not perceived as having merit no relevant question has been 'raised' for the purpose of the preliminary ruling process: Case 283/81 *CILFIT SrL v Ministro della Sanita* [1982] ECR 3415, paras 8–9. In the context of judicial review this will be so where permission is refused or the point is finally determined.

[61] *HP Bulmer Ltd v J Bollinger SA* [1974] Ch 401, 422, per Lord Denning MR.

[62] *R v International Stock Exchange, ex p Else* [1993] QB 534, 545.

[63] [1985] 1 CMLR 6, 10, per Neill J.

[64] Case C–143/94 *Furlanis Costruzioni Generali SpA v Azienda Nazionale Autonoma Strade (ANAS)* [1995] ECR I–3633, para 12.

[65] Case 283/81 [1982] ECR 3415.

[66] There is, however, nothing to prevent the national court from making a new reference even where the issue has been the subject of a judgment of the ECJ: see *CILFIT* (n 65 above) paras 13–15. See, also, Cases C–332, 333 and 335/92 *Eurico Italia v Ente Nazionale Risi* [1994] ECR I–711.

[67] Note the careful analysis of this issue in Anderson and Demetriou (n 28 above) paras 3–100–3–110.

[68] [1999] Eu LR 492.

4.47   The 'judgment' referred to in Article 234 includes interlocutory rulings.[69] Generally, at least, the court making the reference must be the court giving the judgment.[70] This means that where the Court of Appeal grants permission to apply for judicial review on a renewed permission hearing but remits the case to the High Court it ought not to request a preliminary ruling. If the Court of Appeal considers that a preliminary ruling should be requested the safest course is for that court, when granting permission, to assume jurisdiction to hear the substantive application for judicial review.

C. Inadmissible References

What is an inadmissible reference?

4.48   The term 'inadmissible reference' is used here to denote those instances where although the ECJ has strict jurisdiction to give a preliminary ruling it is likely to refuse to do so.

4.49   So far as the Administrative Court is concerned this situation is little different in practice from cases where the ECJ has no jurisdiction. It is not entirely accurate, therefore, to suggest that the Administrative Court has, in such circumstances, *discretion* to refer. Its decision as to whether to request a preliminary ruling is entirely contingent on the position taken or likely to be taken by the ECJ. If the ECJ will (or is overwhelmingly likely to) decline jurisdiction then the Administrative Court does not, in any practical sense, have discretion to make a reference under Article 234.

4.50   Further, there is no clear borderline between those cases in which the ECJ is expressly denied jurisdiction by reference to the terminology of Article 234 and those cases in which the developing case law shows that the court will not accept jurisdiction. For example, the refusal by the ECJ to accept jurisdiction in cases where a claimant had the requisite standing to maintain a direct action under Article 230 but failed to do so timeously (see above) can be seen either as an instance of lack of jurisdiction (impermissible references) or as an instance of the ECJ establishing a uniform policy towards such applications (inadmissible references).

4.51   In general terms, though the categories are by no means exhaustive, the circumstances in which the ECJ will decline jurisdiction so as to render a reference inadmissible fall under four main headings. These are:

(1) Insufficiency of information.
(2) Irrelevancy.
(3) Hypothetical or advisory questions.
(4) Misuse or abuse of ECJ process.

---

[69] Case 107/76 *Hoffman-La Roche v Centrafarm Vertriebsgesellschaft Pharmazeutischer Erzugnisse mbH* [1977] ECR 957, para 4.
[70] Case 338/85 *Pardini Fratelli SpA v Ministero del Commercio con l'Estero* [1988] ECR 2041, applied by the CA in *BLP Group plc v Commissioners of Customs and Excise* [1994] STC 41.

Insufficiency of information and irrelevancy

Although there is no fixed rule as to the degree of information that must be provided in a **4.52**
reference it must be sufficient to achieve the purpose of the Article 234 process. In *Max
Mara*[71] the ECJ observed that:

> The information provided and the questions raised in orders for reference must not only
> enable the Court to give helpful answers but must also give the governments of the Member
> States and other interested parties the opportunity to submit observations pursuant to
> Article 23 of the EC Statute of the Court of Justice.

There is an increasing tendency on the part of the ECJ to decline jurisdiction in cases where **4.53**
there is insufficient detail of the factual and domestic legal context in which the dispute
arises as well as the reasons for the reference.[72]

That context will dictate the amount of detail that is required. For example, in competition **4.54**
cases the ECJ usually expects a greater degree of information because of the complex details
that are frequently involved.[73] On the other hand, it is sometimes said that disputes raising
specific technical issues do not need extensive detail.[74]

From the perspective of the Administrative Court it is, therefore, not merely desirable but also **4.55**
jurisdictionally important to ensure that it has made all findings of fact that are necessary to
achieve compliance with the *Mara* test applied in the context of the dispute before it.[75]

In making a reference the Administrative Court must ensure that the questions are **4.56**
relevant. The ECJ may decline to give a preliminary ruling where the questions asked are
'manifestly irrelevant'.[76]

Although the jurisdiction is sparingly exercised there have been cases where the ECJ has **4.57**
declined jurisdiction on this basis. In *Falciola Angelo SpA*,[77] for example, the question was
directed to the ability of the national court to function in an impartial manner whereas the
dispute before that court concerned Community law public procurement rules.

Hypothetical or advisory questions

In principle it is not the function of the ECJ to provide general and advisory opinions.[78] So, **4.58**
jurisdiction may be declined if the problem is purely hypothetical. This occurred in

---

[71] Case C–307/95 *Max Mara* [1995] ECR I–5083, paras 7–8.
[72] See, especially, Joined Cases C–320 to C–322/90 *Telemarsicabruzzo SpA v Circostel* [1993] ECR I–393.
But the court's power to 'cure' deficiencies in the information by seeking clarification or to examine the documents forwarded with the reference (or added to the written observations of the parties) to supplement the
information may be utilized: see, eg, Case C–316/93 *Vaneetveld v Le Foyer* [1994] ECR I–763; Joined Cases
C–51/96 and 191/97 *Deliege* [2000] ECR I–2549.
[73] See, eg, Case C–157/92 *Pretore di Genova v Banchero* [1993] ECR I–1085, paras 4–5.
[74] Case C–316/93 *Vaneetveld v Le Foyer* [1994] ECR I–763, para 13.
[75] See, also, *Practice Direction (ECJ references: procedure) (Guidance of the Court of Justice of the European
Communities on References by National Courts for Preliminary Rulings)* [1999] 1 WLR 260, 261, para 7 which
states that: 'on any view, the administration of justice is likely to be best served if the reference is not made until
both sides have been heard'.
[76] Case C–343/90 *Dias v Director da Alfandega do Porto* [1992] ECR I–4673, para 20. See, also,
Case C–62/93 *BP Supergrass v Greece* [1995] ECR I–9883.
[77] Case C–286 *Falciola Angelo SpA v Commune di Pavia* [1990] ECR I–191.
[78] See, eg, Case 244/80 *Foglia v Novello* [1981] ECR 3045, paras 18, 20–21.

Meilicke[79] where a preliminary ruling was requested on the compatibility of German case law with the Second Company Law Directive (Directive (EEC) 77/91) in circumstances where that case law was not relevant to the subject matter of the dispute.

4.59   But a question is not necessarily hypothetical or advisory merely because the problem is not immediate. As Advocate General Jacobs observed in his Opinion in *Leclerk-Siplec v TFI Publicite SA*:[80]

> If under the procedural law of a Member State non-hostile litigation is a possible way of bringing an issue before the courts, it would not be appropriate for the Court of Justice to interfere with the procedural autonomy of that Member State by holding that such litigation cannot lead to a reference to the Court.

4.60   There is now a body of case law in judicial review to the effect that where there is a significant public interest element in the claim the case will not be regarded as academic or hypothetical and relief may be granted.[81] It is submitted that similar considerations apply to a decision to seek a preliminary ruling from the ECJ. For example, in the Administrative Court, Newman J was prepared to grant a reference under Article 234 where a question of general importance in the EU arose even though the relevant entitlement, the subject of the declaration sought by the claimant, could have been determined in a concurrent claim for damages.[82]

4.61   Sometimes, too, additional practical considerations may be involved. It is, at least occasionally, possible for questions to contain assumptions of fact that have not yet been substantiated. In *R v Secretary of State for the Home Department, ex p Evans Medical Ltd*[83] Advocate General Lenz pointed out that a preliminary ruling would not, in some such circumstances, be hypothetical. He said:

> It serves the interests of procedural economy to postpone the taking of evidence so long as it is not clear whether the subject-matter of that evidence is material to the proceedings.

4.62   In practice, the ECJ will not reject references on the ground that the questions are academic or hypothetical unless 'it is quite obvious that the interpretation of Community law sought by that Court bears no relation to the actual facts of the main action or its purpose'.[84]

---

[79]   Case C–83/91 *Meilicke v ADV/ORGA FA Meyer AG* [1992] ECR I–4971.

[80]   Case C–412/93 [1995] ECR I–179, 184. It is settled law that a national court has jurisdiction to make a reference to the ECJ relating to the validity of a directive in advance of the adoption of domestic implementing measures and where it considers the arguments relating to invalidity are well founded it must stay the proceedings and make a reference under Art 234: see Case C–344/04 *R (IATA and ELFAA) v Department of Transport* (nyr, 12 January 2006); *R (International Association of Independent Tanker Owners) v Secretary of State for Transport* [2006] EWHC 1577.

[81]   See, of the many cases, *Don Pasquale (A Firm) v Customs and Excise Commissioners* [1990] 1 WLR 1108; *R v Board of Visitors of Dartmoor Prison, ex p Smith* [1987] QB 106; *R v Secretary of State for the Home Department, ex p Mehari* [1994] 2 WLR 349. The House of Lords accepted the principle but declined jurisdiction on the particular facts in *R v Secretary of State for the Home Department, ex p Salem* [1999] 1 AC 450. In HRA cases a 'victim' for the purposes of bringing judicial review proceedings appears to adopt a similar approach given that a victim includes a person who runs the risk of a Convention breach occurring in the future: see *Marckx v Belgium* (1979) 2 EHRR 330: 'Article [34] entitles individuals to contend that a law violates their rights by itself in the absence of an individual measure of implementation if they run the risk of being directly affected by it'.

[82]   *R (Synthon BV) v Licensing Authority* [2006] EWHC 1759.

[83]   Case C–324/93 [1995] ECR I–563, paras 15–17.

[84]   Case C–415/93 *Union Royale Belge des Societes de Football Association v Bosman* [1995] ECR I–4921.

Misuse/abuse of process

There are also certain residual cases where the ECJ may decline jurisdiction to give a pre-   **4.63**
liminary ruling. The underlying rationale in most of these cases is that it is a misuse (sometimes abuse) of ECJ process. Reference has, for example, already been made to the situation
in which a claimant has standing to bring a direct action but fails to do so in time.[85] Such
cases may, perhaps, be regarded as an abuse of ECJ process as an alternative categorization
to the ECJ not possessing jurisdiction under Article 234.

Other instances in which the ECJ has declined jurisdiction to give a preliminary ruling   **4.64**
include those where:

(1) the parties have, in effect, fabricated a dispute for the purpose of obtaining a reference
   to the ECJ;[86]
(2) there is no pending dispute before the national court.[87]

The discretion of the ECJ to decline jurisdiction on the footing of misuse or abuse of   **4.65**
process should not be confused with the quite separate discretions of the national court to:
(a) decline to make a reference by reference to criteria considered in the next section below
or (b) in the case of the Administrative Court decline even to entertain judicial review proceedings on similar but conceptually distinct grounds to those of the ECJ in refusing to give
a preliminary ruling.

So far as declining to hear judicial review proceedings is concerned, there are instances in   **4.66**
which the Administrative Court has for example declined, in its discretion, jurisdiction to hear
applications for judicial review on the basis that the cases were unsuitable for judicial review
and that the complaints should have been brought by way of infraction proceedings under
Article 226 EC.[88] The ECJ does not, however, appear to decline jurisdiction on such a basis.[89]

D. Discretionary References

Introduction

Having decided, by reference to the criteria outlined above, that requesting a preliminary   **4.67**
ruling from the ECJ is neither impermissible nor inadmissible the Administrative Court must

---

[85] See paras 4.34–4.38.
[86] Case 104/79 *Foglia v Novello* [1980] ECR 745 paras 9–11; Case 244/80 *Foglia v Novello* [1981] ECR
3045, para 18; Case C–105/94 *Celestini v Saar-Sektkellerei Faber* [1997] ECR I–2971, para 23; Case C–28/95
Leur-Bloom v Inspecteur der Belastingdienst [1998] QB 182; Case 89/91 *Meilicke v Meyer* [1992] ECR I–4871;
Case C–318/00 *Bacardi-Martini v Newcastle United* [2003] ECR I–905. Contrast Case C–36/99 *Ideal
Tourisme* [2000] ECR I–6049 where the ECJ rejected the suggestion by the defendant Government of a contrived dispute.
[87] For instances see, eg: Case 338/95 *Pardini v Ministero del commercio con l'estero* [1988] ECR 2041, para 11;
Case 176/96 *Lehtonen v FRBSB* [2000] ECR I–000, para 19; Case C–314/96 *Djabali v Caisse d'allocations
familiales de l'Essonne* [1998] ECR I–1149, paras 21, 23.
[88] *R v MAFF, ex p Dairy Trade Federation* [1995] COD 3; *R (Association of Pharmaceutical Importers) v
Secretary of State for Health* [2001] EWCA Civ 1896.
[89] Case 26/62 *Van Gend en Loos v Nederlandse Administratie der Belastingen* [1963] ECR 1, 13.

then decide, *as a matter of discretion*, whether to seek a preliminary ruling under Article 234. In this context reference should also be made to Chapter 19 where tactical considerations from the practical perspective of practitioners, illustrated by case analyses, are examined.

4.68 Importantly, Article 234 places no *obligation* on, for example, the Administrative Court as a national court of first instance to make a reference since that court is one in respect of which there is a judicial remedy, namely the seeking of permission to appeal.[90]

4.69 There are two relevant questions:

(1) Is there a general presumption that a reference should, or should not, be made if the threshold criteria are satisfied?

(2) What are the factors that should, in any event, militate in favour of, or against, a reference?

(1) Is there a general presumption for or against referring once the threshold criteria are met?

4.70 Although the national courts have vacillated about this underlying question it now seems clear that there is no general presumption that a request for a preliminary ruling should or should not issue once the threshold issues of jurisdiction have been determined. There are, rather, certain broad criteria which suggest whether a reference should, or should not, be made and there are more specific criteria that have been enunciated in some of the cases.

4.71 There was, initially, a presumption against referring. In *Bulmer Ltd v Bollinger SA*[91] Lord Denning MR stated that:

> Unless the point is really difficult and important, it would seem better for the English judge to decide it himself . . .

4.72 This approach was, at least ostensibly, subsequently converted into something close to a general presumption in favour of referring. In *R v International Stock Exchange, ex p Else Ltd*[92] Sir Thomas Bingham MR said:

> . . . if the facts have been found and the Community law issue is critical to the court's final decision, the appropriate course is ordinarily to refer the issue to the Court of Justice unless the national court can with complete confidence resolve the issue itself. In considering whether it can with complete confidence resolve the issue itself the national court must be fully mindful of the differences between national and Community legislation, of the pitfalls which face a national court venturing into what may be an unfamiliar field, of the need for uniform interpretation within the Community and of the great advantages enjoyed by the Court of Justice in construing Community instruments. If the national court has any real doubt, it should ordinarily refer.

4.73 The ECJ has itself provided little guidance emphasizing the wide discretion that is vested in the national courts. However, in *Wiener v Hauptzollamt Emmerich*[93] Advocate General

---

[90] Procedural issues can arise on appeals in respect of the *obligation* on certain courts to refer: see paras 4.139 et seq.

[91] [1974] Ch 401, 424F.

[92] [1993] QB 534.

[93] Case C–338/95 [1997] ECR I–6495: see paras 12–20 of the Opinion of 10 July 1997.

Jacobs counselled 'a greater measure of self-restraint' on the part of national courts in exercising their discretion to request a preliminary ruling. His formulation suggests that there is no presumption in favour of referring. He stated:

> A reference will be most appropriate where the question is one of general importance and where the ruling is likely to promote the uniform application of the law throughout the European Union. A reference will be least appropriate where there is an established body of case-law which could readily be transposed to the facts of the instant case; or where the question turns on a narrow point considered in the light of a very specific set of facts and the ruling is unlikely to have any application beyond the instant case. Between those two extremes there is of course a wide spectrum of possibilities; nevertheless national courts themselves could properly assess whether it is appropriate to make a reference.

The formulation of Advocate General Jacobs in *Wiener* was approved by Chadwick LJ in **4.74**
Trinity Mirror plc v Commissioners of Customs and Excise[94] and has, subsequently, also been
endorsed by that court in *Professional Contractors' Group v Commissioners of Inland Revenue*.[95]

These observations suggest that the modern approach to references is one where several **4.75**
different factors may operate and where there is no clear presumption that a request for a
preliminary ruling will be made.

Some of the relevant discretionary criteria are set out below. They are by no means **4.76**
exhaustive.

(2) Discretionary criteria

Difficulty and importance of the point

In strict logic a first instance national court such as the Administrative Court is not bound— **4.77**
as a court of last resort would be —by the doctrine of *acte clair*.[96] It has the widest discretion
in determining whether to request a preliminary ruling and may decide the most difficult
and/or important questions of Community law if it considers that such a course is justified.

However, in practice, national courts considering points of Community law that arise **4.78**
in domestic public law proceedings have often been cautious in their approach and have
tended to refer if they entertain any doubt especially about a point of law with Community-
wide implications.

In *R v Secretary of State for Trade and Industry, ex p Trade Union Congress*,[97] for example, the **4.79**
question at issue was whether the Maternity and Parental Leave Regulations 1999 had

---

[94] [2001] EWCA Civ 65, para 52.

[95] [2001] EWCA Civ 1945.

[96] This doctrine is often misused. It only applies where there is an *obligation* to refer. It absolves the court of the duty to refer provided that the correct application of Community law is so obvious—to the courts of other Member States and the ECJ as well as to the domestic court—as to leave no doubt as to how the question raised should be resolved: see *CILFIT* [1982] ECR 3415, especially paras 15–20.

[97] [2000] IRLR 565. See, also, *R v Pharmaceutical Society of Great Britain, ex p Association of Pharmaceutical Importers* [1987] 3 CMLR 951, 972 (reference where question is one of 'great practical importance for the Community in general'). Contrast, though, *R v Secretary of State for the Home Department, ex p Vitale* [1995] 3 CMLR 605, 612 where a reference was refused despite the issues being of 'general significance for the citizens of each Member State of the European Union'.

lawfully transposed the Parental Leave Directive (Directive (EC) 96/34). The Divisional Court hearing the application for judicial review considered that the arguments advanced by the claimant were likely to prevail. Nonetheless, it decided to request a preliminary ruling because the point affected other Member States and it would be 'inherently undesirable' for a domestic ruling to be given which might be inconsistent with a decision in another Member State or with a future decision of the ECJ.

4.80 The rationale of referring such points is that the ECJ is 'best placed' to decide how the orderly development of the Community should be advanced.[98] As Bingham J observed in *Commissioners of Customs and Excise v Samex ApS*:[99]

> [The Court of Justice] has a panoramic view of the Community and its institutions, a detailed knowledge of the treaties and of much subordinate legislation made under them, and an intimate familiarity with the functioning of the Community market which no national judge denied the collective experience of the Court of Justice could hope to achieve. Where questions of administrative intention and practice arise the Court of Justice can receive submissions from the Community institutions, as also where relations between the Community and non-member states are in issue. Where the interests of member states are affected they can intervene to make their views known ... Where comparison falls to be made between Community texts in different languages ... the multinational Court of Justice is equipped to carry out the task in a way in which no national judge, whatever his linguistic skills, could rival. The interpretation of Community instruments involves very often ... the more creative process of supplying flesh to a spare and loosely constructed skeleton. The choice between alternative submissions may not turn on purely legal considerations. These are matters which the Court of Justice is very much better placed to assess and determine than a national court.

Length of time/cost in obtaining a preliminary ruling

4.81 The delay entailed in seeking a preliminary ruling may be considerable. The average delay in 2001 was 22.7 months.[100] Similarly, added cost is a factor to be taken into account including the effect of such cost upon the Legal Services Commission in legally aided cases.[101]

4.82 As against this, however, is the fact, that delaying a reference may actually increase the time and cost to the parties. As Bingham J stated in *Samex:*[102]

> The reference to the Court of Justice would be unlikely to take longer than appeals have normally taken to reach the Court of Appeal, at least until recently, and unlikely to cost much more. If, at the Court of Appeal stage, a reference were held to be necessary, the delay and expense would be roughly doubled.

4.83 Other considerations may be material especially to the question of delay. It has been observed that a request for a preliminary ruling is more likely to be made where the party

---

[98] *R v Inland Revenue Commissioners, ex p Commerzbank AG* [1991] 3 CMLR 633, 646.

[99] [1983] 1 All ER 1042, 1056.

[100] Anderson and Demetriou (n 28 above) para 5–040. The average delay in 2005 was reduced to 20.4 months: see ECJ 2005 Annual Report, 10.

[101] See, eg, *Evans v Secretary of State for the Environment, Transport and the Regions* [2001] 2 CMLR 10, paras 32 and 43.

[102] [1983] 1 All ER 1042, 1056.

seeking the reference will be the one to suffer the adverse effects of delay.[103] This chimes with the relevance of Article 6 of the European Convention on Human Rights which requires the determination of civil rights and obligations or criminal charges to be heard within a reasonable time and which may have to be considered separately by the Administrative Court when deciding whether to order a reference.[104]

A decision to grant interim relief may also affect the court's view on questions of delay since **4.84** the grant of such relief may ameliorate what would otherwise be prejudicial delay.[105] To contrary effect, the fact that the point at issue will become otiose if there is delay in obtaining a reference may be a powerful factor in the national court not seeking a preliminary ruling.[106]

Wishes of the parties/overloading the ECJ

Neither the wishes of the parties nor the risk of overloading the work of the ECJ should, in **4.85** principle, play a large part in a decision as to whether to request a preliminary ruling.

Analytically, a reference to the ECJ is a reference by the court and not by the parties. Certainly, **4.86** the national court has power to order a reference of its own motion. As Kerr LJ observed in *Portsmouth City Council v Richards*:[107]

> It is very important that the concept of so-called references by consent should not creep into our practice. All references are by the court. The court must itself be satisfied of the need for a reference, that the factual material accompanying the reference is sufficient to provide a proper foundation for it, and that it is of sufficient assistance to the European Court to enable it to reach a decision.

In practice, however, the wishes of the parties will be taken into account. In particular, **4.87** where neither party seeks a reference this will weigh heavily with the national court.[108]

Less obvious is the legitimacy of taking into account the workload of the ECJ. It has been **4.88** doubted whether this is a relevant factor to take into account at all.[109] To the extent that it is a practical reflection of Advocate General Jacobs' plea for restraint in *Wiener* considered above,[110] it seems clear that such consideration could only operate in a straightforward case. Where the point of law is difficult and/or important *Wiener* itself suggests that a reference is appropriate.

---

[103] *Generics UK Ltd v Smith-Kline and French Laboratories Ltd* [1990] 1 CMLR 416, 435.

[104] *Pafitis v Greece RJD* 1998–I, No 66 (European Court of Human Rights), para 95. For the relevance of the ECHR in general to questions of Community law see Chapter 12.

[105] See paras 3.123–3.148 for consideration of interim relief in EC judicial review cases.

[106] See, eg, *R v MAFF, ex p Portman Agrochemicals Ltd* [1994] 3 CMLR 18, 25. Indeed, where the question has become otiose the Administrative Court has jurisdiction to *withdraw* the reference: see *R v Home Secretary, ex p Adams* [1995] 3 CMLR 476, 484.

[107] [1989] 1 CMLR 673, 708.

[108] *R v MAFF, ex p Portman Agrochemicals Ltd* [1994] 3 CMLR 18, 25.

[109] See, eg, per Dyson J in *Commissioners of Customs and Excise v Anchor Food Ltd* (unreported, 26 June 1998); per Sir John Pennycuik VC in *Van Duyn v Home Office* [1974] 1 CMLR 347, 358. Contrast per Lord Denning MR in *HP Bulmer Ltd v J Bollinger SA* [1974] Ch 401.

[110] See n 93 above and text.

Parallel proceedings by the Commission

4.89 Where the Commission has instituted proceedings against a Member State by way of direct action before the ECJ under Article 226 EC there may be competing reasons for and against the making of a reference.

4.90 Whilst the making of a reference may result in consistency as between the national court and the ECJ it may be thought—subject to questions of delay—that a reference is unnecessary because the point at issue can be determined without a preliminary ruling.

Collateral motive

4.91 In *Samex*[111] Bingham J suggested that a reference would be unlikely to be made if:

> the question is raised mischievously, not in the bona fide hope of success but in order to obstruct or delay an almost inevitable adverse judgment, denying the other party his remedy meanwhile.[112]

Particular questions of validity and direct effect

4.92 Importantly, as explained elsewhere, a national court has no power to declare a *Community* measure to be invalid.[113] Whilst this does not prevent the Administrative Court, for example, from determining that the act is *valid*, it does raise an important point of principle as to whether, when such questions of validity are raised, the Administrative Court or other national court is, in practice, under a duty, as opposed to simply possessing a discretion, to request a preliminary ruling since, it may be argued, a claimant loses the prospect of having a Community act such as a directive or regulation declared unlawful unless a reference is ordered.[114]

4.93 Certainly in those circumstances a reference seems almost inevitable.[115] It seems, nonetheless, logical that the national court still retains discretion *not* to refer. If the position were otherwise it would produce anomalous consequences.

4.94 It would, for example, mean that despite the fact that the Treaty itself confers a discretion *not* to refer under Article 234 EC that discretion was qualified in a manner not (at least expressly) recognized in the Treaty. Perhaps more fundamentally it would have the result that a national court such as the Administrative Court would be deprived of its underlying jurisdiction—where an issue of invalidity was raised—to declare the measure in question to be *valid*. Finally, from a practical perspective, if—as soon as issues of invalidity were raised—the Administrative Court was bound to refer the case to the ECJ it would permit

---

111 [1983] 1 All ER 1042, 1056.

112 This has particular resonance in the arena of commercial judicial review where there may be a valuable commercial benefit to be obtained by one commercial competitor over another from the delay involved in the matter being referred to the ECJ.

113 Case 314/85 *Foto-Frost v Hauptzollamt Lubeck-Ost* [1987] ECR 4199, para 17.

114 *R v MAFF, ex p FEDESA* [1988] 3 CMLR 207, 212.

115 See, eg, Case C–491/01 *R (British American Tobacco) v Secretary of State for Health* [2003] All ER (EC) 604. There, the validity of Directive 2001/37 was central to the challenge in the Administrative Court which was directed to 'the intention and/or obligation' of the defendant to transpose the directive into national law. The case was referred to the ECJ under Art 234 which, in due course, upheld the validity of the directive.

claimants to require references in cases of manifest unsuitability in many of the situations canvassed above. So, even if—to take an extreme scenario—the claimant had a collateral motive or the point at issue was otiose, the court would be required to seek a preliminary ruling.

However, where invalidity issues are genuinely raised and are of practical importance the Administrative Court should, ordinarily, refer.[116] In terms of discretion, the reason for this is that—unless that court entertains no doubt as to validity—a reference is likely to be inevitable. So, ordering a reference at an early stage will save both time and costs as well as being consistent with the principle of legal certainty. In jurisdictional terms, the ECJ has recently held that where a national court finds that the arguments in support of the invalidity of a Community act are unfounded it may reject them and conclude that the act was valid. But if it considers that an argument for invalidity is well founded, it was bound to stay proceedings and make a reference to the ECJ.[117] **4.95**

An important exception to this is the situation considered above[118] where a claimant with the requisite standing seeks to raise invalidity issues in judicial review that could and should have been raised in a direct action to the ECJ under Article 230. Here, for reasons earlier analysed, the Administrative Court must, at least in a clear case, refuse to refer under Article 234. **4.96**

In the context of references questions of direct effect sometimes raise similar issues to those posed by invalidity challenges. In those cases where it remains uncertain whether a provision of Community law is directly effective, and so enforceable in the national courts at the suit of an individual, the question arises as to whether there should, automatically, be a reference to the ECJ on the specific question of whether the measure is directly effective. **4.97**

For similar, but rather stronger, reasons to those advanced in the case of invalidity challenges to Community measures[119] it is submitted that the Administrative Court is not obliged to seek a preliminary ruling in cases where direct effect is in issue. Indeed, there have been a number of judicial review applications in which the Administrative Court has ruled as to whether a measure is or is not directly effective. Issues as to direct effect will usually be important given the Community interest in their resolution. But there may, notwithstanding this, be particular discretionary criteria that militate against a reference. In each case where direct effect is in issue it must, it is submitted, be a matter in the discretion of the court as to whether the ECJ is invited to give a preliminary ruling. **4.98**

---

[116] See, eg, *R v Secretary of State for the Environment, ex p IATA No 2* [1999] 2 CMLR 1385, 1388 per Jowitt J .

[117] Case C–344/04 *R (International Air Transport Association) v Department for Transport* The Times, 16 January 2006.

[118] See paras 4.34–4.38.

[119] There is, after all, no prohibition in Community law against a domestic court ruling on questions of direct effect as there is in respect of declarations of invalidity.

E. Procedural Questions

4.99 Seeking a reference

The procedure for seeking a reference from the first instance national court (or often the Court of Appeal)[120] is regulated by RSC Ord 114 as amended and incorporated into Sch 1 to the CPR.[121]

4.100 A reference may be made at one of three stages, namely

(1) on application by application notice by one or both parties[122] prior to the trial or hearing in conformity with CPR Pt 23;[123]

(2) on application by one or both parties at the trial or hearing itself;

(3) by the judge of his or her own motion.[124]

Form of the order for reference

4.101 An order referring a question to the ECJ for preliminary ruling must comply with RSC Ord 114 and the Prescribed Form 'Order for reference to the European Court (Schedule 1— RSC Ord 114, r. 2)'.[125]

4.102 In summary, the reference takes the form of an order:

(1) making a reference to the ECJ for a preliminary ruling in relation to the question(s) recited in a schedule to the order;[126]

(2) staying further proceedings until the preliminary ruling has been delivered;

(3) specifying any consequential orders as, for example, in respect of interim relief;[127]

(4) (where, as in a great many cases, there is no separate judgment of the national court performing the same function) setting out—in the schedule to the order—a statement of case.

---

[120] The position in the House of Lords is less regulated. Application may, as a matter of principle, be made: (1) in the statement of facts and issues and/or in the written case, (2) during the course of oral submission and (3) as the subject of separate petition. The essential procedure as set out below will be the same as for the Administrative Court and the Court of Appeal. Importantly, the House of Lords may be under an obligation to refer in certain circumstances: see paras 4.134 et seq. below.

[121] CPR r 50.1(2).

[122] Apart from the Commission, other Member States, and any relevant EU institution, there is no entitlement to intervene in Art 234 proceedings before the ECJ: see, eg, Case C–181/95 *Biogen v Smith Kline Beecham Biologicals* [1996] ECR I–717. However, parties wishing to intervene in likely ECJ proceedings should ensure that they intervene in the domestic judicial review proceedings at an early stage. For a case in point see *R v MAFF, ex p Anastasiou* [1994] COD 329.

[123] RSC Ord 114 r 2(2).

[124] RSC Ord 114 r 2(1).

[125] There is no further requirement prescribed by Community law which leaves the matter to be regulated by domestic procedural law: see *Practice Direction (ECJ references procedure) (Guidance of the Court of Justice the European Communities on References by National Courts for Preliminary Rulings)* [1999] 1 WLR 260, 261, para 4.

[126] It is now also common practice to include a provision specifying that the reference be transmitted to Luxembourg prior to the period for appeal expiring: if an appeal against the reference were to succeed the ECJ will automatically remove the reference from the register.

[127] As to interim relief, see paras 3.123 et seq.

Drafting the questions

In practice, the questions are either agreed by counsel in advance and submitted to the **4.103** court for its approval or are drafted between counsel on the basis of the court's judgment, or other indication, and then put before the court for final approval.[128]

Consistently with the principles outlined above the questions should be drafted so **4.104** that they:

(1) raise issues within the scope of Article 234 itself in respect of which the ECJ has jurisdiction;
(2) have been raised in the judicial review or other public law proceedings;
(3) are not irrelevant, and do not raise hypothetical or advisory issues;
(4) do not invite the ECJ to give a direct ruling on the compatibility of national measures with Community law;
(5) do not ask the ECJ to apply Community law to the particular facts of the case.

The drafting style should be as simple and as clear as possible having regard to the fact that **4.105** the questions will be translated. In particular, the drafting should not over-complicate the issues by inserting numerous questions and sub-questions reflecting the rival drafts of the parties rather than the true issues.[129] In all likelihood, the ECJ will redraft or decline to address, questions that have been improperly drafted.

Some of the ECJ case law affords examples of how questions ought to be drafted.[130]   **4.106**

The statement of case/judgment

Both the ECJ[131] and the British courts[132] have given guidance as to the appropriate content **4.107** of the reference. The reference will frequently take the form of a statement of case although the same matters may be set out in a separate judgment.

The guidance of the ECJ and the British courts is, materially, identical. Paragraph 12.8.4 **4.108** of the *Queen's Bench Guide* provides that the reference should:

• identify the parties and summarize the nature and history of the proceedings;
• summarize the salient facts and indicate whether these are proved or admitted or assumed;
• give an explanation of the national law (procedural and substantive) relevant to the dispute;
• summarize the arguments of the parties so far as is relevant;

---

[128] It is the responsibility of the national court and not the parties to settle the terms of reference: see *Practice Direction (ECJ references: procedure)* (n 125 above) para 2.
[129] See, eg, the critique of T Koopmans 'The Technique of the Preliminary Question—a view from the Court of Justice' in Schermers et al (eds), *Article 177 EEC—Experiences and Problems* (1987) 328 cited in Anderson and Demetriou (n 28 above) para 7–047.
[130] See, eg, Case C–329/95 *VAG Sverige* [1997] ECR I–2675, paras 16–17.
[131] See *Information Note on References by National Courts* issued by the ECJ, para 6.
[132] See, generally, *Practice Direction (ECJ references: Procedure)* (n 125 above) and *Queen's Bench Guide* at <http://www.hmcourts-service.gov.uk/cms/1444.htm>.

- explain why a preliminary ruling is sought, identifying the EC provisions whose effect is in issue;
- formulate, without avoidable complexity, the question(s) to which an answer is requested.

4.109 In drafting a reference it is important to ensure that the background is fully explained. If insufficient detail is provided, the ECJ may decline jurisdiction.[133] As with the drafting of questions the statement of case/judgment (of which the questions form a necessary part) should be drafted simply and clearly since it will be translated.

Other documents

4.110 Any necessary documents—especially the text of relevant domestic law—should be annexed to the order for reference. However, such annexes are not always translated. For this reason, any passages relied on should be set out in the statement of case/judgment itself.[134]

An outline of the procedure following the making of the reference

4.111 A single copy of the order for reference, and accompanying documents, must be passed to Room E13 for the attention of the Senior Master of the Supreme Court (Queen's Bench Division) for transmission to the ECJ.[135] There is no prescribed time limit for transmission to Luxembourg and it is by no means uniform. In particular, the time taken for the parties to agree the statement of case is likely to protract the reference reaching the ECJ.

4.112 Usually, the referring court will play no further part in the proceedings until delivery of the ECJ's judgment (see below). There may, though, be circumstances where one of the parties seeks to have the reference withdrawn (in whole or in part). In *Royscot Leasing Ltd v Commisioners of Customs and Excise*[136] the Court of Appeal refused an application to withdraw its reference to the ECJ. It observed that withdrawal should only occur where it was clear that the reference would not serve any useful purpose.

4.113 During the preliminary reference procedure the ECJ Registry will remain in direct contact with the parties.[137] It will send them copies of the written observations of the other participants, the report for the hearing,[138] the Advocate General's Opinion and the final judgment (see below). It is, therefore, essential to communicate addresses (including changes of address) of relevant legal representation to the ECJ.

4.114 In the ECJ the preliminary ruling will be registered. Thereafter, a Judge Rapporteur and Advocate General are appointed. The order is notified to the parties, to the Member States,

---

[133] See, eg, Joined Cases C–320/90, C–321/90 and C–322/90 *Telemarsicabruzzo v Circostel* [1993] ECR I–393; Case C–157/92 *Pretore di Genova v Banchero* [1993] ECR I–1085.

[134] *Information Note on References by National Courts* issued by the ECJ, para 6.

[135] CPR r 68.3(1).

[136] [1999] 1 CMLR 903.

[137] In the ECJ the Commission and other Member States who wish to make observations may also intervene as of right as may other institutions where one of their own acts is engaged.

[138] This is a report produced by the Judge Rapporteur summarizing the parties' written observations and produced prior to any oral hearing before the ECJ.

the Commission, and any other potential intervener.[139] Written observations are then requested from the various participants. These must be provided (by being lodged at the Court Registry) within two months of notification of the order. Annexes to the written observations may be (and usually are) lodged at the same time although they are not usually translated. Although there is an automatic extension of 10 days 'on account of distance' the time stipulation is otherwise strict and could only be extended, exceptionally, if the relevant party could establish *force majeure* or unforeseeable circumstances.

Within one month of lodging the written observations (subject to agreed extension of time by the court) a reasoned request in writing should be made if an oral hearing is required. **4.115**

Notes for the Guidance of Counsel, published in May 2006, recommend that written observations should state: (1) the relevant facts and provisions of national law, (2) legal argument including references to the case law of the ECJ,[140] and (3) proposals for answers to be given by the court to the questions submitted by the national court.[141] That apart, the drafting should be as succinct as possible. Because annexes are not usually translated, particular passages relied on should be set out in full in the observations. **4.116**

The written observations will be transmitted by the court to the other parties and interveners. **4.117**

Following the preparation of a confidential[142] preliminary report by the Judge Rapporteur the court may ask the parties further questions or request further information. The ECJ may dispense with an oral hearing if none of the parties have made a reasoned request in writing for a hearing within the time stipulated (see above). **4.118**

The Judge Rapporteur prepares a report for the hearing[143] which is, invariably, circulated in advance to the parties, Member States, and other relevant Community institutions. This summarizes the facts, history of the proceedings, and written observations of the participants. If the report is materially incomplete or inaccurate an affected party should write to the Registrar suggesting amendment. **4.119**

When notified of the date for an oral hearing the parties will be asked to give a *maximum* time estimate. The normal maximum time allowed for oral address is 30 minutes (in the case of a chamber of three 15 minutes).[144] This may be extended but only by special permission from the court. In addition, the parties and interveners will each be permitted to reply to the oral submissions of the other participants. **4.120**

Time estimates are rigorously enforced by the court and some informal pressure is also sometimes exerted immediately prior to the hearing when the participants meet the President and other members of the court. The purpose of the oral hearing is—apart from responding to questions from the court—to focus on essential submissions, any new arguments **4.121**

---

[139] See n 137 above.
[140] Full references should be provided.
[141] See Notes for the Guidance of Counsel, para 14.
[142] This report is for administrative purposes and is not disclosed to the participants.
[143] The same report is prepared even in the absence of a hearing but is then termed the Report of the Rapporteur.
[144] This time is exclusive of the time taken to respond to questions put by the court.

that have been prompted by events following the close of the written procedure, to reply to the arguments in the written observations of the other participants, and to explain or expound on points that require elucidation. [145]

4.122   The court encourages counsel to provide copies of the notes on which their address is based to the interpreters before the hearing. National robes are worn. There is no prescribed form of address to the court. A form of usage becoming increasingly popular is to address the court at the commencement by 'Mr/Madam President, Members of the Court'.

4.123   Ordinarily, the claimant will speak first followed by the defendant. If there are Member States at the hearing (apart from the effective defendant who precedes them) they address the court next. Finally, intervening institutions speak. The Commission usually addresses the court last. There may be questions from the court and each party has a short reply in the original order of speeches.

4.124   Because of problems caused by simultaneous translation it is important to address the court in short, simple sentences. Advocates should not speak too quickly. Their address should be carefully structured. A useful guide[146] is to explain, at the outset, what points it is intended to cover and to explain, as the speech proceeds, when one is moving from one point to the next. The facts in the report do not need to be rehearsed but salient features of the case may be emphasized so as to put the arguments in their proper context. One or two main arguments should then be focused on so as to ensure that the court fully understands them.[147]

4.125   Following the oral hearing the Advocate General usually indicates the date on which his Opinion will be delivered. Delivery of the Opinion (which is pronounced in court)[148] marks the end of the oral procedure. Exceptionally, the oral procedure may be reopened where, for example, there is a material error in the Advocate General's Opinion. Parties should be alert to the possibility of seeking to have the oral procedure reopened.[149] However, the court will not consider further written observations at this stage.[150]

4.126   The court will then proceed to consider its judgment. It meets for the first time only after the Advocate General's Opinion has been received. Judgment is pronounced in open court though the parties are not required to, and usually do not, attend. The ECJ does not award costs of a reference; this is a matter for the national court.[151] Generally, legal aid for the

---

[145] See Notes for the Guidance of Counsel, para C.2.

[146] This is a summary of the helpful views of Judge Edward: see *Practitioners' Handbook of EC Law* (1998) para 3.1.5.33.

[147] For some helpful 'do's and don'ts' see M Hoskins, 'Preliminary References to the ECJ: Some Practical Points' [2002] JR 162, 166.

[148] The parties are not expected to attend.

[149] The Advocate General will, in practice, be willing to correct 'slips' on receipt via the Court Registry of a letter pointing out the error: see Anderson and Demetriou (n 28 above) paras 11–067–11–068.

[150] In Case C–17/98 *Emesa Sugar (Free Zone) NV v Aruba* [2000] ECR I–066 the court rejected the argument that this practice involved a breach of Art 6 ECHR because of its power to reopen the oral procedure in exceptional circumstances.

[151] This is said to be because the ECJ does not apply its rulings to the facts of the case: see *Practice Direction (ECJ references: procedure) (Guidance of the Court of Justice of the European Communities on References by National Courts for Preliminary Rulings)* [1999] 1 WLR 260, 261, para 9.

making of a reference is also a matter for domestic consideration (by the Legal Services Commission). However, where legal aid is refused the ECJ may grant legal aid.

Judicial review proceedings following the ECJ's judgment

After the ECJ has delivered judgment the case is sent back to the referring court. The **4.127** proceedings then continue from the point at which they became stayed (see above).

To the extent that the court determining the application for judicial review decides the case **4.128** on a Community law basis it is bound by the preliminary ruling of the ECJ.[152] If the referring national court (or an appellate court) failed or refused to give effect to the ruling such failure might itself be capable of being brought before the ECJ under Article 226 (ex 169), and Article 227 (ex 170) EC.[153]

There may, nonetheless, be cases where the referring court is dissatisfied with aspects **4.129** of the preliminary ruling because, for example, it is based on findings of fact at variance with those of the national court. If this occurs the court should make a second reference. This has occurred in a few cases.[154] However, it should not be done to test the validity of a judgment.

As noted above, it is for the referring court to determine the costs of the proceedings includ- **4.130** ing the costs of that part of the proceedings occasioned by the reference. In *R v Intervention Board for Agricultural Produce, ex p Fish Producers' Organisation Ltd*[155] the Court of Appeal indicated that the costs of the reference will generally follow the event. The costs of the interveners before the ECJ are borne by themselves.

Appeals against decisions of national courts on requests for preliminary rulings

Appeals may be made against orders to refer or not to refer a case to the ECJ. **4.131**

Appeals from the High Court against a decision to refer lie with permission within 14 days **4.132** after the order in question.[156] Appeals from the same court against a decision not to refer are subject to the ordinary rules for appeal contained in CPR Pt 52.

A decision of the Court of Appeal to refer or not to refer is governed by the same rules that **4.133** apply to civil appeals generally in that appeal lies to the House of Lords with permission

---

[152] Case 29/68 *Milch- Fett- und Eierkontor* [1969] ECR 165, para 3. In the United Kingdom at least this is true for all courts whether the referring court or otherwise. By s 3(1) of the European Communities Act 1972, any question as to the meaning or effect of any of the Treaties or as to the validity, meaning or effect of any Community instrument must, if not referred to the ECJ for a ruling, be decided in accordance with the principles laid down by any relevant decision of the ECJ.

[153] See Case C–224/01 *Kobler v Republik Osterreich* (30 September 2003) at paras 32–34. This case is considered further at paras 5.157 et seq. For a case where the national referring court refused to implement a preliminary ruling but was overturned by the Court of Appeal, see per Laddie J in Case 206/01 *Arsenal Football Club v Reed* [2003] Ch 454.

[154] See, eg, Case 283/81 *CILFIT Srl v Ministro della Sanita* [1982] ECR 3415; Case 77/83 *CILFIT Srl v Ministro della Sanita* [1984] ECR 1457.

[155] [1993] 1 CMLR 707.

[156] RSC Ord 114 r 6.

either of the Court of Appeal or the House of Lords being required. There would appear to be three possible stages in the House of Lords where the question of a reference may be considered. These are: (1) on the hearing of the petition for leave, (2) as a separate interlocutory matter, or (3) during the course of oral argument.

F. Mandatory References

4.134 The House of Lords, as the final appellate court, is in a special position. Article 234(3) EC provides thus:

> Where any such question [that is of a preliminary ruling set out in Article 234(1) above] is raised in a case pending before a court or tribunal of a Member State against whose decisions there is no judicial remedy under national law, that court or tribunal shall bring the matter before the Court of Justice.

4.135 Plainly, therefore, the House of Lords is under a general obligation to seek a preliminary ruling under Article 234 provided, always, that the non-discretionary jurisdictional conditions permitting a reference (considered above)[157] are satisfied.

4.136 However, even the House of Lords is not obliged to refer a case where 'previous decisions of the Court have already dealt with the point of law in question'[158] where the question raised is irrelevant[159] or where 'the correct application of Community law [is] so obvious as to leave no scope for any reasonable doubt as to the manner in which the question raised is to be resolved'.[160]

4.137 The latter is known as the *acte clair* doctrine. It is, though, subject to important qualification. As the ECJ observed in *CILFIT*[161] the national court must be convinced that the answer would be equally obvious to the courts of the other Member States as well as to the ECJ. In determining that question the national court must compare the different language versions of the text. It must bear in mind that the terminology of Community law is different to that employed in national law. Finally, every provision of Community law must be placed in its context and interpreted in the light of Community law as a whole having regard to the objectives of the Community and to its state of evolution at the time at which the provision is being applied. There are, despite these qualifications, instances of the House of Lords refusing to make a reference to the ECJ under Article 234 on *CILFIT* grounds.[162]

4.138 There are other occasions where, in domestic public law proceedings, the national court below the House of Lords may be required (with the qualifications noted above) to

---

[157] See paras 4.08–4.66.
[158] Case 283/81 *CILFIT Srl v Ministro della Sanita* [1982] ECR 3415.
[159] *R v Licensing Authority, ex p Smith-Kline* [1990] 1 AC 64.
[160] *CILFIT* [1982] ECR 3415, para 16. Many commentators have suggested that the *CILFIT* guidelines should be relaxed.
[161] Case 283/81 [1982] ECR 3415. For contrary arguments, see M Demetriou (1995) European Law Review 628, 631.
[162] See, eg, *R v Chief Constable of Sussex, ex p International Trader's Ferry Ltd* [1998] 3 WLR 1260; *MacDonald v Ministry of Defence; Pearce v Governors of Mayfield School* [2004] 1 All ER 339.

make a reference. In respect of mandatory references, Article 234(3) uses the expression 'against whose decisions there is no judicial remedy under national law' for courts that are under an obligation, as opposed to having discretion, to refer.

This appears to mean that a first instance court and/or the Court of Appeal are required to refer when deciding a question against which—as a result of that decision—there is no possibility of seeking permission of a higher court to appeal. **4.139**

In the context of judicial review a refusal by the Court of Appeal to give permission to appeal against a substantive decision or interlocutory ruling of the Administrative court or a refusal by the same court to grant permission to appeal against the Administrative Court's refusal to grant permission to apply for judicial review are the most obvious instances. Similar considerations ought, in principle, to apply to decisions on judicial review in criminal cases by a Divisional Court where there is no appeal to the House of Lords if the Divisional Court refuses to certify a point of law for consideration by the House of Lords.[163] **4.140**

The Court of Appeal does not, however, consider itself as under an obligation to make a reference where permission to appeal may be sought from the House of Lords since, apart from the Court of Appeal then being *functus*, the right to petition the House of Lords is itself a 'judicial remedy' in terms of Article 234.[164] **4.141**

Nonetheless, the recent decision of the ECJ in *Lyckeskog*[165] suggests that if the House of Lords does not grant permission to appeal it is (subject to the above-noted qualifications) required to make a reference on the hearing of the petition for leave to appeal. **4.142**

The important aspect appears to be that there must be some stage during the course of the national proceedings where there is an obligation to refer.[166] **4.143**

---

[163] The point was not resolved in *S A Magnavision N F v General Optical Council (No 2)* [1987] 3 CMLR 262.

[164] See *Chiron v Murex Diagnostics (No 2)* [1994] FSR 187.

[165] Case C–99/00 [2003] 1 WLR 9.

[166] Case 107/76 *Hoffman-La Roche v Centrafarm* [1977] ECR 957.

5

EC LAW REMEDIES IN
JUDICIAL REVIEW

A. Relevant EC Remedy Principles

Introduction

5.01 EC law provides for domestic remedies for violation of EC law in two general ways. First, it requires national laws to provide for a system of remedies, themselves compliant with EC law principles, sufficient to allow for enforcement of EC obligations. Secondly, it imposes a specific State liability in damages (or other comparable mode of reparation) for particularly serious violations of EC law provided that certain conditions are satisfied.

5.02 Whether, in any particular case, an EC law claim derives, at least in the first instance, from national legislation or whether it is to be derived from the doctrine of direct effect[1] EC law does not itself generally prescribe the remedies for breach that a national court should provide.[2] In particular, the EC Treaty contains no express provisions dealing with remedies. However, there is a tension between the need to ensure that Member States possess procedural autonomy in the formulation of their remedial rules and the correlative need to ensure the effective protection of EC rights. The latter consideration has, in particular, sometimes led the ECJ to modify national rules and to introduce new remedies.

5.03 The primary governing EC principles affecting remedies are those of equivalence (itself an aspect of the non-discrimination principle)[3] and effectiveness and these, insofar as they affect remedies for breaches of EC law in the national courts, are outlined below.[4] However, an understanding of all the general principles of EC law discussed in detail in Part II is necessary to an appreciation of the true content of EC remedies.[5]

5.04 Different aspects of equivalence and effectiveness are addressed in Chapter 3 (in relation to their application to the judicial review procedure) and Chapter 7 (in respect of the general principle of non-discrimination). Here, the emphasis is on their relationship to remedies. In essence, equivalence requires, in terms of remedy, that an EC right is not treated less favourably than similar domestic law rights. Effectiveness requires Member States (including national courts) to ensure the full and effective protection of EC rights by appropriate remedies. Importantly, these two criteria (equivalence and effectiveness) operate independently so that even if only one is breached the national remedy (or absence of remedy) remains inadequate and in breach of EC law.

5.05 EC remedial obligations for public law breaches are often applicable to the remedies granted or denied by *all* national courts in respect of EC rights. They have particular

---

  [1] For an explanation of direct effect, see paras 1.60 et seq.
  [2] Slightly different considerations may arise in the context of damages where EC law may require reparation as a remedy but leaves the choice of specific method of reparation to the State. For State liability in damages see, generally, paras 5.85 et seq.
  [3] For non-discrimination as a general principle of EC law see, generally, Chapter 7.
  [4] See, respectively, paras 5.06–5.12 and 5.13–5.22.
  [5] Either alone or in conjunction. Consider, for example, the alliance of protecting fundamental rights, effectiveness and the need for proportionality in fashioning a discrete EC remedy in a particular case. Properly analysed, the principle of effectiveness embraces fundamental rights and the other general EC principles of law since their denial erodes the effective protection of EC rights.

application to the Administrative Court (and appellate courts) in judicial review proceedings, however, because of the vertical effect of directives and the need to define the nature of an emanation of the State for that purpose. They are also important from the perspective of judicial review proceedings because the legality of national remedies in terms of their compliance with EC law is more likely to be challenged in such proceedings as is the Member State's liability in damages.

Equivalence

The principle of equivalence is, in the context of remedies, to the effect that remedies for **5.06** breaches of EC rights should not be less favourable than those for similar domestic rights. It does not translate as a requirement that Member States are obliged to apply their most favourable rules to all actions brought in a particular area of law.[6] In *Levez*[7] the ECJ observed that it was 'for national courts to ascertain whether the procedural rules intended to ensure that the rights derived by individuals from Community law are safeguarded under national law and comply with the principle of equivalence'.[8] It also held that the burden of proving a breach of the principle lay on the person claiming the benefit.

In the absence of a true comparator, therefore, there is no infringement of this principle **5.07** although (see below) there may still be an infringement of the twin principle of effectiveness.

To establish comparability between a domestic remedy and an EC law remedy there must **5.08** be similar objectives and similar essential characteristics.[9] It would, for example, be inappropriate to compare a claim for breach of duty with a claim arising in consequence of passing an unconstitutional law.[10] It is also necessary to ensure that an EC remedy is compared with a separate domestic remedy for the purpose of determining whether there is less favourable treatment. Thus, compliance with the principle is not established by comparing procedural rules that apply to claims arising under directly effective Treaty provisions with claims arising under domestic legislation but implementing EC secondary legislation since, in effect, the same form of action is involved in both.[11]

Whether there is less favourable treatment is part of the court's consideration of equivalence **5.09** and the two issues cannot, sensibly, be separated. The national court must look at the matter contextually. In *Preston*, for example, the ECJ stated that 'the national court must verify objectively, in the abstract, whether the rules at issue are similar taking into account the role played by those rules in the procedure as a whole, as well as the operation of that procedure and special feature of those rules'.[12] Thus, the national court in reviewing the different procedures as a whole will have to weigh the relative advantages and disadvantages

---

[6] See, eg, Case 324/96 *Levez v TJ Jennings (Harlow Pools) Ltd* [1998] ECR I–7835, para 42.
[7] ibid, para 39.
[8] However, as cases such as *Levez* (n 6 above) show, the ECJ has always retained the function of guiding the national courts on the true effect of the principle.
[9] Case C–261/95 *Palmisani v INPS* [1997] ECR I–4025, para 38.
[10] ibid, per Advocate General Cosmas 4034.
[11] See *Levez* [1998] ECR I–7835, paras 47–48; Case C–78/98 *Preston and Fletcher v Wolverhampton NHS Healthcare Trust* [2000] ECR I–3201, paras 51–52.
[12] [2000] ECR I–3201, para 63.

of each taking into account matters such as respective limitation periods, delay in obtaining relief and the costs involved.[13]

5.10 In the domestic cases that have raised equivalence issues, the national courts have looked '... not merely for a domestic action that is similar ... but for one that is in juristic structure very close to the Community claim'.[14] Thus, in *Matra*[15] a case on public procurement,[16] the Court of Appeal rejected the claim that proceedings for breach of the public procurement directives was equivalent to the tort of breach of statutory duty.

5.11 The court similarly rejected the argument that there was equivalence between a claim under the public procurement directives and proceedings for judicial review. As to the latter comparison, the court considered that since the procurement remedy envisaged a claim for damages which was, in English law, a private as opposed to a public law remedy there was insufficient equivalence between the two procedures. In some ways this is a surprising conclusion since damages on a private law basis are encompassed within the judicial review procedure and there may be circumstances in which judicial review lies for breach of EC procurement obligations.[17] Moreover, at least since the passing of the HRA it is possible to claim damages on what is, ostensibly at least, a public law basis for violation of the HRA.

5.12 However, whilst *Matra* exemplifies a strict view on the part of national courts to equivalence, *Levez*[18] itself shows a more liberal approach. Following (and applying) the ECJ's preliminary ruling, the Employment Appeal Tribunal which had referred the case to the ECJ under Article 234 EC held that the two-year limitation period on payment of arrears of damages under the UK Equal Pay Act 1970 was an ineffective remedy and breached the principle of equivalence. This was so because the Act only applied to equal pay claims founded on sex discrimination and compared unfavourably with claims for damages under non-discrimination statutes such as the Race Relations Act 1976 and the Sex Discrimination Act 1975.

Effectiveness

5.13 In the context of remedies, the principle of effectiveness requires that national courts are under an obligation to ensure the full and effective protection of rights derived from EC law by granting appropriate remedies. As with other general principles, it is often used in conjunction with other relevant protections such as fundamental rights.[19] Remedies required by the principle of effectiveness include (where appropriate) not merely some relief for violation of EC law but also a remedy that gives full protection to the right in question and that encompasses the means of obtaining particular relief. Thus, for example, in appropriate circumstances the principle requires (amongst other things) a remedy in

---

[13] *Levez* [1998] ECR I–7835, para 51.
[14] *Matra Communications SAS v Home Office* [1999] 1 WLR 1646, 1658.
[15] [1999] 1 WLR 1646.
[16] For a fuller treatment of the EC public procurement regime and the issues raised by it, see Chapter 15.
[17] See paras 15.84 et seq.
[18] [1998] ECR I–7835.
[19] See n 5 above and text.

effective compensation,[20] interim relief,[21] review by national courts of the implementation of Community decisions by national bodies,[22] and effective judicial review.[23]

However, the principle is not monolithic. Nor has it been entirely consistently applied by the ECJ.[24] As originally introduced, in cases on domestic limitation periods, the effectiveness principle required that an effective remedy was one that did not make it 'impossible in practice' for a claimant to exercise his EC rights.[25] The scope of the principle was subtly expanded by the later formulation that national remedies must not make it 'virtually impossible' or 'excessively difficult' to do so.[26]   **5.14**

Effectiveness was put rather differently in *Von Colson*.[27] There, in a case concerning sex discrimination, the ECJ said: **5.15**

> Although ... full implementation of the Directive does not require any specific form of sanction for unlawful discrimination, it does entail that that sanction be such as to guarantee real and effective judicial protection. Moreover, it must also have a real deterrent effect on the employer. It follows that where a Member State chooses to penalise the breach of the prohibition of discrimination by the award of compensation, that compensation must in any event be adequate in relation to the damage sustained.

The explanation for the more expansive approach to the effectiveness principle in cases such as *Von Colson* may be the relevant context. Provided that a time limit is not unreasonable there is no obvious basis for the ECJ to intrude on national procedural limitation rules in order to secure effective remedial protection. That is probably why the ECJ has retreated from its bold approach in *Emmott*.[28] where it held that the national time limits for claiming that the provisions of a directive were directly effective did not start to run until the Member State had lawfully transposed the directive. This ruling has, as noted elsewhere, been effectively restricted to its own facts.[29]   **5.16**

On the other hand, there are many areas of EC law (sex discrimination being a prime example)[30] where (for example) prevention is an important consideration and where, therefore, remedies should be directed to that end in order to provide full and effective protection.   **5.17**

This is why the early ECJ cases on limitation periods cannot be regarded as a comprehensive statement of the scope of the principle of effectiveness. The broadest formulation of the principle in terms of remedy was articulated by the court in *Simmenthal*[31] a case that was   **5.18**

---

[20] See, eg, Case 79/83 *Harz v Deutsche Tradax* [1984] ECR 1921.
[21] See paras 3.123 et seq.
[22] Case 94/00 *Roquette Freres v Commission* [2002] ECR I–9011.
[23] See, eg, paras 3.09 et seq.
[24] See, further, T Tridimas, *The General Principles of EU Law* (2nd edn, 2006) ch 9, especially 422.
[25] See, eg, Case 45/76 *Comet BV v Produktschap voor Siergerwassen* [1976] ECR 2043; Case 33/76 *Rewe* [1976] ECR 1989.
[26] See, eg, Case 312/93 *Peterbroeck van Campenhout & Cie SCS v Belgium* [1995] ECR I–4599. This case was heard on the same day by the same court as the *Van Schijndel* cases (see para 5.20).
[27] Case 14/83 *Von Colson and Kamann v Land Nordrrhein-Westfalen* [1984] ECR 1891. To similar effect see Case 222/84 *Johnston v Chief Constable of the RUC* [1986] ECR 1651.
[28] Case C-208/90 *Emmott v Minister for Social Welfare and Attorney General* [1991] ECR 4269.
[29] See paras 3.100 et seq.
[30] Compare, also, areas such as public procurement and environmental law at (respectively) Chapters 15 and 14.
[31] Case 106/77 *Amministrazione delle Finanze dello Stato v Simmenthal SPA* [1978] ECR 629.

built on in subsequent case law to fashion important new remedies for breaches of EC law. In *Simmenthal* the ECJ observed:

> Any provision of a national legal system and any legal, administrative or judicial practice which might impair the effectiveness of Community law by withholding from the national court having jurisdiction to apply such law the power to do everything necessary, at the moment of its application, to set aside provisions which might prevent, even temporarily, Community rules having their full force and effect, are incompatible with these requirements, which are the very essence of Community law.

5.19 It would, however, be fallacious to conclude that the *Simmenthal* formulation will always be applied where the ECJ (and, hence, the national court) seeks to apply the principle of effectiveness. As with equivalence (see above) the ECJ generally prefers a balancing approach looking at the national rules in question rather than laying down broad statements of principle.

5.20 Thus, for example, in the *Van Schijndel*[32] cases, decided long after *Simmenthal*, the ECJ, in giving a preliminary ruling on the effect of a national measure preventing a reference to the ECJ by the court of its own motion ruled, materially, as follows:

> A national provision [that] renders application of Community law impossible or excessively difficult must be analysed by reference to the role of that provision in the procedure; its progress and special features, viewed as a whole, before the various national instances. In the light of that analysis the basic principles of the domestic judicial system, such as the protection of the rights of the defence, the principle of legal certainty and the proper conduct of procedure must, where appropriate, be taken into consideration.

5.21 So, the principle of effectiveness must, in the same way as the principle of equivalence, usually be applied to the facts of particular cases or at least to the specific national procedural frameworks involved. Unsurprisingly, this can sometimes produce ostensibly inconsistent formulations of principle.

5.22 As fundamentally, the way in which the principle of effectiveness has been applied in many of the cases permits national variations in the extent of protection of EC rights. The wide variation in national limitation periods for enforcement of EC rights has, for example, often been the subject of academic commentary.[33] This, however, may be a necessary price to pay for a measure of domestic procedural autonomy. Commenting on the then recent cases in which the ECJ appeared to be engaging in judicial activism so far as EC remedies were concerned, Weiler has observed that:

> In the past the European Court was always careful to present itself as primus inter partes and to maintain a zone of autonomy of national jurisdiction even at the price of non-uniformity of application of Community law. If the new line of cases represents a nuanced departure from that earlier ethos, the prize may be increased effectiveness, but the cost may be a potential tension in the critical relationship between European and national courts.[34]

---

[32] Case C–430, 431/93 [1995] ECR I–4705.

[33] See, eg, J Bridge, 'Procedural Aspects of the Enforcement of European Community Law through the Legal Systems of the Member States' (1984) 9 EL Rev 28, 34.

[34] J Weiler, 'Journey to an Unknown Destination: a Retrospective and Prospective of the European Court of Justice in the Arena of Political Integration' (1993) 31 JCMS 417, 443.

B. Categories of Case Where EC Law Remedy May Be Needed

The preceding discussion shows that distinct public law remedies to give effect to EC rights   **5.23**
are required to be granted by the national courts. It also shows that in certain instances new
relief, sometimes inconsistent with expressly stated national remedies, will be required
in order to comply with EC general principles of law.

All cases in which it is contended that a particular national judicial remedy is defective as   **5.24**
not complying with those EC general principles involve public law considerations because
what is in issue is whether or nor the court as an emanation of the State is required, as a matter
of EC law, to accord a particular remedy to the claimant. Thus, there exists the necessary
vertical relationship between the exercise of public power and the State that founds the
basis of domestic public law.[35]

This work is mainly concerned with judicial review (whether in the Administrative Court   **5.25**
or elsewhere). However, in order to have a full understanding of the categories of case
in which EC public law remedies may be relevant the private law dimension is also relevant
because the issue of adequate remedy for breach of EC law may occur in a private law forum
as well as in the Administrative Court.

The categories of cases in which EC domestic public law remedies will need to be considered   **5.26**
are, principally, these:

- Those cases where specific issues as to EC remedy occur in *private* law proceedings
  between individual litigants.
- Those cases where specific issues of EC remedy occur in *public* law proceedings
  (primarily judicial review in the Administrative Court) between the citizen and the
  State.[36]
- Those cases where the purpose of judicial review proceedings is to challenge the alleged
  deficiency of an EC remedy or to provide an EC remedy where one is lacking.
- Those cases where particular remedial issues arise in respect of the enforcement of
  directives.
- Those cases where issues arise as to State liability in damages.
- Those cases where EC remedial issues may arise in the context of collateral challenges.

As can be seen, the above categories are neither necessarily exhaustive nor distinct. Nor can   **5.27**
they be compartmentalized into the straitjacket of domestic judicial review. On the other
hand, each of them is capable of raising significant public law issues in which the principles
of domestic judicial review are likely to be important. There follows a discussion of the first
five of these categories (collateral challenges are separately considered in Chapter 19).

---

[35] See, generally, Chapter 1, especially para 1.44.
[36] The same issues may sometimes overlap with issues in private law proceedings either because:
(1) consideration of the principle of equivalence in a public law context may require consideration of whether
a particular private law provision is 'equivalent' or (2) the compliance of a particular public law remedy with
EC law may arise in judicial review proceedings but have equal application to private law proceedings (as, for
example, interim injunctive relief against the Crown or damages). The same is, of course, true in reverse.
Note that the EC public law principles relating to interim relief are separately analysed: see paras 3.123 et seq.

C. Category 1—Private Law Cases

5.28   Some instances of specific EC remedial issues arising in private law disputes have been given in the above outline of the principles of equivalence and effectiveness at paras 5.06 et seq. These will, for the most part, be cases where—as in *Levez*[37]—an individual brings a claim against another private party (there through the mechanism of a statutory procedure before a domestic tribunal) and an issue as to EC remedy arises. In *Levez* the issue was whether or not the statutory limitation on an award of damages for violation of EC law was lawful. In the event, following a reference to the ECJ for a preliminary ruling, the Employment Appeal Tribunal held that it was not and made an award of damages that was not subject to the ostensible statutory ceiling.

5.29   Where statute does not afford a clear right to bring proceedings to enforce EC rights questions may arise, in the EC context, of whether—and how—particular EC rights are to be enforced in domestic private law. Such questions will usually arise in the context of directly effective EC rights that have not been transposed into domestic law and that sound against individuals rather than against public bodies. In general, such claims are regarded as civil claims in the nature of a breach of statutory duty.[38] There may be instances where particular domestic torts may be able to be modified so as to accommodate a claim for a breach of an EC right.[39]

5.30   There are also certain cases in which even though there appears to be a public law element to the claim, only private law domestic law remedies and not public law remedies may be obtained in respect of violations of EC law. For example, Articles 81 and 82 (ex 85 and 86) EC on competition apply to 'undertakings' and not, generally at least, to public bodies performing public functions.[40] To that extent, of course, EC remedial issues will still arise in the context of an essentially 'private' law dispute.

5.31   However in all these cases, as noted earlier, the national court or tribunal as an emanation of the State will itself be required to comply with EC remedial principles in much the same way as national courts being required to act in a manner that is compatible with the European Convention on Human Rights under HRA, s 6.[41]

---

[37] [1998] ECR I–7835.

[38] See, especially, *Garden Cottage Foods v Milk Marketing Board* [1984] AC 130. In this case, decided many years before *Factortame*, Lord Diplock considered that injunctive relief alone without the availability of damages could not lie to prevent a breach of directly effective rights under Art 86 (now 82) EC because only if damages were available could there be an actionable breach of statutory duty in domestic law. It is submitted that this approach cannot survive *Factortame* or, indeed, the developed expression of the EC principle of effectiveness considered above.

[39] As yet, possibly because such claims can be treated as akin to a breach of statutory duty there is no developed case law on domestic EC torts. In *Cato v Minister of Agriculture, Fisheries and Food* [1989] 3 CMLR 513 in an action for negligent misstatement founded on EC law it was held that a duty of care was owed but that there had not been any breach of that duty.

[40] See, eg, Case 136/86 *BNIC v Aubert* [1988] 4 CMLR 331. However, this proposition is not necessarily of uniform application. See, eg, paras 13.82 et seq.

[41] Article 10 (ex 5) EC requires the Member State (including, therefore, its courts) to take all appropriate measures to ensure the fulfilment of Treaty obligations. There is, thus, a close parallel between this provision and HRA, s 6(1) which stipulates that public authorities (including courts) must not act in a manner that is incompatible with Convention rights.

Sometimes the forum for a claim will be private law as opposed to judicial review as where,   **5.32**
for example, damages are claimed against an emanation of the State outside the scope of
judicial review.[42] There, as is the case for other remedies such as restitution, it is immaterial
to EC law which court has jurisdiction in domestic law.[43] The EC remedial principles
still fall to be applied by the national court hearing the case as an emanation of the State.
For this reason particular remedies such as damages and restitution that may overlap with
judicial review proceedings in the Administrative Court are addressed below.

D. Category 2—Public Law Cases

Overview

Most public law issues are ventilated by means of judicial review in the Administrative   **5.33**
Court. However, the principles of judicial review (and, hence, the remedial issues that
may arise) are now also ventilated before some tribunals (most notably the Competition
Appeal Tribunal)[44] and EC remedial issues may also arise in the course of a collateral
challenge before other national courts or tribunals.[45]

State liability in damages is treated separately, as are the particular EC remedial issues   **5.34**
arising in respect of the enforcement of directives.[46] What is under consideration here,
however, is the operation of EC remedial issues insofar as they are, otherwise, likely to arise
in cases where public law issues arise—particularly before the Administrative Court.

There are three possible stages during judicial review proceedings where the question of   **5.35**
EC remedies may arise. These are:

(1) Issues relating to procedural rules, especially those in respect of time limits.
(2) Issues relating to interim relief.
(3) Issues relating to the relief to be awarded if the claimant has succeeded.

The first two stages were examined in Chapter 3.[47] However, even where the claimant   **5.36**
has succeeded on the legal issues, questions of EC remedy may well be relevant to the final
order to be made by the Administrative Court.

Remedy depends upon the EC violation alleged

As discussed in Chapter 2,[48] there are certain grounds for seeking judicial review in an   **5.37**
EC case that are not available in either a purely domestic or even HRA context. It is

---

[42] For consideration of when this might be appropriate, see paras 1.100 et seq. By contrast, there are also
cases where what are, essentially, private law disputes have been allowed to continue to be litigated in the
Administrative Court more for practical convenience than for reasons of principle. See, eg, *R (Dengleet) v NHS
Purchasing Authority* [2005] Eu LR 526.

[43] See, eg, *Comet* [1976] ECR 2043, 2053.

[44] See paras 13.154 et seq.

[45] See paras 1.120 et seq.

[46] See paras 5.66 et seq.

[47] See paras 3.81–3.122 and 3.123–3.148.

[48] See, especially, para 2.30.

important to separate the different types of case for the purpose of understanding the potential domestic remedies that apply and that the Administrative Court can grant.[49] In terms of remedies, the three main types of case are:

(1) Claims against public bodies on the basis that the acts or omissions of such bodies are in breach of either directly effective EC rights or, alternatively, of transposing or other relevant domestic legislation. Here, the assumption is that the underlying EC and/or domestic legislation under which the relevant powers have been exercised are EC compliant.

(2) Claims against public bodies on the basis that either primary or subordinate domestic legislation is invalid and/or that a public body is in breach of EC law by giving effect to such defective national law. Here, the assumption is that the underlying EC legislation is valid but that the transposing or other relevant legislation is invalid.

(3) Claims against national measures and/or public bodies on the basis that the European legislation permitting or compelling performance of the function in question violates EC law.

Type 1—Administrative public law breach alleged but underlying EC legislation not challenged

5.38 The first type of case presents few general problems. It is clear that administrative acts or omissions that violate EC law may be the subject of quashing or prohibitory orders or, indeed, of declaratory relief. Many of the illustrative judicial review cases in Part III exemplify the grant of such relief. It should be noted that the acts or omissions of public bodies may derive from a domestic statute and/or subordinate legislation[50] or (by reason of the doctrine of direct effect) from EC regulations or directives.[51]

5.39 The source of a public body's exercise of power in this respect is unimportant. In *R v Hammersmith and Fulham London Borough Council, ex p Council for Protection of Rural England*[52] Harrison J had correctly held that Articles 10 and 249 EC were designed to ensure, amongst other things, that a Member State correctly implemented directives into national law so that the purpose of the directive might be achieved. However, he went on to hold that the consequence of the correct transposing of a directive was that a claimant was confined to his remedies under the domestic legislation and there remained no individually enforceable rights under the directive. This proposition was rejected by the ECJ in the *Marks & Spencer* case.[53] There, the ECJ ruled that claimants may rely on the content of a directive before the national courts wherever the directive is not being fully implemented as, for example, where national measures correctly transposing the directive are not being implemented so as to achieve the objective intended by the directive.

---

[49] It is, of course, possible that overlapping issues will arise in the same proceedings.

[50] See, eg, *R v Attorney General, ex p ICI plc* [1987] 1 CMLR 72.

[51] See, eg, *R v Intervention Board for Agricultural Produce, ex p Fish Producer's Organisation Ltd* [1987] 3 CMLR 473.

[52] [2001] 81 P & CR 73.

[53] Case C–62/00 *Marks & Spencer Plc v Commissioners of Customs and Excise* [2002] ECR I–6325.

Further, in any case within the scope of EC law[54] a public body must act in a manner **5.40** that is compliant with EC law. This may mean that even if statutes fail to transpose EC obligations into domestic law that are not directly effective, there remains a subsisting EC law obligation.[55]

In certain cases a specialized EC remedy of damages may also be available as a remedy **5.41** for such breaches (see below). In the context of EC remedies, damages should not simply be viewed as a private law remedy even though that is their status in domestic law. As will be seen, damages are available under EC law only for very serious breaches of EC law by the State or an emanation of the State. The fact that there is no equivalent for domestic public law default is, logically, immaterial.[56]

Occasionally, there may also be the need for other specialized remedies to fit the circum- **5.42** stances of the case and to ensure that the principle of effectiveness is complied with. In those circumstances such remedies would have to be granted by the Administrative Court in judicial review proceedings even though they were not traditionally regarded as administrative law remedies.

A good example is the remedy of restitution. There is an EC right not to be subjected to **5.43** unlawful charges by the State and a commensurate right to repayment of sums paid out under an unlawful levy.[57] Formerly, it was thought that money paid under a mistake of law was not recoverable. Had that exclusion been applied in EC cases it would, undoubtedly, have breached the principle of effectiveness. However, in line with the EC approach, the House of Lords has accepted that domestic charges levied and paid out pursuant to an unlawful demand should, even as a matter of domestic law, also be recoverable.[58]

In many, if not most, cases the legality under EC law of a charge levied by a public body will **5.44** be challenged by way of judicial review. If the charge is unlawful then restitution would be an appropriate remedy in the form of either a mandatory order or declaratory relief. In principle, since domestic law recognizes that interest may be awarded in a claim for restitution the same should be true of a claim founded on EC law; if the position were otherwise there would be a breach of the principle of equivalence.[59]

Type 2—Challenge to transposing or other relevant legislation and/or to a public law breach derived from such unlawful legislation

EC law may be transposed into domestic law by means of primary or subordinate legislation **5.45** or be otherwise relevant to such legislation. In purely domestic judicial review the doctrine

---

[54] This concept is not without its complications: see paras 6.24 et seq.
[55] *Quaere* the extent to which obligations that are not directly effective may be enforced in the Administrative Court: see paras 2.151 et seq. See also, paras 5.51 et seq. below.
[56] There is a similarity between State liability in EC law for damages and liability of public authorities under the HRA for damages.
[57] See Case 199/82 *Amministrazione delle Finanze dello Stato v San Giorgio* [1983] ECR 3595.
[58] *Woolwich Building Society v Inland Revenue Commissioners (No 2)* [1993] AC 70. The House of Lords was heavily influenced by the fact that if the citizen had a right in EC law to recover payment of an unlawfully levied charge, it would be surprising if there were not an equivalent right to recover payment of an unlawful domestic levy. This case is, therefore, an interesting example of EC law affecting the progress of domestic law. For another instance, see *M v Home Office* [1994] 1 AC 377.
[59] For the application of domestic rules to EC damages claims see paras 5.126 et seq.

of parliamentary sovereignty precludes any challenge to the validity of *primary* legislation (or, therefore, to any challenge for a public body acting in conformity with the statute), although subordinate legislation may be declared to be unlawful if it is ultra vires the enabling statute. Even under the HRA the validity of primary legislation may not be directly challenged although there is provision for the national court to make a declaration of incompatibility with the ECHR under HRA, s 4 if it is unable to interpret the statute, under HRA, s 3, in a manner that is compatible with the Convention.

5.46 In EC law, the position is somewhat different. Under EC law it is now well established that where a statute relevant to the enforcement of directly effective EC rights is inconsistent with Community law and cannot be interpreted to operate consistently with Community law then the statute has the effect of being automatically 'inapplicable'.[60]

5.47 In such circumstances the Administrative Court is required to disapply the offending statutory provision.[61] This, though, is not quite the same as declaring the statute to be unlawful; a remedy that the courts have, thus far, not been prepared to grant. In *R v Secretary of State for Employment, ex p Equal Opportunities Commission*[62] the Equal Opportunities Commission (EOC) brought judicial review proceedings seeking a declaration against the Secretary of State that certain provisions of the Employment Protection (Consolidation) Act 1978 infringed EC law. Further, essentially mandatory, relief was also sought that would have required the Secretary of State to amend the Act.[63] EOC applied for judicial review even though it did not have any directly effective rights itself.

5.48 The EOC's application was dismissed in the High Court and, by a majority, in the Court of Appeal. In the Court of Appeal the mandatory relief was said by Kennedy LJ to be 'wrong and unconstitutional' and 'an attempt to enforce obligations which if they existed did so only in international law'.[64] Whilst the House of Lords allowed EOC's appeal it did not address the question of mandatory relief. What it did, however, was to hold that although primary legislation cannot be quashed by virtue of its incompatibility with EC law a declaration to that effect may be obtained by way of judicial review.[65]

5.49 Lord Keith (with whom there was unanimous agreement on this point) also held that it was unnecessary to declare that the United Kingdom or the Secretary of State were in breach of their obligations under EC law. It was sufficient for EOC's purposes to declare that the relevant provisions of the 1978 Act were *incompatible* with EC law. Nor would this involve an attempt by EOC to enforce international Treaty obligations.[66]

---

60 See *Simmenthal* [1978] ECR 629.

61 It is submitted that, in those circumstances, there can be no objection to the court granting a quashing order in respect of any administrative decision or act effected pursuant to the statutory provision in question. This is all the more so given the duty of a public body as a State emanation itself to disregard the statute if it is incompatible with directly effective rights: see Case C–103/88 *Fratelli Costanzo SpA v Commune di Milano* [1989] ECR 1839.

62 [1995] 1 AC 1.

63 The mandatory relief took the form of a declaration and/or mandamus to compel the Secretary of State to take the requisite action.

64 [1995] 1 AC 1.

65 Ibid, especially per Lord Keith of Kinkel, 26–27; per Lord Browne-Wilkinson, 35.

66 *EOC* [1995] 1 AC 1, 27.

The practical consequence of *EOC* is that although the Administrative Court is most unlikely **5.50** to grant quashing orders in respect of infringements of EC law by primary legislation giving effect to directly effective rights this will not matter because of the wide power to grant declaratory relief. Nor is a declaration that UK primary legislation is incompatible with EC law one that leaves the statute with full force and effect (as would be the case with a declaration of incompatibility under the HRA). As noted above, the Administrative Court must, in such a case, disapply the offending provisions.

Different considerations may engage where primary legislation is not giving effect to directly **5.51** effective rights. As Moses J observed at first instance in *R v HM Treasury, Commissioners of Customs & Excise and Attorney General, ex p Shepherd Neame Ltd*[67] there is no case where directly effective rights have not been involved in successful EC challenges to primary legislation.

However, as Moses J also pointed out in the same case, the national courts have—as in **5.52** *EOC* itself—been prepared to entertain applications for judicial review by claimants who could not, themselves, claim the benefit of the directly effective right in question. Although the EOC had standing in the broad sense allowed for in domestic judicial review it could not claim to have a directly effective right in EC law but was, rather, promoting the interests of other individuals who did enjoy such rights. In *Shepherd Neame*[68] when the case reached the Court of Appeal, that court having held that there was no relevant incompatibility expressed no view as to whether the court might issue a declaration if there had been incompatibility albeit that no directly effective rights were found to be involved.

The point is important since it greatly limits the effectiveness of EC law (and the notion **5.53** of indirect effect)[69] if only primary legislation addressing directly effective rights can be challenged in the national courts. It is submitted that the issue is to be resolved as one of jurisdiction. Even though the EOC had no directly effective rights of its own the Administrative Court still had jurisdiction to hear its application for judicial review.[70] In such circumstances, the Administrative Court is—in exercising its jurisdiction—bound by Article 10 (ex 5) EC so that it should, in terms of remedy, comply with its remedial obligations in conformity with the principle of effectiveness by declaring primary legislation to be incompatible with EC law.

But if that analysis is right in a case such as *EOC* then, it is submitted, it applies equally **5.54** in a case where no directly effective rights are engaged provided, always, that the claimant has standing to bring the case. Standing is now very widely accorded in domestic judicial review proceedings. There is no reason, in principle at least, why a claimant does not have standing to bring the State's attention to an incompatibility between domestic primary legislation and EC law. Once the claimant is accorded standing then the national court has equal obligations under Article 10 EC whether or not directly effective rights are engaged. That is, indeed, the rationale of indirect effect.

---

[67] [1998] 1 CMLR 1139, 1153.
[68] [1998] I CMLR 1139. The Court of Appeal's decision is reported at (1999) 11 Admin L Rep 517.
[69] For an outline of indirect effect, see paras 1.86–1.90.
[70] It is submitted that the EOC clearly had sufficient proximity to the directive to bring the proceedings as a matter of EC law: see paras 5.68 et seq.

5.55   In the same way, under the HRA (see below) there is no prior requirement that a claimant in judicial review proceedings must be a 'victim' before the court has jurisdiction to make a declaration of incompatibility under HRA, s 4 or before its interpretative obligations engage under s 3. If this is right for claims under the HRA it should, *a fortiori*, apply to obligations under EC law. However, it is almost certainly the case (see below) that the *remedy* available to a claimant who cannot assert a directly effective right is more limited than if directly effective rights are in play. It is one thing to grant a declaration that legislation is incompatible with EC law but another to disapply such legislation in circumstances where there are no directly effective rights asserted at all.

5.56   So far as subordinate legislation is concerned there is no difficulty in the Administrative Court making a declaration of invalidity if the statutory instrument or relevant provision thereof violates EC law.[71] Specific considerations may arise in respect of regulations made under s 2(2) of the European Communities Act 1972.[72] In particular, since that enabling power is conferred for the purpose of implementing EC obligations there may be a successful ultra vires challenge to the extent that the legislation *exceeds* what EC law requires.[73]

Type 3—Underlying challenge to the validity of EC legislation

5.57   Although a public body must disregard *domestic* legislation (whether primary or subordinate) that is incompatible with EC law[74] such body is not entitled to disregard invalid EC legislation on which domestic legislation may depend. But, challenges by way of judicial review may be brought *indirectly* to the validity of Community legislation.

5.58   There is no express provision in the Treaty preventing national courts from determining the validity of Community legislation. However, the ECJ in *Foto-Frost*[75] observed that whilst Community legislation may be declared to be *valid* by domestic courts, such legislation may not be declared to be invalid.

5.59   This means that challenges either to primary or subordinate legislation or derivative domestic administrative decisions and other acts that are entirely contingent on the establishing that the underlying EC legislation is invalid may be brought by way of judicial review. If the Administrative Court considers that the EC legislation is, in fact, valid it may make a declaration to that effect. In practice it would be more likely simply to dismiss the application for judicial review.

5.60   However, if the Administrative Court considers that the EC legislation is or might be invalid, the proper course is to refer the matter to the ECJ for a preliminary ruling under

---

[71] Though similar issues will arise as in the case of primary legislation in respect of whether the subordinate legislation is addressing directly effective obligations and whether EC obligations that are not directly effective may be enforced (see above). The legality of Orders in Council under s 1(3) of the European Communities Act 1972 may also be challenged by way of judicial review: see *R v HM Treasury, ex p Smedley* [1985] QB 657.

[72] See also paras 2.31 et seq.

[73] See the discussion at paras 2.36–2.47.

[74] See n 61 above.

[75] Case 314/85 *Foto-Frost v Hauptzollamt Lubeck-Ost* [1987] ECR 4199.

Article 234 EC.[76] Particular issues, considered elsewhere, may arise in respect of the granting of interim relief[77] and standing.[78]

E. Category 3—Judicial Review to Create an EC Law Remedy

5.61 As the above discussion has shown, EC obligations may be procedural or substantive in nature. In many cases what is at issue is an EC remedial obligation where domestic legislation has provided no, or no adequate, remedy for established violations of EC law.

5.62 Sometimes the issue of lack of remedy will be fought out in the proceedings that have been brought. *Levez*[79] affords a good example of this as do the cases on interim relief that have arisen in the context of judicial review.[80]

5.63 In some instances, however, judicial review proceedings may be brought either as a default remedy or for the specific purpose of challenging the lack of an appropriate EC remedy in national law.

5.64 There are many examples of this. Such cases are most likely to occur in practice where there is an existing EC remedies regime but where one or more aspects of that regime are said to be non-compliant with EC law. A possible example of this is the EC public procurement regime.[81] There, although provision is made under the EC Remedies Directives ((EEC) 89/775 and (EEC) 92/13) for specific remedies for breach of the regime, implementation is left to the Member States.

5.65 If, and to the extent that, the remedies provided for in national law under the various procurement directives are defective in respect of particular breaches of the regime then judicial review may itself be required to take the place of the absent remedy. This might be the case, for example, where withdrawal of a tender is made by a contracting authority under the procurement directives. Currently, there is no obvious remedy provided under the regime in respect of that occurring but it is submitted that judicial review would be available in order to provide an effective remedy under the regime.[82]

F. Category 4—Enforcement of Directives

5.66 EC directives pose special problems so far as remedies are concerned. Assuming that a directive is directly effective,[83] the crucial and related points so far as remedies are concerned are that:

(1) An individual may only rely on the directly effective rights conferred by the directive as against the State or an emanation of the State.
(2) The State may not rely on the directive as against individual persons.

---

[76] See paras 4.92 et seq.
[77] See paras 3.123 et seq.
[78] See paras 3.67 et seq.
[79] [1998] ECR I–7835, see text at n 6 above.
[80] See paras 3.123 et seq.
[81] See Chapter 15.
[82] See para 15.95.
[83] As to this, see paras 1.67 et seq.

5.67   This is the logical consequence of directives having so-called 'vertical' as opposed to 'horizontal' direct effect. However, the position is not quite as straightforward as this as the following three issues demonstrate.

Directives and standing issues

5.68   This difficult issue has already been touched upon.[84] In *EOC* the House of Lords was able to grant a declaration in favour of the EOC even though the EOC itself had no directly effective rights. In effect it was 'treated as acting as, or on behalf of, private individuals'.[85] This is unsurprising and, it is submitted, not in any way inconsistent with the principle that directives have only vertical effect.

5.69   More problematic is the position where the claimant is not acting on behalf of an individual who could assert directly effective rights but is, rather, acting on his own behalf and claiming an interest as opposed to a right. There is some scope for arguing that, in such a case, the claimant has standing to claim the same relief as the person who enjoyed a directly effective right.

5.70   Thus, in *Becker*[86] the ECJ observed that:

> provisions of Directives can be invoked by individuals insofar as they define rights which individuals are able to assert against the State.

5.71   In *Verholen*[87] the ECJ clarified this statement by limiting its scope to a person with a direct interest in the application of the directive. There, the ECJ held that Mr Verholen could rely on a directive concerning equal treatment in respect of social security in circumstances in which his wife fell within the scope of the directive and he suffered consequential discriminatory effects.

5.72   Whether or not every direct 'interest' (as opposed to 'right') enables a claimant to claim the same relief as a person asserting a directly effective right is not entirely clear. For present purposes, however, it is submitted that there is a distinction between, on the one hand, standing to claim a particular remedy said to be derived from the directive and, on the other, standing to apply for declaratory relief in respect of provisions of domestic legislation that are argued to be incompatible with the provisions of a directive. In the latter situation, on the assumption that the claimant had standing to challenge the national legislation (or to ask the national court to interpret it) the claimant ought, at least generally, to have the requisite standing to bring the incompatibility of the national legislation with the terms of a directive to the attention of the national court despite the fact that he was not claiming directly effective rights.[88]

---

[84]   See paras 5.51 et seq.

[85]   See Case C–468/93 *Gemeente Emmen v Belastingsdienst Grote Ondernemingen* [1996] ECR I–1721, 1636.

[86]   Case 8/81 *Becker v Finanzamt Munster-Innenstadt* [1982] ECR 53.

[87]   Joined Cases 87–89/90 *Verholen v Soziale Vezekeringsbank Amsterdam* [1991] ECR I–3757.

[88]   See also, paras 5.54–5.55.

Meaning of State emanation[89]

In order to give vertical effect to directives it is important to understand that, as with domes-   **5.73**
tic judicial review, there is a necessary relationship with the State and the body against which
the directive is sought to be enforced before a remedy can be obtained. In domestic public
law the relevant concept is that of a 'public body'. Under the HRA the relevant concept is
that of a 'public authority'. In the context of enforcing directives the relevant concept is that
of an emanation of the State.

In *Foster v British Gas*[90] the ECJ considered, at para 18 of its judgment, that there was an   **5.74**
emanation of the State (though the court did not, in fact, use those words) where:

> . . . the body was subject to the authority or control of the State or had special powers beyond
> those which result from the normal rules applicable to relations between individuals.

As formulated, that test appears to comprise two disjunctive elements, namely: (1) a source of   **5.75**
powers test and (2) a functions test. Provided, therefore, that one or other element is satisfied
there is an emanation of the State. As with other related issues, however, the position is far
from obvious. Albeit in the specific context of proceedings against British Gas (then a nationalized undertaking) the ECJ observed in *Foster*, at para 20 of its judgment, as follows:

> A body, whatever its legal form, which has been made responsible, pursuant to a measure
> adopted by the State, for providing a public service under the control of the State and has
> for that purpose special powers beyond those which result from the normal rules applicable
> in relations between individuals is included in any event among the bodies against which the
> provisions of a Directive capable of having a direct effect may be relied upon.

That formulation puts State authority or control for a particular purpose *and* special powers   **5.76**
as independent requirements, *both* of which must be satisfied before there can be an emanation of the State. This was the approach adopted by the Court of Appeal in *Rolls-Royce plc v
Doughty*.[91] There—purporting to apply *Foster*—the court held that Rolls Royce, even
though (then) a nationalized body, was not an emanation of the State. This was because it
was neither providing a 'public' service[92] nor did it possess special powers.[93]

However, this may be too restrictive an approach. The ECJ jurisprudence, taken overall,   **5.77**
does not suggest that the test in *Foster* was intended to be exhaustive but, rather, that there
are a series of indications that need to be considered broadly in determining whether there
is an emanation of the State in any given case. Indeed, this has been stressed by the Court
of Appeal in another case.[94]

---

[89] See, also, paras 2.17 et seq. where the concept of an emanation of the State is discussed in greater detail
in the treatment of general EC doctrines. The rationale of the requirement for there to be an emanation of the
State as a prerequisite of obtaining remedies in respect of directives would appear to lie in the EC law prohibition of directives having horizontal effect for which, see paras 5.80 et seq.

[90] Case C–188/89 [1990] ECR 3313.

[91] [1992] ICR 538.

[92] The court apparently considered that services to the State in the form of military production were not
'public' services in the sense that they were not services to the public.

[93] Contrast *Griffin v South West Water Services Ltd* [1995] IRLR 15 where the High Court held that a privatized
water company was a State emanation.

[94] *National Union of Teachers v Governing Body of St Mary's Church of England (Aided) Junior School* [1997]
ICR 334 (*held*: the governing body of a voluntary aided school that was largely funded by the State and had
been integrated into the state education sector was an emanation of the State).

5.78   On that basis, the ECJ has held a number of different entities to be emanations of the State including the Equal Opportunities Commission,[95] tax authorities,[96] area health authorities,[97] and a Chief Constable,[98] as well as all bodies that 'exercise legislative, executive and judicial powers' within the State.[99]

5.79   In many, if not most, instances it seems clear that a State emanation for the purposes of enforcing directives will be similar to a public body that is amenable to domestic judicial review or that is a 'public authority' within the meaning of HRA, s 6. However, some caution is needed in merely assimilating these notions. The relatively broad formulation in para 18 of *Foster*, as augmented by the ECJ case law, suggests that there may be cases where an entity (as, for example, the EOC and possibly universities and some privatized entities) would be amenable to judicial review in cases with an EC element but not otherwise. It seems unlikely, however, that the process would work in reverse.

Remedies where challenge to a directive affects individual third parties

5.80   There are situations in which a successful challenge, most notably by way of judicial review, to a directive could have consequential effects on individual third parties. The question then arises whether or not the grant of relief would offend against the bar on the horizontal effect of directives. This important issue is discussed in more detail in Chapter 2.[100] As that discussion shows, care is needed to distinguish between the effect of a challenge where horizontal effect would be breached and the separate situation of a challenge where there are merely incidental effects on individual third parties. In the latter case, the courts have held that horizontal effect is not violated and that relief can be applied for and granted.

5.81   The point arose directly for consideration in *Huddleston*.[101] In that case judicial review was sought by the claimant to require a local mineral planning authority to obtain an environmental statement pursuant to directly effective rights under the Environmental Impact Assessment Directive (Directive (EEC) 85/337). In order for a statement to be required it was necessary for the authority to disregard a statutory provision under which the developer was entitled to deemed planning permission even without an environmental statement.

5.82   At first instance, Richards J, relying on *R v Secretary of State for Employment, ex p Seymour-Smith*[102] held that relief could not be granted because the effect of disapplying the statutory provision in question would, in effect, be to permit a claim by one individual (the claimant affected by the development) against another (the developer) thereby investing the directive with horizontal effect.

---

[95] Case C–411/96 *Boyle v EOC* [1998] ECR I-6401.
[96] Case 8/81 *Becker v Finanzamt Munster-Innenstadt* [1982] ECR 53.
[97] Case 152/84 *Marshall v Southampton and South West Hampshire Area Health Authority* [1986] ECR 723.
[98] Case 224/84 *Johnston v Chief Constable of the RUC* [1986] ECR 1651.
[99] Case C–232/96 *Commission v Belgium* [1998] ECR I–5063.
[100] See paras 2.161 et seq.
[101] *R v Durham County Council, ex p Huddleston* [2000] 1 WLR 1484.
[102] [1997] 1 WLR 473.

However, the Court of Appeal allowed the claimant's appeal. It held, first, that there was no **5.83** relationship in private law as between the claimant and the developer so that no horizontal effects were created. Secondly, it held that 'enforcement of a Directive by an individual against the State is not rendered inadmissible solely by its consequential effects on other individuals'.

The Court of Appeal's reasoning in *Huddleston* has recently been confirmed by the ECJ **5.84** in *R (Delena Wells) v Secretary of State for Transport, Local Government and the Regions*[103] (another case on the EIA regime).

G. Category 5—State Liability in Damages for Breach of EC Law

Legal basis of State EC liability in damages

Outline

There is no reference in the EC Treaty to Member States bearing potential liability in **5.85** damages for violations of EC law. Prior to the landmark decision of the ECJ in *Francovich*[104] the matter was thought to be regulated solely by rules of national law subject, always, to EC general principles of law—especially the principle of effectiveness.[105]

However, in *Francovich* the ECJ outlined a juridical basis to be derived from two separate **5.86** strands of EC law for there being a substantive and specific EC Member State liability in damages where EC law is breached. First, the court held that the general principle of effectiveness would be impaired if injured parties could not obtain redress for violations of EC law by the State.[106] Secondly, the ECJ considered that Article 10 (ex 5) EC required Member States to nullify the unlawful consequences of such violations.[107] Thus, so the court reasoned, 'the principle whereby a State must be liable for loss and damage caused to individuals as a result of breaches of Community law for which the State can be held responsible is inherent in the system of the Treaty'.[108]

As explained below, despite *Francovich,* the precise scope of State EC liability in damages **5.87** remained unclear. It was not clarified more precisely until the ECJ's rulings in *Brasserie du Pecheur* and *Factortame*[109] and—even then—the position was (see below) not entirely clear.

Since these two seminal decisions, however, the principles regulating State liability in damages **5.88** in EC cases have been derived from these two cases and applied in a variety of situations. The starting point is, therefore, *Francovich* and *Brasserie du Pecheur* after which a number of particular aspects of EC damages liability of Member States will be considered.

---

[103] Case C–201/02 [2004] ECR I–723.
[104] Joined Cases C–9/90 *Francovich and Bonifaci v Italy* [1991] ECR I–5357.
[105] See, eg, Case C–189/89 *Foster v British Gas Corporation* [1990] ECR I–3313, 3341, per Advocate General Van Gerven, describing Member State damages liability as '... in principle a question that must be answered in accordance with the national law of the Member State'.
[106] [1991] ECR I–5537, para 33.
[107] ibid para 36.
[108] ibid para 35.
[109] Joined Cases C–46 and C48/93 *Brasserie du Pecheur SA v Germany, R v Secretary of State for Transport, ex p Factortame Ltd* [1996] ECR I–1029.

5.89 *Francovich* In *Francovich* the complaint was that Italy had failed to implement a directive (Directive (EEC) 80/987) providing for the creation of institutions to guarantee salaries on an employer becoming insolvent. Mr Francovich was unsuccessful in his claim (on his employer becoming insolvent) for payment of unpaid salary by the State said to arise as a directly effective right under the directive.[110]

5.90 Importantly, however, the ECJ held that a denial by the State of a right to claim payment of outstanding salary payments *could* give rise to a damages claim against the State.[111] This was for the two reasons set out above, namely that otherwise the EC general principle of effectiveness would be impaired and that, in any event, a duty to nullify the consequences of a breach of EC law was to be derived from Article 10 (ex 5) EC.[112]

5.91 Crucially, *Francovich* was a case involving non-implementation of a Community measure that was *not* directly effective. It is in that light that the principles there said to govern State liability in damages may have to be seen. As the court observed, the precise conditions of State liability arising would 'depend on the nature of the breach giving rise to the loss and damage'.[113] In the particular context of that case—non-implementation of a directive that was not directly effective—the ECJ held that EC State liability in damages arose if the following conditions were satisfied:

(1) Rights were conferred on an individual under a directive.
(2) The content of such rights was identifiable by reference to the terms of the directive.
(3) There was a causal link between the breach of EC law by the State and the damage suffered by the injured person.[114]

5.92 On the particular facts of the case, those conditions were held to be satisfied. First, although the directive was not directly effective, it was intended to confer on individuals the right to a guarantee of payment by the State (through a specified State institution) for unpaid salary. Secondly, the content of that right could be identified by reference to the terms of the directive. Finally, the fact that the right was not available to Mr Francovich was because the State had failed to implement the directive and nominate the institution liable to pay the unpaid salary. Thus, the requisite causal link was established.

5.93 It is, though, by no means obvious that the ECJ, in *Francovich*, was intending to lay down rules of general application in respect of State EC liability in damages. Several questions remained unanswered after the ruling. For example, although the court held that conditions of State liability would depend upon the nature of the breach, this formulation did not explain whether, at least in principle, *all* breaches of EC law by the State provided a foundation for the State being held to be liable to pay damages to affected parties or only serious breaches of EC law gave rise to State liability. Further, the judgment did not clarify whether—even if it was intended only to apply to breaches of directives—the principles laid down referred to breaches by the State of directives generally or were intended to apply only to those cases

---

110 [1991] ECR I–5357, para 5.
111 Similar, though not identical, issues arose in the joined case *Bonifaci*.
112 For consideration of the effectiveness principle in this context, see para 5.13.
113 [1991] ECR I–5357, para 38.
114 See para 40 of the court's judgment.

where directives that were not directly effective were not implemented. In particular, the judgment did not explain whether the principles laid down were intended to cover the case of a directive that did confer directly effective rights.

Following *Francovich*, then, there was a period of uncertainty. However, the principles **5.94** relating to State EC liability in damages were clarified further in the cases that followed.

***Brasserie du Pecheur* and *Factortame*[115]** *Brasserie du Pecheur*[116] involved a claim by **5.95** a French company against the German Government. At issue was whether or not a domestic prohibition on importation of beer because of failure to comply with national purity requirements was a breach of free movement of goods under Article 28 (ex 30) EC. The claim succeeded before the ECJ[117] and the subsequent question was whether the French company could recover damages against the State for losses sustained by reason of the prohibition before the ECJ ruling.

In *Factortame*[118] the applicants sought judicial review of Pt II of the Merchant Shipping **5.96** Act 1988 as being incompatible with, amongst other provisions, Article 43 (ex 52) EC directed to freedom of establishment. Again, the challenge succeeded[119] and the subsequent question was whether damages could be claimed against the State for the violation of EC law for losses incurred prior to the amendment of national law to comply with EC law.

In both cases (each of which involved directly effective rights) the ECJ, in essence, moulded **5.97** the *Francovich* criteria to fit a much wider class of case. The court noted that in each of the cases before it the Member State possessed a 'wide discretion'. In those circumstances, at least,[120] it specified the following conditions necessary to found State liability in damages:

(1) The rule of law infringed must have been intended to confer rights on individuals.
(2) The breach of such rule must have been 'sufficiently serious'.
(3) There must have been a 'direct causal link' between the breach and the damage sustained. [121]

The first and third conditions appear to be similar to national law requirements and the **5.98** court in *Brasserie du Pecheur* gave no further guidance on them. In particular, the first condition resembles the requirement in the domestic tort of breach of statutory duty that, for a cause of action to arise, it must be established that the statutory obligation was intended to give rise to such cause of action and to protect a class of persons that includes the claimant. However, there is an important difference between the approach of the ECJ (and,

---

[115] These conjoined decisions are referred to hereafter as *Brasserie du Pecheur*.
[116] [1996] ECR I–1029.
[117] See Case 178/84 *Commission v Germany* [1987] ECR 1227.
[118] Case C–221/89 *R v Secretary of State for Transport, ex p Factortame Ltd* [1991] ECR I–3905.
[119] ibid.
[120] Where there is no discretion it seems that illegality coupled with loss and causation is sufficient to found an EC damages claim against the State: see, eg, Cases C–258, 259/90 *Pasquerias De Bermeo SA and Naviera Laida SA v Commission* [1992] ECR I–2901. See also para 5.121.
[121] [1996] ECR I–1029, paras 48–51.

hence, that of the national courts in an EC case) to State liability and that of national courts in a purely domestic cause of action. As Caranta has observed:

> Community law is much more generous than English law in so far as the protective character of the infringed provision ... is considered. Up to now, no decision by the Court of Justice on Member States' liability has found this requirement wanting. Under Community law, no lengthy inquiry into the legislative intention is made. It is sufficient that the citizen can derive some benefit from the application of a given provision. Conferring rights does not need to be the only or even the main purpose ... It would be mistaken to address the purpose of the Community provision question in the same way it is addressed by English courts with reference to breach of statutory duty.[122]

5.99 However, in its judgment the ECJ did give specific guidance in respect of the second condition—not expressly articulated in *Francovich* — on how the question of whether a breach is 'sufficiently serious' should be approached. It said:

> the factors which the competent court should take into consideration include the clarity and precision of the rule breached, the measure of discretion left by that rule to the national or Community authorities, whether the infringement and the damage caused was intentional or involuntary, whether any error of law was excusable or inexcusable, the fact that the position taken by a Community institution may have contributed towards the omission, and the adoption or retention of national measures or practices contrary to Community law.[123]

5.100 In laying down these conditions the ECJ made it clear that they corresponded, in substance, to the conditions laid down by the ECJ as being necessary to found damages liability on the part of the Community institutions under Article 288 (ex 215) EC.[124] This was because, as the court observed, Article 288 was:

> simply an expression of the general principle familiar to the legal systems of the Member States that an unlawful act or omission gives rise to an obligation to make good the damage caused. That provision also reflects the obligation on public authorities to make good damage caused in the performance of their duties.[125]

5.101 For this reason it may be inferred from the court's judgment in *Brasserie du Pecheur* that State liability would arise, in the circumstances there contemplated, whether or not the breach was caused by legislative action on the part of the State. Administrative or executive action would suffice.[126]

5.102 Finally, the ECJ also made it clear that it did not matter which State institution caused the breach since all organs of the State were required, when undertaking their functions, to comply with EC law.[127]

---

[122] See R Caranta, 'Public Law Illegality and Governmental Liability' in D Fairgrieve, M Andenas, and J Bell (eds), *Tort Liability of Public Authorities in Comparative Perspective* (2002) 348.

[123] [1996] ECR I–1029, para 56.

[124] ibid para 53.

[125] ibid para 29. It should, however, be noted that no such 'general principle' currently exists in English law.

[126] Importantly, the Art 288 EC test is expressed to apply '*particularly*' in relation to liability for legislative measures' (emphasis added): [1996] ECR I–1029, paras 43–44.

[127] [1996] ECR I–1029, para 34.

Towards a general State EC damages liability

It can readily be seen that the approaches in *Francovich* and *Brasserie du Pecheur* were, at least **5.103** potentially, complementary. Nonetheless, in each of the cases, the ECJ had provided a formulation of State EC damages liability that was heavily dependent on the factual context. Whether a more general formulation was intended by the court was, even after *Brasserie du Pecheur*, not entirely clear. Indeed, in both *Francovich*[128] and in *Brasserie du Pecheur*[129] the ECJ had emphasized that the necessary conditions for State liability would differ according to the nature of the breach of EC law occasioning the damage.

In the event, the ECJ sought to reconcile its respective approaches in *Dillenkofer*[130] and, **5.104** in so doing, arrived at a general statement as to State EC liability in damages that has provided the foundation for later decisions of both the ECJ and national courts on State liability.

As explained above, no mention had been made in *Francovich* of the threshold requirement **5.105** that State violation of EC law must be 'sufficiently serious' in order to attract liability. However, in *Dillenkofer* the ECJ said that this requirement, although it had not been referred to expressly in *Francovich*, '. . . was evident from the circumstances of that case'.[131]

The court then laid down three prior requirements for State liability: **5.106**

(1) The rule of law infringed must have been intended to confer rights on individuals and the content of the rights in question must be identifiable on the basis of the provisions of the directive.[132]
(2) The breach must be sufficiently serious.
(3) There must be a direct causal link between the breach of obligation by the State and the damage suffered by the injured party.[133]

These conditions were, the court said, to be applied 'according to each type of situation' **5.107** so that the same principles were, it was now made clear, engaged whatever the nature of the breach. Future cases would expand upon those criteria but their general applicability to State liability in damages where discretion was involved was now established.

Analysing conditions of State damages liability where State exercises an EC discretion

First condition—rights on individuals

As has been seen, in order to be liable in damages in EC cases where the State is exercising **5.108** discretion[134] there must be an intention to confer rights on individuals which can be identified from the terms of the relevant directive or Treaty provision. In the case of directly effective rights, there ought, in principle, to be no difficulty because, by definition, directly

---

[128] [1991] ECR I–5357, para 35.
[129] [1996] ECR I–1029, para 31.
[130] Joined Cases C–178–179, C–188–190/94 *Dillenkofer v Germany* [1996] ECR I–4845.
[131] Ibid para 23.
[132] Or, on similar principles, it is to be assumed, the Treaty.
[133] [1996] ECR I–4845, paras 21–24.
[134] *A fortiori* where the State is under a *duty:* see para 5.121.

effective rights confer rights on individuals which are, plainly, derived from the provisions of a directive or Treaty provision. *Brasserie du Pecheur* and *Factortame* were cases in which the rights in question were directly effective.

5.109 However, it seems that State liability may also arise even where the rights in question are *not* directly effective. This is clear from *Francovich*.[135] There,[136] the ECJ held that the directive was not sufficiently precise and unconditional to create a directly effective right but only because there was no specification in the directive of which State institution or institutions should provide the requisite guarantees to individuals where an employing firm became insolvent. Had there been such specification there would have been a directly effective right.

5.110 Whilst, then, as a matter of formal analysis it is not necessary for the national court to find a directly effective right before being able to hold the State liable in damages it is by no means clear that non-directly effective provisions of a directive (or the Treaty) will, in practice, generally be sufficient to afford a basis for State liability.

5.111 There have been suggestions that the test for the creation of individual rights sufficient to found a claim for damages against the State is quite broad. It appears, for example, to be capable in some circumstances of encompassing the protection of general as well as individual interests.[137] In *Francovich*, Advocate General Mischo observed that it was 'in general difficult to imagine a situation in which an individual has suffered if the purpose of the rule was not to protect his interests'.[138] However, recent indications from the ECJ suggest that the individual interest requirement may be more restrictive than this.[139] In any event, the position is less certain for State institutions acting in a non-public capacity. There is, as yet, no authority clearly establishing that such bodies may claim damages against the State.

5.112 Importantly, loss does not, of itself, confer an individual right. For example, if the State has unlawfully given state aid to an undertaking, a competitor of that undertaking has no right to recover damages against the beneficiary of the unlawful aid.[140] However, the fact that a claimant may have behaved unlawfully and contrary to EC law does not necessarily preclude his relying on EC rights in a damages claim.[141]

Second condition—breach must be 'sufficiently serious'

5.113 The second condition of State EC damages liability is directed towards the nature of the breach. It must be 'sufficiently serious'. Some guidelines were given as to the meaning of this expression in *Brasserie du Pecheur*.[142]

---

135 [1991] ECR I–5357, see paras 5.89 et seq.

136 For the factual context, see paras 5.89 et seq.

137 See *Brasserie du Pecheur* [1996] ECR I–1029, 1107 per Advocate General Tesauro.

138 [1991] ECR I–5357, 5398.

139 Case 222/02 *Peter Paul* (unreported, 12 October 2004). See, also, *Three Rivers Case* [2000] 3 CMLR 205.

140 *Betws Anthracite Ltd v DSK Anthrazit Ibben buren GmbH* [2004] Eu LR 241.

141 See, eg, Case 453/99 *Courage Ltd v Crehan* [2001] 3 WLR 1646 where the ECJ held that the general principle of effectiveness of the Treaty competition provisions enables a claimant, in certain circumstances, to seek damages for breach of an anti-competitive contract to which he was a party. This case sounded in private law but the overall principle must be the same where the State is a contracting party or in some other contexts engaging State liability in damages.

142 See paras 5.99–5.102 above.

There has been extensive case law on the second condition. As Lord Clyde observed in **5.114**
Factortame (No 5):[143]

> No single factor is necessarily decisive. But one factor by itself might, particularly where there
> was little or nothing to put into the scales on the other side, be sufficient to justify a conclusion
> of liability.

In that case, Lord Clyde enunciated the following eight factors which have carried weight **5.115**
with the ECJ and are, therefore, relevant to decisions of national courts.[144] These comprise:

(1) The importance of the principle which has been breached.[145]
(2) The clarity and precision of the rule breached.[146]
(3) The degree of excusability of an error of law.[147]
(4) The existence of any relevant judgment on the point.[148]
(5) The state of mind of the infringer and, in particular, whether the infringer was acting
     intentionally or involuntarily.[149]
(6) The behaviour of the infringer after it has become evident that an infringement has
     occurred.
(7) The identity of the persons affected by the breach.[150]
(8) The position (if any) taken by one of the Community institutions in the matter.

Third condition—need for direct causal link between breach and damage
The third condition—a causation requirement—is similar to that prevailing in the English
law of tort. It has been observed of this condition that:

> So far ... the Court has not elaborated any systematic principles of causation but has approached   **5.116**
> the issues that arise on a case by case basis.[151]

---

[143] *R v Secretary of State for Transport, ex p Factortame (No 5)* [2000] 1 AC 524, 554.
[144] Although, ultimately, the decision is one of 'fact and circumstance', per Lord Clyde ibid.
[145] See, eg, *R v Secretary of State for Transport, ex p Factortame* [1997] Eu LR 475, 514.
[146] See, eg, Joined Cases C–283, C–291–292/94 *Denkavit International v Bundesamt fur Finanzen* [1996]
ECR I–5063, paras 50–51.
[147] The taking of legal advice does not necessarily render a breach excusable: see *Factortame* (n 143 above)
544 (per Lord Slynn), 548 (per Lord Hoffmann), 551 (per Lord Hope).
[148] *Brasserie du Pecheur* [1996] ECR I–1029, para 57.
[149] Thus a breach will be 'sufficiently serious' where the State has manifestly and gravely disregarded the
constraints on its discretionary powers. See *Brasserie du Pecheur* [1996] ECR I–1029, para 55. See, also, Case
C–392/93 *R v HM Treasury, ex p British Telecommunications plc* [1996] ECR I–1631, 1668–9; *Bourgoin v
MAFF* [1986] 1 QB 716, 777, per Oliver J. Where the State is not exercising a discretion or has very limited
discretion, any infringement of EU law may be enough to amount to a 'sufficiently serious' breach: see
Dillenkofer [1996] ECR I–4845, para 25. The other conditions will, of course, still apply before the State is
liable in damages. See, further, paras 5.121 et seq.
[150] Violations affecting a finite group are more likely to be considered to be 'sufficiently serious' than
breaches affecting the world. Even here, much may depend on the particular effect so that purely procedural
breaches with no discernible effect are unlikely to be classified as grave: see *R v Secretary of State for the Home
Department, ex p Gallagher* [1996] 2 CMLR 951.
[151] T Tridimas, 'Liability for Breach of Community Law: Growing Up or Mellowing Down?' in
D Fairgrieve, M Andenas, and J Bell (eds), *Tort Liability of Public Authorities in Comparative Perspective*
(2002), 158.

5.117 At least initially, the ECJ was content to leave questions of causation to the national court by reference only to EC general principles such as non-discrimination and effectiveness.[152]

5.118 More recently, however, there are signs that the ECJ is prepared to lay down principles as to whether a direct link between breach and loss has been established. For example, in *Brinkmann*[153] the question was whether there was a direct link between the failure of the Danish Government to implement Directive (EC) 79/32 on taxes and other turnover taxes and loss suffered by Brinkmann in the form of higher taxes than would have been required had the directive been implemented.

5.119 The ECJ held that no direct link had been established. This was, so it was held, because the Danish authorities had purported to give effect to the (then unimplemented) directive albeit that the relevant provisions had not been interpreted correctly.

5.120 In another case, the ECJ held that the fact that the loss suffered was itself unforeseeable did not preclude the existence of a direct link where the loss was caused by non-implementation of a directive.[154]

Conditions of State damages liability where State does not exercise an EC discretion

The distinguishing feature—absence of need to prove breach as 'sufficiently serious'

5.121 Where EC law is breached in circumstances in which the State has *no* discretion then it appears that all that may sometimes be required to establish liability in damages is the existence of: (1) individual rights to be derived from the EC measure in question, (2) the fact of a breach and (3) a direct causal link between breach and loss. There may, in other words, be no prior threshold to surmount of the breach being 'sufficiently serious' because the gravity of the breach may be inferred from the fact that the State was obviously required to comply with the EC obligation in question.[155]

5.122 This is exemplified by the facts of *R v MAFF, ex p Hedley Lomas*.[156] There, the United Kingdom refused to grant an export licence to persons seeking to export live sheep for slaughter to Spain. This was directly contrary to Article 29 (ex 34) EC which contained a prohibition against such bans. Further, there was a directive (Directive (EEC) 74/577) containing uniform standards for slaughter. The United Kingdom argued that Spain was in breach of this directive and that, accordingly, its refusal to grant an export licence was justified.

---

[152] See, eg, *Brasserie du Pecheur* [1996] ECR I–1029, para 65. See, also, F Smith and L Woods, 'Causation in Francovich: the Neglected Problem' (1997) 46 ICLQ 925. In the EU context national legal rules have assessed direct link on the balance of probabilities: see *R v Secretary of State for the Home Department, ex p Gallagher* [1996] 2 CMLR 951.

[153] Case C–319/96 *Brinkmann Tabakfabriken GmbH v Skatteministeriet* [1998] ECR I–5255.

[154] Case C–140/97 *Rechberger and Greindl v Austria* [1999] ECR I–3499. See, most recently, Case C–295/03 *P–Alessandrini Srl v Commission EC (Second Chamber)* (unreported, 30 June 2005).

[155] For similar reasoning see *Brasserie du Pecheur* [1996] ECR I–1029, paras 67 and 80 per Advocate General Tesauro.

[156] Case C–5/94 [1996] ECR I–2553.

The ECJ rejected the argument. It held that the threefold test enunciated in *Brasserie du* **5.123**
Pecheur for determination of State liability in damages was appropriate.[157] However, so far
as the requirement of a breach being 'sufficiently serious' was concerned, the court said:[158]

> . . . where at the time when it committed the infringement, the Member State in question was
> not called upon to make any legislative choices and had only considerably reduced, or even
> no discretion, the mere infringement of Community law may be sufficient to establish the
> existence of a sufficiently serious breach.

> In that respect, in this particular case, the United Kingdom was not even in a position to
> produce any proof of non-compliance with the Directive by the slaughterhouses to which the
> animals for which the export licence was sought were destined.

Failure to transpose directives

Where the State completely fails to transpose a directive into domestic law, similar principles **5.124**
apply to those where the State does not exercise discretion at all. Indeed, failure to transpose
a directive may be viewed as a sub-set of the State committing an obvious breach of EC law
and not exercising discretion in any true sense.

The underlying vice here (as in other cases) is that the gravity of the breach of EC law **5.125**
is *manifest*.[159] Difficult issues may, however, arise where there is some mitigating factor such
as, for example, that the State incorrectly assumes that domestic law already satisfies
the provisions of the directive.[160] In such instances, it would appear that the gravity of the
breach is not necessarily manifest and that the court would have to decide whether the
failure to transpose was 'sufficiently serious' to attract State liability in damages.

EC or domestic rules of damages liability—which apply?

From the perspective of the national court, it is important to distinguish between the separate **5.126**
application of EC and domestic rules of damages liability and the relationship between the two.

Rules as to the *conditions* of State EC damages liability are, plainly, a matter of EC law. **5.127**
The regulating principles are those already outlined. However, once those conditions are
satisfied, national law—at least generally—prescribes the scope and ambit of the *remedy*
by which reparation will be made by the State.

Nonetheless, although national rules dictate the 'shape' of the remedy, EC general principles **5.128**
of law circumscribe the permissible limits of the remedy. In particular, as explained earlier in
this chapter, the EC general principles—especially those of equivalence and effectiveness—
mean (respectively) that a remedy (including that of damages) for breach of EC law must
not be less favourable than a remedy relating to comparable domestic claims and that such
remedy (including that of damages) must not make it impossible in practice or excessively
difficult to secure reparation in respect of the EC law breach.[161]

---

[157] ibid para 25.
[158] ibid paras 28–29.
[159] Case C–392/93 *R v HM Treasury, ex p British Telecommunications plc [1996]* ECR I–1631, 1652,
per Advocate General Tesauro.
[160] This example is given by Tridimas (n 151 above) 506. See, eg, Case C–63/01 *Evans v Secretary of State
for the Environment, Transport and the Regions and the Motor Insurers' Bureau* [2003] ECR I–4447.
[161] *Brasserie du Pecheur* [1996] ECR I–1029, para 67.

5.129 This distinction may, therefore, make it necessary on occasion for the national courts, including the Administrative Court, to scrutinize domestic rules as to State liability in damages in order to determine their legality; specifically, their compliance with EC law as a remedy that satisfies these general imperatives of EC law. Such rules will obviously include procedural rules such as relevant limitation periods in respect of damages claims,[162] and rules of evidence for such claims.[163]

5.130 But the ECJ has made it clear that rules of national law may—subject to the need for compliance with EC general principles—also govern some *substantive* issues affecting damages claims at least where there is an absence of specific—especially contrary — EC provision. As has been seen, causation has, with that *caveat*, largely, been left to the development of national rules.[164] Matters such as mitigation of loss, and contributory negligence[165] are also largely subject to national rules[166] as is the amount of damages consequent upon liability being proved.[167]

5.131 All this is, however, subject to the important qualification that national damages rules— whether procedural or substantive—must not stray beyond the permissible ambit of EC law and, in particular, must not stray beyond the permissible limits of the general principles of equivalence and effectiveness. Where national rules go beyond those limits, the ECJ has shown itself prepared to hold them to be incompatible with EC law.

5.132 Thus, the ECJ in *Brasserie du Pecheur* ruled that State EC damages liability cannot be made dependent on proof of misfeasance in public office as UK national rules had previously required.[168] The court has also held as incompatible with EC law national rules designed to place a 'ceiling' on damages.[169] The overall principle is that the amount of damages awarded by the national court 'must be commensurate with the loss or damage sustained'.[170] On that basis, for example, although national rules may, generally, provide for heads of liability, loss of profits may not be totally excluded as a legitimate head of claim.[171]

5.133 It seems safe to assume that, as the substantive content of EC law develops, the ECJ will make more statements of principle in areas formerly governed by national rules. As this occurs, the national court must be familiar with these statements of principle and not act incompatibly with them when formulating or applying national rules. As exemplified

---

[162] See, eg, Case C–261/95 *Rosalba Palmisani v Instituto Nazionale della Providenza Sociale (INPS)* [1997] ECR I-4025 (one-year limitation period for damages claims for loss for delayed transposition of a directive upheld by ECJ).

[163] Case 199/82 *Amministrazione delle Finanze v San Giorgio* [1983] ECR 3595 (national rules of evidence requiring elaborate documentary proof from traders to establish that burdens of charges had not been passed on to consumers held by ECJ to make EU damages claim 'virtually impossible or excessively difficult' to enforce.

[164] See paras 5.116 et seq.

[165] Importantly, mitigation of loss and contributory negligence are two different things. Contributory negligence involves avoiding the loss whereas mitigation of loss involves reducing the loss that has occurred. Nonetheless, the ECJ routinely addresses the two concepts together.

[166] *Brasserie du Pecheur* [1996] ECR I–1029, para 84.

[167] ibid paras 82–83, *Palmisani* [1997] ECR I–4025, para 26.

[168] *Brasserie du Pecheur* [1996] ECR I–1029 I, paras 71–73.

[169] Case C–271/91 *Marshall v Southampton and Southwest Hampshire Area Health Authority* [1993] ECR I–4367, paras 26 and 30.

[170] *Brasserie du Pecheur* [1996] ECR I–1029, paras 82–83.

[171] ibid para 87.

immediately below, sometimes a statement of principle from the ECJ may itself encompass a new area of case law. Nowhere is this more true in the damages context than in the ECJ's incorporation, into questions of State EC damages liability, of its case law under Article 288 (ex 215) EC on the liability in damages of the Community institutions.

State liability and liability under Article 288 (ex 215) EC compared

It is clear from the ECJ's ruling in *Brasserie du Pecheur* that the court intended that there **5.134** should, to say the least, be a very similar test for the triggering of EC damages liability whether the breach of EC law was occasioned by the exercise of State discretion or by a Community institution.[172]

Article 288 EC provides: **5.135**

> In the case of non-contractual liability, the Community shall, in accordance with the general principles common to the laws of the Member States, make good any damage caused by its institutions or by its servants in the performance of their duties.

Nothing in the terminology of Article 288(2) compels any particular approach to the **5.136** triggering of EC damages liability on the part of the Community institutions. However, as long ago as its decision in *Schoppenstedt*,[173] the ECJ held that where the legislature was exercising a complex discretion, liability in damages did not automatically follow from the fact that, in the event, it acted unlawfully. This was because in many instances the illegality could not reasonably have been foreseen. So, there was no true 'fault' on the part of that legislature. The court held in that case that where legislation took the form of measures of economic policy involving broad discretion, liability in damages would only arise if there was 'a sufficiently flagrant violation of a superior rule of law for the protection of the individual'.[174]

That starting point for EC damages liability has obvious affinity with the later formulation **5.137** of 'sufficiently serious' to be developed by the ECJ in its subsequent case law on State liability in damages. However, the principle in *Schoppenstedt* was interpreted restrictively in later cases so that in order to succeed in a damages action against the institutions of the Community, a claimant had to prove both that the *manner* and the *effect* of the breach were wholly exceptional. In one decision, the ECJ held that the conduct of the institution in question (ie the *manner* of breach) must be verging on the arbitrary to trigger liability.[175] In another case, the ECJ held that the loss suffered by a claimant (ie the *effect* of the breach) must extend further than the ordinary risk of loss for the activity in question.[176]

A simple transposition of the conditions of liability under Article 288(2), as initially developed **5.138** in the ECJ case law, to the conditions of liability for State liability was never possible and

---

172 ibid para 51. Where the State has no discretion the issue does not arise because (see below) the case law on the necessary conditions for Art 288 liability on the part of the Community institutions presupposes the exercise of a complex discretion.

173 Case 5/71 *Aktien-Zuckerfabrik Schoppenstedt v Council of the European Communities* [1971] ECR 975.

174 ibid para 11.

175 Case 116/77 *GR Amylum NV and Tunnel Refineries Ltd v Council and Commission of the European Communities* [1979] ECR 3497.

176 Joined Cases 83, 94/76, 4, 15 and 40/77 *Bayerische HNL Vermehrungsbetriebe GmbH & Co KG v Council and Commission of the European Communities* [1978] ECR 1209.

was probably not intended. For one thing, the Community legislature—like a sovereign Parliament—is a primary legislature. It is, therefore, unsurprising that the constraints on its freedom of action should be limited to exceptional cases where it should be required to make reparation. The same may not be true in relation to *national* legislatures where the Community legislature has reduced the scope of Member State discretion to legislate. Further, although Community institutions may, undoubtedly, violate EC law their violations are usually those that conflict with the general principles of EC law and in a different way to the more specific State breaches of (say) directly effective rights. There may also be policy reasons for limiting claims that can be brought against the institutions in a way that would be inappropriate in cases of a breach by the State.

5.139 It is perhaps unfortunate, therefore, that the ECJ has, to date, not articulated the undoubted contextual differences that exist between the liability of the Community institutions on the one hand and that of the Member States on the other. Despite this, the ECJ has, in respect of liability under Article 288, adopted a less rigid approach in recent years. It has, for example, extended the scope of Article 288(2) to administrative (as well as legislative) acts.[177] It now accepts—as it originally did not—that the prospect of numerous claimants seeking damages does not preclude proceedings for damages under Article 288.[178] In practice, it seems improbable that a claim for damages against the State should (or would) be refused by rigid adherence to the rules that have grown up in relation to Article 288. It seems probable that the Article 288 case law should be treated by the national court as a guide rather than a mantra.

Analysing classes of State EC damages liability where discretion is exercised

The issue

5.140 The first and third conditions of State liability (individual rights and direct causal link) rarely cause difficulty beyond the facts of the individual case or the interpretation of the Community measure in question. It is in respect of the second condition of State damages liability ('sufficiently serious') that issues of more general principle are most likely to arise.

5.141 The question is whether a particular breach is 'sufficiently serious' to attract State liability. The issue addressed here is whether specific *types* of breach may (or even must) attract the rubric of their being 'sufficiently serious'. It has already been noted[179] that simple failure to transpose a directive into domestic law is, almost invariably, regarded as a sufficiently serious breach because the State has no discretion not to transpose but is, rather, under a direct EC law duty to do so.

---

[177] Case C–352/98 *Laboratoires Pharmaceutiques Bergaderm SA and Jean-Jacques Goupil v Commission of the European Communities* [2000] ECR I–5291.

[178] Joined Cases C–104/89 and C–37/90 *JM Mulder, WH Brinkoff, JMM Muskens, T Twijnstra and Otto Heinemann v Council of the European Union and Commission of the European Communities* [1992] ECR I–3061.

[179] See paras 5.124–5.125.

Defective transposition

Sometimes, the State purports to transpose a directive into domestic law but fails to do **5.142** so accurately. Issues of State liability in damages may arise where individuals have suffered loss in consequence of the State's breach of EC law.[180]

The problem arose for consideration in *R v HM Treasury, ex p British Telecommunications*.[181] **5.143** There, the ECJ held that the UK Government had misinterpreted the relevant provisions of Directive (EEC) 90/531 which was concerned with public procurement. However, in the court's view, the breach was not sufficiently serious to render the State liable in damages.

At stake in BT's claim for damages was whether or not it was for BT or the State to deter- **5.144** mine whether or not particular services were subject to competition. The ECJ decided the point in favour of BT. But, in rejecting BT's argument on liability, it distinguished between those cases where there was a total failure to implement a directive (see above) and cases, such as the present, where a genuine interpretation of the directive had been reached by a Member State in company, as it happened, with other Member States and where the provision in question was 'imprecisely worded'. Further, the interpretation given to the directive was not obviously contrary to the purpose of the directive.[182]

What *British Telecommunications* suggests is that the ECJ will—where a directive has been **5.145** incorrectly transposed—look with some care at the nature of the breach. Where, in its turn, the national legislature has to make a complicated judgment the ECJ will take a fairly stringent approach broadly in line with the general approach taken to breaches of EC law by the Community legislature under Article 288 EC. However, the narrower the judgment to be made by the State the more likely is it that incorrect transposition will give rise to an actionable claim in damages against it.[183]

State breaches following transposition

There is an important distinction between transposition and implementation which has been **5.146** touched on elsewhere.[184] The provisions of a directive may have been lawfully *transposed* into domestic law but there may remain further duties of *implementation*. Most commonly, the duties of implementation will vest on a State administrative body rather than on the national legislature. If the State, despite having lawfully transposed a directive, commits breaches of EC law in the implementation of the directive a damages claim may, in certain circumstances, lie against the State by an affected person.

---

[180] Defective transposition is usually more accurately described as an error of law on the part of the State rather than a failure of discretion though some errors of law are reflected in the State exceeding the discretion it possesses as to how to transpose directives into national law whereas in other cases there is minimal discretion being exercised (see below).

[181] Case C–392/93 [1996] ECR I–1631.

[182] See, also, Joined Cases C–283, C–291 and C–292/94 *Denkavit International BV v Bundesamt fur Finanzen* [1996] ECR I–5063.

[183] For a case in point see Case C–150/99 *Stockholm Lindopark AB v Sweden* [2001] ECR I–493, para 40.

[184] See paras 2.159–2.160.

5.147   The relevant conditions triggering State liability would appear to be essentially similar to those engaged where the State unlawfully transposes a directive and to apply in the same way whether the national legislature or an administrative body is involved.

5.148   In such cases a national court determining a claim for damages should ask itself—as the ECJ has done—whether or not a broad discretion is being exercised. If such discretion is being exercised then the court will have to address the further question of whether the breach is sufficiently serious. If, by contrast, no discretion (or very limited discretion) is being exercised then the element of sufficient seriousness is likely to be inferred.

5.149   This issue arose in *Norbrook*.[185] There, directives on the authorization of veterinary products had been lawfully transposed into domestic law. However, the complaint in the damages claim was that they had not been implemented correctly in that the rules laid down in the directives in respect of applications for marketing authorizations had been breached by the competent State authority (the Licensing Authority).

5.150   The ECJ stated the governing principle as follows:

> Where ... the Member State was not called upon to make legislative choices, and had considerably reduced, if no discretion, the mere infringement of Community law may be sufficient to establish the existence of a sufficiently serious breach.[186]

5.151   This repeats the formulation in *Hedley Lomas*.[187] In the circumstances prevailing in *Norbrook*—that is, the laying down of extremely detailed rules in the directive for national transposition and implementation—there were no real legislative choices involved on the part of the national administrative authorities. That being so, the breach of EC law was treated as being 'sufficiently serious' without the need to address this criterion explicitly and separately.[188]

Transposing or implementing an invalid Community measure

5.152   Although the context is different, it would appear that similar considerations ought, in principle, to apply to the situation where the State legislature transposes a directive that is held by the ECJ to be invalid or where State administrative action is founded upon an illegal Community measure. As has been seen, whether there is exposure to an action in damages against the State depends, in large measure, on whether the State is truly 'at fault'. Where broad discretion is being exercised, the court looks carefully at the circumstances to see if the discretion has been exercised in a way that invites censure. Where, however, there is no (or only limited) discretion and the State has simply breached EC law the ECJ has usually inferred that the breach is 'sufficiently serious'. The reason for such inference being drawn is, of course, that the State could (and should) have complied with EC law. Its breach is not excusable.

---

[185] Case C–127/95 *Norbrook Laboratories Ltd v MAFF* [1998] ECR I–1531.

[186] Case C–75/94 [1996] ECR I–2553, para 109.

[187] See n 156 above and text at para 5.122.

[188] But the position would be likely to be different where there was considerable administrative discretion. For the policy implications of exposing State administrative authorities to damages claims in such circumstances, see *Brinkmann* [1998] ECR I–5255, point 34, per Advocate General Jacobs.

However, properly analysed, it is not so much the absence of discretion that compels the **5.153** conclusion that the State's breach is of sufficient seriousness but, rather, the culpability to be attached to there being a breach of EC law.

So, where the State has—whether with discretion or not—transposed a directive or **5.154** (as the case may be) implemented a Community measure that is subsequently declared to be invalid, it is difficult to see how the State can be said to be at fault. It has simply complied with its *ostensible* EC obligation to transpose and implement EC law.

There is a distinction to be drawn, in public law terms, between the State being liable **5.155** to other public law remedies in proceedings for judicial review and the State being liable in damages. Irrespective of 'fault' the State has no power to transpose or to implement an illegal directive or other Community measure. However, it by no means follows that such unlawful transposition or implementation affords a right of action against the State in damages where the illegality is the responsibility of the Community legislature.

Here, therefore, it is suggested that the inference should be drawn that a breach of EC law **5.156** on the part of the State that is occasioned by prior legislative action on the part of the Community legislature is not 'sufficiently serious' to justify the award of damages.[189] Further, to encourage damages claims in such circumstances would, arguably, be to bypass the constraints of actions under Article 288 EC against the relevant Community institution.[190]

State liability for decisions of the national courts

A new class of case has recently emerged in respect of the failure by a national court to apply **5.157** EC law correctly. Whether or not the State should be exposed to claims for damages in such circumstances raises different issues from those categories of case considered above. This is because in domestic law there is, at least generally,[191] exclusion of liability for judicial acts.

However, following *Brasserie du Pecheur*[192] it was clear that, in principle, there was no immunity **5.158** from State EC damages liability in respect of judicial decisions. As the ECJ there observed:[193]

> ... in international law a State whose liability for breach of an international commitment is in issue will be viewed as a single entity, irrespective of whether the breach which gave rise to damage is attributable to the legislature, the judiciary or the executive. This must apply *a fortiori* in the Community legal order since all State authorities, including the legislature, are bound in performing their tasks to comply with the rules laid down by Community law directly governing the situation of individuals.

---

[189] This is the mirror-image of the *Hedley Lomas* situation where—there being no relevant discretion— a direct breach of EC law caused by the State is usually inferred by the court as being 'sufficiently serious' (see paras 5.121 et seq.). It may also be that the requisite element of direct causal link is absent in such a case because, in reality, it is the Community legislature that has caused the loss. *Quaere*, though, whether this is right given the State's obligations under Art 10 (ex 5) EC to comply with EC law: see, eg, Case 103/88 *Fratelli Constanzo SPA v Commune di Milano* [1989] ECR 1839.

[190] Since the relevant considerations may not be identical to those engendering State liability: see paras 5.134–5.139. See, also, *Francovich* [1991] ECR I–5357, 5387, per Advocate General Mischo.

[191] There are limited exceptions most notably under the HRA 1998, s 8 and in limited circumstances in respect of certain decisions of magistrates: see *Re McC* [1985] AC 528.

[192] [1996] ECR I–1029.

[193] ibid para 34.

5.159 Thus, in its general observation as to the existence of State liability in damages regardless of the identity of the particular institution concerned, the ECJ (whether intentionally or not) created the basis of an argument that judicial decisions were as amenable to a claim for damages against the State as any other act or omission of the State that violated EC law.

5.160 This argument came directly before the ECJ in *Kobler*.[194] In that case the claimant brought an action for damages against the State alleging loss occasioned by a judgment of the Austrian Supreme Administrative Court denying him a special increment for length of service allegedly contrary to EC law. One of the questions referred by the national court (the Regional Civil Court in Vienna) was whether the principle of State liability covered judicial decisions of a supreme court.

5.161 The ECJ held:

> In the light of the essential role played by the judiciary in the protection of the rights derived by individuals from Community rules, the full effectiveness of those rules would be called in question and the protection of those rights would be weakened if individuals were precluded from being able, under certain conditions, to obtain reparation when their rights are affected by an infringement of Community law attributable to a decision of a court of a Member State adjudicating at last instance.[195]

5.162 So, *Kobler* provides a potential jurisdictional basis for State liability in damages in circumstances in which judgments of national courts of last instance are contrary to EC law and cause loss to relevantly affected individuals. The conditions under which liability is triggered are, nominally at least, the same as those for State damages liability generally.

5.163 As might be expected, however, there are strong policy considerations that militate against the award of damages against the State in such cases save in highly exceptional circumstances. Many of these considerations were, unsuccessfully, urged on the ECJ by Member States in *Kobler* as a reason for conferring immunity from damages in relation to judicial decisions. It is, for example, hard to see how awards of damages will be made in practice. Presumably, the award would have to be made by an inferior court against the court of last instance contravening EC law. That prospect raises the spectre of a lack of independence argument against the inferior court under Article 6 ECHR if either the award is not made—because the breach is not considered to be 'sufficiently serious'—or if it is thought to be too low.[196]

5.164 However, whilst rejecting policy criteria as the basis for excluding liability, the ECJ did accept that State liability in damages for judicial error would be highly exceptional. It said:

> regard must be had to the specific nature of the judicial function and to the legitimate requirements of legal certainty ... State liability for an infringement of Community law by a decision of a national court adjudicating at last instance can be incurred only in the exceptional case where the court has manifestly infringed the applicable law.[197]

---

[194] Case C–224/01 [2004] QB 848.

[195] ibid para 33.

[196] For a fuller analysis see M Hoskins, 'Suing the HL in Damages: Career Suicide or Community Law Right?' [2004] JR 278.

[197] Case C–224/01 *Kobler* [2004] QB 848, para 53.

The question of whether, within that class of *'exceptional case'*, the EC breach by the court **5.165** of last instance was 'sufficiently serious' was one to be answered by the injunction of the ECJ to the national court awarding damages to 'take account of all the factors which characterise the situation put before it'. The ECJ said that:

> Those factors include, in particular, the degree of clarity and precision of the rule infringed, whether the infringement was intentional, whether the error of law was excusable or inexcusable, the position taken, where applicable, by a Community institution and non-compliance by the court in question with its obligation to make a reference for a preliminary ruling under the third paragraph of Article 234 EC.[198]

There will perhaps, in view of this formulation, be very few cases capable of founding **5.166** a claim for damages against the State because of judicial error leading to a breach of EC law. In particular, the notion of the House of Lords *intending* to infringe EC law is a surprising one. In practice it seems unlikely that any but highly exceptional cases will succeed. But there would now seem to be a likelihood of damages claims being brought in a new litigation culture in respect of adverse (and arguably incorrect) EC decisions being made at least by the House of Lords in cases where permission to appeal from the Court of Appeal is contended to have been unjustifiably refused or where the House of Lords rejects an EC claim without a request for a preliminary ruling.[199]

Inevitably, this brings the further possibility of increased pressure being put on the ECJ **5.167** which may have to determine, by way of preliminary ruling, references made by national courts hearing claims for damages against decisions of the House of Lords despite the fact that the House of Lords refused to refer the case. It is an unsettling prospect.[200]

Other EC monetary claims against the State

Closely allied to claims for damages for breach of EC law by the State are other monetary **5.168** claims arising out of such a breach. As noted earlier, it is generally for the State to determine— subject to general principles of EC law—the nature of the remedy governing reparation.[201] This means that the State may choose, or provide, other means of obtaining reparation than a claim for damages.[202]

In that respect, the remedy of restitution is sometimes used to enable the recovery of money **5.169** by an individual who has paid money in response to a demand by the State that was made contrary to EC law.

---

[198] ibid paras 54–55.

[199] It seems unlikely that damages claims could or would be brought against defective decisions of inferior courts in the majority of (even exceptional) cases given the possibility of appeal.

[200] Indeed, the potential for damages claims raises the spectre of dissatisfied litigants using the damages route to challenge decisions of the House of Lords with which they disagree in an endeavour to get the case before the ECJ. The unanswered conundrum is whether the ECJ is itself susceptible to a damages claim as a court of last resort.

[201] See para 5.02.

[202] Remedies may, of course, be complementary. For example, permitting recovery of money paid pursuant to an unlawful demand may not afford full reparation for the breach of EC law since the unlawful demand may have occasioned further loss—a fact noted by the ECJ in Cases C–192–218/95 *Société Comateb v Directeur Général des Douanes et Droits Indirects* [1997] ECR I–165, para 34.

5.170   As with damages, there are limitations on the extent to which the State can, in such circumstances, lawfully seek to limit the amount of money recoverable. Thus, in *San Giorgio*[203] the ECJ had to consider a domestic rule that sought to limit unjust enrichment (and, hence, recovery of moneys paid) by establishing a presumption that the burden of taxes that had been unduly levied had been passed on when the goods, the subject of the taxes, had been transferred to a third party. The ECJ held that the passing on of a charge was a legitimate consideration for limiting recovery of moneys paid but that it would offend against EC law if the burden of proof made recovery excessively difficult or virtually impossible in practice.[204]

5.171   Other means of obtaining compensation that bear an affinity to damages include the obtaining of a declaration in judicial review proceedings of entitlement to be paid interest on payments due under an EC directive,[205] and, where appropriate, a declaration that the exercise of statutory powers is contrary to EC law because of failure to provide a scheme of compensation in respect of the power so exercised.[206] These are obviously not exhaustive of the duty on public law courts to fashion a compensatory payment where that is necessary so as to afford proper reparation for loss suffered in consequence of a breach of EC law by the State.[207]

State EC liability in damages—what is the correct procedure?

5.172   Difficult questions can arise as to the appropriate procedure for commencing claims in respect of EC damages. Ordinarily, a claim for damages sounds in private rather than in public law. However, as explained elsewhere,[208] many areas of claims for damages in EC law involve claims against emanations of the State in circumstances where there is increasing recognition by the court that—depending on the particular circumstances—a remedy for *public* law default on the part of the State may be (or may include) damages.

5.173   This can result in issues of limitation and/or abuse of process. It may be argued that intrinsically public law EC claims should, if they include a damages element, be brought by way of judicial review under CPR Pt 54 and within the strict time limits mandated by

---

[203] Case C–199/82 *Amministrazione delle Finanze dello Stato v San Giorgio* [1983] ECR 3595.

[204] See, also, Cases C–192–218/95 *Société Comateb v Directeur Général des Douanes et Droits Indirects* [1997] ECR I–165 where the ECJ observed that repayment must be made unless the charge was entirely borne by a third party and that repayment would not necessarily constitute unjust enrichment even where a charge had been passed on because the unlawful tax may have had a consequential effect on sales. In that event, a damages claim might also lie.

[205] *R v MAFF, ex p Lower Burytown Farms Ltd* [1999] Eu LR 129.

[206] *Booker Aquaculture Ltd v Secretary of State for Scotland* The Times, 24 September 1998 where the Scottish Outer House held that the exercise of particular statutory power to destroy property without a compensation scheme was unlawful. Contrast *R v MAFF, ex p Country Landowners' Association* [1996] 2 CMLR 193 where the ECJ held that a change in national legislation requiring payment of meat premiums to producers rather than landowners without scheme of compensation to affected landowners was not contrary to EC law.

[207] There may, of course, be instances in which the remedial choice to secure reparation for a breach of EC law by the State will be between some form of compensatory remedy or a non-compensatory remedy. See, eg, Case C–201/02 *R (Wells) v Secretary of State for Transport, Local Government and the Regions* (unreported, 7 January 2004) where the State had, according to the ECJ, the choice of revoking or suspending a development consent already granted or (if the claimant consented) awarding compensation for loss sustained by reason of a development consent granted without a prior environmental impact assessment.

[208] See paras 1.100 et seq.

CPR r 54.5.[209] On that footing, it would be an abuse of process to commence such claims by a private law action under CPR Pt 7 in order to bypass the time requirements of judicial review.

On the other hand, the counter-argument is that a claimant ought not to be compelled to **5.174** institute a claim for judicial review before being able to claim damages. Thus, for example, claims for damages for negligence in the exercise of statutory powers are not required to be brought in judicial review proceedings even though they contain an implicit public law dimension.[210] Plainly, if that is the correct approach to EC damages claims, it has important implications for limitation because the judicial review time limits are simply not engaged.

The correct starting point appears to be that State liability for damages for a breach of **5.175** EC law is (at least usually) best understood as a breach of statutory duty. This was the view of Hobhouse LJ in the Divisional Court in *Factortame No 5*.[211] In reaching that view Hobhouse LJ relied on dicta of Lord Diplock in *Garden Cottage Foods v Milk Marketing Board*[212] and the reasoning of Mann J in *Bourgoin v MAFF*[213] to the effect that the duty on the State was, in a case involving breach of a directive, imposed by the relevant provision of the directive and under s 2(1) of the European Communities Act 1972.

As such, claims of this nature are 'founded in tort' and there is, at least in principle, a limitation **5.176** period of six years 'from the date on which the cause of action accrued' prescribed by s 2 of the Limitation Act 1980.[214]

Further, many such claims are continuing and give rise to a fresh cause of action on each **5.177** occasion that the claimant suffers consequential damage. That was held to be the position in *Phonographic Performance Ltd v Department of Trade and Industry*.[215] There, the claimant alleged that the Crown was in breach of EC law in failing to implement Council Directive (EEC) 92/100 as amended by Council Directive (EC) 2001/29 so as to provide for a single equitable remuneration in respect of the public performance and broadcast of sound recordings in the circumstances prescribed by the Copyright, Designs and Patents Act 1988, ss 67 and 72.

In that case, the Vice Chancellor—ruling on a number of preliminary issues—held that **5.178** the cause of action was not statute-barred and that causes of action accrued each time that the claimant sustained damage as a result of the violation of EC law. He cited with approval the approach of Colman J in *Arkin v Borchard Lines Ltd*[216] a case concerning the operation of agreements alleged to infringe Articles 81–82 EC. Colman J had observed:

> . . . it is important to recognise that there are different ways in which such a breach may cause damage. Thus, an isolated event amounting to such a breach may cause a chain of damage

---

[209] See, generally, Chapter 3.
[210] See, eg, *X (Minors) v Bedfordshire CC* [1995] 2 AC 633, 736G, per Lord Browne-Wilkinson.
[211] [1998] 1 CMLR 1353. The case was appealed unsuccessfully to the Court of Appeal and House of Lords but the basis of State liability in domestic law was not addressed.
[212] [1984] AC 130, 141.
[213] [1986] QB 716, 733.
[214] See *Factortame (No 7)* [2001] 1 WLR 942.
[215] [2004] 8 Eu LR 1003.
[216] [2000] Eu LR 232, 242.

development commencing when the effects of the breach first affect the claimant, and those [effects] may continue for a long period of time. If that period commences prior to the cut-off date for the purpose of the period of limitation, the claim will prima facie be time-barred notwithstanding that the effects of the breach may continue beyond that date. The position is similar to a claim in tort for negligence.

By contrast, there may be a continuing or repeated breach of statutory duty, over an extended period such as an unlawful emission of toxic fumes which continues to affect and injure those exposed to it over the whole period of that breach. In such a case, if the limitation cut-off date occurs during the period, the claimant's cause of action for the damage suffered after the date in question will not be time-barred.

5.179 Importantly, however, the fact that a damages claim against the State for breach of EC law may, in principle, be subject to ordinary limitation periods applicable to private law actions does not mean that such a claim cannot be brought by way of judicial review (with the damages claim being decided in those proceedings) or that a claimant who could have instituted judicial review proceedings may necessarily rely on a six-year limitation period to bring the claim in private law proceedings. Such delay may, depending on the circumstances of the case, be held to constitute an abuse of process.

5.180 This was the defendant's argument in *Phonographic Performance* where, instead of proceeding by way of judicial review, the claimant brought private law proceedings for declaratory relief and damages and relied on the six-year limitation period under s 2 of the 1980 Act. Although, on the facts, the Vice Chancellor held that the claimant's private law proceedings were not an abuse of process he did not exclude the prospect of such a finding in a different case. In terms of principle he held, essentially, as follows:

(1) It was common ground that the proceedings could have been brought either by judicial review or by ordinary action.

(2) Accordingly, the judgments of Lord Woolf MR and Sedley LJ in *Clark v Humberside University*[217] applied. Those judgments showed that, in a case such as the present, the choice of either judicial review or an ordinary action may constitute an abuse of process depending on the particular facts.[218]

(3) How to exercise the abuse of process jurisdiction will depend on all the relevant circumstances including matters occurring before the proceedings were instituted and which remedy is, in the circumstances, the most appropriate.

(4) However, there is no necessary abuse merely because proceedings involve a consideration of the duties of the Crown under EC law and might have been brought by an application for judicial review.

5.181 As can be seen, the Vice Chancellor relied heavily on the judgments in *Clark* which analysed the relationship between judicial review and private law in some detail albeit nor from the perspective of an EC damages challenge. Since *Phonographic Performance* involved allegations

---

[217] [2000] 1 WLR 1988.

[218] It seems clear from *Clark* (see n 217 above) that it is not the wrong choice of procedure that matters. What matters is the substantive consequences and obtaining of a procedural advantage (as, eg, time limits) flowing from the particular choice of procedure. If, eg, a claimant has brought proceedings well in time it will not matter that the procedure chosen should have been different. The court will look at the matter as one of substance rather than procedure: see *Clark*, per Lord Woolf MR paras 34–38.

of breach of EC law engaging State liability that case is authority for the proposition that the principles stated in *Clark* apply equally in an EC context. The most accurate formulation of legal principle in *Clark* was enunciated by Sedley LJ at para 17 who said:

> ... the CPR now enable the Court to prevent the unfair exploitation of the longer limitation period for civil suits without resorting to a rigid exclusionary rule capable of doing equal and opposite injustice. Just as on a judicial review application the Court may enlarge time if justice so requires, in a civil suit it may now intervene, notwithstanding the currency of the limitation period, if the entirety of circumstances—including of course the availability of judicial review—demonstrates that the Court's processes are being misused, or if it is clear that because of the lapse of time or other circumstances no worthwhile relief can be expected.

This formulation suggests that a claim for damages for breach of EC law against a State **5.182** emanation that could have been (but was not) commenced by way of judicial review but that is brought well within a six-year limitation period is unlikely, in many if not most instances, to be struck out as an abuse of process provided that there is no obvious unmeritorious conduct involving misuse of the court's process. Circumstances in which this might well occur, however, are where a damages claim is brought merely to avoid the operation of judicial review time limits. However, even where a claim is brought genuinely, it cannot be assumed that a claimant has the full six years to bring the claim. In deciding the appropriate limita-tion period the court will, as *Clark* shows, have regard to all the circumstances including the availability of judicial review.

The flexible approach articulated in *Clark* has particular resonance in the sphere of alleged **5.183** breaches of EC law where the State is, as a matter of EC law, at least in principle under a continuing duty pursuant to Article 10 (ex 5) EC to nullify the unlawful consequences of a breach of EC law[219] and where an over-restrictive limitation period could affect the effectiveness of ensuring that this duty is fulfilled. Nonetheless, the Court of Appeal in *Noble*[220] has recently held that a judicial review challenge to an administrative decision that is contended to violate EC law will be out of time if the decision is itself dependent on the legal validity of earlier decisions that have not themselves been challenged by way of judicial review. This decision sits uneasily with the approach taken in cases such as *Clark* and *Phonographic Performance* since the effectiveness of the court's control of State reparation for breaches of EC law ought not, it is submitted, to depend in terms of time limits solely on whether a claimant has or does not have a claim in damages.

Comparing HRA and domestic causes of action for damages for public law default

In purely domestic (ie non-HRA) public law there is currently,[221] no cause of action for **5.184** damages for misuse of public power. This is unsatisfactory but, if a case is outside the scope of EC or HRA law, the only available remedy in respect of financial loss occasioned by administrative acts or omissions is that afforded by a private law cause of action on the

---

[219] See Case C-201/02 *R (Wells) v Secretary of State for Transport, Local Government and the Regions* [2004] ECR I–723, para 64. cf also the related notion of continuing duty: see paras 5.178–5.179.

[220] *R (Noble Organisation) v Thanet District Council* [2005] EWCA Civ 782, [2006] Env LR 8.

[221] The Law Commission is including claims against public authorities as part of its ninth programme of law reform.

same facts. If there is no private law cause of action there is no remedy. If there is a private law cause of action then damages may be awarded in judicial review proceedings as a procedural convenience.

5.185   There are three potential torts likely to be available in respect of loss arising from public law default, These are: (1) misfeasance in public office,[222] (2) breach of statutory duty, and (3) negligence. However, the first two are of limited utility. Misfeasance in public office is a rare event and, in the context of breach of statutory claims, Scott Baker J has pointedly observed that there is 'a considerable reluctance on the part of the courts to impose upon local authorities any liability for breach of statutory duty other than that expressly imposed in the statute'.[223]

5.186   Negligence as a tort against public bodies is a complex subject and beyond the scope of this book. However, the principal hurdle is that of establishing a duty of care. In the context of exercise of public power this is not necessarily easy to establish and relies on the threefold test enunciated by the House of Lords in *Caparo Industries v Dickman*[224] namely: (1) the harm suffered by the claimant must have been a foreseeable consequence of the act complained of, (2) there must have been a sufficient proximity between the parties, and (3) it must have been fair, just, and reasonable to impose a duty of care in the circumstances of the case.

5.187   As far as the HRA is concerned, claims for damages for public default are likely to arise by virtue of a public authority's acts or omissions in the public law arena that infringe Convention rights. Importantly, however, damages are not automatically awarded for Convention breaches (as they would be if a private law cause of action were established).

5.188   There is, as with EC law, a threshold requirement although that requirement is not whether the breach is 'sufficiently serious'. As the Court of Appeal formulated the test in *Anufrijeva v London Borough of Southwark*[225] (see para 56 of the court's judgment):

> In considering whether to award compensation and, if so, how much, there is a balance to be drawn between the interests of the victim and those of the public as a whole . . . The court has a wide discretion in respect of the award of damages for breach of human rights . . . Damages are not an automatic entitlement but . . . a remedy of 'last resort'.

5.189   In summary, it is, at least in the public law context, easier to secure an award of damages for a breach of EC law than it is either as a matter of domestic law (where it is only available as a private law cause of action) or under the HRA (where it is predominantly discretionary). This should be carefully borne in mind when formulating grounds for a damages claim with potentially overlapping EC, HRA, and domestic law elements.

---

[222] See, especially, *Three Rivers District Council v Bank of England (No 3)* [2003] AC 1.
[223] *T v Surrey County Council* [1994] 4 All ER 577, 597.
[224] [1990] 2 AC 605.
[225] [2003] EWCA Civ 1406, [2004] 2 WLR 603. The generally restrictive approach suggested in *Anufrijeva* was approved by the House of Lords in *R v Secretary of State for the Home Department, ex p Greenfield* [2005] UKHL 14. See, especially, paras 9 and 30, per Lord Bingham.

Part II

UNDERLYING GENERAL PRINCIPLES IN EC LAW JUDICIAL REVIEW CHALLENGES

6

GENERAL PRINCIPLES OF EC LAW—
AN OVERVIEW

A. What Are General Principles of EC Law?

From the perspective of national courts in public law cases interpreting and applying national **6.01**
measures and/or omissions falling within the scope of EC law, EC law has, for practical purposes, two clear sources. These are: (1) the EC Treaty itself and (2) EC secondary legislation.
However, in a subtly different way, certain so called 'general principles of law' identified and
developed by the ECJ now constitute an important further source of EC law that must be
carefully borne in mind in the conduct of domestic judicial review proceedings.

These general principles are those drawn from the 'constitutional traditions common to the **6.02**
member states' or from 'international treaties for the protection of human rights on which
the member states have collaborated or of which they are signatories'.[1] As explained in more
detail below, these principles essentially represent norms by which the content and legality
of Community legislation and derivative national measures and administrative or executive
acts and decisions are to be interpreted and/or applied.

---

[1] Case 4/73 J. *Nold KG v Commission* [1974] ECR 491.

6.03 The development of such general principles is probably an inevitable result of the need to create rules of law to determine issues not provided for in existing Community legislation. The influence of the national systems of law of different Member States on the expanding jurisprudence of the ECJ has, apart from providing an obvious analytical framework for the resolution of these issues, served to reduce the potential for conflict between the Community legal order (doctrinally supreme)[2] and the legal order of the Member States. This is, perhaps, especially so in the case of national laws deriving from international treaties outside the ostensible scope of EC law as, most notably, in the fields of public international law and human rights and appears to be one reason for the ECJ in *Nold*[3] placing emphasis on international human rights treaties as a source of general principles.

6.04 However, despite the close connection between EC general principles of law and the legal values and protections accorded by at least some of the Member States there are a number of important distinctions that must be understood when seeking to apply these general principles in EC public law cases before the Administrative Court and other national courts

6.05 First, and most obviously, the general principles represent standards by which *EC* law must be interpreted and applied. This means that, unlike a new *intra vires* EC legislative provision, the general principles do not themselves extend the scope of EC law. They are constrained in their legal effect in that they operate only within the proper scope of EC law. Thus, for example, the fact that a national measure may contravene a general principle of EC law is not, of itself, sufficient to invalidate the national measure unless it is a measure that is within the scope of application of EC law. The proper scope of EC law has not been authoritatively determined but it is significant in that it affects the practical operation of each of the general principles and may be decisive in resolving whether a particular principle can be deployed in an application for judicial review or other proceedings before national courts where public law issues are ventilated.

6.06 Secondly, general principles of EC law have functions that, whilst complementary to the purposes of EC legislation, do not replicate those purposes. In effect, so far as domestic public law is concerned there are at least five functions of such principles being to:

(1) assist in, and sometimes to determine, the proper interpretation of EC legislation (ie Treaty provisions[4] and secondary legislation[5]);[6]

(2) assist in, and sometimes to determine, the proper interpretation of national measures;[7]

---

[2] See paras 2.60–2.89.

[3] See n1 above and text.

[4] See, eg, Case 6/72 *Europemballage Corp and Continental Can Co Inc v Commission* [1973] ECR 215, 244–5.

[5] See, eg, Case 155/79 *AM & S Europe Ltd v Commission* [1982] ECR 1575, 1610–12.

[6] Importantly, the national courts may not pronounce EC legislation to be invalid but they may interpret Treaty provisions and/or pronounce Community secondary legislation to be valid or refer to the ECJ under Art 234 (ex 177) EC for a preliminary ruling as to validity. It follows that in undertaking these various tasks the national court will need to be aware of this aspect of the interpretative functions of EC general principles of law and also, of course, of the way in which the ECJ has used general principles to interpret EC Treaty provisions and secondary legislation in cases such as those referred to in nn 4–5 above. See, further, paras 6.51–6.62.

[7] The term 'national measures' encompasses, of course, primary and secondary legislation as well as administrative decisions and other acts and omissions.

(3) provide a basis for challenging the legality of EC legislation;[8]
(4) provide a basis for challenging the legality of national measures;[9]
(5) provide a basis for establishing State liability in damages.[10]

In this fashion, general principles of EC law afford both a *structure* for interpreting the nature **6.07** and scope of Treaty and other Community legislative obligations (including national measures within the scope of EC law) *and* a *standard* by which the legality of such obligations/measures can be assessed.

Finally, it is relevant to note the sources and status of general principles of EC law in the **6.08** Community legal order itself. Not only does that facilitate an understanding of the contrasting functions of the principles outlined above; it also enables material distinctions to be drawn between: (1) general principles and fundamental Treaty rights, and (2) general principles and similar, but by no means identical, concepts in national law, public international law and under the ECHR. For present purposes it is to be observed that—as with the autonomous nature of certain ECHR concepts—it should not be assumed that general principles of EC law are synonymous with domestic public law (or ECHR) concepts even if they are referred to by the same generic label.

This has particular significance in judicial review proceedings where, as has been emphasized, **6.09** the Administrative Court will frequently have to examine arguments in the same case based on three different jurisdictions (EC, ECHR, and domestic law). Each of those jurisdictions may require deployment of a concept such as, for example, equal treatment. However, as will be seen, this notion does not have the same substantive content in either ECHR or domestic law as it does as a general principle of EC law.[11]

So, in utilizing EC general principles of law in public law cases, the national court must **6.10** undertake the following exercise. It must:

(1) identify the EC general principle or principles of law (and its/their true content) at issue;
(2) decide whether the case is one to which the principles are engaged: that is, whether or not, in particular, the case is one within the scope of EC law;
(3) use the relevant principle(s) to interpret,[12] or (as the case may be) determine the legality of, a national measure (including administrative acts and omissions) and/or to interpret the scope of an EC measure or determine that EC secondary legislation is valid;[13]
(4) insofar as there is an associated damages claim use the relevant principle(s) to determine State liability in damages.[14]

---

[8] For the reasons outlined in n 6 above, the nature of such challenge will in domestic public law proceedings be indirect and will, in practice, amount to the claimant seeking a reference to the ECJ under Article 234 (ex 177) EC unless a direct challenge can be made to the ECJ under Article 230 (ex 173) EC if the requisite *locus standi* can be shown: see, further, paras 3.67–3.80.

[9] See n 7 above.

[10] Whether such a claim should be commenced by way of judicial review or in a damages action is considered separately at paras 5.172–5.183.

[11] See Chapter 7 generally.

[12] This exercise of interpretation may, of course, require interpretation of a Treaty provision which will itself be interpreted consistently with general principles of EC law.

[13] Subject, always, to the important proviso that the court cannot pronounce on the *invalidity* of a Community measure: see n 6 above.

[14] As to which, see paras 5.85–5.171.

6.11 The content of the general principles of law enunciated, thus far, by the ECJ is covered in some detail in Chapters 7–12. This Chapter addresses the relevant functions of the national court, especially the Administrative Court in respect of those principles where public law issues are engaged.

B. Identifying the General Principles

6.12 The ECJ has identified a number of general principles. However, these categories are not closed and are likely to increase as new issues are raised in the cases.

6.13 At present, the main general principles[15] accepted by the ECJ include:

(1) The principle of *equal treatment* or *non-discrimination* (Chapter 7 below). This reflects the fact that, apart from specific Treaty provisions and other instruments relating to particular aspects of discrimination as, for example, nationality (Article 12 (ex 6) EC) and pay (Article 141(ex 119) EC) there is a general principle that comparable situations ought not to be treated differently without some objective justification.[16] This principle is of potentially very broad scope and has been interpreted generously by the ECJ. It contains both procedural[17] and substantive elements.

(2) The principle of *legal certainty*[18] which is sometimes subdivided into: (a) *legitimate expectations* (Chapter 8 below), and (b) *non-retroactivity* (Chapter 9 below). Legitimate expectations,[19] a concept derived from German law, entails the consequence that a measure must not, absent an overriding public interest, violate the reasonable expectation of the party or parties concerned engendered by conduct on the part of the EC institutions or the State. There are important differences between the EC concept of legitimate expectations and the domestic concept bearing the same name. In particular, in EC law an expectation that is not a *reasonable* one is not recognized as a *legitimate* expectation.[20] The principle of non-retroactivity, in general terms, prevents a measure from having legal effect before its publication.[21] Non-retroactivity is, however, rather more complicated than that and includes, for example, consideration of measures having effects on transactions that are not yet complete by the time that the measure comes to be published.

---

[15] There are many other principles which are sometimes referred to as general principles of EC law. These include the principles of effectiveness and equivalence which underpin a number of procedural and substantive guarantees. They may also include, where appropriate, other well-established principles such as those of subsidiarity (decisions to be taken at the lowest level of authority for effective decision-making).

[16] See, eg, Cases 103 and 145/77 *Royal Scholten-Honig (Holdings) Ltd v Intervention Board for Agricultural Produce* [1978] ECR 2037. Similarly, on the same basis, dissimilar cases ought not to be treated in the same way without such justification.

[17] Both the procedural principles of equivalence and effectiveness are founded, at least in some measure, on the principle of equal treatment: see paras 7.12 et seq.

[18] The principle of legal certainty may also be said to encompass the principle of legality which requires the acts of EC institutions and national authorities to be in accordance with law.

[19] See, eg, Case 112/77 *August Topfer & Co GmbH v Commission* [1978] ECR 1019.

[20] See, eg, Cases 95–98/74, 15, 100/75 *Union Nationale des Cooperatives Agricoles de Cereales v Commission* [1975] ECR 1615.

[21] See, eg, Case 88/76 *Société pour l'Exportation des Sucres v Commission* [1977] ECR 709.

As with most, if not all, of the general principles exceptional cases (or classes of case) may justify measures or acts that would, otherwise, constitute a breach of EC law.

(3) A number of procedural principles (Chapter 10 below) taking the overall form of the right to a fair hearing.[22] These are closely akin to the due process rights under Article 6 ECHR and the protection accorded under domestic natural justice rules although, as will be seen, there are some differences of emphasis. These rights include a duty to give reasons,[23] as well as the right to 'pursue ... claims by judicial process after possible recourse to the competent authorities'.[24] They also include a limited protection against self-incrimination.[25]

(4) The proportionality principle (Chapter 11 below). This very important principle, again derived from German law, prevents interference with a Community right save to the extent that the interference is strictly necessary to attain a legitimate Community purpose.[26] This general principle is now referred to expressly in the Treaties (see Article 5(3) (ex Article 3b(2)) EC).[27] There is a considerable overlap between EC proportionality and the protection of fundamental human rights since the proportionality principle is often invoked by public bodies as justification for interference with such rights. Proportionality is also highly relevant to the legality of derogation from Treaty rights by Member States. It is often a competing general principle justifying non-compliance with another general principle. For example, the principle of equal treatment may be departed from if there is objective justification. One of the means by which objective justification may be established is that the discriminatory treatment is proportionate to the Community interest sought to be achieved.[28] In EC law there is a different intensity of review of the proportionality of measures depending on the context. In general, EC legislation is accorded a wider measure of deference by reference to proportionality than is a domestic measure.

(5) The protection of fundamental human rights (Chapter 12 below). As can be seen from the general principles already mentioned, many of the principles articulated by the ECJ overlap with the protection of fundamental human rights. Yet there is a difference in that each of the principles mentioned are as relevant to the protection of fundamental *Treaty* rights as they are to fundamental *human* rights. The two are not synonymous. However, the ECJ has increasingly recognized that fundamental human rights constitute a relevant standard by which the interpretation of EC legislation should be judged and the legality of measures taken in pursuance of, or derogation from, EC law rights should be determined. In this respect although it is not a direct source of EC law the ECHR has a 'special significance'.[29] The provisions of the ECHR are now frequently referred to in the jurisprudence of the ECJ. Although there have been occasions on which the ECJ has interpreted ECHR provisions differently from the European Court of Human

---

[22] See, eg, Case 17/74 *Transocean Marine Paint Association v Commission* [1974] ECR 1063.

[23] Case 222/86 *UNECTEF v Heylens* [1987] ECR 4097.

[24] Case 222/84 *Johnston v Chief Constable of the RUC* [1986] ECR 1651.

[25] Case C–60/92 *Otto BV v Postbank NV* [1993] ECR I–5683.

[26] Of the many cases see, eg, Case 62/70 *Werner A Brock KG v Commission* [1971] ECR 897.

[27] It should also be noted that Art 5(3) (ex 3b(2)) embraces the principle of subsidiarity. It provides that the Community may take action 'only if and in so far as' the objectives of the proposed action cannot be sufficiently achieved by the Member States. This principle is, however, really an aspect of proportionality albeit one that determines whether Community action is necessary in the first place.

[28] See, generally, Chapter 11.

[29] See *Opinion 2/94 on Accession by the Community to the ECHR* [1996] ECR I–1759 para 33.

Rights in Strasbourg[30] this is not normally intentional. However, there is at least the potential for conflict between Luxembourg and Strasbourg case law. This, in turn, presents a jurisdictional conundrum for the Administrative Court. The problems that can occur are separately examined.[31]

C. A Structured Approach to Understanding the Source and Content of the Principles

6.14 There are three Treaty provisions that provide a theoretical basis for application of general principles of law and an understanding of how to approach their true content. They are:

(1) Article 220 (ex 164) EC. This stipulates that: 'The Court of Justice shall ensure that in the interpretation and application of this Treaty the law is observed.' That provision referring, as it does, to an undefined corpus of law, ostensibly free-standing from the Treaty, has been interpreted by the ECJ as conferring jurisdiction on it to draw inspiration from the laws of the Member States.[32] It is to be noted that Article 220 itself expressly picks up the twin functions of general principles of law, namely interpretation and determination of the legality of administrative acts and omissions purporting to be in conformity with EC law. Equally, however, (see also below) Article 220 makes it clear that the role of general principles is limited to interpreting and applying *the Treaty* so that such principles cannot be utilised as a separate source of EC law divorced from their relationship with Community rights created by the Treaty.

(2) Article 230 (ex 173) EC. This confers jurisdiction on the ECJ to judicially review the legality of acts of the Community by annulment of the act in question if invalid. The grounds for such review by way of direct action before the ECJ include 'infringement of [the] Treaty, or of any rule of law relating to its application'. Once again, therefore, the text presupposes a free-standing body of law to be applied by the ECJ albeit one that relates to the application of the Treaty. Further, Article 230 must be read in conjunction with Article 220 (above). So, if general principles of law are (see Article 220) relevant to interpretation of the Treaty it follows that they are equally relevant to determining whether there has been an infringement of the Treaty.

(3) Article 288 (ex 25) EC (second paragraph). This is concerned with State liability in tort (non-contractual liability). It contains a direct reference to the general principles providing that such liability is to be decided 'in accordance with the general principles common to the laws of the Member States'.

6.15 Thus, the source of the general principles of law appears to be Treaty-based. It may be inferred that the legal status of such principles is higher than, since logically prior to, both Community secondary legislation and national measures. Further, although the general principles of law are jurisdictionally to be derived from the Treaty, the proper interpretation and scope of the Treaty is itself, in large measure, founded on application of those principles.

---

[30] See para 12.100.

[31] See paras 12.128–12.139.

[32] See Joined Cases C–43 and C–48/93 *Brasserie du Pecheur v Germany, R v Secretary of State for Transport, ex p Factortame Ltd* [1996] ECR I–1029, paras 27 and 41.

For these reasons it seems clear, first, that the content of the general principles is not **6.16** dependent on some minimum, but universal, content of the national systems of law of the Member States. As explained by Advocate General Lagrange:[33]

> ... the case law of the Court, in so far as it invokes national laws (as it does to a large extent) to define the rules of law relating to the application of the Treaty, is not content to draw on more or less arithmetical 'common denominators' between the different national solutions, but chooses from each of the Member States those solutions which, having regard to the objects of the Treaty, appear to be the best or, if one may use the expression, the most progressive ...

This has significant implications for resolving EC public law issues in the domestic courts **6.17** especially in judicial review applications. If the content of a general principle is selected for EC law purposes by the ECJ by reference to the most preferable solutions adopted by the national courts of different Member States, it follows that different—but in the ECJ's view less preferable—formulations of the same principle by the courts of other Member States will not form the content of the EC general principle.[34] This is, for example, true of the EC general principle of equal treatment which has a strong substantive (as well as procedural) content that has no precise analogue in domestic public law.[35] Similarly, the general principle of legitimate expectations is different from the principle of the same name espoused in domestic law in that the EC general principle is, without doubt, substantive in nature (as well as procedural) but is limited to legitimate expectations that are reasonable.[36]

A second, and crucial, aspect to bear in mind when examining the content of general prin- **6.18** ciples is that the same principle may be different and/or have to be applied differently in particular contexts. Certain principles may, in fact, not even be relevant (or have limited relevance) in other contexts.

For example, although general principles may, *as a class*, be used both to interpret and to apply **6.19** EC law (including national measures), procedural principles—such as the right to a fair hearing—are usually inapposite to interpret or to determine the legality of an EC legislative provision. Presumably, though, a Community or national legislative provision would, in an appropriate case, have to be interpreted so as to accord the right to a fair hearing and/or its legality have to be determined by reference to whether or not it complied with such principle.[37]

Similarly, as earlier explained, some general principles, most notably proportionality, bear **6.20** a different intensity of review depending on the context. So far as proportionality is concerned, the Community legislature is, for example, given a particularly broad discretionary area of judgment in macro areas of activity such as economic and social policy. The Community legislature generally enjoys, in any event, a degree of proportionality

---

[33] Case 14/61 *Hoogovens v High Authority* [1962] ECR 253, 283–4.

[34] It seems, though, that the ECJ does require observance by all Member States of at least some common core of principle before it is capable of constituting a general principle of law: see, eg, Cases 46/87 and 227/88 *Hoechst AG v Commission* [1989] ECR 2859.

[35] See paras 7.103–7.127.

[36] The parallels and differences between the EC and national doctrines are explored more fully at paras 8.01–8.17.

[37] Consider, eg, Case 98/79 *Pecastaing v Belgium* [1980] ECR 691 where, though there was no challenge to the legality of that provision, the ECJ observed that Art 8 of Directive (EEC) 64/221 fulfilled the requirements of a 'fair hearing' within the meaning of Art 6 ECHR.

deference from the ECJ greater than that of the Member States who are, by their national measures, most commonly responsible for implementing Community law or for justifying particular derogations from it. The area of penalties or sanctions is, however, one where—affecting as they do particularly strong fundamental human rights—both Community and national authorities are subject to a higher intensity level of judicial review by reference to the proportionality principle.[38]

6.21 A further, important, contextual aspect is that EC general principles will be applied stringently in relation to derogation from provisions of EC law of national measures.[39]

6.22 In summary, the process of identifying the content of a general principle of EC law is not unlike that engaged in comparative law where, for example, the fact that a human right is given the same name by a different legal system does not necessarily mean that the right engaged has the same legal content. Consideration must be given to the terms of the Constitution of the legal system in question and the overall context in which the right has been conferred.

D. Are EC General Principles of Law Engaged?

6.23 Having ascertained the relevant EC general principle of law and its content there is a further prior question, namely whether the domestic court has jurisdiction to apply the principle in question. Here, two broad issues arise which are: (1) whether the case is within the scope of EC law and (if so) (2) if, and how, the principle can be applied to the parties before the court or private third parties affected by the court's judgment. The first question is, in terms of precise definition, by far the most difficult. Only once each is answered, however, can EC general principles of law properly be applied to the particular case.

Cases clearly within the scope of EC law

6.24 The same problem arises, albeit sometimes in differently expressed form, in relation to each of the general principles. As has been seen, the jurisdiction to develop general principles appears to be derived from specific Treaty provisions. However, the general principles have a direct relationship to the Treaty provisions in that they are the means by which such provisions are to be interpreted and applied.

6.25 This is another way of saying that unless the case is, in some way, affected by the scope of a Treaty provision it is not a case within the scope of EC law and the general principles are not capable of engaging.

6.26 Certain categories of case are obviously within the scope of EC law so as to attract the operation of EC general principles of law. These categories comprise those cases:

(1) involving the interpretation of a Treaty provision;
(2) where issues of interpretation of EC legislation arise;

---

[38] See generally Chapter 11, especially paras 11.56–11.63.
[39] This issue is, by definition, only likely to arise in the context of *national* legislative, administrative or executive measures. As to the case law see, eg: *Thomas v Adjudication Officer* [1991] 2 QB. 164; *R v MAFF, ex p Portman Agrochemicals Ltd* [1994] 3 CMLR 18; *Consorzio del Prosciotto di Parma v Asda Stores Ltd* [1998] 2 CMLR 215.

(3) challenging the legality of Community legislation or other acts (including omissions) of the Community institutions;

(4) raising the proper interpretation, and/or legality, of national measures purporting to implement, or derogate from, a Treaty provision or other Community legislation;

(5) raising the legality of acts or omissions of an emanation of the State that are *directly* based upon a Community law or national measure purporting to implement EC law[40] (as, for example, an environmental impact assessment undertaken—or (as the case may be) *not* undertaken—by a local authority prior to the grant of planning permission).

The Administrative Court may, on an application for judicial review, have to consider the relevance of EC general principles of law in each of the above cases. Cases where the role of that court in utilizing general principles of law is clear are those involving consideration of national measures (see (4) and (5) immediately above).   **6.27**

Sometimes, however, the role of the national court in relation to general principles of EC law is more oblique. The proper interpretation of a national measure may, for example, be contingent on the proper interpretation of an underlying Community measure such as a directive. The Administrative Court in particular has jurisdiction to pronounce on the *legality* of a Community measure though not on its *invalidity*.[41] Therefore, in such a case, the court might seek (and be able) to interpret the Community measure consistently with the general principles. The resulting interpretation would be likely, in such a case, to determine the meaning of the national measure.   **6.28**

Or, the court may be faced with a straightforward challenge to the legality of a national measure where the legality of that measure is entirely dependent on the legality of an EC measure.[42] In reality, such a challenge is a disguised challenge to the validity of EC legislation. If the national court takes the view, by reference to EC general principles of law, that the Community measure may itself be unlawful then it will usually decide to refer the case to the ECJ under Article 234 (ex 177) EC for a preliminary ruling.[43]   **6.29**

In all these instances, however, there is no doubt that the case is one to which EC general principles of law may apply. Jurisdictional problems will arise where the case is not so clear-cut.   **6.30**

Cases that are outside the scope of EC law—the principle

The ECJ has not confronted directly the principle that regulates whether a case is within or outside the scope of EC law. As a preliminary observation, the problem appears to arise only in respect of *national* measures since, *ex hypothesi*, a Treaty provision and dependent Community legislation are within the scope of EC law.   **6.31**

---

[40] The Treaty provisions themselves are, as the foundation of EC law obligations, of course not susceptible to annulment by any court (including the ECJ).

[41] See, further, paras 5.57–5.60.

[42] For the issues that this can give rise to in respect of interim relief, see paras 3.137–3.142.

[43] As to this, see paras 4.92–4.98.

6.32   First principles suggest that a case will fall outside the boundaries of EC law (and so not be amenable to application of the EC general principles) where a national measure is not, in some fashion, directed towards implementing, fulfilling, or derogating from, a provision of EC law. But such a formulation begs the question of the nature of the connection required to be established between the measure and the Treaty before finding that the case is within the scope of Community law.

6.33   The issue arose directly in *R v MAFF, ex p First City Trading*.[44] This case is analysed in other chapters where it arises specifically in respect of the general principle of law at stake.[45] It is, however, of significance in the analysis of the overall boundaries of such principles.

6.34   *First City Trading* involved a judicial review challenge to the legality of the Beef Stocks Transfer Scheme. The claim arose because of the UK Government's compensation scheme for emergency financial assistance to the slaughtering industry consequent upon financial losses suffered following a Commission decision banning exports of British beef in response to the BSE crisis.[46]

6.35   The claimants were meat exporters who, because they lacked slaughtering and cutting facilities, were not entitled to compensation under the national scheme. The claim was brought on the basis that the national scheme was in violation of the EC general principle of equality.

6.36   Such argument assumed that the national measure (the compensation scheme) was within the scope of EC law. But this premise was rejected. In respect of general principles of law, Laws J observed that:

> It is by no means self-evident that their contextual scope must be the same as that of Treaty provisions relating to discrimination or equal treatment—which are statute law taking effect according to their own, express terms.[47]

6.37   That passage is, perhaps, surprising given the fact that at least in respect of certain Treaty provisions (including Article 12 (ex 6) EC—prohibition of discrimination on grounds of nationality) the ECJ has held that the Treaty provision is merely a particular aspect of the general principle.[48] It is also surprising because the scope of Article 12 itself has consistently been applied very broadly by the ECJ.[49]

6.38   However, the fact that Laws J's rejection of the argument that the UK compensation scheme was outside the scope of EC law may be open to criticism does not mean that the *principles* that he enunciated in *First City Trading* are wrong. In particular, it is submitted that he was surely correct in holding that:

> ... There is no legal space for the application of the general principles of law to any measure or decision taken otherwise than in pursuance of Treaty rights or obligations. No court can expand the Treaty provisions. The position is altogether different where a measure is adopted *pursuant* to Community law; ... Then, the internal law of the Court of Justice applies.

---

[44] [1997] 1 CMLR 250.
[45] See paras 7.88–7.104.
[46] That is, Decision 96/239 (see [1996] OJ L78/47).
[47] [1997] I CMLR 250, para 39.
[48] See, eg, Case 147/89 *Hochstrass v European Court of Justice* [1980] ECR 3005, para 7.
[49] See paras 7.73–7.78.

First City Trading is to be contrasted with the earlier case of *R v MAFF, ex p Hamble Fisheries* **6.39** *(Offshore) Ltd.*[50] There, a judicial review challenge was issued by the claimants who relied on the EC general principle of legitimate expectations to support the argument that they were entitled to qualify for a licence. In 1984 MAFF had published a policy permitting the transfer of fishing licences in respect of EC quotas from one vessel to another. However, in 1992 MAFF changed its policy and refused to permit such transfers. In 1987 the claimants had purchased a vessel in the expectation that they would qualify for a licence.

Although, in the event, the judicial review challenge was dismissed the Administrative **6.40** Court applied the EC general principle of legitimate expectations to the facts of the case. This was because, as Sedley J observed:

> although the exercise is the formulation of policy within a discretion conferred entirely by domestic legislation, the purpose of legislation and policy alike is to permit the UK, under the principle of subsidiarity,[51] to exercise its powers for the purposes of implementing the common fisheries policy of the European Community.

So, in *Hamble*, unlike *First City Trading*, the relevant context was one in which a national **6.41** measure was taken in pursuance of EC law to the extent that such measure was necessary to give effect to EC law. This was so even though EC law did not require the particular measure to be adopted.

Importantly, then, it is the *context* that will—at least in cases where the connection with EC **6.42** law is not obviously remote[52]—determine whether or not the case is one falling within the scope of EC law. *First City Trading* suggests that reference to the general context of a specific Treaty provision does not necessarily compel the conclusion that a complementary general principle of EC law is engaged. That may be so though whether it is so in the case of a Treaty provision such as Article 12 (ex 6) EC is, perhaps, open to question. However, the relevant point appears to be that there must be a sufficiently strong contextual relationship between a requirement of EC law on the one hand and a national measure on the other. That is, it is submitted, the true meaning of the phrase, emphasized by Laws J in *First City Trading*, 'measure … adopted pursuant to Community law'.

Properly understood, therefore, *Hamble* and *First City Trading* are reconcilable. On that **6.43** basis neither case appears to preclude instances where national measures may be said to be within the ambit of EC general principles of law despite the fact that the discretion on the public body in question is one conferred entirely by national law and even though EC law does not require that the national measure be adopted.[53]

It may be—though the issue has not been clarified by the ECJ—that national measures **6.44** will have a sufficiently strong contextual relationship with Community law (so as to engage

---

[50] [1995] 2 All ER 714.

[51] As to subsidiarity, see n 27 above.

[52] For such a case see, eg, Case C–299/95 *Kremzow v Austria* [1997] ECR I–2405 where the applicant claimed compensation for unlawful detention consequent upon a sentence of life imprisonment imposed after a trial found to be in breach of Art 6 ECHR. The claim was held to fall outside the scope of EC law. The ECJ held that the purely hypothetical prospect of exercising the right of free movement did not establish a sufficient connection with EC law. Further, the applicant's sentence was under a domestic law which was not designed to secure compliance with any rule of EC law.

[53] This is supported by the principle of subsidiarity: see n 27 above and para 6.13.

the general principles) where, for example, such measures have an impact on interests that are within the ambit of specific Community legislation.

6.45 In this and other respects the effect of Article 10 (ex 5) EC[54] should be borne in mind. That provision requires Member States:

> to take all appropriate measures ... to ensure fulfilment of the obligations arising out of this Treaty or resulting from action taken by the institutions of the Community ... They shall abstain from any measure which could jeopardise the attainment of the objectives of this Treaty.

6.46 So, national measures which have the potential to jeopardize Treaty objectives fall within the scope of Community law and are to be interpreted by reference to general principles of EC law.[55]

6.47 In cases involving consideration of national measures where the issue of EC jurisdiction arises, the task of the national (in most cases the Administrative) Court is to assess the nature and purpose of the measure. The fact that a discretion may be conferred by national law, as opposed to being derived directly from a specific Treaty provision or other Community legislation, does not necessarily mean that the measure is outside the scope of Community law. It is submitted that the regulating principle is whether or not there is a sufficiently strong link with the Treaty to justify interpreting or determining legality by reference to EC general principles of law. In deciding that question reference may properly, it is submitted, be made to the case law of the ECJ on the scope of Treaty provisions such as Article 12 (ex 6) EC which have, in the light of EC general principles, been interpreted broadly.[56]

Parties within the scope of the principles

6.48 As with other provisions of EC law, public bodies, as emanations of the State,[57] are—if the case is otherwise within the scope of Community law (see above)—bound to comply with EC general principles of law.

6.49 So, all national legislative measures—if they are otherwise within the scope of Community law—are amenable to application of the relevant EC general principles. Subject to the same caveat, administrative decisions, acts, and defaults susceptible to domestic judicial review are also likely to be within the ambit of the principles as, at least generally, are other functions over which the State exercises some control. At present, therefore, the notion of a State emanation for the purposes of Community law control appears to be wider than under the domestic judicial review jurisdiction or the court's jurisdiction under the HRA, s 6 in relation to 'public authorities'.[58]

---

[54] This important Treaty provision itself reflects what might be termed a general EC principle of solidarity.

[55] Thus where, eg, the Member State is acting in an area outside the scope of EC law but its act is likely adversely to affect the application of an EC measure, the general EC principle of proportionality is engaged: Cases C–286/94, C–340/95, C–401.05 and C–47/96 *Garage Molenheide v Belgium* [1997] ECR I–7281, paras 41–48.

[56] As to this see paras 7.73–7.78.

[57] For examination of this concept, see paras 2.17–2.29.

[58] See paras 2.28–2.29.

Care is needed where private third parties are affected by the interpretation of Community **6.50**
or national legislative provisions on a judicial review challenge. As has been explained[59]
certain Treaty provisions as, for example, Article 12 (ex 6) EC can, as a matter of interpretation, create directly effective obligations on private parties. It is, however, well established
that directives cannot directly impose obligations on third parties. But directives, properly
interpreted, may result indirectly in obligations being imposed on individuals. Subject to
these points it follows, therefore, that in terms of interpretation general principles of law are
not necessarily excluded because directives or national provisions deriving authority from
such directives will create effects on individual third parties. However, the effect that such
provisions have on individual third parties may well be relevant to the interpretation that
the court reaches and that effect may itself have to be assessed by reference to general principles of law. For example, the effects that a national measure has on individual third parties may constitute a breach of the legitimate expectations of those parties or it may produce
discriminatory effects or, otherwise, be disproportionate in respect of such parties.

E. Using the General Principles of EC Law

Role of the national court in respect of general principles of law

The final task of the national court is to apply the general principle or principles of EC law **6.51**
that it has identified as being engaged, to the particular case. This involves two possible and
separate stages, namely: (1) a process of interpretation, and (2) a process of determination
of legality or illegality of the measure in question (in the case of Community legislation
potential illegality).[60]

The stages are not, necessarily, cumulative. There is a parallel here, with HRA, ss 3–4. The **6.52**
national court is, under HRA, s 3, required to strive to interpret primary and subordinate
legislation compatibly with the ECHR insofar as it is possible to do so. Accordingly, resort
to a declaration of incompatibility under HRA, s 4 only becomes relevant where it is
impossible to avoid it.[61]

In the same way, the national court may, when resorting to general principles of EC law, need **6.53**
only engage in the process of *interpretation*. Indeed, its task may also be limited to one of
interpretation because there is no challenge to the legality of the measure but only competing interpretations of the parties as to what the provision in question actually means.

Alternatively, the national court may only be concerned with the second stage—that of **6.54**
determining legality. This is because questions of interpretation will often apply only in
respect of Treaty provisions, Community legislation or national legislative measures. It will
not arise, any more than it would in the domestic or HRA context, in relation to administrative or executive acts or defaults unless such acts or defaults involve, as they may well, the
interpretation of Community legislation or national legislation derived from EC law.

---

[59] See paras 1.60 et seq.
[60] See paras 5.57 et seq.
[61] See, especially, *R v A (No 2)* [2001] 2 WLR 1546, especially paras 58 and 106.

There, the issue is not one of interpreting such acts or omissions but, rather, of deciding whether they are lawful.

6.55 In many instances, though, the processes will go together. An administrative act or default is alleged to be unlawful because the public body has complied with unlawful Community or national legislation. There, the Administrative Court on a judicial review challenge may have to interpret the allegedly offending legislation and then decide, in the light of its interpretation, whether the public body has acted unlawfully. In these cases the general principles of EC law will be relevant but they will be deployed differently according to whether they are being used to interpret a particular legislative measure or to determine the legality of an administrative act or omission by reference to EC general principles.

Using general principles to interpret Community and national measures

6.56 So far as *interpretation* is concerned the cardinal principle is that Community legislation deriving, as it does, from the Treaties, must be interpreted *so far as is possible* consistently with the general principles of law. This principle extends, first, to the Treaty provisions themselves. Here, the interpretative exercise is not so much one of possibility (since the Treaty provisions are *ex hypothesi* consistent with EC law) as of ensuring that Treaty interpretation does not conflict with a general principle or principles of law.

6.57 Secondly, the principle of interpretation extends to Community legislation including, most notably, regulations and directives. Such Community legislation is, necessarily, subordinate to EC law that—as has been seen—includes the general principles of law. Since those principles are here used to *apply* the Treaty it follows that Community legislation that cannot be interpreted to conform to the general principles is unlawful.

6.58 In its interpretation of Community legislation the ECJ has frequently been able to interpret EC legislative measures so as to comply with general principles of law. Numerous instances of legislation being so construed are referred to in succeeding chapters in respect of each of the general principles covered.

6.59 Finally, general principles are equally relevant to the interpretation of national legislative measures that are within the scope of EC law.

6.60 There are, however, certain constraints on interpretation that have the effect of limiting the clear operation of general principles of law. Some of the relevant constraints are material to arriving at an interpretation that best serves the objectives of the Treaty. Other constraints reflect the fact that there is a necessary limit to the process of interpretation and that if a legislative provision cannot be interpreted to comply with the general principles overall then it will be unlawful.

6.61 The principal limitations on the use to be made in respect of general principles in relation to interpretation of EC and national measures are these:

(1) The general principles are not absolute in nature. Certain principles, such as proportionality, reflect the fact that there may have to be interferences with other general principles (as, for example, with fundamental human rights) provided that the interference is no more than is strictly necessary to achieve a legitimate Community objective. So, for

example, a legislative provision may have to be interpreted as permitting interference with a fundamental human right provided that such interference is proportionate.

(2) Similarly, there may be competing general principles (as, for example, between legal certainty and equal treatment). In order to enable the general principles to work in tandem constraints may have to be placed, *as a matter of interpretation*, on the operation of one or more of the general principles in particular instances.

(3) As will be seen, in many cases the ECJ accords a wide measure of deference to the Community legislature when, for example, legislating in respect of matters of economic or social policy or when evaluating uncertain future effects of legislative provisions.[62] Thus, the use to be made of the general principles themselves in interpreting the content of legislation will, in such instances, be subject to interpretative variation depending on the context.

(4) The general principle of legal certainty may, itself, compel an interpretation of national measures that, *as a matter of interpretation*, denies a national measure from being construed so as to give effect to EC law. Thus, the express wording of a national measure excluding its having effect in particular areas covered by a directive cannot be interpreted otherwise than that the directive remains unimplemented.[63] This is but a sub-set of the more general *contra legem* principle, that applies both to Community and national measures, to the effect that interpretation 'does not oblige a national court to interpret a specific rule . . . *contra legem*'.[64]

(5) Nor, for similar reasons, may Community or national legislation be interpreted so as to be consistent with general principles by adding amendments to 'cure' the plain meaning where, on that plain meaning, such legislation would be invalid.[65]

(6) Special considerations also attach to the interpretation of national legislative measures. Even if such a measure is within the scope of EC law, general principles of law[66] will themselves compel an interpretation of the national measure that neither determines nor aggravates criminal liability on the part of an individual for breaching EC law unless such liability is clearly provided for in the national legislation. So, even if a directive requires Member States to criminalize certain conduct, national 'implementing' legislation will only be interpreted to the precise extent that it creates a specific criminal offence.[67]

In reality, therefore, there are significant limitations on the power of the national court when interpreting Community and national legislative measures by reference to the general principles of law. It is, in particular, not open to the court simply to rewrite legislation or to legislate as opposed to interpret legislation. These constraints run in parallel to similar constraints under the HRA[68] and circumscribe the boundaries of possible interpretation in

6.62

---

63 Case C–111/97 *EvoBus Austria GmbH v Novog* [1998] ECR I–5411, Advocate General Fennelly.
64 See Case C–271/91 *Marshall v Southampton and South West Area Health Authority* [1993] ECR I–4367, 4368, per Advocate General Van Gerven. See also, in relation to Community secondary legislation, Case C–37/89 *Weiser* [1990] ECR I–2395, 2415, per Advocate General Darmon.
65 See Case C–85/90 *Dowling v Ireland* [1992] ECR I–5305, 5319, per Advocate General Jacobs.
66 That is, the principle of legality as a fundamental human right, recognized (eg) in Art 7 ECHR.
67 Case C–106/89 *Marleasing SA v La Comercial Internacional de Alimentacion SA* [1990] ECR I–4135, 4147, per Advocate General Van Gerven. Similar principles may apply to 'civil' sanctions ibid.
68 See, eg, *R v A (No 2)* [2001] 2 WLR 1546.

similar vein to how far it is 'possible' to interpret primary or subordinate domestic legislation compatibly with the ECHR under HRA, s 3.

Using general principles to apply EC law under the Treaty

6.63 As outlined above at paras 6.56 et seq. interpretation is an important aspect of the national court's functions in relation to general principles of law. As important a function, however, is that of using the principles to *apply* EC law in the sense of *determining* whether: (1) a national legislative measure is lawful or unlawful, or (2) an administrative or executive act or default is lawful or unlawful, or (3) EC legislation itself is lawful or *may* be unlawful.

6.64 Determination of whether a national legislative measure is unlawful is, of course, also largely a function of interpreting the measure in question. The relevant principles have been discussed immediately above. However, having interpreted the legislation the question may still arise as to whether the measure is in breach of EC law.

6.65 This could require resolution of other questions beyond simply answering the issues of interpretation. It may, if the point is unclear, be necessary to decide whether there is a binding EC obligation contained in the Treaty or other Community legislation, the nature of that obligation and whether it has been fulfilled in the legislation. It may require the national court to determine whether or not any discretion in terms of implementing Community legislation has been exercised lawfully in the sense of ensuring that the objectives of the Community legislation have, both generally and specifically, been achieved in full.[69] To answer that is itself likely to compel analysis of the relevant Community legislation and/or Treaty provision and a separate application of the general principles of law. For example, in the context of sex discrimination, issues have arisen as to adequacy of remedy.[70] This requires interpreting relevant Community and national law by reference to the general principles as well, then, of assessing the legality of national purported compliance by reference to those principles.

6.66 In determining the legality of national legislative measures by reference to EC law it should not be forgotten that there may also be higher domestic or HRA standards that affect interpretation and/or legality. The fact, for example, that a national law is valid as a matter of EC law does not necessarily mean that it has the same validity under the HRA.[71]

6.67 The Administrative Court in particular will not be concerned with a *direct* challenge to the legality of *Community legislation* but it is frequently required, in judicial review challenges, to examine the legality of Community legislation *indirectly*. This is because national legislative measures or administrative or executive acts or defaults may be based on invalid Community legislation. Here, as has been observed, the Administrative Court cannot pronounce the Community legislation to be *invalid* though it may, if it so determines, pronounce it to be *valid*.[72] Only the ECJ may pronounce on the invalidity of Community legislation.

---

[69] See, eg, Case C–337/89 *Commission v UK* [1992] 1 ECR 6103. For further analysis of these issues in the context of transposition, see paras 11.52–11.55.

[70] See paras 7.28–7.41.

[71] See, further, para 12.138. The converse is not true: a lower national or HRA standard cannot deprive a claimant of the protection of EC law (see para 6.74 and n 75 below).

[72] See para 1.57.

Although, therefore, the Administrative Court will undertake essentially the same functions by reference to general principles of law as in the case of national legislation that purports to implement or derogate from valid EC law it would, in such a case, have to refer the proceedings to the ECJ under Article 234 (ex 177) EC before even being able to find that the *national* legislation was unlawful.

Finally, *provided that the case is within the scope of EC law* (see above) the EC general principles **6.68** of law also play an important role so far as the legality of executive or administrative acts and omissions are concerned. Public bodies are, in such circumstances, themselves under an obligation to comply with those principles in exercising their functions.

This distinctive obligation is exemplified by the facts of *Wachauf*.[73] The applicant, a tenant **6.69** dairy farmer, sought compensation from the German authorities arising out of the discontinuing of milk production on the expiry of his lease by his lessor. The national authority refused compensation on the basis that the national compensation rules were required by Community legislation. However, on a reference under Article 177 (now 234) EC the ECJ held that, properly interpreted, the Community legislation neither precluded nor required compensation.

Importantly, the ECJ held that the Community regulations conferred a power to award com- **6.70** pensation and that this had not been exercised. The national compensation system was, so it was held, 'unacceptable' in that it had the effect of 'depriving the lessee ... of the fruits of his labour'. This was so because the lessor, who had never engaged in milk production, was— under the national scheme—entitled to receive the benefit of the outgoing tenant's 'reference quantities' (a levy-free benefit calculated by reference to a specified period of milk production).

Wachauf is significant because the court held that although the relevant Community *legisla-* **6.71** *tion* did not require the setting up of a compensation system by the national authority, the national scheme was 'incompatible with the requirements of the protection of fundamental rights in the Community legal order'—in other words, incompatible with the general principles of EC law. This was because, as the ECJ observed, Community rules that had the effect that the national scheme had on Mr Wachauf would breach these requirements. The court continued:

> Since those requirements are also binding on the Member States when they implement Community rules, the Member States must, as far as possible, apply those rules in accordance with those requirements.

The *ratio* of *Wachauf* is clear. Amongst other things, the national authority of a Member **6.72** State acts as the agent of the Community institutions. Community legislation must comply with the general principles of EC law. So, in implementing Community rules the Member State is not empowered to act in such a way as to breach those general rules. As with the Community institutions, there is a qualification in that the obligation is to comply with the general principles 'as far as possible'. It follows, for example, that in some instances there may be a balancing exercise that the public body must engage in as between competing rights.[74]

---

[73] Case 5/88 *Wachauf v Germany* [1989] ECR 2609.
[74] See the principles of interpretation at paras 6.56–6.62 above which, *mutatis mutandis*, appear to be apposite to the legality of acts and defaults of public bodies in respect of the general principles.

6.73 In determining the legality of executive or administrative acts or defaults by reference to EC general principles of law the Administrative Court will, apart from interpreting the underlying legislative provisions in accordance with such principles, have to consider whether:

(1) there is any different standard of protection (whether higher or lower) in domestic or HRA law in respect of the general principle in question;

(2) the national authority has been conferred with discretion.

6.74 To the extent that national law imposes a *higher* standard of judicial review protection than EC law it would appear that the hypothetical 'higher' national standard would still permit the Administrative Court, at least as a matter of theory in some cases, to pronounce the national act or default to be unlawful. This follows from the fact that an EC challenge operates only *qua* EC law.[75] But any higher national standard must itself comply with EC law in the sense that it does not offend against general principles of EC law as, for example, being discriminatory and favouring—in its operation—areas of national law outside the scope of EC law.[76]

6.75 However, to the extent that national law imposes a *lower* standard of judicial review protection then EC law, in its own sphere, prevails and must in any event be complied with.

6.76 The acts or omissions of national authorities may involve the exercise of discretion. So far as discretion is concerned, it may be that EC law itself confers a particular discretion on national authorities. The legality of the exercise of that discretion is then, of course, also to be determined by reference to the general EC law principles.

6.77 It appears that *Bostock*,[77] a case sometimes said to be at odds with *Wachauf*, is, properly analysed, a decision of the ECJ that turned on the legality of exercise of the Member State's discretion as opposed to undermining the principle, accepted in *Wachauf*, that general principles of law were equally binding on the Member States as the Community institutions.

6.78 There, another tenant dairy farmer brought judicial review proceedings also seeking compensation for the loss of reference quantities that had been transferred to his lessor on the expiry of his lease which he, unlike the lessee in *Wachauf*, had terminated. His unsuccessful claim for compensation was brought against his landlord, rather than the national authority, and it should be noted that he had increased milk production on the holding rather than its being a case—as in *Wachauf*—of the claimant having been entirely responsible for such production.

6.79 Against that particular factual background, the ECJ, on an Article 234 (ex 177) EC reference held that Community law (including general principles):

did not include the right to dispose, for profit, of an advantage, such as the reference quantities allocated in the context of the common organisation of the market, which did not derive from the assets or occupational activity of the person concerned.

6.80 So, if Community law did not confer such a right, it followed that any discretion exercisable by the national authority was one necessarily to be exercised under purely domestic law principles.

---

[75] See, by way of comparison, HRA, s 11 which clarifies that HRA protection is a 'floor' and not a 'ceiling' and that where domestic protection is stronger than that conferred by the ECHR then domestic protection applies. Domestic protection now, of course includes, EU protection.

[76] Case C–63/93 *Duff v Minister for Agriculture and Food, Ireland and Attorney General* [1996] ECR I–569, 583. See also, paras 7.09–7.39.

[77] Case C–2/92 *R v MAFF, ex p Bostock* [1994] ECR I–955.

It could not, at least as a matter of EC law, avail the claimant that the national law was subsequently changed by statutory amendment to provide for the award of compensation in future cases. In the view of the ECJ this:

> could not bring about retroactive modification of the relations to the parties to a lease to the detriment of a lessor by imposing on him an obligation to compensate the outgoing lessee, whether under national provisions which the member state in question might be required to adopt, or by means of direct effect.

Remedies by reference to general principles of EC law

If a national measure or act/default is unlawful it follows that, in principle, there should be an available remedy. This issue is separately examined in detail.[78] **6.81**

Here—in respect of the relationship between EC general principles and remedies—it is simply noted that there are at least four aspects of remedies (see Chapter 5) that the Administrative or other national court in a public law case may—-by reference to general principles of EC law—have to consider once a finding of illegality is a practical prospect, or has been made by the ECJ: **6.82**

(1) Particular difficulties arise in the context of damages. Given that Member States are themselves under a duty, as agents of the Community institutions, to comply with general principles of EC law, it follows that there may be a liability on the part of the Member State, or an emanation of the State, to pay damages if general principles are breached in a case falling within the scope of EC law. However, as with any other area of EC law, an award of damages does not ensue as a matter of course. The conditions precedent for general State liability in damages must, first, be fulfilled.

(2) As outlined above, the illegality of a national measure, act or omission may stem from an underlying EC law illegality. Interim relief (see paras 3.123 et seq.) must always be considered where the court considers that there is such a prospect. Indeed, the grant of such relief may itself be conditioned by reference to general principles of EC law such as proportionality or legal certainty.

(3) Where underlying Community legislation is unlawful, the question of relief will, inevitably, come before the national court following its initial reference under Article 234 (ex 177) EC after the ECJ has annulled the Community measure in question in exercise of its jurisdiction under Article 230 (ex 173) EC. Aside from declaring the national measure, act or omission to be unlawful (or quashing it) there may be other relief that—by reference to general principles of EC law—the national court should grant pursuant to its own duties, as an emanation of the State, under Article 10 (ex 5) EC. It may, for example, be required as a matter of EC law general principles to consider questions such as restitution caused as the result of the offending measure. The guiding consideration is that the national court is required to apply EC law in the light of the ECJ's ruling.[79] However, that general statement may raise complex questions of remedy in the individual case as where, for example, there is no specific EC law mechanism to cater for what has happened and/or there is no replacement legislation in place.

---

[78] See, generally, Chapter 5.
[79] Case C–127/94 *R v MAFF, ex p Ecroyd* [1996] ECR I–2731, para 58.

(4) Finally, the existence of different remedies for breach of national or HRA provisions of law should also be taken into account. Although, in general terms, EC law (including the application of general principles of EC law) provides the most far-reaching remedies the possibility cannot, necessarily, be excluded that greater remedies may be available outside the scope of EC law on the facts of a particular case.

7

EQUAL TREATMENT

A. What Is Equal Treatment in EC Law?

7.01 In EC law the general principle of equality, equal treatment, or non-discrimination,[1] means that 'similar situations should not be treated differently and that different situations should not be treated identically unless such differentiation is objectively justified'.[2] Essentially, the principle gives protection against arbitrary treatment. The principle has application in many different contexts. As its starting point it operates—as the citation suggests—in a formal sense. But its more concrete expression is reflected in procedural protections, specific Treaty rights (most notably Article 12 (ex 6) EC) and in particular substantive status areas such as prohibitions on sex, race, and age discrimination,[3] EU citizenship protections,[4] and prevention of arbitrary treatment in relation to fundamental economic freedoms.[5]

---

[1] The terms are, here, used interchangeably.

[2] Case C–479/93 *Francovich v Italy* [1995] ECR I-3843, para 43. For a domestic statement of the principle see per Laws J in *R v MAFF, ex p First City Trading Ltd* [1997] 1 CMLR 250: 'Once it is shown that the classes involved are *prima facie* in a comparable position . . . the question will be whether the factual differences which nevertheless exist between them are such as to justify the discrimination practised by the decision-maker.'

[3] See Chapter 18 for a fuller treatment.

[4] See Chapter 16.

[5] See Chapter 12.

7.02 Discriminatory treatment is generally prohibited and, whether the discrimination is direct or indirect,[6] it is permissible only if there is objective justification,[7] including compliance with the principle of proportionality.[8] The EC general principle, like its ECHR counter-part, has a positive element in that there is a positive obligation to remove unlawful discrimination where it exists.[9]

7.03 Where the EC principle of equality is breached, judicial review proceedings may be brought to challenge defective relevant national legislative (including primary legislation) or administrative measures (including omissions) that are said to infringe the principle. Such proceedings may be brought at the instance of the relevant statutory commission.[10] Cases involving an asserted breach of the equality principle may be referred by the national courts to the ECJ under Article 234 (ex 177) EC where necessary.

7.04 The principle of equal treatment is easy to state but it is not always easy to apply. A number of relevant distinctions should be made which are addressed in greater detail below.

7.05 First, as outlined at para 7.01 above, equality in EC law is a notion that, as a general principle, has both procedural and substantive content. It extends to the way in which the law must be applied and, in that context, creates procedural guarantees to prevent arbitrary discrimination between subjects.[11] It also extends to affording substantive protection against discriminatory treatment because the content of substantive Treaty and legislative EC obligations (and, through them, national legislative and administrative measures) must comply with that general principle.

7.06 Secondly, equality may be approached somewhat differently where a challenge by way of judicial review is, albeit to a national decision, in reality directed towards the legality of an underlying Community measure. As has been noted elsewhere,[12] whilst only the ECJ may pronounce on the invalidity of Community legislation there are many circumstances in which the Administrative Court may, in that context, have to consider legality issues.[13]

---

6 Indirect discrimination is where there is disadvantageous effect on the affected group by a measure which is ostensibly neutral. For specific instances in the field of sex discrimination, see paras 18.22–18.23.

7 Consider, eg, Case C–280/93 *Germany v Council* [1994] ECR I–4973 where unequal rules relating to the common organization of the market in bananas was held to be objectively justified by reason of the legitimate aim of integrating national markets.

8 See Chapter 11. See, eg, Case C–29/95 *Pastoors and Trans-Cap* [1997] ECR I–285, paras 24–26.

9 See, eg, Joined Cases 56–60/74 *K Kampffmeyer v Muhlenvereinigung KG v Commission and Council* [1976] ECR 711, 744.

10 *R v Secretary of State for Employment, ex p EOC* [1995] 1 AC 1. Importantly, the Commission for Equality and Human Rights created by the Equality Act 2006 will be established by 2007 and has particular functions relating to equal treatment. It will have the power to bring and intervene in judicial review proceedings relating to its functions. Although an individual person will frequently have standing to bring judicial review proceedings against primary legislation on the basis that the legislation is discriminatory, this is not always so. See the *EOC* case itself where although EOC had standing to bring the judicial review proceedings, Mrs Day (the other claimant) did not. Her remedy was one in private law and a matter for the Industrial Tribunal.

11 Thus, in legal proceedings both sides should be treated equally so far as procedural rules are concerned and neither party should be accorded an unfair advantage: see, eg, Case T–52/90 *Volger v European Parliament* [1992] ECR II–121, para 41. The general principle of equivalence exemplifies one aspect of the more general principle of equal treatment (see paras 7.12–7.27).

12 See para 2.08.

13 As, eg, in deciding whether to make a reference under Art 234. See paras 4.92 et seq.

Where the legality of Community measures is engaged then—as noted in other contexts[14]—the Community institution, as legislator, is recognized as possessing generally wide discretion. Although the legislative context may dictate how much deference is paid by the ECJ to that discretion (see paras 7.44–7.68 below) the approach of the Administrative Court in domestic judicial review where there is an indirect challenge to underlying EC legislation on equal treatment grounds must (consistently with the ECJ approach) generally be to accept that in certain areas—such as those involving macro-economic judgment—the ECJ would not be likely in most cases on a reference to it under Article 234 (ex 177) EC to interfere with the exercise of such EC legislative discretion. Context is, though, always important.

However, where the challenge is purely to the legality of a *national* measure that is   **7.07** argued to be discriminatory then the Administrative Court is more likely to be required to examine the actual effect of the national measure.[15] This is, in essence, because the national legislature is generally accorded less discretion than the Community legislature[16] and may be pursuing a legitimate EC purpose but by unlawful means. There will, of course, in some cases be equal treatment arguments that are directed to the legitimacy of both the underlying Community legislation and the national decision or measure in question. In those instances a combination of the respective approaches may be required.

The third point is that equality has a particularly wide application. It is sometimes embod-   **7.08** ied separately as a general principle of EC law but appears, more commonly, in specific Treaty and other legislative provisions that are expressly directed towards protecting equal treatment as a substantive obligation in its own right. Here, although there is an overlap with equality as a general principle of EC law, equality is surfacing as a discrete obligation irrespective of the fact that it is also a general principle of EC law. There are a number of such specific provisions.[17]

Finally, it is important to distinguish the application of equality as a general principle and   **7.09** (as appropriate) discrete obligation of EC law from its separate application in domestic law and, more predominantly, in the case law both domestically and in Strasbourg relating to Article 14 ECHR. The EC law principle of equal treatment is far broader than either of these and, in particular, encompasses social and economic matters that are, at least currently, far outside the ambit of the ECHR or domestic law.

So, in applying the EC general principle of equality in proceedings for domestic judicial   **7.10** review the Administrative Court must resolve a number of questions. These are:

(1) Is the issue before the court one of procedure or substance? If procedural, what aspect of the equality principle is engaged?

---

[14] cf, eg, proportionality discussed in Chapter 4.

[15] As to the distinction between Community and national measures in the context of the equality principle see, especially, T Tridimas, *The General Principles of EC Law* (2nd edn, 2006) 84 et seq.

[16] See paras 7.67 et seq.

[17] As, eg, Arts 2–3 (equality between men and women as part of the general purposes and activities of the Community), Art 12 (ex 6) EC (requirement of non-discrimination on nationality grounds); Arts 39, 43 and 49 (ex 48, 52 and 59) EC (requirement of non-discrimination in respect of freedom of movement provisions); Art 137 EC (equality in the area of social protection), Article 141 (ex 119) EC (equal pay for men and women for equal work). Some of these obligations are considered separately. Note, also, the inclusion of equal treatment obligations in the EU Charter of Fundamental Rights. The Charter is outlined at paras 12.19 et seq.

(2) If there is a challenge to a substantive provision is the challenge one to the legality of Community legislation or to a national measure or to both and what should the approach of the court be to each?

(3) To the extent that the challenge involves consideration of specific Treaty provisions or Community legislation specifically directed towards protection against discrimination and/or more general legislative or Treaty obligations to what—if any—extent is the interpretation of such legislation affected by the content of the general principle of equality?

(4) How will the application of the EC general principle of equality be different to that in the purely domestic or EHCR context?

B. Equality and Procedural Protection

Relationship between procedural protection and equal treatment

7.11 It is now well established that:

> In the absence of Community rules it is for the domestic systems of each Member State to designate the courts having jurisdiction and the procedural conditions governing actions at law intended to ensure the protection of the rights which subjects derive from the direct effects of Community law, it being understood that such conditions cannot be less favourable than those relating to similar actions of a domestic nature nor render virtually impossible or excessively difficult the exercise of rights conferred by Community law.[18]

7.12 Both the procedural principles of *equivalence* and of, at least in some instances, *effectiveness* are aspects of the general principle of equality of treatment. The application of these principles is also addressed in the specific context of the judicial review procedure and EC remedies and, for the fullest consideration of these principles in relation to the procedural aspects of equal treatment in EC law, reference should also be made to those sections.[19]

Equivalence

7.13 Equivalence obliges the Member State to adopt procedural rules that are no less favourable in respect of the exercise of EC law rights than those governing similar domestic actions. Its relevance to remedies is considered in more detail in Chapter 5 (see paras 5.06–5.12).

7.14 In order for there to be a breach of equivalence (and, hence, lack of equal treatment) there must, first, be an appropriate comparator.[20] The ECJ's approach to comparators has varied according to the context. In general, the ECJ has *in the context of limitation periods* been cautious in finding a comparator.

---

[18] Case 33/76 *Rewe Zentralfinanz v Landwirtschaftskammer fur Saaralnd* [1976] ECR 1989; Case 45/76 *Comet BV v Productschap voor Siergewassen* [1976] ECR 2043; Case 130/79 *Express Dairy Foods Ltd v Intervention Board for Agricultural Produce* [1980] ECR 1887; Case C–312/93 *Peterbroeck v Belgian State* [1995] ECR I–4599. See, also, *Preston v Wolverhampton Healthcare NHS Trust (No 2)* [2001] 2 WLR 148, para 4 per Lord Slynn; *R v MAFF, ex p Hedley Lomas (Ireland) Ltd* [1997] QB 139, 204E.

[19] See paras 3.09–3.31 and 5.06–5.22.

[20] There may, depending on the circumstances, be a breach of effectiveness (see below) or of some other general principle relevant to the legality of specific procedural rules (as, eg, proportionality).

In *Palmisani*,[21] for example, the applicant claimed unsuccessfully that there was a breach **7.15** of the equivalence principle by reason of a one-year limitation period for delayed transposition of a directive compared to the five-year period allowed by the Italian Civil Code in relation to the non-contractual liability of the State available in other similar domestic actions.

However, the specific domestic actions relied on as comparators were rejected by the court. **7.16** Neither domestic law applications to enforce the directive nor actions under national law for obtaining social security benefits (for which a five-year period was allowed) were truly comparable because their objectives were different to the attempt to trigger the compensation scheme under the directive. In order, the ECJ reasoned, for there to be a proper comparator it was necessary to examine 'the essential characteristics of the domestic system of reference'. This was, at least in the instant case, a task for the national court given that the ECJ did not have sufficient information before it.

The ECJ concluded:[22]

7.17

> If the ordinary system of non-contractual liability were to prove incapable of serving as a basis for an action against public authorities for unlawful conduct for which they can be held responsible in the exercise of their powers and the national court were unable to undertake any other relevant comparison between the time-limit at issue and the conditions relating to claims of a similar nature, the conclusion would have to be drawn ... that Community law does not preclude a Member State from requiring any action for reparation of the loss or damage sustained as a result of the belated transposition of the Directive to be brought within a limitation period of one year from the date of its transposition.

As *Palmisani* shows, the search for a true comparator does not involve a straight comparison **7.18** between time limits. A more subtle exercise is required. In *Matra Communications*[23] the Court of Appeal was faced with a challenge to the three-month limitation period for damages claims flowing from a breach of the rules on public procurement. The court rejected suggested comparators in other areas with more generous time limits as, for example, in claims for breach of statutory duty. The court emphasized that:

> the domestic court ... must look not merely for a domestic action that is similar ... but for one that is in juristic structure very close to the Community claim.[24]

Similar conclusions have been reached in relation to national limitation periods in respect **7.19** of claims for the recovery of unlawfully levied charges,[25] and of claims for the recovery of interest arising from having had to pay the unlawful charge.[26]

Even where there is an appropriate comparator by reference to other domestic procedures **7.20** it does not follow that a national limitation period will, by failing the comparison, be in

---

[21] Case C–261/95 *Rosalba Palmisani v Istituto Nazionale della Providenza Sociale (INPS)* [1997] ECR I–4025.
[22] ibid paras 38–39.
[23] *Matra Communications SAS v Home Office* [1999] 1 WLR 1646.
[24] ibid 1658.
[25] See, eg, Case C–231/96 *Edis v Ministero delle Finanze* [1998] ECR I–4951.
[26] Joined Cases C–279/96, C–280/96 and C–281/96 *Ansaldo Energia v Amministrazione della Finanze* [1998] ECR I–5025.

violation of the equivalence principle. It is also necessary, to establish a breach of equivalence, that the limitation period operates less favourably to the claimant.

7.21   Thus, in *Preston*[27] Lord Slynn in the House of Lords was prepared to accept that a contractual damages claim with a limitation period of six years was an appropriate comparator to a claim under the Equal Pay Act 1970 (as amended). However, he observed that when one compared the respective advantages and disadvantages to a claimant of the different procedures, he was not satisfied that it could be said that the rules of procedure for a claim under the 1970 Act were less favourable than those applying to a claim in contract. On a reference, in the same case, to the ECJ that court observed (following its approach in *Palmisani*) that:

> the national court must verify objectively, in the abstract, whether the rules at issue are similar taking into account the role played by those rules in the procedure as a whole, as well as the operation and special features of those rules.[28]

7.22   Exceptionally, however, a national limitation rule may violate the principle of equivalence. A conclusion to that effect will usually require a careful analysis of the particular facts. This occurred in *Levez*.[29]

7.23   *Levez* concerned a claim for damages to the Employment Appeal Tribunal in respect of sex discrimination under Aricle 119 (now 141) EC and Directive (EEC) 75/117. In the result, the ECJ held that the statutory two-year limitation period provided for by the Equal Pay Act 1970 'in these particular circumstances' breached equivalence by reference to other domestic procedures.

7.24   In reaching this conclusion the court reiterated many of the principles analysed above. It emphasized that equivalence requires that a national rule must be applied without distinction 'where the purpose and cause of action are similar'.[30] It also observed the principle espoused in earlier cases that Member States were not obliged to extend their most favourable rules to Community law rights.[31] However, on the facts the limitation period, if applied, would have the effect in the instant case of depriving an employee who had been deliberately misled by her employer 'of the means provided by the Directive of enforcing the principle of equal pay before the Court'.

7.25   It was no answer, contrary to the UK Government's submission, that the limitation period contained in s 2(5) of the Equal Pay Act 1970 applied equally to purely domestic sex discrimination claims or that the statutory restriction could have been circumvented by a county court action alleging sex discrimination. As the ECJ observed, the restriction in s 2(5) applied solely to equal pay claims whereas claims based on domestic law rights were not so limited. Further, an action before the Tribunal was simpler and less costly. In those circumstances the principle of equivalence was breached.

---

[27]   Case 78/98 *Preston and Fletcher v Wolverhampton NHS Healthcare Trust* [2000] ECR I–3201.
[28]   ibid para 63.
[29]   Case C–326/96 *Levez v TH Jennings (Harlow Pools) Ltd* [1998] ECR I–7835.
[30]   ibid para 41.
[31]   ibid para 42. See, eg, to similar effect, *Edis* [1998] ECR I–4951 para 36.

Levez, then, shows that there may be exceptional cases in which a national limitation rule **7.26** may violate equivalence. It is, though, the exception rather than the rule.

Procedural non-discrimination, as reflected in the equivalence principle, also operates in **7.27** other contexts. For example, albeit under the aegis of Article 12 (ex 6) EC, equal treatment has been held to prevent a procedural requirement to provide security for costs from being imposed on community nationals conducting litigation in Member States outside their state of residence.[32] In *Shingara and Radiom*[33] the ECJ held that legal remedies relating to, amongst other things, entry and expulsion decisions must be equally available to non-nationals as well as nationals of the Member State concerned. Finally, in *Draehmpaehl*[34] a ceiling on damages for sex discrimination breached the equivalence principle where infringements of German domestic law of a similar nature were not so limited.

Effectiveness

Many of the cases on equivalence will contain overlapping issues on effectiveness. If a **7.28** procedure or remedy[35] breaches the equivalence principle it will, at least in many cases, not comply with the principle of effectiveness whereby the exercise of rights conferred by Community law must not be made impossible or excessively difficult in practice.

However, the principle of effectiveness provides separate procedural protection.[36] In **7.29** substance it bears a strong relationship to the procedural rights conferred by Articles 6 and 13 ECHR. So, even if a procedural rule survives a judicial review challenge founded on the principle of equivalence as, for example, because there is no appropriate comparator (see above) it may still violate effectiveness.

In relation to the principle of equal treatment there are now several cases in which national **7.30** procedures have been held to violate effectiveness in the sense of failing to provide an effective remedy for alleged discrimination, especially in the context of sex discrimination.

Von Colson,[37] for example, concerned a directive on sex discrimination. The ECJ said: **7.31**

> Although ... full implementation of the directive does not require any specific form of sanction for unlawful discrimination, it does entail that that sanction be such as to guarantee real and effective judicial protection. Moreover, it must also have a real deterrent effect on the employer. It follows that where a Member State chooses to penalize the breach of the prohibition of discrimination by the award of compensation, that compensation must in any event be adequate in relation to the damage sustained and must therefore amount to more than purely nominal compensation such as, for example, the reimbursement only of the expenses incurred in connection with the application.[38]

---

[32] Case C–43/95 *Data Delecta Aktieborg v MSL Dynamics Ltd* [1996] ECR I–4661.
[33] Cases C–65/95 and C–111/95 *R v Secretary of State for the Home Department, ex p Shingara and Radiom* [1997] ECR I–3343.
[34] Case C–180/95 *Draehmpaehl v Urania Immobilienservice* [1997] ECR I–2195.
[35] For separate consideration of the principle of effectiveness in relation to procedure and remedies see (respectively) paras 3.09–3.17 and 5.13–5.22.
[36] See, further, paras 5.13–5.22.
[37] Case 14/83 *Von Colson and Kamann v Land Nordrhein-Westfalen* [1984] ECR 1891.
[38] ibid para 26.

7.32 Importantly, *Von Colson* demonstrates that a relevant aspect of securing procedural compliance with the principle of effectiveness in the context of prohibiting discriminatory treatment is the deterrent effect of available sanctions. In similar fashion, the ECJ held in *Dekker*[39] that a Member State may not derogate from the prohibition against sex discrimination contained in a directive by imposing a 'fault' requirement as a necessary condition of civil liability. As the court observed: 'any infringement of the prohibition ... suffices in itself to make the person guilty fully liable'.

7.33 In *Marshall (No 2)*[40] the ECJ developed the effectiveness doctrine in the discrimination context even further. In the first *Marshall* case[41] the ECJ held that Miss Marshall had been the victim of sex discrimination under the Equal Treatment Directive. Subsequently, she was awarded damages and interest that exceeded both the statutory maximum available under the Sex Discrimination Act 1975 and the jurisdiction of the Industrial Tribunal to award interest at all.

7.34 The ECJ, in reference proceedings, held materially thus:

> Where financial compensation is the measure adopted in order to achieve the objective ... it must be adequate, in that it must enable the loss and damage actually sustained as a result of the discriminatory dismissal to be made good in full in accordance with the applicable national rules.

> ... the fixing of an upper limit of the kind at issue in the main proceedings cannot, by definition, constitute proper implementation of Article 6 of the Directive, since it limits the amount of compensation *a priori* to a level which is not necessarily consistent with the requirement of ensuring real equality of opportunity through adequate reparation for the loss and damage sustained as a result of discriminatory dismissal.

> With regard to ... the award of interest ... full compensation for the loss and damage sustained as a result of discriminatory dismissal cannot leave out of account factors, such as the effluxion of time, which may in fact reduce its value. The award of interest, in accordance with the applicable national rules, must therefore be regarded as an essential component of compensation for the purposes of restoring real equality of treatment.

7.35 So, *Marshall (No 2)* envisages the prospect of a procedural guarantee of *full* compensation in order to preserve the integrity of the principle of equal treatment. A similar result obtained in *Draehmpaehl*.[42] That case (see above) exemplifies how equivalence and effectiveness can overlap in the field of equal treatment imperatives. There, the ECJ held that a ceiling on the damages that could be paid to the claimant, Mr Draehmpaehl, for sex discrimination breached the principle of equivalence. However, the court also held that the damages ceiling was in violation of the principle of effectiveness. This was because if, but for the discrimination, the claimant would have been employed the compensation limit (of three months) would obviously not have constituted anything like adequate compensation.

---

[39] Case C–177/88 *Dekker v Stichting Vormingscentrum voor Jong Volwassenen* [1990] ECR I–3941, especially para 26.
[40] Case C–271/91 *Marshall v Southampton and South West Hampshire Area Health Authority* [1993] ECR I–4367.
[41] Case 152/84 *Marshall v Southampton and South West Hampshire Area Health Authority* [1986] ECR 723.
[42] See n 34 above and text.

However, the ECJ has been careful to limit the circumstances in which a Member State's **7.36** procedural rules relating to the moneys payable for discriminatory treatment may be interfered with on the ground of non-compliance with the effectiveness principle. The court's ruling in *Sutton*[43] suggests a distinction between compensation claims on the one hand and, on the other, claims for payment of sums due from the State for a breach of Community law.

In that case, Mrs Sutton was refused invalidity care allowance by reason of her having **7.37** reached retirement age. This was an error of law following the court's earlier ruling in *Thomas*.[44] Accordingly, the Social Security Commissioner awarded Mrs Sutton a backdated allowance. She claimed interest on arrears of benefit under Directive (EEC) 79/7 or (in the alternative) damages against the State for its breach of EC law.

The court refused to apply its ruling in *Marshall (No 2)* (above). It held that the right to **7.38** receive interest on social security benefits was not compensatory in nature so that the payment of interest could not be viewed as an essential component of the right to equal treatment. It may be doubted whether such a distinction can be justified given the rationale underlying the principle of effectiveness.[45] In any event, the ECJ did not fully address Mrs Sutton's alternative claim for damages preferring to leave the issue of entitlement to reparation for loss to the national court to determine.[46]

As with equivalence (see above) the principle of effectiveness has been used in respect of **7.39** national limitation rules in the context of according procedural protection against discriminatory treatment. Most notably, in *Emmott*[47]—a case concerned with the refusal of the Irish authority to pay Mrs Emmott disability benefit in alleged contravention of Directive (EEC) 79/7 on equal treatment—the ECJ held that until a directive has been fully transposed into the domestic law of the Member State that Member State may not rely on national limitation rules to defeat a challenge. This was held to be the position even though the applicant could, at any time, have brought proceedings in the national court based on her directly effective rights stemming from the directive in question.

The court's decision in *Emmott* is, however, probably of limited effect. In two other cases— **7.40** *Steenhorst-Neerings*[48] and *Johnson*[49]—the ECJ ruled that a slightly different type of national limitation period, namely one placing a time limit on the retrospective payment of benefit, was permissible.

The distinction appears to be between a limitation period that has the effect of preventing **7.41** a claimant from relying on a directive at all and, by contrast, one that gives the directive

---

[43] Case C–66/95 *R v Secretary of State for Social Security, ex p Sutton* [1997] ECR I–2163.
[44] Case C–328/91 *Secretary of State for Social Security v Thomas* [1993] ECR I–1247.
[45] See, eg, P Oliver, 'State Liability in Damages following Factortame III: A Remedy Seen in Context' in J Beatson and, T Tridimas (eds), *New Directions in European Public Law* (1998).
[46] For further consideration of Directive (EEC) 79/7, see paras 18.36–18.44.
[47] Case C–208/90 *Emmott v Minister for Social Welfare* [1991] ECR I–4269. To similar effect, see Case C–246/96 *Magorrian v Eastern Health and Social Services Board* [1997] ECR I–7153; Case C–78/98 *Preston v Wolverhampton NHS Healthcare Trust* [2000] ECR I–3201.
[48] Case C–338/91 *Steenhorst-Neerings v Bestuur van de Bedrijfsvereniging voor Detailhandel* [1993] ECR I–5475.
[49] Case C–410/92 *Johnson v Chief Adjudication Officer* [1994] ECR I–5483.

some effect.[50] This is a somewhat uncertain application of the effectiveness principle and there is a tension between the time limit cases, founded on effectiveness, and the court's more generous approach, based on the same principle, to the compensation cases considered earlier. In terms of giving proper protection to the requirements of equal treatment the different strands of reasoning in the cases cannot easily be reconciled.

C. Equality and Substantive Protection

Different types of protection

7.42 It is important to understand that the notion of equality in EC law is not monolithic. As has already been explained in relation to procedural protection (see paras 7.11 et seq.) the principle of equal treatment operates to different effect in different contexts.

7.43 There are, in that respect, two basic distinctions to be made, namely those between:

(1) EC and national measures in the field of equal treatment.
(2) Specific Treaty and EC legislative provisions protecting equality of treatment as a substantive right and the over-arching general principle of equality which both operates to separate effect as well as informing interpretation of those and other Treaty obligations.

Community measures and equality of treatment

7.44 There are instances in which the legality of a national measure is dependent upon the underlying legality of the triggering Community legislation. In such circumstances the Administrative Court cannot declare the Community measure to be invalid.[51] However, it may need to examine the strength of the contention that such measure is invalid for interim relief purposes and in order to decide whether to refer the case to the ECJ under Article 234 EC or, indeed, whether to hold that the measure is valid.[52]

7.45 It is, therefore, relevant for domestic judicial review purposes to examine the general approach that the ECJ takes in relation to the legality of certain types of Community measure in the field of equal treatment where the principle is most likely to arise in terms of an indirect challenge in the national courts to Community legislation.

7.46 Thus, certain EC legislative measures such as those in respect of the adoption of harmonization directives and in respect of agricultural law may not operate equally. The fact that they may not operate equally does not, however, mean that the equality principle is breached. This is because a wide measure of discretion vests in the Community legislator in such areas.[53]

---

[50] ibid para 26.
[51] Case 314/85 *Foto-Frost v Hauptzollamt Lubeck-Ost* [1987] ECR 4199.
[52] See, especially, paras 3.137–3.142 and 4.92–4.98.
[53] In this respect, the approach of the ECJ (and national courts) to particular types of EC legislative measure is paralleled in HRA cases by the notion of deference. See, eg, *International Transport Roth GmbH v Secretary of State for the Home Department* [2002] 3 WLR 344, 376–8, per Laws LJ.

The ECJ's approach to these areas illustrates how different thresholds can apply to the **7.47** intensity of review of Community legislation in certain contexts as opposed to that applied to national measures purporting to implement, or derogate from, EC law where the threshold of review is more intense.

Community measures—equal treatment and harmonization

It is clear that the requirement of harmonization of rules may, in many instances, result in **7.48** unequal treatment. However, there are at least three reasons why such requirement is unlikely—save in an extreme case—to represent a breach of the equality principle.

First, expanding on the conventional deference accorded to the Community legislature[54] it **7.49** is recognized that there is a wide discretion vested in the legislature to legislate so as to achieve broad social and economic objectives. It is probable that the relevant Community institution must be *manifestly incorrect* in its assessment of the effects of its legislation before the ECJ will interfere.[55]

Secondly, the transitional difficulties inherent in harmonization have led to the ECJ being **7.50** prepared to treat necessary inequalities stemming from the intrinsic nature of the harmonization process as providing objective reasons for any difference in treatment. This will occur typically in circumstances in which the Community institutions exercise discretion to take a step-by-step approach having regard to the problems of harmonizing complex areas of law.

Thus, in the context of harmonizing provisions, in *Assurances du Credit v Council and* **7.51** *Commission*[56] the amending directive (Directive (EC) 87/343) to the First Insurance Directive (Directive (EEC) 73/239) imposed additional obligations on private insurance companies but left public undertakings materially excluded from those obligations. A claim for damages was brought against the Community alleging discriminatory treatment against the private sector. The ECJ observed as follows:

> The implementation of harmonizing provisions of this kind is generally difficult because it requires the competent Community institutions to draw up, on the basis of diverse, complex national provisions, common rules which conform to the objectives laid down by the Treaty and obtain, as appropriate, either the unanimous agreement of the Council or the agreement of a qualified majority of its members.

> It is because of that difficulty in particular that the competent Community institutions must be recognized as enjoying a discretion in relation to the stages in which harmonization is to take place, having regard to the particular nature of the field subject to co-ordination.[57]

In *Francovich (No 2)*[58] the ECJ was concerned with the effects of partial harmonization **7.52** created by Directive (EEC) 80/987 which approximated laws relating to the protection of

---

[54] See, eg, para 7.06.
[55] See, eg, Joined Cases C–267–C–285/88 *Wuidart v Laiteries Cooperative Eupenoise Socit Cooperative* [1990] ECR I–0435 especially paras 16–18.
[56] Case C–63/89 [1991] ECR I–1799.
[57] ibid paras 11–12.
[58] Case C–479/93 *Francovich v Italian Republic* [1995] ECR I–3843.

employees in the event of the insolvency of their employer. The court rejected the argument that because the directive applied solely to those employees whose employers were subject to claims for the collective satisfaction of creditors this breached the principle of equal treatment. Whilst accepting that there was a difference in treatment as between two categories of employees the ECJ held that there was objective justification given the discretion accorded to the Community institutions as outlined above.

7.53 The third reason why, at least generally, harmonization rules will not violate the equality principle is because other general principles will, in this instance, be capable of 'trumping' equal treatment. Here, for example, considerations of proportionality,[59] and the principle of legal certainty[60] may provide objective justification for what would otherwise be discriminatory treatment.

Community measures—equal treatment and agricultural law

7.54 Equally, in the context of the Common Agricultural Policy the Community legislature enjoys a wide measure of discretion. As with harmonization (above) this connotes a relatively low intensity of review. However, it should be noted that the principle of equality is well recognized in relation to agricultural law both in terms of Treaty provision and general principle.

7.55 Thus, Article 34(2)(ex 40(3)) EC stipulates that the common organization of agricultural products must exclude discrimination as between producers or consumers. This is supplemented by the general principle of equal treatment which extends the express Treaty prohibition on discriminatory treatment in agricultural matters to other economic groupings such as importers and exporters.[61]

7.56 In summary, the approach of the ECJ to challenges to the legality of Community legislation in this field has been to focus on the objectives of the measure in question and to assess those objectives by reference to a deferential standard of review.

7.57 In this context the ECJ has not, however, always distinguished precisely whether a measure is justified in terms of its compliance with the equality principle because there is no true comparator (so that there can be no differential treatment) or whether the measure is objectively justified (so that the difference in treatment does not breach the general principle or Treaty prohibition).

7.58 So far as comparisons are concerned the question of whether undertakings or products are in a comparable situation is determined by recourse to whether their respective positions place them in competition with each other. If, for example, there is a material difference in the structure of particular undertakings or undertakings are subject to different risks then there may be found to be no relevant competition so as to trigger the operation of the equality principle.

---

[59] See, eg, Case 5/88 *Wachauf v Bundesamt fur Ernahrung und Forstwirtschaft* [1989] ECR 2609, para 18.
[60] Case 84/87 *Erpelding v Secretary of State for Agriculture and Viticulture* [1988] ECR 2647, para 30.
[61] See, eg, Case 8/78 *Milac Case* [1978] ECR 1721.

This is exemplified by *Denkavit*.[62] There, a Council regulation made provision for compensation for losses sustained by agricultural producers following revaluation of the national currency. However, the distinction made by that regulation between two different types of agricultural producers did not, so the court held, involve comparing like with like. This was because the first set of producers (agricultural livestock breeders) used their own produce and were subject to the risks attendant on working the soil. By contrast, the second set of producers (industrial breeders) dealt in the international market and were not subject to the same risks. They could, in particular, act so as to prevent loss by purchasing abroad at advantageous prices. So, there was no differential treatment involved in compensating the first as opposed to the second group.   **7.59**

In relation to objective justification, in respect of agricultural Community legislation, the ECJ looks to the particular circumstances of the case with emphasis on the objectives underlying the measure.   **7.60**

There is, in particular, recognition of the fact that the Community institutions have a wide discretion in respect of agricultural legislation and measures taken pursuant thereto.[63] This is especially so with regard to financial compensatory measures and decisions. In *Merkur*,[64] for example, a case on financial compensation, the ECJ made it clear that before a breach of the principle of non-discrimination could be established something more would have to be shown than that a decision was debatable on economic grounds. 'Manifestly erroneous' considerations would have to be demonstrated to have been taken into account.   **7.61**

Similar criteria attach to the situation in which the Community legislature is required to strike a legislative balance in terms of assessing the future effects of a particular measure. If the effects cannot be predicted accurately then it seems that the assessment will not be capable of judicial review by the ECJ on the basis of a breach of equal treatment unless it was 'manifestly incorrect' by reference to the information available to it at the time.[65]   **7.62**

The overriding principle is, in the context of the equal treatment principle that Community measures in the field of the Common Agricultural Policy will not be challengeable unless they are, in some fashion, shown to be arbitrary. Further, in determining whether a measure is arbitrary due deference is shown to the broad discretion possessed by the Community institutions.   **7.63**

Notwithstanding this, there will be circumstances in which Community legislation does result in discriminatory treatment. This may, for example, occur where the circumstances justifying the measure initially have ceased to exist.[66]   **7.64**

It is also instructive to consider the facts in *Royal Scholten-Honig*.[67] There, the applicants— producers of isoglucose (a new product)—brought a challenge, in common with other   **7.65**

---

62 Case 139/77 *Denkavit v Finanzamt Warendorf* [1978] ECR 1317.
63 See, eg, Case 179/84 *Bozetti v Invernizzi* [1985] ECR 2301 especially para 30.
64 Case 43/72 *Merkur v Commission* [1973] ECR 1055.
65 See, eg, Case 59/83 *Bivolac v EEC* [1984] ECR 4057.
66 Joined Cases T–177 and T–377/94 *Altmann v Commission* [1996] ECR II–2041 para 119.
67 Joined Cases 103 and 145/77 *Royal Scholten-Honig v Intervention Board for Agricultural Produce* [1978] ECR 2037.

isoglucose producers, to the legality of certain production levies resulting in the subsidising of sugar producers at the expense of isoglucose producers.

7.66   The Council regulation in question was said to breach the equality principle by placing the isoglucose producers in a disadvantageous position in relation to the sugar producers. The ECJ (on an Article 234 reference) agreed. It held that the producers in question were in competition with each other so that there was a relevant comparison to be made. It then went on to rule that there was no objective justification for the levy. In so ruling, the ECJ accepted that the objective of the measure—to ensure the sharing of production costs— was legitimate. However, the allocation of burdens was, so it was held, unequal.

National measures and the equal treatment principle

7.67   In understanding the threshold of judicial review applicable to national measures in the context of the equal treatment principle, it is emphasized that the legality of a national measure will, *if any underlying Community measure on which it depends is lawful*, generally be determined by reference to more stringent criteria than will the legality of Community legislation.

7.68   This is, essentially, because the Member State does not possess the wider (and sometimes very wide) discretion that is vested in the Community institutions. In part, this flows from the supremacy of EC law and the fact that the discretion vested in Member States is frequently directed to establishing national measures that implement the often wide discretion already exercised by the Community legislator. For these reasons, judicial review of national measures by the Administrative Court (or, where appropriate, the ECJ on an Article 234 reference)[68] by reference to the general principle of equal treatment is usually subject to more intensive review than a Community measure.

7.69   There are also a number of possible areas in which the legality of a national measure (including omission)[69] in terms of its compliance with the Community law principle of equal treatment will—aside from the unchallenged legality of the underlying Community measure—fall to be tested. In essence these are where:

   (1) A national measure purports to implement a Treaty obligation or otherwise to be in conformity with such obligation.
   (2) A national measure purports lawfully to derogate from a Treaty provision or Community measure.
   (3) The interpretation of a national measure is founded on the general principle of equal treatment.
   (4) A national measure is argued to be within the scope of Community law as being linked to a Treaty provision either directly or indirectly.

---

   [68] As explained in Chapter 2, at paras 2.08 et seq. the ECJ may not decide questions of national law directly.
   [69] There are, eg, instances of the State failing to abolish discriminatory national legislation contrary to Directive (EEC) 76/207: see, eg, Case 165/82 *Commission v United Kingdom (Re Equal Treatment for Men and Women)* [1983] ECR 3431.

National measures—implementing, derogating, and conformity provisions

Examples of Treaty provisions directly relating to equal treatment are these:[70] **7.70**

(1) Article 141 (ex 119) EC ('[e]ach Member State shall ensure that the principle of equal pay for male and female workers for equal work or work of equal value is applied').

(2) Article 12 (ex 6) EC ('[w]ithin the scope of application of this Treaty, and without prejudice to any special provisions contained therein, any discrimination on grounds of nationality shall be prohibited').[71]

(3) Article 34(2) (ex 40(3)) EC (common organization of agricultural markets 'shall exclude any discrimination between producers or consumers within the Community').[72]

Clearly, a national measure that conflicts with (or fails properly to implement) one of the **7.71**
above Treaty provisions is unlawful. Thus, in *R v Secretary of State for Employment, ex p Equal Opportunities Commission*,[73] a statutory requirement for a five-year minimum period in relation to part-time workers (as opposed to the two-year period for full-time workers) for redundancy/unfair dismissal protection was held to be incompatible with Article 141 and, so, unlawful because the overwhelming majority of part-time workers were women.[74] Similarly, at the level of administrative decision-making, in *Harmon*[75] an unsuccessful European tenderer whose bid for work at the House of Commons had been rejected on a 'buy British' basis succeeded in a damages claim founded, in part, on a breach of Article 12 EC.

The same principles apply, of course, to national measures that are in conflict with (or do not **7.72**
implement) lawful *secondary* Community legislation aimed at protecting against discriminatory treatment.[76] In *R v Secretary of State for Social Security, ex p Taylor*,[77] for example, certain winter fuel payments that discriminated between men and women were held not to be objectively justified and, therefore, to be in breach of the Equal Treatment Directive

It is particularly important to note that Article 12 (ex 6) EC has very wide application. The **7.73**
ECJ has, in particular, used that Treaty provision to determine the legality of national rules with other Treaty obligations by reference to the equality principle.

In *Gravier*,[78] for example, the applicant was, as a foreign student, charged a fee in respect of **7.74**
a four-year art course. This charge was not levied on home students. The ECJ held that the charge was in breach of Community law. It observed that although educational organization and policy were not matters vested in the Community institutions 'access to and

---

[70] See, also, eg Arts 2–3, 13 (below) and 137. Importantly, too, subordinate Community legislation,whether made under these or other more general Treaty provisions, will also provide the basis for national measures: see below.

[71] Note, too, the new Art 13 EC empowering the Council to 'take appropriate action to combat discrimination based on sex, racial or ethnic origin, religion or belief, disability, age or sexual orientation'.

[72] See, also, paras 7.54–7.66.

[73] [1995] 1 AC 1.

[74] According to the EOC's calculations, some 90 percent of part-time workers were women.

[75] *Harmon CFEM Facades (UK) Ltd v Corporate Officer of the House of Commons* (1999) 67 Con LR 1.

[76] Such legislation may be based on another more general Treaty-making power. Consider, materially, Directive (EEC) 76/207 on equal treatment which was issued under Art 308 (ex 235) rather than under Art 141.

[77] [2000] All ER (EC) 80.

[78] Case 293/83 *Gravier v City of Liege* [1985] ECR 593.

participation in . . . vocational training are not unconnected with Community law'. The court went on to hold that such matters fell within Art 151 (ex 128) EC relating to cultural diversity. On that footing the court considered that the charge was discriminatory and contrary to Article 12 (ex 6) EC. This judgment exemplifies the broad scope of Article 12 and the fact that the principle of non-discrimination is capable of extending to areas—such as education—that had not previously been thought of as being obviously affected directly by Community law.

7.75 National measures purporting to *derogate* from Community obligations—whether in the context of discrimination or otherwise—are usually to be construed narrowly.[79] The legitimacy of any derogation is itself assessed by reference to the general principles of Community law.[80]

7.76 In the context of discrimination there are many specific provisions permitting derogation. In general, they have been interpreted restrictively. An example is afforded by Article 2(2) of Directive (EEC) 76/207. This provides for exemption from the principle of equal treatment for 'activities . . . for which . . . the sex of the worker constitutes a determining factor'.

7.77 The principles governing derogation in Article 2(2) were considered and formulated in *Johnston*.[81] Essentially, the ECJ held that: (1) derogation under Article 2(2) was limited to specific duties as opposed to activities in general, (2) the situation would have to be reviewed periodically so as to ensure that any permitted derogation was still justified and (3) any derogation was subject to the general principle of proportionality.[82] In *Sirdar*,[83] and exceptionally, derogation under Article 2(2) was permitted so as to allow the army board to refuse to transfer a female chef to the Royal Marines—albeit that she would then be made redundant—in circumstances where such transfer would expose her to serious danger. However, the court emphasized the special nature of the case and expressly observed that derogation from fundamental Treaty rights is construed narrowly and must satisfy the proportionality principle.

7.78 Even though it contains no express legislative provision permitting derogation it seems probable that limited derogation is allowed from the provisions of Article 12 (ex 6) EC. This is because the notion of objective justification is intrinsic to the notion of unlawful discrimination. However, as with any derogation from fundamental Treaty rights the circumstances in which derogation will be allowed are narrow (see above).

National measures—problems of interpretation

7.79 The process of domestic judicial review does not require the Administrative Court merely to determine the legality of national measures by reference to whether such measures are in conformity, or conflict, with the principle of equal treatment in the abstract. Since the equality principle is a general principle of EC law, the Administrative Court must also

---

[79] See, generally, para 2.111.
[80] See Case C–260/89 *ERT* [1991] ECR I–2925.
[81] Case 222/84 *Johnston v Chief Constable of the Royal Ulster Constabulary* [1986] ECR 1651.
[82] See Chapter 18.
[83] Case C–273/97 *Sirdar v Army Board* [1999] ECR I–7403.

interpret the underlying Community provisions and contingent national measures by reference to that principle in so far as it is possible to do so. That means that in so far as it is possible to do so the Administrative Court when invited to determine the legality of national measures that depend for their legality upon an underlying Community measure must seek to interpret the underlying Community measure consistently with the principle of equal treatment.

As has already been seen,[84] the ECJ has shown itself prepared to find a link between **7.80** a national measure and a Treaty provision so as to give effect to the principle of equal treatment at least as enshrined in Article 12 (ex 6) EC. It does this by according a broad interpretation to the Treaty provision in question and then, indirectly at least, subjecting the national rule to the relevant Treaty provision as interpreted by reference to equal treatment criteria.

A further example is afforded by the facts of *Cowan*.[85] There, it was held that an EC **7.81** national who was the victim of violent crime was entitled to claim compensation under a national compensation scheme. The ECJ reached this conclusion because it gave a wide meaning to the freedom to provide services under Article 49 EC. The court ruled that it included 'the freedom for the recipients of services to go to another Member State in order to receive a service there, without being obstructed by restrictions, and that tourists, among others, must be regarded as recipients of services'.[86]

In the light of that reasoning, the court observed thus: **7.82**

> When Community law guarantees a natural person the freedom to go to another Member State the protection of that person from harm in the Member State in question, on the same basis as that of nationals and persons residing there, is a corollary of that freedom of movement . . . Although in principle criminal legislation and the rules of criminal procedure, among which the national provision in issue is to be found, are matters for which the Member States are responsible, the Court has consistently held . . . that Community law sets certain limits to their power. Such legislative provisions may not discriminate against persons to whom Community law gives the right to equal treatment or restrict the fundamental freedoms guaranteed by Community law.

So, too, when interpreting Community measures that are specifically directed towards equal **7.83** treatment the ECJ, in order to give effect to the general principle of equality, generally gives a broad interpretation to those measures often extending beyond the plain meaning of the words used. It is, then, in that context that contingent national measures will fall to be interpreted and applied by the national court. This is exemplified by those cases dealing with issues in the context of gender reassignment and sexual orientation that stretch the traditional understanding of 'sex' and discrimination on the ground of 'sex'.[87]

For example, in *P v S and Cornwall County Council*[88] the ECJ held that, without objective **7.84** justification, the dismissal of a transsexual for a reason relating to his decision to have

---

[84] See Case 293/83 *Gravier v City of Liege* [1985] ECR 593 and at para 7.72.
[85] Case 186/87 *Cowan v Tresor Public* [1989] ECR 195.
[86] ibid para 15.
[87] For more detailed consideration of these issues, see Chapter 18.
[88] Case C–13/94 [1996] ECR I–2143, especially paras 21–22.

gender reassignment by surgical operation was in breach of the Equal Treatment (Directive (EEC) 76/207). The court ruled that discrimination by reason of gender reassignment is based essentially, if not exclusively, on the sex of the person concerned. Where this occurs 'he or she is treated *unfavourably* by comparison with persons of the sex to which he or she was deemed to belong before undergoing gender reassignment'. The court also observed that: '[t]o tolerate such discrimination would be tantamount, as regards such a person, to a failure to respect the dignity and freedom to which he or she is entitled, and which the Court has a duty to safeguard'.

7.85 The significance of the case is that the ECJ accorded an ostensibly broader meaning to the term 'sex' than suggested by the (then unamended) directive itself.[89] For practical purposes the ECJ approached the case from the wider perspective of the equal treatment principle than that of the plain wording of the directive. The court held, in substance, that the meaning of the directive should not be restricted so as to narrow discrimination protection on grounds of gender given the equality principle that it reflected. In so ruling, the Court implicitly endorsed the reasoning of Advocate General Tesauro who supported:

> a rigorous application of the principle of equality so that . . . any connotations relating to sex and/or sexual identity cannot be in any way relevant.[90]

7.86 It may be thought that the ECJ took a somewhat narrower view of the scope of the equality principle in *Grant v South West Trains*.[91] That was a case concerned with sexual orientation. There, a female employee with a female partner unsuccessfully claimed rail benefits to which married couples were entitled. However, the ECJ held that there was no discrimination because travel concessions were also refused to partners of gay men.

7.87 More recently, however, in *KB v The National Health Service Pensions Agency and Secretary of State for Health*[92] the ECJ has returned to a broader view of the principle of equal treatment in the context of sexual orientation. *KB* raised the issue of the right of transsexuals to marry and, thereby, to claim a survivor's pension when one of them died. The court held that Article 141 EC, properly interpreted, precludes legislation preventing the threshold requirement of marriage for conferment of such benefit.

National measures—the scope of Community law

7.88 Finally, in unravelling the breadth of the general principle of equality it is important to understand that, at least currently, however broadly the ECJ (and, therefore, the Administrative Court) is prepared to interpret Treaty provisions or other Community measures upon which the legality of national measures depend, there is a distinction between a national measure being *within* the scope of EC law (and so subject to the

---

89 The directive has been amended to reflect the broader approach of the ECJ to discrimination issues. See paras 18.29–18.32 and 18.55–18.57.

90 Case C–13/94 [1996] ECR I–2143, 2154, para 19.

91 Case C–249/96 [1998] ECR I–621.

92 Case C–117/01 (unreported, 7 January 2004). And see, most recently, Case C–423/04 *Richards v Secretary of State for Work and Pensions* The Times, 5 May 2006 (*held*: Art 4(1) of Directive (EEC) 79/7 precluded legislation which denied a person who had undergone male-to-female gender reassignment entitlement to a retirement pension on the ground that she had not reached the age of 65 when she would have been entitled to such pension at the age of 60 if held to be a woman as a matter of domestic law).

standards of the EC general principle of equality) and a national measure being *outside* the scope of EC law (and so *not* subject to the EC general principle of equality).[93]

This distinction is explored elsewhere, especially in the context of human rights.[94] It is a distinction that is, in fact, relevant to the application of *any* general principle of EC law but has a particular resonance given the wide substantive scope of the equal treatment principle (especially as developed under Article 12 EC) and the consequent potential for giving EC law, in the equality context, an extremely wide 'reach'. **7.89**

The case law, to date, suggests that there are particular situations in which the EC equality principle under Article 12 EC may apply even though there is no specific link to a Treaty provision but where, at least, the national measure in question affects inter State trade or economic activity. **7.90**

This extended approach to the equality principle began in *Phil Collins*.[95] That was a case in which Phil Collins commenced proceedings in Germany challenging the distribution of unauthorized recordings of concerts that he had given in the United States. There was a national statutory remedy accorded to German nationals but not to non-nationals. The issue before the ECJ, on a preliminary reference, was whether there was a violation of Community law. **7.91**

No Treaty provision was argued to be engaged other than Article 12. The ECJ accepted that it was for the Member States to establish the conditions and detailed rules for the protection of literary and artistic property. Nonetheless, the court reasoning that '[c]opyright and related rights are ... economic in nature in that they confer the right to exploit commercially the marketing of the protected work' went on to hold that such rights 'are by their nature such as to affect trade in goods and services and also the competitive relationships within the Community. For that reason ... those rights, although governed by national legislation, are subject to the requirements of the Treaty and therefore fall within its scope of application.' **7.92**

So, in that context, the ECJ held that copyright and related rights fell within the scope of Community law not because, as previously, of any direct link to another Treaty provision such as free movement of goods or services, or any of the competition provisions but, rather, because of the general effect of such rights on trade in goods and services affecting Community activity. That was sufficient, so it was said, to bring the case within the direct application of Article 12. **7.93**

Such an approach is, of course, extremely far-reaching. It was followed in the subsequent case of *Data Delecta*.[96] At issue there was the legality of a Swedish national measure requiring a foreign claimant not resident in Sweden to furnish security of costs for the bringing of legal proceedings in the Swedish courts. **7.94**

---

[93] In those circumstances the national measure may be subject to a domestic or, at least, ECHR principle of equality (see below).
[94] See paras 12.62–12.68. The distinction is also touched on in Chapter 6: see, especially, paras 6.31–6.47.
[95] Cases C–92/92 and C–326/92 *Collins v Imtrat Handelsgesellschaft mbH* [1993] ECR I–5145.
[96] Case C–43/95 *Data Delecta and Forsberg* [1996] ECR I–4661.

7.95   On the face of it this was a national procedural rule outside the scope of Community law. However, the ECJ found that its effect was to impact upon the economic activities of traders from other Member States and was caught by Article 12 EC. This was because:[97]

> [a]lthough it is, as such, not intended to regulate an activity of a commercial nature, it has the effect of placing such traders in a less advantageous position than nationals of that State as regards access to its courts. Since Community law guarantees such traders free movement of goods and services in the common market, it is a corollary of those freedoms that they must be able, in order to resolve any disputes arising from their economic activities, to bring actions in the courts of a Member State in the same way as nationals of that State.

7.96   Thus, *Phil Collins* and *Data Delecta* show that a national measure having an entirely *indirect* effect on inter-State trade in goods and services is capable of falling within Article 12 and, so, within the scope of Community law.

7.97   Beyond this type of extension of the need for a direct link between a Treaty provision and a national measure before EC law is engaged, however, it is unlikely that a national measure would be subject to an EC general principle such as that of equal treatment. It would be likely to be held to be outside the scope of Community law.

7.98   Although the scope of equal treatment as a general principle and under Article 12 EC, is very broad and is still evolving the Administrative Court has, thus far at least, been careful to distinguish those cases which are outside the scope of Community law and so not subject to its 'reach'.

7.99   The distinction was clearly made in *R v MAFF, ex p First City Trading*.[98] There, an issue was raised as to whether the Beef Stocks Transfer Scheme complied with the EC law general principle of equality. The argument was that the legality of a national measure is subject to the general principle of equality if it affects intra-Community trade in goods or services.

7.100   However, Laws J held that the general principles of law adumbrated by the ECJ are narrower in their application than those contained in the Treaty itself (such as Article 12) and only extend to decisions taken *pursuant* to Community law. He said this:

> The power of the ECJ, as it seems to me, to apply (whether on an [Article 234] reference or otherwise) principles of public law which it has itself evolved cannot be deployed in a case where the measure in question, taken by a member state, is not a function of Community law at all. To do so would be to condition or moderate the internal law of the member state without that being authorised by the Treaty. Where action is taken, albeit it under domestic law, which falls within the scope of the Treaty's application, then of course the court has the power and duty to require that the Treaty be adhered to. But no more precisely because the fundamental principles elaborated by the ECJ are not vouchsafed by the Treaty, there is no legal space for their application to any measure or decision taken otherwise than in pursuance of Treaty rights or obligations.

7.101   Thus, however broadly Treaty provisions—such as Article 12—and other Community legislative provisions may be interpreted so as to bring them within the scope of the general principle of equality, the Community law general principle of equality itself can only be applied to interpreting and applying Community law.

---

[97]   ibid para 13.
[98]   [1997] 1 CMLR 250.

That reasoning may be right. However, in *R v MAFF, ex p British Pig Industry Support* **7.102**
Group[99] Richards J expressed 'real doubts' as to its correctness. One of the difficulties is that
the general principles of EC law are themselves derived from the constitutional traditions
common to the Member States and from international human rights Treaties to which the
Member States are parties. It follows that: 'the fundamental principles of national legal
systems . . . contribute to forming that philosophical, political and legal substratum common to the Member States from which through the case-law an unwritten Community law
emerges'.[100]

There is, for example, an incongruity between elevating the importance to be accorded to **7.103**
discrimination on the ground of nationality (prohibited by Article 12 EC and so extending
to indirect effects on inter-State trade: see above) over other forms of discrimination
(founded, for example, on social policy or the environment which are Community activities
under Article 3 EC).

On the distinction drawn by Laws J in *First City Trading* an equal treatment principle is **7.104**
given primacy where it can be read into a Treaty or derivative legislative provision such as
Article 12 EC but not otherwise. It is, however, at least arguable that equal treatment has a
broader application and *as a matter of Community law* that it extends to all national measures having effects in an area of Community law albeit that such measures have not been
taken pursuant to Community law.[101] However, the implications of such an approach are
applicable to all general principles of law and would result in a considerable broadening of
the presumed extent of Community law. It remains to be seen whether the ECJ will take
such a course.

D. Other Aspects of Equal Treatment in Judicial Review

Equal treatment as a domestic ground of challenge

It is undoubtedly the case that domestic public law has drawn inspiration from the increasing **7.105**
European dimension to public law requiring application of both ECHR and EC principles
of review. In a number of instances, domestic courts have overtly recognized that it is undesirable to have different and contradictory review principles regulating the parallel public
law jurisdictions that now exist.[102]

So far as purely domestic judicial review is concerned there is some basis for arguing that a **7.106**
substantive principle of equality, comparable to the EC general principle, already exists in
administrative law. The *locus classicus* is *Kruse v Johnson*.[103] There, a local authority enacted
a byelaw prohibiting singing or music being played within 50 yards of a dwelling house.

---

[99]   [2000] Eu LR 724.
[100]   Case 11/70 *Internationale Handelsgesellschaft* [1970] ECR 1125, per Advocate General de Lamothe.
[101]   Consider, eg, Advocate General Van Gerven in Case C–159/90 *Society for the Protection of Unborn
Children (SPUC) v Grogan* [1991] ECR I–4685, 4723, para 31.
[102]   See, especially, *M v Home Office* [1994] 1 AC 377, 407, per Lord Woolf; *Woolwich Equitable Building
Society v Inland Revenue Commissioners* [1993] AC 70, 177E per Lord Goff.
[103]   (1889) 2 QB 291.

The byelaw was challenged, by way of defence to a criminal prosecution, as being unreasonable. Although a Divisional Court dismissed an appeal by way of case stated against conviction, Lord Russell observed that byelaws could, in principle, be held to be unreasonable because of 'partial and unequal treatment in their operation as between different classes'.

7.107 However, despite this clear (though *obiter*) statement, subsequent cases have not articulated a general principle of substantive equality that would, as in the EC context, justify the quashing of the *content* of national measures including subordinate legislation on the broad basis of discriminatory treatment.

7.108 Despite the absence of a clear principle of *substantive* equality in the case law there exists, nonetheless, in domestic judicial review a set of principles that is closely akin to recognition of *formal* equality in the sense of equal *application* of the law or consistent treatment.

7.109 Even this proposition needs to be stated with care since, at least *eo nomine*, the Administrative Court has not recognized a general principle of consistency of treatment in administrative decision-making.[104]

7.110 In substance, though, equality is frequently given practical effect (albeit not as a formal principle) in the application of other principles by which the legality of administrative decisions and other national measures will be judged.[105] Most commonly, this will find expression in the application of well-established review principles such as abuse of power,[106] fair treatment,[107] or the requirement that all material considerations must be taken into account.[108]

7.111 Properly analysed, however, there is no discrete principle of substantive equality available to claimants in purely domestic judicial review proceedings that is truly comparable to the EC general principle of equality discussed in this chapter. There are a number of formal rules that enable the Administrative Court, in appropriate cases, to hold that particular decisions are unlawful on the ground of arbitrariness by virtue of discriminatory treatment. However, for the most part (subject, always, to specific express or implied statutory provision) there would appear to be no purely domestic principle that subjects a national measure to judicial review on the basis of its unequal or discriminatory *content*.

---

104 *R v Aylesbury Vale DC, ex p Chaplin* The Times, 23 July 1996, where Keene J rejected the submission that public law had reached the stage 'where it will require public bodies to act consistently, at least in relation to the same person or the same set of facts'. The decision was upheld on appeal: see [1997] 3 PLR 55.

105 See eg, of the many cases, *R v Immigration Appeal Tribunal, ex p Jeyeanthan* [1998] Imm AR 369, 374 (CA reported at [2000] 1 WLR 354) per Sedley J where he observed in relation to immigration appeal notices to 'the principle of equality before the law' being 'jeopardised if the State as appellant is placed or is allowed to place itself in a materially different position from any other appellant'. Note, too, *Matadeen v Pointu* [1999] 1 AC 98 where the PC concluded that there was (*in casu*) no relevant *constitutional* right to equality but that there was a relevant common law principle subject to conventional principles of judicial review.

106 See, eg, *HTV Ltd v Price Commission* [1976] ICR 170, 185 per Lord Denning MR.

107 *R v Inland Revenue Commissioners, ex p Unilever Plc* [1996] STC 681, 692, per Sir Thomas Bingham MR.

108 As, eg, *R v Secretary of State for the Home Department, ex p Golam Mowla* [1992] 1 WLR 70.

Equal treatment under the HRA

In cases where the HRA applies[109] but where there is no relevant EC element there is a more **7.112** limited principle of substantive equality. Article 14 ECHR provides:

> The enjoyment of the rights and freedoms set forth in this Convention shall be secured without discrimination on any grounds such as sex, race, colour, language, religion, political or other opinion, national or social origin, association with a national minority, property, birth or other status.

So, unlike the EC principle of equal treatment, Article 14 ECHR does not represent a **7.113** general prohibition on discrimination. It enjoys no 'independent existence'[110] from the other Convention rights because it stipulates only that there must be no discrimination in the 'enjoyment of' those rights.

Despite this, it is not necessary for Article 14 to engage that there be an actual breach of **7.114** a separate Convention right. What is required is that the facts of the case 'fall within the ambit' of one or more of the other Convention rights.[111] Thus, for example, in *Inze v Austria*[112] the European Court of Human Rights, faced with a challenge to an Austrian law depriving the applicant of an inheritance because of his illegitimate birth, held that the case fell within the ambit of Article 1 of Protocol No 1 (right to peaceful enjoyment of property) and that, taken together with Article 14, a Convention breach was established.

Importantly, as with its EC counterpart, even if there is relevant discriminatory treatment **7.115** under the ECHR it may be objectively justified. If it is, then there is no violation of Article 14 ECHR.[113]

It can be seen that although Article 14 contains a substantive principle of equality it is **7.116** somewhat more restricted than the EC general principle. In particular, a matter falling outside the scope of the substantive Convention rights takes the case outside Article 14. In the sphere of EC law the general principle of equality has a far wider scope extending, as has been explained, to any discrimination having even indirect effect on inter-State trade provided, only, that it falls within the province of Community law.

Recent case law has given rise to particular issues in the context of ECHR law that will not **7.117** necessarily arise in an EC equality case unless, perhaps, the ECJ were drawing directly from the ECHR and applying it to the case before it.

The House of Lords has endorsed a five-stage test for whether Article 14 ECHR is engaged and **7.118** breached. Paraphrasing Baroness Hale in *Ghaidan v Godin-Mendoza*[114] (see para 133–134 of the judgment) the stages are:

(1) Do the facts fall within the ambit of one or more of the Convention rights?
(2) Was there a difference in treatment in respect of that right between the complainant and others put forward for comparison?

---

[109] See, especially, para 2.25.
[110] *Belgian Linguistics Case* (1979–80) 1 EHRR 252, Pt B1, para 9.
[111] *Rasmussen v Denmark* (1985) 7 EHRR 371, para 29; *Marckx v Belgium* (1979–80) 2 EHRR 330, para 32.
[112] (1988) 10 EHRR 394.
[113] See, eg, *Belgian Linguistics Case* (1979–80) 1 EHRR 252.
[114] [2004] UKHL 30, [2004] 2 AC 557.

(3) Were those others in an analogous situation?

(4) Was the difference in treatment objectively justifiable?

(5) Was the difference in treatment based on one or more of the grounds proscribed (whether expressly or by inference) in Article 14?[115]

7.119 Though added late to the list of relevant questions,[116] it is the final test encompassing consideration of the phrase 'other status' in Article 14 that has given rise to particular difficulty in some of the cases. But the House of Lords has, in two recent cases, evinced some interest as to its proper scope and application.

7.120 *R (S and Marper) v Chief Constable of West Yorkshire*[117] involved the fundamental question of whether DNA samples may be retained from persons from whom such samples have been taken during the process of investigation but who have subsequently been acquitted.

7.121 One of the grounds of challenge was made under Article 14. An important issue was whether or not (even assuming there was a relevant comparator) there was discrimination by virtue of 'other status'.[118] The House of Lords held that there was not. As to the meaning of 'other status' Lord Steyn said:[119]

> The list of grounds in article 14 is not exhaustive, and necessarily includes each of the specifically proscribed grounds as well as 'other status'. The European Court of Human Rights has interpreted 'other status' as meaning a personal characteristic: *Kjeldsen, Busk Madsden and Petersen v. Denmark* (1976) 1 EHRR 711, 732–733, para 56 ... On the other hand, the proscribed grounds in article 14 cannot be unlimited, otherwise the wording of article 14 referring to 'other status' beyond the well-established proscribed grounds, including things such as sex, race or colour would be unnecessary. It would then preclude discrimination on any ground. That is plainly not the meaning of article 14.
>
> . . .
>
> By way of summary the position is as follows. The difference in treatment is not analogous to any of the expressly proscribed grounds such as sex, race, gender or religion. The fact that the police are now in possession of fingerprints and samples which were previously lawfully acquired as a result of a criminal investigation does not give rise to a 'status' within the meaning of article 14. The appellants, and other individuals in their position, are as fully entitled to the presumption of innocence as the general body of citizens.

7.122 In *R (Carson) v Secretary of State for Work and Pensions*[120] Article 14 issues arose because of the claimant's residence in South Africa at the date of her retirement. Although she was a

---

[115] As Baroness Hale makes clear, the first four tests are derived from the judgment of Brooke LJ in *Wandsworth LBC v Michalak* [2003] 1 WLR 617, 625, para 20, as amplified by the Court of Appeal in *R (Carson) v Secretary of State for Work and Pensions* [2003] EWCA Civ 797. The fifth test was common ground between the parties and accepted by the House of Lords in *Godin-Mendoza*.

[116] See para 7.118 above. Other issues in respect of 'other status' than those canvassed here are likely to arise. Most notably, there is an issue over the intensity of judicial review for particular types of status even if Art 14 is engaged. See A Baker, 'Comparison Tainted by Justification: Against a "Compendious Question" in Article 14 Discrimination' [2006] PL 476.

[117] [2004] 1 WLR 2196.

[118] The *chosen* comparator was the class of acquitted persons but the *relevant* comparator was held to be those who had been through the police investigation process (ie whether acquitted or convicted). However, independently of this, the 'status' namely that of acquitted person, was held not to constitute a personal characteristic as identified by the House of Lords.

[119] [2004] I WLR 2196, paras 48 and 51.

[120] [2005] UKHL 37; [2005] 2 WLR 1369.

British citizen Ms Carson was, under subordinate legislation, only entitled to a pension at a lower (2001) level than she would be entitled to were she resident in this country. She brought proceedings for judicial review claiming (amongst other things)[121] a breach of Article 14 by virtue of alleged discrimination by reference to her 'status' as a resident of South Africa.

The House of Lords held that there was no breach of Article 14. In doing so, there are important statements of principle about the scope of 'other status'. **7.123**

Only Lord Hoffmann and Lord Walker adverted to the narrow *Kjeldsen* test of 'status' as denoting a personal characteristic. **7.124**

Lord Hoffmann observed (para 13 of his speech) as follows: **7.125**

> In *Kjeldsen, Busk Madsen and Pedersen v Denmark* (1976) 1 EHRR 711, 732-733, para 56 the court said that article 14 applied *only* if the discrimination was on the basis of a personal characteristic. That is the construction which has recently been adopted by the House of Lords: *R (S) v Chief Constable of the South Yorkshire Police* [2004] 1 WLR 2196, 2213, para 48 (Lord Steyn). On the other hand, in *Wandsworth London Borough Council v Michalak* [2003] 1 WLR 617, 628, para 34 Brooke LJ said that Strasbourg seemed to have moved on since Kjeldsen's case and had applied article 14 in cases in which it was hard to say that the ground of discrimination was in any meaningful sense a personal characteristic. As the House of Lords has recently adopted the Kjeldsen test, I need not discuss the later Strasbourg jurisprudence. I am content to assume that being ordinarily resident in South Africa is a personal characteristic. (emphasis supplied).

On that point Lord Walker made the following observations (paras 53 and 54 of the judgment): **7.126**

> In *Kjeldsen, Busk Madsen and Pedersen v Denmark* (1976) 1 EHRR 711, an early Strasbourg decision concerned with compulsory sex education in state primary schools, the court (at pp 732–733, para 56) interpreted 'status' in article 14 as 'a personal characteristic . . . by which persons or groups of persons are distinguishable from each other.' The fact that a number of parents objected to their children receiving sex education at school was not accepted as equivalent to a religious belief so as to make the complainants a group for the purposes of a claim under article 14 taken together with article 2 of the First Protocol.
>
> It was suggested in argument that the *Kjeldsen* test of looking for a personal characteristic is no longer part of the Strasbourg jurisprudence. But it has recently been followed by the Fourth Section of the European Court of Human Rights in two admissibility decisions, *Budak v Turkey* (unreported), 7 September 2004 (App No 57345/00) and *Beale v United Kingdom* (unreported), 12 October 2004 (App No 6743/03). In *Budak* the only relevant difference was in the criminal procedure adopted for two different types of offence. In *Beale* it was the different investigatory procedures appropriate for the police (on the one hand) and trading standards officers (on the other hand). In neither case was there any personal characteristic of the claimant which could be a ground for discrimination contrary to article 14. Moreover this House has recently applied *Kjeldsen* in *R (S) v Chief Constable of the South Yorkshire Police* [2004] 1 WLR 2196, 2213, para 48 (Lord Steyn).

It seems, therefore, (for the present at least) that Article 14 ECHR is considerably more restrictive and poses greater difficulties for claimants in public law cases than relying on the EC general principle of equal treatment where that principle is capable of being engaged. **7.127**

---

121 She also claimed a breach of Art 1 of Protocol 1.

8

LEGITIMATE EXPECTATIONS

A. The EC Principle Outlined

Legitimate expectations is well known as a doctrine of public law in both domestic and **8.01** HRA law. It is, nonetheless, a distinctive general principle of EC law. As such, the Administrative Court is bound to observe the EC general principle of legitimate expectations, as articulated by the ECJ, in its discrete form. Precisely because it has the same name and essentially similar content to its domestic counterpart, care is needed on the part of those conducting and determining judicial review and other domestic proceedings in which public law issues arise to ensure that the separate EC dimension of the legitimate expectations doctrine is preserved in a case falling within the scope of EC law.

The principle, simply stated, is that Community and national institutions must not, save **8.02** where there is an overriding matter of public interest, breach the legitimate expectations of those in whom such expectations have been engendered in terms of the legal effect of a Community measure such as previous legislation, a specific assurance or specific past practice. The expectation may also arise out of national measures provided that such measures are within the scope of EC law.

Expressed thus, there is a circularity that can only produce a satisfactory definition by exam- **8.03** ining what is meant by, and what is excluded from, the concept of a *legitimate* expectation.

In understanding the differences between, in particular, the domestic conception of legitimate expectation and the EC doctrine it is relevant to emphasize that the EC rationale for the principle and the context in which that principle operates are not the same as in national law.

8.04 The legal foundation for the EC principle of legitimate expectations is closely related to the separate general EC principle of legal certainty.[1] That principle has both a procedural and a substantive content. However, its overall aim is to ensure that the content and application of Community law are certain. This, in turn, involves the twin features, familiar to ECHR practitioners as embodied in Article 6 ECHR protections, of: (1) accessibility and (2) foreseeability.[2] Accessibility is, in essence, procedural and connotes the need for the law to be adequately accessible to the citizen. This aspect of legal certainty is separately considered in Chapter 10.

8.05 Foreseeability means that persons affected by particular legal requirements must be made aware, so that they know, with certainty, what their legal rights and obligations are at any given time.[3]

8.06 It is sometimes difficult to separate this aspect of legal certainty—requiring, as it does, clarity and precision in the drafting of legal measures—from the potentially wider principle of legitimate expectations as espoused by the ECJ. As Advocate General Cosmas observed in *Duff*:[4]

> Particularly for the individual the principle of legality would in many ways lose its significance as a guarantee of a sphere of freedom, if the temporal succession of legal provisions concerning him was not governed by an elementary consistency and coherence sufficient to enable him to discern the consequences (legal and financial) of his activities.

8.07 If, therefore, either the Community institutions or national authorities, as their agents,[5] engender an expectation that is a legitimate one on the part of those affected by it that a measure will have particular consequences, then that *may* have a *substantively* binding effect. There are certain qualifications to be made to this proposition. Nonetheless, this aspect of the rationale for EC legitimate expectations is that of *substantive* as well as procedural legal certainty. As will be seen, the principle of legitimate expectation in domestic law is largely based on fairness which is essentially (though not always) procedural in nature.[6]

8.08 Although, of course, fairness is an important aspect of legal certainty, the latter principle carries with it a clear substantive content which has, until relatively recently, been entirely

---

[1] Case C-83/99 *Commission v Spain* [2001] ECR I–445, para 24.

[2] See, eg, *Silver v United Kingdom* (1983) 5 EHRR 347.

[3] The doctrine of EC legitimate expectations is not necessarily confined to individual decisions although that is its usual application: see Case 81/72 *Commission v Council* [1973] ECR 575.

[4] Case C–63/93 *Duff v Minister for Agriculture and Food, Ireland and Attorney General* [1996] ECR I–569, Opinion, para 24.

[5] National authorities applying EC law are equally bound by the doctrine of EC legitimate expectations: see, eg, Joined Cases C–31–44/91 *Alois Lageder SpA v Amministrazione delle Finanze* [1993] ECR I–1761, para 33.

[6] Fairness may, exceptionally, create a substantive content to legitimate expectation in domestic law as where there is an abuse of power on the part of the public body. See paras 8.81–8.91.

lacking from the domestic enunciation of legitimate expectation. EC jurisprudence has, by contrast, seen no difficulty on the level of principle in recognizing substantive legitimate expectation and the case law of the ECJ does not distinguish, as the English cases most certainly do, between substantive and procedural expectation.

The second point of difference between the development of legitimate expectation in EC **8.09** law and that in domestic law is the different contexts in which the principle has been nurtured.

English public law has, traditionally, been developed in terms of a series of piecemeal **8.10** protections for the individual against the State. Indeed, the doctrine of legitimate expectation was originally cast as the means by which an individual citizen fell within the ambit of judicial review rather than as a separate review doctrine.[7]

The EC context is different. In addressing legitimate expectations the ECJ has always given **8.11** great weight to the public interest and, in particular, to the dynamic way in which the Community operates. Whilst recognizing that there may be circumstances where a legitimate expectation may prevail, the ECJ has been careful to limit the operation of the principle by reference to practical considerations such as the fast-changing nature of Community rules.

Thus, for example, the ECJ has accepted that the concept of legitimate expectations does **8.12** not prevent new rules from being able to be made in order to deal with the future effects of situations arising under earlier rules.[8] The court has been particularly careful to restrict such expectations from prevailing in respect of the common organization of markets that is, necessarily, subject to frequent change.[9]

It is against that background that the subtle but important differences between (in par- **8.13** ticular) EC and domestic legitimate expectation need to be understood. Whilst the ambit of EC legitimate expectations is probably broader than in domestic law because it places fewer restrictions on the notion of *substantive* expectation,[10] the burden of establishing breach of a legitimate expectation in EC law appears to be greater than in domestic law because of the particularly strong competing public interest imperatives in EC law.

Finally, in approaching the general principle of EC legitimate expectations it is important **8.14** to distinguish between: (1) the rules applying to legitimate expectations created by the *conduct* of a Community or national institution from (2) the rules applying to legitimate expectations created by Community or State *legislative measures*. The former bear a relationship to domestic law whereas the latter (in company, at least to some extent, with ECHR law) bring into play the legality of the legislation itself.

---

[7] *Council of Civil Service Unions v Minister for the Civil Service* [1985] AC 374, 408–9, per Lord Diplock.

[8] See, eg, Case 84/78 *Tomadini* [1979] ECR 1801; Case 278/84 *Germany v Commission* [1987] ECR 1.

[9] See, eg, Case 245/81 *Edeka v Germany* [1982] ECR 2745, para 27. See, also, the similar domestic application of this aspect of EC legitimate expectations in *R v Secretary of State for the Environment, ex p Omega Air Ltd* [2000] 2 CMLR 167, 183.

[10] As will be seen, this is not, invariably, the case. For example (see below) EC law requires an expectation to be reasonable whereas, at least in theory, domestic law does not.

8.15   There is, of course, often a close connection between the conduct of the legislator who may have legislated in breach of legitimate expectations and the legislative measures enacted. However, care is needed in addressing legitimate expectations in domestic judicial review in the context of EC and EC derived national legislation. There is an important analytical difference between lawful Community or national EC legislation the non-enforcement of which cannot, generally, give rise to a legitimate expectation of non-enforcement (see below) and Community or national EC legislative measures that it would be unlawful to enforce precisely because such measures breach the EC general principle of legitimate expectations.

8.16   Further, as noted elsewhere, the national court may not hold *Community* legislation to be invalid.[11] In domestic judicial review proceedings a reference under Article 234 (ex 177) EC would be necessary for such purpose. This applies as much to challenges to Community legislation founded on an alleged breach of legitimate expectation as it does to other such challenges.

8.17   Community or State legislation frequently offends against EC legitimate expectations because it breaches the general principle of non-retroactivity which is sometimes considered to be a sub-set of legitimate expectations. The principle of non-retroactivity is separately considered in Chapter 9.

B. EC Legitimate Expectation—Necessary Elements

Nature of expectation

Expectation must be reasonable

8.18   The ECJ will, generally, determine the legitimacy of the expectation and whether it has been induced before examining whether there is an overriding matter of public interest justifying departure from it. These issues are, therefore, considered separately.

8.19   As a threshold requirement, for an expectation to be legitimate it must be *reasonable*. In determining this question the relevant issue is whether an informed, 'prudent and discriminating' person would have had such expectation.[12] This is an objective test and all relevant factual circumstances must be considered by the national court. Where necessary, therefore, extrinsic evidence may be required.

8.20   It can readily be seen that whether or not an expectation is legitimate, in the sense of being reasonable, is a flexible process. It may, for example, require some *assumed* understanding by the person affected of the nature of the Community legislative framework in question. Where that framework necessarily involves the exercise of a broad discretion and frequent adjustment (as, for example, in respect of the common agricultural policy) then a legitimate expectation is less likely to be established.

8.21   In *Delacre*,[13] for example, the applicants, who manufactured pastry products, had applied for aid for butter following an invitation to tender. However, the amount of aid that they

---

[11]   See paras 5.57–5.60.
[12]   See, eg, CFI decision in Case T–336/94 *Efisol SA v Commission* [1996] ECR II–1343.
[13]   Case 350/88 *Delacre v Commission* [1990] ECR I–395.

sought was more than the maximum fixed by the Commission albeit after their application for aid had been lodged. They claimed that they enjoyed a legitimate expectation that the market regulatory system in force at the time of their application would be applied to their application. This argument was rejected. The ECJ held that changes in the applicable rules were to be expected and that, as prudent and well-informed traders, they ought to have foreseen a fall in the level of aid consequent upon an increase in the selling price of butter.[14]

As so often, however, the legislative context is usually highly relevant. Whilst the introduc- **8.22** tion of new pension measures without appropriate transitional provisions may violate a legitimate (that is, reasonable) expectation that there will at least be a suitable transitional period before new measures are introduced,[15] the court has held that it is not a reasonable expectation that there can never be any introduction of legislation with immediate effect merely because certain interests are affected. In *Tomadini*,[16] for example, a regulation introducing compensation was held not to apply to exports made under contracts adopted prior to its adoption. The position, said the ECJ, is otherwise where specific rules have been laid down to enable traders to protect themselves against the shifting effects of particular agricultural measures.

Aspects of reasonableness—motive

The motive of a claimant may sometimes be relevant to determining whether there is a rea- **8.23** sonable expectation. This is not a retreat from the objective test of the 'prudent and discriminating' person referred to above for such a person would not act with improper motive.

So, if a person is seeking to make a speculative profit or, in some other way, to take **8.24** advantage of the Community system his expectation that he will be allowed to do so will not be legitimate. The 'prudent and discriminating' person would appreciate that the Community or relevant national authorities would take immediate action to prevent the loophole from being exploited.

A good example of this is afforded by the court's ruling in *EVGF v Mackprang*.[17] There, a **8.25** German grain dealer sought to take advantage of low grain prices in France in order to sell on to the intervention agency in Germany. A Commission decision was introduced to prevent this after the applicant had purchased grain in France but before he was able to offer it to the German agency. He claimed to have a legitimate expectation that he would be able to sell on to the German agency since at the time of purchase there was no law in force preventing him from doing so.

However, the ECJ held that the Commission decision, which covered grain in transit, was **8.26** simply 'a justified precaution against purely speculative activities'. As Advocate General Warner had observed in his Opinion in the same case:

> No trader who was exploiting that situation in order to make out of the system profits that the system was never designed to bestow on him could legitimately rely on the persistence of

---

[14] To similar effect see, eg, Cases 95–98/74, 15, 100/75 *Union Nationale des Cooperatives Agricoles de Cereales v Commission* [1978] ECR 57.
[15] Case 127/80 *Grogan v Commission* [1982] ECR 869.
[16] Case 84/78 [1979] ECR 180, see para 8.12 above.
[17] Case 2/75 [1975] ECR 607.

the situation. On the contrary, the only reasonable expectation that such a trader could have was that the competent authorities would act as swiftly as possible to bring the situation to an end.

Aspects of reasonableness—non-enforcement or breach of Community law

8.27 The fact that a Community (or national) institution has created or permitted violation of Community law by the position that it adopts towards a third party undertaking does not, of itself, engender a legitimate expectation in that undertaking that any consequent violation of Community law by it will not be enforced at a later stage.[18]

8.28 Thus, for example, the grant of unlawful state aid by a national authority to an undertaking in relation to a product that has not been included in prohibitory state aid guidelines issued by the Commission does not operate either against the State or the Commission, on the footing of legitimate expectation, to prevent the Commission from ordering the national authority to recover the unlawfully paid aid.[19] Similarly, undertakings to which aid has been granted may not, in principle, entertain a legitimate expectation that the aid is lawful unless it has been granted in compliance with the procedure laid down in Article 88 EC and a diligent businessman should normally be able to determine whether that procedure has been followed.[20] The rationale is that neither Commission guidelines nor contingent state action can derogate from the Treaty provisions as to state aid.[21]

8.29 In the same way, a promise not to enforce Community law does not create any legitimate expectation.[22] Nor can mere silence in response to a query as to entitlement under Community law engender such expectation[23] or even incorrect confirmation of entitlement.[24] In other words, it is not a reasonable expectation to seek to rely on Community or State assurances or practices that are themselves in breach of Community law.

8.30 At least in the context of legitimate expectation, the relevant distinction is between Community or State assurances or practices that are precluded by Community law and those that are not.[25] An assurance or practice that is contrary to Community law can never create a legitimate (or reasonable) expectation in an economic operator.[26] For this purpose it is, without more, irrelevant whether or not the Community institution itself has failed to take the necessary steps to ensure that the State complies with Community law.[27]

---

[18] This is, of course, different from the situation where the Community or State measure is itself unlawful *because it breaches a legitimate expectation*. Here, the legislation itself may fall to be quashed: see para 8.15.

[19] See, eg, Case 52/84 *Commission v Belgium* [1986] 1 ECR 89.

[20] See Joined Cases C–183/02 P and C–187/02 P (2004) *(1) Daewoo Electronics Manufacturing Espana SA (Demesa) and (2) Territorio Historico de Alava—Diputacion Foral de Alava v Commission* (unreported, 11 November 2004).

[21] Case 310/85 *Deufil v Commission* [1987] ECR 901.

[22] Case T–2/93 *Air France v Commission* [1994] ECR II–323, para 102.

[23] Case T–123/89 *Chomel v Commission* [1990] ECR II–131, para 26.

[24] Case 188/82 *Thyssen AG v Commission* [1983] ECR 3721, para 11.

[25] For example, Commission guidelines on the method of setting fines did not engender a legitimate expectation that the Commission would not exceed the level of fines previously imposed: see Case C–189/02 P *Dansk Robindustri A/S v Commission* (unreported, 28 June 2005).

[26] See, eg, Case 316/86 *Hauptzollamt Hamburg-Jonas v Krucken* [1988] ECR 2213, para 23.

[27] Case 5/82 *Hauptzollamt Krefeld v Maizenac* [1982] ECR 4601. But see immediately below.

However, Community law does not, at least in the context of agricultural aids, prevent **8.31** domestic law from recognizing a legitimate expectation that payment will not be recovered provided that: (1) recovery of unlawfully paid *national* benefits are made subject to the same rules, and (2) Community interests are fully taken into account.[28]

Further, there may be particularly egregious aspects of a State's or community institution's **8.32** conduct in relation to non-enforcement that do raise a legitimate expectation that enforcement of a Community law obligation will not take place. For example, in *RSV v Commission*[29] the Commission's delay of some 26 months in requiring the Netherlands to recover unlawfully paid state aid was held to have created a legitimate expectation that RSV (the recipient of the unlawful payment) was entitled to retain the aid.

Expectation must be induced

Need for specificity

The requirement that an expectation must, in order to be legitimate, be reasonable is a **8.33** necessary but not a sufficient condition before a breach of such expectation needs to be justified by reference to a matter of overriding public interest (see below). What is also required is that such expectation has been *induced* by the assurance, practice, or legislation of the Community or State body in question.[30]

In examining whether or not there has been a relevant inducement the most important **8.34** consideration is whether or not the conduct of the Community/State—be it in the form of previous legislation, assurance, or practice—is sufficiently *specific* in relation to a particular individual or undertaking. Thus, merely general statements cannot constitute a sufficient inducement. In *Lefebvre v Commission*[31] the CFI said:

> There is an important difference between a statement made by the Commission in general terms which cannot engender any valid expectations, and an assurance in precise terms, on which expectations may legitimately be based.

Although the analogy is far from exact it has been observed that there is usually something **8.35** in the nature of a contract characterizing the relationship between the Community or State institution and the party seeking to raise a legitimate expectation before there can be an inducement in the above sense.[32]

Certainly, proximity of relationship is necessary to establish specificity. As has been suggested **8.36** by one commentator:

> ... Adequate grounds for a solid expectation can be provided on the one hand by the fact of having entered into certain obligations towards the authorities, or on the other hand by a course of conduct on the part of the authorities giving rise to specific expectations—which in certain circumstances may arise out of a commitment entered into by the authorities.[33]

---

[28] Joined Cases 205 to 215/82 *Deutsche Milchkontor v Germany* [1983] ECR 2633, para 33.
[29] Case 223/85 [1987] ECR 4617.
[30] See the helpful summary of Advocate General Cosmas in Case C–183/95 *Affisch BV v Rijksdienst voor de Keturing van Veen en Vlees* [1997] ECR I–4315, 4349.
[31] Case T-571/93 [1995] ECR II–2379, para 74.
[32] See, eg, Advocate General Mischo in Case C–331/88 *R v MAFF, ex p FEDESA* [1990] ECR I–4023, 4048.
[33] J Schwarze, *European Administrative Law* (1992) 1134–5.

8.37 A notable instance of proximity of relationship founding legitimate expectation in the context of previous Community legislation is afforded by the ECJ's decision in the first *Mulder*[34] case. There, a milk quota regulation was held to breach the legitimate expectations of certain milk producers.

8.38 Milk quotas were introduced as a means of curbing excess milk production. Under Council Regulation (EEC) 1078/77, a payment was offered to producers who undertook not to engage in milk production for a period of five years. A subsequent Council Regulation ((EEC) 857/84) created a levy on quantities of milk that were produced over and above a so-called 'reference quantity'. But the new Council Regulation did not allocate any reference quantity to those, such as Mr Mulder, who had discontinued milk production in the year preceding his application. That meant that he was, in practice, unable to take up milk production again. This violated his legitimate expectations. The ECJ observed:

> where such a producer, as in the present case, has been encouraged by a Community measure to suspend marketing for a limited period in the general interest and against payment of a premium he may legitimately expect not to be subject, upon the expiry of his undertaking, to restrictions which specifically affect him precisely because he availed himself of the possibilities offered by the Community provisions.

8.39 The cases following the *Mulder* decision are equally instructive. As a result of the ECJ decision in the first *Mulder* case[35] the Council introduced a further Regulation allowing the affected farmers a special reference quantity of 60 per cent of the quantity of milk marketed in the year preceding that in which they had undertaken to discontinue milk production. That, too, was held to violate the producers' legitimate expectations. The ECJ said:

> It must be made clear . . . that where a reduction . . . is applied, the principle of the protection of legitimate expectations precludes the rate of reduction from being fixed at such a high level, by comparison with those applicable to producers whose reference quantities are fixed pursuant to . . . Regulation No. 857/84, that its application amounts to a restriction which specifically affects them by very reason of the undertaking given by them under Regulation No. 1078/77.[36]

8.40 As these milk quota decisions illustrate, a State or Community institution (there the Council) may have a sufficiently close relationship with a *class* of persons (there milk producers who had undertaken to discontinue production for a particular period) to engender a specific legitimate expectation.

8.41 The inducement engendering such expectation may take the form of legislative provisions (in *Mulder*, for example, the relevant inducement was contained in Regulation (EEC) 1078/77 and the concomitant expectation that producers would only be prevented from producing milk for a specified period). In effect the previous legislation in *Mulder* creating the premium for the producers amounted to a practice of encouraging producers to suspend production for a five year period and no more. It could also be classified as an assurance to such producers that they would only be required to suspend production for five years. So, the decisions also show that challenges to legislation founded on legitimate expectations by reference to the content of previous legislation cannot easily be separated from challenges

---

[34] Case 120/86 *Mulder v Minister van Landbouw en Visserij* [1988] ECR 2321.
[35] ibid.
[36] Case C–189/89 *Spagl* [1990] ECR I–4539, para 22.

to the conduct of State or Community institutions whether by reason of a specific assurance or past practice.

Inducement must be breached by the Community or State body

An inducement may be specific but still not give rise to the need to justify its frustration in **8.42** terms of the legitimate expectations doctrine unless the Community or State body is responsible for the breach. In particular, neither legal certainty nor fairness—which underpin this general principle—requires that the Community or State should bear responsibility for acts of third parties.

In *Anglo-Irish Beef Processors International v MAFF*,[37] for example, the ECJ held that a trade **8.43** embargo imposed by the UN rather than a Community measure preventing trade was the underlying cause of goods failing to reach their destination. Accordingly, the traders' forfeited security did not constitute any breach of legitimate expectation *by the Community institution.*

Fairness and EC legitimate expectations

Although (see above) legal certainty is the mainspring of EC legitimate expectations, **8.44** fairness also plays an important part in determining whether an expectation has been engendered and the strength of the legitimacy that should be accorded to it.

The proper role of the Administrative Court vis-à-vis a domestic public law decision-maker **8.45** in an EC context was fully explained by Sedley J in *R v MAFF, ex p Hamble (Offshore) Fisheries*:[38]

> The legal alchemy which gives an expectation sufficient legitimacy to secure enforcement in public law is the obligation to exercise powers fairly which permits expectations to be counterposed to policy change, not necessarily in order to thwart it but—as in the present case—in order to seek a proper exception to the policy. While policy is for the policy-maker alone, the fairness of his or her decision not to accommodate reasonable expectations which the policy will thwart remains the court's concern (as of course does the lawfulness of the policy) ... It is the court's task to recognise the constitutional importance of ministerial freedom to formulate and to reformulate policy; but it is equally the court's duty to protect the interests of those individuals whose expectations of different treatment has a legitimacy which in fairness outtops the policy choice which threatens to frustrate it ... Legitimacy was a function of expectations induced by government and of policy considerations which militated against their fulfilment. The balance in the first instance was for the policy-maker to strike; but if the outcome was challenged by judicial review, the court's criterion was not the bare rationality of the policy-maker's conclusion and its task was not only to recognise the constitutional importance of ministerial freedom to formulate and to reformulate policy, but also to protect the interests of those individuals whose expectations of different treatment had a legitimacy which in fairness outweighed the policy choice which threatened to frustrate it.

---

[37] Case C–299/94 [1996] ECR I–1925.
[38] [1995] 2 All ER 714, 731. *Hamble* involved the application of MAFF's policy permitting the transfer of fishing licences in respect of EC quotas. Thus, consideration of the doctrine of legitimate expectation by the Administrative Court in that case was, necessarily, consideration of the EC doctrine of legitimate expectation as opposed to the domestic law doctrine.

8.46 This important passage suggests that the legitimacy of an expectation, at least in the EC context, is to be derived from: (1) the fact of a reasonable expectation induced by the public body concerned[39] and (2) the fairness of that expectation being allowed to trump subsequent policy choices. Thus, the unfairness of not adhering to a legitimate expectation that has been created is a highly relevant indication of the true legitimacy of that expectation.

8.47 Viewed in that light, the test of legitimate expectation is, ultimately, objective. It is for (usually) the Administrative Court, in domestic judicial review proceedings, to decide on whether a reasonable expectation has been induced by the Community or State institution and whether or not it is an expectation possessing sufficient legitimacy to require enforcement.

8.48 So, matters such as whether an undertaking has relied to its detriment on the inducement may, depending on the particular facts, be persuasive evidence of the existence of and/or strength to be accorded to a legitimate expectation. Detrimental reliance is also necessary to found a claim for damages based on breach of legitimate expectations.[40] However, such reliance is not in principle determinative in establishing the right to have a legitimate expectation enforced.[41] *A fortiori*, Community or State knowledge or ignorance as to whether there has been such reliance ought to be irrelevant. This was certainly the view of Sedley J in *Hamble*. He said:

> It is precisely because public authorities have public duties to perform that they can no more be estopped from performing them than they can contract out of them. This is why the decision-maker's knowledge or ignorance of the extent of reliance placed by the applicant upon the factors upon which the expectation is founded has no bearing upon the existence or legitimacy of the expectation. It is upon the practices or promises of the public authority that any such expectation will be built: whether it stands up depends not at all on how much the decision-maker knew of the applicant's reliance on the practice or promise . . . [42]

C. Justifying Breaches

Overview

8.49 In reaching, and reviewing, decisions relating to EC legitimate expectations there are, as suggested above, two possible and distinct stages. Stage one is deciding whether there is a legitimate expectation at all. Stage two, if it arises, is deciding whether there is justification for breaching the expectation. As will be seen, this may simply depend upon a factual state of affairs rather than on any real balancing exercise.

8.50 If a balancing exercise arises there is, analytically at least, a difference between stages one and two even though, as *Hamble Fisheries*[43] suggests, considerations of fairness may often

---

[39] As to which, see para 8.19.
[40] See, eg, Case 74/74 *CNTA v Commission* [1975] ECR 533.
[41] Although, as in domestic law, there are cases where the ECJ has not accepted the application of the legitimate expectation doctrine where the applicant has not changed its position in reliance on State conduct: see, eg, Case C–110/97 *Netherlands v Commission* [2001] ECR I–8763, para 117.
[42] [1995] 2 All ER 714, 725.
[43] [1995] 2 All ER 714, see para 8.45.

be as relevant to the legality of a decision to breach a legitimate expectation as to defining the *strength* of that expectation.

The question of whether there is a matter of overriding public interest needs, therefore, to **8.51** be separated from the determination of whether a legitimate expectation has been engendered at all. Whereas the existence or otherwise of a legitimate expectation is, in part, a matter of objective ascertainment by the court, in accordance with the principles discussed in the previous section, a decision as to whether such expectation may lawfully be breached may depend upon: (1) correct identification of the public interest and (2) lawful exercise of power conforming to the proportionality principle. So, proportionality—striking the balance between the public interest and the legitimate expectation—is fundamental to stage two. It is not directly relevant to stage one.

Thus, for example, proportionality is not relevant to deciding whether an ultra vires assurance **8.52** that cannot be given pursuant to Community law should be honoured because of a claimant's asserted legitimate expectation. It cannot be honoured because it would be unlawful to do so. Similarly, proportionality is not material to the question of whether an asserted expectation is *reasonable*. An expectation may, on the facts of a given case, be reasonable but whether or not it is reasonable does not depend upon the proportionality principle. The same considerations apply to whether or not there has been a relevant inducement.

Identifying the relevant public interest

The Community or State institution must correctly identify the nature of the public **8.53** interest. Whether or not it is an *overriding* public interest engages proportionality but if there is, in law, no relevant public interest then there can be no justification for breaching a legitimate expectation.

Identification of a relevant public interest is, like the search for a legitimate aim in ECHR **8.54** law, unlikely to prove controversial. It is, nonetheless, as important a starting point as identifying a legitimate expectation since, without such identification, the proportionality exercise cannot lawfully engage.[44]

Further, it is the public interest identified by the Community or State institution that is, **8.55** in principle, determinative. So, for example, the fact that as a matter of theory the Administrative Court might be able to infer a relevant public interest justifying breach of an EC legitimate expectation ought not to be relevant to determining an unlawful breach if such public interest was not the true basis of the decision challenged by way of judicial review.

The importance of the decision-maker identifying a relevant public interest is to be **8.56** inferred from the ECJ's ruling in *Sofrimport*.[45] There, the ECJ held that the Commission had 'failed completely' to take the legitimate expectations of the applicants into account when suspending importation by two Council regulations. By a previous Council regulation the Commission was required in adopting protective measures to take into account the 'special position of products in transit'. This provision, in the court's view, created

---

[44] cf Richard Gordon QC, 'Legitimate Aim—A Dimly Lit Road' (2002) 4 EHRLR 421–7.
[45] Case C–152/88 *Sofrimport v Commission* [1990] ECR I–2477.

a legitimate expectation that no importer with goods in transit would be subject to importation being suspended unless there was an overriding public interest that compelled breach of the expectation.

8.57 In the event, the Commission's argument that there was no legitimate expectation in play because the prospect of future suspensory measures was heralded in its legislation was rejected. The ECJ held that the Commission was obliged to state in advance what overriding public interest could require the applicants' legitimate expectations to be defeated. It had not done so and had, in the circumstances, not shown any overriding public interest to exist.

8.58 *Sofrimport* offers a particular instance of the importance, at least in some cases, of informing affected persons in advance of what constitutes an overriding public interest. Whilst this is, plainly, not a general requirement on Community or State institutions it is incumbent on those bodies to be able to establish that they have addressed the circumstances in which an identified legitimate expectation is said to be justifiably breached when seeking to defend their decisions.

8.59 It is, however, also true (see below) that there are cases in which the questions of identifying a relevant public interest and/or deciding whether such interest is overriding are somewhat artificial since the authority's prior conduct may, of itself, render it illegitimate to breach a legitimate expectation.

Is there an overriding public interest?

8.60 Proportionality is not an exact science. As *Hamble*[46] indicates the balancing exercise is one 'in the first instance' for the Community or State body concerned. Having identified a legitimate expectation and a countervailing public interest those two elements have to be balanced one against the other in order to determine whether the public interest is *overriding*—that is, a public interest that is sufficiently strong to outweigh the legitimate expectation. As with proportionality generally[47] a measure of deference on the part of the court is required before the proportionality exercise conducted by the decision maker will be held to be unlawful or, if appropriate, referred under Article 234 (ex 177) EC for a ruling by the ECJ. There are, though, certain qualifications that need to be made to this.

8.61 First, if—as in *Sofrimport*[48]—the institutions have 'failed completely' to take the applicants' legitimate expectations into account then there is non-compliance with proportionality because no balancing exercise has been undertaken. In such a case the national court is not required to show deference to the decision-maker or to decide whether there is some overriding public interest justifying breach of the legitimate expectation that has occurred.

8.62 Secondly, the question of 'balancing' the expectation against the public interest may not arise because the conduct of the authority in creating a legitimate expectation effectively rules out such an exercise. In such a case, again, proportionality will not engage. The authority is bound to fulfil the expectation.

---

[46] See para 8.45.
[47] See Chapter 11.
[48] Case C–152/88 [1990] ECR I–2477, see paras 8.56–8.59.

In *Interhotel*,[49] for example, the CFI ruled that the Commission could not refuse to make a **8.63** payment from the European Social Fund on the ground of a breach of an approval condition that it had not ensured was communicated to the undertaking concerned. The Commission's conduct in approving the application without reference to that condition created a legitimate expectation that it would not act inconsistently with its stated approval. So, too, in *Opel*[50] the CFI held that a deposit of Treaty instruments gave rise to a specific representation and, hence, legitimate expectation that the Commission would not act inconsistently prior to the entry into force of the Treaty obligation.

These cases exemplify a situation in which the conduct of the Community or State institution **8.64** seems, at least for practical purposes, to exclude any further balancing exercise.

Where, however, the court is concerned with alleged justification for breaching a legitimate **8.65** expectation it has been observed that:

> Overall, the cases on milk quotas[51] indicate that the principle of protection of legitimate expectations imposes more severe restraints on the discretion of Community institutions than the principle of equal treatment, and a trader who is able to establish that somehow he has a legitimate expectation is more likely to succeed in his claim.[52]

Despite this, as with other instances engaging proportionality,[53] very few cases based on an **8.66** alleged breach of legitimate expectation succeed in areas where economic policy judgments have to be made. As Sharpston has commented in respect of the legitimate expectations principle:

> ... the general rule appears to be that the European Court will usually be prepared to back the Council and/or the Commission and to hold that they are entitled to have a fairly wide margin of manoeuvre in market management, even where the chosen scheme has been subjected to fairly heavy criticism.[54]

In the cases where the ECJ has held that there has been a breach of an undertaking's legitimate **8.67** expectations the situation has usually involved the court balancing, in favour of the undertaking, the need of the Community to change its policy for the future with the adverse impact that the altered policy will have on an undertaking that has based its commercial arrangements on the pre-existing situation. Legitimate expectation has, for example, as shown above been successfully invoked in a number of instances including those involving milk quotas, and the grant of state aid.

A further example is afforded by the facts of *CNTA*.[55] There, the applicant was an undertaking **8.68** that had entered into export contracts in reliance on the availability of monetary compensation amounts. These were payments designed to provide compensation for fluctuations in exchange rates.

After the export contracts had been concluded, but before they were to be performed, the **8.69** Commission introduced legislation abolishing monetary compensation amounts in the

---

[49] Case T–81/95 *Interhotel v Commission* [1997] ECR II–1265.
[50] Case T–115/94 *Opel Austria GmbH v Council* [1997] ECR II–39.
[51] See paras 8.37–8.41.
[52] T Tridimas, *The General Principles of EU Law* (2nd edn, 2006) 279.
[53] See paras 11.24–11.31.
[54] E Sharpston, 'Legitimate Expectations and Economic Reality' (1990) 15 EL Rev 103, 108.
[55] Case 74/74 [1975] ECR 533.

relevant sector. The ECJ held that, in the circumstances, a legitimate expectation had been created and that a prudent undertaking might reasonably expect not to have to cover itself against the risks protected by the compensation payments and that, in the absence of an overriding public interest (which did not exist) transitional measures should have been adopted to protect the applicant's position.

8.70   The ECJ said:

> In these circumstances, a trader might legitimately expect that for transactions irrevocably undertaken by him because he has obtained, subject to a deposit, export licences fixing the amount of the refund in advance, no unforeseeable alteration will occur which could have the effect of causing him inevitable loss, by re-exposing him to the exchange risk.[56]

8.71   As can be seen from the cases discussed above on the prudent and discriminating trader,[57] there will often be a close relationship between the reasonableness of the expectation creating a *legitimate* expectation and the issue of whether there is an *overriding* public interest enabling it to be defeated. Part of the determination of whether the expectation is reasonable may depend upon whether the trader ought to have foreseen the circumstances that have arisen. To some extent, at least, (though in *CNTA* they were treated separately) the question of whether subsequent acts of the Community or State institution ought to have been foreseen by a trader or undertaking claiming a legitimate expectation will be highly relevant to the conceptually separate question of whether or not there is an overriding public interest.

D. Legitimate Expectation in the Domestic and HRA Contexts

8.72   Legitimate expectation is a doctrine that applies not only to EC law but is also well established in domestic law and under the ECHR.[58] It follows that in approaching judicial review challenges founded on an alleged breach of a claimant's legitimate expectations the national court may be faced with overlapping jurisdictional notions of the precise content of the doctrine. Since legitimate expectation is very similar as between the jurisdictions it is particularly important to isolate the points of difference in order to apply the principle appropriately.[59] In particular, it would be impermissible for a national court in a case falling within the scope of EC law to accept as a legitimate expectation in domestic law that which would not constitute a legitimate expectation in EC law since, otherwise, the interests of the EU would effectively be bypassed.[60]

8.73   The starting point is, however, the common features underlying legitimate expectation. In EC, domestic, and HRA law it is necessary for there to be: (1) a legitimate expectation that

---

[56] ibid. para 42.
[57] See paras 8.19–8.32.
[58] The literature on domestic legitimate expectation is now immense. See, generally: C Forsyth, 'The Provenance and Protection of Legitimate Expectations' (1988) 47 CLJ 238; R Clayton, 'Legitimate Expectations, Policy and the Principle of Consistency' (2003) 62 CLJ 93; P Sales and K Steyn, 'Legitimate Expectations in English Public Law: An Analysis' [2004] PL 564; I Steele, 'Substantive Legitimate Expectations: Striking the Right Balance?' (2005) 121 LQR 300; P Sales, 'Legitimate Expectations' [2006] JR 186.
[59] A point well made, in the domestic/HRA context by Paul Craig and Soren Schonberg. See, 'Substantive Legitimate Expectations after Coughlan' [2000] PL 684, 700–1.
[60] See, eg, Case C–5/89 *Commission v Germany* [1990] ECR I–3437, paras 13–19.

has (2) been engendered by a public authority, and that (3) cannot be breached save where there is a matter of overriding public importance.

Is there a legitimate expectation?—contrasting the position in domestic and HRA law

In EC law, as has been seen, the legitimacy of an expectation is largely determined by its **8.74** *reasonableness*. The question of what is a reasonable expectation is flexible but is certainly sufficiently broad to enable the court to find that no legitimate expectation exists in a wide range of situations by reference to objective criteria, most notably that of the person who is 'prudent and discriminating'.[61] The flexibility of the EC approach means, for example, that the ECJ has never found difficulty in accommodating the notion of substantive expectation. To that extent it has, sometimes, proved more expansive than the traditional domestic approach. On the other hand, under the rubric of *reasonableness* the court has denied expectations the requisite legitimacy in circumstances in which domestic law[62] might well have operated differently.

It is certainly true that domestic law recognizes that the fact that an expectation has been **8.75** engendered does not necessarily render that expectation *legitimate*. Thus, in *Re Findlay*,[63] Lord Scarman asked:

> It is said that the refusal to except [the claimants] from the new policy was an unlawful act on the part of the Secretary of State in that his decision frustrated their expectation. But what was their legitimate expectation?[64]

However, domestic law does not formulate the scope of that which may constitute a legit- **8.76** imate expectation in the same way as in EC law. The purpose of legitimate expectations in EC law '. . . is not the furtherance of consistency of conduct by public bodies but avoidance of prejudice by inconsistency of conduct'.[65]

In domestic law the principle has developed slightly differently. There is an emphasis on con- **8.77** sistency of conduct and avoidance of abuse of power.[66] For example, in *Begbie*[67] Sedley LJ said:

> I have no difficulty with the proposition that in cases where government has made known how it intends to exercise powers which affect the public at large it may be held to its word irrespective of whether the [claimant] had been relying upon it. The legitimate expectation in such a case is that government will behave towards its citizens as it says it will.

It is certainly the position that in a great many instances the context will require a specific **8.78** and unambiguous promise or assurance.[68] Frequently, there will also be a need to establish

---

[61] See paras 8.19 et seq.
[62] The phrase 'domestic law' is used here, unless otherwise qualified, to reflect the position in domestic cases outside the confines of the HRA.
[63] [1985] AC 318.
[64] ibid 338. To similar effect, see *R v Department for Education and Employment, ex p Begbie* [2000] 1 WLR 1115, 1125, per Peter Gibson LJ.
[65] *Milk Marketing Board of England and Wales v Tom Parker Farms Ltd* [1999] Eu LR 154, 164G.
[66] See, further, *R (Rashid) v Secretary of State for the Home Department* [2005] EWCA Civ 744 and the analysis by Mark Elliott 'Legitimate Expectation, Consistency and Abuse of Power: the *Rashid* Case' [2005] JR 281.
[67] [2000] 1 WLR 1115, 1133E.
[68] See, most notably, *R v Inland Revenue Commissioners, ex p MFK Underwriting Agents Ltd* [1990] 1 WLR 1545.

detrimental reliance on the part of the claimant.[69] However, neither communication nor knowledge on the part of the claimant is, inevitably, required before a legitimate expectation can be created in domestic law. In *R v Secretary of State for the Home Department, ex p Ahmed*,[70] for example, it was held that there was, even in the absence of knowledge or communication, a legitimate expectation vested in the claimant that the Secretary of State would not act inconsistently with a ratified Convention.

8.79 The rationale for this is that legitimate expectation in domestic law is increasingly underpinned by a conception of administrative fairness and lawful exercise of power rather than by (as in the EC context) an overall framework of reasonableness.[71]

8.80 This slightly different perspective has its strengths and weaknesses. One of the weaknesses is that English administrative law, in sharp contrast to its EC counterpart, has found it particularly difficult to embrace a concept of *substantive* legitimate expectation; that is, a legitimate expectation of a substantive benefit as opposed to an expectation of procedural fairness. The focus has, until recently, been on *procedural* legitimate expectation presumably because procedural fairness has a clear association with the lawful exercise of administrative power and because judicial review has, traditionally, been concerned with the legality of the decision-making process; that is, with process rather than with outcome.

8.81 However, it is now accepted that, at least in some instances, domestic law recognizes the principle of substantive legitimate expectation.

8.82 The leading case is the decision of the Court of Appeal in *R v North and East Devon Health Authority, ex p Coughlan*.[72] There, the claimant had been seriously injured in a road traffic accident. For many years she resided at a particular hospital (Newcourt Hospital). Ms Coughlan, and the other patients, agreed to be moved to a different hospital (Mardon House) which was a modern, long-term, purpose-built NHS facility said to be more appropriate to meet their needs. They were induced to leave because of the Health Authority's promise that they could live at Mardon House 'for as long as they chose'.

8.83 In the event, only a few years after giving its promise, the Health Authority made a decision to close Mardon House and to move the patients to different facilities. The patients were consulted and the Authority went through a process that was, as the Court of

---

[69] See, especially, *R v Jockey Club, ex p RAM Racecourses* [1993] 2 All ER 225 where per Stuart-Smith LJ at 236–237 this was said to be a necessary requirement. However, subsequent decisions have made it clear that detrimental reliance, though usually highly relevant, is not a necessary precondition of a legitimate expectation: see, eg, *Begbie* [2000] 1 WLR 1115, 1124, per Peter Gibson LJ.

[70] [1999] Imm AR 40.

[71] This may be why the concept of private law estoppel has been rejected in the domestic public law context: see *R (Reprotech (Pebsham) Ltd) v East Sussex County Council* [2003] 1 WLR 348. It has been suggested that *Reprotech* is an opportunity for the Administrative Court to expand the notion of domestic law legitimate expectation: see M Elliott, 'Unlawful Representations, Legitimate Expectations and Estoppel in Public Law' [2003] JR 71, 80.

[72] [2001] QB 213. See, most recently, *R (Abdi and Nadarajah) v Secretary of State for the Home Department* [2005] EWCA Civ 1363, especially paras 67–71, where the Court of Appeal comes closer to EC legitimate expectation by emphasizing the relevance of proportionality whether the legitimate expectation in question is procedural or substantive.

Appeal held,[73] procedurally fair. The decision-making process was not criticized as irrational but it was, nonetheless, held to breach the claimant's legitimate expectation of being able to remain at Mardon House in the absence of a contrary overwhelming public interest. The court found that there was no such interest.

Coughlan is a landmark decision because it settles the long-standing debate as to whether a **8.84** substantive expectation is a concept known to English law. Unlike the position in EC law, however, the classes of case in which the Administrative Court is prepared to find a substantive legitimate expectation are limited.

The Court of Appeal designated three classes of case in *Coughlan* in which legitimate **8.85** expectation may engage in domestic law. They are:

(1) Those cases where a public authority is required merely to have regard to its previous policy before adopting a different policy. Here, the Administrative Court will only review a decision to change course on rationality grounds. In such a case 'the individual can claim no higher expectation than to have his individual circumstances considered by the decision-maker in the light of the policy then in force'.[74]

(2) Those cases where there is a legitimate expectation of consultation before a particular decision is taken. Here 'it is uncontentious that the court itself will require the opportunity for consultation to be given unless there is an overriding reason to resile from it . . . in which case the court will itself judge the adequacy of the reason advanced for the change of policy, taking into account what fairness requires'.[75] The Administrative Court is, in such a case, exercising a 'full review' jurisdiction.[76]

(3) Those cases where a substantive legitimate expectation is created. As the Court of Appeal observed in *Coughlan*:

> Where the court considers that a lawful promise or practice has induced a legitimate expectation of a benefit which is substantive, not simply procedural, authority now establishes that here too the court will in a proper case decide whether to frustrate the expectation is so unfair that to take a new and different course will amount to an abuse of power. Here, once the legitimacy of the expectation is established, the court will have the task of weighing the requirements of fairness against any overriding interest relied upon for the change of policy.[77]

Whilst the first two classes of case identified in *Coughlan* involve consideration of a procedural **8.86** legitimate expectation, the last category is avowedly substantive. Difficulty arises, however, in specifying the circumstances necessary for the creation of a substantive as opposed to a procedural legitimate expectation in domestic law. In *Coughlan* the Court of Appeal adopted a pragmatic approach providing indicia but no clear statement of principle. It was, for example, suggested that most fairness cases are 'likely in the nature of things to be cases where the expectation is confined to one person or a few people, giving the promise or

---

[73] At first instance, Hidden J had categorized the process as procedurally unfair holding, in particular, that the consultation process was unlawful.

[74] [2001] QB 213, para 73.

[75] ibid para 57(b).

[76] ibid para 62.

[77] ibid para 57(c).

representation the character of a contract'.[78] Further, on the facts of *Coughlan* a substantive expectation was capable of being created because the consequences of having to honour the promise were purely financial.[79]

8.87 A more structured approach to identifying substantive expectation was provided by Laws LJ in *Begbie*[80] He observed as follows:

> As it seems to me the first and third categories explained in the *Coughlan* case . . . are not hermetically sealed. The facts of the case, viewed always in their statutory context, will steer the court to a more or less intrusive quality of review. In some cases a change of tack by a public authority, though unfair from the [claimant's] stance, may involve questions of general policy affecting the public at large or a significant section of it (including interests not represented before the court); here the judges may well be in no position to adjudicate save at most on a bare *Wednesbury* basis, without themselves donning the garb of policy-maker, which they cannot wear . . . In other cases the act or omission complained of may take place on a much smaller stage, with far fewer players . . . There may be no wide-ranging issues of general policy, or none with multi-layered effects, upon whose merits the court is asked to embark. The court may be able to envisage clearly and with sufficient certainty what the full consequences will be of any order it makes. In such a case the court's condemnation of what is done is an abuse of power, justifiable . . . only if an overriding public interest is shown of which the court is the judge, offers no offence to the claims of democratic power. There will of course be a multitude of cases falling within these extremes, or sharing the characteristics of one or other.

8.88 It can be seen, therefore, that although domestic law now recognizes the concept of a substantive legitimate expectation it is a restricted one. The position would appear to be somewhat different in an HRA context. In that context, a legitimate expectation to a substantive benefit may arise from the nature of the Convention right claimed to be affected.

8.89 In one respect, at least, the approach to substantive legitimate expectation adopted by the European Court of Human Rights may be more generous than that prevailing in either EC or domestic law in that the fact that the public authority has acted ultra vires does not appear to prevent the creation of a substantive legitimate expectation. This is shown by the facts in *Stretch*.[81]

8.90 There, the applicant's building lease, granted by the Borough Council, contained an option to renew. The applicant gave notice to the Council's successor of his wish to exercise the renewal option. However, this request was refused because the original grant of the option had been made ultra vires. In domestic proceedings the applicant sought declarations and specific performance but his claim and appeal were dismissed. He applied to the European Court of Human Rights alleging a breach of Article 1 of the First Protocol. The Strasbourg Court held that he had a legitimate expectation of exercising the option. The Council was not obliged in law to renew so its refusal could not amount to interference with the

---

[78] ibid para 59.
[79] ibid para 60.
[80] [2000] 1 WLR 1115, 1130.
[81] *Stretch v United Kingdom* (2004) 38 EHRR 12. As was noted by Mance LJ in *Rowland v Environment Agency* [2003] EWCA Civ 1885, [2005] Ch 1, para 55, 'it can no longer be an automatic answer under English law to a case of legitimate expectation, that the Agency had no power ...'. The context suggests that this observation was made in a case engaging Convention rights. See, also, *Pine Valley Developments v Ireland* (1991) 14 EHRR 319.

applicant's possessions. However, it was held that the Council's actions did deprive the applicant of part of the consideration which he gave in entering the original agreement. That was an interference with peaceable enjoyment of his possessions and the interference was disproportionate. This was, therefore, a violation of his Article 1 rights and compensation was awarded for pecuniary and non-pecuniary damage (that is, for frustration and inconvenience).

Cases like *Coughlan* and *Stretch* illustrate the different approaches that may be taken to the scope of legitimate expectation outside EC law and, in particular, to whether a legitimate expectation has been created. As has been emphasized repeatedly, judicial review proceedings may involve overlapping challenges founded on each of the relevant jurisdictions and the concept of legitimate expectation may result in a different outcome depending on the jurisdiction being exercised. **8.91**

Inducing the expectation—public bodies, public authorities, and emanations of the State

The distinctions between a public body susceptible to domestic judicial review, a 'public authority' under the HRA and an emanation of the State sufficient to attract the protection of EC law have already been addressed.[82] In general, at least on the cases thus far, the test of whether a body is an emanation of the State for EC purposes appears to be broader in scope than for that of being a public authority under the HRA (or in domestic law). **8.92**

For present purposes it is important to bear in mind that, at least in the current state of domestic law, a legitimate expectation may be created by a particular authority because it is considered to be a relevant public authority for domestic judicial review or HRA purposes. A very similar body may, however, not create such an expectation because it is considered by the courts to be outside the scope of a 'public authority' and so is not susceptible to judicial review at all. **8.93**

This is demonstrated by *Coughlan* discussed above[83] taken together with two very similar cases that led to a different outcome. In *Coughlan* it was not contested that a health authority was a public body susceptible to domestic judicial review. Accordingly, the issue of whether it had created a substantive legitimate expectation was justiciable by reference to the principles of legitimate expectation in domestic law analysed earlier. **8.94**

Servite[84] involved very similar facts to *Coughlan*. It was a pre-HRA case. The claimants were residents in a residential care home managed by Servite, a charitable housing association. Wandsworth LBC had assessed the residents as being in need of residential accommodation. Instead of providing the care directly, as it might have done, Wandsworth discharged its statutory duty by making indirect provision and entering into an arrangement with Servite. **8.95**

---

[82] See paras 2.17–2.29.
[83] See paras 8.82–8.86.
[84] *R v Servite Houses and Wandsworth LBC, ex p Goldsmith and Chatting* [2000] 2 LGLR 997.

8.96   Just as in *Coughlan* a specific promise was made to the residents by Servite that they could live in the residential care home for the rest of their lives. However, Moses J held that—unlike the Health Authority in *Coughlan*—Servite was not amenable to domestic judicial review. It followed that no valid legitimate expectation was created even though, had Wandsworth made the promise, an enforceable legitimate expectation would have resulted.

8.97   A similar result prevailed in *Leonard Cheshire*.[85] That was a post-HRA case. The facts were virtually identical to those in *Servite*. Leonard Cheshire, a private charity, contracted with the local authority—as had Servite—to manage a residential care home in order to provide care that the local authority had assessed elderly and disabled residents as being in need of. It was assumed for the purposes of argument that a specific home for life promise had been given to the claimants by Leonard Cheshire. The question was whether Leonard Cheshire was a 'public authority' for the purposes of the HRA or was otherwise amenable to judicial review.

8.98   The Court of Appeal, upholding Stanley Burnton J at first instance, held that Leonard Cheshire was neither a 'public authority' nor otherwise amenable to domestic judicial review. Accordingly, no valid legitimate expectation had been created.

8.99   It is outside the scope of this work to analyse the post-*Coughlan* cases further. They produce obvious anomalies and have been subject to academic criticism.[86] However, they show that in all cases involving legitimate expectation that come before the Administrative Court the nature of the body inducing the claimed expectation may need to be carefully examined before it can be established that a valid legitimate expectation has been created. A public body for the purposes of domestic judicial review may or may not be a 'public authority' for HRA purposes or a State emanation for EC purposes.

The basis of review

8.100   Once a legitimate expectation is established it becomes necessary to decide whether or not there is a matter of overriding public importance that justifies breaching the expectation. As has been observed, the relevant standard of review of a decision to breach a legitimate expectation in EC law is that of proportionality.[87] Proportionality is also applied in HRA cases.[88] However, application of EC proportionality has recently been held by the Court of Appeal to involve a more stringent test than HRA proportionality.[89] Proportionality,

---

85   *R (Heather) v Leonard Cheshire Foundation* [2002] 2 All ER 936. See, though, *Aston Cantlow v Wallbank* [2003] UKHL 37, [2004] 1 AC 546. For the relationship between these cases see paras 2.17–2.29.

86   See, eg, PP Craig 'Contracting Out, the Human Rights Act and the Scope of Judicial Review' (2002) 118 LQR 551. See, also, the Seventh Report of the Joint Committee on Human Rights, 'The Meaning of Public Authority under the Human Rights Act', HL 39/HC 382, 2003–2004 which is critical of the approach taken by the courts to the meaning of the term 'public authority'. For a contrary view see, eg, D Oliver [2004] PL 329.

87   See para 8.51. See, also, S J Schonberg, *Legitimate Expectations in Administrative Law* (2000) 149–50.

88   See, eg, *Stretch v United Kingdom* (2004) 38 EHRR 12.

89   *R (Countryside Alliance) v (1) Attorney General and (2) Secretary of State for Environment, Food and Rural Affairs* [2005] EWHC 1677 (judgment 23 June 2006). For analysis of this case including the Court of Appeal's important pronouncement on the different scope of proportionality in EC law, see Ch 17 paras 17.98–17.129.

in whatever form, may well produce a different outcome to other less intensive methods of judicial review.[90]

In domestic law the standard of review appropriate to protecting substantive legitimate expectations has not yet been precisely delineated. *Coughlan* approached the question by reference to principles of 'full review' to prevent an abuse of power. However, this does not provide a precise set of criteria comparable to those contained in the proportionality principle. In a non-HRA case that is outside the scope of EC law the Administrative Court has not yet embraced proportionality explicitly.[91] It is submitted, however, that in substantive legitimate expectation cases some form of balancing process, akin to proportionality, is likely to be undertaken in practice.[92] **8.101**

---

[90] See paras 11.84–11.85.

[91] See the reservations as to proportionality expressed by the House of Lords in *R v Home Secretary, ex p Brind* [1991] 1 AC 696, 767. See, though, *R (Abdi and Nadarajah) v Secretary of State for the Home Department* [2005] EWCA Civ 1363. For a critical analysis of this case, see P Sales, 'Legitimate Expectations' [2006] JR 186.

[92] See Craig and Schonberg (n 59 above) 698–700.

9

NON-RETROACTIVITY

A. Non-retroactivity as a General Principle

Non-retroactivity is a general principle of EC law. As with other general principles, it is **9.01** used both as a principle of interpretation and as one conferring substantive protection.

This means that the Administrative Court—or other national court where public law **9.02** issues are raised—must apply non-retroactivity in its discrete EC form in those judicial review challenges falling within the scope of EC law.[1] Although (see para 9.86 et seq.) both domestic and HRA law have a similar principle there are distinctions and constraints on non-retroactivity in EC law that do not find formal recognition elsewhere.

In essence, non-retroactivity—*where it operates as a legal constraint*[2]—prevents a Community **9.03** or relevant national legislative measure from having effect in respect of a period prior to its publication.[3]

---

[1] The definitional scope of EC law in the context of general principles of EC law is analysed separately: see para 6.31 et seq.

[2] The qualification is important since (see below) a legislative measure may sometimes be retroactive yet perfectly lawful.

[3] The principle of non-retroactivity applies, most commonly, to legislative measures but is, in principle, equally applicable to other administrative decisions falling within the scope of EC law. The expression 'legislative measures' is used here for convenience.

9.04 That is a statement of what non-retroactivity as an EC general principle entails. However, it should be appreciated that there is, save in relation to the criminal law, no general *prohibition* against retroactivity. There is, in certain instances, a *presumption* against it. But the presumption may be displaced if particular conditions are satisfied. Occasionally, indeed, there may be a requirement that a particular measure be made retroactive.

9.05 As will be seen, the general principle of non-retroactivity in EC law has strong affinities with certain other general principles; most notably, those of legal certainty and legitimate expectations. Legal certainty provides the rationale for non-retroactivity since if laws could, generally, operate to retroactive effect those subject to the law could not plan their activities and legal certainty would be eroded. Legitimate expectations are also highly material to non-retroactivity since the presence of a legitimate expectation may operate to prevent a legislative measure from having retroactive effect if such effect would infringe the legitimate expectation in question.

9.06 The EC principle of non-retroactivity may affect domestic judicial review proceedings in a number of ways. It may, in particular, be relevant to:

(1) the interpretation of Community and national legislative measures;
(2) the legality of Community[4] and national legislative measures;
(3) consideration of those cases where:
    (a) unlawful legislative measures are revoked retroactively, and/or
    (b) a Community measure is annulled or a national measure quashed by the ECJ or Administrative Court.

9.07 Thus, a number of different situations may arise where non-retroactivity has to be grappled with. Before embarking on these, there are a number of basic principles, in relation to non-retroactivity, that must be understood.

B. The Basic Rules

Distinction between true and apparent retroactivity

9.08 The non-retroactivity principle as such extends only to cases of 'true retroactivity', namely to events already completed before the legislative measure was published but to which the legislation is expressed to apply or where the date of implementation of a measure precedes the date of publication.

9.09 So, the principle is not designed to address what is sometimes called 'apparent retroactivity'[5] as, for example, the consequences of situations arising under previous legislation that have

---

[4] As emphasized elsewhere in this work, Community legislation may not be declared to be invalid by the Administrative Court. However, a reference under Art 234 (ex 177) EC may be made to the ECJ so that issues of potential non-compliance of a Community measure with the EC general principles of law will still fall to be addressed by the Administrative Court: see, generally, paras 4.92–4.98.

[5] Apparent retroactivity is sometimes termed 'quasi-retroactivity', or 'material retroactivity' or 'immediate application': see, generally, T Tridimas, *The General Principles of EU Law* (2nd edn, 2006), 266 et seq.

not been resolved by the time of the new legislation and that are, therefore, necessarily affected by the new legislation.[6]

The central distinguishing feature between true and apparent retroactivity is that in the **9.10** latter case the actions and events to which the new legislation is expressed to apply are still in the course of completion.[7]

Effect of the distinction

The dividing line between true and apparent retroactivity is sometimes difficult to draw. **9.11** Legislation that is retroactive in either sense is, of course, capable of causing hardship and unfairness to individuals and undertakings.

Importantly, the ECJ does not always distinguish between true and apparent retroactivity. **9.12** However, there is an important analytical difference between the two concepts. The EC general principle of non-retroactivity, at least outside the criminal context, does not apply to cases of apparent retroactivity at all. This does not mean that third parties whose interests are unfairly affected by such legislation are left unprotected. What it means, though, is that in such cases they will have to establish that the legislation has offended against a separate general principle usually that of legitimate expectations. They will, for practical purposes, bear the burden of proving a breach of their legitimate expectations.

The effect of the principle of non-retroactivity applying is that the presumption against **9.13** non-retroactivity engages. The effect of the presumption is, at least for practical purposes, that the State bears the burden of displacing the presumption. It is, therefore, somewhat easier for an affected undertaking to establish a breach of its legitimate expectations in a case where the non-retroactivity principle applies than it would be if the principle were not in play.

Scope of the principle

As explained above, the principle of non-retroactivity contains both an interpretative and **9.14** a substantive aspect. The rule of interpretation, *so far as substantive non-criminal legislation is concerned*, is that such legislation is presumed, in the absence of clear contrary wording, not to be retroactive.[8]

There are, however, certain points that require emphasis. First, the above interpretative rule **9.15** may not apply to *procedural* legislation. Certainly, in *Salumni*[9] the ECJ limited the above formulation of the principle against retroactivity to rules of substantive law.

Secondly, there is an absolute prohibition against any type of retroactivity so far as *crimi-* **9.16** *nal* legislation is concerned. This was made clear by the ECJ in *R v Kent Kirk*[10] where the

---

[6] See, eg, Case 1/73 *Westzucker v Einfuhr-und Vorratsstelle fur Zucker* [1973] ECR 723, para 5.
[7] ibid 739, per Advocate General Roemer.
[8] Of the many cases see, eg, Case 100/63 *Kalsbeek v Sociale Verzekeringsbank* [1964] ECR 565, 575.
[9] Joined Cases 212–17/80 [1981] ECR 2735.
[10] Case 63/83 [1984] ECR 2689, paras 21–22: see, also, paras 9.51–9.52.

ECJ aligned the non-retroactivity principle as a general principle of EC law with the protection accorded by Article 7 of the ECHR.

9.17 However, the fact that the absolute prohibition against retroactivity in respect of the criminal law derives from Article 7 of the ECHR does not affect the remedial application of the principle insofar as it can be derived separately from EC law. If the Administrative Court cannot interpret domestic legislation in question compatibly with Article 7 ECHR then, in a case within the scope of EC law, it must disapply the provision. However, in a case founded solely on the HRA it would be limited to granting a declaration of incompatibility under HRA s 4.[11] In either event, the legality of the provision in question would not depend upon any form of balancing exercise.[12]

9.18 Thirdly, and in contrast to the position in respect of criminal legislation, the rule is that even where a substantive legislative provision must be interpreted as being truly retroactive in nature it may still be lawful if two conditions are fulfilled, namely that: (1) the legislative purpose requires such retroactivity, and (2) the legitimate expectations of those affected by the measure are respected.[13]

9.19 It is at this point that the doctrine of legitimate expectations, examined in Chapter 8, engages to slightly different effect. Ordinarily, the burden of establishing a legitimate expectation lies on the claimant. This is still the position in relation to truly retroactive legislation. Nonetheless, as explained above, the fact that a legislative provision is retroactive is likely, in practice, to make it easier for a legitimate expectation to be established since the fact of true retroactivity itself in respect of an identified person or undertaking suggests an interference with established interests. Similarly, the burden of justifying a breach of a legitimate expectation by reference to an overriding matter of public importance is, in practice, likely to be more difficult given the interpretative presumption against legislation of that type.

9.20 So, non-retroactivity is an important interpretative and substantive principle. Its application in the cases is examined below. There are two other aspects to the principle that will also require consideration and that may sometimes arise in domestic judicial review proceedings.

9.21 The first special situation involves the retroactive revocation of unlawful measures. There are occasions where either a Community or national measure may be unlawful but where legal effects have been created.

9.22 In certain circumstances such measures may be revoked retroactively even though rights of third parties are engaged. The general rule is that revocation must take place within a

---

[11] See paras 3.38–3.40.

[12] The position would, in terms of remedy, be different if allegedly offending EC legislation was under consideration. There, the Administrative Court could not declare the EC legislation to be invalid but would have to refer to the ECJ under Art 234 (ex 177) EC. If the legality of the national legislation was contingent on the validity of the underlying EC legislation then any decision as to the national legislation would have to await the outcome of such reference: see paras 4.92–4.98.

[13] See, eg, Case 108/81 *Amylum v Council* [1982] ECR 3107; Case C-376/02 *Stichting 'Goed Wonen' v Staatssecretaris van Financien* [2005] ECR 1-3445. However (see below) care is needed since it seems unlikely that the two conditions are always cumulative.

reasonable time. Further, the principle of legality and the principle of legal certainty will have to be balanced.[14] As explained at para 9.53 et seq. the principles governing retroactivity generally may require some modification in the context of retroactive revocation of unlawful acts and it may be doubted whether, in such cases, the presumption against retroactivity applies or applies with equal force as in the case of pre-existing acts or policies that are lawful.

The second special situation involves the question of retroactive effect of judgments of the EC courts or of the Administrative Court annulling or quashing legislative measures within the scope of EC law. As will be seen,[15] so far as judgments of EC courts are concerned particular rules apply and such judgments will have retroactive effect unless they are temporally qualified. There seems to be no reason why, at least in principle, judgments of the Administrative Court do not have a similar effect although a general rule of this nature would mean that judgments of the Administrative Court in EC cases might operate differently from the way that they do in domestic judicial review proceedings. **9.23**

C. Non-retroactivity and Legislative Measures

Non-retroactivity as a principle of interpretation

As outlined above, there is, in general, an interpretative presumption against true retroactivity[16] in *substantive* legislation.[17] The ECJ held, in *Salumni*,[18] that such legislation will only be interpreted as having retroactive effect if this clearly follows from the terms of the legislation, or from the objectives of the general scheme of which the provisions form a part. **9.24**

The presumption is a strong one. As the ECJ observed in *Racke*:[19] **9.25**

> A fundamental principle in the Community legal order requires that a measure adopted by the public authorities shall not be applicable to those concerned before they have the opportunity to make themselves acquainted with it.

Thus, in *Société pour l'Exportation des Sucres v Commission*,[20] for example, the regulation in question was published in an issue of the Official Journal *dated* 1 July 1976. However, publication was delayed by a strike so that the regulation was not *published* until the following day. On 1 July 1976 the applicant sought cancellation of certain licences which was refused on the basis of the regulation. Applying the presumption against retroactivity, and consistently with the 'fundamental principle' subsequently to be clarified in *Racke*, the ECJ **9.26**

---

[14] See, eg, Joined Cases 7/56 and 3-7/57 *Algera v Common Assembly* [1957–58] ECR 39. See, also, the cases discussed at paras 9.37–9.50.

[15] See para 9.77 et seq.

[16] For the meaning of this term, see para 9.08.

[17] This, of course, includes the *interpretation* of criminal legislation that, as explained above, will be invalid if retroactive in its effect: see para 9.16.

[18] Joined Cases 212–17/80 [1981] ECR 2735, para 9.

[19] Case 98/78 *Racke v Hauptzollamt Mainz* [1979] ECR 69, para 15.

[20] Case 88/76 [1977] ECR 709.

interpreted the regulation as not coming into force until its actual publication (2 July 1976) so that it did not cover the applicant's situation.

9.27 Importantly, the interpretative presumption against retroactivity does not apply to:

(1) procedural measures;[21]
(2) apparent retroactivity.

9.28 It may also be doubted whether the interpretative presumption against retroactivity applies to those cases where a conflicting general principle of EC law or other binding obligation of EC law is engaged.

9.29 Thus, for example, transitional measures may have to be introduced with retroactive effect in order to protect identified legitimate expectations.[22] Legislation has also been interpreted as being retroactive in order to give effect to the principle of proportionality.[23] And it seems improbable that a national measure lawfully implementing a directive, but doing so retrospectively so as to remedy the State's default in implementing the directive on time, would be presumed as a matter of interpretation not to be intended to be retroactive in its operation.

Substantive protection against retroactivity

Substantive measures outside the sphere of criminal law

9.30 A measure may, consistently with the presumption against retroactivity, have to be interpreted as being retroactive in nature yet still be lawful. This is because, even though the presumption has been displaced by reason of the language or general scheme, the EC general principle of non-retroactivity has a substantive as well as an interpretative element.

9.31 The distinction between interpretative and substantive protection against retroactivity is important. The fact that the underlying legislative scheme compels the interpretation that the measure in question is retroactive means that the Administrative Court has, then, to engage in the second stage of analysis and involves examining whether the measure is unlawful precisely because it is retroactive in nature. Different rules apply to criminal cases and they are examined separately.

9.32 Materially, this is no longer solely a process of interpretation. A measure that is interpreted as retroactive in nature may be held to be lawful where:

(1) the purpose of the measure demands retroactivity; and,
(2) the legitimate expectations of those affected are respected.[24]

9.33 So, in the case of substantive measures outside the sphere of criminal law, the Administrative Court must look, at least in part, to the reasons for the passing of the measure and to its effect on third parties.

---

[21] Joined Cases 212–17/80 *Salumni* [1981] ECR 2735.
[22] See, eg, Case 127/80 *Grogan v Commission* [1982] ECR 869, para 37.
[23] Case C–345/88 *Butterabsatz Osnabruck-Emsland* [1990] ECR I–159.
[24] See n 13 above and text.

The conditions are sometimes said to be cumulative. If however that is right, then: **9.34**

(a) a measure that demands retroactivity for the fulfilment of its hypothetically legitimate purpose will not be lawful if third-party legitimate expectations are not respected, *and*
(b) a measure whose legitimate purpose does not require it to be retroactive will be unlawful even if it respects legitimate expectations.

The first of these consequences is, surely, right. If a measure were held to be lawful purely **9.35**
because there was a legitimate aim and a compelling reason for that aim being fulfilled it would mean that the necessary balancing exercise in order to give proper respect to legitimate expectation would not have been undertaken. But if a balancing exercise is undertaken the second consequence would not always appear to follow.

Tridimas has persuasively argued[25] that the conditions for retroactivity are 'inextricably **9.36**
linked' and that, in reality, a balancing exercise is undertaken. It is, indeed, not easy to see how, if legitimate expectations are respected, and a proper balancing exercise is undertaken, the Community or State institution should necessarily be deprived of a policy choice. If a measure respects the interests of all concerned then, whether or not the legislative purpose could be fulfilled by non-retroactive means, the underlying rationale of the non-retroactivity principle—legal certainty—is not obviously offended.

A number of ECJ decisions have recognized the legality of substantive non-criminal meas- **9.37**
ures that are necessarily retroactive in nature and that do not fail to respect any legitimate expectations. In *FEDESA*,[26] for example, a directive was introduced to replace an earlier directive that had been annulled on purely procedural grounds. The later directive was made retroactive so that the substance of the earlier directive was continued. In such circumstances the court held that there was permissible retroactivity since:

(a) the legislative purpose (the need to preserve the substance of the first directive) required retroactivity,[27] and
(b) no relevant legitimate expectations had been created in that the applicants could not reasonably have supposed that the later directive would be substantively different from its predecessor.

FEDESA can also be seen as a case that validates, in practice, the proposition that **9.38**
procedural retroactive measures are, at least generally, not subject to the application of the EC general principle against retroactivity. Such measures may operate unlawfully so as, for example, to defeat legitimate expectations or by violating the proportionality principle but there is no discrete protection in terms of non-retroactivity. Although the second directive in *FEDESA* was substantive in content its legislative aim was, in essence, procedural, namely to ensure the continuity of legislation annulled on procedural grounds.

---

[25] Tridimas (n 5 above) 256–7.
[26] Case C–331/88 *R v MAFF, ex p FEDESA* [1990] ECR I–4023.
[27] Though *quaere*, see above, whether this was a necessary criterion to surmount.

9.39 There are, in fact, many examples of the ECJ upholding *substantive* legislative aims that require retroactive application. In *Affish*,[28] for instance, the court ruled that imperatives of public health justified retroactive application of protective measures on imports from third countries.[29]

9.40 In that context in *Amylum*,[30] the ECJ specified, as being a necessary element of a lawful retroactive provision, a legislative aim to be achieved 'in the general interest'.[31] *Amylum* was a similar case to *FEDESA* though the legislative aim in question was expressed somewhat differently and in substantive terms. In that case an earlier Council regulation had been annulled by the court because the Council had failed to consult the European Parliament. The regulation was concerned with the imposition of a quota system in respect of isoglucose producers. Following annulment, the Council passed a second regulation reimposing the same quota system retroactively.

9.41 The ECJ held that the second regulation was lawful and did not offend against the retroactivity principle. This was because:

(a) the legislative purpose was to subject producers of isoglucose to the same quota system as other sugar producers—a purpose that required the measure to be retroactive, and

(b) the legitimate expectations of the producers of isoglucose had been respected because it was entirely foreseeable that such retroactive measure would be passed.

9.42 However, the ECJ has also shown itself prepared to annul retroactive legislation that offends against third-party legitimate expectations without a sufficiently compelling legislative purpose. This is especially so where adverse financial consequences will result. It is submitted that the same consideration applies to the validity of national measures as determined by the Administrative Court. In *Commission v France*,[32] for example, the ECJ said this:

> Certainty and foreseeability are requirements which must be observed all the more strictly in the case of rules liable to entail financial consequences.

9.43 Thus, in *Crispoltoni I*,[33] a retroactive Council regulation designed to curb tobacco production was applied to cases—such as that of the applicant—where producers had already received payment in respect of decisions that they had made relating to the harvesting of tobacco. Mr Crispoltoni resisted proceedings for repayment based on the regulation.

9.44 The ECJ held that the regulation could not be enforced. It was invalid because it contravened the general principle of non-retroactivity. The requisite legislative purpose was absent because retroactivity was not required in a case where harvesting had started prior to publication of the measure. The applicant's legitimate expectations had not been respected

---

[28] Case C–183/95 *Affish BV v Rijksdienst voor de Keuring van Veen en Vlees* [1997] ECR I–4315.
[29] See, also, Case C–459/02 *(1) Willy Gerekens, (2) Association Africole Procola v Luxembourg* (unreported, 15 July 2004).
[30] Case 108/81 *Amylum v Council* [1982] ECR 3107.
[31] ibid paras 6 and 8.
[32] Case C–30/89 [1990] ECR I–691, para 23.
[33] Case C–368/89 [1991] ECR I–3695.

because producers were entitled to expect that they would receive notification in good time of any measure having effects on their investments.

A slightly different situation arose in *Kloppenburg*.[34] There, the question that arose was **9.45** whether the Ninth VAT directive could lawfully extend time for the implementation of the Sixth VAT directive retroactively. In the circumstances of the case the ECJ held that the measure was lawful in that it was not, properly interpreted, designed to alter the position of economic operators. However, the court observed as follows:

> It is necessary to emphasise ... that Community legislation must be unequivocal and its application must be predictable for those who are subject to it. Postponement of the date of entry into force of a measure of general application, although the date initially specified has already passed, is in itself liable to undermine that principle. If the purpose of an extension is to deprive individuals of the legal remedies which the first measure has already conferred upon them, such an effect in practice raises the question of the validity of the amending measure.[35]

An important formal requirement of substantive protection against non-retroactivity is **9.46** that a Community legislative measure must specify in its statement of reasons why retroactive effect is said to be necessary.[36] Whilst the ECJ has not always applied this requirement where there is justification for the measure,[37] it has sometimes done so.

For example, in *Diversinte*[38] the ECJ annulled a Commission regulation to such extent as **9.47** it applied retroactively. The statement of reasons claimed justification in terms of urgency in order to combat speculative transactions. However, the ECJ held that such reasoning was inadequate.

The extent to which equivalent retroactive *domestic* legislative measures are required to **9.48** contain independent reasoned justification is unclear. Plainly, to the extent that such domestic measures are compelled by, or dependent for their legality on, Community legislation, that legislation will already contain a statement of reasons justifying its retroactive operation. This should, ordinarily, be sufficient for parallel domestic justification.

However, the requirement for a statement of reasons in respect of Community legislation **9.49** is one laid down by the Treaty. Article 253 (ex 190) EC specifically provides that:

> Regulations, directives and decisions adopted jointly by the European Parliament and the Council, and such acts adopted by the Council or the Commission, shall state the reasons on which they are based and shall refer to any proposals or opinions which were required to be obtained pursuant to this Treaty.

There is no related requirement for a statement of reasons for domestic legislation. In practice, **9.50** explanatory notes to statutes are now treated as an interpretative aid. But it is doubtful that there exists a procedural requirement that domestic legislation contain a statement of

---

[34] Case 70/83 *Kloppenburg v Finanzamt Leer* [1984] ECR 1075.
[35] ibid para 11.
[36] Case 1/84 R *Ilford v Commission* [1984] ECR 423, para 19.
[37] See, eg, Case C–244/95 *Moskof v Ethnikos Organismos Kapnou* [1997] ECR I–6441.
[38] Joined Cases C–260 and C–261/91 *Diversinte and Iberlacta* [1993] ECR I–1885.

reasons justifying its retroactive operation.[39] However, if the underlying EC legislation contained insufficient reasons then that would provide the basis for an indirect challenge to the EC legislation in a challenge to the contingent national measures by way of judicial review.

Substantive criminal measures

9.51 In *R v Kent Kirk*[40] the master of a Danish fishing vessel was fined retrospectively for fishing in prohibited waters. At paras 21 and 22 of its judgment, the ECJ held as follows:

> Without embarking upon an examination of the general legality of the retroactivity … of that Regulation, it is sufficient to point out that such retroactivity may not, in any event, have the effect of validating *ex post facto* national measures of a penal nature which impose penalties for an act which, in fact, was not punishable at the time at which it was committed. That would be the case where at the time of the act entailing a criminal penalty, the national measure was invalid because it was incompatible with Community law.
>
> The principle that penal provisions may not have retroactive effect is one which is common to all the legal orders of the Member States and is enshrined in Article 7 of the European Convention for the Protection of Human Rights and Fundamental Freedoms as a fundamental right; it takes its place among the general principles of law whose observance is ensured by the Court of Justice.

9.52 As this case illustrates, then, the prohibition of retroactive application of *criminal* laws is absolute.

D. Retroactive Revocation of Unlawful Measures

9.53 Thus far, the general principle of non-retroactivity in EC law has been considered in relation to retroactive changes by reference to a pre-existing law or policy that was itself entirely *lawful*. As has been seen, the legality of such subsequent non-criminal retroactive measure is generally dependent upon that measure having a legitimate purpose requiring retroactivity and the measure also respecting relevant legitimate expectations.[41]

9.54 Particular considerations arise in respect of a pre-existing law or policy that was *unlawful*. At first sight retroactive revocation of such law or policy might seem to be unobjectionable. However, unless that law or policy was void so as to create no legal effects[42] there is no clear analytical difference between the legality of a subsequent retroactive measure that alters the

---

[39] An administrative decision on the other hand is likely to require reasoned justification for purported lawful retroactive effect: see para 10.47 et seq.

[40] Case 63/83 [1984] ECR 2689. The scope of Art 7 ECHR in the context of precluding retroactivity is, however, not entirely clear. Two modern domestic cases restate the relevant principles: (1) no person should be convicted under a law unless it is sufficiently clear to enable him to know what conduct is prohibited before he commits the act; (2) no one should be subject to penal sanction unless the sanction was clearly and ascertainably in force when the act was committed: see *R v Misra* [2005] 1 Cr App R 21, paras 28–36, per Judge LJ and *R v Rimmington* [2005] UKHL 63, [2005] 3 WLR 982, paras 33–35, per Lord Bingham.

[41] But see paras 9.34–9.36.

[42] Whether a law or policy creates legal effects is, at least as far as the ECJ is concerned, in part a matter of judicial discretion. See discussion at para 9.77 et seq.

effect of a pre-existing lawful law or policy from one that alters the effect of a pre-existing unlawful law or policy. In both cases legal effects have been created that it may be unfair in the interests of legal certainty or legitimate expectations to affect.

This is confirmed by the case law of the ECJ though the applicable principles appear to be slightly different (if only because the fact of prior illegality has had to be factored into the court's reasoning) than in the case of a prior policy or law that is not tainted by illegality. **9.55**

There appear to be at least two relevant constraints on retroactive revocation in respect of unlawful measures that have created legal effects. First, such revocation to be lawful must usually be effected within a reasonable time.[43] **9.56**

Secondly, in such instances, the principle of legal certainty and the separate principle of legality may have to be balanced so as to produce an outcome that is fair. **9.57**

These considerations are exemplified in two factually related cases concerning the functioning of the ECSC. **9.58**

In the first case, *SNUPAT v High Authority*[44] the applicant, a steel producer, requested the Commission to revoke retroactively particular levy exemptions granted by decisions made in favour of two firms. When the Commission failed to reply, SNUPAT commenced annulment proceedings before the ECJ in respect of the Commission's implied decision to reject its request. **9.59**

The ECJ held that the exemptions had been granted unlawfully. The question then arose whether the Commission ought to have revoked them retroactively pursuant to SNUPAT's application. Unsurprisingly, the two firms in question contended that retroactive revocation would violate the principle of legal certainty. However, the ECJ observed that this was not the only principle in play. The public interest in legality was also relevant and fell to be balanced against the principle of legal certainty. In particular, retroactive revocation would be appropriate where an unlawful decision was the product of incorrect or incomplete information being supplied by the person affected or where, on the facts, the public interest in legality outweighed legal certainty. **9.60**

In the event, the ECJ held that the balancing exercise involved was, at least in the first instance, one for the Commission to make. **9.61**

The second case, *Hoogovens v High Authority*,[45] was the result. The Commission, on the matter being remitted back to it by the ECJ, decided that it should revoke the exemptions retroactively. One of the two affected firms (Hoogovens) in its turn brought annulment proceedings in respect of the Commission's new decision. **9.62**

Hoogovens contended both that it had not supplied misleading or incomplete information to the Commission and that retroactive revocation of the Commission's unlawful exemption **9.63**

---

[43] See, eg, Case 15/85 *Consorzio Cooperative d'Abruzzo v Commission* [1987] ECR 1005.
[44] Cases 42, 49/59 [1961] ECR 53.
[45] Case 14/61 [1962] ECR 253.

had, in any event, been unreasonably delayed by some three and a half years. The first ground was uncontroversial but it was necessary to succeed on each. Hoogovens lost on its delay argument.

9.64 As to delay, the ECJ concluded that this did not necessarily preclude retroactive revocation of an unlawful decision. Much would depend on the nature of the decision. Here, the decision merely declared what the Commission erroneously believed the law to be. It was not a decision constitutive of legal rights. A purely declaratory decision was of less significance than a decision creating legal rights. This distinction may, however, be difficult to apply in practice since any unlawful decision capable, in principle, of being retroactively revoked must have had at least some legal *effects* (see above). It is, perhaps, questionable whether classifying those effects as legal rights or as something less than legal rights is meaningful where the decision-maker has, *ex hypothesi*, erred in law.

9.65 It is also apparent from the ECJ's approach in *Hoogovens* that the national court should also examine the effect of the delay. There, the ECJ held that the applicant must have been aware for some time that the legality of the exemptions was contested by SNUPAT.

9.66 In the context of retroactive revocation of unlawful decisions other cases have emphasized additional aspects of the overall balance to be effected between the respective principles of legal certainty and legality. In *Lemmerz-Wercke v High Authority*[46] the ECJ suggested that one important consideration was whether the party affected was justified in believing that the decision in question was final and definitive.

9.67 That general question, of course, feeds back into issues such as the conduct of the claimant and delay. If, for example, the claimant has provided misleading information it cannot reasonably suppose the resulting decision to be definitive. Similarly, the less the delay that there has been between an ostensibly final (and apparently lawful) decision and any purported retroactive revocation by reason of its illegality the less justified a party may be in believing the decision to be final.

9.68 In these instances it may be thought that the principle of legal certainty has not been infringed at least to any great extent. However, even if legal certainty is not infringed, decision-makers may still be penalized by not being permitted to revoke an unlawful measure retroactively if the illegality reflects 'a breach of their duty to act with care and accuracy'.[47] In *Hoogovens*,[48] in contrast, the Commission was found not to have been culpable in granting the relevant exemptions since the law was complex and the proper interpretation had 'proved to be very debatable'.

9.69 Finally, as with retroactive revocation of lawful measures, legitimate expectations may still have a relevant and separate role to play in the legality of retroactive revocation of unlawful measures. For example, in *De Compte v Parliament*[49] the CFI had permitted retroactive revocation of a decision by the European Parliament that the applicant suffered from an occupational disease. The decision was unlawful when viewed against the individual

---

[46] Case 111/63 [1965] ECR 677.
[47] ibid 692.
[48] Case 14/61 [1962] ECR 253.
[49] Case C–90/95 P [1997] ECR I–1999.

circumstances but its illegality and purported retroactive revocation were communicated to the applicant within three months of the decision being taken. The CFI considered that any reliance placed on the decision by the applicant was, therefore, undermined and that there was no continuing legitimate expectation.

The ECJ, however, overruled the CFI. It observed that once a legitimate expectation as to **9.70** the legality of a favourable administrative act had been engendered it could not be undermined by subsequent events.

De Compte is, perhaps, illustrative of the fact that the concept of legitimate expectation may **9.71** not be an entirely satisfactory concept in explaining the legality of retroactive revocation of an unlawful act.

The difficulty is that of articulating the notion of what a *legitimate* expectation comprises **9.72** in the present context. Luxembourg's more flexible approach to the potential continuing effect of unlawful acts is, it is submitted, at least in principle to be preferred to the more rigid approach of English administrative law to illegality where a legitimate expectation can rarely, if ever, be derived from an unlawful act.[50]

However, there are difficulties in the idea that ostensible legality is capable of creating legi- **9.73** timate expectations in relation even to administrative acts that are intrinsically unlawful. On that footing, unless an affected party has provided misleading information or is otherwise on notice of the illegality it is not easy to conceive of circumstances in which the beneficiaries of favourable, albeit unlawful, administrative decisions cannot claim to be entitled to relevant legitimate expectations.

The resolution may be that such expectations can be 'trumped' by the public interest in **9.74** lawful decision-making (the principle of legality) when balanced against the expectation. What that could entail, though, is that a decision-maker would still have to justify retrospective retroactivity in respect of unlawful decisions since there is a legitimate expectation that arises from the ostensible legality of the act in question.

Whether that is a necessary consequence of the case law is doubtful. The principle of legal- **9.75** ity is of equal importance to the principle of legal certainty and, as the cases suggest, they have to be balanced against each other when retroactive revocation of unlawful decisions is being concerned. It is by no means obvious, therefore, that the general presumption against retroactivity analysed earlier applies, or applies with equal force, to unlawful decisions that are proposed to be revoked retroactively.

Finally, it is emphasized that the retroactive revocation of unlawful measures by national **9.76** authorities is necessarily subject to the same considerations as in the case of Community institutions. This means that in a case falling within the scope of EC law[51] it is by no means

---

[50] See, especially, the powerful critique of the domestic ultra vires principle advanced by PP Craig *Administrative Law* (5th edn, 2003), 671–80 referred to with approval by May LJ in *Rowland v Environment Agency* [2003] EWCA Civ 1885, [2005] Ch 1. For a spirited defence of the traditional domestic principle, see S Hannett and L Busch, 'Ultra Vires Representations and Illegitimate Expectations' [2005] PL 729.

[51] As to this, see further paras 6.31 et seq.

an answer to a challenge to retroactive revocation founded on (for example) legitimate expectation—as it might be in domestic law—to assert that since the public body had no power to adopt the revoked measure there can be no valid interest to be protected.

E. Retroactive Effect of Judicial Decisions

9.77 Judicial decisions necessarily involve at least the potential prospect of retroactive application. It is, though, a special type of retroactivity and one that, as with retroactive revocation of unlawful acts, has its own particular difficulties.

9.78 So far as the ECJ itself is concerned, Article 231 (ex 174) EC, reciting the powers of the ECJ in respect of annulment applications made under Article 230 (ex 173) EC contains specific provision relevant to retroactivity. It provides that where the application is successful, the court shall declare the act in question to be void. It then continues as follows:

> In the case of a regulation, however, the Court of Justice shall, if it considers this necessary, state which of the effects of the regulation which it has declared void shall be considered as definitive.

9.79 So, for Article 231 purposes, there is—contrary to the general rule—a presumption *in favour* of retroactivity. Importantly, although Article 231 is expressed to apply only to regulations the ECJ has applied the power to directives by analogy and on the basis that Article 231 reflects the general principle of legal certainty. That being so, as Advocate General Jacobs reasoned in *European Parliament v Council*,[52] the power is as applicable to indirect proceedings under Article 234 (ex 177) EC as it is to direct proceedings under Article 230.

9.80 The power of the ECJ to limit the retroactive effect of its judgments or rulings by imposing a temporal limitation on their effect is one that the court has said must be used only exceptionally.[53] In this respect, the retroactive effect of the judicial rulings of the ECJ does not appear to be confined by concepts such as legitimate expectations or even a straightforward balancing exercise as between the principles of legal certainty and legality.

9.81 Thus, in *Defrenne v Sabena (No 2)*[54] the ECJ declared that Article 141 (ex 119) EC (guaranteeing equal pay for equal work) was directly effective. It then had to decide whether to limit the temporal effect of its ruling. Whilst taking into account the enormous financial consequences (including multiple bankruptcies for affected firms) of its ruling if made retroactive that would not, according to the court, have been sufficiently exceptional to justify a limitation of the ruling's temporal effect. What persuaded the court to limit the effect of its ruling was that the Commission had led Member States to believe that Article 141 was not directly effective. Also material was that it was impossible to know the general level at which pay would have been fixed.

---

[52] Case C–295/90 [1992] ECR I–4193, 4227–8.
[53] See, eg, Case 43/75 *Defrenne v Sabena (No 2)* [1976] ECR 455, para 72; Case C–294/99 *Athinaiki Zithopiia AE v Greece* [2001] ECR I–6797, para 36.
[54] Case 43/75 [1976] ECR 455, paras 69–75.

The ECJ has shown itself especially prepared to lay down temporal limitations in respect of **9.82** its judgments or rulings where there would be widespread detrimental effects at the Member State level if there were retroactive effect.

In *European Parliament v Council*,[55] for example, the European Parliament brought annul- **9.83** ment proceedings in relation to a directive that had been implemented by Member States. The ECJ held that, although the directive should be annulled, the annulment would operate only from the date that a new directive had been lawfully adopted.

The ECJ took a similar course in *Agreement on the Transfer of PNR Data*.[56] There, follow- **9.84** ing the terrorist attacks of 11 September 2001 the USA had adopted legislation requiring disclosure of passenger names records in respect of flights crossing USA territory. The European Parliament brought an action before the ECJ seeking to annul two Decisions approving transfer of such records. The ECJ annulled the Decisions but, for reasons of legal certainty, the legal effect of the Decisions was preserved until 30 September 2006 (ie four months after the court's ruling).

As explained below, the position so far as purely domestic judgments are concerned is more **9.85** complex. However, in an EC case it is submitted that the Administrative Court may enjoy a similar power to that of the ECJ and that where a case is within the scope of EC law[57] there is a power in the Administrative Court (albeit one to be exercised, like the ECJ, only exceptionally) to limit the temporal scope of that court's judgment.[58]

F. Non-retroactivity in Domestic Law

There is, in domestic law as in EC law, a general presumption against retroactivity. This **9.86** presumption applies in purely domestic cases as well as in cases under the HRA. However, the HRA context may more often require retroactivity.

The issue of retroactivity of the HRA arose in *Wilson v First County Trust (No 2)*.[59] **9.87** In January 1999 Mrs Wilson borrowed £5,000 from the pawnbrokers First County Trust using her car as security. She was charged a small administration fee that was repayable at the end of the credit period. The credit agreement, which was regulated by the Consumer Credit Act 1974 (CCA), wrongly stated the amount of credit as £5,250. It included the administration fee of £250 when it should not have done. The effect, on the face of the statute, was to render the agreement unenforceable. Mrs Wilson did not keep up repayments and sought a declaration that the credit agreement was unenforceable against her.

---

[55] Case C–295/90 [1992] ECR I–4193.

[56] Joined Cases C–317/04, C–318/04 *European Parliament v Council; European Parliament v Commission (Re Agreement on the Transfer of PNR Data)* (not yet reported, 30 May 2006).

[57] For further analysis of this concept, see paras 6.31 et seq.

[58] There is a difference between limiting the temporal effect of the court's judgment and postponing the granting of a quashing order in judicial review proceedings to a future date. The latter power was exercised in *R (Rockware Glass Ltd) v Chester City Council and Quinn Glass Ltd* [2006] EWCA Civ 240 (15 June 2006).

[59] [2003] UKHL 40, [2003] 3 WLR 435.

9.88 At first instance (September 1999) the county court judge rejected Mrs Wilson's arguments. He held that the administration fee was part of the credit. However, this finding was overturned in the Court of Appeal. The question of whether CCA, s 127(3)—rendering, as it did, the credit agreement unenforceable—was in breach of Article 6 (right of access to a court) and/or Article 1 of Protocol 1 (peaceful enjoyment of property) ECHR was raised by the Court of Appeal and, eventually, decided in favour of the pawnbrokers. Materially, the Court of Appeal, granting a declaration of incompatibility under HRA s, 4 (in respect of CCA, s 127(3)) considered that, on the facts, the HRA applied since the Court of Appeal was seised of the matter after the entry into force of the HRA on 2 October 2000.

9.89 However, the House of Lords, allowing the appeal, considered that such a conclusion militated against the general presumption against retroactivity in English law.

9.90 The House of Lords' general conclusions on retroactivity were as follows:

(1) In any proceedings the court's power under HRA, s 4 to make a declaration of incompatibility did not arise unless it had first construed the legislation in accordance with s 3(1) and concluded that it was not possible to read and give effect to it in a way which was compatible with the Convention rights.

(2) It could not have been Parliament's intention that the application of s 3(1) should have the effect of altering the existing rights and obligations of the parties to an agreement made before s 3 came into force. This was consistent with the general presumption against retrospective operation of statutes.

(3) CCA, s 127(3), if construed in a way which was favourable to the defendant, would deprive the claimant of the protection she acquired when entering into the agreement in 1999 and, therefore, for the purposes of identifying the parties' rights and obligations under the agreement the 1974 Act was to be interpreted without reference to HRA, s 3(1). Since s 3 was not available to the court as an interpretative tool the court's powers under s 4 did not arise and there was, therefore, no jurisdiction to make the declaration.[60]

9.91 As *Wilson* clarifies, therefore, the general presumption in domestic law is that legislative measures do not operate retroactively. The various speeches that addressed retroactivity recognize, however, that the human rights context is important and that there may be exceptional cases where retroactivity ought to operate so as to enable the HRA to be applied to protect particularly strong fundamental rights.

9.92 This point was addressed most fully in the speech of Lord Rodger at paras 209–210. He said:

> The operative provisions of the 1998 Act must all apply in the same way when used to give effect to the same Convention right. But they may apply differently when used to give effect to different Convention rights. Article 6 embodies rights in relation to matters of procedure. When the 1998 Act is used to give effect to those article 6 rights in our domestic law, it provides remedies for defects in procedure. There is no presumption against purely procedural

---

[60] ibid paras 10–27 (per Lord Nicholls); paras 88–102 (per Lord Hope); paras 126–134 (per Lord Hobhouse); paras 152–162 (per Lord Scott); paras 179–220 (per Lord Rodger).

statutory provisions applying generally on commencement since no-one has a vested right to any particular form of procedure. It follows that, given its unqualified language, the 1998 Act applies generally from the date of commencement in so far as it gives effect to article 6 rights. That is only what one would expect. Suppose, for instance, that during the hearing of the appeal in this case the Court of Appeal had done something—such as refusing to listen to submissions on behalf of First County—which was incompatible with their rights under article 6(1). There can be no doubt that section 6(1) would have applied and that the Court of Appeal would have acted unlawfully in terms of it. Similarly, section 7(1)(b) would have applied and under it First County could have relied on their article 6(1) rights. Sections 3 to 5 would also have applied to the appeal for this purpose. So, if the alleged infringement of First County's article 6(1) rights had arisen out of a statutory provision regulating the procedure in the appeal, section 3 would have bound the Court of Appeal. Depending on how the statutory provision could be read under section 3, the Court of Appeal could also have used the mechanism in sections 4 and 5 to make a declaration of the incompatibility of the provision with article 6(1) rights.

In so far as articles of the Convention contain substantive rather than procedural rights, the presumption would be that Parliament did not intend that, when used to give effect to them, the operative provisions should interfere with vested rights or pending actions. It is, however, unnecessary, and would be unwise, to go through the various articles with a view to identifying those Convention rights in respect of which Parliament would or would not have intended the 1998 Act to apply generally on commencement. For example, I reserve my opinion on whether, because of the overwhelming importance and the absolute nature of articles 2, 3 and 4, Parliament would have intended that on commencement the Act would apply generally for the purpose of giving effect to them.[61]

The particular retroactivity issues that have arisen in relation to the operation of the HRA itself are unlikely to recur since they have, largely, been resolved.[62] In addressing them, however, the national courts have shown a similar approach to that prevailing in EC law. As with EC and domestic law, there is a general presumption against retroactivity. As also with EC law, however, the presumption may sometimes be overridden. The national courts have not, as yet, articulated detailed principles for permitting retroactivity although—like the ECJ—they have generally made a distinction between procedural provisions (not subject to the presumption) and substantive provisions (subject to the presumption). **9.93**

In criminal law, Article 7 ECHR is now part of domestic law and this makes the same distinction as does EC law between the criminal context where retroactivity is always prohibited and the non-criminal context where it is, at least sometimes, permitted. Article 7(1) prohibits both conviction for a retroactive offence and the imposition of a retroactively increased penalty except where the conduct complained of was, in any event, a crime under international law (see Article 7(2)). **9.94**

There remain potential differences between domestic administrative law and EC law in relation both to the retroactive revocation of unlawful measures and to the retroactive effect of judicial decisions. **9.95**

---

[61] It has also been held that acts of courts or tribunals which took place before 2 October 2000 which they were required to do by primary legislation and were done according to the meaning which was to be given to the legislation at that time are not affected by HRA, s 22(4): see *R v Kansal (No 2)* [2002] 2 AC 69, para 84.
[62] There have, though, been further cases. See, eg, *Re McKerr* [2004] 1 WLR 807.

9.96   As to unlawful acts, the ostensible legality of which could in EC law be held to engender a legitimate expectation, the national courts have been careful not to permit any form of legitimate expectation to be created by detrimental reliance as to the legality of an unlawful act. It has consistently been held that a public body may resile from an undertaking given outside its authorized powers since, otherwise, it would be extending its powers by estoppel.[63]

9.97   In this respect EC law is somewhat more flexible than domestic law *simpliciter* but there are recent signs that the European Court of Human Rights may, at least in some instances, also be more amenable to holding a public body to its undertakings even if such undertakings were made without legal authority.[64]

9.98   As to the retroactive effect of judicial decisions, there is no reason why, in principle at least, the national courts could not make the effect of judicial decisions entirely retroactive or, depending on the nature of the case, limit the operation of the court's ruling to the future as a matter of discretion. Although national courts have sometimes been prepared to accept that certain legislative measures and other acts are presumed to be valid unless and until they are set aside by the courts,[65] that does not, of itself, mean that a quashing order by the Administrative Court could not operate retroactively so as to deny future (but not past) legal effect to the measure in question.[66]

9.99   However, the temporal effect of judicial decisions in domestic law has still not been authoritatively clarified. In *R v Governor of Brockhill Prison, ex p Evans (No 2)*[67] the respondent prisoner was kept in prison for 59 days longer than she should have been. The Governor was blameless. He relied on a Home Office explanation of the legal position of prisoners in the position of the appellant. The Home Office was also blameless. The Home Office view of the position was founded on a clear line of Divisional court decisions. But the courts had erred. On the respondent's application for judicial review the Divisional court overruled the earlier decisions. It was held that the respondent was unlawfully detained.

9.100   The Governor immediately released the respondent. The respondent pursued a claim for false imprisonment against the Governor. The Court of Appeal, by a majority (Lord Woolf MR and Judge LJ), took the view that a defendant may be liable for false imprisonment of a claimant in circumstances where the defendant acts in good faith on a view of the law which appears to be settled by precedent but which subsequently turns out to have been wrong.

---

63   Of the many cases see, eg, *Rootkin v Kent County Council* [1981] 1 WLR 1186.

64   See, eg, paras 8.89 et seq.

65   See, eg, *McEldowney v Forde* [1971] AC 632, 655, per Lord Pearson; *Hoffman-La Roche (F) & Co AG v Secretary of State for Trade and Industry* [1975] AC 295, 466, 368; *R v Inland Revenue Commissioners, ex p Rossminster* [1980] AC 952, 1013.

66   This is not uncontroversial. See, especially, per Lord Irvine LC in *Boddington v British Transport Police* [1999] 2 AC 143, 155 who considered that unlawful subordinate legislation once quashed never had any legal effect. cf, though, per Lord Browne-Wilkinson at 164 and Lord Slynn at 165 who preferred to leave open this question.

67   [2001] 2 AC 19. Most recently, the House of Lords has suggested (though Lords Steyn and Scott were doubtful) that there could be circumstances in which it would be justifiable to overrule an earlier decision with prospective effect only: *Re Spectrum Plus Ltd* [2005] UKHL 41, [2005] 3 WLR 58.

In the House of Lords, analysing the question of whether the courts could as a matter of domestic law limit the temporal effects of their judgments (in a fashion similar to that of the ECJ: see above) Lord Steyn said this: **9.101**

> There was an interesting debate about the merits and elements of introducing a system of prospective overruling. For my part I am satisfied that such a power, if created, could not be appropriately used in order to relieve the Crown of an obligation to pay damages to the respondent in the present case. It is therefore not necessary to consider whether the House should alter the existing practice to allow for prospective overruling. Without shutting the door on the possibility of such a development by a decision or practice statement of the House, I would say that it is best considered in the context of a case or cases where the employment of such a power would serve the ends of justice.[68]

Lord Slynn, a former Advocate General at the ECJ, observed: **9.102**

> The judgment of the Divisional Court in this case follows the traditional route of declaring not only what was the meaning of the section at the date of the judgment but what was always the correct meaning of the section. The court did not seek to limit the effect of its judgment to the future. I consider that there may be situations in which it would be desirable, and in no way unjust, that the effect of judicial rulings should be prospective or limited to certain claimants. The European Court of Justice, though cautiously and infrequently, has restricted the effect of its ruling to the particular claimant in the case before it and to those who had begun proceedings before the date of its judgment. Those who had not sought to challenge the legality of acts perhaps done years before could only rely on the ruling prospectively. Such a course avoided unscrambling transactions perhaps long since over and doing injustice to defendants.

> But even if such a course is open to English courts there could in my view be no justification for limiting the effect of the judgment in this case to the future. The respondent's case has established the principle and she is entitled to compensation for false imprisonment; there could it seems in any event be no compensation for the period after the Divisional Court's decision since she was released immediately.[69]

In Lord Hope's view resolution of the issues posed by retroactivity are, largely, contextual. He observed as follows: **9.103**

> Mention was made of the differens of opinion which were expressed in your Lordships' House in *Kleinwort Benson Ltd. v. Lincoln City Council* [1999] 2 A.C. 349 as to the application of the declaratory theory in the context of a claim for restitution where money had been paid under a mistake: contrast Lord Browne-Wilkinson at pp. 357G–362H and Lord Lloyd at pp. 390F and 393B–394A for the view that the fact that a decision was overruled did not mean that the law as stated in the overruled case should not be considered as the law at the time of the payment, with the contrary view as expressed by Lord Goff of Chieveley at pp. 377D–381G and by myself at pp. 410E–411E. I doubt whether much is to be gained from an analysis of those differences of view in the present context. As I tried to make clear in my own speech, the critical issue where a claim is made for money paid under a mistake on the ground of unjust enrichment is one of fact—would the payer have made the payment if he had known the true state of the law or the facts at the time of the payment? The function of mistake in this context is to show that the benefit which was received when the payment was made was an unintended benefit. The principles which underlie the law of unjust enrichment enable this matter to be examined retrospectively. The declaratory theory is consistent with

---

[68] ibid 29.
[69] ibid 26–7.

those principles. That is not to say that it may not be appropriate in another context to depart from this theory. But an examination of that matter is best left over until another day.[70]

9.104   That retroactivity may have to be answered differently according to the context is not in doubt in an EC context. EC law distinguishes between procedural and substantive measures and between criminal and non-criminal contexts. EC law also recognizes that whether to limit the temporal effect of a judicial decision or whether not to permit unlawful acts to be revoked retroactively will depend upon the circumstances of the case and that there is no bright-line rule. In this respect it is submitted that EC law is, at the same time, both more pragmatic and more principled than its domestic law counterpart.

9.105   In any event, in a case falling within the scope of EC law the Administrative Court will have to apply the principles discussed in this chapter when addressing questions of retroactivity in its judgments even if they conflict with that principle as applied by that court in domestic judicial review proceedings.

---

[70]   ibid 37.

10

DUE PROCESS

A. Development of Due Process as a General Principle

There is no Treaty provision conferring the right to a hearing or, indeed, to most of the **10.01** rights encompassed by what are now regarded as EC administrative law requirements of due process. However, such rights have become well established under the general rubric of 'the rights of the defence'. In general terms, the EC expression 'the rights of the defence' equates to natural justice in domestic judicial review. As so often, however, there are differences—sometimes significant—between the protections accorded by the two doctrines. Importantly, too, there is (as with natural justice) equivalent protection, in most instances, to *both* sides as opposed merely to the defence.

Analytically, these EC procedural guarantees, form part of the general principles of EC law **10.02** discussed throughout this section. The starting point is the decision of the ECJ in *Alvis*[1] where the court observed that:

> According to a generally accepted principle of administrative law in force in the Member States . . . the administration of these States must allow their servants the opportunity of replying to allegations before any disciplinary decision is taken concerning them.

> This rule which meets the requirements of sound justice and good administration must be followed by Community institutions.

---

[1] Case 32/62 *Alvis v Council* [1963] ECR 49, 55.

10.03 *Alvis* was concerned with disciplinary proceedings. However, the accession of the UK to the EEC in 1973 soon resulted in the elaboration of the rights of the defence in a much wider set of fairness principles.

10.04 The leading case is *Transocean Marine Paint Association*.[2] There, the Commission made its extension of an exemption to the prohibition of cartels under Article 81(3) (ex 85(3)) EC subject to new and stringent conditions. The Association successfully appealed to the ECJ on the footing that the Commission had imposed the new conditions on it without obtaining and considering its views.

10.05 Central to the Association's complaint was that the Commission had acted in breach of a Commission regulation. However, Advocate General Warner provided a broader analysis.[3] He pointed out that, in English law, the right to be heard is a 'rule of natural justice'. This was so even if there was no written obligation to provide a hearing. Further, the notion of *audi alteram partem* was a general principle that was recognized in the legal orders of all the Member States. Accordingly, it should be recognized as a general principle of EC law.

10.06 This analysis was endorsed by the ECJ. The court held that the Commission regulation applied:

> ... the general rule that a person whose interests are perceptibly affected by a decision taken by a public authority must be given the opportunity to make his point of view known. This rule requires that an undertaking be clearly informed, in good time, of the essence of conditions to which the Commission intends to subject an exemption and it must have the opportunity to submit its observations to the Commission. This is especially so in the case of conditions which, as in this case, impose considerable obligations having far-reaching effects.[4]

10.07 Since *Transocean,* the ECJ has developed a number of other 'natural justice' principles. Apart from the right to be heard, the rights of the defence include (at least) the following:[5]

(1) The right to legal representation.[6]
(2) Confidentiality of lawyer and client communications.
(3) A form of privilege against self-incrimination.
(4) A right to reasons.
(5) The right to a hearing within a reasonable time by an independent and impartial court or tribunal.
(6) A right of access to documents.

---

[2] Case 17/74 *Transocean Marine Paint Association v Commission* [1974] ECR 1063.
[3] ibid especially at 1088–90.
[4] ibid para 15.
[5] However (see below), all these 'separate' rights are, in truth, aspects of the right to a hearing. Some of them (eg the right to reasons for a decision) may be classed as an aspect of the general principle of effectiveness: see paras 10.25 and 10.54.
[6] See, eg, Case 115/80 *Demont v Commission* [1981] ECR 3147.

B. Due Process in EC Law—The Questions to Ask

The following structure is relevant to consideration of EC 'rights of the defence' in a   **10.08**
domestic public law context:

(1) Identifying the specific content of the EC right.
(2) Determining the scope of judicial protection if the right is infringed.
(3) Comparing the position in EC law with that in purely domestic and HRA law.

Before addressing these matters, however, there is a threshold question which is whether or   **10.09**
not EC rights of the defence can be invoked directly in domestic judicial review (or other
public law) proceedings at all[7] or whether they are confined to proceedings involving
Community institutions.

As a matter of principle it should be clear that EC rights of the defence *can* be invoked   **10.10**
against public bodies in domestic judicial review. This is so for at least three reasons.

First, as stated above, rights of the defence constitute a general principle of EC law. General   **10.11**
principles, insofar as they affect public law proceedings before national courts, are principles
that apply to such proceedings falling *within the scope of EC law*. Although the meaning of this
expression is complex[8] it undoubtedly encompasses judicial review proceedings against public bodies (or other proceedings where such public law issues arise) where the body in question is charged with implementing EC law or is purporting lawfully to derogate from EC law.

Secondly, procedural guarantees are frequently contained in both primary and subordinate   **10.12**
EC legislation. Principles that were, initially, not reduced to writing but that have been
enunciated by the ECJ have now been incorporated in many secondary legislative provisions. It would be anomalous, and antithetical to the uniformity of EC law, if the rights of
an individual differed merely because the ECJ had expressly articulated a fairness principle
in the context of dealings with a Community rather than a national institution. There is a
parallel here with a domestic statutory regime where it is now well established that the
requirements of fairness (such as the giving of reasons) apply whether or not there is an
express requirement in the statute itself.

Finally, the rights of the defence are themselves an application of the underlying principle   **10.13**
of effectiveness to which reference has been made elsewhere.[9] The principle of effectiveness
does not depend for its engagement upon whether EC rights are being enforced against a
Community institution.

---

[7] Of course, default by the Community institutions in complying with the rights of defence may be
invoked *indirectly* in domestic judicial review proceedings since a Community measure (leading to a national
measure) may be unlawful because of violation of the rights of defence. Whilst the Administrative Court cannot itself declare the Community measure to be unlawful it may (see paras 4.92–4.98) refer the proceedings
to the ECJ for a preliminary ruling under Art 234. References are addressed in detail in Chapter 4 and, from
a tactical perspective, in Chapter 19.
[8] See paras 12.62–12.80.
[9] See paras 3.09–3.17 and 5.13–5.22. See, eg: *R (USA Government) v Bow Street Magistrates Court and
Others* [2006] EWHC 2256 (Admin) (*held*: Article 13 ECHR applies to extradition hearings under the
European Arrest Warrant extradition procedure).

10.14 It is however, undoubtedly, the case that the decisions of the ECJ have addressed fairness principles in relation to the Community institutions rather than in respect of hearings before national authorities. This is, perhaps, unsurprising given the fact that instances of alleged infringement of EC due process rights are much more likely to come before the ECJ as direct actions under Article 230. To the extent that natural justice issues are raised in EC cases before domestic courts they will usually be addressed by domestic principles of fairness without differentiating between their domestic and EC content.

10.15 In practice this may not, at least in most cases, be detrimental to the interests of the party seeking to invoke relevant rights of the defence. However, as developed below, it is important to bear in mind that there are discrete EC elements of due process and that it will sometimes be important to identify them both because of the stronger remedies available for breaches of EC law,[10] and also because the scope of EC due process protection may sometimes be different than in the case of domestic or HRA law. For this reason, it is important for the Administrative Court, in domestic judicial review cases, to be conversant with decisions of the ECJ and CFI in regard to due process rights.

C. Identifying the Right

The right to a hearing

10.16 The right to a hearing was the earliest of the rights of the defence to be clarified by the ECJ. Reference has already been made to *Alvis* and *Transocean*.[11] Later decisions have built on those cases and expanded on the nature of the right. In *Michelin v Commission*,[12] for example, in the context of competition proceedings, the ECJ said:

> The necessity to have regard to the rights of the defence is a fundamental principle of Community law which the Commission must observe in administrative procedures which may lead to the imposition of penalties under the rules of competition laid down in the Treaty. Its observance requires *inter alia* that the undertaking concerned must have been enabled to express its views effectively on the documents used by the Commission to support its allegation of an infringement.[13]

10.17 There is no precise demarcation between the threshold right to a hearing and the subsequently developed rights of the defence encompassing closely associated entitlements such as a right to reasons. This is because it is intrinsic to the right to a hearing that it should be a *fair* hearing. There are, thus, two questions relevant to consideration of the assertion of the right to a hearing, namely:

(1) Is there, in any given case, a right to a hearing at all?
(2) (If so) what are the obligations of fairness required by that hearing?

---

10 See Chapter 5, especially at paras 5.37 et seq.
11 See paras 10.02 and 10.04.
12 Case 322/81 [1983] ECR 3461.
13 ibid para 7.

Is there always a right to a hearing?

As adumbrated by the ECJ in *Transocean,* there is a general rule that there is a right to **10.18**
a hearing where the undertaking or other party claiming the right has interests that are
'perceptibly affected' by the decision of a public body.[14]

It follows from this formulation that not every decision of a public body will be challenge- **10.19**
able on this ground. Further, even if the decision is potentially challengeable by the party
directly affected it may not be capable of challenge by a party who has standing, in the
widest sense, to seek domestic judicial review of the decision.

Certainly, it is widely accepted that proceedings that are 'initiated against a person which **10.20**
are liable to culminate in a measure adversely affecting the person'[15] requires a hearing.
So, too, it appears does a public law decision-making process that has the potential to affect
a claimant detrimentally where the claimant is part of a limited class. That is the rationale
of cases such as *Technische Universitat Munchen,*[16] where, despite the absence of legislative
provision for a hearing, the importer of scientific apparatus was held to be entitled to
a hearing in circumstances involving the refusal by the Commission of exemption from
customs duty under criteria specified in Community legislation.

However, the notion of interests being 'perceptibly affected' appears to be sufficiently flex- **10.21**
ible to be capable of excluding from its ambit cases where the measure in question is one of
general application and where the interests of the claimant are not, at least in comparison
with others, detrimentally affected.[17] Notably, the ECJ in *Mollett v Commission*[18] referred
to a 'measure which is liable gravely to prejudice the interests of an individual'.

In order for interests to be 'perceptibly affected' it is not necessary for there to be a *final* deci- **10.22**
sion. However, the ECJ has not reviewed merely preparatory acts on rights of defence
grounds. There must, at least in general, be some irreversible legal effect. For example, in
IBM[19] the court refused to rule on the commencement of a procedure and the statement of
objections because of the lack of legal consequences. The court said:

> A statement of objections does not compel the undertakings concerned to alter or reconsider
> its marketing practices . . . Whilst a statement of objections may have the effect of showing
> the undertaking in question it is incurring a real risk of being fined by the Commission, that
> is merely a consequence of fact and not a legal consequence . . .[20]

By contrast, an intermediate decision may produce legal consequences. In *AKZO*[21] a decision **10.23**
by the Commission to transmit documents was treated by the ECJ as definitive and as

---

[14] See para 10.06.
[15] Case C–135/92 *Fiscano v Commission* [1994] ECR 1–2885 para 39.
[16] Case C–269/90 [1991] ECR I–5469.
[17] There is no case articulating such exclusion. However, the European courts have shown a reluctance to
accept that decisions of public bodies that affect an indeterminate number of undertakings give rise to myriad rights of individual hearings: see, eg, Case T–260/94 *Air Inter SA v Commission* [1997] ECR II–997 where
the CFI left open the question of whether or not rights of defence are engaged when an indeterminate number of undertakings are affected by a Commission decision.
[18] Case 75/77 [1978] ECR 897, para 21.
[19] Case 60/81 *International Business Machines Corporation v Commission* [1981] ECR 2639.
[20] ibid para 19.
[21] Case 53/85 *AKZO Chemie v Commission* [1986] ECR 1965, para 20.

producing perceptible legal consequences. Limiting review to the final decision did not, in the court's view, afford an adequate degree of protection.

10.24   On the other hand, the creation of legal effects does not always subject a decision to review on rights of defence grounds. In *Philip Morris*[22] the Commission decided to institute proceedings before courts in the USA in respect of manufacturers' alleged involvement in the bringing of cigarettes into the EU. The ECJ held that although the commencement of such proceedings was not without legal effects, the effects concerned the procedure before the court that was seized of the proceedings. As the ECJ observed:

> ... When it decides to commence proceedings, the Commission does not intend (itself) to change the legal position in question, but merely opens a procedure whose purpose is to achieve a change in the position through a judgment...[23]

What are the requirements of a fair hearing?

10.25   There is no rigid set of indicia of that which constitutes a fair hearing.[24] The rationale of the requirement—the enabling of the affected party to advance its case and make known its views—dictates the content in each case. However, the main elements of a fair hearing (most of which are considered below separately) are those identified at para 10.07.

10.26   The different constituent elements of a fair hearing are necessary in order that the affected party is given the opportunity to make known its views on the truth and relevance of the facts, charges, and circumstances relied on by the decision-maker.[25] Accordingly, as fundamental requirements, that party must: (1) be provided with a clear statement of the case against it,[26] (2) be permitted to comment on all the information to be taken into account by the decision-maker.[27] These twin requirements, designed to ensure 'equality of arms', have been deployed to justify disclosure of documents from the Commission in several competition cases.[28]

10.27   Although (as will be seen) Article 6 ECHR is not coterminous with EC due process safeguards, it is apparent that the ECJ regards the procedural autonomy of national courts as being derived, at least in part, from Article 6(1).[29] Article 6 is often referred to in ECJ judgments where the rights of the defence are in issue. Indeed, the ECJ has shown itself prepared to assess the fairness of its own proceedings by reference to Article 6.[30]

10.28   Article 6 distinguishes between, on the one hand, the determination of a *criminal charge* and, on the other, the determination of *civil rights and obligations*. In general terms, the

---

[22]   Joined Cases T–377, 379–380/00 and 260 and 272/01 *Philip Morris International v Commission* [2003] 1 CMLR 21.

[23]   ibid para 79.

[24]   See, eg, Case C–342/89 *Germany v Commission* [1991] ECR I–5031, para 17.

[25]   See, eg, Case 85/76 *Hoffmann-La Roche v Commission* [1979] ECR 461, paras 9 and 11.

[26]   See, eg, Joined Cases 48/90 and 66/90 *Netherlands v Commission* [1992] ECR I–565.

[27]   *Hoffmann-La Roche* [1979] ECR 461, para 14.

[28]   See, eg, Cases 100–103/80 *Musique Diffusion Francaise v Commission* [1983] ECR 1825, para 14.

[29]   Joined Cases C–174/98 P and C–189/98 P *Netherlands and Van der Wal v Commission* [2000] ECR I–0001.

[30]   Case C–17/98 *Emesa Sugar (Free Zone) NV v Aruba (No 1)* [2000] ECR I–0665.

former is governed not merely by the overall due process requirements in Article 6(1) but also by the additional procedural safeguards contained in Article 6(2)–(3) (presumption of innocence, right to cross-examine, etc). Importantly, what constitutes a 'criminal charge' or the charging of a 'criminal offence' are autonomous Convention concepts.

Thus, it is possible that different species of EC administrative procedures may fall into the category—at least in ECHR terms—of criminal rather than civil proceedings and, from a purely Convention perspective, carry with them further attendant safeguards as set out in Article 6(2)–(3). In such cases—if the ECJ were to apply Article 6—the content of a fair hearing would be rather different than has formerly been the position. **10.29**

This prospect has already been accepted in the context of competition law. The starting point was the Opinion of the European Commission of Human Rights in *Societe Stenuit v France*.[31] There, the Commission considered that penalties levied for breaches of French competition law constituted a criminal charge within the meaning of Article 6. In the event, it was unnecessary for the ECJ to rule on the issue because the applicant withdrew its application. **10.30**

In a subsequent case the point was corrected. In the light of *Stenuit* the Commission has not disputed that competition proceedings amount to a criminal cause or matter under Article 6. **10.31**

Confidentiality of lawyer and client communications

The ambit of legal professional privilege is, in an EC case, founded on the *confidentiality* of lawyer–client communication as part of the rights of the defence. **10.32**

The EC principle that communications between lawyer and client are privileged was first approved by the ECJ in *AM & S Europe v Commission*.[32] That case involved a Commission investigation into an alleged cartel of zinc producers in the course of which the Commission demanded to see the company's business records which included correspondence and records of legal consultations with both independent and in-house lawyers. AM & S refused disclosure of those documents claiming that they were privileged. **10.33**

In the Commission's view it was entitled under the relevant Council Regulation (Regulation (EEC) 17/62) to check all documents and reach a judgment as to its relevance to the investigation. Such unlimited power included, so it determined, correspondence and records of legal consultations with AM & S's independent and in-house lawyers. AM & S brought an action for annulment of the Commission's decision before the ECJ. **10.34**

The ECJ held that—in the case of independent lawyers—EC law recognizes a general principle of confidentiality of correspondence as between those lawyers and their clients. However, the court also ruled that there were two qualifications: (1) this general principle did not extend to in-house lawyers who were in a relationship of employment with the **10.35**

---

[31] (1992) 14 EHRR 509.
[32] Case 155/79 *AM & S Europe Ltd v Commission* [1982] ECR 1575.

client, and (2) the principle was confined to the communication in question being for the purpose of the client's rights of defence.

Privilege against self-incrimination

10.36   There is at least a qualified privilege against self-incrimination in EC law. However, its current limits appear to be narrower than under the ECHR. In *Orkem*[33] and *Solvay*[34]the ECJ had to consider whether in the absence of a right to silence in Council Regulation (EEC)17/62—empowering the Commission to require undertakings to supply information during an investigation into anti-competitive practices—there was, nonetheless, a general principle of EC law recognizing the right of an undertaking not to supply information that could be used against it in order to establish an infringement of competition law.

10.37   The court drew a distinction between: (1) information that the Commission is entitled to compel for the purposes of its investigation including disclosure of relevant documents even if those documents may be deployed to prove anti-competitive conduct, and (2) information that undermined the rights of the defence. The latter was precluded. Whilst purely factual information could be compelled, information could not be demanded as to the objects behind the company's actions. Nor could the Commission seek an acknowledgement by the undertaking of its participation in anti-competitive practices.

10.38   Importantly, the ECJ observed:

> As far as Article 6 of the European Convention is concerned, although it may be relied upon by an undertaking subject to an investigation relating to competition law, it must be observed that neither the wording of that article nor the decisions of the European Court of Human Rights indicate that it upholds the right not to give evidence against oneself.[35]

10.39   This reasoning, though not necessarily the outcome, requires revision in the light of the subsequent decision of the European Court of Human Rights in *Funke v France*.[36] There, the Strasbourg Court ruled that the applicant's conviction was obtained in breach of a privilege against self-incrimination conferred by Article 6(1) since he was convicted of a failure to provide documents in an attempt to secure evidence of offences that he was alleged to have committed. This was held to infringe his right to remain silent and, thereby, not to incriminate himself.

10.40   The interplay between EC and ECHR law, in the context of the privilege against self-incrimination, was prayed in aid by the claimants in domestic judicial review proceedings considered by the House of Lords in *R v Hertfordshire County Council, ex p Green*

---

[33] Case 374/87 *Orkem v Commission* [1989] ECR 3283, paras 28–29.
[34] Case 27/88 *Solvay & Cie v Commission* [1989] ECR 3355.
[35] *Orkem* [1989] ECR 3283, para 30.
[36] (1993) 16 EHRR 297. See, also, *Saunders v United Kingdom* (1997) 23 EHRR 313; *Murray v United Kingdom* (1996) 22 EHRR 29; *Serves v France* (1999) 28 EHRR 265; *Shannon v United Kingdom (App No 656/03)* The Times, 12 October 2005.

Environmental Industries Ltd.[37] That was a case engaging s 33(1)(a) of the Environmental Protection Act 1990 implementing an EC Council Directive. It was a criminal offence to fail, without reasonable excuse, to answer a request for information under s 71(2) of the 1990 Act. The appeal to the House of Lords concerned the refusal of Hertfordshire County Council to confirm that a response to the request would not be used in a subsequent prosecution.

Lord Hoffmann delivered the principal speech in the House of Lords. His analysis of the   **10.41**
Strasbourg case law was to the effect that Article 6(1) only came into play if the information provided was used in *criminal* proceedings. This, he demonstrated, was clarified in *Saunders v United Kingdom*[38] at paras 67 and 74 of the court's judgment which distinguished between the legitimacy of compulsory questions in a non-judicial investigation from compulsory questions in a criminal trial. Nothing, he observed, in *Funke v France*[39] eroded that distinction or was considered by the Strasbourg Court in the later case of *Saunders* to have eroded the distinction. On that basis, the appellants were rightly convicted.

In the light of the Strasbourg jurisprudence it is not easy to sustain the reasoning in   **10.42**
Orkem.[40] Whilst Strasbourg appears clearly to have distinguished between purely investigatory processes and a criminal trial it has not narrowed the availability of the privilege against self-incrimination in the manner suggested by the ECJ in *Orkem*.

However, that conclusion does not necessarily suggest that the outcome, in *Orkem,* would   **10.43**
be any different.[41] As developed by the European Court of Human Rights, there is a distinction between a non-judicial investigation and the criminal trial process. Although (see above) certain types of non-judicial investigations—notably competition proceedings—appear to constitute the determination of a criminal charge under Article 6 ECHR it may be that there is a further distinction to be drawn (at least in the EC context) between two different types of 'criminal' proceedings under the ECHR, namely: (1) criminal proceedings of a judicial nature, and (2) criminal proceedings of a non-judicial nature (such as competition investigations). Whilst the latter would attract wider procedural safeguards in Article 6(2)–(3) the privilege of self-incrimination would attach only in the qualified form envisaged in *Orkem*.

It is emphasized that the above reasoning has not been developed by the ECJ. However, the   **10.44**
most recent domestic and Strasbourg case law tends to blur the distinctions between 'criminal' and 'civil' proceedings for the purposes of Article 6 ECHR and to lay stress on the fact that there is a spectrum of proceedings which require fairness to be looked at more broadly.[42]

---

[37] [2000] 1 All ER 773.
[38] (1997) 23 EHRR 313.
[39] (1993) 16 EHRR 297.
[40] (1989) ECR 3283.
[41] Thus far, at least. neither the CFI nor the ECJ have been prepared to qualify the reasoning in *Orkem*. See, eg, Joined Cases C–238, 244–245, 247, 250, 251, 252 and 254/99 P *PVC II Cases* [2002] ECR I–8375.
[42] See, eg, in the domestic courts *Official Receiver v Sterm* [2000] UKHRR 332; *International Transport Roth GmbH v Secretary of State for the Home Department* [2003] QB 728; *R v Securities and Futures Authority* (2002) IRLR 297. See, also, *Albert Le Compte v Belgium* [1983] 5 EHRR 533, paras 30, 39.

If that is the correct approach, it seems likely to be adopted by the ECJ so as to permit the eliciting of factual information in Commission investigations into anti-competitive practices and other EC investigations of a similar nature (whether conducted by Commission or national authorities).

10.45 The importance of a case such as *R v Hertfordshire County Council, ex p Green Environmental Industries Ltd*[43] is that it illustrates the way in which domestic judicial review proceedings may involve consideration of domestic law, HRA law, and EC law. The House of Lords first analysed the 1990 Act from a purely domestic standpoint before addressing the separate question of whether HRA or EC law made a difference.

10.46 Although the House of Lords appeared to consider, at least for the purposes of that case, that EC and HRA law were the same it cannot always be assumed that this is so. In particular, in the context of the privilege against self-incrimination the significance of competition inquiries in the EC legal system might well produce a different result—along *Orkem* lines—were Strasbourg to conclude, say, that a domestic competition investigation engaged the privilege against self-incrimination under Article 6 ECHR in the same way as in a criminal trial. As the ECJ observed in *Orkem*:[44]

> This Court may ... adopt, with respect to the provisions of the Convention, an interpretation which does not coincide exactly with that given by the Strasbourg authorities, in particular the European Court of Human Rights. It is not bound, in so far as it does not have systematically to take into account, as regards fundamental rights under Community law, the interpretation of the Convention given by the Strasbourg authorities ...

A right to reasons

10.47 There is a wide-ranging duty to give reasons in EC law. The duty derives both from the Treaty and from the case law of the ECJ. The latter is a facet of the general principle of effectiveness and its development in the cases affords a good example of why not merely Community institutions but also national bodies implementing (or purporting to implement) or derogating (or purporting to derogate) from EC law are bound by the rights of the defence: here, the requirement to give reasons for their decisions.

Reasons under the Treaty—Community institutions

10.48 Article 253 (ex 190) EC stipulates that:

> Regulations, directives and decisions adopted jointly by the European Parliament and the Council, and such acts adopted by the Council or the Commission, shall state the reasons on which they are based ...

---

[43] [2000] 1 All ER 773.
[44] [1989] ECR 3283, para 140. This approach is, it is submitted, consistent with Case T–112/98 *Mannesmannrohren-Werke AG v Commission* [2001] ECR II–729 in which the CFI held, at para 77 of its judgment, that EC law offered: 'protection equivalent to that guaranteed by Article 6 of the Convention'. Certainly, to date neither the ECJ nor CFI have indicated a change of stance on *Orkem*: see, eg, Joined Cases T–305–307, 313–316, 318, 325, 328–329 and 335/94 *Re the PVC Cartel No II* [1999] ECR II–0931. cf Case C–185/95 P *Baustahlgewebe GmbH v Commission* [1999] 4 CMLR 1203.

The Treaty obligation to give reasons is, thus, general in character extending, as it does, **10.49** both to administrative and legislative measures. As such, it goes well beyond the requirements of purely domestic law,[45] and even the HRA.[46] There is a threefold justification for the obligation. In *Germany v Commission*[47] the ECJ expressed it thus:

> In imposing upon the Commission the obligation to state reasons for its decisions, Article 253 [190] is not taking mere formal considerations into account but seeks to give an opportunity to the parties of defending their rights, to the Court of exercising its supervisory functions and to the Member States and to all interested nationals of ascertaining the circumstances in which the Commission has applied the Treaty.

In terms of what the court requires, the ECJ has observed that: **10.50**

> . . . the statement of grounds required by Article 190 of the EEC Treaty [now Article 253 EC] must disclose in a clear and unequivocal fashion the reasoning followed by the Community authority which adopted the measure in question in such a way as to make the persons concerned aware of the reasons for the measure and thus enable them to defend their rights and the Court to exercise its supervisory jurisdiction.[48]

As might be expected, the extent of the duty is dependent on the circumstances of the indi- **10.51** vidual case. It will depend, amongst other things, on matters such as the content of the measure, the nature of the reasons provided and the interest that the parties have in obtaining explanations.[49]

Thus, for example, it will usually be sufficient in the case of a legislative measure of general **10.52** application, such as a regulation, to indicate in the preamble the general situation leading to its adoption and its general objectives.[50] On the other hand, an individual decision will require greater specificity. A decision is likely to be annulled if it is insufficiently precise to enable those concerned to exercise their rights of defence.[51] In general terms, the reasons given need not examine all the issues of law and fact raised by all parties at all stages of the decision-making process.[52]

The principles governing the Treaty obligation on Community institutions to give reasons **10.53** for their decisions are important and need to be understood by the Administrative Court. In particular, especially in the case of secondary legislation, they may become relevant to domestic judicial review proceedings where the underlying Community legislation underpins the legal validity of a subsequent national measure.[53]

---

[45] *R v Secretary of State for the Home Department, ex p Doody* [1994] 1 AC 531, 564, per Lord Mustill.
[46] Materially, Art 6(1) ECHR only requires reasons in respect of rhe determinations of 'civil rights and obligations' or of the determination of a criminal charge.
[47] Case 24/62 [1963] ECR 63, 69.
[48] Case 350/88 *Société Francaise des Biscuits Delacre e.a. v Commission* [1990] ECR I–395, para 15.
[49] Case C–113/00 *Spain v Commission* [2002] ECR I–7601, paras 47 et seq.
[50] See, eg, Case 5/67 *Beus* [1968] ECR 83, 95.
[51] For an instance of this, see Case 24/62 *Germany v Commission* [1963] ECR 63.
[52] See, eg, Case T–114/92 *Bemim v Commission* [1995] ECR II–147, para 41.
[53] Issues may, however, then arise as to whether—if rights of defence are asserted—those issues should have been brought before the ECJ by means of a direct action under Art 230: see paras 3.69–3.80. Procedural issues relating to underlying Community legislation are not, of course, confined to reasons. See, eg, Case 138/79 *Roquette Freres SA v Council* [1980] ECR 3333.

The wider duty to give reasons in EC law

10.54 It is well established that the general principle of effectiveness[54] requires the giving of reasons in respect of decisions that adversely affect Community rights. In *Sodemare*[55] Advocate General Fennelly said:

> The obligation to give reasons for national decisions affecting the exercise of Community law rights does not arise from any extension of Article 190 of the Treaty, but from the general principle of Community law, flowing from the constitutional traditions of the Member States, that judicial remedies should be available to individuals in such cases.[56]

10.55 The same principle has now been applied, and a duty to give reasons imposed, by the ECJ in a variety of contexts involving EC rights.[57]

10.56 In the light of these authorities it would appear that the Court of Appeal decision in *R v Secretary of State for the Environment, Transport and the Regions, ex p Marson*[58] was decided *per incuriam*. There, the Court of Appeal upheld the decision of Jowitt J to the effect that there was no obligation on the Secretary of State to give reasons for refusing to undertake an environmental impact assessment under the Town and Country Planning (Assessment of Environmental Effects) Regulations 1988 implementing the Environmental Impact Assessment Directive (Directive (EEC) 85/337).

10.57 Although the court cited the opinion of the Advocate General in *Sodemare* it appeared to consider that because there was no 'fundamental' right engaged, there was no duty on the Secretary of State to give reasons. The House of Lords refused permission to appeal.

10.58 It is, however, submitted that the principle in *Sodemare* reflects the fact that it is the giving of reasons itself that constitutes the fundamental right because it reflects a general principle of EC law that effective judicial remedies should be available to individuals in respect of national decisions affecting the exercise of their EC law rights. Having accepted that the claimant, Mr Marson, had a right derived from EC law to consideration of whether an environmental impact assessment should be carried out there is no obvious basis for the Court of Appeal then requiring the EC right in question to be of a so-called 'fundamental' character.

10.59 *Marson* was, however, followed by Richards J in *Gillespie v First Secretary of State*[59] who observed that:

> Although the judgment of the Court of Appeal in *Marson* was on a permission application, it was a detailed judgment and is of strong persuasive authority.

10.60 Since *Marson* and *Gillespie* it should be noted that in *Commission v Italy*[60] the ECJ had to consider a case where the Italian authorities had given approval for a road scheme and

---

[54] For which, see paras 3.09–3.17 and 5.13–5.22.
[55] Case C–70/95 *Sodemare SA v Regione Lombardia* [1997] ECR I–3395.
[56] ibid 3405.
[57] See, most notably, Case 222/86 *UNECTEF v Heylens* [1987] ECR 4097, para 15 (free access to employment).
[58] Unreported, 8 May 1998.
[59] [2003] EWHC 8, especially para 94.
[60] Case C–87/02 [2004] ECR I–5975.

subsequently decided that it did not require an environmental impact assessment (EIA). The Commission argued that 'clear and precise reasons' had to be given for any decision not to require EIA and that this had not occurred. The ECJ found, amongst other things, that the screening opinion of the Italian authorities as to whether there should be an EIA 'is based on a cursory statement of reasons and merely refers to the favourable opinion of the Coordinating Committee'. It would appear that, at least by implication, the ECJ considered that there is a duty to give reasons for decisions not to require an EIA. If that is a correct interpretation of *Commission v Italy* it is clear that *Marson* is, in any event, no longer a reliable precedent. The reliability of *Marson* is currently under challenge in a judicial review challenge due to be heard by the Court of Appeal.[61]

Right to a hearing within a reasonable time

The right to a hearing connotes, as provided for expressly under Article 6 ECHR, a hearing within a reasonable time before an independent court or tribunal.[62] This aspect of due process safeguards has itself been recognized by the ECJ as constituting a general principle of EC law.[63] In *Baustahlgererbe GmbH v Commission*,[64] for example, it was held that the general principle was breached in a case that had been pending before the CFI for five-and-a half years. **10.61**

As with similar principles directly applied by the European Court of Human Rights in cases under Article 6 ECHR, what constitutes a reasonable time is to be determined by reference to all the circumstances of the specific case. In particular, the context and complexity of the proceedings, its importance to the parties involved and the conduct of the respective parties may all be relevant factors.[65] **10.62**

Right of access to documents

Equality of arms is a separate facet of the right to a hearing. In principle, this denotes that a party is entitled to equal access to relevant material and it has, indeed, been recognized that the 'right to information' is a general principle of EC law.[66] In *Solvay*[67] a competition case, the CFI clarified, however, that there is at least one limit to such entitlement which is that the material in question must be capable of making a difference **10.63**

---

[61] Permission to apply for judicial review was refused at first instance by Burton J in *R (Probyn) v First Secretary of State* [2005] EWHC 398 who, however, observed that 'it is plain that the drift of the European Courts—or, at any rate, those arguing before the European Court—is flowing in the other direction from *Marson*'.

[62] For the element of independence and impartiality see, eg, Cases C–174/98 P and C–189/98 P *Netherlands and van der Wal v Commission* [2000] ECR I–1, para 17.

[63] Joined Cases C–238, 244, 245, 247, 250–252 and 254/99 P *Limburgse Vinyl Maatschappij NV (LVM) v Commission* [2002] ECR I–8375, paras 164 et seq.

[64] Case C–185/95 P [1998] ECR I–8417, paras 26 et seq.

[65] See paras 10.25–10.27.

[66] Case 58/94 *Netherlands v Council* [1996] ECR I–2169. Further, access to documents may not be denied on the ground that disclosure will place a disproportionate burden. Where it is not obvious whether access should be granted or refused, it is necessary to examine each document in order to decide whether partial access should be granted: see Case T–2/03 *Verein für Konsumentinformation v Commission* [2005] 1 WLR 3302.

[67] Case T–30/91 *Solvay SA v Commission* [1995] ECR II–1175.

to the decision-making process. The burden of establishing that non-disclosure has affected the rights of defence lies upon the undertaking asserting it.[68]

10.64 But the burden is not, necessarily, a high one.[69] As the ECJ has put it (at para 68 of its judgment in *Solvay*):[70]

> ... In order to find that the rights of the defence have been infringed, it is sufficient for it to be established that the non-disclosure of the documents in question might have influenced the course of the procedure and the content of the decision to the applicant's detriment ...

10.65 There is, at first sight, a tension between this principle and the discrete obligation of professional secrecy on Community and national institutions towards undertakings. Article 287 (ex 214) EC imposes an obligation on members and servants of institutions of the Community 'not to disclose information of the kind covered by the obligation of professional secrecy, in particular information about undertakings, their business relations or their cost components'.

10.66 Moreover, the Article 287 obligations of confidence are also owed to individuals because they, too, constitute a wider general principle of confidentiality recognized by EC law. In *Stanley Adams v Commission*[71] the ECJ held that information supplied by Mr Adams to the Commission as to certain anti-competitive practices on the part of his former employer Hoffmann-La Roche ought not to have been disclosed at least so as to enable Hoffmann-La Roche to ascertain the identity of Mr Adams as the source of the information. It was held that the Commission owed a duty of confidentiality to Mr Adams and that it was, accordingly, liable in damages to him for the consequences of its breach of duty.

10.67 The tension between the respective obligations of disclosure and non-disclosure must be (and has been) resolved by recourse to a third and somewhat more complex principle. This is that an EC decision-maker must not act to the detriment of a person or undertaking by using information that it is under an obligation not to disclose where the omission to disclose—consistent with that obligation—affects the rights of defence of the undertaking in question.[72] In this fashion, the legitimate interest of Hoffmann-Le Roche in obtaining access to the information on which the Commission's decision against it was based is reconciled with the equally legitimate interest of Mr Adams in keeping his identity secret from the company.[73]

D. Scope of Judicial Protection

10.68 Great importance is attached to due process guarantees in EC law because of the limited basis on which the exercise of discretionary powers by bodies implementing EC law—especially EC institutions—can, in practice, be reviewed.

---

[68] See, eg, Joined Cases 209–15 and 218/78 *Van Landewyck v Commission (FEDETAB)* [1984] ECR 3125, para 39.

[69] See, also, paras 10.69 et seq.

[70] Case T–30/91 [1995] ECR II–1175.

[71] Case 145/83 [1985] ECR 353, para 34.

[72] See, eg, Case 234/84 *Belgium v Commission* [1986] ECR 2263, para 29.

[73] See, further, J Schwarze, 'The Administrative Law of the Community and the Protection of Human Rights' [1996] CML Rev 401.

This was explained by the ECJ in *Technische Universitat Munchen*.[74] The court said: **10.69**

> It must be stated first of all that, since an administrative procedure entailing complex techni-
> cal evaluations is involved, the Commission must have a power of appraisal in order to be
> able to fulfil its tasks. However, where the Community institutions have such a power of
> appraisal, respect for the rights guaranteed by the Community legal order in administrative
> procedures is of even more fundamental importance. Those guarantees include, in particu-
> lar, the duty of the competent institution to examine carefully and impartially all the relevant
> aspects of the individual case, the right of the person concerned to make his views known and
> to have an adequately reasoned decision. Only in this way can the Court verify whether the
> factual and legal elements upon which the exercise of the power of appraisal depends were
> present.

The corollary of this is that provided that it can be shown that the formal infringement of **10.70**
a procedural guarantee *might* have made a difference to the outcome the court will not scrutinize the detail of the case in order to determine whether the decision can be supported.
We have already seen the operation of this principle in relation to the right to information.
In that context, in *Solvay*[75] (cited for a similar purpose above) the CFI also observed that:

> ... it is not for the Court of First Instance to rule definitively on the evidential value of all the
> evidence used by the Commission to support the contested decision ... The possibility [that
> the infringement might have affected the outcome] can therefore be established if a provi-
> sional examination of some of the evidence shows that the documents not disclosed might—
> in the light of that evidence—have had a significance which ought not to have been
> disregarded. If it were proved that the rights of the defence were infringed, the administrative
> procedure and the appraisal of the facts in the decision would be defective.

So, the threshold for interference by the ECJ (and, it is submitted, the Administrative **10.71**
Court) for infringement of the rights of defence requires more than a merely formal breach.
There must be a breach of substance as opposed to form. However, the court does not
require more than the possibility that the infringement in question could have influenced
the result.

This is further exemplified by two decisions of the CFI in respect of challenges brought **10.72**
under Article 230 EC for annulment on the ground of 'infringement of an essential procedural requirement'.[76] In a recent staff case the CFI observed that the right to be heard is
materially infringed in the above sense if 'it cannot be reasonably precluded that that irreg-
ularity could have had a particular impact on the content of that act'.[77] So, too, in *Schneider
Electric*[78] the CFI held that if a fair hearing had taken place the undertaking would have
been in a position to suggest remedies for the Commission's competition concerns. Its decision might, in that event, have been different.

---

[74] Case C–269/90 *Technische Universitat Munchen v Hauptzollamt Munchen-Mitte* [1991] ECR I–5469,
paras 13 et seq.

[75] Case T–30/91 [1995] ECR II–1175, para 68.

[76] In practice, infringement of due process rights will be governed by the same principles whether proceedings are brought under Art 230 or in the Administrative Court and/or (thereafter) the ECJ on a preliminary
ruling.

[77] Case T–237/00 *Patrick Reynolds v European Parliament* [2002] ECR II–163, para 112.

[78] Case T–310/01 *Schneider Electric v Commission* [2002] ECR II–4071.

10.73   The second consequence of the need for effective EC due process guarantees, as explained in *Technische Universitat Munchen*[79] is that unlike the position in domestic and HRA law (see below) it is, at least generally, not possible to 'cure' defects of process that have occurred. In *Solvay*,[80] for example, the CFI ruled that the Commission's unjustified failure to disclose information was not capable of being 'cured' in the proceedings before it. Exceptionally, however, the court has been prepared to remedy defects of process where the interests of the affected person or undertaking have not been prejudiced.[81]

E.   Comparing EC Due Process with Domestic and HRA Law

10.74   The evolution of due process rights in domestic law has been greatly accelerated by the advent of the HRA. However, as earlier explained, purely domestic UK principles of natural justice heavily influenced the recognition of due process rights as a general principle of EC law.[82] As Willes J observed in an early domestic case:[83]

> ... a tribunal which is by law invested with power to affect the property of one of Her Majesty's subjects, is bound to give each subject an opportunity of being heard before it proceeds: and that the rule is of universal application and founded on the plainest principles of justice.

10.75   These principles were expanded and clarified by the House of Lords in *Ridge v Baldwin*.[84] There, it was recognized that any decision affecting a person's rights or interests—not merely property rights—was subject to natural justice (or due process) imperatives.

10.76   In reality, therefore, most of the due process rights recognized by EC law are also recognized in domestic law; certainly in domestic law as augmented by the coming into force of the HRA which has itself greatly influenced the development of EC general principles including rights of the defence.[85]

10.77   Where differences occur it is usually the result either of the special nature of EC law or of a different interpretation being placed by the ECJ to that of the European Court of Human Rights on a particular provision of the ECHR.

10.78   The special nature of EC law arguably implies a different, and somewhat more restrictive, approach to certain Article 6 ECHR due process safeguards. A potential instance of this, in the field of the privilege against self-incrimination in competition investigations, has been noted above where it was suggested that the privilege may be more circumscribed in that EC context than in general.[86]

---

79 Case C–269/90 [1991] ECR I–5469.
80 Case T–30/91 [1995] ECR II–1175, para 98.
81 See, eg, Case 85/76 *Hoffmann-La Roche v Commission* [1979] ECR 461, para 15.
82 See paras 10.05–10.06.
83 *Cooper v Wandsworth Board of Works* (1863) 14 CB (NS) 180, 190.
84 [1964] AC 40.
85 See generally Chapter 12.
86 See paras 10.36–10.46.

Another field where EC law may, because of its special nature, be less protective of due **10.79**
process safeguards is that relating to the imposition of sanctions. Sanctions represent an
important instrument for implementing EC law in areas such as antitrust law or merger
control where fines are regularly levied and also in other areas—though for rather different
purposes—such as the agricultural sector where unduly awarded benefits may be reclaimed
and a sanction imposed such as an additional fee.

The potential size of fines coupled with their intended deterrent nature suggests that crim- **10.80**
inal protections and standards such as (for example) the specific fair trial safeguards under
Article 6(2) ECHR or the principle of *nullum crimen sine lege* to be found in Article 7
ECHR—applicable under the ECHR to substantively criminal accusations—are appropriate to at least a number of sanctions levied under EC law whether by EC or national
institutions.

However, thus far, the ECJ has proved resistant to the notion of treating even ostensibly **10.81**
penal sanctions as deserving of all criminal due process safeguards. In *Kaserei
Champignon*,[87] for example, the ECJ addressed the legality of a regulation providing for a
sanction without proof of fault in circumstances where the sanction (an additional penalty
for making an inaccurate export refund application and receiving the refund) did not
assume fault.[88]

The court's rationale for holding that the regulation in question was valid was that the leg- **10.82**
islation was not criminal in nature. It was merely intended to counter the many irregulari-
ties perpetrated when seeking agricultural aid. It was simply part of the export refund
system to which the applicant was a voluntary participant.

Such a result may be justified by the fact that, in EC law, objectives characterizing criminal **10.83**
penalty may overlap with genuinely administrative objectives where to require proof of
fault would subvert those objectives. It has, nonetheless, been cogently argued that the EC
rights of defence principles governing the imposition of sanctions are, currently, less than
clear and may demand special attention.[89]

Finally, in the special context of EC law, it should—a point noted earlier—be emphasized **10.84**
that although a broad discretion is frequently conferred by EC law on those institutions or
authorities responsible for undertaking often complex and technical appraisals this does
not mean, as it does in many areas of domestic law, that the intensity of judicial review is
necessarily lowered. This is because the ECJ has recognized that without laying down stringent due process safeguards (whether in terms of a duty to give reasons or requiring a full
scrutiny by way of judicial review) the factual and legal elements informing an EC law decision would escape judicial control.

---

[87] Case C–210/00 *Kaserei Champignon Hofmeister GmbH & Co KG v Hauptzollamt Hamburg-Jonas*
[2002] ECR I–6453, especially paras 38–43.
[88] For the stringent approach taken to sanctions see, further, Case C–397/03 P *Archer Daniel Midland v
Commission* (not yet reported judgment 18 May 2006).
[89] See J Schwarze, 'Judicial Review of European Administrative Procedure' [2004] PL 146, 166.

10.85   As has for example been observed, by the CFI:

> It seems that although the courts traditionally grant broad discretionary powers to the administration, especially in respect of the complex economic analyses in merger control, the CFI today is nevertheless willing to review the Commission's reasoning in great detail.[90]

10.86   The second aspect that may sometimes indicate a difference between application of due process principles in HRA cases and in EC cases is that whilst many of the EC law due process safeguards are modelled on the ECHR (and, in particular, on Article 6) the ECJ, at least in constitutional terms, merely takes account of the ECHR albeit that it occupies a special place in the general principles common to Member States.[91] So, the ECJ is not bound by the ECHR. This is why it is, for example, open to the ECJ to take a different view of the scope of the privilege of self-incrimination than does the European Court of Human Rights or the domestic courts.

10.87   Because of the supremacy of Community law, the Administrative Court and appellate courts are bound by decisions of the ECJ. In judicial review proceedings falling within the scope of EC law[92] the Administrative Court is, therefore, likely to be required to follow an ECJ due process ruling even if it conflicts with a decision of the European Court of Human Rights.[93] As explained above, there may sometimes be good reason for the difference of approach. However, even if the reason is simply because the ECJ has not anticipated the way in which the Strasbourg jurisprudence has subsequently developed it is not open to the Administrative Court to disregard the inconsistent ECJ ruling. In such circumstances it is submitted that a reference to the ECJ for a preliminary ruling would be the most appropriate course to take.

---

[90] See Schwarze (n 89 above) 160–1.

[91] For further discussion, see paras 12.13–12.18.

[92] For further analysis of this term, see paras 12.62–12.80.

[93] For further analysis, see paras 12.106 et seq. If and to the extent that the case includes a non–EC dimension, the Strasbourg ruling may often be followed to the extent of its applicability. But care must be taken to ensure that by doing so the scope and extent of EC law is not impeded. To that extent, the Administrative Court would not be able to follow the Strasbourg ruling. Importantly, the House of Lords accepted in *Kay v London Borough of Lambeth Council* [2006] UKHL 10 that s 3(1) of the European Communities Act 1972—which requires national courts to follow rulings of the ECJ—was different to the effect of HRA decisions (see per Lord Bingham, para 28).

11

PROPORTIONALITY

A. EC Law Proportionality in Judicial Review

Proportionality, as one of the general principles of EC law, may be relied on in domestic public law proceedings where issues arise as to (either or both) the legality of EC measures and of national measures (including administrative acts and omissions) intended to implement or derogate from EC law.[1] The exercise required to be undertaken by the Administrative Court or other national court potentially involves (depending on the context) both interpretation of EC and domestic legislative measures (including Treaty provisions) and—where necessary—applying the legislation as interpreted to the legality of administrative decision-making. **11.01**

In very general terms EC law proportionality operates to prevent obligations being imposed by legislative measure or administrative act save to the extent to which such obligations are necessary in the public interest to attain the purpose of the measure/decision in question.[2] **11.02**

---

[1] Instances of application of the EC proportionality principle by the Administrative Court are given throughout this work. Specific examples include *R (Hoverspeed) v Commissioners of Customs and Excise* [2002] Eu LR 668; *International Transport Roth v Secretary of State for the Home Department* [2003] QB 728. Both these cases are analysed elsewhere: see paras 17.72 et seq.

[2] Case 11/70 *Internationale Handelsgesellschaft* [1970] ECR 1125, 1146, per Advocate General de Lamothe.

11.03   In *R (Omega Air Ltd) v Secretary of State for the Environment, Transport and the Regions*[3] the
ECJ in giving a preliminary ruling under Article 234 (ex 177) EC on the validity of an EC
regulation observed as follows:

> [I]t should be remembered that it is settled case-law that the principle of proportional-
> ity, which is one of the general principles of Community Law, requires that measures
> adopted by Community institutions should not exceed the limits of what is appropriate
> and necessary in order to attain the objectives pursued by the legislation in question, and
> where there is a choice between several appropriate measures, recourse must be had to
> the least onerous and the disadvantages caused must not be disproportionate to the aims
> pursued.

11.04   In domestic judicial review proceedings with an EC law element the EC proportionality
principle may arise in one or more of a number of ways. It may, for example, arise:

(1) as part of the necessary application of EC law in a public law context, and/or
(2) in the context of discrete or overlapping proportionality arguments founded on the
     Human Rights Act 1998 (HRA) because proportionality is an important doctrine in
     HRA cases,[4] and/or
(3) in the context of discrete or overlapping arguments founded on the common law.[5]

11.05   As has been emphasized[6] both the grounds for domestic judicial review (even if, as with
proportionality, sometimes *nominally* the same) and the available remedies may differ
according to whether the legal regime in question sounds in EC and/or HRA and/or purely
domestic law.

11.06   As far as proportionality is concerned these differences are, in part, a question of the practical application of the doctrine over the years in the various international jurisdictions.
These differences then become embedded in domestic administrative law via the national
statutory incorporation provisions (HRA/European Communities Act 1972) into ostensibly different approaches to proportionality. For example, in respect of the application of
proportionality, the European Court of Human Rights in Strasbourg (a statutory source of
law for domestic public law decisions under the HRA)[7] has been described as—compared
to the ECJ—'cautiously inhibited'.[8]

---

[3] Joined Cases C–27/00 and C–122/00 [2002] ECR I–2569, para 62. See, also, Joined Cases C–286/94,
C–340/95, C–401/95 and C–47/96 *Garage Molenheide BVBA v Belgian State* [1997] ECR I–7281,
paras 46–49.

[4] The most concise formulation of the ECHR proportionality requirements is contained in the formulation of Gubbay CJ as approved by Lord Clyde in *De Freitas v Permanent Secretary of Ministry of Agriculture,
Fisheries, Lands and Housing* [1999] 1 AC 69, PC in the following threefold test: (i) 'the legislative objective is
sufficiently important to justify limiting a fundamental right; (ii) the measures designed to meet the legislative objective are rationally connected to it; and (iii) the means used to impair the right or freedom are no more
than is necessary to accomplish the objective'.

[5] Currently, at least, proportionality is not a discrete head of challenge in judicial review outside
Community and ECHR grounds or perhaps associated constitutional grounds (see below).

[6] See, eg, para 2.30.

[7] HRA, s 2.

[8] Lord Lester of Herne Hill QC, *General Report,* 8th International Colloquy on the ECHR (Budapest,
20–23 September 1995), Council of Europe, 234–6.

However, there is also a difference of substantive approach to the proportionality doctrine **11.07** in the different jurisdictions. There is a continuing debate as to whether proportionality even exists as an independent head of judicial review in terms of most *domestic* grounds of challenge.[9] Also, the Court of Appeal has recently held that in EC law the doctrine of proportionality may require more stringent justification than proportionality in an HRA context.[10]

Further, the remedies available for a successful EC law challenge are more draconian (even) **11.08** than for an HRA challenge in that primary legislation may have to be disapplied if an existing statutory provision contravenes an EC law requirement such as the EC proportionality principle. In terms of remedy, under the HRA there can, at most, be a (discretionary) declaration of incompatibility. In domestic public law the doctrine of parliamentary sovereignty prevents any challenge, even indirectly, to an Act of Parliament.

It should also be borne in mind that, in the EC law context, the range and scope of propor- **11.09** tionality falls to be applied by reference to a different constitutional order. As will be seen,[11] there is an important overlap between cases where fundamental rights are in issue. But even here, although its effect is now very strong, the European Convention on Human Rights (ECHR) does not regulate EC law directly. There have been occasions when the ECJ and the Strasbourg Court have reached different interpretations of the same Convention provision.[12]

Finally, in EC law proportionality is applied in many contexts beyond that of fundamental **11.10** rights. It is (see below) one of the principal ways in which the general legitimacy of both Community measures and national implementation thereof, or derogation therefrom, can be tested. In such cases the doctrine of supremacy of Community law[13] may imply that, at least in principle, some higher degree of stringency may be involved in examining whether a measure is necessary as a matter of general application of EC law than in the context of 'Convention rights' under the HRA where the State has a margin of appreciation or discretionary area of judgment or than in the field of domestic law where, at least until recently, irrationality in the *Wednesbury* sense[14] has been a relatively high threshold to the success of an application for judicial review.

---

[9] It seems now to be recognized that proportionality is relevant to grounds of challenge founded on domestic law constitutional rights (though these are, in any event, akin to 'Convention rights' under the HRA): see *R (Daly) v Secretary of State for the Home Department* [2001] UKHL 26, [2001] 2 AC 532.

[10] *R (Countryside Alliance) v (1) Attorney General and (2) Secretary of State for Environment, Food and Rural Affairs* [2006] EWCA Civ 817. For a case analysis, see paras 17.98 et seq.

[11] See Chapter 12.

[12] See para 12.100.

[13] See, eg, Case 6/64 *Costa v ENEL* [1963] ECR 585, 594.

[14] *Associated Provincial Picture Houses Ltd v Wednesbury Corporation* [1948] 1KB 223. The *Wednesbury* doctrine has been criticized but is still a relevant ground of domestic judicial review: see *R (Association of British Civilian Internees (Far East Region)) v Secretary of State for Defence* [2002] EWHC 2119.

B. Applying EC Law Proportionality in Judicial Review Cases

11.11 The first express reference by the ECJ to proportionality was in the *Internationale Handelsgesellschaft* case.[15] Although the principle was derived by the ECJ from the general principles of Community law it has subsequently been given recognition in the Treaties. Thus, Article 5(3) (ex 3b(3)) EC provides that: '[a]ny action by the Community shall not go beyond what is necessary to achieve the objectives of this Treaty'. Although formal embodiment in the Treaty goes no further than the ECJ case law it demonstrates the significance of proportionality in the EC constitutional regime.

11.12 There are, broadly, two types of judicial review grounds for challenge before the Administrative Court in which the proportionality principle *in its EC law form* is likely to arise.[16] These are proceedings where it is used as a ground of challenge to:

(1) the validity of particular Community measures; or,

(2) the legality of national measures implementing Community measures or purporting to derogate from them.[17]

11.13 It is, now, well established that only the ECJ has jurisdiction to declare a *Community* measure to be *invalid*.[18] In many instances, therefore, the question of whether such measure is invalid by reason of contravening the proportionality principle will come before the ECJ (without troubling the Administrative Court) on a direct action under Article 230 (ex 173) EC.

11.14 However, the Administrative Court may, in proceedings for judicial review, sometimes be confronted either with what is in effect a direct challenge to the validity of a Community measure on proportionality grounds or (more usually) to a challenge to a national measure the legality of which is, necessarily, dependent upon the validity or invalidity of underlying Community legislation. The court will then be required to address proportionality in the context of *considering* the validity of the Community legislation because either: (1) the *validity* of such legislation is being asserted (since the court has jurisdiction to make declarations as to validity); or more commonly (2) it is contended that a Community measure is *invalid* and that there should be a preliminary reference to the ECJ under Article 234 (ex 177) EC.

11.15 In such cases the Administrative Court is not required (or empowered) to declare that the Community measure in question lacks validity by reason of being disproportionate but must, rather, assess whether the proportionality arguments as to invalidity are sufficient to

---

[15] Case 11/70 [1970] ECR 1125. Earlier cases may be said to have applied the principle indirectly: see, eg, Case 8/55 *Fedechar v High Authority* [1956] ECR 292, 299.

[16] Similar public law issues may arise in the course of a collateral challenge: see paras 1.20–1.23. Reference here to the Administrative Court in judicial review cases is generally intended to include such collateral challenge cases although (see Chapter 5) the jurisdiction of the Administrative Court is wider than that of other first instance national courts in terms of the relief that it may grant.

[17] Such measures may, of course, include administrative acts or omissions taken in purported pursuance of Community law as, for example, the acts of a public body alleged to be discriminatory under Community law: see, eg, Case C-330/90 *R v IRC, ex p Commerzbank* [1993] ECR I–4017.

[18] See, especially, Case 314/85 *Foto-Frost v Hauptzollamt Lubeck-Ost* [1987] ECR 4199, paras 15–20.

warrant a reference to the ECJ under Article 234.[19] Even so, the principles governing the manner in which the proportionality doctrine may operate to invalidate Community legislation are important for this purpose.

The court may decide that it is unnecessary to make a reference because—having regard to the relevant standards of proportionality—the measure is proportionate. Importantly, in reaching its decision the court may have to operate a different standard, or intensity, of review depending upon the legislative measure under consideration. In particular, the court will have to decide whether the standard is one of: (1) the least restrictive alternative or (2) manifest inappropriateness.[20]   **11.16**

In deciding, in such cases, whether to make a reference there are at least two possible approaches and the ECJ has not definitively pronounced on either. First, the court may decide to refer whenever there is a doubt as to validity. This seems to have been the approach favoured in *Foto-Frost*.[21] Alternatively, the Administrative Court may take the view (unless there are well-founded arguments as to invalidity) that the Community legislation should be taken to be valid unless declared to be invalid by the ECJ. This would allow the Administrative Court to exercise its general discretion as to whether or not to request a preliminary ruling leaving it to the court of last instance to make a mandatory reference under Article 234(3) EC. In either case, though, the court will have to be fully aware of the legal relationship between proportionality and validity.   **11.17**

By contrast, so far as *national* measures—including administrative decisions purporting to apply (or derogate from) Community law—are concerned the Administrative Court undoubtedly possesses jurisdiction to make declarations of invalidity (or to quash the measure/act in question).[22] National legislative measures may, for example, incorrectly purport either to: (1) implement/apply Community law (as, for example, in the transposition of a directive) or (2) derogate from Community law (as, for example, in unlawfully immunizing certain activities from the Community provisions as to freedom of movement of goods or services).   **11.18**

Where national measures of this kind are concerned the Administrative Court may, in the context of proportionality, have to address three issues: **11.19**

(1) the appropriate standard/intensity of review (in general a higher intensity of review applies to derogations than to implementations);
(2) whether or not to make a preliminary reference to the ECJ;[23]
(3) (if not making a reference) the legality or otherwise of the measure in question.

---

[19] For the criteria regulating whether a reference is permitted/required see Chapter 4, especially paras 4.12–4.47.

[20] See paras 11.20–11.35.

[21] Case 314/85 [1987] ECR 4199, 4223, para 9(1) in the Opinion of the Advocate General and the academic views cited by him at 4219–20. See, also, paras 14–15 of the ECJ's judgment at 4230–1. See also paras 4.92 et seq.

[22] If, however, the legality of the national measure is contingent on the validity of prior Community legislation then—so far as the validity of Community legislation is concerned—the same issues will arise and the Administrative Court will not be empowered to declare such legislation to be invalid.

[23] This causes particular problems, considered below, since the ECJ does not, ordinarily, determine questions of fact which are for the national courts.

C. EC Law Proportionality and the Validity of Community Measures

The general test

11.20 As noted at para 11.13 above, only the ECJ may pronounce on the *invalidity* of a *Community* measure. According to that court's standard formulation as to the requisite elements of proportionality:

> In order to establish whether a provision of Community law is consonant with the principle of proportionality it is necessary to establish, in the first place, whether the means it employs to achieve the aim correspond to the importance of the aim and, in the second place, whether they are necessary for its achievement.[24]

11.21 This formulation contains two elements, namely: (1) appropriateness or suitability of the means employed to achieve the desired objective, and (2) the necessity of employing those means.

11.22 A slightly different expression was given to proportionality in *FEDESA*.[25]

> The principle of proportionality ... [requires] that the prohibitory measures are appropriate and necessary in order to attain the objectives legitimately pursued by the legislature in question; when there is a choice between several appropriate measures recourse must be had to the least onerous, and the disadvantages caused must not be disproportionate to the aims pursued.

11.23 It is, therefore, sometimes suggested that the proportionality test contains three, as opposed to two, constituent elements; the third element being that the measure in question must not have a disproportionate effect on a claimant's interests. Notwithstanding this, the ECJ seems, in practice, to have adopted a relatively pragmatic approach without seeking carefully to distinguish between the various possible elements. In reality, the ECJ conducts a balancing exercise weighing up individual interest against legislative aim and the importance of achieving that aim via the measure under scrutiny.

Deference as part of the proportionality standard

11.24 The most significant indicator of how the ECJ approaches proportionality in the context of Community measures is that of how much deference that court pays to the Community legislator having regard to the legislative context.[26]

---

[24] Case 66/82 *Fromancais v FORMA* [1983] ECR 395, para 8.

[25] Case C–331/88 *R v MAFF, ex p FEDESA* [1990] ECR I–4023, para 13.

[26] Deference is equally apposite to judicial review of the validity of national measures with Community law (see paras 11.47 et seq.). Deference to the Community legislature should not be confused with the ECJ determining that the Community legislature has exceeded its powers. Here, proportionality is not the issue though there may be an overlap where the lack of jurisdiction is caused by excessive regulation: see, eg Case C–378/98 *Germany v Parliament and the Council* [2000] ECR I–8419 where the ECJ annulled the Tobacco Advertising Directive on the ground of excess of jurisdiction.

In purely domestic judicial review deference is emerging as an important concept in the **11.25** intensity of review undertaken by the Administrative Court. In his dissenting judgment[27] in *International Transport Roth Gmbh v Secretary of State for the Home Department*[28] Laws LJ distilled a number of general principles in relation to the deference which the court will accord to an Act of Parliament. He observed:

> . . . greater or lesser deference will be due according to whether the subject matter lies more readily within the actual or potential expertise of the democratic powers or the courts. Thus . . . government decisions in the area of macro-economic policy will be relatively remote from judicial control.

A similar approach is, in fact, adopted by the ECJ to certain areas of Community legislative **11.26** competence (see below). This is the underlying rationale of the 'manifestly inappropriate' test as to whether particular Community legislative measures are proportionate.

This test, which presupposes a lower intensity of review than the general formulation of **11.27** proportionality, is (as with deference) especially relevant to cases involving legislative pol- icy measures.[29] For example, in *Fedesa*[30] the applicants challenged the validity of a Council directive prohibiting substances having a hormonal action in livestock farming. Having laid down the general approach to proportionality (in para 13 of its judgment) the ECJ went on, in para 14, to say:

> However . . . it must be stated that in matters concerning the common agricultural policy the Community legislature has a discretionary power which corresponds to the political respon- sibilities given to it by Articles [34] 40 and [37] 43 of the Treaty. Consequently, the legality of a measure adopted in that sphere can be affected only if the measure is manifestly inappro- priate having regard to the objective which the competent institution is seeking to pursue.

Similarly, in *United Kingdom v Council (Working Time Directive)*[31] the ECJ held that 'the **11.28** Council must be allowed a wide discretion in an area which, as here, involves the legislature in making social policy choices and requires it to carry out complex assessments'. On that footing, review would only be appropriate if there were 'manifest error or misuse of powers'.

The reasons for employing this more limited form of review in certain legislative contexts **11.29** are not difficult to discern. If the ECJ were to adopt a high-intensity proportionality review of macro-economic policy choices by the Community legislature it would be faced with endless challenges by applicants who sought to argue an alternative balancing of potentially conflicting factors.

As a doctrine, what proportionality offers, whether at the level of high or low intensity judicial **11.30** review, is a more sharply focused method of examining the legality of the decision-making process than the traditional domestic *Wednesbury* approach.[32]

---

[27] Nothing that Laws LJ had to say about deference was disagreed with by the majority ruling (see the respective judgments of Simon Brown LJ and Parker LJ).
[28] [2002] 3 WLR 344, 376–8.
[29] See, eg, T Tridimas, *The General Principles of EU Law* (2nd edn, 2006) who concludes, at 146, that 'in relation to policy measures, the [Luxembourg] Court does not apply the less restrictive alternative test scrupulously, relying instead on reasonableness or arbitrariness of conduct'.
[30] Case C–331/88 [1990] ECR I–4023.
[31] Case C–84/94 [1996] ECR I–5755, especially para 58.
[32] M Elliott, 'The HRA 1998 and the Standard of Substantive Review' [2002] JR 97.

11.31   However, from the perspective of the Administrative Court determining whether to refer a proportionality judicial review challenge to the underlying validity of Community legislation to the ECJ under Article 234 EC, the most critical point to understand is the context. In particular, if the context is legislative there is (although even that context has different shades) likely to be a wide discretion in the Member State and the ECJ. Some concrete examples of the different standards of proportionality review in different legislative contexts are given below.

Community measures and proportionality

Community legislation and fundamental rights

11.32   In a series of cases, culminating in the ECJ's Opinion 2/94, the ECJ has authoritatively stated that:

> It is well settled that fundamental rights form an integral part of the general principles of law whose observance the Court ensures. For that purpose, the Court draws inspiration from the constitutional traditions common to the Member States and from the guidelines supplied by international treaties for the protection of human rights on which the Member States have collaborated or of which they are signatories. In that regard, the Court has stated that the [European] Convention [on Human Rights] has special significance ...

11.33   The wider arena of the required approach of the Administrative Court generally to fundamental human rights in a Community context is separately considered.[33] For present purposes it should be noted that proportionality plays a potentially important part in determining the validity or otherwise of a Community measure on the alleged ground of its incompatibility with fundamental rights as recognized in EC law.

11.34   In practice, however, it has proved to be extremely difficult to challenge Community legislation directly on this basis. This is because, where the protection of fundamental rights is concerned, most Community measures involve legislative choices of policy at the macro level and, therefore, attract a wide measure of judicial deference (see above). This is to be contrasted with (for example) the exercise of administrative discretions in individual cases where, at least in respect of fundamental rights, there is generally more intensive proportionality scrutiny by way of judicial review.[34] The practical effect of this limitation in domestic judicial review proceedings is that national measures (including administrative decisions) that are challenged on the basis of the underlying invalidity of EC legislative measures in contravening fundamental rights will often be difficult to mount on the basis of the incompatibility of the EC legislation with the principle of proportionality.

11.35   This difficulty of challenging Community measurers via proportionality in the human rights context is shown by cases such as *Ter Voort*.[35] There, the ECJ rejected a proportionality challenge to Council Directive (EEC) 65/65 based on an alleged breach of freedom

---

[33] See Chapter 12.

[34] See paras 11.58 et seq. and, generally, Chapter 12. It is also to be contrasted with many national implementing transposing legislative measures—especially measures of derogation where the standard of proportionality review is usually more stringent for the reasons set out at paras 11.54–11.55.

[35] Case 219/91 *Criminal Proceedings against Ter Voort* [1992] ECR I–5485.

of expression. The court held that freedom of expression fell to be assessed against 'the requirements of the objective protection of public health'[36] which was the aim of the directive. In that and similar contexts the test for whether a measure complies with the proportionality principle has sometimes been expressed as being whether the measure effects 'a disproportionate and intolerable interference which infringes the very substance of the rights guaranteed'.[37]

Detailed administrative measures

By contrast the ECJ has been more prepared to apply the proportionality doctrine in its more intrusive form to Community administrative measures containing detailed regulation of the market. **11.36**

Thus, for example, in the Skimmed-Milk Powder case[38] the Council attempted to reduce, by regulation, the surplus of skimmed-milk powder by requiring producers to purchase it instead of soya. But skimmed-milk powder was required to be purchased at a price approximately three times its value as animal feed. The ECJ held, in part,[39] that the regulation was disproportionate because it was unnecessary to require skimmed-milk powder to be purchased in this way in order to reduce the surplus. A similar standard of proportionality review was applied by the ECJ when holding Council Regulation (EC) 1796/81 to be invalid insofar as it set a charge levied on imports of preserved mushrooms at an excessively high level.[40] **11.37**

In these types of case proportionality can readily be employed by means of high-intensity review because the principle is capable of being applied with precision. This is also true of those Community administrative measures which impose sanctions or penalties or forfeiture. Here, there is no inhibitory range of choices to constrain the 'reach' of proportionality. **11.38**

An example of how the higher intensity level of proportionality review by the ECJ in relation to this kind of case can be relevant to public law cases before the Administrative Court is afforded by the facts of *R v Intervention Board, ex p Man (Sugar) Ltd*.[41] There, the claimant in judicial review proceedings before a Divisional Court sought repayment of a security deposit of £1,670,370 that had been forfeited by the Intervention Board when it failed by four hours to complete the necessary paperwork. **11.39**

The underlying ground for judicial review was the alleged invalidity of the EC regulation on which the forfeiture had been based. Forfeiture appeared to be required for breach both **11.40**

---

[36] ibid para 38.

[37] Case 265/87 *Schrader HS Kraftfutter GmbH & Co KG v Hauptzollamt Gronau* [1988] ECR 2237, para 15.

[38] Case 114/76 *Bela-Muhgle Josef Bergman v Grows Farm* [1977] ECR 1211. See, also, Case 116/76 and Cases 119, 120/76 at (respectively) ECR 1247 and 1269.

[39] The regulation was also invalidated on the basis of a breach of the principle of equality: see, generally, Chapter 7.

[40] Case C–295/94 *Hupeden v Hauptzollamt Hamburg-Jonas* [1996] ECR I–3375. See, also, the similar fate of the subsequent Council regulation in Case C–296/94 *Pietsch v Hauptzollamt Hamburg-Waltershof* [1996] ECR I–3409.

[41] Case 181/84 [1985] ECR 2889.

of the primary obligation to export goods as agreed with the Commission *and* for breach of the secondary obligation to submit a licence application within the stipulated time period. The ECJ, on a request for a preliminary ruling, held that blanket forfeiture for breach of both primary and secondary obligation was disproportionate and that, to the extent that the regulation required such forfeiture, it was invalid.[42]

Gradations within policy choices

11.41 So far as proportionality is concerned the general distinction between detailed regulation (high-intensity review) and policy choices (low-intensity review) has been emphasized and is important to an understanding of how the proportionality doctrine works in practice in domestic public law.

11.42 However, there is an important caveat. As with most principles of public law, even the relationship between proportionality and Community measures that give effect to policy choices should not be treated dogmatically as one involving solely marginal review by the ECJ.

11.43 The cases in which, for the purposes of applying proportionality, the low-intensity 'manifestly inappropriate' test (see above) has been deployed are mainly in the agricultural and harmonization spheres and other macro-economic areas of policy such as social and health policy and transport policy which, plainly, involve very wide economic choices on which courts are ill equipped to adjudicate. Whilst those areas are generally characterized by low-intensity review the position is not necessarily the same for fields in which Community measures are drafted on narrower grounds more easily reviewable by a court. Where this is so it is difficult to see why proportionality should not be applied at a high (or at least relatively high) intensity review level.[43]

Approach of the Administrative Court to the proportionality of Community measures

11.44 As explained above (see para 11.14) the Administrative Court may often be called upon to examine proportionality questions of validity of Community measures in judicial review proceedings where the validity of a national measure is being defended by reference to the validity of an EC measure or where a claimant contends that the underlying EC measure is invalid.

11.45 In practice, the issues will be similar since they are mirror images of the other. The Administrative Court cannot declare that a Community measure is invalid.[44] However, it may pronounce it to be valid. Where, however, a serious question arises as to invalidity it will often be sensible to refer the case to the ECJ for a preliminary ruling under Article 234 (ex 177) EC (see above).

---

[42] See, also, Case C–161/96 *Sudzucker Mannheim/Oschenfurt AG v Hauptzollamt Mannheim* [1998] ECR I–281.

[43] One technique that the court has used in contrast to higher intensity of review is to lay down more stringent process requirements. See paras 10.68–10.73. Note also the judgment of the ECJ in Joined Cases C–154 and C–155/04 *R (Alliance for Natural Health) v Secretary of State for Health* (not yet reported, judgment 12 July 2005). See, generally, Tridimas (n 29 above) 145–9.

[44] See para 11.13.

Whether pronouncing on the proportionality (and, hence, validity) of a Community **11.46**
measure or deciding whether to refer a question to the ECJ as to its invalidity by reason of its
being allegedly disproportionate it will be relevant for the Administrative Court to consider
a number of questions. These include (but are not necessarily confined to) the following:

(1) What is the legislative/administrative context? In particular, is the measure in question
    the product of policy choices or is it confined to matters of regulatory detail or a nar-
    row focused discretion (see above)?

(2) In the light of (1) what is the appropriate review standard by which to assess propor-
    tionality? Is it one of low-intensity review (the general standard for policy choices) or
    high-intensity review (the general standard for regulatory detail or narrowly focused
    discretion) (see above)?

(3) Applying the appropriate review standard, is it desirable for the Administrative Court
    to declare the Community measure to be *valid?* If so, a declaration may be made. If not,
    the Administrative Court should carefully consider referring the case to the ECJ for a
    preliminary ruling.[45] Difficult questions may arise as to whether the Administrative
    Court should refer in cases of doubt as to the validity of a Community measure
    (see above).

(4) Is the legality of any national measure under challenge severable from the validity of
    underlying Community legislation? If so, it may be possible for the Administrative
    Court to address the legality of the national measure in isolation. The relevant princi-
    ples are outlined below. However, if the legality of the national measure is, properly
    analysed, entirely dependent upon the validity of particular Community legislation
    then—subject to the Administrative Court being able to declare the Community
    legislation to be valid—it can only address the issues by reference to the underlying
    legality of the Community legislation.[46]

D. EC Law Proportionality and the Legality of National Measures

Varieties of national measures

Many EC judicial review challenges in which proportionality is raised will be to the legal- **11.47**
ity of national measures alone. Such measures include, of course, the transposition or
implementation of Community law,[47] derogations from Community law in exceptional
cases and the exercise of an administrative discretion. As with challenges to the validity of

---

[45] For the general criteria involved in determining whether a reference should be made, see Chapter 4.

[46] An instance is afforded by *FEDESA* (n 25 above) where the legality of domestic regulations adopted in
order to implement Council Directive (EEC) 88/146 was challenged in judicial review proceedings. The
argument was that the regulations were unlawful by reason of the directive being invalid on, amongst other
grounds, contended violation of the proportionality principle.

[47] In respect of implementing measures, proportionality will often be the most relevant of the general EC
principles in a fundamental rights context (for which see Chapter 12). Fundamental rights aside, the EC
general principles (other than proportionality) most commonly relevant to challenging implementing national
measures appear to be equality (Chapter 7) and legitimate expectation (Chapter 8).

Community legislation, considered above, there are different thresholds of review depending upon the context.[48]

11.48 In general—from the perspective of the proportionality principle—there appears to be an expressly stated higher intensity of review where the Member State is derogating from, as opposed to implementing, Community law.[49] However, the position is complicated by the fact that the legality of domestic implementation of Community law—especially by transposing Community legislation into national law and implementing it—is, at least in principle, itself regulated by a higher intensity of review than that affecting the validity of Community legislation.[50]

11.49 When considering challenges to national measures (without reference to the legality of underlying Community measures) the Administrative Court is not, at least in practice,[51] constrained by jurisdictional limitations. It may therefore—unlike the position in respect of Community legislation—declare a national administrative (or subordinate legislative) measure to be unlawful by reason of breach of the proportionality principle or may disapply primary legislation for the same reason.

11.50 However, it will always be relevant to consider whether proceedings for judicial review of a national measure that raises an EC proportionality question should be referred to the ECJ. Resolution of this question (see below) is not without difficulty because proportionality, as a doctrine, can be heavily fact-laden and inherently unsuitable for determination by the ECJ.

11.51 There is now a considerable amount of jurisprudence from the ECJ, in the form of preliminary rulings, on the application of proportionality to national measures. Much of the case law may be of assistance to the Administrative Court in particular cases in deciding whether to seek a preliminary ruling.

National measures and proportionality

Transposition: general principles

11.52 It is well established that whilst an EC directive prescribes the result to be achieved it leaves the Member States a discretion—unless it specifies the method of implementation—as to the form and method of implementation.[52]

---

[48] For example, it does not follow that a national measure, to be proportionate, cannot be more restrictive than an EC measure: see Case C–510/99 *Tridon* [2001] ECR I–7777, para 59. It will depend on the particular context. There is even in the EC context a broader margin of appreciation enjoyed by Parliament when enacting parliamentary legislation than in other contexts. But there is also a relatively wide margin of appreciation when acting (for example) in urgent public health circumstances: see *R v Secretary of State for Health, ex p Eastside Cheese Company* [1999] Eu LR 968. However, these wider margins of appreciation should not be confused with the deference to be paid to the Community legislature: see *R (Countryside Alliance) v (1) Attorney General and (2) Secretary of State for Environment, Food and Rural Affairs* [2006] EWCA Civ 817.

[49] Even here, care is needed. There is, for example, no clear distinction drawn in the case law so far as proportionality is concerned between derogation simpliciter and a Member State's acts in purporting to define the scope of application of a directive. However, the latter question requires interpretation of the directive (ie the threshold of proportionality review will be that relevant in the particular context to the Community institutions).

[50] See paras 11.54–11.55.

[51] Though there are constitutional implications attached to declaratory relief and provisions of primary legislation that are incompatible with EC law: see further at paras 5.45–5.50. Other national courts do not have so wide a declaratory jurisdiction.

[52] Article 249 (ex 189) EC.

This means that there is usually some latitude accorded to the Member States in 'transpos- **11.53** ing' the directive into national law. In particular, different wording may be used in the domestic implementing provision.[53]

However, the process of transposition is subject to the requirements of Community law **11.54** including, apart from the specific requirements of the directive itself, the provisions of the Treaty,[54] and the general principles of Community law.[55] Because of the priority accorded to EC law there is, therefore, an important constitutional difference between, on the one hand, deferring in sometimes wide terms to the discretion of the Community institutions in legislating and, on the other, requiring Member States, within a limited discretionary area of judgment, to give effect to the relevant Community intent.

In the context of transposition (and implementation)[56] proportionality represents a signif- **11.55** icant general principle of EC law. The proportionality test for determining the compatibil- ity of national implementing measures with Community law ought, generally, to be closer to the higher threshold necessity approach earlier considered as opposed to the more defer- ential standard of 'manifest inappropriateness'. This is because the Member State is, in the context of implementation, purporting to implement the results of judgments already reflected in EC legislation (see also above). A heightened threshold of proportionality review is certainly exemplified in a number of areas as set out below although the ECJ has not always been explicit as to the threshold test to be applied.

Transposition/implementation in exemplary contexts

A common area where proportionality becomes relevant in evaluating the legality of trans- **11.56** position/implementation of Community law into domestic legislation is that of the enforcement of criminal penalties.

Directives do not give rise directly to criminal penalty since criminal law is within the area **11.57** of competence of the Member States.[57] However, the directive may itself require a penal enforcement regime for infringement of its terms or, more commonly, penalties for breach may be imposed by a Member State so as to ensure the effectiveness of the directive.

It is, however, clear that—at least in order to protect the integrity and supremacy of **11.58** Community law—the imposition of penalties is subject to strict application of the propor- tionality principle. As the ECJ observed in *Casati*:[58]

> In principle, criminal legislation and the rules of criminal procedure are matters for which the Member States are still responsible. However, it is clear from a consistent line of cases decided by the Court, that Community law also sets certain limits in that area as regards the control measures which it permits the Member States to maintain in connection with the free movement of goods and persons. The administrative measures or penalties must not go

---

[53] See, eg, Case C–300/95 *Commission v United Kingdom* [1997] ECR I–2649, para 12.
[54] Case C–410/96 *Criminal Proceedings against Ambry* [1998] ECR I–7875.
[55] Case C–2/97 *Societa Italiana Petroli SpA v Borsana Srl* [1998] ECR I–8597, para 48.
[56] As to the distinction between transposition and implementation, see para 2.159.
[57] See, eg, Case C–316/93 *Vaneetveld v Le Foyer SA* [1994] ECR I–731, 776, per Advocate General Jacobs.
[58] Case 203/80 *Criminal Proceedings against Guerruno Casati* [1981] ECR 2595, para 27.

beyond what is strictly necessary, the control procedures must not be conceived in such a way as to restrict the freedom required by the Treaty and they must not be accompanied by a penalty which is so disproportionate to the gravity of the infringement that it becomes an obstacle to the exercise of that freedom.

11.59 As this case shows, the principle is stated in terms of 'necessity' because the rationale is that the penalties imposed must not be disproportionate in the sense that they affect the proper exercise of Community law rights. Thus, for example, in *Skanavi*[59] the German national court fined Mrs Skanavi and her husband, two Greek nationals, because they had failed to exchange their driving licences within a year of their taking up residence in Germany as required by German law pursuant to Directive (EEC) 80/1263. Under the directive, although a licence had to be exchanged within one year it remained valid in the State which issued it after that period.

11.60 The question was whether the fine was compatible with fundamental freedoms under the Treaty, most notably freedom of establishment. On a preliminary ruling the ECJ held that the obligation to exchange driving licences was, essentially, an administrative requirement only and that it could not be equated with the right to drive a motor vehicle in the territory of the host state. It was merely evidence of the existence of such right. A criminal penalty, such as a fine, was an obstacle to free movement, and hence disproportionate, because it could have serious consequences for the exercise of a trade or profession by an employed or self-employed person.

11.61 In similar fashion an imbalance in the penalties imposed as between domestic and non-domestic VAT transactions could, the ECJ held, 'have the effect of jeopardising the free movement of goods within the Community'. In the instant case the court held that the different penalties did not have this effect because the two categories of offence were sufficiently distinguishable in terms of their constituent elements and enforcement. In terms of proportionality, the critical question was whether or not the difference in penalty was disproportionate to the dissimilarity between the offences.

11.62 Another example of implementation where proportionality may be relevant is where the Member State imposes more stringent requirements than a directive requires. Sometimes the object and purpose of the directive will prevent additional requirements from being imposed at all.[60]

11.63 However, in other instances, the directive may confer discretion on the Member State. It is well established that such discretion must be exercised in accordance not only with the provisions of the Treaty and the object and purpose of the directive but also in conformity with general principles of Community law including proportionality. So, for example, in *Booker Aquaculture Ltd v Secretary of State for Scotland*[61] slaughter orders without compensation

---

[59] Case C–193/94 *Criminal Proceedings against Sofia Skanavi and Konstantin Chryssanthakopoulos* [1996] ECR I–929.

[60] This is a matter of interpreting the directive in question. For a case in point see Case 103/88 *Fratelli Costanzo SPA v Commune di Milano* [1989] ECR 1839 where the Member State's exclusion of abnormally low tenders effectively removed the right granted by the directive to provide an explanation for a low tender.

[61] [1999] 1 CMLR 35.

made pursuant to national implementing measures were held to be unlawful as a disproportionate interference with the fundamental right to freedom of property.

Derogations

There is sometimes provision for derogation from EC law allowing for departure by **11.64**
Member States from Community legislation in limited and usually carefully identified
circumstances.

The ECJ has consistently observed that derogations must be interpreted strictly. This is **11.65**
because they constitute exceptions to a Community scheme and will, therefore, generally
require an autonomous Community interpretation unless Community legislation itself
has left the task of definition to the Member States.[62] There must be express provision permitting derogation from the provisions of the Treaty itself.[63] The burden of establishing the
circumstances said to justify derogation lies on the party seeking to rely on them.[64]

Proportionality is often woven into the language of derogation provisions as, for example, **11.66**
that a derogation measure must be 'strictly necessary'[65] or that it must 'cause the least
disturbance of the common market'.[66]

Equally often, however, whilst derogation may be provided for more generally, proportion- **11.67**
ality in any derogation will be implicit. For example,[67] Article 30 (ex 36) EC provides thus:

> The provisions of Articles 28 and 29 [on freedom of movement] shall not preclude prohibi-
> tions or restrictions on imports, exports or goods in transit justified on grounds of public
> morality, public policy or public security; the protection of health and life of humans, ani-
> mals or plants; the protection of national treasures possessing artistic, historic or archaeolog-
> ical value; or the protection of industrial and commercial property. Such prohibitions or
> restrictions shall not, however, constitute a means of arbitrary discrimination or a disguised
> restriction on trade between Member States.

In such cases proportionality is intrinsic to the validity of derogation. So, although Article 30 **11.68**
(ex 36) EC permits Member States to determine national derogation measures for (say) the
protection of health, such measures must not be more restrictive than is necessary to
achieve the State's legitimate objective.[68] Further, it has been held that a national derogation measure under Article 30 (ex 36) EC must not restrict trade between Community
Member States more than is absolutely necessary.[69]

---

[62] Case C–468/93 *Gemeente Emmen v Belastingdienst Grote Ondernemingen* [1996] ECR I–1721,
para 25.
[63] Case 222/84 *Johnston v Chief Constable of the Royal Ulster Constabulary* [1986] ECR 1651, para 26.
[64] See, eg, *Commission v Italy* [1995] ECR I–1249, para 23.
[65] Article 120 (ex 109) EC.
[66] Article 134 (ex 115) EC.
[67] There are, of course, many other Treaty provisions with a similar structure to Art 30 that are equally subject to the proportionality principle. cf, eg, Arts 46 and 55 on the right of establishment and freedom to provide services. See, also, cases such as Case 36/75 *Rutili v Minister of the Interior* [1975] ECR 1219 (derogation
under Art 39(3)).
[68] Of the many cases illustrative of this proposition under Art 30 (ex 36) EC see, eg, Case 153/78
Commission v Germany [1979] ECR 2555, para 5.
[69] Case 72/83 *Campus Oil Ltd v Minister for Industry and Energy* [1984] ECR 2727, para 37.

11.69   An example of proportionality in the context of the free movement of goods is afforded by the well-known *Cassis de Dijon* case.[70] There, the ECJ had to examine a German rule that laid down the minimum alcohol content for an alcoholic beverage. The issue before the court was whether the rule constituted an impediment to free movement under Article 30 (now 28) and, if so, whether—as contended by the German Government—the rule was necessary for the purpose of consumer protection. The court found that the rule did constitute an impediment to free movement and was an unjustified derogation because consumer interests could be protected in less restrictive ways as, for example, by displaying the alcohol content on the packaging of the drinks.

Article 234 references

11.70   It is well established that the ECJ does not, generally, make findings of fact in respect of domestic proceedings in which a reference has been made by the national court under Article 234 (ex 177) EC.[71] As has been seen, however, a reference may have to be made to the ECJ because of a challenge to the validity of a Community measure since only the ECJ may pronounce such measure to be invalid.[72] Where that happens, the ECJ may be called upon to determine matters of fact raised by application of proportionality considerations.

11.71   The problem of fact-finding by the ECJ also (and more commonly) arises where the challenge is made to the validity of a national measure on proportionality grounds. Here there may be strong policy reasons for the Administrative Court to determine contested proportionality issues itself rather than seeking a preliminary ruling. Indeed, the ECJ may require it to do so even if the case is referred to Luxembourg under Article 234 (ex 177) EC.

11.72   The ECJ has taken different views in different contexts about the discretionary area of judgment left to the national court in relation to determination of the proportionality of national measures. An instance of the difficulties is illustrated by the litigation in England over whether the law on Sunday trading was in breach of Article 28 (ex 30) EC.

11.73   In *Torfaen*[73] the ECJ held, amongst other things, that Article 28 did not apply to national rules prohibiting retailers from trading on Sunday where the restrictive effect of those rules on Community trade did not exceed 'the effects intrinsic to rules of that kind'. It also held that 'the question whether the effects of specific national rules do in fact remain within that limit is a question for the national court'.

11.74   Despite this, the ECJ gave preliminary rulings in proceedings from other national courts raising similar issues. In giving such rulings, it ruled on the issue of proportionality. In consequence, the House of Lords decided to make a further reference. On that reference the ECJ determined whether the Shops Act 1950 complied with the proportionality principle.[74]

---

[70] Case 120/78 *Rewe-Zentrale AG v Bundesmonopolverwalrung fur Branntwein* [1979] ECR 649.
[71] See, generally, Chapter 4, especially at para 4.39.
[72] See para 11.13.
[73] Case 145/88 *Torfaen Borough Council v B&Q plc* [1989] ECR 3851.
[74] Case C–169/91 *City of Stoke-on-Trent v B&Q*, Case 306/88 *Rochdale Borough Council v Anders*, Case 304/90 *Reading Borough Council v Payless DIY* [1993] 1 CMLR 426, para 905, [1993] 1 All ER 481. For the ECJ's judgment in all cases, see [1992] ECR I–6635.

It is by no means obvious, however, that the ECJ will feel able to decide issues of fact relat-   **11.75**
ing to the proportionality of national measures in most cases. Nor, analytically, is it obvious that it is generally appropriate for it to do so. Institutionally at least, the Administrative
Court is frequently far better equipped to undertake proportionality scrutiny of national
measures.

Careful consideration will, therefore, have to be given by the Administrative Court as to   **11.76**
whether to refer a case to the ECJ if the primary ground for judicial review of a national
measure is an alleged violation of the proportionality principle. The general discretionary
criteria for whether to refer have already been considered in Chapter 4. However, the
Administrative Court—and even higher courts on appeal—will be required to consider
whether the ECJ would consider itself to be jurisdictionally competent to undertake the
proportionality balancing exercise in respect of national legislation. If, as a matter of jurisdiction, the ECJ confers the judgment on the national court then it would, correspondingly,
not be open to the national court to refer.

The difficulty is that no obvious principles have been laid down by the ECJ. Much   **11.77**
depends on the nature of the issues in the case and the factual circumstances. The proportionality of criminal penalty or other sanction is an area where the ECJ is highly likely to
defer to the judgment of the national court.[75] The position appears to be similar where
questions of indirect discrimination arise in relation to Article 141 EC.[76] On the other
hand, there will be cases such as *Clinique*[77]—not always easy to predict in advance—
where the ECJ had no difficulty in deciding for itself that a national prohibition on the
marketing of products under the brand 'Clinique' was not justified on the ground of consumer protection.

E. EC Law Proportionality Compared with Other Judicial Review Grounds

The most obvious contrast, in terms of judicial review proceedings, is that between EC pro-   **11.78**
portionality and *Wednesbury* unreasonableness.[78] The distinction may be important since
whereas in domestic judicial review proceedings the Administrative Court will not apply
proportionality (see below) in a Community law case it must.[79]

In a conventional domestic challenge, founded on the merits and shorn of human rights   **11.79**
or Community law proportionality, the discretionary decision of a public authority is
liable to be quashed only if it is 'so unreasonable that no reasonable authority could ever

---

[75] See, eg, Case C–367/89 *Criminal Proceedings against Aime Richardt* [1991] ECR I–4621, para 25.
[76] See, eg, Case C–167/99 *R v Secretary of State for Employment, ex p Seymour-Smith* [1999]
ECR I–623.
[77] Case C–315/92 *Verband Sozialer Wettbewerb v Clinique Laboratories and Estee Lauder* [1994]
ECR I–317.
[78] *Associated Provincial Picture Houses Ltd v Wednesbury Corporation* [1948] 1 KB 223.
[79] *Thompson v Chief Adjudication Officer* [1991] 2 QB 164. Proportionality is also, of course, intrinsic to
all HRA challenges on human rights grounds.

come to it'.[80] The essential difference between this and proportionality is that although both doctrines permit the Administrative Court to review the balance struck by a public authority between competing interests, only proportionality allows the balance to be assessed by reference to an objective standard (whatever the variations in intensity of review considered above).

11.80   Although *Wednesbury* appears to be falling out of favour, even in domestic cases,[81] the English courts have yet to embrace proportionality as a discrete head of review in such cases. Most notably, in *R v Secretary of State for the Home Department, ex p Brind*[82] the House of Lords, by a majority, held that proportionality in domestic law does not subsist as an independent legal doctrine. In *R v Chief Constable of Sussex, ex p International Trader's Ferry Ltd*[83] the House of Lords examined a judicial review challenge brought under *Wednesbury* and Community law proportionality criteria separately.

11.81   In *Brind* Lord Lowry, in particular, considered that importation of European proportionality into domestic law would constitute an abuse of the High Court's supervisory function and jeopardize stability and certainty, as well as greatly increasing the number of judicial review applications. He also thought that judges were not equipped with the requisite knowledge and expertise to embark on an investigation of administrative reasonableness involving a lower threshold test than that of *Wednesbury* unreasonableness.

11.82   The Court of Appeal, in *R (Association of British Civilians—Far Eastern Region) v Secretary of State for Defence*[84] reviewed the cases since *Brind* and noted the support for a separate domestic doctrine of proportionality expressed by Lord Cooke in *R (Daly) v Secretary of State for the Home Department*[85] and by Lord Slynn in *R (Alconbury Ltd) v Secretary of State for the Environment, Transport and the Regions*.[86]

11.83   However, although the Court of Appeal appeared (see para 34 of the court's judgment) to consider that the *Wednesbury* test no longer had much to commend it, it pointed out, at para 35, that it was 'not for this court to perform its burial rites'.

11.84   In a human rights context under the HRA the position is different and similar to that prevailing in EC law (at least in the context of fundamental rights protection) in that proportionality rather than *Wednesbury* irrationality is the touchstone for review by the Administrative Court. As Lord Steyn observed in *Daly*,[87] whilst the outcome of many cases would be the same, the court's determination may, at least in some cases, be different on a

---

[80] Note the modification to *Wednesbury* as formulated by Lord Diplock in *Council of Civil Service Unions v Minister for the Civil Service* [1985] AC 374, 410: '. . . a decision so outrageous in its defiance of logic or of accepted moral standards that no sensible person who had applied his mind to the question to be decided could have arrived at it . . .'.

[81] For a comprehensive survey of the decline of *Wednesbury*, see A le Sueur, 'The Rise and Ruin of Unreasonableness?' [2005] JR 32.

[82] [1991] 1 AC 696.

[83] [1999] 2 AC 418.

[84] [2003] EWCA Civ 473, [2003] 3 WLR 80.

[85] [2001] UKHL 26, [2001] 2 AC 532, para 32.

[86] [2001] UKHL 23 [2001] 2 WLR 1389, 1406.

[87] [2001] 2 AC 532, 547.

proportionality review than on a *Wednesbury* review.[88] Lord Steyn identified three differences between proportionality and *Wednesbury* review in the arena of Convention protection. He said:

> First, the doctrine of proportionality may require the reviewing court to assess the balance which the decision-maker has struck, not merely whether it is within the range of rational or reasonable decisions. Secondly, the proportionality test may go further than the traditional grounds of review inasmuch as it may require attention to be directed to the relative weight accorded to interests and considerations. Thirdly, even the heightened scrutiny test developed in *R v Ministry of Defence, ex p. Smith* [1996] QB 517, 554 is not necessarily appropriate to the protection of human rights ...

Importantly, too, in *Smith and Grady v United Kingdom*[89] despite the heightened scrutiny **11.85** test—where fundamental human rights are concerned—developed by the national courts in *R v Ministry of Defence, ex p Smith*[90] (and cited by Lord Steyn in *Daly*) the European Court of Human Rights upheld a challenge to the Government's ban on homosexuals serving in the armed forces which had been litigated unsuccessfully before the national courts in *Ex p Smith*. It contrasted the traditional (albeit heightened) *Wednesbury* approach of the Administrative Court and the Court of Appeal with that of proportionality under the European Convention on Human Rights. It said:

> [T]he threshold at which the High Court and the Court of Appeal could find the Ministry of Defence policy irrational was placed so high that it effectively excluded any consideration by the domestic courts of the question of whether the interference with the applicants' rights answered a pressing social need or was proportionate to the national security and public order aims pursued, principles which lie at the heart of the Court's analysis of complaints under Article 8 of the Convention.[91]

The doctrine of proportionality in Community law cases is, essentially, similar to that under **11.86** the European Convention. However, it is important to bear in mind the intrinsic differences between Community and Convention law insofar as they are likely to affect application of the proportionality principle. Further, in the recent challenge to the hunting ban, the Court of Appeal remarked on a number of institutional differences between EC and HRA law and considered that these differences meant that there were circumstances in which EC law required a higher threshold of justification for infringement of EC law than for violation of Convention rights.[92]

As has been seen, one of the overriding principles in the EU is that EC law is supreme.[93] **11.87** The position is otherwise so far as the European Convention on Human Rights is concerned.

---

[88] For a case in domestic judicial review where ECHR proportionality made a significant difference to the outcome in one of the conjoined appeals, see *R (P and Q) v Secretary of State for the Home Department* [2001] EWCA Civ 1151, [2001] 1 WLR 2002. For other indications of the domestic court's approach to ECHR proportionality issues, see especially: *R v Shayler* [2002] UKHL 11, [2003] 1 AC 247; *A v Secretary of State for the Home Department* [2004] UKHL 56, [2005] 2 WLR 87; *South Bucks District Council v Porter* [2003] UKHL 26, [2003] 2 AC 558; *R (SB) v Headteacher and Governors of Denbigh High School* [2005] EWCA Civ 199, [2005] 2 All ER 396.

[89] (1999) 29 EHRR 493.

[90] [1996] QB 517, 554.

[91] (1999) 29 EHRR 493, para 138.

[92] See *R (Countryside Alliance) v (1) Attorney General and (2) Secretary of State for Environment, Food and Rural Affairs* [2006] EWCA Civ 817.

[93] See paras 2.60 et seq.

The subsidiarity principle in ECHR law is to the effect that it is the Member States who have the primary role in safeguarding human rights within their jurisdiction.[94] As the European Court of Human Rights observed in *Handyside v United Kingdom*:[95]

> ... the machinery of protection established by the Convention is subsidiary to the national systems of safeguarding human rights.

11.88 So, the European Court of Human Rights has, in order to give effect to subsidiarity, developed the notion of the State's margin of appreciation. As the majority judgment in *Handyside* observed:

> By reason of their direct and continuous contact with the vital forces of their countries, state authorities are in principle in a better position than the international judge to give an opinion on the exact content of those requirements as well as on the 'necessity' of a 'restriction' or 'penalty' intended to meet them ...[96]

11.89 The role of margin of appreciation in domestic human rights litigation was given detailed consideration by the House of Lords in *R v Director of Public Prosecutions, ex p Kebilene*.[97] Lord Hope pointed out that although margin of appreciation was, as an international principle, not directly applicable to national disputes it reflected the same principle as the courts would apply in domestic disputes under the Human Rights Act 1998, namely that the courts would 'defer, on democratic grounds, to the considered opinion of the elected body or person whose act is said to be incompatible with the Convention. . .'.

11.90 In Community law it is less clear that the scope of the proportionality principle is as open-textured. There is undoubtedly—as the case law shows—a role for deference when applying proportionality in Community law. But the doctrine of the supremacy of Community law makes it arguably less likely that the Administrative Court can operate in as deferential a fashion as it would in a challenge under the HRA—in at least most areas of application of Community law *affecting the validity of domestic legislation*—where alleged violations of Community law are raised by reference to the principle of proportionality.

11.91 The position is, as noted above, rather different in the case of *Community* legislation. There, the ECJ will defer to the Community institutions to a greater extent although the principle of proportionality is still enshrined in Article 5(3)(ex 3b(3)) EC which provides that '[a]ny action by the Community shall not go beyond what is necessary to achieve the objectives of the Treaty'.

11.92 When examining the scope of EC proportionality in any given case it is also important to bear in mind that proportionality is often used in combination with other general EC principles, most notably the principle of equality.[98] Its use in this way may circumscribe the ambit of those principles or reflect the contextual limits of what may be regarded as a proportionate State measure.

---

[94] Note, though, the terms of Art 5(2) EC which requires the Community to take action 'only if and in so far as' the relevant objectives cannot be achieved by the Member States. The principle, also called subsidiarity, is not inconsistent with the supremacy of EC law since the Member States have to apply EC law in its entirety.
[95] (1979–80) 1 EHRR 737, para 48.
[96] ibid para 48.
[97] [2000] 2 AC 326.
[98] See para 6.61.

12

FUNDAMENTAL RIGHTS
PROTECTION

A. Introduction

Fundamental rights protection, in the context of EC law, is related to—though distinct **12.01** from—the protection now accorded in domestic law to fundamental rights under the European Convention on Human Rights (ECHR) through the medium of the Human Rights Act 1998 (HRA) that came into force on 2 October 2000. The HRA has had a considerable impact on judicial review but the relationship between fundamental rights and EC law and, in turn, between EC law and the HRA is not always appreciated by practitioners.

There are close parallels between the respective regimes and, indeed, between those regimes **12.02** and the position pre-HRA under domestic law which will still apply in judicial review challenges brought by 'victims' in respect of pre-HRA events[1] and, generally, by non-victims even after the HRA came into force.[2]

12.03 However, there may be significant substantive differences in particular cases between the various regimes. Nor is Community law protection of fundamental rights confined to the 'Convention rights' protected by the ECHR in national law.[3] The greater 'reach' of Community law fundamental rights will acquire especial significance if the EU Charter of Fundamental Rights becomes binding under the proposed Constitution.[4]

12.04 Irrespective of the distinctiveness of substantive protection of fundamental rights in Community law there are important remedial differences. Where a challenge is brought to domestic primary legislation that is alleged to contravene fundamental rights guaranteed by EC law the national court has jurisdiction to disapply the legislation.[5] This follows from the supremacy of Community law.[6] Further, a national court may—where necessary—even suspend domestic primary legislation by way of interim relief and any national rules prohibiting such relief would be incompatible with EC law.[7] The position is very different under the HRA where (see HRA, s 6(6)) even after the grant of a declaration of incompatibility primary legislation continues to have full force and effect.

B. Fundamental Rights in EC Law

Absence of specific rights in the Treaties

12.05 There is, at least currently, no equivalent in Community law to the ECHR or USA Bill of Rights. The position may change if the EU Charter of Fundamental Rights becomes binding (see below).

12.06 This has resulted in the ECJ developing, incrementally, protection of human rights in the case law. To begin with, however, the ECJ suggested that the protection of fundamental rights, as recognized in the constitutions of certain Member States, was neither intrinsic to the EC Treaty nor part of the general principles of Community law.[8]

---

[1] The term 'victim' (see HRA, s 7) is restrictively defined and, under HRA, s 7(7), bears the same meaning as under Art 34 ECHR. See, also, paras 12.111 et seq. In general the HRA is not retrospective: see *Wilson v First County Trust* [2003] UKHL 40, [2004] 1 AC 816. It bears retrospective effect, in limited circumstances, under HRA, s 22(4).

[2] There are, at least potentially, circumstances in which a non-victim may mount a (horizontal) HRA claim as, eg, when a statute is being interpreted in any proceedings before the court. HRA, s 3 requires the court to interpret the Act 'so far as possible' to be compatible with the ECHR. See para 12.123.

[3] It should be noted that not all the rights in the ECHR fall within the Administrative Court's jurisdiction under the HRA. The term 'Convention rights' is a term of art (see HRA, s 1(1)) and does not, eg, include Art 13 ECHR (right to an effective remedy). Thus, there is potential dissonance between such omission and the EC general principle of effectiveness discussed (in the context of remedy) at paras 5.13–5.22.

[4] See paras 12.19 et seq.

[5] *R v Secretary of State for Employment, ex p Equal Opportunities Commission* [1995] 1 AC 1.

[6] See paras 2.60 et seq.

[7] *R v Secretary of State for Transport, ex p Factortame (No 2)* [1991] 1 AC 603.

[8] See, eg, Case 1/58 *Stork v High Authority* [1959] ECR 17.

This reflected the tension, as between domestic law and Community law, inherent in the **12.07**
then developing concepts of Community law supremacy[9] and direct effect[10] as enunciated
by the ECJ. If constitutional fundamental rights protection could 'trump' Community law
then, axiomatically, Community law could not be supreme.

Severe reservations were expressed by national constitutional courts in different Member **12.08**
States as to the implications of a doctrine of supremacy of Community law that failed
to accord guarantees of fundamental rights. It was this, more than anything, that led to
the ECJ edging its way towards a recognition that fundamental rights formed part of
the general principles of Community law.

Development of fundamental rights by the ECJ

In *Stauder v Ulm*,[11] although Mr Stauder's claim was dismissed, the ECJ stated that the **12.09**
allegedly offending Community provision did not infringe 'the fundamental human rights
enshrined in the general principles of Community law and protected by the Court'.
A similar approach was taken in *Internationale Handelsgesellschaft*[12] where the court observed,
at para 4 of its judgment, that '... respect for fundamental rights forms an integral part of
the general principles of law protected by the Court of Justice. The protection of such
rights, whilst inspired by the constitutional traditions common to the Member States,
must be ensured within the framework of the structure and objectives of the Community'.

Nold[13] was the first case in which the ECJ made direct reference to international human **12.10**
rights treaties to which Member States were signatories as affording guidelines (see para 13
of the judgment). In *Rutili*[14] the ECJ made its first reference both to the ECHR and to
specific Convention provisions.

The present position

Article 6 of the Treaty on European Union provides as follows: **12.11**

1. The Union is founded on the principles of liberty, democracy, respect for human rights
   and fundamental freedoms, and the rule of law, principles which are common to the
   Member States.
2. The Union shall respect fundamental rights as guaranteed by the European Convention
   for the Protection of Human Rights and Fundamental Freedoms signed in Rome on
   4 November 1950 and as they result from the constitutional traditions common to the
   Member States, as general principles of Community law.

Article 6(2) is qualified by Article 46(d) EU which limits the ECJ's competence over **12.12**
matters falling within Article 6(2) to 'the acts of the institutions, insofar as the Court
has jurisdiction under the Treaties establishing the European Communities and under

---

[9] See, eg, Case 6/64 *Costa v ENEL* [1964] ECR 585; Case 92/78 *Simmenthal v Commission* [1979] ECR 777.
[10] Case 26/62 *Van Gend en Loos* [1963] ECR 1.
[11] Case 29/69 [1969] ECR 419.
[12] Case 11/70 *Internationale Handelsgesellschaft mbH v Einfuhr- und Vorratsstelle für Getreide und Futtermittel* [1970] ECR 1125.
[13] Case 4/73 *Nold v Commission of the European Communities* [1974] ECR 491.
[14] Case 36/75 *Rutili v Ministre de l'Interieur* [1975] ECR 1219.

this Treaty'. This would appear to be a restatement of the pre-existing position so far as the EU Treaty is concerned.

12.13 The above formulation makes it clear that the protection afforded by Community law is potentially wider than under the ECHR since it encompasses, by reference, international instruments such as the ICCPR and the European Social Charter.

12.14 However, it appears that the ECJ considers that the ECHR has a distinctive importance in the protection of fundamental rights in Community law. Although the ECJ has advised, in Opinion 2/94 on Accession by the Community to the ECHR,[15] that the Community lacks competence to accede to the ECHR, that Opinion contains a clear summary of the status of the ECHR in Community law. The ECJ observed (para 33):

> It is well settled that fundamental rights form an integral part of the general principles of law whose observance the Court ensures. For that purpose, the Court draws inspiration from the constitutional traditions common to the Member States and from the guidelines supplied by international treaties for the protection of human rights on which the Member States have collaborated or of which they are signatories. In that regard, the Court has stated that the Convention has special significance.

12.15 Three essential propositions can be derived from this formulation. The first is that the ECHR is not, of itself, a source of Community law. It is, rather, an indicator of common values of the Member States. That means that it is not formally binding.[16]

12.16 Secondly, the corollary is that the ECJ treats its fundamental rights doctrine as autonomous. As Advocate General Trabucchi observed in *Watson v Belmann*:[17]

> ... some learned writers have felt justified in concluding that the provisions of the said Convention [on Human Rights] must be treated as forming an integral part of the Community legal order, whereas it seems clear to me that the spirit of the judgment [in *Rutili*] did not involve any substantive reference to the provisions themselves but merely to the general principles of which, like the Community rules with which the judgment drew an analogy, they are a specific expression.

> In fact, in that judgment, the Court substantially reaffirmed the principle which had already emerged from its previous decisions that the fundamental human rights recognized under the constitutions of the Member States are also an integral part of the Community legal order.

> The extra-Community instruments under which those states have undertaken international obligations in order to ensure better protection for those rights can, without any question of their being incorporated as such in the Community order, be used to establish principles which are common to the states themselves.

12.17 Thirdly, the ECHR has a 'special significance'.[18] Its significance, however, lies in the assistance in interpreting the fundamental rights which are themselves part of the

---

[15] [1996] ECR I–1759.

[16] Contrast Lord Browne-Wilkinson, 'The Infiltration of a Bill of Rights' [1992] PL 397, 401, who suggested that, in the Community law context, the ECHR had already been directly incorporated into English domestic law prior to the coming into force of the HRA.

[17] Case 118/75 [1976] ECR 1185, 1207.

[18] Apart from Opinion 2/94 see, eg, Case C–219/91 *Ter Voort* [1992] ECR I–5485; Case C–17/98 *Emesa Sugar (Free Zone) NV v Aruba* [2000] ECR I–0665.

Community legal order.[19] As with Convention rights, EC fundamental rights are subject to the proportionality principle and may, therefore, be subject to restrictions provided that they comply with that principle.[20]

In reality, the ECJ has greatly expanded the scope and breadth of its fundamental rights **12.18** jurisdiction (and, hence, the scope of EC law itself) since it first recognized the inclusion of those rights as part of EC law. In *Schmidberger*[21] the court appeared to consider fundamental rights to be on an equal footing with the fundamental freedoms discussed in Chapters 16 and 17 in the context of permitting restrictions on free movement which were considered to be justified on fundamental rights grounds (*in casu* the omission by the national authorities to prevent demonstrators in the interest of freedom of expression and assembly). This is an important decision (and considered in the *Roth* case study in Chapter 19) because it has led to many ECJ decisions in which the emphasis in freedom of movement cases has shifted perceptibly from economics to the individual or undertaking affected by particular restrictions.[22]

Future possible developments

At Nice, in December 2000, the Charter of Fundamental Rights of the European Union **12.19** was 'solemnly proclaimed'. At that time it was not said to be binding. Indeed, it was negotiated outside the framework of the Treaties and currently enjoys no formal status in Community law.[23]

However, the fourth paragraph of the preamble to the Charter (as contained in Part II **12.20** of the draft Constitutional Treaty) is expressly stated to reaffirm 'the rights as they result, in particular, from the constitutional obligations common to the Member States, the European Convention for the Protection of Human Rights and Fundamental Freedoms, the Social Charters adopted by the Union and by the Council of Europe and the case law of the Court of Justice of the European Unions and the European Court of Human Rights . . .'.

Even, therefore, if the Charter were not to be given formal status it is likely to become **12.21** increasingly significant in the interpretation of EC fundamental rights protection.

---

[19] Hence the fact that EC fundamental rights are applied in relation to their social function: see, eg, Case C–62/90 *Commission v Germany* [1992] ECR I–2575, para 23.

[20] Case C–292/97 *Karlsson* [2000] ECR I–2737, para 58. Exceptionally, too, fundamental rights may be subject to the imperatives of public international law: see Case T–306/01 *Yusuf v Commission* (unreported, 21 September 2005).

[21] Case C–112/00 [2003] ECR I–5659.

[22] This point and many of these cases are considered in Chapters 16–17. Note, especially: Case C–60/00 *Carpenter v Secretary of State for the Home Department* [2002] ECR I–6279; Case C–413 *Baumbast v Secretary of State for the Home Department* [2002] ECR I–7091; Case C–109/01 *Secretary of State for the Home Department v Akrich* [2003] ECR I–9607. For a case where fundamental rights have been overridden by a competing legitimate aim, see *R (British American Tobacco) v Secretary of State for Health* [2004] EWHC 2493.

[23] See G de Burca, 'The Drafting of the European Charter of Fundamental Rights' (2001) 26 EL Rev 126.

12.22   In practice, the CFI has already taken account of the Charter.[24] So, too, have a number of Advocates General.[25] In addition, both the European Court of Human Rights[26] and the High Court[27] have cited it.

12.23   In *BECTU*[28] Advocate General Tizzano (at para 27 of his Opinion) said:

> Admittedly ... the Charter of Fundamental Rights of the European Union has not been recognised as having genuine legislative scope in the strict sense. In other words, formally, it is not binding. However, without wishing to participate here in the wide-ranging debate now going on as to the effects which, in other forms and by other means, the Charter may nevertheless produce, the fact remains that it includes statements which appear in large measure to reaffirm rights which are enshrined in other instruments ...

12.24   He then recited the preamble (see above) and at para 28 observed:

> I think therefore that, in proceedings concerned with the nature and scope of a fundamental right, the relevant statements of the Charter cannot be ignored; in particular, we cannot ignore its clear purpose of serving, where its provisions so allow, as a substantive point of reference for all those involved—Member States, institutions, natural and legal persons—in the Community context. Accordingly, I consider that the Charter provides us with the most reliable and definitive confirmation of the fact that the right to paid annual leave constitutes a fundamental right.

12.25   To similar effect, in *Booker Agriculture*[29] Advocate General Mischo stated as follows:

> I know that the Charter is not legally binding, but it is worthwhile referring to it given that it constitutes the expression, at the highest level, of a democratically established political consensus on what must today be considered as the catalogue of fundamental rights guaranteed by the Community legal order.

12.26   To some extent the Charter overlaps with the rights contained in the ECHR. However, even then, the language is often different. For example, Article 5 ECHR (right to liberty and security) is a more complex provision than Article 6 of the Charter which simply provides that: 'Everyone has the right to liberty and security of person.'

12.27   This is because, as stipulated by Article 52(3), where the rights that the Charter contains correspond to those guaranteed by the ECHR then 'the meaning and scope of those rights shall be the same as those laid down by the said Convention'. Article 52(3) also makes it clear, however, that it does not operate so as to prevent EU law providing more extensive protection.

12.28   In certain instances, however, the Charter goes beyond rights that are obviously justiciable in English domestic judicial review or under the ECHR. Its scope is sometimes broader

---

[24] Case T–54/99 *Max-Mobil Telekommunication Service GmbH* [2005] ECR I–1283.

[25] Apart from the cases cited below, see also, eg, Case C–313/99 *Mulligan v Ministry of Agriculture and Food, Ireland* [2002] ECR I–5719, Opinion of Advocate General Geehoed, para 28; Case C–413/99 *Baumbast and R v Secretary of State for the Home Department* [2002] ECR I–7091, Opinion of Advocate General Geelhoed, para 59; Case C–270/99 *Z v European Parliament* [2001] ECR I–9197, Opinion of Advocate General Jacobs, para 40.

[26] *Goodwin v United Kingdom* (2002) 35 EHRR 18.

[27] *R (Robertson) v Wakefield MDC* [2001] EWHC Admin 915, [2002] QB 1052, 1070; *R (Howard League for Penal Reform) v Secretary of State* [2002] EWHC 2497, [2003] 1 FLR 484.

[28] Case C–173/99 *Broadcasting, Entertainment, Cinematographic and Theatre Union (BECTU) v Secretary of State for Trade and Industry* [2001] ECR I–4881.

[29] Joined Cases C–20 and C–64/00 *Booker Aquaculture Ltd and Hydro Seafood GSP v Scottish Ministers* [2003] ECR I–7411.

than that of the ECHR, encompassing many economic and social rights including such matters as social security and social assistance provisions as well as workers' and health care rights.

Under Article 35, for example: **12.29**

> Everyone has the right of access to preventive health care and the right to benefit from medical treatment under the conditions established by national laws and practices ...

And Article 13 provides that: 'The arts and scientific research shall be free of constraint.' **12.30**

In December 2001 a declaration was adopted by the European Council. This set up a **12.31** Convention on the Future of Europe to take forward the post-Nice agenda. As part of the work for this Convention a draft Constitution was, on 18 July 2003, submitted to the President of the European Council.

Currently, the Charter is included as Part II of the Constitution.[30] However, given the **12.32** rejection of the Constitution (and, hence, the Charter) by France and the Netherlands in national referendums its final provisions (even if it is subsequently ratified) remain uncertain. Certainly, no final decisions have been taken as to content or legal status.

In its current form Article 51(1) of the Charter provides that: **12.33**

> The provisions of this Charter are addressed to the institutions, bodies and agencies of the Union with due regard for the principle of subsidiarity and to the Member States only when they are implementing Union law. They shall therefore respect the rights, observe the principles and promote the application thereof in accordance with their respective powers and respecting the limits of the Union as conferred on it in the other Parts of the Constitution.

It is to be noted that Article 51(1) appears to be intentionally limited in its potential **12.34** effect. It is, at most, a consolidating measure and ostensibly confined to the situation where Member States are *implementing* EU law as opposed to being a general charter of fundamental rights. It may even be that, at least in one respect, the Charter is more restricted than the general respect paid by the ECJ to fundamental rights in its case law.[31] The ECJ has consistently ruled that national rules subject to the general principles of respect for fundamental rights encompass rules of *derogation* as well as rules of implementation.[32] Further, the ECJ has subjected national rules to the same general principle where such rules fall 'within the scope of Community law'.[33] This may be a broader formulation that that contained in Article 51(1).

Apart from incorporating the Charter, the draft Constitution provides—by Article 7(2)— **12.35** that the Union 'shall seek accession' to the ECHR. If this were to happen (or if the Charter were to be incorporated) new judicial remedies might be required in particular cases.

---

[30] The Articles cited in the text are, as they appear in the draft Constitution, preceded by the section number (II) in which they appear as, eg, Article II–1 etc.

[31] However, Art 53 of the Charter suggests that the general authority of the ECJ to apply Community law, including its fundamental rights doctrine, is not intended to be affected by the Charter.

[32] See para 12.50.

[33] See paras 12.49 et seq.

12.36 Article 47(1) of the Charter provides that '[e]veryone whose rights and freedoms guaranteed by the law of the Union are violated has the right to an effective remedy before a tribunal in compliance with the conditions laid down in this Article'. Article 47(1) itself is modelled on Article 13 ECHR (right to an effective remedy). Article 47(2) is modelled on Article 6 ECHR (due process). Article 47(3) is concerned with legal aid. However, Article 47 is wider in its scope than Article 6 ECHR in that it is not confined to an applicant's 'civil rights and obligations' but extends to the rights and freedoms guaranteed by EC law.

12.37 At the present time it is by no means clear that the draft Constitution will ever receive final approval or that, therefore, the Charter will be incorporated. As outlined above, however, it is—despite this—still likely that the provisions of the Charter will become increasingly important in the jurisprudence of the ECJ.

C. Current Scope of EC Fundamental Rights Protection

The regulating principle

12.38 It is clear that the scope of the doctrine of fundamental rights in Community law extends to the legality of *Community* measures.[34]

12.39 The doctrine also applies to domestic law insofar as domestic law is itself within the scope of Community law. In *ERT*,[35] the ECJ said:

> As the Court has held, it has no power to examine the compatibility with the European Convention on Human Rights of national rules which do not fall within the scope of Community law. On the other hand, where such rules do fall within the scope of Community law, and reference is made to the Court for a preliminary ruling, it must provide all the criteria of interpretation needed by the national court to determine whether those rules are compatible with the fundamental rights the observance of which the Court ensures and which derive in particular from the European Convention on Human Rights.

12.40 Properly analysed, therefore, fundamental rights protection in Community law will affect domestic judicial review in two different ways: (1) in informing the interpretation to be given by the Administrative Court to Community Treaty or legislative measures that affect national measures, (2) in the interpretation or application to be given by the Administrative Court to national measures that are within the scope of Community law.[36]

Fundamental rights doctrine as it affects Community measures

12.41 Although the Administrative Court may find a Community measure to be *valid* it has no power to make a finding of invalidity.[37] The doctrine of fundamental rights is, however,

---

[34] *Opinion 2/94 on Accession by the Community to the ECHR* [1996] ECR I–1759, para 34.

[35] Case C–260/89 *Elliniki Radiophonia Tileorassi AE v Dimotiki Etairia Pliroforissis* [1991] ECR I–2925, para 42. See, also, Case C–94/00 *Roquette Freres v Directeur general de la concurrence, de la consommation et de la repression des fraudes* [2003] 4 CMLR 1, para 25; Case C–276/01 *Steffensen* [2003] CMLR 13.

[36] There is a further way in which fundamental rights are relevant in Community law: the doctrine must itself be applied to the procedures of the ECJ and CFI. See, eg, Case C–199/92P *Huls AG v Commission* [1999] 5 CMLR 1016, para 127; Case C–17/98 *Emesa Sugar (Free Zone) NV v Aruba (No 1)* [2000] ECR I–0665.

[37] Case 314/85 *Foto-Frost v Hauptzollamt Lubeck-Ost* [1987] ECR 4199.

still relevant to domestic judicial review proceedings involving a challenge to the legality of Community measures since the *validity* of such measures may determine the issue of whether a national measure is lawful. Importantly, where the wording of a provision of Community law is open to more than one interpretation, preference should be given to the interpretation that renders it consistent with fundamental rights.[38]

Further, where the Administrative Court has serious doubts as to the validity of a Community **12.42** measure on fundamental rights grounds it may well decide to refer the case to the ECJ for a preliminary ruling under Article 234 EC.[39]

For the most part the issue of validity or invalidity of a Community measure on funda- **12.43** mental rights grounds will be ventilated before the Administrative Court where a national implementing measure sought to be challenged is argued to be unlawful because the Community measure on which it depends is said to be unlawful. Judicial review proceedings have, however, been brought in respect of a Community measure even before national implementing measures have been passed.[40] In *Royal Scholten-Honig v Intervention Board*[41] the claimants simply sought a declaration that a Council regulation was invalid.

Fundamental rights in domestic EC law—general

So far as is possible, Member States must implement and apply Community measures in **12.44** accordance with the fundamental rights recognized in Community law.[42]

Although, as a principle of interpretation, fundamental rights (and the other relevant gen- **12.45** eral principles) are engaged where the Administrative Court has to interpret Community law—including *relevant* national measures—difficulty arises where the national measure (including administrative action) bears only an indirect relationship to the Community. As seen above, national measures are subject to Community fundamental rights protection only where such measures 'fall within the scope of Community law'.

There is an important constitutional issue here. As Advocate General Gulmann observed **12.46** in *Bostock*:[43]

> The issue is one of fundamental significance because it is determinative for the division of powers between the Court of Justice and national courts as regards the protection of basic rights and the question is a difficult one to answer. The issue lies within an area where the Court must tread carefully. Similar questions may arise in the most diverse situations and it is important that the Court develop its case law in the light of the cases that are submitted to it.

The question as to what falls within the scope of Community law in the human rights con- **12.47** text has not yet been decisively resolved. There are, however, decisions at both Community and national level that provide some illumination.

---

[38] See, eg, per Lord Hope in *Shanning International Ltd (In Liquidation) v Lloyds TSB Bank Plc* [2001] UKHL 31, 1 WLR 1462.
[39] See, generally, Chapter 4.
[40] See, especially, judgment of Turner J in *R v Secretary of State for Health, ex p Imperial Tobacco Ltd* (unreported, 16 December 1998).
[41] Cases 103 and 145/77 [1978] ECR 2037.
[42] See, eg, Case 5/88 *Wachauf v Germany* [1989] ECR 2609.
[43] Case C2/92 *R v MAFF, ex p Bostock* [1994] ECR I–955.

12.48 It is proposed, first, to examine the ECJ decisions that exemplify (respectively) whether a national measure is, or is not, within the scope of Community law. Those decisions suggest that a measure will be within the scope of Community law if it is a measure that implements or derogates from Community law. A measure will not be within the scope of Community law where there is no real connection with Community law. The separate issue, considered last, is whether or not there is a borderline or residual category of cases that fall within the scope of Community law. This has given rise to decisions at ECJ and national level that are not altogether easy to reconcile.

Measures falling within the scope of Community law

12.49 It is well established that Member States' measures (including administrative action) may be assessed on the basis of Community fundamental rights in two situations. The first is where the measure in question implements Community measures. As the ECJ has stated:

> . . . the requirements flowing from the protection of fundamental rights in the Community legal order are also binding on Member States when they implement Community rules and that the Member States must therefore, as far as possible, apply those rules in accordance with those requirements.[44]

12.50 Secondly, Community law fundamental rights doctrine also seems to apply where a Member State applies measures to derogate from Community provisions.

12.51 In *ERT*,[45] for example, the ECJ was asked to consider a reference seeking a preliminary ruling as to the lawfulness of a television monopoly which the Member State sought to justify under Articles 46 and 55 (ex 56 and 66) EC. At para 43 of its judgment, the ECJ observed:

> In particular, where a Member State relies on the combined provisions of Articles 56 and 66 in order to justify rules which are likely to obstruct the exercise of the freedom to provide services, such justification, provided for by Community law, must be interpreted in the light of the general principles of law and in particular of fundamental rights. Thus the national rules in question can fall under the exceptions provided for by the combined provisions of Articles 56 and 66 only if they are compatible with the fundamental rights the observance of which is ensured by the Court.

12.52 It should be borne in mind that to the extent that a Community measure confers discretion (as opposed to imposes a duty) on the Member State then the Member State or emanation of the State[46] must exercise that discretion in accordance with Community law. In that event, Community law fundamental rights protection will be relevant in determining the legality of exercise of the discretion.

12.53 An instance of this is afforded by the ECJ ruling in *P v S & Cornwall County Council*.[47] There, the ECJ held that the Equal Treatment Directive could not be interpreted so as to limit protection against discrimination on the ground of gender. It therefore held

---

[44] ibid para 16; Cases 201 and 202/85 *Marthe Klensch v Secretaire d'Etat à l'Agriculture et à la Viticulture* [1986] ECR 3477, para 8; Case 5/88 *Wachauf v Germany* [1989] ECR 2609, para 19.

[45] Case C–260/89 [1991] ECR I–2925.

[46] For consideration of the meaning of a State emanation in EC law, see, further, at paras 2.17 et seq.

[47] Case C–13/94 [1996] ECR I–2143.

that domestic legislation—in the form of the Sex Discrimination Act 1975—had failed lawfully to transpose the directive because it did not prohibit discrimination against transsexuals.[48]

Measures falling outside the scope of Community law

Community law fundamental rights protection may not be relied upon with respect to a purely internal situation.[49]   **12.54**

Further, a connection with Community law that is considered to be contrived or incidental falls outside Community law fundamental rights protection. It is though unclear, at least in terms of principle, how strong the connection with Community law must be to afford such protection. The ECJ appears to approach the issue on an incremental, case-by-case basis.[50]   **12.55**

In *Kremzow*,[51] for example, Mr Kremzow's claim for compensation for unlawful detention consequent upon a sentence of life imprisonment imposed after a trial found to be in breach of Article 6 ECHR was held not to fall within the scope of Community law.   **12.56**

The Austrian court that rejected the compensation claim referred the case to the ECJ on the basis of Mr Kremzow's argument that his right to freedom of movement under the EC Treaty had been infringed by his sentence of imprisonment. The ECJ held that the purely hypothetical prospect of exercising the right of free movement did not establish a sufficient connection with Community law. Further, Mr Kremzow's sentence was under a domestic law which was not designed to secure compliance with any rule of Community law.   **12.57**

To similar effect, in *Demirel*,[52] the ECJ held that it did not possess jurisdiction to determine whether the wife of a Turkish worker must be allowed to remain with her husband whose residence in the Member State was regulated by the subsidiary legislation of the EEC/Turkey Association Agreement. The asserted breach of Article 8 ECHR was not within the scope of Community law because rights to family reunification were not, at that time, covered by the Agreement and the national law lay outside the court's jurisdiction.   **12.58**

The closest that the ECJ has probably come to explaining its approach to whether a national measure falls within 'the scope of Community law' is in *Annibaldi*.[53] That was a case in which the applicant sought planning permission to plant an orchard on land that he owned falling within a national park. His application was refused by the municipal authority. The applicant contended that his fundamental right to property had been   **12.59**

---

[48] The ECJ's case law on discrimination has, however, not always been consistent. cf, eg, Case C–249/96 *Grant v South-West Trains Ltd* [1998] ECR I–621. For further discussion, see paras 18.14 et seq.

[49] Case C–132 *Volker Steam v Deutsche Bundespost (No 2)* [1994] ECR I–2715.

[50] See, eg, M Demetriou, 'Using Human Rights through European Community Law' [1999] EHRLR 484, 487.

[51] Case C–299/95 *Kremzow v Austria* [1997] ECR I–2405.

[52] Case 12/86 *Demirel v Stadt Schwabisch Gmund* [1987] ECR 3719.

[53] Case C–309/96 *Daniele Annibaldi v Sindaco del Commune di Guidonia and Presidente Regione Lazop* [1997] ECR I–7493.

infringed and that the national measure (refusal of permission) was in breach of the Community prohibition against discrimination under Article 40(3) (now 34(3)) EC.

12.60   On a preliminary reference the ECJ ruled that national legislation creating a national park did not fall within the scope of Community law and that, from a Community perspective, the legislation did not attract fundamental rights protection. In reaching that conclusion the ECJ took into account the fact that there was nothing to suggest that the legislation was intended to implement Community law. Further, the legislation was general in nature and pursued objectives other than those covered by the Treaty. There were no Community rules on expropriation of property and a common organization of the market had no effect on systems of agricultural property ownership.

12.61   *Annibaldi* is suggestive of the fact that the ECJ will require a relatively close connection between the national measure and Community law before deciding that it falls within the scope of Community law. The difficulty lies in defining what that connection entails as a question of principle.

Borderline categories

12.62   An important question arises as to whether it is only national measures implementing, or derogating from, Community measures that are capable of falling within the scope of Community law for the purposes of Community fundamental rights protection. Underlying this is whether it is the ECJ or the national courts that determine that question.

12.63   The constitutional position is not entirely free from doubt. However, by s 3(1) of the European Communities Act 1972 the meaning or effect of Treaty provisions is to be treated 'as a question of law ... for determination ... in accordance with the principles laid down by and any relevant decision of the European Court'. Article 220 (ex 164) EC makes the ECJ the final arbiter of Community law by providing, as it does, that the ECJ 'shall ensure that in the interpretation and application of the Treaty the law is observed'.

12.64   That suggests that it is, ultimately, the ECJ that determines whether a measure deriving from a Treaty provision is or is not within the scope of Community law. As Advocate General La Pergola put it in *Kremzow*[54] the interpretative task facing the Community by recognition of fundamental rights 'came into play and may be carried out only in regard to provisions connected with Community law, of which the Court is the supreme interpreter according to the Treaty'.

12.65   The ECJ case law on Article 12 EC may be relevant here. In *Phil Collins*[55] the recordings of singers Phil Collins and Sir Cliff Richard had been distributed in Germany without permission. German nationals were protected against breach of copyright but this prohibition did not extend to foreigners.

---

[54] Case C–299/95 [1997] ECR I–2405, 2635.
[55] Joined Cases C–92/92 and C–326/92 *Phil Collins v Imtrat Handelsgesellschaft mbH* [1993] ECR I–5145.

Article 12 (ex 6) EC provides: **12.66**

> Within the scope of application of this Treaty, and without prejudice to any special provisions
> contained therein, any discrimination on grounds of nationality shall be prohibited.

The issue was whether or not German copyright law fell within the discrimination prohi-   **12.67**
bitions of Article 12 EC. True it was that there were no Community provisions harmonizing national laws with respect to protecting literary and artistic property. However, the
ECJ held that:

> Like the other industrial and commercial property rights, the exclusive rights conferred by
> literary and artistic property are by their nature such as to affect trade in goods and services,
> as well as competitive relationships within the Community. For that reason, and as the
> Court has consistently held, those rights, although governed by national law, are subject
> to the requirements of the Treaty and therefore fall within its scope and application . . .
>
> It follows from what has been said that copyright and related rights, which by reason in
> particular of their effects on intra-Community trade in goods and services fall within the scope
> of application of the Treaty particularly by reason of their effect on trade in goods or services
> in the Community, are necessarily subject to the general principle of non-discrimination laid
> down by [Article 12].[56]

Phil Collins, therefore, gives rise to a possible argument that national measures with a   **12.68**
merely indirect relationship to Treaty provisions (*in casu* freedom of movement) could,
by parity of reasoning, lead to an extension of what is within the scope of Community
law for the purpose of applying a Community fundamental rights doctrine.[57]

However, the basis for such extension remains controversial and there is no decision of   **12.69**
the ECJ directly in point. *Phil Collins* was unsuccessfully relied on by the claimants in
R v MAFF, ex p First City Trading.[58] There, the claimants sought judicial review of the
Beef Stocks Transfer Scheme that had been introduced following the fall in demand for
British beef consequent upon the BSE crisis.

The scheme provided for compensation to those who operated slaughterhouses and   **12.70**
cutting equipment. However, it excluded exporters. Relying on *Phil Collins* the claimants
argued that the legality of a national measure is subject to general principles of Community
law—here equal treatment—if it affects intra-Community trade in goods or services. By
contrast, the Government argued that fundamental rights protection only applied where
the national measure was exercising a power or duty imposed by Community law.

Laws J held that the general principles enunciated by the ECJ are narrower in scope than   **12.71**
those measures specifically contained in the Treaty. He said:

> These fundamental principles . . . are not provided for on the face of the Treaty of Rome.
> They have been developed by the Court of Justice . . . out of the administrative law of
> the Member States. They are part of what may perhaps be called the common law of
> the Community. That being so, it is to my mind by no means self-evident that their cont-
> extual scope must be the same as that of Treaty provisions relating to discrimination or
> equal treatment, which are statute law taking effect according to their express terms . . .

---

[56] ibid, paras 22 and 27.
[57] See, also, Case C–279/93 *Finanzamt Koln-Alstadt v Schumacker* [1995] ECR I–225, paras 21–22;
Case C–107/94 *Asscher v Staatssecretaris van Financien* [1996] ECR I–3089.
[58] [1993] ECR I–5145.

Like any statute law containing orders or prohibitions, the Treaty is dirigiste; it is ... to be sharply distinguished from law which is made by a court of limited jurisdiction, such as the Court of Justice.

The powers of the Court of Justice ... to apply ... principles of public law which it had itself evolved cannot be deployed in a case where the measure in question, taken by a Member State, is not a function of Community law at all ... Where action is taken, albeit under domestic law, which falls within the scope of the Treaty's application, then of course the Court has the power and the duty to require that the Treaty be adhered to. But no more precisely because the fundamental principles elaborated by the Court of Justice are not vouchsafed by the Treaty, there is no legal space for their application to any measure or decision taken otherwise than in pursuance of Treaty rights or obligations.[59]

12.72   This analysis may be circular. Laws J accepts that a domestic measure will, if it falls within the scope of the Treaty's application, be subject to Community law fundamental rights protection. The difficulty, as always, is in drawing the line. In *Phil Collins* the line was drawn so far as application of the Treaty was concerned in terms of the effect of discrimination on inter-State trade. In *First City Trading* the link with the Treaty was, perhaps, less clear.

12.73   Similar issues were addressed by a Divisional Court in *R v Customs and Excise Commissioners, ex p Lunn Poly*.[60] There, an Insurance Premium Tax, imposed by the UK Government in 1994, was thought to be being avoided by (amongst others) travel agents. In 1997, therefore, the Government introduced a dual band tax with a higher rate applying to certain goods and services.

12.74   A travel agent, Lunn Poly, claimed that the dual band tax contravened general principles of Community law. It argued that national measures could be challenged on Community law principles in four situations. These were where:

(1)   national authorities implement Community law by fulfilling an obligation to act;

(2)   national authorities implement Community law by purporting to act within the scope of a Community enabling provision or authorization,

(3)   national authorities rely on a Community derogation in order to justify a measure which restricts the fundamental freedoms protected by the Treaty, or

(4)   there is a sufficient Community context for the general principle to apply.

12.75   In the Divisional Court Maurice Kay J considered and approved the reasoning of Laws J in *First City Trading*. He rejected the argument for Lunn Poly that the state measure in question fell under category (2) above. He also rejected the argument that category (4) could be deployed to apply Community fundamental rights protection. To do this, he held, would be 'a wholly unwarranted encroachment on sovereign powers'. He said that '[i]t would be as if Article [12] prohibited breach of all the fundamental principles within the scope of the Treaty's application, and not merely discrimination on the grounds of nationality'.

12.76   However, Laws J's reasoning in *First City Trading* (and its approval in *Lunn Poly*) has come under attack. In *British Pig*[61] judicial review proceedings were brought in respect

---

[59] ibid paras 39–42.
[60] [1998] Eu LR 438, 444–6. The case went to the Court of Appeal on a different basis: see [1999] 1 CMLR 1357.
[61] *R v MAFF, ex p British Pig Industry Support Group* [2000] Eu LR 724, 745–7.

of BSE support measures. On this occasion financial aid was given to the beef and sheep industries as opposed to pig farmers. The pig farmers claimed that this violated the general principle of equality of treatment.

Amongst other things, the claimants argued that *First City Trading* was wrongly decided. **12.77** The context in which the aid had been granted was that of assistance being given to an agricultural sector governed, in part at least, by a common organization of the market (COM).

Richards J expressed 'real doubts' about the correctness of *First City Trading* and *Lunn Poly*. **12.78** He said this:

> ... although the grant of state aid cannot in my view be said to amount to 'implementation' of the COM or to be done 'pursuant' to Community law, I think it is well arguable that the grant of aid by a Member State falls within the scope of Community law to the extent that the fundamental principles of Community law apply to it. I also see some substance in [the] challenge to the validity of the distinction drawn in *First City Trading* between Treaty law and the fundamental principles of Community law as developed in the case law of the ECJ.

However, in the event, Richards J decided the case on its facts against the claimants **12.79** whilst accepting—for the purposes of argument—the incorrectness of Laws J's analysis in *First City Trading*. Accordingly, the point was not made the subject of a reference under Article 234.[62]

At present, the ECJ has not decided the possible further scope of Community law in terms **12.80** of applying its fundamental rights/general principles protection. Nor, in the absence of such a ruling, have the national courts necessarily pronounced finally on the matter.

D. Extent of Substantive ECHR Protection in the ECJ Cases

The general position

It should not be assumed that the content of the fundamental rights recognized by **12.81** Community law is the same as the content of similar fundamental rights contained in the ECHR. This is so for at least three reasons.

First, Community law may contain fundamental rights principles recognized by the **12.82** ECHR but that are not intrinsically coextensive with those in the ECHR. A notable example is discrimination. Article 14 ECHR prohibits discrimination but only in the enjoyment of another Convention right. So, in order for Article 14 to apply via the ECHR it must be established that the discrimination complained of 'falls within the ambit' of another Convention right.[63] Community law, however, contains no such limitation. There is a general prohibition on discrimination.

Secondly, it is important to have regard to the fact that the ECHR is, so far as Community **12.83** law is concerned, being mediated through a legal system with its own distinct priorities.

---

[62] For further consideration of these issues, see paras 6.34 et seq. and 7.88 et seq.
[63] *Rasmussen v Denmark* (1985) 7 EHRR 371, para 29.

12.84   Thus, in *Commission v Germany*,[64] the ECJ was careful to observe that:

> ... such [fundamental] rights are not absolute privileges, but may be subject to restrictions, provided that the latter actually promote the objectives of general interest pursued by the Community and are not, by reference to such objectives, disproportionate and intolerable to such an extent that they would interfere with the very substance of the rights thus safeguarded ...

12.85   It is, therefore, by reference to Community objectives that the legality of interference with Convention rights will be evaluated. For example, in *National Panasonic v Commission*,[65] the ECJ had to consider whether Article 8(2) ECHR justified infringement of the right to privacy. After citing Article 8(2), the ECJ applied it against the Community background and held that:

> ... The exercise of the powers given to the Commission by Regulation 17 contributes to the maintenance of the system of competition intended by the Treaty which undertakings are absolutely bound to comply with. In these circumstances it does not therefore appear that Regulation 17, by giving the Commission the powers to carry out investigations without previous notification, infringes the right invoked by the applicant.

12.86   Further, whilst Community and ECHR protection of fundamental rights may often coincide, in Community law concepts such as 'margin of appreciation' and 'proportionality' may have a different meaning to that applied by the Strasbourg Court.[66]

12.87   The Strasbourg Court has itself addressed the question as to the priority that should be afforded to Convention rights as against Community law provisions. In *Matthews v United Kingdom*[67] the applicant, a British citizen resident in Gibraltar, successfully complained to the Strasbourg Court that she had been unable to vote in the 1994 elections to the European Parliament and that, in consequence, there had been a violation of Article 3 of Protocol No 1. The UK Government submitted that her real objection was to a Council Decision and to a Community act which governed the elections to the European Parliament.

12.88   In constitutional terms, the issue was whether, despite the fact that the Convention extended to Gibraltar, the quality of elections to the European Parliament (itself an organ of the EC) could be challenged before the Strasbourg Court. Strasbourg held that although the acts of the EU, as such, could not be challenged before the court—since the EU was not a Contracting Party—and although nothing in the Convention prevented the transfer of competences to international organizations, the United Kingdom was, as an individual Contracting Party, still bound under its Convention obligations to comply with Article 3 of Protocol No 1.

12.89   Thus, the Strasbourg Court's view, at least, is that it is no answer to a breach of a person's rights under the Convention to assert that such breach is either permitted or required by Community law. This raises the possibility of a direct conflict between Strasbourg and Luxembourg should the ECJ reach a contrary view as to the content of the rights at issue.

---

[64] Case C–62/90 [1992] ECR I–2575.

[65] C–136/79 [1980] ECR 2033.

[66] This can produce different outcomes: see para 12.100. See, also, Case 44/79 *Hauer v Land Rheinland-Pfalz* [1979] ECR 3727.

[67] (1999) 28 EHRR 361, especially paras 30–32.

This leads, logically, to the third reason why Community law protection of (even the same) **12.90** fundamental rights may differ from that accorded by the Strasbourg Court. The ECJ and the European Court of Human Rights in Strasbourg may, and sometimes have, simply come to different conclusions as to the proper scope of particular Convention rights.

Overall, for example, the Strasbourg Court has tended to be more circumspect than **12.91** the ECJ in relation to the adequacy of judicial review as an effective remedy for alleged breaches of Articles 6 and 13 ECHR.[68] In cases such as *Bryan v United kingdom*[69] and *Soering v United Kingdom*[70] the Strasbourg Court has found domestic judicial review, with its traditional restrictions on permitting examination by the Administrative Court of the merits, sufficient to satisfy the Convention's requirements.

In contrast, albeit in the context of espousing the Community principle of effectiveness, **12.92** the ECJ has emphasized the importance of effective judicial review scrutiny including review of the merits where this is necessary to protect Community rights.

In *Factortame*,[71] or example, Advocate General Tesauro observed that Community law **12.93** requires that national courts:

> ... afford complete and effective judicial protection to individuals on whom enforceable legal rights are conferred under a directly effective Community provision ... from this it follows that any national provision or practice which precludes those courts from giving 'full effect' to the Community provision is incompatible with Community law.

In similar vein, Advocate General Colomer stated in *Shingara*[72] (at para 64) that: **12.94**

> ... if judicial review of government decisions concerning the entry or expulsion of foreign nationals did not allow the courts to undertake complete and effective examination of such decisions, as a result of restrictions on judicial activity such as to render nugatory their review of the substance of such decisions, Community law would require such restrictions to be set aside and the applicants to be afforded adequate judicial protection.

And (at para 131) he continued: **12.95**

> Community nationals who have had an expulsion order made against them or have been refused entry to a Member State, on grounds of public health, public security or public policy, are entitled to challenge such measures before a judicial authority in that Member State by means of an effective remedy which ensures that the entire administrative decision, including its substantive grounds, is subjected to judicial review.

Observations such as these exemplify the potential for tension, if not for outright conflict, **12.96** between the respective approaches of the ECJ and the European Court of Human Rights in interpreting the proper scope of fundamental rights protection.

However, the Strasbourg Court has managed, thus far, to avoid direct conflict with the **12.97** ECJ. For example, in its recent judgment in the *Bosphorus* case,[73] which came in the wake

---

[68] Article 13 (right to an effective remedy for ECHR breaches) is not a 'Convention right' under the HRA.
[69] (1996) 21 EHRR 342.
[70] (1989) 11 EHRR 439.
[71] *Factortame Ltd v Secretary of State for Transport (No 2)* [1990] ECR I–2433, para 15.
[72] Cases C–65 and 111/95 *R v Secretary of State for the Home Department, ex p Shingara* [1997] ECR I–3343.
[73] *Bosphorus Hava Yollari Turizm ve Ticaret ASI v Ireland* (2006) 42 EHRR 1.

of an earlier ruling from the ECJ as to the legality of Article 8 of Regulation (EEC) 990/93 which was held to permit impounding of vessels, freight, vehicles and aircraft on a very broad basis,[74] the Strasbourg Court concluded that the seizure of aircraft by the Irish Government under that Community regulation amounted to a control on the use of property within the meaning of Article 1 Protocol 1 ECHR but that compliance by the Irish Government with its obligations under EC law was, in the circumstances of the case, a legitimate interest objective under that Convention right which complied with the proportionality principle.

12.98   Nonetheless, the Strasbourg Court's ruling in *Bosphorus* lays down a number of extremely important principles concerning the relationship between the Strasbourg and Luxembourg Courts. The material part of the ruling (paras 151–156) of the European Court of Human Rights (which, in essence, endorses *Matthews)* is, therefore, cited in full below:

> The question is therefore whether, and if so to what extent, that important general interest of compliance with EC obligations can justify the impugned interference by the State with the applicant's property rights.

> The Convention does not, on the one hand, prohibit Contracting Parties from transferring sovereign power to an international (including a supranational) organisation in order to pursue co-operation in certain fields of activity (the *M. & Co.* decision, at p. 144 and *Matthews* at § 32, both cited above). Moreover, even as the holder of such transferred sovereign power, that organisation is not itself held responsible under the Convention for proceedings before, or decisions of, its organs as long as it is not a Contracting Party (see *CFDT v European Communities*, no. 8030/77, Commission decision of 10 July 1978, DR 13, p. 231; *Dufay v European Communities*, no. 13539/88, Commission decision of 19 January 1989; the above-cited *M. & Co.* case, at p. 144 and the above-cited *Matthews* judgment, at § 32).

> On the other hand, it has also been accepted that a Contracting Party is responsible under Article 1 of the Convention for all acts and omissions of its organs regardless of whether the act or omission in question was a consequence of domestic law or of the necessity to comply with international legal obligations. Article 1 makes no distinction as to the type of rule or measure concerned and does not exclude any part of a Contracting Party's 'jurisdiction' from scrutiny under the Convention (*United Communist Party of Turkey and Others v Turkey* judgment of 30 January 1998, Reports, 1998-I, § 29).

> In reconciling both these positions and thereby establishing the extent to which State action can be justified by its compliance with obligations flowing from its membership of an international organisation to which it has transferred part of its sovereignty, the Court has recognised that absolving Contracting States completely from their Convention responsibility in the areas covered by such a transfer would be incompatible with the purpose and object of the Convention: the guarantees of the Convention could be limited or excluded at will thereby depriving it of its peremptory character and undermining the practical and effective nature of its safeguards (*M. & Co.* at p. 145 and *Waite and Kennedy*, at § 67). The State is considered to retain Convention liability in respect of treaty commitments subsequent to the entry into force of the Convention (*mutatis mutandis*, the above-cited *Matthews v the United Kingdom* judgment, at § 29 and 32–34, and *Prince Hans-Adam II of Liechtenstein v Germany* [GC], no. 42527/98, § 47, ECHR 2001–VIII).

---

[74] Case C–84/95 *Bosphorus Hava Yollari Turizm ve Ticaret AS v Minister of Transport and Attorney General* [1996] ECR I–3953.

In the Court's view, State action taken in compliance with such legal obligations is justified as long as the relevant organisation is considered to protect fundamental rights, as regards both the substantive guarantees offered and the mechanisms controlling their observance, in a manner which can be considered at least equivalent to that for which the Convention provides (see the above-cited *M. & Co.* decision, at p. 145, an approach with which the parties and the European Commission agreed). By 'equivalent' the Court means 'comparable': any requirement that the organisation's protection be 'identical' could run counter to the interest of international co-operation pursued (paragraph 150 above). However, any such finding of equivalence could not be final and would be susceptible to review in the light of any relevant change in fundamental rights' protection.

If such equivalent protection is considered to be provided by the organisation, the presumption will be that a State has not departed from the requirements of the Convention when it does no more than implement legal obligations flowing from its membership of the organisation.

However, any such presumption can be rebutted if, in the circumstances of a particular case, it is considered that the protection of Convention rights was manifestly deficient. In such cases, the interest of international co-operation would be outweighed by the Convention's role as a 'constitutional instrument of European public order' in the field of human rights (*Loizidou v Turkey* (preliminary objections), judgment of 23 March 1995, Series A no. 310, § 75).

12.99 For its part, the ECJ also seeks to avoid inconsistency with the European Court of Human Rights. In *Prais v Council*,[75] Advocate General Warner regretted the absence from the ECHR of any power in the ECJ or in national courts to refer questions of interpretation of the Convention for a preliminary ruling comparable to that allowing references to the ECJ under Article 234 (ex 177) EC.[76]

12.100 Inevitably, though, inconsistencies have occurred. For example, in *Grogan*,[77] Advocate General Van Gerven considered that a prohibition against dissemination of information in Ireland about UK abortion services would not (even if justiciable in EC law) be a breach of Article 10 ECHR. By contrast, the European Court of Human Rights—on substantially the same facts—held exactly the opposite in *Open Door Counselling and Dublin Well Women v Ireland*.[78] In *Hoechst*,[79] the ECJ held that Article 8 ECHR did not extend to business premises. The opposite conclusion was reached by the European Court of Human Rights in *Niemeitz v Germany*.[80]

12.101 As will be seen,[81] the potential for different approaches towards the protection of fundamental rights by the ECJ and the European Court of Human Rights is compounded by the further scope for divergence by the Administrative Court seeking to interpret and/or apply the case law of those courts. In particular, jurisdictional issues may arise in domestic

---

[75] Case 130/75 [1976] ECR 1589.

[76] See Chapter 4 for detailed consideration of the reference procedure under Article 234 (ex 177) EC.

[77] Case C–159/90 *SPUC v Grogan* [1991] ECR I–4685.

[78] (1993) 15 EHRR 97.

[79] Cases 46/87 and 227/88 *Hoechst AG v Commission* [1989] ECR 2859.

[80] (1993) 16 EHRR 97. It is, though, fair to observe that in its recent decision in Case C–94/00 *Roquette Freres v Directeur general de la concurrence, de la consommation et de la repression des fraudes* [2002] ECR I–9011 the ECJ has now accepted that Art 8 does extend to business premises.

[81] See paras 12.106 et seq.

judicial review with a Community law element where the case law of Luxembourg and Strasbourg is in conflict.

ECHR protection in the ECJ cases

12.102 The fact that Community law confers protection of fundamental rights in particular areas does not mean that a Community national thereby becomes entitled to the full benefit of ECHR protection.

12.103 It is, nonetheless, relevant to note that in *Konstantanidis*[82] Advocate General Jacobs said this:

> In my opinion, a Community national who goes to another state as a worker or self-employed person under Articles 48, 52 or 59 of the Treaty is entitled not just to pursue his trade or profession and to enjoy the same living and working conditions as nationals of the host state; he is in addition entitled to assume that, wherever he goes to earn his living in the European Community, he will be treated in accordance with a common code of fundamental values, in particular those laid down in the European Convention on Human Rights. In other words, he is entitled to say 'civis europeus sum' and to invoke that status in order to oppose any violation of his fundamental rights.

12.104 However, nothing in the ECJ's judgment endorsed such a broad approach; a fact noted by Advocate General Gulman when disagreeing with Advocate General Jacobs and giving his Opinion in *R v MAFF, ex p Bostock*.[83] The true analysis would appear to be that any applicable ECHR protection, as part of Community law fundamental rights doctrine, extends only as far as is necessary to protect the Community right in question. If the position were otherwise, Community fundamental rights protection would extend beyond the proper scope of Community law as analysed above.[84] Notwithstanding this, as explained above, the ECJ has expanded its fundamental rights protection considerably. In particular, the case law on EU citizenship has subsequent to the ECJ's ruling in *Konstantinidis* developed in its own right and is separately considered.[85]

12.105 Table 12.1 provides examples of cases in which provisions of the ECHR (or their substantive content) have been referred to by the ECJ.

Table 12.1 Examples of reference to the ECHR by the ECJ

ECHR provision	ECJ case reference
Article 2 (right to life)	Case C–159/90 *SPUC v Grogan [1991] ECR I–4605;* Case C–62/90 *Commission v Germany* [1992] ECR 2575.
Article 3 (protection from torture etc)	Joined Cases 115 and 116/81 *Adoui v Belgian State* [1982] ECR 1665.
Article 5 (right to liberty/security)	Case C–299/95 *Kremzow v Austria* [1997] ECR I–2629.

---

[82] Case C–168/91 *Konstantinidis v Stadt Altensteig-Standesamt and Landratsamt Calw, Ordnungsamt* [1993] ECR I–1191, para 46.

[83] [1994] ECR I–955, 971.

[84] See paras 12.49 et seq.

[85] See paras 16.71 et seq.

Table 12.1 *Cont.*

ECHR provision	ECJ case reference
Article 6 (right to a fair hearing)	Case 322/81 *Michelin v Commission* [1983] ECR 3461; Case 222/84 *Johnston v Chief Constable of the Royal Ulster Constabulary* [1986] ECR 1651; Case 222/86 *UNECTEF v Heylens* [1987] ECR 4097; Case C–17/98 *Emesa Sugar (Free Zone) NV v Aruba (No 1)* [2000] ECR I–0665.
Article 7 (non-retroactivity)	Case 63/83 *R v Kent Kirk* [1984] ECR 2689; Case 14/86 *Pretore di Salo v Persons Unknown* [1987] ECR 2545; Case C–331/88 *R v MAFF, ex p FEDESA* [1991] ECR I–4023.
Article 8 (right to respect for private and family life etc)	Case 136/79 *National Panasonic v Commission* [1980] ECR 2033; Case 53/85 *AKZO Chemie BV and AKZO Chemie UK Ltd v Commission* [1986] ECR 2565; Case 46/87 *Hoechst AG v Commission* [1989] ECR 2859; Case C–404/92P *X v Commission* [1994] ECR I–4737; Case C–94/00 *Roquette Freres v Directeur general de la concurrence, de la consummation and de la repression des fraudes* [2002] ECR I–9011.
Article 9 (freedom of thought etc)	Case 36/75 *Rutili v Minister for the Interior* [1975] ECR 1219; Case 130/75 *Prais v Council* [1976] ECR 1589.
Article 10 (freedom of expression)	Case C–353/89 *Commission v The Netherlands* [1991] ECR I–4069.
Article 11 (freedom of assembly and association)	Case C–415/93 *Union Royale Belge des Societes de Football v Bosman* [1995] ECR I–4921.
Article 12 (right to marry)	Case 236/87 *Bergemann v Bundesanstalt fur Arbeit* [1988] ECR 5125.
Article 13 (right to an effective remedy)	Case 33/76 *Rewe-Zentralfinanz eG and Rewe-Zentral AG v Landwirtschaftskammer fur das Saarland* [1976] ECR 1989; Case 45/76 *Comet v Produktschap voor Siergewassen* [1976] ECR 2043; Case 222/86 *UNECTEF v Heylens* [1987] ECR 4097; Case C–70/88 *Parliament v Council (Radioactive Food)* [1991] ECR I–4529; Case 213/89 *R v Secretary of State for Transport, ex p Factortame Ltd (No 2)* [1990] ECR I–2433; Cases C–6 and 9/90 *Francovich and Bonifaci v Italy* [1991] ECR I–5357.
Article 14 (non-discrimination)	Case 149/77 *Defrenne v SABENA* [1978] ECR 1365.
Article 1 Protocol 1 (right to property)	Case 44/79 *Liselotte Hauer v Land Rheinland-Pfalz* [1979] ECR 3727; Case 5/88 *Wachauf v The State* [1989] ECR 2609.
Article 2 Protocol 4 (liberty of movement within territory of Contracting State)	Case 36/75 *Rutili v Ministeur de l'Interieur* [1975] ECR 121.
Article 3 Protocol 4 (prohibition of expulsion of nationals)	Case 41/71 *Van Duyn v Home Office* [1974] ECR 1337; Case 370/90 *R v IAT and Surinder Singh, ex p Secretary of State for the Home Department* [1992] ECR I–4265; Joined Cases C–65/95 and C–111/95 *Shingara and Radiom* [1997] ECR I–3343; Case C–348/96 *Criminal Proceedings against Calfa* [1999] ECR I–0011.

E. Relationship between EC Law, the ECHR, and the HRA

Judicial review—resolving jurisdictional conflicts

12.106 As noted at para 12.100 above, there may sometimes be important differences between the approach to fundamental rights of the ECJ and the European Court of Human Rights. The Administrative Court may itself take a different view of the law than that taken in particular cases by one or both of those courts.

12.107 The jurisdictional conflict that may occur in these situations can only be resolved by asking, and answering, the following questions:

(1) Is the case one within the scope of Community law? This requires the analysis outlined above.[86]

(2) If the case is *not* within the scope of Community law is the case one to which the HRA applies? In such a case what are the relevant jurisdictional principles to apply (see below)?

(3) If the case is not within the scope of Community law and is not one to which the HRA applies what are the relevant jurisdictional principles to apply (see below)?

(4) If the case *is* within the scope of Community law and the case is also one to which the HRA applies what are the relevant jurisdictional principles to apply (see below)?

(5) If the case *is* within the scope of Community law but the case is not one to which the HRA applies what are the relevant jurisdictional principles to apply (see below)?

12.108 Identification of whether the case is within the scope of Community law is—as has been seen—not always obvious. Even in such a case the extent of Community law protection may be limited.

12.109 These difficulties have already been examined. However, resolving questions (2) to (4) above raises jurisdictional problems. Questions (2) and (3) do not raise issues of Community law and are, therefore, addressed in outline only. Similarly, question (5) addresses, in substance, issues that are addressed throughout this book and is, therefore, not separately examined.

In a non-EC case is the HRA engaged and, if so, what are the relevant jurisdictional principles?

12.110 In a case that raises fundamental rights issues but is outside the scope of EC law[87] it is important to identify whether or not the HRA is engaged. This is because the HRA gives greater protection and affords wider scope for legal submission than domestic law outside the HRA.

---

[86] See paras 12.49 et seq.
[87] See paras 12.54 et seq.

In order for the HRA to apply, at least generally, a person must be a 'victim'. HRA, s 7(1) **12.111** provides that:

[a] person who claims that a public authority has acted (or proposes to act) in a way which is made unlawful by section 6(1) may—

(a) bring proceedings against the authority under this Act in the appropriate court or tribunal; or

(b) rely on the Convention right or rights concerned in any legal proceedings, but only if he is (or would be) a victim of the unlawful act.[88]

HRA, s 7(7) provides that for the purposes of s 7 'a person is a victim of an unlawful act only if he would be a victim for the purposes of Article 34 of the Convention if proceedings were brought in the European Court of Human Rights'.

A 'victim' under Article 34 ECHR is embodied in the description of those who may apply to **12.112** the European Court of Human Rights in respect of alleged human rights violations. It states that: '[t]he Court may receive applications from any person, non-governmental organisation or group of individuals claiming to be the victim of a violation by one of the High Contracting Parties of the rights set forth in the Convention or the protocols thereto …'.

The Strasbourg case law demonstrates that the 'victim' test is applied in a similar way to **12.113** that of standing to bring judicial review in domestic law. For example, the potential rather than actual effect of a measure on a claimant is sufficient to confer 'victim' status.[89]

There are, however, two areas in which the 'victim' test is undoubtedly narrower than **12.114** that for standing in judicial review. These are: (1) corporate or group challenges and (2) challenges by public bodies.

Although groups or associations are themselves capable of being 'victims' the group must be **12.115** able to show that it is itself a 'victim'.[90] This is exemplified by the facts of *Greenpeace Schweiz v Switzerland*.[91] There, the applicants included a number of associations and individuals who brought an Article 6 challenge in respect of the renewal of a permit to operate a nuclear power plant. The individual complaints were held to be admissible. However, the group applicants' complaints were declared to be inadmissible. This was because they had 'failed to indicate whether they own, or lease, property, within the vicinity of the nuclear power plant'.

Similarly, although in domestic judicial review public bodies may bring as well as defend **12.116** claims for judicial review,[92] the restriction in Article 34 ECHR to 'non-governmental organisations' suggests that many public authorities will lack the requisite standing under the HRA.

---

[88] Note that under the HRA an 'act' includes a failure to act (see s 6(6)).

[89] See, eg, *Dudgeon v United Kingdom* (1982) 4 EHRR 149, *Open Door Counselling and Dublin Well Women Centre v Ireland* (1993) 15 EHRR 244. For a more detailed analysis of the 'victim' test in the Strasbourg cases see R Clayton and H Tomlinson, *The Law on Human Rights* (2000) paras 22.14 et seq.

[90] The position is, of course, otherwise on a purely domestic law judicial review where the rules of standing for public interest groups are more relaxed: see, eg, *R v Secretary of State for Foreign and Commonwealth Affairs, ex p World Development Movement Ltd* [1995] 1 WLR 386.

[91] (1996) 23 EHRR CD 116.

[92] See, eg, *R v Secretary of State for Transport, ex p Richmond LBC (No 1)* [1994] 1 WLR 74.

12.117   Apart from 'victim' status it seems likely that the HRA may also be deployed in cases where an Act of Parliament is being interpreted including those cases where a declaration of incompatibility is sought.[93] Part of the rationale is that HRA, s 3(1) places an interpretative obligation on the courts to read and give effect to primary and subordinate legislation 'in a way which is compatible with the Convention rights'.

12.118   This may have the effect that even in a domestic judicial review where the claimant is not a 'victim' in the Convention sense[94] the interpretation of a particular statutory provision may engage the HRA at least in the way in which the Administrative Court is required to construe that provision.[95]

12.119   The second aspect of whether or not the HRA is engaged is whether or not there is a relevant act or omission by a 'public authority' within the meaning of HRA, s 6. The question here is whether or not the individual or body in question is exercising relevant 'public functions'[96] and is the subject of a considerable number of domestic law cases which have yet to be entirely satisfactorily resolved.[97]

12.120   Where the HRA is engaged then the Administrative Court is required, by s 2, to take into account the relevant Strasbourg jurisprudence in giving effect to the 'Convention rights' as referred to in s 1(1) and set out in Sch 1. The s 2 obligation is important. As Lord Slynn observed in *R (Amin) v Secretary of State for the Home Department*:[98]

> ... In my opinion, even if the United Kingdom courts are only to take account of the Strasbourg Court decisions and are not strictly bound by them (section 2 of the Human Rights Act 1998), where the Court has laid down principles and, as here a minimum threshold requirement, United Kingdom courts should follow what the Court has said. If they do not do so without good reason the dissatisfied litigant has a right to go to Strasbourg where existing jurisprudence is likely to be followed.

12.121   Importantly, the case law of the European Court of Human Rights is relevant not merely to analysing the substantive content of Convention rights but also to understanding the principles of law that infuse the ECHR. Just as much of the detailed application of EC law is underpinned by general principles of law so, too, is fundamental rights protection under the ECHR.

---

[93] This point has not been as clearly determined as it might. In *Rusbridger v Attorney General* [2004] 1 AC 357 the House of Lords held that a claim for a declaration of incompatibility might be made under the HRA without the need for victim status under HRA, s 7.

[94] Or, even, in private law proceedings. See below.

[95] In *Wilson v First County Trust* [2003] UKHL 40, [2004] 1 AC 816 the House of Lords interpreted provisions of the Consumer Credit Act 1974 in litigation involving private parties with no public law element and without any 'victim' therefore being able to take proceedings under the HRA directly. However, none of the parties suggested that the HRA was not engaged and the House of Lords never considered the issue.

[96] See also paras 2.25–2.28.

[97] See, especially *Aston Cantlow and Wilmcote Parochial Church Council v Wallbank* [2003] UKHL 37, [2004] 1 AC 546; *R (Heather) v Leonard Cheshire Foundation* [2002] EWCA Civ 366, [2002] All ER 936; *Poplar Housing and Regeneration Community Association v Donoghue* [2001] EWCA Civ 595, [2002] QB 48; *R (Bear) v Hampshire Farmers' Markets Ltd* [2003] EWCA Civ 1056, [2004] 1 WLR 233; *R (West) v Lloyd's of London* [2004] EWCA Civ 506, [2004] 3 All ER 251; *R (Johnson) v Havering LBC* [2006] EWHC 1714.

[98] [2003] UKHL 51, [2003] 3 WLR 1169, para 44. For statements to similar effect, see *R (S) v Chief Constable of South Yorkshire* [2004] UKHL 39, [2004] 1 WLR 2196, para 66, per Lord Rodger. *Pelling v Bruce-Williams* [2004] EWCA Civ 845, [2004] 3 All ER 875, para 35, per Thorpe LJ. For a rather more diluted view of the HRA s 2 obligation see *R v Lyons* [2002] UKHL 44, [2003] 1 AC 976, para 46, per Lord Hoffmann.

A notable example is the principle of proportionality. As yet, proportionality is not a **12.122** developed principle in domestic law.[99] However, the application of ECHR proportionality, ostensibly similar in form and content to EC proportionality, may produce a very different result in judicial review proceedings to that obtained under domestic principles.[100]

By HRA, s 3, the court must seek to read and give effect to both primary and subordinate leg- **12.123** islation in a way which is compatible with the Convention rights. HRA, s 6 makes it unlawful for a 'public authority'[101] to act in a way which is incompatible with a Convention right.

So, an HRA challenge by way of judicial review has a wider 'reach' in terms of the argu- **12.124** ments that may be advanced than a purely domestic challenge. Further, the remedies are more extensive. Thus, damages may be claimed if a public authority acts in violation of a Convention right[102] whereas damages for a domestic public law default do not lie save on an available private law basis.[103] So, too, in an HRA challenge an Act of Parliament may be subject to a declaration of incompatibility (see below) whereas in a conventional domestic challenge the doctrine of parliamentary sovereignty means that a statutory provision is— subject to its proper interpretation—immune from judicial criticism.

In a non-EC case and a non-HRA case what are the relevant jurisdictional principles?

Heightened intensity of review will apply to a case in which neither EC law nor the HRA **12.125** has application.

In practice, with the long-delayed incorporation of the ECHR, fundamental rights pro- **12.126** tection had already developed apace in domestic judicial review. The coming into force of the HRA has increased that tendency. Domestic law developments in the context of proportionality and the decline in practice of *Wednesbury* irrationality are separately examined.[104] In addition, where fundamental rights issues arise in domestic law, principles such as anxious scrutiny[105] and the principle of legality[106] are likely to be invoked often to similar effect to the application of HRA principles.

---

[99] See further para 11.78.

[100] *R (Daly) v Secretary of State for the Home Department* [2001] UKHL 26, [2001] 2 WLR 1622. See, also, the case study at paras 17.98 et seq. which shows that in some cases the application of EC proportionality may produce a different outcome from the application of proportionality under the ECHR and HRA.

[101] This term (see HRA, s 6(3)(a)) includes courts and tribunals. It also includes (s 6(3)(b)) 'any person certain of whose functions are functions of a public nature'. The intention appears to be to make many defendants amenable to judicial review also amenable to HRA obligations although the case law on the subject is by no means unambiguous: see, especially, *Aston Cantlow and Wilmcote Parochial Church Council v Wallbank* [2004] 1 AC 546.

[102] See HRA, s 8. In practice, HRA damages have not to date proved a particularly successful add-on to damages subsisting at common law: see, especially, *Marcic v Thames Water Utilities* [2003] UKHL 66, [2003] 3 WLR 1603. However, there have been cases where they have made a significant difference as, eg, in *R v Enfield LBC, ex p Bernard* [2003] HRLR 4. See, also, *Anufrijeva v LB of Southwark* [2003] EWCA Civ 1406, [2004] 2 WLR 603.

[103] See CPR r 54.3(2) and Supreme Court Act 1981, s 31(4).

[104] See paras 11.82 et seq.

[105] The doctrine that the court has a responsibility to subject an administrative decision to more rigorous scrutiny where fundamental rights are in issue: see, eg, *R v Secretary of State for the Home Department, ex p Bugdaycay* [1987] AC 514, 531, per Lord Bridge.

[106] A principle of statutory construction whereby it is presumed that words in primary and subordinate legislation are intended to be subject to the basic rights of the individual unless there are express words to the contrary or a necessary implication to the contrary: see, most notably, *R v Secretary of State for the Home Department, ex p Simms* [2000] 2 AC 115.

12.127   However, a fundamental rights challenge that has to be founded on domestic principles alone certainly lacks the wider remedies under the HRA (see above). It also lacks the clear scope of ECHR proportionality and the substantive Convention rights. In all cases where fundamental rights issues arise there is rarely a case where domestic protection is greater than that afforded under the HRA and ECHR. For these reasons, therefore, it is always wise—if at all possible—to run a domestic human rights challenge in tandem with the HRA.

In an EC and HRA case what are the relevant jurisdictional principles?

12.128   There will be many situations in which EC and ECHR principles overlap. In such cases there is potential for conflict as between the two jurisdictions. This, in turn, may create jurisdictional difficulty for the Administrative Court.[107]

12.129   The difficulty arises where the ECJ has interpreted the ECHR in a manner that is different to that of the European Court of Human Rights or where there is an ostensible conflict between Community law and the ECHR itself. Instances where this has occurred are outlined above.[108]

12.130   In such cases, which are likely to be exceptional, which source of law should the Administrative Court follow? There are duties imposed on the national court under both EC law and under the HRA. To act under one, to the detriment of the other, places that court in an invidious position.

12.131   In terms of jurisdiction, it would seem that the Administrative Court is bound by EC law rather than by the HRA. This is, in part, because of the nature of Community law but also because of the substantive content of the HRA.

12.132   By virtue of Article 220 (ex 164) EC the ECJ requires the ECJ itself to 'ensure that in the interpretation and application of this Treaty the law is observed'. It has been observed that this general mandate would be 'seriously impaired' if a parallel fundamental rights jurisdiction could be set up by the Member States.[109]

12.133   Further, the ECJ has emphasized that it is not obliged, in any event, to follow rulings of the Strasbourg Court. In *Orkem v Commission*[110] the ECJ noted:

> This Court may . . . adopt, with respect to provisions of the Convention, an interpretation which does not coincide exactly with that given by the Strasbourg authorities, in particular the

---

[107] The difficulties set out here are compounded where a higher court has interpreted EC law in a particular way. Notwithstanding that in an HRA case the doctrine of precedent applies (*Kay v Lambeth London Borough Council* [2006] UKHL 10, [2006] 2 WLR 570 the House of Lords accepted in *Kay* that s 3(1) of the European Communities Act 1972 was different to the effect of ECHR decisions: see per Lord Bingham of Cornhill, para 28.

[108] See para 12.100.

[109] See N Reich (1996) 7 EJIL 103, 110–11. See, also, the Opinion of Advocate General Jacobs in Case C–168/91 *Konstantinidis v Stadt Altensteig-Standesamt and Landratsamt Calw, Ordngsamt* [1993] ECR I–1191, para 50, which emphasizes that the Strasbourg Court has always accepted that its jurisdiction is subsidiary and that it is primarily for the national authorities and the national courts to apply the ECHR. The Strasbourg doctrine of subsidiarity is exemplified by cases such as *Handyside v United Kingdom* (1979–80) 1 EHRR 737.

[110] [1989] ECR 3283, para 140.

European Court of Human Rights. It is not bound, in so far as it does not have systematically to take into account, as regards fundamental rights under Community law, the interpretation of the Convention given by the Strasbourg authorities.

Finally, s 3(1) of the European Communities Act 1972 requires the court to treat questions as to the meaning and effect of Treaty provisions 'as a question of law . . . for determination . . . in accordance with the principles laid down by and any relevant decision of the European Court'. **12.134**

By contrast, the HRA is less absolute in its terms and structure. As stated above, HRA, s 2 requires the court (including the Administrative Court) to 'take into account' the Strasbourg case law. Whilst the obligation is an important one it appears to confer on UK judges the power to give a different interpretation to the ECHR to that accorded by the European Court of Human Rights. Similarly, HRA, s 3 enjoins the court 'so far as it is possible to do so' to interpret legislative provisions to be Convention-compatible. **12.135**

Importantly, too, although HRA, s 6(1) makes it unlawful for a public authority—which includes the Administrative Court—to act in a way which is incompatible with a Convention right, s 6(2)(a) provides, materially, that s 6(1) does not apply to an act if 'as the result of one or more provisions of primary legislation, the authority could not have acted differently'. **12.136**

So, given the existence of s 3(1) of the European Communities Act 1972, the Administrative Court would not be acting unlawfully under HRA, s 6(1) in interpreting a statutory provision consistently with ECJ case law because (see s 6(2)) it could not have acted differently. **12.137**

However, the conflict may be more apparent than real. Where the Administrative Court is seeking to decide whether a breach of fundamental rights *in Community law* has occurred it seems clear that—for the reasons set out above—s 3(1) of the 1972 Act and the ECJ's case law prevails.[111] Nevertheless, the same facts may give rise to an allegation that a breach of Convention rights has also taken place. In determining the latter claim, the Administrative Court must apply the HRA principles outlined above. It is at least possible, therefore, that a challenge involving overlapping EC and HRA issues may lead to different conclusions. **12.138**

For this reason it is, tactically, sensible for overlapping fundamental rights claims to be couched—where possible—both in terms of Community law and under the HRA.[112] So far as the basis of review is concerned a Community law challenge may sometimes afford **12.139**

---

[111] There is a theoretical argument to the effect that even Community law should defer to Strasbourg. This is because Art 307 (ex 234) EC stipulates that the Treaty is subject to pre-existing international obligations and at the time of ratifying the EC Treaty, the UK had already ratified the ECHR. It would, of course, be for the ECJ—as opposed to Strasbourg—to determine this issue which has never been decided. The argument, raised in R Gordon and T Ward, *Judicial Review and the Human Rights Act* (2000), is analysed in depth in L Mulcahy (ed), *Human Rights and Civil Practice* (2001), paras 6.52–6.60.

[112] For an instance of such a claim, see *International Transport Roth GmbH v Secretary of State for the Home Department* [2002] EWCA Civ 158, [2002] 3 WLR 344 (see case analysis in Chapter 17). The claims were framed against the Secretary of State in both EC law and under the HRA. At first instance, Sullivan J decided both issues in favour of the claimants. On appeal, however, the Court of Appeal allowed the Secretary of State's appeal on the EC points but dismissed the appeal (by a majority) on the HRA points. Note that an EC judicial review of a State measure will lie only against the State or an emanation of the State: there may, therefore, be cases where an EC claim is narrower than an HRA claim against a 'public authority'.

a broader scope than under the HRA. Fundamental rights in Community law are directly effective. This means that they are not dependent on the canons of interpretation under the HRA.[113] Also, as earlier observed, the scope of fundamental rights protection in EC law embraces international instruments other than the ECHR.[114]

12.140 In any event, in remedial terms, an EC law fundamental rights challenge has far greater potential than an HRA challenge. EC damages are likely to be more readily available than under the HRA. The ECJ case law on the assessment of damages is more developed than that under the HRA which applies the rather arbitrary 'just satisfaction' measure of damages of the Strasbourg Court.[115] In particular, under EC law a failure to legislate may be challenged by judicial review and, in some cases, damages may be awarded for a failure to legislate.[116] Under the HRA a failure to legislate is expressly excluded from protection (see s 6(6)).

12.141 Most importantly, the principle of effectiveness[117] in EC law requires the national court to provide an effective remedy for established violations of Community obligations including relevant fundamental rights obligations.. Further, Article 10 (ex 5) EC requires national courts to ensure the effective protection of individual Community rights.[118]

12.142 Under the HRA, though, Article 13 ECHR (right to an effective remedy) has not been incorporated into English law. The basis for this was, no doubt, that the HRA itself was designed to provide an effective remedy for breaches of Convention rights.

12.143 However, the HRA does not allow primary legislation to be disapplied and, by s 4, only permits the Administrative Court to make a declaration of incompatibility in respect of it. In many, if not most, cases such declaration will not avail the claimant in the particular case. This is because a declaration of incompatibility does not affect the validity, continuing operation or enforcement of any incompatible primary legislation (HRA, s 4(6)(a)). Nor is it binding on the parties to the proceedings in which it is made (s 4(6)(b)). Further, where a declaration of incompatibility has been made, there is only limited power to take remedial action. By HRA, s 10 a Minister of the Crown may consider that there are compelling reasons to make such amendments to the statutory provision as he considers necessary to remove the incompatibility. However, he is not *required* so to act.[119]

12.144 The position is very different in EC law where it is now well established that domestic rules and judicial practices (including primary legislation) must be disapplied by the court insofar as they impede the full effectiveness of Community law rights.[120]

---

113 In practice whilst EC and HRA review is often similar there can be crucial differences. For a striking example, see the case study at paras 17.98 et seq., especially at paras 17.117 et seq.

114 But the Strasbourg Court has itself often referred to international instruments in reinforcing the substantive content of a Convention right. Those cases must be taken into account by the Administrative Court under HRA, s 2.

115 For an analysis of the EC damages case law, see Chapter 5. See, also, n 102 above on the HRA damages case law.

116 Joined Cases C-6 and 9/90 *Francovich and Bonifaci v Italy* [1991] ECR I–5357. The breach must, though, be sufficiently serious to attract damages. For a case in point, see Case C–48/93 *Factortame and Brasserie du Pecheur* [1996] ECR I–1029; *Factortame (No 5)* [2000] 1 AC 524.

117 See, in the context of remedy, paras 5.13–5.22.

118 Of the many cases see, eg, Case 33/76 *Rewe v Landwirtschaftskammer Saarland* [1976] ECR 1989, para 5.

119 *Quaere* whether domestic judicial review would lie against a Minister's refusal to act.

120 *R v Secretary of State for Transport, ex p Factortame (No 2)* [1991] AC 603: *R v Secretary of State for Employment, ex p Equal Opportunities Commission* [1995] 1 AC 1.

PART III

EC LAW AND JUDICIAL REVIEW
IN PRACTICE

13

STATE AID AND COMPETITION

A. Introduction—State Aid and Competition Compared

The state aid provisions of the EC Treaty are contained in Articles 87 and 88. They prohibit **13.01** the State from distorting competition by aiding undertakings unless the aid has been notified to, and approved by, the European Commission. Articles 81 and 82 of the Treaty prohibit undertakings from distorting competition by concluding anti-competitive agreements or abusing a dominant position.

Although the two sets of provisions (respectively, state aid and competition) complement **13.02** each other, state aid, properly understood, forms a sub-set of the competition rules contained in the EC Treaty. However, from the perspective of domestic public law, it is the state aid cases which are more likely to feature in a domestic judicial review challenge in the Administrative Court. Relevant parts of the state aid Treaty rules are directly effective (although have not been incorporated into domestic law) and affect many exercises of discretion by public bodies which result in the conferment of financial benefit to a third party.

13.03 State aid judicial review challenges are particularly likely to be brought by competitors who wish to prevent their rival companies from being financially advantaged. But many public bodies may grant a state aid without, necessarily, being aware of the relevant EC dimension.[1] Thus, what appears at first sight to be a purely domestic set of facts may contain a disguised EC state aid element. It should be borne in mind that in state aid cases there may be a breach of the relevant prohibitions without having to show a material effect on inter-state trade as in a pure competition case.

13.04 In contrast, EC competition disputes under Articles 81–82 are more likely to occur in a private law context although as will be seen the relevant principles may also be deployed by the Administrative Court or, more probably, by the Competition Appeal Tribunal in a public law context. The Competition Appeal Tribunal has a specialist review jurisdiction which is often very similar to that of judicial review as exercised in the Administrative Court. The nature of that specialist jurisdiction is separately examined below.

B. The Real Question in State Aid Cases

13.05 Importantly, once notification of a state aid has been given to the Commission the aid cannot generally be challenged in domestic judicial review proceedings. Any challenge must then be mounted in the European Court.[2] This is because it is the notification requirement, contained in Article 88(3) that creates directly effective rights. There may, though, be limited potential for a judicial review challenge in respect of acts by the State—following notification—that do offend against directly effective rights and which are related to the aid.[3]

13.06 In substance the real issue facing the Administrative Court will be whether the measure in question constitutes a state aid as defined in Article 87(1) (see below). Unless that question is determined affirmatively there can be no requirement to notify. Thus, the existence of a state aid is a condition precedent triggering the obligation to notify the Commission under Article 88(3). Where the Commission has not been notified, a decision by a public body to grant aid is unlawful and subject to judicial review in the Administrative Court. If there is an unlawful state aid the Administrative Court must, consistent with general principles of EC law, grant an effective remedy to the claimant (see below).

---

[1] As, eg, there may be state aid involved in selective local authority charges or taxes imposed by regulatory or other bodies. For an example of an unsuccessful state aid challenge in the context of art exports, see *R v Secretary of State for the National Heritage, ex p Getty Trust* [1997] Eu LR 407. *Quaere*, too, state aid in the context of public procurement: see paras 15.121 et seq.

[2] Case C–188/92 *TWD Textilwerke Deggendorf GmbH v Germany* [1994] ECR 1–833.

[3] As, eg, seeking to recover the aid before the conclusion of proceedings before the ECJ: see *Department of Trade v British Aerospace* [1991] 1 CMLR 65.

C. The Definition of an Aid—Essential Elements

The definition of state aid is ostensibly contained in Article 87(1)[4] EC which (materially) **13.07**
prohibits:

> any aid granted by a Member State or through State resources in any form whatsoever which
> distorts or threatens to distort competition by favouring certain undertakings or the produc-
> tion of certain goods . . . insofar as it affects trade between Member States.

However, the terminology is elliptical and the Administrative Court has found it necessary **13.08**
to develop a more systematic approach to the necessary constituent elements of state aid.

The Court of Appeal in *Professional Contractors Group Ltd v Commissioners of Inland Revenue*[5] **13.09**
endorsed the following criteria as being necessary to establish the existence of state aid:

(1) an aid in the sense of a benefit or advantage;
(2) which is granted by the State or through state resources;
(3) which favours certain undertakings over others (the 'selectivity' principle);
(4) which distorts or threatens to distort competition;
(5) which is capable of affecting trade between the United Kingdom and at least one other
    Member State; and,
(6) which has not been notified to the Commission.

D. Aid in the Sense of a Benefit or Advantage

The question of whether there is an aid in the sense of a benefit or advantage is, at least **13.10**
often, analytically separate from other issues. It is, in particular, frequently to be distinguished from the selectivity principle considered below.[6] At this stage, all that is—in
effect—under consideration is whether a particular state measure is (if other conditions are
satisfied) capable of being an aid at all.

It is important to bear in mind that an 'aid' in EC law is broad. It is not, for example, con- **13.11**
fined to a direct subsidy—such as a cash payment to a company—but is apt to include
measures such as tax-breaks 'which, in various forms, mitigate the charges which are
normally included in the budget of an undertaking'.[7] It may even include an omission.[8]

But there will not necessarily be a benefit or advantage merely because, following state **13.12**
measures, the budget of an undertaking has increased (or its charges have been lowered).
The essential concept is that of state activity which confers a relevant advantage.

---

[4] Note that by virtue of Art 87(2) EC certain types of aid *shall* be compatible with the common market
(non-discriminatory aid granted to individual consumers for a social purpose) and certain types of specified
aid may be considered to be compatible with the common market (as, eg, aid to remedy a serious economic
disturbance in the economy of a Member State).
[5] [2001] EWCA Civ 1945, para 28, per Robert Walker LJ adopting the formulation of Burton J at first
instance at [2001] Eu LR 514, para 55.
[6] Though not, perhaps, where the state is acting in a purely public as opposed to a market participant capacity:
see paras 13.30 et seq.
[7] Case 30/59 *Steenkolenmijnen* [1961] ECR 1, 19.
[8] See paras 13.22 et seq.

13.13 Certainly, where the State is itself in whole or in part a market participant, both the ECJ and the Administrative Court have adopted the so-called 'market investor', 'market creditor', or 'market conditions' test. The court asks itself whether, on the available evidence, the undertaking has received an economic advantage which it would not have secured 'under normal market conditions'.[9]

13.14 In *R v Secretary of State for Trade and Industry, ex p BT3G and One2One, (BT3G)*[10] for example, the Court of Appeal observed that '[t]he normal market conditions test involves comparing the position of the State with that of a commercial entity'.[11]

13.15 Clearly, the comparison between the State's position and that of a commercial entity may involve disputes of fact. More often, though, the issue will be whether such comparison can usefully—or as a matter of analysis—be made. *BT3G* was such a case. There, the much publicized auction of licences for third generation mobile phones resulted in an ostensible benefit to Vodafone and Orange by reason (applying the auction rules) of a deferment of payment by those two successful bidders until Vodafone had divested itself of Orange following the acquisition by Vodafone of Mannesmann AG which owned Orange. The considerable sums of money that the auction produced meant that the payment advantage thereby conferred was substantial.

13.16 BT3G and One2One brought judicial review proceedings against the Secretary of State claiming that this significant advantage constituted a state aid. As observed above, the Court of Appeal found it possible to apply a 'market conditions test'. It rejected the claimants' arguments that the test was inappropriate because the State was, in the conduct of the auction, acting not as a market participant but, rather, as a regulator. The court found that although the Secretary of State was, indeed, undertaking regulatory functions he was also acting in a commercial capacity because he was selling a valuable asset, namely the licences. On that footing a market conditions test could be used and—applying that test—there was no relevant benefit or advantage conferred on Vodafone and Orange.

13.17 But where there is no scope for employing a 'market conditions' test because the State's functions are (for example) entirely regulatory or otherwise sovereign or public then there may be little to separate the benefit/advantage element of state aid from the selectivity principle.[12]

13.18 Although the concept of state aid is wide certain measures have been held to fall outside its scope. Thus (albeit, in one sense, benefits) measures held not to be state aids on the facts of the particular case have included:

(1) a state benefit designed to compensate an undertaking for the costs of its public service obligations;[13]

---

[9] Case C–342 *Demenagements-Manutention Transport* [1999] ECR 1–3913, para 22. See, also, *Application by Peninsula Securities Ltd for Judicial Review* [1998] Eu LR 699.

[10] [2001] Eu LR 325.

[11] ibid para 71.

[12] See Advocate General Fennelly in *Banks v Coal Authority* Opinion, paras 18–20.

[13] Case 53/00 *Ferring v ACOSS* [2001] ECR I–9067. cf, though, Advocate General Leger's contrary reasoning in Case C–280/00 *Altmark*, Opinion 19 March 2002.

(2) a 'special charge' (as opposed to an 'aid') such as the selective imposition of a tax;[14]

(3) the removal of a pre-existing distortion of competition;[15]

(4) cases where the benefit is attributable not to an aid but, rather, to a particular set of facts.[16]

E. Granted by the State or through State Resources

In order to qualify as a state aid the measure must involve—whether by act or omission—either a direct grant by the State or a grant effected through state resources. **13.19**

The first aspect is straightforward—direct grants by the State are easy to identify and are capable of constituting state aid provided that the other criteria are satisfied. **13.20**

For a benefit to be granted through state resources there must be some relevant economic advantage gained through state, as opposed to third party, resources. **13.21**

So, the non-imposition of tax on a competitor undertaking is—whilst not amounting to a direct grant by the State—at least *capable* of constituting a state aid because it represents an economic advantage to the competitor secured through state resources being the loss of revenue to the State occasioned by its omission to tax. **13.22**

This analysis is borne out by two cases—one in Luxembourg, the other in the Court of Appeal (on appeal from the Administrative Court). **13.23**

In *R v Commissioners of Customs & Excise, ex p Lunn Poly*[17] the claimants sought judicial review in respect of differential rates of Insurance Premium Tax (IPT) on insurance contracts contained in the Finance Act 1997 contending that these differential rates were a state aid. **13.24**

One of the arguments advanced by Customs & Excise was that there could be no state aid because the lower rate of IPT was the standard rate. The higher rate, so the argument ran, did not therefore involve any transfer of state resources or a foregoing of tax revenue. **13.25**

This argument was rejected both at first instance and on appeal. In particular, in the Court of Appeal Clarke LJ observed that it was purely a 'matter of form' whether tax was expressed to be at 4 per cent standard rate with a higher rate of 17.5 per cent or, alternatively, at 17.5 per cent standard rate with a lower rate of 4 per cent.[18] **13.26**

---

[14] See, eg, *Professional Contractors Group Ltd v Commissioners of Inland Revenue* [2001] EWCA Crim 1945, para 34: 'For the State to confer a benefit on an identifiable group of undertakings is at first sight state aid. For the state to impose a detriment (for instance, a "windfall" tax on privatised utilities) can be state aid only if it can be seen as occasioning a corresponding advantage to identifiable business competitiors of those who have to bear the detriment.' In the latter case it would be the *omission* to charge that would constitute the state aid.

[15] See *R v Commissioners of Customs & Excise, ex p Lunn Poly Ltd* [1999] STC 350, 361, per Lord Woolf MR.

[16] See, eg, *BT v Director General of Telecommunications* (unreported, 4 August 2000) (greater costs borne by BT by virtue of a change in the statutory scheme); *R v Secretary of State for Trade and Industry, ex p BT3G and One2One* [2001] Eu LR 325 (fortuitous operation of the effect of contractual conditions benefiting one party rather than another).

[17] [1999] STC 350.

[18] [1999] Eu LR 653, 667–668.

13.27   Similarly, in *Ferring v ACOSS*[19] where tax had been imposed on one group of undertakings but not on another competitor group the ECJ held that there was a necessary tax exemption on the second group which amounted to an economic advantage granted through state resources.

13.28   But where the State requires one undertaking to subsidize another the position is less clear. The decision of the ECJ in *Preussen Elektra AG v Schleswag AG*[20] suggests that no economic advantage is, thereby, conferred through state resources.

13.29   In *Preussen Elektra* a German law required suppliers of electricity to purchase electricity from renewable energy sources at minimum prices. This was held by the ECJ not to involve any transfer of state resources to the producers. Thus, although the law conferred a clear economic advantage to the producers the advantage lacked the necessary connection with state resources to be capable of amounting to a state aid.[21] The court's reasoning in *Preussen Elektra* has not escaped criticism.[22]

F. The Selectivity Principle

13.30   As already observed the conferment of a benefit on one or more undertakings is not, of itself, sufficient to create a state aid. There is, nonetheless, a connection between the requirement of benefit and that of selectivity. Before a benefit can be said to have the potential for state aid the relevant benefit must favour certain undertakings over others.

13.31   The favouring of particular undertakings is to be contrasted with a 'general measure'. A general measure is intrinsically incapable of constituting an aid because it is, by definition, non-selective in nature.[23] The difficulty is, however, that the term 'general measure' has never been defined with any precision and that, in reality, there is often a de facto favouring.

13.32   Analytically, therefore, although the sole question should be whether or not there is a 'favouring' of certain undertakings such an approach would, in practice, undermine the importance of 'general measures' as an exception to the 'favouring' rule.

13.33   It has been suggested, with some force, that there are two issues to be considered when resolving selectivity.[24] These are whether:

(1) there is a de facto favouring of certain undertakings or the production of certain goods; and whether,

(2) the measure in question is a general measure.

---

[19] [2001] ECR I–9067.

[20] Case C–379/98 [2001] ECR 1–2099.

[21] ibid paras 59–61.

[22] See, eg, M Bronkers and R van der Vlies, 'The European Court's Preussen Elektra Judgment: Tensions Between EU Principles and National Renewable Energy Initiatives' [2001] ECLR 458.

[23] *Professional Contractors Group Ltd v Commissioners of Inland Revenue* [2001] EWCA Civ 1945, para 30.

[24] K Bacon, 'The Concept of State Aid: The Evolving Jurisdiction in the European and UK Courts' (2003) 24 ECLR 54–61.

De facto favouring is relatively easy to identify. As Lord Woolf MR succinctly put it (in the **13.34** context of taxation measures) in *R v Commissioners of Customs & Excise, ex p Lunn Poly*:[25]

> You can have a State aid in relation to a group of taxpayers where you have the position . . . of one body of taxpayers receiving a benefit which another body of taxpayers does not receive.

Thus, there will be at least potential selective favouring where, for example, a state measure **13.35** is available only to undertakings in one industrial sector,[26] or where only certain industries benefit from it.[27] Favouring may also occur in respect of differential treatment in favour of small over large undertakings or vice versa.[28]

Having ascertained that there is *prima facie* favouring the court must then examine **13.36** whether or not the measure in question is or is not a 'general measure'. Here, the case law suggests two categories.[29]

First, there is likely to be a general measure where a broad policy measure is applied on **13.37** objective criteria without regard to factors such as location, sector or undertaking. Even here, however, caution is needed. A measure that is potentially open to all undertakings may still amount to state aid in circumstances where only certain undertakings may, in practice, benefit from the measure. Thus, the Commission decided that tax relief contained in Italian legislation was not a general measure but was, rather, intended to benefit only certain undertakings and was, accordingly, a state aid.[30]

Secondly, there may still be a 'general measure' in the context of a particular measure as part **13.38** of a general system where certain undertakings are more affected by its operation than others but where this consequence is the product of some inherent feature of that general system. This follows from the reasoning in a series of cases in the ECJ on permissible derogations from general measures.

In *Sloman Neptun Schiffarts AG v Seebetriebsrat Bodo Ziesemer*[31] Advocate General Darmon[32] **13.39** considered that for such a measure to be general in nature it had to be a derogation that, by its very nature, derived from the scheme of the general measure in which it was set. Similarly, in *Italy v Commission*[33] the ECJ analysed a reduction in social security contributions for undertakings in the textiles industry in terms of whether the reduction could be justified by reference to an exemption from the normal operation of the system on the basis of the nature or general scheme of the system. It held that it could not. And in *Tierce Ladbroke v Commission*[34] the ECJ held that there was no relevant benefit accruing from a difference in treatment as the result of a state measure which could be justified by reasons relating to the logic of the system.

---

[25] [1999] Eu LR 653, 665.
[26] Case C–169/84, *Cdf Chimie AZF v Commission* [1990] ECR 1–3083, paras 22–23.
[27] Case 203/82, *Commission v Italy* [1983] ECR 2525, para 4.
[28] cf, eg, Case T–55/99 *CETM v Commission* [2000] ECR II–3207, para 40 and Case C–200/97 *Ecotrade* [1998] ECR 1–7907.
[29] Bacon (n 24 above).
[30] *Twentieth Report on Competition Policy* (1990), Pt 305; Commission Decision 92/389/EEC [1992] OJ L207/47.
[31] Cases C–72–73/91 [1993] ECR 1–887.
[32] Ibid 915.
[33] Case 173/73 [1974] ECR 709, para 15.
[34] Case C–353/95P, [1997] ECR 1–7007, paras 33–35.

13.40   As the above cases show it is important to identify the general system first before considering whether the contended state aid, by creating differential effect, still conforms to the logic of the general system. As Bacon has convincingly demonstrated[35] the English courts on judicial review have sometimes confused the particular measure with the general system and treated the former as if it were the latter.[36] The flaw in logic is that the court is then abandoning any necessary frame of reference by which to analyse the general system.

13.41   Further, there have been conflicting observations in the English courts as to the relevance of 'objective justification' in determining the existence of a general measure. Whilst it is, of course, permissible on objective grounds to evaluate whether or not a particular state measure is a justified derogation from a general system by virtue of the logic of the system it would seem clear that this does not mean that the choice of policies underlying the general system should be examined by the Administrative Court in order to determine whether they are objectively justified. The crucial factor in deciding whether there is a relevant general measure is the absence of an illegitimate differential effect as opposed to the choice of policy creating the general system in the first place.[37]

13.42   Finally, and importantly, the selectivity principle will always extend to a benefit that is derived from discretion. This means that a state measure that depends for its effect on particular undertakings on whether discretion is exercised is, necessarily, to be regarded as selective. Thus, in *Kimberley Clark*[38] French legislation under which redundancy payments could be made at the discretion of a public body was held to be state aid.

G. Distorts or Threatens to Distort Competition

13.43   In order to amount to state aid the measure in question must distort or threaten to distort competition by favouring certain undertakings or the production of certain goods.

13.44   In judicial review proceedings the claimant need not prove actual distortion of competition. It is enough merely to establish that the measure threatens to distort competition. This appears both from the express wording of Article 87(1) (above) and also from the case law.[39]

13.45   Distortion, or threat of distortion, of competition is easily presumed. Thus, in *Philip Morris v Commission*[40] the ECJ ruled that where a measure strengthens the position of an

---

[35] See n 24 above.

[36] See, eg, *Professional Contractors Group Ltd v Commissioners of Inland Revenue* [2001] EWCA Civ 1945, paras 49–51.

[37] *R (British Aggregates Association) v HM Treasury* [2002] 2 CMLR 51, paras 106–115, per Moses J. Contrast, though, the reasoning in *R v Commissioners of Customs & Excise, ex p Lunn Poly* [1999] Eu LR 653; *R v Secretary of State for Trade and Industry, ex p BT3G and One2One* [2001] Eu LR 325, paras 83–85 and *Professional Contractors Group Ltd v Commissioners of Inland Revenue* [2001] EWCA Civ 1945, paras 49–51.

[38] Case C–241/94 *France v Commission* [1996] ECR 4393, para 37. See, also, Case C–200/97, *Ecotrade Srl v AFS* [1998] ECR 1–7907, para 40; Case C–295/97 *Piaggio SpA v Ilfitalia SpA* [1999] ECR 1–3735, para 39.

[39] Case T–288/97, *Regione Autonoma Friuli Venezia Giulia v Commission* [2001] ECR II–1169, paras 49–50; Case T–35/99 *Keller SpA v Commission* [2002] ECR II–261, para 85.

[40] Case 730/79 [1980] ECR 2671, para 11.

undertaking compared with other undertakings competing in intra-Community trade, the latter are properly to be regarded as being affected.

Two cases show the operation of the presumption in action. In *Belgium v Commission*[41] the recipient of a state benefit exported some 40 per cent of its output to Member States. Given that excess production capacity existed in the relevant market the ECJ concluded that the Commission had been entitled to infer a distortion or threatening of distortion of competition by reason of aid which had the effect of reducing the recipient's financial costs in comparison with those of its competitors. **13.46**

In *Regione Autonoma Friuli Venezia Giulia v Commission*[42] the CFI ruled that even a modest amount of 'aid' in the context of the road haulage sector containing, as it did, a large number of small undertakings, was liable to strengthen the position of the recipient compared to its competitors and so distorted or threatened to distort competition. **13.47**

H. Capable of Affecting Trade

As with threatened distortion of competition considered immediately above, it is unnecessary for the claimant to establish an actual effect on inter-state trade. All that is required is that the measure, argued to be a state aid, is capable of affecting inter-state trade.[43] So even if there is no intra-Community trade when the state measure is effected, if it is foreseeable that exports will shortly be directed towards other Member States, then the measure is capable of amounting to an aid.[44] **13.48**

Moreover, it should not be assumed that only measures relating to exports and imports as between Member States are caught by Article 87(1). A relevant benefit may, for example, constitute a state aid because whilst enabling increase in production of a purely domestic product it thereby reduces opportunities for undertakings in other Member States to export to the market of the Member State concerned.[45] It is, therefore, capable of affecting inter-state trade. **13.49**

But Article 87(1) does not extend to trade with third countries. In *R v Secretary of State for National Heritage, ex p Getty Trust*[46] the Court of Appeal held that a state grant to two British museums to enable them to make a purchase of a work of art that would otherwise have been sold to a museum in California did not affect inter-Community trade. **13.50**

It has been held by the ECJ that, in theory at least, the *de minimis* rule does not apply in the state aid context. On that footing there is no particular threshold below which intra-Community trade is unaffected by an aid.[47] **13.51**

---

[41] Case 234/84 [1986] ECR 2263.
[42] Case T–288/97 [2001] ECR II–1169, para 46.
[43] See, eg, Case T–105/95 *FFSA v Commission* [1997] ECR II–229, para 169; Case T–206/97 *Alzetta Mauro v Commission* [2000] ECR II–2319, paras 79–80; *R v Secretary of State for the National Heritage, ex p Getty Trust* [1997] Eu LR 407, 417, per Neill LJ.
[44] Cases T–447–449/93 *AITEC v Commission* [1995] ECR II–1971, paras 139–140.
[45] See, eg, *France v Commission* [1988] ECR 4067, para 19.
[46] [1997] Eu LR 407.
[47] Case C–142/87 *Belgium v Commission* [1990] ECR 1–959, para 43. See also Case 730/79 *Philip Morris Holland BV v Commission* [1980] ECR 2671, 2699, per Advocate General Capotorti.

13.52   However, in practice, everything will depend on the context. In *France v Commission*[48] the ECJ also held that whether or not a state measure affects trade sufficiently to attract the operation of Article 87(1) is less a matter of quantity than of the particular factual circumstances. Thus, even aid of a relatively small amount could materially affect intra-Community trade where there was strong competition in the relevant sector.[49]

I. State Aid Challenges and Judicial Review

13.53   Challenge to an alleged state aid engages the vertical relationship between citizen and state where the State is, plainly, exercising public functions. In principle, therefore, judicial review is the appropriate procedure to employ.[50] It is the usual means of challenging alleged state aid to a competitor.[51] If the challenge succeeds the normal remedy will be an order requiring the aid to be repaid. But, as suggested below, the remedy sought may sometimes determine the nature of the proceedings.

13.54   Further, in terms of the above-mentioned elements of state aid, it is possible that some at least will involve complex disputes of fact. Certain criteria such as the existence of a benefit or advantage granted by the state or the favouring of certain undertakings over others are more likely to involve the application of law to agreed fact. But questions as to whether there is actual or threatened distortion of competition or the potentiality for relevant interstate trade being affected may well require disclosure and cross-examination.

13.55   The appropriateness of judicial review for the resolution of such issues in state aid cases should always be considered. Sometimes the existence of an alternative remedy such as a statutory appeal may need to be considered. Occasionally, as where the investigative process would distort the nature of the procedure, then judicial review may be avoided. This will, predominantly, be the position where some form of restitutionary relief is being sought. In some instances, however, the Administrative Court has—in the state aid context—been prepared to order disclosure or cross-examination[52] and the seeking of these and similar directions may be necessary. In perhaps the majority of such cases, though, the Administrative Court will seek to resolve factual issues on the evidence. As Lord Woolf MR observed in *R v Commissioners of Customs & Excise, ex p Lunn Poly Ltd*:[53]

> While the task may be difficult, the Divisional Court, and this court on appeal, is usually well able to decide the relevant facts without the need for cross-examination of the evidence which was given by affidavit.

13.56   Sometimes, the forum will enable or even require state aid issues to be litigated outside judicial review. Thus, in *GIL Insurance Ltd v Commissioners of Customs & Excise*[54] claims for

---

[48]   Case 259/85 *France v Commission* [1987] ECR 4393, para 24.

[49]   For other indications that the Commission does not treat minor 'aid' as constituting state aid, see, eg, Council Regulation (EC) 994/98, Art 2(1), Commission Regulation (EC) 69/2001, Art 2(1) and Commission Guidelines at [1996] OJ C213/4.

[50]   For the general reasons why this is so, see paras 1.100 et seq.

[51]   Plainly, however, the competitor recipient is an interested party and must be joined to the proceedings.

[52]   See, eg, *R v Attorney General, ex p ICI plc* [1987] 1 CMLR 72, 90.

[53]   [1999] STC 350, 360.

[54]   [2001] Eu LR 401.

restitution in respect of contended state aid were brought before the VAT tribunal. Similarly, in *Banks v Coal Authority*[55] state aid issues were canvassed by way of collateral challenge in defending a private law action for payment of a fee in respect of a licence to mine coal.

There have, nonetheless, now been several state aid challenges brought in judicial review **13.57** proceedings. The majority of these have involved the argument that particular state financial measures constitute a state aid but that such measures have neither been notified to, nor approved by, the European Commission.

There are, though, other possibilities. For example, a recipient of state benefit may wish to **13.58** act pre-emptively so as to obtain declaratory relief to the effect that the benefit is not an 'aid' and should not, therefore, be notified to the Commission. Or, a competitor may be able to seek judicial review to compel the State to take enforcement proceedings to recover aid where the Commission has ordered the recovery of unlawfully paid state aid.[56] Judicial review may also be possible to seek relief in respect of notified aid which is sought to be recovered before the conclusion of proceedings before the ECJ.[57] In *R v MAFF, ex p First City Trading*[58] the relevant scheme sought to be challenged by way of judicial review had been notified to the Commission but had not been decided upon by the Commission.

As outlined above, whether or not state aid issues are raised within judicial review proceed **13.59** ings the essential issue, according to the relevant principles of what constitutes an aid, is whether an unlawful state aid has been granted. It is, therefore, immaterial whether in conventional review terms the State acted rationally (or even fairly). As Lord Woolf MR put it in *R v Commissioners of Customs & Excise, ex p Lunn Poly*:[59]

> Whether or not there has been a contravention of the final sentence of art [88(3)] can only fall to be determined if the court decides for itself whether or not these matters complained of constitute an aid which should have been notified to the Commission. The fact that the commissioners believed that they have acted legitimately in promoting the legislation cannot affect this issue.

In other words, the Administrative Court must determine the existence or otherwise of a **13.60** state aid objectively.[60] If the court has doubts about the matter it is entitled to seek clarification from either the Commission or the ECJ. The Commission in its notice on co-operation between national courts and the Commission in the state aid field actively encourages this course.[61] The Commission's answer will not bind the Administrative Court but, of course, that court is always entitled to request a preliminary ruling if it still entertains doubt as to how to resolve any of the applicable principles.

---

[55] Case C–390/98 [2001] 3 CMLR 51.

[56] The State is under a duty to take steps to recover unlawfully paid state aid in such circumstances: see Council Regulation (EC) 659/1999, Art 14(1). It seems probable that the regulation creates directly effective rights in this respect.

[57] See n 3 above.

[58] [1997] Eu LR 195.

[59] [1999] STC 350, 358.

[60] Of the many cases see, eg, Cases T–195/01 R and T–207/01 R, *Government of Gibraltar v Commission* [2001] ECR II–3915, para 75.

[61] OJ [1995] L312/8.

J. State Aid Remedies in Judicial Review Cases

13.61 In principle the Administrative Court must do all in its power to give full and effective protection where it finds there to be an unlawful state aid. This obligation, resting on all national courts, has been described by the ECJ as 'a duty to provide protection in the final judgment it gives ... in a case against the consequences of unlawful implementation of aid'.[62]

13.62 The conventional orders obtainable on judicial review are well suited to providing such relief in many, perhaps most, cases. Thus, where aid has been paid out, a declaration that the aid has been granted in violation of Article 88(3) requires—in the majority of instances—recovery by the State of the moneys so paid.[63] In addition, or as an alternative, to declaratory relief the court may make a mandatory order to similar effect. Damages may also lie for loss sustained by virtue of any competitive advantage lost through payment of the aid.

13.63 Although, in such cases, the State is in breach of its duty of notification under Article 88(3) this does not entitle the recipient of the aid to refuse to make repayment. The State's obligation is to ensure that no benefit is obtained from the illegal payment.

13.64 There may, however, be exceptional cases where the recipient of aid is entitled to contend that repayment should not be ordered. This will be so, primarily, where a general principle of EC (or domestic) law, such as that of legitimate expectation, comes into conflict with the state aid rules. So, a recipient of unlawful aid may be able to argue that it had been entitled to rely, and did rely, on a legitimate expectation engendered by the State that the aid was lawful and, on that footing, to argue that it should not be required to repay the aid.[64]

13.65 In such circumstances the Administrative Court will be required to weigh up the various interests involved.[65] But the way in which the court conducts this exercise must not render the recovery required by EC law practically impossible and it must ensure that the interests of the European Community are fully considered.[66]

13.66 Orders directed towards recovery of payment of aid are by no means the sole remedy available to the Administrative Court. In some instances, of course, the aid will not yet have been paid. A declaration that an unlawful aid is proposed and/or a prohibitory order or an injunction preventing the payment of aid will, then, usually be the appropriate relief.

13.67 However, there will be cases in which unlawful aid has been paid out where further or other remedies than recovery may be required. For example, where the court determines that unlawful aid has been granted through differential taxation, with the effect that certain competitors have been advantaged by having to pay a lower tax rate, the court must be

---

[62] Case C–39/94 *SFEI v La Poste* [1996] ECR 1–3547, para 67.

[63] ibid para 72, per Advocate General Jacobs.

[64] Case C–5/89 *Commission v Germany* [1990] ECR I–3437, para 16; Case C–310/99 *Italy v Commission* [2002] ECR I-2289 para 103.

[65] Case 94/87 *Commission v Germany* [1989] ECR 175, para 12.

[66] Case C–142/87 *Belgium v Commission* [1990] ECR 1–959, para 61; Case C–480/98 *Spain v Commission* [2000] ECR I–8717, para 34.

astute not to make an order for recovery that has as its only objective placing of competitors on an equal footing following the making of the order. The obligation on the State (and the court) is a different one. It is to recover the aid so as to restore the competitive situation to that prevailing before the aid was granted.

In *Banks v Coal Authority*[67] the ECJ held that, in such a case, the court should determine **13.68** the normal application of tax charges under the general tax system and then order those who were charged at the unlawful lower rate to pay an amount to compensate for their previous tax reduction.

What the Administrative Court could not do, on that analysis, would be to order that the **13.69** claimant be refunded for having to pay tax at the higher rate in the past so as to eliminate the distortion of competition. Such an order would merely be to effect state aid being granted to additional operators.[68] Different considerations may, however, attach to future measures since the differential element responsible for producing an unlawful aid can, presumably, then be eliminated.

Other relief which may be afforded by the Administrative Court includes damages against **13.70** the State.[69] The circumstances in which an award may be made are those which prevail for any award of damages for breach of Community law and are considered separately in more detail.[70] Essentially, there are three necessary conditions for such an award:

(1) the rules of law infringed must be intended to create rights for individuals,
(2) the breach must be sufficiently serious, and
(3) there must be a direct causal link between the relevant breach of obligation and the damage suffered by the parties in question.[71]

In the state aid context it is clear that, as a matter of principle, damages are capable of being **13.71** awarded by a breach of the State's duty under Article 88(3) since (see above) that provision creates directly effective rights.

Provided that the other two necessary conditions are satisfied it seems that disadvantaged **13.72** competitors may seek damages at least where repayment of aid cannot be recovered.[72] Persons other than competitors may also be able to seek damages.[73] For such damages to be

---

[67] Case C–390/98 [2001] 3 CMLR 51, para 75.

[68] ibid para 80. See, also, analysis of the Court of Appeal in *R v Secretary of State for Trade and Industry, ex p BT3G and One2One* [2001] Eu LR 325.

[69] This is, however, to be distinguished from damages against a private body based on a Commission decision that the private body had unlawfully used state aid. In the latter case there is no available cause of action since Commission decisions on state aid were always directed to the state: see *Betws Anthracite Ltd v DSK Anthrazit Ibbenburen GMBH* [2003] EWHC 2403, [2004] 1 All ER 1237.

[70] See paras 5.85–5.167.

[71] Cases C–46 and 48/93 *Brasserie du Pecheur SA v Germany* [1996] ECR 1–1029, para 51.

[72] *Banks v Coal Authority* [2001] ECR I–6117, para 80. See, also, Case 142/87, *Belgium v Commission* [1990] ECR 1–959, 985, per Advocate General Tesauro.

[73] See, eg, Case 52/84 *Commission v Belgium* [1986] ECR 89, 99, per Advocate General Lenz, suggesting that third parties such as creditors of an affected undertaking if it had to go into liquidation because of recovery of unlawfully paid aid might be able to claim damages in the national courts. *Quaere* whether the recipient of unlawful aid may be able to claim damages against the State: contrast per Advocate General Tesauro in Case 142/87 *Belgium v Commission* [1990] ECR 1–959, 986 with Advocate General Slynn in Cases 106–120/87 *Asteris v Greece* [1988] ECR 5515, 5530.

capable of being awarded in judicial review proceedings persons who wish to claim them should, at least ordinarily, seek to be made parties to the proceedings as an interested party.[74]

13.73 Questions of interim relief are also likely to arise in state aid judicial review cases. This will usually occur where a state measure, contended to be an unlawful 'aid', has not been notified to the Commission. There may be a lengthy delay before a full judicial review hearing and the Administrative Court may, for example, have sought clarification from the Commission[75] or made a reference to the ECJ under Article 234 EC thereby increasing the delay before the matter is finally resolved. In such cases the Commission has observed that the national court can usually adopt appropriate interim measures.[76] Further, Council Regulation (EC) 659/1999, Article 14(3) requires the Member State to take all necessary steps, including provisional measures, where there are proceedings to recover unlawful aid.

13.74 Whether a measure should be suspended or recovery ordered ad interim will depend upon the usual factors relevant to the grant of interim relief in EC cases which have been separately considered.[77]

13.75 The position is more complicated where the Commission has declared an aid to be unlawful but where the Commission's decision is itself subject to challenge by annulment before the ECJ.

13.76 This is what occurred in *Department of Trade v British Aerospace*.[78] In that case the court made an interim order suspending recovery on the footing that if—as happened[79]—the action for annulment succeeded it would mean that the claim by the United Kingdom authorities for recovery would be struck out. However, to the extent that this was the sole rationale for making the order it means that the merits of the case were not considered. This is, arguably, wrong in principle.[80]

K. Approach of the Administrative Court in State Aid Cases

13.77 Most of the judicial review cases before the Administrative Court on state aid, to date, have been challenges brought in respect of unnotified and unapproved state aid.[81] There have also been isolated challenges to other forms of contended state aid.[82]

---

[74] As in the *BT3G* case, for which see paras 13.14 et seq. and also n 51 above.

[75] See para 13.60.

[76] See Notice on Co-operation between National Courts and the Commission in the State Aid Field, para 13.

[77] See paras 3.123–3.148.

[78] [1991] 1 CMLR 165.

[79] Case C–294/90 *British Aerospace v Commission* [1992] ECR I–493.

[80] See, eg, T Sharpe, 'The Role of National Courts in relation to Community Law of State Aids' in I Harden (ed), *State Aid: Community Law and Policy* (1993).

[81] Note, especially, *R v Attorney General, ex p ICI plc* [1987] 1 CMLR 72; *R v Secretary of State for National Heritage, ex p Getty Trust* [1997] Eu LR 407; *R v Commissioners of Customs & Excise, ex p Lunn Poly Ltd* [1999] STC 350; *R v Secretary of State and Industry, ex p BT3G and One2One* [2001] Eu LR 325; *Professional Contractors Group Ltd v Commissioners of Inland Revenue* [2001] EWCA Civ 1945. There has also been one statutory appeal to the Administrative Court in respect of a state aid: see *BT v Director General of Telecommunications* (unreported, 4 August 2000).

[82] See, eg, *R v MAFF, ex p First City Trading* [1997] Eu LR 195 (challenge to notified but unapproved aid); *R v Secretary of State for Trade and Industry, ex p Isle of Wight Council* (unreported, 4 April 2000) (challenge to decision to exclude an area of the United Kingdom from eligibility for state aid under an approved scheme).

Two challenges—those in *R v Attorney General, ex p ICI plc*[83] and *R v Commissioners of*   **13.78**
Customs & Excise, ex p Lunn Poly Ltd[84]—have been successful. In the first of these, ICI succeeded in challenging a decision of the Inland Revenue to give preferential tax treatment to
its principal competitors. In *Lunn Poly*[85] the claimants succeeded in challenging primary
legislative provisions in the Finance Act 1997. The Court of Appeal (endorsing the
approach of the Divisional Court) held that differential rates of Insurance Premium Tax
introduced in the 1997 Act amounted to a state aid to those taxpayers charged at the lower
rate of tax.

Since *Lunn Poly*, state aid challenges have been advanced in a series of cases. These chal-   **13.79**
lenges have largely been directed to state measures (not notified as state aids to the
Commission) which have been alleged to be discriminatory and, hence, in breach of the
selectivity principle (see above).

The approach of the Administrative Court has, so far at least, been unreceptive. This may   **13.80**
be because of the unfamiliarity of domestic courts with the difficult concepts that state aid
principles create. Most notably, as suggested above,[86] the English courts have not found it
easy to apply the selectivity principle and have sometimes confused the meaning of a 'general measure' with the measure under challenge as well as seeking to import inappropriate
notions of objective justification into that principle.

The practitioner should, therefore, certainly resort to Luxembourg case law in this area   **13.81**
rather than over-relying on the previous cases in the Administrative Court and above. For
reasons developed elsewhere, the Administrative Court is required to follow Luxembourg
jurisprudence in the event of conflict with domestic decisions.[87]

L. Competition Law in a National Context— the Administrative Court and the Competition Appeal Tribunal Compared

EC competition law is regulated by Articles 81–82 (ex 85–86) EC. Essentially, Article 81   **13.82**
prohibits restrictive trade practices on the part of undertakings or associations of undertakings which may affect trade between Member States and which have as their object or effect
the prevention, restriction or distortion of competition within the Community. Article 82
prohibits the abuse of a dominant position by an undertaking which affects or may affect
intra-Community trade. Both Articles are: (1) directed to undertakings, and (2) directed
to the effect of anti-competitive practices on inter-Member State trade. These prohibitions
are mirrored, albeit in a domestic context, in the Chap I and Chap II prohibitions in the
Competition Act 1998.

---

[83] [1987] 1 CMLR 72.
[84] [1999] STC 350.
[85] See, also, paras 13.24 et seq.
[86] See paras 13.30–13.42.
[87] See paras 2.60 et seq.

13.83   The detail of the ECJ case law on Articles 81–82 is outside the scope of this work and is, in any event, peripheral to any discussion of domestic public law.[88] However, judicial review of competition decisions having *national,* as opposed to inter-State, effect is increasingly likely to take place in a statutory context. It is here that the EC competition rules and the principles of domestic judicial review interact.

13.84   UK competition decision-making now consists, largely, of review by the Competition Appeal Tribunal[89] (CAT) under a new statutory judicial review jurisdiction directed towards monopolies, mergers, and restrictive trade practices both generally and in respect of particular regulatory sectors. Although, as explained above, the developing area of state aid also represents a decision-making process that affects competition, state aid is concerned with inter-State trade, is not governed by discrete statutory review procedures and judicial review proceedings in respect of most state aid issues take place (as did the former monopoly/merger control)[90] in the Administrative Court in the usual way.

13.85   UK competition law is primarily—though not exclusively—founded on two statutes that are largely reflected in CAT jurisdiction. These are the Enterprise Act 2002 (enacted on 7 November 2002) and the Competition Act 1998. Also relevant is the Communications Act 2003 which creates a new sectoral regulator—Ofcom—in the field of communications and which is subject to a similar statutory judicial review regime, also applied by CAT, to that created under the Enterprise Act.

13.86   The specialized jurisdiction of CAT is outlined below. As will be seen, the principles of Administrative Court judicial review (including HRA principles where relevant) continue to apply to certain hearings before CAT. For this reason much of the earlier judicial review case law under RSC Ord 53 and CPR Pt 54, mainly in relation to monopoly/merger control, remains of relevance. That case law is examined below.

13.87   However, CAT's jurisdictional remit is usually broader than that of the Administrative Court since it may (and usually will) under certain statutory provisions[91] consider the factual merits of decisions, which of itself,[92] generally, remains a dubious ground of review in judicial review cases in the Administrative Court.[93]

---

[88]   It should, nonetheless, be borne in mind that by Article 86—subject to an exception for services of general economic interest or activities having the character of a revenue-producing monopoly—the EC competition obligations apply equally to 'public undertakings and undertakings to which Member States grant special or exclusive rights'. This has at least potential implications for public law challenges founded on alleged violation of EC competition obligations by State entities and is mirrored in the Competition Act 1998, Sch 3, para 4. The public law question at issue (which has been considered by the new Competition Appeal Tribunal: see below) is whether, in the circumstances of a particular case, a public body susceptible to judicial review is subject to EC and/or national competition prohibitions.

[89]   There is an appeal to the Court of Appeal (see below).

[90]   Restrictive trade practices came before the Restrictive Trade Practices Court and rarely led to conventional judicial review since there was a direct appeal from that court to the Court of Appeal.

[91]   See, eg, Communications Act 2003, s 192(6).

[92]   Even as augmented by proportionality (for which see Chapter 11) judicial review defers to the discretionary area of judgment of the decision-maker. That is why judicial review of competition decisions has rarely been successful being seen largely as an illegitimate challenge to the merits of regulatory decisions: see *R (T-Mobile, Vodafone) v Competition Commission, Director General of Telecommunications* [2003] EWHC 1566, para 132, per Moses J.

[93]   See paras 1.111–1.119.

Detailed examination of competition disputes, even against public undertakings, is not **13.88** generally a process suited to traditional judicial review involving, as it does, economic assessment, a large amount of evidence and the implementation of detailed economic criteria. However, this is exactly the rationale for a specialist tribunal such as CAT which has the legal and specialist expertise to move between the public law issues that arise in competition disputes as well as being in a position to investigate the evidence in much greater detail than would the Administrative Court.

M. Relationship between UK Competition Rules under Articles 81–82 EC and EC Law in Domestic Judicial Review Competition Cases

There is an important relationship between the EC competition rules under the Treaty and **13.89** competition decisions made by UK regulators and reviewed by CAT (or, in appropriate cases, the Administrative Court). Despite the fact that EC competition law is concerned with the effect on 'trade between member states' there are three over-arching aspects to understand that bring the EC and domestic law competition regimes together.

First, there may be a factual overlap leading to issues of EC law and the relationship of EC **13.90** law with national law. This is so because the effect of anti-competitive practices may distort both national trade and trade between Member States. The question of enforcement of national law may thus be dependent in part on EC principles.

In the event of a conflict between EC and national law, EC competition rules will prevail. **13.91** This follows, inevitably, from the principle of supremacy of Community law.[94]

However, this does not prevent national competition laws from being applied in conjunc- **13.92** tion with Community law. As the ECJ observed in *Walt Wilhelm v Bundeskartellamt*[95] national authorities may:

> intervene against an agreement, in application of their national law, even when the examination of the position of that agreement with regard to the Community rules is pending before the Commission subject, however, to the proviso that such application of the national law may not prejudice the full and uniform application of the Community law.[96]

This has the consequence (subject, however, to Regulation (EC) 1/2003 below) that, even **13.93** following Community approval, national law may legitimately prohibit at least certain activity on competition grounds.

A new competition enforcement regime (Regulation (EC) 1/2003) came into force in **13.94** May 2004. This places more obvious competition enforcement responsibilities on national authorities, including the national courts, and thereby enables the Commission to concentrate on the more serious cartels. In particular, national courts now have power under Article 6 of the regulation to exempt agreements which infringe Article 81(1).

---

[94] See paras 2.60 et seq.
[95] Case 14/68 [1966] CMLR 100.
[96] ibid para 7. See, also, R Galinsky 'The Resolution of Conflicts between UK and Community Competition Law' (1994) 15 ECLR 16.

13.95   Regulation (EC) 1/2003 makes it clear that Articles 81–82 EC must be applied by national courts where national competition law is being applied to Article 81 and 82 prohibitions and that the application of national law should not result in a different outcome than that produced by applying Article 81. By virtue of Article 3(2) of Regulation (EC) 1/2003 permitted agreements under Article 81 cannot be prohibited under national law. Agreements which are precluded under Article 81 cannot be permitted under national law.[97] As far as Article 82 is concerned, there does not have to be the same convergence between EC and national law as under Article 81 but, consistent with the principle of the supremacy of EC law, national courts must disapply national competition provisions that are inconsistent with EC law.[98]

13.96   In cases where the EC Commission is taking action in respect of an overlapping infringement, the national courts have obligations in EC law not to take action that would conflict with a Commission decision,[99] and (at least generally) not to take a decision that is inconsistent with a Commission decision.[100] Importantly, where appropriate and to ensure consistent application of EC enforcement, the national court should consider seeking a preliminary ruling from the ECJ.

13.97   Secondly, where—as with the Communications Act 2003—a statute is enacted to reflect requirements of Community law or where—as in the Competition Act 1998 (as amended by the Enterprise Act 2002)—a statute expressly incorporates Community competition principles and compatibility of national practice with Community law[101] then the relationship between national law and Community competition law is obvious.

13.98   Thirdly, Articles 81–82 are directly effective.[102] This means that individuals may invoke their provisions before the national courts (including the Administrative Court). According to Article 9(3) of the former Regulation (EEC) 17/62:

> As long as the Commission has not initiated any procedure under Articles 2 [negative clearance], 3 [investigation either on application of third parties or on own initiative], or 6 [exemption] the authorities of the Member States shall remain competent to apply Article 85(1) [now 81(1)] and Article 86 [now 82].

13.99   However, at least as important in reviewing domestic competition decisions with an EC public law element are the domestic judicial review principles and the approach formerly taken by the Administrative Court in competition cases especially those relating to monopolies and mergers. These cases are relevant to an understanding of the way in which public law issues in competition cases will have to be addressed under the new statutory regimes.

---

   [97] See para 13.91 and n 94 above.
   [98] Case C–198/01 *Consorzio Industrie Fiammiferi (CIF) v Autorita Garante della Concorrenza e del Mercato* [2003] ECR I–8055, para 49.
   [99] Regulation (EC) 1/2003, Art 15. But the national courts need not follow a Commission decision where the legal and factual context of the case being examined by the Commission was not completely identical to that before the national court: see *Crehan v Inntrepreneur Pub Co (CPC)* [2006] UKHL 38, The Times, 20 July 2006. See also Advocate General Cosmas in Case C–344/98 *Masterfoods Ltd v HB Ice Cream Ltd* [2000] ECR I–369, para 16, distinguishing Case C–234/89 *Delimitis v Henninger Brau AG* [1991] ECR I–935, 995.
   [100] See, eg, Regulation (EC) 1/2003, Art 16.
   [101] See Competition Act 1998, ss 10 and 60.
   [102] They have both horizontal and vertical effect and so may be used in private law causes of action as well as in public law proceedings.

N. Relationship between Administrative Law Principles and the Review of Competition Decisions

This section focuses, principally, on judicial review cases in respect of the former monopolies and mergers regime since that is where most of the public law challenges were directed against. It should, however, be borne in mind that the effect of the Enterprise Act 2002 is to replace the monopoly and merger control regime that had previously existed under the Fair Trading Act 1973 and Competition Act 1998[103] with an entirely new regime; the first major change since the introduction of merger control in 1965. CAT will decide cases—so far as monopolies and mergers are concerned—under the new rather than the old regime. **13.100**

Under the 1973 Act there was, essentially, a three-stage decision-making process. The Director General of Fair Trading (DGFT) was required to carry out a preliminary investigation of monopolies/mergers (whether or not they had actually taken place) so as to advise the Secretary of State whether there were outstanding competition questions that should be investigated by the Competition Commission (CC).[104] The Secretary of State, in turn, decided whether to refer the case to the CC. If the CC considered that there was a monopoly or merger likely to operate against the public interest then the Secretary of State had to decide what remedial action to take. **13.101**

Traditionally, grounds for domestic judicial review challenges in this area have embraced: (1) error of law, (2) irrationality, (3) procedural unfairness. Other potential bases for review need, also, to be considered (especially in the light of human rights or EC law overlap). These include proportionality[105] and no evidence/error of fact. Each of these grounds is considered below. **13.102**

Error of law

An error of law may result from a public body acting outside its jurisdiction so that its decision is ultra vires. Alternatively, it may result from such body failing to interpret a statutory provision correctly or failing to take relevant considerations into account or taking irrelevant considerations into account. **13.103**

---

[103] There was an overlap between monopoly investigation under the 1973 and 1998 Acts. Most single firm monopolies were investigated under the 1998 Act whereas industry-wide investigations were conducted under the Fair Trading Act 1973.

[104] CC was itself formerly known as the Monopolies and Mergers Commission. The new regime is governed by the Enterprise Act 2002. The initial investigation into a merger is carried out by the OFT. If the OFT decides that a merger has resulted or may be expected to result in a substantial lessening of competition, then the OFT is required to make a reference to the CC. If the CC, following its investigation, reaches the same conclusion as the OFT it must, in its report, state what action (if any) it proposes to take. A parallel regime applies to market investigations where the OFT or other sectoral regulator may make a reference to the CC to investigate a particular market where there is a suspicion that an aspect of the market is affecting competition. In certain circumstances the Secretary of State may become involved in decision-making in respect of mergers or the making of references to the CC in respect of market investigation.

[105] If and to the extent that the issues raised fall within the scope of EC law then, of course, all the general principles discussed in Part II may be relevant. For discussion of whether issues fall within the scope of EC law, see paras 6.31 et seq.

13.104   An instance of a challenge raising lack of jurisdiction is afforded by the facts, arising out of rival bidding for Distillers, in *R v Monopolies and Mergers Commission, ex p Argyll Group plc*.[106] In that case, Guinness's proposal was referred by the Secretary of State to the Monopolies and Mergers Commission (later to become CC) for inquiry and report under s 75 of the Fair Trading Act 1973.

13.105   Before the Commission had organized, in accordance with its usual procedure, a group of members for the purposes of investigating the proposal, representatives of Guinness met with the Chairman of the Commission. Information was provided as to certain of Distillers' activities which might not form part of a Guinness take-over. As a result the Chairman alone decided that the proposal had been 'abandoned' within the meaning of s 75(5) of the 1973 Act and recommended to the Secretary of State that the reference be laid aside. Guinness then made a revised bid for Distillers. The claimants, who were bidding in competition with Guinness, applied for judicial review of the Commission's decision that the proposal had been abandoned. At first instance Macpherson J refused the application.

13.106   However, the Court of Appeal held that although the decision on the abandonment of the proposal was well founded, the Chairman—acting alone—had no power to take the decision and the Commission did not have power tacitly to approve the Chairman's decision. The decision had to be taken by a properly constituted group of members of the Commission.

13.107   Nonetheless, although the vires challenge was correctly made, the Court of Appeal, in the event, refused relief to the claimant as a matter of discretion. Discretion to refuse relief is an important aspect of the Administrative Court's jurisdiction in judicial review cases especially in a commercial context. It is examined in more detail below.

13.108   Although it is also, clearly, an error of law to fail to interpret a statute correctly, care is needed in the context of financial regulation such as that arising in respect of monopoly/merger control. There, the regulator has often been held to enjoy a discretionary area of judgment in the interpretation of particular statutory phrases.

13.109   In *R v Monopolies and Mergers Commission, ex p South Yorkshire Transport*,[107] for example, one question for the House of Lords was the proper interpretation of the phrase 'a substantial part of the United Kingdom' in s 64(3) of the 1973 Act.

13.110   The Secretary of State had made a reference to the MMC under s 64 following the acquisition by South Yorkshire of certain other bus companies. The area defined in the reference represented 1.65 per cent (area), 3.2 per cent (population) and 4.04 per cent (vehicle mileage) of the United Kingdom. The Commission's Report concluded, amongst other things, that the defined area represented a 'substantial part of the United Kingdom' so as to satisfy a necessary statutory precondition of its jurisdiction. The House of Lords held that the Commission's approach was 'broadly correct' and disclosed no misdirection in law. Whilst the question was one of jurisdiction the test was 'broad enough to call for the exercise of judgment'.

---

[106] [1986] 1 WLR 763.
[107] [1993] 1 WLR 23.

In particular, Lord Templeman said:[108]   **13.111**

> Even eliminating inappropriate senses of 'substantial' one is still left with a meaning broad
> enough to call for the exercise of judgment rather than an exact quantitative measurement.
> Approaching the matter in this light I am quite satisfied that there is no ground for interfer-
> ence by the court, since the conclusion at which the Commission arrived was well within the
> permissible field of judgment.

A similarly broad approach has been applied in judicial review applications where the   **13.112**
alleged error of law is founded on a challenge to the content of Commission reports in
merger cases on the basis that irrelevant considerations have been taken into account.
In *R v Monopolies and Mergers Commission, ex p Visa International Service Association*[109]
Hodgson J observed, in respect of one such challenge, that:

> the Report must not be read as if it were a statute or a judgment ... It should be read in a gen-
> erous not a restrictive way and the Court should be slow to disable [the Commission] from
> recommending action considered to be in the public interest or to prevent the Secretary of
> State from acting thereon unless any perceived errors of law are both material and substantial.

Irrationality

The courts have, generally, been unwilling to interfere with the exercise of judgment or dis-   **13.113**
cretion by a monopolies regulator on the basis of *Wednesbury* irrationality.[110] So, the fact of
either an adverse or a favourable Commission Report has not been considered to circumscribe the freedom—in terms of rationality—of the Secretary of State to act differently.

Thus, in *R v Secretary of Trade and Industry, ex p Anderson Strathclyde plc*[111] the Secretary of   **13.114**
State refused to take action following an adverse Commission Report. Dunn LJ observed
as follows:

> In my judgment, the Act read as a whole shows that the Secretary of State is not bound by the
> conclusions of the majority of the Commission, that he has a wide discretion in deciding
> whether to make any order at all, and in exercising that discretion he is entitled to take into
> account all the relevant circumstances, and to consider the opinion of the minority of the
> Commission, and also representations and advice from persons other than members of the
> Commission ... it was a matter for the minister, in his unfettered discretion, to choose
> between those two views, taking into account any other relevant matters including the advice
> which he received from the Director General. He preferred the view of the minority. Whether
> he was right or wrong about that is a matter of political judgment, and not a matter of law.[112]

A comparable situation arose in *Lonrho plc v Secretary of State for Trade and Industry*.[113]   **13.115**
There, the Secretary of State failed to publish a report by inspectors and by the Serious
Fraud Office or to make a reference to the Monopolies and Mergers Commission following
Al Fayed's take-over of Harrods despite being asked to do so by Lonhro. An irrationality

---

[108] ibid 32–3.
[109] [1991] CCLR 13. This case was further considered in *R v MMC and Secretary of Trade and Industry, ex p Ecando* [1993] COD 89.
[110] See, further, at paras 11.79–11.80.
[111] [1983] 2 All ER 233.
[112] ibid 241–2.
[113] [1989] 1 WLR 525.

challenge failed even though no reasons were given. In the House of Lords Lord Keith stated that 'whether or not a particular commercial activity is or is not in the "public interest" is very much a matter of political judgment'. He said that 'the courts must be careful not to invade the political field and substitute their own judgment for that of the minister. The courts judge the lawfulness, not the wisdom, of the decision.'

13.116 But there are necessary limits to the deference that the Administrative Court will show to a regulator's judgment even in the context of an irrationality challenge. As Kay J has observed:

> Whilst accepting that in matters of judgment on technical aspects of a matter, the court will be slow to interfere with the conclusions of an expert tribunal, when it is submitted that the whole process of assessment is on a fundamentally flawed basis and the conclusion has resulted in decisions adverse to the applicant, the Court has a duty to consider such arguments and cannot shirk its responsibilities by saying 'this is all very technical' and bow to the 'wisdom' of the expert tribunal. To do so . . . would be to put the expert tribunal above the scrutiny of judicial review.[114]

Procedural fairness

13.117 There are a number of cases that have addressed the application of procedural fairness in the context of the Fair Trading Act 1973. In *Hoffmann-La Roche v Secretary of State for Trade and Industry*[115] Lord Diplock held as follows:

> The Commission makes its own investigation into facts. It does not adjudicate upon a lis between contending parties. The adversary procedure followed in a court of law is not appropriate to its investigations. It has a wide discretion as to how they should be conducted. Nevertheless, I would accept that it is the duty of the Commissioners to observe the rules of natural justice in the course of their investigation—which means no more than that they must act fairly by giving to the person whose activities are being investigated a reasonable opportunity to put forward facts and arguments in justification of his conduct of these activities before they reach a conclusion which may affect him adversely.[116]

13.118 He also observed that:

> Even in judicial proceedings in a court of law, once a fair hearing has been given to the rival cases presented by the parties the rules of natural justice do not require the decision maker to disclose what he is minded to decide so that the parties may have a further opportunity of criticising his mental processes before he reaches a final decision.[117]

13.119 In *R v Monopolies and Mergers Commission, ex p Matthew Brown plc*[118] McPherson J said:

> The timetable and conduct of the case by the commission must be looked at as a whole. It is wrong in my judgment to seek to impose on the commission any such uniform requirement that every piece of material put before the commission which may in any way influence its report must go to all parties or even to the opposing main participants in the bid. The commission establishes, within the framework of the Fair Trading Act 1973, its own procedure and its own approach to each individual reference. Of course it must heed all representations

---

[114] *R v Monopolies and Mergers Commission, ex p Milk Marque Ltd* (unreported, 10 December 1999).
[115] [1975] AC 295.
[116] ibid 368.
[117] ibid 369.
[118] [1987] 1 WLR 1235.

made either way. But it has a discretion which is broad and which should not be prescribed or inflexible. The concept of fairness is itself flexible and should not be subject to the court laying down rules or steps which have to be followed. The question in each case is whether the commission has adopted a procedure so unfair that no reasonable commission or group would have adopted it, so that it can be said to have acted with manifest unfairness. Provided each party has its mind brought to bear upon the relevant issues it is not in my judgment for the court to lay down rules as to how each group should act in any particular inquiry. Of course neither side must be faced with a bolt from the blue and no party may be kept in the dark and prevented from putting its case.

These very broad statements require some qualification in the light of more recent decisions. In *R v Monopolies and Mergers Commission, ex p Stagecoach Holdings plc*[119] Collins J observed as follows:

> No doubt the [Commission] will in future consider most carefully whether it has given full opportunity to an interested party to deal with any matter on which it intends particularly to rely. There should be a good reason not to put back any such material, especially if it arrives after a hearing.

He also tempered, to some extent, the suggestion in *Matthews Brown* that procedural fairness should be judged purely on *Wednesbury* principles:

> I entirely accept that the Court will be slow to intervene [in procedural matters]. That is because regard must be had to the nature of the MMC and the knowledge that having directed itself properly on the requirements of fairness it will be unlikely that none the less it will be unfair. As Lloyd L.J. said at page 184D [of *R v Panel on Takeovers and Mergers, ex p Guiness plc* [1990] 1 QB 146] the Court will give great weight to the tribunal's own view of what is fair. No doubt, this will mean that in the vast majority of cases the Court will be unlikely to regard what the MMC has reasonably believed to be fair as unfair so that in practice the adoption of the *Wednesbury* test will make little difference.

However, the *Wednesbury* test as a touchstone for fairness has now been rejected in the important decision of Moses J in *Interbrew SA*.[120] In that case Interbrew challenged, by judicial review, the Secretary of State's decision to accept the recommendation of the Competition Commission that Interbrew should be required to divest itself of its recently acquired interest in Bass plc since such acquisition could, in CC's opinion, be expected to operate against the public interest.

The case is an interesting example of the overlap between EC and domestic competition regimes referred to above. The acquisition of Bass had been notified to the European Commission as being within the potential scope of the EC Merger Regulation (Regulation (EEC) 4064/89). In the event, the Commission cleared the merger but referred the matter back to the UK authorities in respect of that part of the merger which affected the supply of beer in the UK itself pursuant to Article 9 of the EC Regulation.

Shortly before acquiring Bass, Interbrew—whose major activity was then licensing of Stella Artois—had acquired another UK brewer Whitbread which was the licensee for

13.120

13.121

13.122

13.123

13.124

---

[119] The Times, 23 July 1996.
[120] *Interbrew SA and Interbrew UK Holdings Ltd v Competition Commission and Secretary of State for Trade and Industry* [2001] EWHC Admin 367, [2001] UKCLR 954.

Stella Artois. The effect of the acquisitions was, as the CC believed, to create an effective duopoly between Interbrew and Scottish and Newcastle in the market as a whole.

13.125 Interbrew's challenge was founded on an alleged breach of the proportionality principle and on procedural unfairness. Its proportionality challenge failed (see below). However, the challenge based on procedural unfairness was successful.

13.126 Interbrew complained that it had not been given a fair opportunity to deal with the issue of remedy. Whilst it accepted that CC had requested and received submissions on the potential alternative remedies of Interbrew being required to divest itself of Whitbread on the one hand or Bass on the other, it complained that it had not been invited to comment on CC's reasoning for considering that a divestment of Whitbread would be ineffective because of the Stella Artois licence. As Moses J observed: 'I can see no reason why the simple and, as it seems to me, clear point should not have been put to Interbrew: "do you accept that your capacity as owner of Bass and licensor of Stella Artois will inhibit the competitiveness of Whitbread with Stella Artois?"'

13.127 The following principles were clarified:[121]

 (1) CC owed a duty of fairness in conducting its investigation as to the merger.
 (2) The content of the duty would vary from case to case but, generally, it would require the decision-maker to identify in advance areas which were causing him concern in reaching the decision in question.[122]
 (3) Where Convention rights were at stake those adversely affected should be involved in the decision-making progress to a degree sufficient to provide them with the 'requisite protection of their interests'. Without such participation the interference would not be regarded as 'necessary'.[123]
 (4) The same was true of rights protected by Community law.[124]
 (5) The test of whether the procedure was fair was not simply one of *Wednesbury* unreasonableness.

13.128 In the light of these principles Moses J distinguished *Hoffman-La Roche* and *Matthew Brown* (above). He observed that in both those cases the claimants' complaints were directed at matters which were plainly in issue. Here, by contrast, although Interbrew was under an obligation to put forward its full case it could not be expected to have appreciated that the foundation for any view that the divestment of Whitbread with Stella Artois would not provide an effective remedy would be Interbrew's dual capacity. The effect of that dual capacity upon the viability and independence of Whitbread with Stella Artois was never raised by CC. Accordingly, both the CC's recommendation and the Secretary of State's decision were procedurally unfair.[125]

---

 [121] ibid 973–4.
 [122] See, to similar effect, eg, *R v Secretary of State for the Home Department, ex p Fayed* [1998] 1 WLR 763, 773–774.
 [123] See, eg, *McMichael v United Kingdom* (1995) 20 EHRR 205, para 87.
 [124] Case T–42/96 *Eyckeler and Malt AG v European Commission* [1998] ECR II–401, para 78: '[a]ny person who may be adversely affected by a decision should be placed in a position in which he may effectively make his views known, at least as regards the matters taken into account by the Commission as the basis for its decision'.
 [125] Moses J made the point that the decisions were not necessarily irrational. In the event, the DGFT conducted further investigations and reported that there was an alternative remedy to divestment of Bass.

Procedural fairness has also been considered in two public law cases with a competition ele-   **13.129**
ment outside the monopolies and mergers regime (or other statutory competition regimes
that are within the remit of CAT) but with obvious parallels for the type of administrative
law issues that the Administrative Court and CAT have to address in competition cases
where there may be an EC element.

In *R v National Lottery Commission, ex p Camelot Group plc*[126] Camelot successfully chal-   **13.130**
lenged, by way of judicial review, a decision of the National Lottery Commission to permit
one competitor bidder to Camelot to continue to negotiate with it after making a prior
decision that neither that bidder nor Camelot met the statutory criteria for the award of a
licence to operate the national lottery. The Commission's reason for negotiating with the
other bidder was said to be that the other bidder would, in its view, be more capable of
addressing its concerns over the licence application.

Richards J in the Administrative Court held that this was procedurally unfair and demon-   **13.131**
strated a 'marked lack of even-handedness'. In his judgment he held that the Commission
had abused its power and, thereby, acted unlawfully by terminating the competition before
either bidder had succeeded. The case exemplifies the difficulties that can face commercial
regulators in competitive situations such as this. Richards J accepted that the Commission
was conscious of the need to adopt a fair procedure and had acted as it did in what it
thought to be the interests of fairness. Nonetheless, he considered that the Commission's
course of action was wrong in principle.[127]

The second public law case in the wider competition context is the decision of the Court   **13.132**
of Appeal, upholding the first-instance ruling of Lightman J, in *R (Asha Foundation)
v Millennium Commission*.[128]

There, the Millennium Commission—a statutory body responsible for distributing lottery   **13.133**
money after a competitive round of applications—gave as its reasons for rejecting the
claimant's application for lottery funding that it considered the application before it to be
'less attractive than the others'. On being asked to expand its reasons, it essentially repeated
the reasons already given.

The Court of Appeal (endorsing the reasoning of Lightman J) held that it would be imprac-   **13.134**
ticable in terms of good administration for the Millennium Commission to be required to
give further reasons than it had. This was so for the following reasons (para 29):

> First, the preference for a particular application may not be the same in the case of each
> commissioner. Secondly, in order to evaluate any reasons that are given for preferring one
> application to another, the full nature and detail of both applications has to be known ... the
> Commission would have had to set out in detail each commissioner's views in relation to
> each of the applications and to provide the background material to Asha so that they could
> assess whether those conclusions were appropriate. This would be an undue burden on any
> commission. It would make their task almost impossible.

The Secretary of State made a fresh decision in September 2001 and final approval was given in January 2002
to the alternative remedy agreed to by Interbrew.

[126] [2001] EMLR 43.

[127] *Quaere*, though, whether the National Lottery Commission could have devised a process from the
outset that would have enabled it to act as it did.

[128] [2003] EWCA Civ 88, [2003] ACD 50.

13.135 It seems unlikely that (where they are engaged) EC general principles of law, most notably that of effectiveness, would compel any different application of principle.

Proportionality

13.136 As has been seen, in *Interbrew* one of the grounds raised in the judicial review proceedings was that of proportionality. Proportionality does not yet exist as a separate ground of challenge in a purely domestic judicial review context.[129]

13.137 However, proportionality may be relevant in monopoly/merger cases before the Administrative Court (or now CAT) raising Community law issues and in challenges alleging violation of the European Convention on Human Rights under the HRA. Sometimes, as in *Interbrew*, both jurisdictions are engaged.

13.138 There, proportionality was potentially relevant *as a matter of Community law* because the obligation on Member State authorities to act proportionately was expressly imposed by Article 9(8) of the EC Merger Regulation which imposed a requirement only to take those measures which were strictly necessary to safeguard or restore effective competition. Proportionality was also potentially relevant *as a matter of Convention law* because it was contended that the Secretary of State's decision violated Article 1 Protocol 1 ECHR (right to peaceful enjoyment of possessions).

13.139 In the event Moses J found it unnecessary to determine the proportionality issue separately from a consideration of whether the reasons given by the CC were sufficiently cogent and had an evidential basis. Since he found that they were cogent and had an evidential basis the proportionality challenge necessarily failed. However, though he declined the opportunity, he observed that there may be cases where it is essential to identify the correct approach to proportionality.

13.140 In the present context, the requisite *test* for proportionality is probably similar whether considering the challenge from a Community or Convention perspective. Thus, in Community law terms Article 9(8) of the EC Merger Regulation called for the least restrictive measure to be adopted. This is similar to the test applied in cases concerning Article 1 Protocol 1 ECHR where the European Court of Human Rights looks for a 'reasonable relationship of proportionality between the means employed and the legitimate objectives pursued'.[130]

13.141 The more difficult question is that of intensity of review. Difficult issues can arise as to whether, in any given context, the proportionality review conducted by the national court should be intense or low level in the sense of according a wide latitude to the Member/Contracting State authority. These problems are examined elsewhere.[131]

13.142 In *Interbrew* the claimants submitted that there should be high intensity review. This was because although the right enshrined in Article 1 Protocol 1 ECHR was not as

---

[129] See paras 11.80–11.83.
[130] See, eg, *James v United Kingdom* (1986) 8 EHRR 123.
[131] See generally Chapter 11, especially paras 11.85–11.92.

fundamental as other rights it was, nonetheless, important. Also, there was an alleged restriction on the right of establishment under Articles 43 and 56 (ex 52, 73B) EC.

The counter-argument, advanced by CC and the Secretary of State, was that the correct **13.143** standard was that of low-intensity review. In the circumstances of the case this would appear to be the better view because this is the approach that would have been adopted in respect of the European Commission had it not referred the merger to the United Kingdom.

That test would have afforded to the European Commission a wide margin of appreciation **13.144** given that it would have been addressing questions of economic policy and evaluation. An example of the ECJ's approach is provided by that court's ruling in *Upjohn v Medicines Licensing Authority*[132] where (at para 34) it said:

> According to the Court's case law, where a Community authority is called upon, in the performance of its duties, to make complex assessments, it enjoys a wide measure of discretion, the exercise of which is subject to a limited judicial review in the course of which the Community judicature may not substitute its assessment of the facts for the assessment made by the authority concerned. Thus, in such cases, the Community judicature must restrict itself to examining the accuracy of the findings of fact and law made by the authority concerned and to verifying, in particular, that the action taken by that authority is not vitiated by manifest error or misuse of powers and that it did not clearly exceed the bounds of its discretion ...

Similarly, whilst it is at least arguable that merger decisions are subject to Article 1 Protocol **13.145** 1 ECHR and that, in consequence, proportionality is available as a head of review under the rubric of the HRA it is probable that the Administrative Court would accord to the Secretary of State a relatively wide margin of appreciation when such decisions were being challenged by way of judicial review.[133]

No evidence/error of fact

There is a difference between, respectively, 'no evidence' and error of fact[134] as a basis for **13.146** obtaining judicial review.

If there is no evidence to support a conclusion, there is a necessary error of law in the deci- **13.147** sion reached.[135] But that is conceptually different from an error of fact where judges have, traditionally, been reluctant to grant judicial review for fear of appearing to exercise a function conferred by Parliament on the decision-maker. The question, therefore, of whether an error of fact can constitute a ground of judicial review is a developing one.

In *Interbrew* Moses J was dealing only with 'no evidence'. He examined the reasons given for **13.148** the decisions. He observed that '[i]f the reasons make no sense and are without foundation

---

[132] C–120/97 [1999] ECR I–233.

[133] See, eg, R Clayton and H Tomlinson, *The Law of Human Rights* (2000).

[134] However, error of fact is often a ground of statutory appeal and, in such cases, is clearly available. See, eg, *BT v OFTEL* (unreported, 4 August 2000) where the regulator's finding of fact was quashed on an appeal under s 46B of the Telecommunications Act 1984, as inserted the Telecommunications Appeals Regulations 1999 (SI 1999/3180), reg 3.

[135] See, especially, *Edwards v Bairstow* [1956] AC 14; *Re Islam (Tafazzul)* [1983] 1 AC 688, 717–18, per Lord Lowry.

then I should so rule'. Notwithstanding this, having analysed the reasons he concluded that there was a relevant evidential basis for them.

13.149   However, error of fact (not considered in *Interbrew*)—although not well established as a ground of review—may be sufficiently closely related to other grounds of challenge (most notably, relevancy) as sometimes to afford a basis for judicial review. The clearest authority, to date, is the decision of the House of Lords in *R (Alconbury Developments Ltd) v Secretary of State for the Environment, Transport and the Regions*.[136] There, Lords Slynn (para 53), Nolan (paras 61–62) and Clyde (para 169) appeared to contemplate the possibility of error of fact vitiating a decision at least in some circumstances as where, for example, the decision-maker has taken account of facts that are irrelevant or mistaken or misunderstood or ignored an established and relevant fact.[137]

13.150   In this sense, error of fact could be of obvious potential importance in the regulatory context. In the present context, in *R v Director General of Electricity Supply, ex p Scottish Power Plc*[138] the Director General imposed supply price controls in the licences of Scottish Power and its principal competitor Scottish Hydro-Electric. Only Scottish Hydro-Electric asked for a reference to the Monopolies and Mergers Commission. This led to a modification of the controls (as adjudicated by the MMC) as against Scottish Hydro-Electric which was refused as against Scottish Power. The Court of Appeal held that there was no valid factual basis for treating the competitors differently. In the new monopolies and mergers regime, the scope of error of fact as a doctrine of Administrative Court judicial review may, however, be of less importance given the new and wider jurisdiction of CAT referred to above.[139]

Discretion to refuse relief

13.151   Importantly, judicial review is a discretionary remedy. The remedy sought (or, indeed, any remedy) may, generally, be refused as a matter of discretion. Reference has already been made to the court's decision in *Argyll*.[140] There, the claimant succeeded in challenging the MMC's decision on the basis that the Commission Chairman had no power to make the decision on his own. But, in the event, the court refused to grant a remedy because it considered that had the full panel been seized of the matter it would, inevitably, have come to the same result.

13.152   In reaching this conclusion, the regulatory context was clearly of importance to the court. Amongst other things, Sir John Donaldson MR said:

> Good public administration is concerned with speed of decision, particularly in the financial field . . . If relief is granted, it must be some days before a new decision is reached.

> Good public administration requires a proper consideration of the public interest. In this context, the Secretary of State is the guardian of the public interest. He consented to the reference being laid aside, although he need not have done so if he considered it to be in the public interest that the original proposals be further investigated. He could have made a further reference of the new proposals, if such they be, but has not done so.

---

[136] [2001] UKHL 23, [2001] 2 WLR 1389.
[137] See, also, *R v Criminal Injuries Compensation Board, ex p A* [1999] 2 AC 330, 344–5, per Lord Slynn.
[138] Unreported, 3 February 1997.
[139] See, also, paras 13.154 et seq.
[140] See para 13.104.

Good public administration requires a proper consideration of the legitimate interests of individual citizens, however rich and powerful they may be and whether they are natural or juridical persons. But in judging the relevance of an interest, however legitimate, regard has to be had to the purpose of the administrative process concerned. Argyll has a strong and legitimate interest in putting Guinness in baulk, but this is not the purpose of the administrative process under the Fair Trading Act 1973. To that extent their interest is not therefore of any great, or possibly any, weight.

Lastly good public administration requires decisiveness and finality, unless there are compelling reasons to the contrary. The financial public has been entitled to rely upon the finality of the announced decision to set aside the reference ... [A]ccount must be taken of the probability that deals have been done in reliance upon the validity of the decisions now impugned.

However, discretion to refuse relief is, in the context of application of EC law, almost **13.153** certainly more restricted than it would be in the case of a purely domestic dispute because of the EC general principle of effectiveness.[141] In those cases in which EC law falls to be applied by the Administrative Court or CAT even indirectly, it will be more difficult to justify refusing relief in the court's discretion.[142]

O. Special Public Law Review Jurisdiction of the Competition Appeal Tribunal

CAT was originally the Competition Commission Appeal Tribunal, and cases up to **13.154** 31 March 2003 were decisions of that body. From 1 April 2003 decisions of the Tribunal are those of CAT as a result of the Enterprise Act 2000, s 12 and the Enterprise Act 2002 (Commencement No 2, Transitional and Transitory Provisions) Order 2003 (SI 2003/766). CAT has jurisdiction under a number of statutes. A summary of its specialist jurisdiction is set out in Table 13.1 below.

CAT is an 'expert and specialist tribunal'[143] with an appeal to the Court of Appeal on points **13.155** of law. Because of this, only in the most exceptional circumstances should the Administrative Court entertain applications for judicial review instead of requiring a claimant to proceed through CAT.[144]

CAT is required by s 60 of the Competition Act 1998 to ensure that there is no incon- **13.156** sistency between its decisions and the EC Treaty. This means that the law that will be

---

[141] See paras 14.76 et seq.

[142] But discretion to refuse relief is sometimes exercised in State aid and competition judicial review cases. See, eg, *R (Great North Eastern Railway) v Office of Rail Regulation* [2006] EWHC 1942 where having held that the differential charging regime used by the Office of Rail Regulation which charged some but not all operators a fixed track charge was not discriminatory and did not constitute an unlawful State aid, Sullivan J also held that he would have refused relief in his discretion in any event because of the claimant's delay and also because to grant relief would be to render the application process pointless from the outset.

[143] *Napp Pharmaceutical Holdings Ltd v Director General of Fair Trading* [2002] EWCA Civ 796, at para 34. *Napp* was an unsuccessful application for permission to appeal to the Court of Appeal against a decision of CAT. However, Brooke LJ observed that the judgment of the Court of Appeal contained important guidance on practice and so may be cited notwithstanding the terms of para 6.1 of *Practice Direction (Citation of Authorities)* [2001] 1 WLR 1001.

[144] See, eg, *R v Financial Services Authority, ex p Davies* [2003] EWCA Civ 1128.

Table 13.1 Specialist jurisdiction of the Competition Appeal Tribunal

Source of jurisdiction	Nature of CAT jurisdiction
Competition Act 1998 (CA)	(1) To hear appeals in relation to the merits of decisions made under CA by the OFT and the sectoral regulators in telecommunications, electricity, gas, water, railways, and air traffic services (see ss 46–47). Such decisions include whether there are infringements of either UK or EC competition law.
	(2) To hear actions for damages and other monetary claims under the CA relating to infringements of either UK or EC competition law (ss 47A and 47B).
Enterprise Act 2002	To review decisions of the Secretary of State, CC and OFT relating to merger and market references or possible references (see n 104 above and ss 120(1) and (4) and 179(4) of the Enterprise Act 2002).
Communications Act 2003	To hear appeals on the merits against certain decisions made by Ofcom and the Secretary of State in respect of Ofcom's exercise of functions under EA 2002, Pt 2 (networks, services, and the radio spectrum) and ss 290–294 and Sch 11 (networking arrangements for Channel 3) of the 2003 Act (see s 192).
EC Competition Law (Articles 84–85) Enforcement Regulations 2001 (SI 2001/2916) as amended	To hear appeals relating to particular enforcement decisions made by the OFT.

applied is 'likely to be largely or entirely the law of the European Union' and that those appearing before CAT and appeals from it have 'a particular responsibility to identify clearly what in the jurisprudence of the European Union is truly a principle or decision, in the terms of s 60, and what is not such'.[145]

13.157 As explained above, the jurisdiction of CAT is a mix of public law review as well as, in most areas, fact finding. In terms of its public law jurisdiction, the relevant provisions of the Enterprise Act 2002 make it clear that part of CAT jurisdiction sounds exclusively in public law where many of the principles discussed above will be applicable and where broader fact finding will not. However, even in areas where CAT is dealing with an appeal on the merits, public law principles may be required to be applied in order for CAT to dispose of the appeal satisfactorily and for recourse to CAT to be a true alternative remedy to judicial review.

13.158 The scope and ambit of s 120 of the Enterprise Act 2002 relating to the nature of CAT's public law jurisdiction was the subject of careful analysis by the Court of Appeal in an appeal against a CAT decision in *Office of Fair Trading v IBA Health Ltd*.[146]

---

[145] *Napp Pharmaceutical Holdings Ltd v Director General of Fair Trading* [2002] EWCA Civ 796, para 14.
[146] [2004] EWCA Civ 142, [2004] 4 All ER 1103.

That case involved an important point of statutory interpretation as to the proper con-   **13.159**
struction of s 33(1) of the 2002 Act in relation to when the OFT is required to refer a
merger to the Competition Commission. CAT had formulated a two-part test—for
the OFT's evaluation as to the effect of a merger and whether a reference was necessary to
the Competition Commission—which the Court of Appeal held to be erroneous.[147]

The second point in the appeal raised the question of whether CAT had properly   **13.160**
applied the principles of judicial review as required by s 120. Section 120(1) enables any
person aggrieved by a decision (amongst other bodies) of the OFT to apply to CAT 'for a
review of that decision'. Section 120(4) provides:

> In determining such an application the Competition Appeal Tribunal shall apply the same
> principles as would be applied by a court on an application for judicial review.

CAT had interpreted s 120 as giving it a broad spectrum of review because of its constitution   **13.161**
as a specialist tribunal. The OFT, on appeal, contended that CAT had misdirected itself and
that it had reversed the normal burden of proof in judicial review cases (the burden generally falling on the claimant)[148] as well as failing to apply the conventional *Wednesbury* test
of reasonableness and applying a higher intensity of review.

It was common ground that the principles to be applied by CAT were the ordinary   **13.162**
principles of judicial review. In the event, the Court of Appeal rejected the criticisms of the
approach taken by CAT.

In a supplementary judgment, Carnwath LJ analysed the deeper questions of principle as   **13.163**
to the standard of review to be applied by CAT. His judgment repays careful re-reading
because he was critical of certain aspects of the approach that CAT had taken to its task
of review. He endorsed CAT's observation that its approach to review should reflect the
particular context in which it had been created as a specialist tribunal. However, he stated
that it was wrong for CAT to suggest that this permitted it to discard established case
law relating to unreasonableness (see para 90).

Carnwath LJ's analysis contains the following important elements which are highly rele-   **13.164**
vant to the approach to be taken to judicial review both by specialized tribunals but also
by the Administrative Court when dealing with a particular type of case:

(1) The reasonableness test is a flexible one and is dependent on the statutory context
    (para 90).[149]
(2) At one end of the spectrum—most notably, cases depending essentially on political
    judgment—a low intensity of judicial review is applied, whereas at the other end of the
    spectrum—where fundamental rights are engaged—a high intensity of review will be
    applied (para 91).[150]

---

[147] Note CAT's adoption of the correct test in its subsequent ruling in *Celestio AG v OFT* [2006] CAT 9.
[148] This is, though, not always so. For example, in an HRA case it is for the State to justify the interference
with a particular Convention right.
[149] *R v Secretary of State, ex p Brind* [1991] 1 AC 696, 765 et seq., per Lord Lowry.
[150] cf *R v Secretary of State, ex p Nottinghamshire CC* [1986] AC 240 and *R v Secretary of State, ex p
Hammersmith and Fulham LBC* [1991] 1 AC 521 (low-intensity review) with *R (Daly) v Secretary of State for
the Home Department* [2001] 2 AC 532 (high-intensity review).

(3) A further factor relevant to the intensity of review is whether the issue before CAT (or the Administrative Court) is one properly within the province of the court (para 92).

(4) In a case (such as the present) involving factual judgment on the part of the OFT (rather than policy or discretion) the court is entitled to inquire whether there was adequate material to support that judgment (para 93).

(5) Even in relation to issues relating to factual matters, the cases show considerable variation in the intensity of review (paras 94–99).[151]

13.165   This analysis shows that whether in the Administrative Court or in a specialist tribunal such as CAT, a review jurisdiction may permit quite careful evaluation of the facts underpinning a decision sought to be challenged in order to determine whether there was adequate material to support the decision-maker's conclusions.[152] In competition cases which generally do not involve questions of policy or political judgment, the statutory context allows a relatively high intensity of review. As Carnwath LJ observed (para 100):

> ... the Tribunal did not need to rely on some special dispensation from the ordinary principles of judicial review. Those principles, whether applied by a court or a specialised tribunal, are flexible enough to be adapted to the particular statutory context ... the essential question was no different from that which would have faced a court dealing with the same subject-matter. That question was whether the material relied on by the OFT could reasonably be regarded as dispelling the uncertainties highlighted by the issues letter. That question was wholly suitable for evaluation by a court. It involved no policy or political judgment, such as would be regarded as inappropriate for review by the Administrative Court.

13.166   The review jurisdiction of CAT consists, therefore, of several elements dependent on the nature of the proceedings before it. Even in a merits appeal, public law issues (involving the application of EC law) may arise in the sense that CAT may have to decide points of law affecting the status or activities of a public body. Thus, for example, in *Bettercare*[153] CAT's predecessor had to determine whether the Director General of Fair Trading had been right to decline to investigate the applicant's complaint of a breach of the Competition Act. The basis for the refusal was that the DGFT considered that a public

---

[151] cf, especially, *Edwards v Bairstow* [1956] AC 14, 38–39 per Lord Radcliffe (intrusive review), *R v Hillingdon LBC, ex p Puhlhofer* [1986] AC 485 (low-intensity review). Note the regulating principle articulated by Lord Hoffmann in *Moyna v Secretary of State* [2003] UKHL 44, para 27 (citing his own judgment in *Re Grayan Building Services* [1995] Ch 242, 254–5): '... as long as it is understood that the degree to which an appellate court will be willing to substitute its own judgment for that of the tribunal will vary with the nature of the question'.

[152] This has been noted by CAT in its later decision in *Unichem Ltd v OFT* [2005] CAT 8. Note also the not dissimilar exercise conducted by the CFI (a comparable court to CAT) in competition judicial review cases before it: see Case 12/03P *Commission v Tetra Laval BV* (Case 12/03 P) (not yet reported, judgment 15 February 2005). For further analysis, see B Kennelly, 'Judicial Review and the Competition Appeal Tribunal' [2006] JR 160.

[153] *Bettercare Group Ltd v (1) Director General of Fair Trading, (2) Registered Homes Confederation of Northern Ireland and (3) Bedfordshire Care Group (Interveners)* [2002] CAT 7. Further, even in a so-called merits review it is by no means entirely clear whether CAT has an entirely de novo fact-finding jurisdiction or whether it is required, at least in some instances, to show a wide measure of deference to the specialist regulator. cf *Napp Pharmaceuticals v Director General of Fair Trading* [2002] CAT 1 (which suggests a full review of the merits in such cases) with Case C–120/97 *Upjohn Ltd* [1999] ECR I–223, para 34 (which suggests a wide discretionary area of judgment in the specialist regulator). See, further, the discussion in Kennelly (n 152 above). See, also, *Freeserve* [2002] CAT 5 where, at least in general, CAT demonstrated a reluctance to revisit in detail issues of fact that had already been decided by the regulator.

body *(in casu* a health trust) fell outside the concept of an undertaking within the meaning of s 18(1) of the Competition Act 1998 (corresponding to Articles 81–82) because although a public body could be an undertaking if carrying out an economic activity it was not an undertaking when carrying out a public interest activity (here offering contract prices and terms for the purchase of health care services).

The tribunal, having reviewed the ECJ case law,[154] came to the conclusion that applying **13.167** the relevant ECJ principles the fact that the health trust's activities were funded by taxation did not determine whether its activities were 'economic' or not. The functions in the present case did not involve decisions taken in the exercise of the State's sovereign authority and the fact that the health trust had been entrusted with tasks in the public interest or had a social dimension did not mean that its activities were not economic. In the circumstances, there was a relevant economic activity and the health trust was an undertaking. The complaint ought to have been investigated.

In exercising its review functions CAT (and its predecessor) has had to consider public **13.168** law issues including public law points of potentially wide ambit (including HRA and EC issues) on a number of occasions. Table 13.2 gives a few examples with the relevant CAT citation.[155] As these examples demonstrate, CAT has had to address general principles of EC law such as the rights of the defence as well as HRA and traditional domestic judicial review principles in the increasing number of cases that come before it. The examples set out below do not include the myriad appeals where CAT has to address substantive points of EC competition law such as those raised in *Bettercare* (above) many of which involve hard-edged legal questions which insofar as they affect public bodies (as in that case) involve issues of public law.

Similarly, Table 13.2 does not address the detail of the HRA points that may be canvassed **13.169** before CAT in, for example, competition enforcement cases (or in the Court of Appeal on appeal from CAT). In such cases, the EC enforcement regime applied by CAT must be compatible with the ECHR as well as with general principles of EC law. CAT will, thus, be required to observe the ECHR (and, if and when binding, the EU Charter of Fundamental Rights) in respect of matters such as the right to a fair trial (Article 6 ECHR), including (where appropriate) the presumption of innocence and the privilege against self-incrimination, and the right to respect for private and family life, home and correspondence (Article 8 ECHR). Important questions that may arise in EC fundamental rights cases are addressed in Chapter 12.

---

[154] See, especially, Case C–41/90 *Hofner and Elser v Macroton* [1991] ECR I–1979.

[155] Many other CAT cases not tabulated here simply involve application of conventional administrative law principles. Consider, eg, *Somerfield plc v Competition Commission* [2006] CAT 4, a judicial review of a decision by the Competition Commission under the Enterprise Act 2002 where CAT found that CC had acted reasonably, set out fair criteria, and that its decision was adequately reasoned.

Table 13.2 Examples of principles addressed by the Competition Appeal Tribunal

Point of principle	CAT citation
The tribunal is constituted as an independent and impartial tribunal within the meaning of Article 6 ECHR and proceedings before it are judicial and not administrative.	[2002] 2
For the purposes of Article 6 ECHR, proceedings before CAT are *criminal* in nature by analogy with *Montecatini v Commission* [1999] ECR I–4575.	[2001] 3 [2002] 1
The rights of defence are not necessarily infringed by the fact that continuing conduct after the start of an investigation may be a more serious offence.	[2002] 1
There is no human rights principle that would preclude the Director from reconsidering a remitted decision	[2002] 4
Despite the fact that some appeals are on the merits, it does not follow that application to CAT is not an appropriate remedy or that judicial review should be sought.	[2002] 6; [2003] 3
The exercise of discretion by a regulator not to proceed to a decision or even conduct an investigation might still be susceptible to judicial review on the basis of *Ex p Perceval* [1990] 3 WLR 323.	[2002] 6
There is an equivalent public law duty on those appearing before CAT to that of a public body in the Administrative Court to put information fully before CAT.	[2003] 27
If it is open to CAT to interpret a statute in a manner which would avoid procedural unfairness, it should do so.	[2003] 3
In a penalties case, it is of overriding importance that parties should be able to exercise their rights of defence without having possibly relevant material held back or inaccessible.	[2003] 26
In the event of a conflict between rights of the defence and other claims to confidentiality, there is a presumption that the rights of the defence prevail.	[2003] 26
There is a public interest in encouraging public authorities to make and stand by honest, reasonable and apparently sound administrative decisions made in the public interest without fear of exposure to undue financial prejudice if the decision is successfully challenged (*Bradford MDC v Booth* (2000) 164 JP 485, per Lord Bingham CJ).	[2002] 2
Where the OFT or a concurrent regulator has expressly indicated that they will consider a complaint on its merits, CAT will expect that investigation to reach an outcome.	[2003] 17
Breach of a legitimate expectation does not transform something that is not an appealable decision into one that is appealable.	[2003] 17

14

ENVIRONMENTAL CHALLENGES

A. Overview

Environmental protection has become increasingly important in terms of EC obligations.[1] **14.01**
For example, Article 2 EC now requires the Community to promote, amongst other
things, 'a harmonious and balanced development of economic activities' together with
'a high level of protection and improvement of the quality of the environment'.
Article 3 EC now recognizes the development of 'a policy in the sphere of the environment'.
Articles 174–176 (ex 130) EC contain provision for express legislative environmental
measures on the part of Member States. Regulation of areas such as pollution of water and
air were quickly established. National environmental measures were required to be harmonized
for the purposes of environmental and health protection and so as to prevent distortion of
intra-Community trade and competition.

---

[1] The original Treaty of Rome contained no express provision for environmental measures. Such legisla-
tion was enacted on the basis of general powers as, most notably, under Art 308 (ex 235) EC. However the
Single European Act 1986 added Art 174–176 (see text) and the Maastricht Treaty amended Art 2–3 EC
(see text). However, these powers must be exercised carefully. The ECJ has recently annulled a Council
Framework Decision on the ground of excess of power: see Case C–176/03 *Re Framework Decision on
Protection of the Environment: Commission of the European Communities v Council of the European
Communities* [2005] 3 CMLR 20.

14.02 It has been estimated that:

> At this point in time, hundreds of measures relating to the environment have been established, having an influence on almost all aspects of national environmental law. More than half of national environmental law of the Member States is at present influenced or prescribed by Brussels in this way.[2]

14.03 Against that background, much of domestic environmental judicial review has been concerned with the interpretation of EC law, especially environmental directives and/or whether they have been lawfully transposed and/or implemented[3] into national law. As the cases have increased, the Administrative Court in particular has also been required to examine ECJ case law (as well as its own case law) and apply it to national legislative provisions as best it can referring, in cases of difficulty, to the ECJ for a preliminary ruling under Article 234 (ex 177) EC. Areas of particular importance in the EC domestic public law context include waste,[4] habitats,[5] and environmental impact assessment.[6]

B. Applying EC Law in Environmental Judicial Review Cases

Some basic EC environmental principles

Doctrine of practical compliance

14.04 As noted elsewhere,[7] directives are (under Article 249 (ex 189) EC) 'binding as to the result to be achieved'.

14.05 The strength of the obligation lies in the proper interpretation of both Article 249 EC itself and Article 10 (ex 5) EC which stipulates that Member States:

> must take all appropriate measures, whether general or particular, to ensure fulfillment of the obligations arising out of this Treaty or resulting from action taken by institutions of the Community . . . [and] abstain from any measure which could jeopardize the attainment of the objectives of the Treaty.

---

[2] See European Environmental Law (EEL) website at <http://www.eel.nl>.

[3] For the distinction between transposition and implementation of a directive into national law, see para 5.146.

[4] A number of domestic public law cases have involved the definition of *'waste'* under different directives and in different contexts. Consider, eg, *Castle Cement v Environment Agency* [2001] Env LR 45; *Parkwood Landfill v Customs & Excise* [2003] Env LR 19; *Mayer Parry Recycling Ltd v Environment Agency* [1999] Env LR 489; *Attorney General's Reference (No 5 of 2000)* [2002] Env LR 580. The outcome of these cases, in turn, have sometimes depended upon an analysis by the national courts of ECJ decisions: see (apart from the cases at n 11 below) Case C–304/94 *Euro Tombesi* [1998] Env LR 59; Case C–418/97 *Arco Chemie Nederland Ltd v Minister van Volkshuivesting and EPON* [2003] Env LR 40. The meaning of the term 'deposit' is also important to EC waste law and has featured in a number of domestic public law cases: see, eg *R v Metropolitan Stipendiary Magistrate, ex p London Waste Regulation Authority* [1993] All ER 113; *Thames Waste Management v Surrey County Council* [1997] Env LR 148.

[5] For an interesting domestic decision involving both the waste and habitat regimes, see *R (Friends of the Earth) v Environment Agency* [2004] Env LR 31 (the USA 'ghost ships' case).

[6] See paras 14.44–14.64.

[7] See para 1.67.

As applied to environmental law, at least, these obligations appear to require practical compliance as opposed to the Member State merely doing its best. **14.06**

This is exemplified by the ECJ decision in the first UK drinking water case.[8] There, the question was whether or not the UK Government was in breach of the Drinking Water Directive 1980 by exceeding the maximum standards permitted in the directive for concentration of nitrates in drinking water. The Government contended that it had done everything within its power to comply with the directive's requirements. However, the ECJ held that this was insufficient. Practical compliance was an absolute rather than a relative requirement.[9] **14.07**

This conclusion follows from the clear wording of both Article 249 and Article 10 which (respectively) require a particular result to be achieved and for all appropriate measures to be taken in fulfilment of the State's obligations. It also has a particular relevance so far as environmental considerations are concerned because any lesser obligation on the part of the Member State would entirely frustrate the purpose of the EC legislation. **14.08**

However, articulation of the principle is important because it is the touchstone for interpretation in judicial review proceedings by the Administrative Court of environmental obligations more generally. The principle is to be contrasted with the somewhat less onerous obligations that may arise in purely domestic public law cases.[10] **14.09**

The precautionary principle

The EC precautionary principle is of potential importance to domestic environmental judicial review because whereas it exists in EC law there is no clear basis for it in domestic law. Nonetheless, this means that, in domestic judicial review proceedings falling within EC law, the precautionary principle has some scope for application. **14.10**

There is, however, no clear consensus on the full scope of the principle or on how it can be deployed in domestic challenges. For practical purposes, its exposition in Principle 15 of the Rio Declaration on Environment and Development captures its essential elements. Article 15 provides as follows: **14.11**

> In order to protect the environment, the precautionary approach shall be widely applied by States according to their capabilities. Where there are threats of serious or irreversible damage, lack of full scientific certainty shall not be used as a reason for postponing cost-effective measures to prevent environmental degradation.

It is probably in that sense that the expression should be understood as it finds its way into the formulation of Community policy in the EC Treaty in Article 174(2). This states that: **14.12**

> Community policy on the environment shall . . . be based on the precautionary principle and on the principles that preventative action should be taken, that environmental damage should as a priority be rectified at source and that the polluter should pay.

---

[8] Case C–337/89 *Commission v United Kingdom* [1992] ECR I–6103.

[9] Lawful derogation from the requirements would, of course, have been permitted but that was not an issue in the case.

[10] Albeit not in the environmental context, see, eg, *Meade v London Borough of Haringey* [1979] 1 WLR 637.

14.13 The principle exists both explicitly and implicitly[11] as a discrete obligation on Member States in at least some cases. For example, the Environmental Impact Assessment Directive (Directive (EEC) 85/337) expressly refers to the principle. Other directives implicitly adopt the principle.[12]

14.14 The principle appears also to be recognized more generally as a principle outside a specific legislative context. Thus, in *Bettati*[13] the ECJ had to consider whether an EC measure itself violated, amongst other things, the precautionary principle. Given the law-making context, the ECJ accorded a wide measure of discretion. It said:

> In view of the need to strike a balance between certain of the objectives and principles mentioned in Article [174(2)] and of the complexity of the implementation of those criteria, review by the Court must necessarily be limited to the question whether the Council, by adopting the regulation, committed a manifest error of appraisal regarding the conditions for the application of Article [174(2)] of the Treaty.

14.15 The importance of *Bettati* is, though, that it recognized the existence of the principle in EC environmental law as a general principle of law in the environmental context. Similarly, the precautionary principle was (even more explicitly) accepted as a principle of general application in the environmental context by the CFI in *Pfizer*[14] where that court, in endorsing the taking into account by the Commission of expert scientific advice given to it, held that the principle covered even the case where a risk could not be completely made out.

14.16 Despite this, the precautionary principle appears to have no clear binding effect on an emanation of the State outside the ambit of a specific measure. In *Duddridge*,[15] for example, an application for judicial review brought on behalf of children living near newly laid power lines was dismissed. The Administrative Court held that there was no obligation on the State arising from the precautionary principle as a general principle of EC law to protect the children from a risk of personal injury because of radiation emitted from the lines.

14.17 There may, of course, be cases where there is a domestic statutory provision, outside the scope of EC law altogether, which contains an obligation to take precautionary measures. However, in such a case the obligation arises as a matter of statutory interpretation as opposed to being derived from the EC precautionary principle.[16]

---

[11] The precautionary principle is, eg, the rationale for the ECJ defining 'waste' very broadly for the purposes of control under the Waste Framework Directive (Directive (EEC) 75/442). See, eg, Case C–9/00 *Palin Granit Oy v Vehmassalon kansanterveyston kuntayhtyman hallitus* [2002] Env LR 35, para 23; Case C–126/96 *Inter-Environment Wallonie v Regione Wallone* [1996] Env LR 625. See, also, Case C–127/02 *Landelijke Vereniging tot Behoud van de Waddenzee, Nederlandse Vereniging tot Bescherming van Vogels v Staatssecretaris van Landbouw, Natuurbeheer en Visserij* (judgment 7 September 2004) para 58 where the ECJ treats the precautionary principle as central to the proper interpretation of the authorization criterion in Art 6(3) of the Habitats Directive (Directive (EEC) 92/43).

[12] Note, eg, the Pesticides Directive (Directive (EEC) 91/414).

[13] Case C–341/95 *Bettati v Safety Hi-Tech Srl* [1998] ECR I–4355.

[14] Case T–13/99 *Pfizer v European Commission* [2002] ECR II–3305.

[15] *R v Secretary of State for Trade and Industry, ex p Duddridge* [1995] Env LR 151.

[16] See, eg, the Water Resources Act 1991 which contains powers to serve notices requiring the prevention of water pollution.

Sustainable development

The principle of sustainable development connotes, in essence, development that is sustainable **14.18** in the long term and that does not compromise the environmental needs of future generations.

Sustainable development is enshrined as a principle in the EC Treaty, Article 2 of which **14.19** provides, materially, that:

> The Community shall have as its task, by establishing a common market and an economic and monetary union and by implementing policies or activities referred to in Articles 3 and 4, to promote throughout the Community a harmonious, balanced and sustainable development of economic activity . . .

Further reference to sustainable development is contained in Article 6 EC which requires **14.20** integrating requirements of environmental protection into other policy areas 'in particular with a view to promoting sustainable development'.

There has been little discussion of the principle in either the ECJ or domestic case law. **14.21** However, the concept of sustainable development is implicit in ECJ decisions such as that in *R v Secretary of State for the Environment, Transport and the Regions, ex p First Corporate Shipping Ltd* [17] in which the ECJ held that the special areas of conservation regime under the Habitats Directive was exclusively ecological in nature and that, therefore, economic criteria could not be taken into account by the Member State when submitting candidate areas for Commission approval under the directive.

There are explicit references to the principle of sustainable development in various domestic **14.22** statutes.[18] However, the recognition of the principle in EC law means that in a case falling within the scope of EC law[19] the principle will be relevant to the interpretation of EC and domestic legislative measures even where the principle is not referred to expressly. Further, a legislative or administrative measure that violates the principle—where it applies in an EC case—will be subject to the full panoply of EC relief.[20]

Polluter pays principle

The polluter pays principle is well established as an obligation in EC law and is expressly **14.23** enshrined in Article 174(2) EC. However, there is no clear or developed definitional content to the principle. Polluter pays was considered by the European Court of Justice in *R v Secretary of State for the Environment, ex p Standley* [21] in the context of the Nitrates Directive (Directive (EEC) 91/676) and whether farmers should pay for the costs of abatement. The court noted as follows:

> The Directive does not mean that farmers must take on burdens for the elimination of pollution to which they have not contributed . . . Viewed in that light, the polluter pays principle reflects the principle of proportionality.

---

[17] Case C–371/98 [2001] ECR I–9235.
[18] See, eg, Local Government Act 2000, s 4.
[19] As has been pointed out elsewhere, however, the scope and reach of EC law is still not entirely clear. See, especially, paras 12.62–12.80.
[20] See, especially, paras 2.60–2.89.
[21] Case C–293/97 [1999] ECR I–2603.

General (non-environmental) principles of EC law in the environmental context

14.24   Whilst there are discrete principles that have application mainly, if not exclusively, in an environmental context, it is important to bear in mind that most of the other EC general principles of law discussed in Part II of this book may also be highly relevant to an environmental challenge. Indeed, they have as much application to EC environmental judicial review cases as they do to all other fields of EC activity that are potentially susceptible to challenge in the Administrative Court.[22]

14.25   For example, fundamental rights under the ECHR may be central to an environmental challenge. Importantly, the ECHR—whilst not a direct source of EC law—has assumed great importance in ECJ judgments which treat it as having a 'special significance' in interpreting fundamental rights as one of the general principles of EC law.[23] So, provided that a case falls within the scope of EC law, deploying the ECHR may be a gateway to the wider relief afforded in EC cases generally.[24]

14.26   Although the ECJ may not always decide the ambit of an ECHR provision in the same way as the European Court of Human Rights in Strasbourg,[25] the likelihood is that, in practice, it will do so. Thus, environmental decisions of the European Court of Human Rights may be as relevant to an EC challenge as they are to an HRA challenge.

14.27   By far the most likely ECHR provision to apply in environmental cases is Article 8 (respect for private and family life). An interesting example of the relevance of that provision to environmental litigation is afforded by the facts of a case (decided in Strasbourg) *Guerra v Italy*.[26]

14.28   There, the applicants lived approximately 1 kilometre from a chemical factory which produced fertilizers and other chemicals. In 1988 the factory was classified as high risk according to criteria set out by Presidential Decree. The complaint was that the authorities had not taken appropriate action to reduce the risk of pollution by the factory and to prevent the risk of accident.

14.29   In the event, although other ECHR provisions were argued, the European Court of Human Rights decided in the applicants' favour only on Article 8. The court held that Article 8 does not merely compel the State to abstain from interference by public authorities but also imposes a positive obligation. The court reiterated the point that severe environmental pollution may affect individuals' well-being and prevent them from enjoying their homes in such a way as to affect their private and family life adversely. There was, in the instant case, a violation of the positive obligation under Article 8 as a result of the

---

[22] Such general principles will, therefore, be relevant both to interpretation and application of domestic environmental measures founded on EC law, the exercise of administrative discretion in an EC environmental case, and EC environmental law itself: see, especially, paras 6.05–6.11. They may also affect wider procedural issues including availability of remedy: see paras 5.01–5.22.

[23] See Chapter 12 generally and, especially, paras 12.14–12.18 which deal with the relationship between the ECHR and EC law in some detail.

[24] For which see paras 5.01–5.22.

[25] See para 12.100.

[26] (1998) 26 EHRR 357.

authorities' failure to provide them with relevant information about risk and how to proceed in the event of an accident when (as happened) toxic emission occurred.

However, whether or not Article 8 is either engaged or gives rise to an unjustified interference is as much a question of degree in the environmental context as it is in other contexts. The facts of a serious case such as *Guerra* above, or *Lopez Ostra*,[27] have been held both to engage and to violate Article 8.   **14.30**

By contrast, a complaint of violation of Article 8 by reason of excessive dust caused by construction of the Limehouse Link was held by the European Commission of Human Rights in *Khatun and 180 Others v United Kingdom* [28] to be inadmissible albeit that Article 8 was engaged. In that case the Commission noted that there was no complaint of adverse health effects and the disruption to use of property was limited to the duration of the works.   **14.31**

Similarly, in *Hatton v United Kingdom* [29] the Grand Chamber of the European Court of Human Rights ultimately[30] rejected a challenge founded on Article 8 that had commenced in domestic judicial review alleging significantly disturbed sleep patterns of affected residents in consequence of night flights at Heathrow Airport. The court accepted the UK Government's submission that the economic necessity of the flights justified any interference with Article 8 rights. It also observed that the degree of harm suffered was not severe. In context, therefore, a fair balance had been achieved.   **14.32**

The Strasbourg ruling was picked up in the speech of Lord Nicholls in *Marcic v Thames Water Utilities Ltd* [31](see para 63):   **14.33**

> The court [in *Hatton*] emphasized 'the fundamentally subsidiary nature' of the Convention. National authorities have 'direct democratic legitimation' and are in principle better placed than an international court to evaluate local needs and conditions. In matters of general policy, on which opinions within a democratic society may reasonably differ widely, 'the role of the domestic policy maker should be given special weight' … A fair balance must be struck between the interests of the individual and the community as a whole.

Challenging environmental directives and national measures based on them

Types of challenge to directives/national measures

By far the largest amount of EC environmental law takes the form of directives (see above). In general terms, as explained elsewhere,[32] there are various potential forms of non-compliance   **14.34**

---

[27] *Lopez Ostra v Spain* (1995) 20 EHRR 277 (*held*: construction of a waste treatment plant close to the applicant's home was a breach of Art 8 because, on the facts, a fair balance had not been struck between the interest of the town's economic well-being and the applicant's effective enjoyment of her right to respect for her home and her private and family life. The facts there included health problems caused by nauseating smells, pestilential fumes, and persistent noise emanating from the waste treatment plant).
[28] Application No 3838/97, 1 July 1998.
[29] (2003) 37 EHRR 28.
[30] The challenge had succeeded before a single chamber of the court.
[31] [2004] 2 AC 42.
[32] See para 1.107.

with directives by the Member State that will give rise to the possibility of an application for judicial review. Most notably, these include:

(1) failure to transpose the directive and/or material provisions of the directive within the permitted time,

(2) failure to transpose the directive correctly into domestic law, and

(3) failing to implement a correctly transposed directive by (for example) misinterpreting the directive and/or implementing national legislation or exercising an administrative discretion in such a way as not to apply the material terms of the directive as required by EC law.

14.35 In each of these instances, the use of general principles of EC law or the discrete environmental principles referred to above are likely to be highly relevant. But there are other issues that may arise deriving both from the nature of directives themselves and also from specific aspects of domestic judicial review

Direct effect not always essential

14.36 When mounting an EC-based judicial review challenge it is important to understand, in an environmental context, that directives are often very generally phrased. Sometimes, the level of generality precludes the provision of the directive in question from having direct effect.[33]

14.37 But that does not necessarily mean that judicial review is unavailable. Reference has already been made to the duties of the court under Article 10 (ex 5) EC and the concept of *indirect* effect thereby produced. In the light of the breadth of EC obligation on the court itself there have been a number of judicial review decisions where, in environmental cases, the absence of direct effect has not prevented a successful claim.

14.38 For example, in *R (Murray) v Derbyshire County Council* [34] the Court of Appeal held that the objectives in Article 4 of the Waste Framework Directive (Directive (EEC) 75/442)—a provision that had earlier held by the ECJ not to have direct effect[35]—must always be kept in mind when making a decision even while the decision-maker had regard to other material considerations. There was, in the court's view, a difference between the concept of an objective under an EC directive and a material consideration. The former is an end at which to aim and not a mere material consideration to which no weight need be attached.

14.39 As Pill LJ there observed:

> An objective . . . is something different from a material consideration . . . it is an end at which to aim, a goal. A material consideration is a factor to be taken into account when making a decision, and the objective to be attained will be such a consideration, but it is more than that. An objective which is obligatory must always be kept in mind when making a decision even while the decision maker has regard to other material considerations.

---

[33] Consider, eg, Art 4 of the Waste Framework Directive which has been held by the ECJ *not* to have direct effect: see Case C–236/92 *Comitato di Coordinamento per la Difesa della Cava v Regione Lombardia* [1994] ECR I–483.

[34] [2002] Env LR 28. For a decision to similar effect on the role of (environmental) objectives in decision-making, see the CA ruling in *R (Blewett) v Derbyshire County Council* [2005] Env LR 15.

[35] See n 33 above.

Importantly, too, both the domestic courts and, now, the ECJ have held, in the context of   **14.40**
the 1985 Environmental Impact Assessment Directive, that the challenge by an individual
to failure by the State to require an environmental impact assessment does not fall foul of
the principle that directives only have direct effect and do not have horizontal effect, that is
an adverse effect on third-party private individuals. This is so even where the effect of a successful challenge will be to require a third-party to produce an environmental statement.[36]
The rationale for this is that if the position were otherwise, an individual could not enforce
directly effective provisions of a directive against the State.

Issues of interpretation

Where the terms of a directive are alleged to have been misinterpreted by the Member State   **14.41**
(or as an emanation of the State an administrative body), this may afford a basis for judicial
review. Such issues may involve EC general principles or discrete principles but they need
not. Environmental domestic judicial review challenges have sometimes succeeded
because the domestic decision-maker has simply misinterpreted the true objectives
of a directive in arriving at an administrative decision, act, or omission.

R v Secretary of State for the Environment, ex p Royal Society for the Protection of Birds [37] is a case in   **14.42**
point. There, the Secretary of State excluded Lappel Bank from designation as a special protec-
tion area for birds under the Wild Birds Directive (Directive (EEC) 79/409). This was because
he took into account the economic effect (unemployment) that would be caused by designation. The RSPB argued successfully on a reference to the ECJ under Article 234 (ex 177) EC
that, on a proper interpretation of the directive, economic considerations were irrelevant.

Similarly, in *R v Secretary of State for the Environment, ex p Kingston upon Hull City*   **14.43**
Council,[38] proceedings for judicial review brought by two local authorities in respect of
decisions taken by the Secretary of State under the Urban Waste Water Treatment Directive
(Directive (EEC) 91/271) succeeded on the ground that the Secretary of State had misinterpreted the directive and wrongly taken into account the cost of designation in determining
the meaning of the term 'estuary'.

Environmental impact assessments—the cases considered

The environmental impact assessment (EIA) regime has generated the largest number of   **14.44**
domestic EC judicial review environmental challenges and provides an insight into how
the Administrative Court must, in determining judicial review challenges in EC-based
cases, pay careful regard to the terms of the relevant EC directives and ECJ decisions. Many
of the cases on EIA before national courts have resulted in references by national courts to
the ECJ under Article 234 (ex 177) EC.

---

[36] *R v Durham CC, ex p Huddleston* [2000] JPL 409; Case C–201/02 *R (Wells) v Secretary of State for
Transport, Local Government and the Regions* [2004] ECR I–723.
[37] Case C–44/95 [1997] QB 206. Contrast *R v Secretary of State for the Environment, Food and Rural
Affairs, ex p (1) Friends of the Earth and (2) Greenpeace Ltd* [2002] Env LR 24 where the claimants' suggested
interpretation of Council Directive (EC) 96/29/EURATOM requiring the decision-maker to take account of
sunk costs was rejected on a common-sense basis.
[38] [1996] Env LR 248.

14.45   EIAs were introduced into the United Kingdom by the EIA Directive (Directive (EEC) 85/337).[39] This was later amended in certain respects by the 1997 Directive (Directive (EC) 97/11). The EIA Directive was transposed into domestic law by domestic regulations starting with the Town and Country Planning (Assessment of Environmental Effects) Regulations 1988 (SI 1988/1199). There were amending regulations in 1994 and (to transpose the 1997 Directive) in 1999.[40] EIA is a comprehensive process of collecting information from the developer and other bodies in order that the local planning authority can assess that information before coming to a decision as to whether the development should be allowed to proceed. The report produced from the information that has been collected is known as the environmental statement. That statement must contain information about the development (see Sch 4 to the 1999 Regulations) as follows:

(1) A description of the project including its site, design, and size.
(2) Information necessary to identify its main effects.
(3) The measures to be taken to remedy, avoid, or reduce any significant adverse effects.
(4) A description of any alternatives studied by the applicant or appellant and the reason for the choice having regard to the environmental effects.
(5) A non-technical summary.

14.46   What the EIA Directive (as amended) does[41] is to require certain EIA procedures to be followed before the grant of 'development consent'. The term 'development consent' is defined (see Article 1(2)) as 'the decision of the competent authority or authorities which entitles the developer to proceed with the project'. Article 2(1) requires Member States to adopt a requirement of development consent in respect of projects likely to have significant effects on the environment together with an EIA assessment in respect of such projects.

14.47   The meaning of the term 'development consent' has been the subject of domestic judicial review proceedings. It has been construed purposively. In *R v North Yorkshire County Council, ex p Brown* [42] neighbouring landowners sought judicial review of a decision determining planning conditions in relation to proposed quarrying activities which were the subject of an old mining permission. Whilst no planning permission was given, new conditions were required as a prerequisite to development being allowed to continue. The House of Lords held that this was sufficient to constitute 'development consent' within the meaning of the directive. *Brown* was, in effect, a challenge to the lawful transposition of the EIA Directive although the case was fought on the basis that the EIA Directive conferred directly effective rights so that the local planning authority's decision in the instant case was unlawful.

---

[39] It should also be noted that the Strategic Environmental Assessment Directive (Directive (EC) 2001/42) came into force in June 2004 and has been transposed into domestic law by the Assessment of Plans and Programmes Regulations 2004 (SI 2004/1633). This requires an EIA to be carried out by the relevant statutory authorities when preparing certain plans and programmes.

[40] SI 1999/293. The 1999 Regulations have, in their turn, been subject to further amendment.

[41] The EIA Directive has been held to be directly effective: see *Twyford Parish Council v Secretary of State for the Environment* [1993] 3 Env LR 37.

[42] [2000] 1 AC 397.

A similar approach was adopted by the ECJ in *Wells* [43] a subsequent judicial review application which was referred to it by the Administrative Court under Article 234 (ex 177) EC. The ECJ observed as follows:

> It would undermine the effectiveness of [the EIA Directive] to regard as mere modifications of an existing consent the adoption of decisions which . . . replace not only the terms but the very substance of a prior consent, such as an old mining permission.

The expression 'projects' is defined generally in Article 1 and applied specifically in Article 4. There are two classes of projects falling within EIA requirements, namely (see Article 4) those listed in either Annex I or Annex II of the directive. Annex I projects are those which require EIA. Annex II consists of those projects that are subject to EIA requirements on either (see Article 4(2)) a case-by-case basis or by reference to thresholds or criteria set by the Member State.

The 1999 Regulations have transposed Annexes I and II of the directive into (respectively) Schs 1 and 2 of the 1999 Regulations. Consistent with the directive, an EIA is required for all developments listed in Sch 1. These encompass the largest developments such as motorways, crude oil refineries, and larger thermal power stations. Schedule 2 developments only require EIA if the project will have a significant effect on the environment.

Selection criteria for the screening of possible Sch 2 projects for a mandatory EIA are set out in Sch 3 to the Regulations. Judicial review challenges on this aspect of EIA have, though, tended to focus not on the underlying meaning of whether a particular development is or is not a 'project' but, rather, on whether a particular development is or is not a Sch 2 project.

Such cases most usually involve challenges to a local planning authority's failure to require EIA because the authority concludes that the development does not involve any significant effect on the environment.

In *Malster* [44] a judicial review challenge was brought on precisely this basis. The authority had concluded that an EIA was not required because, in its view, the development was not a Sch 2 project because it would not have a significant effect on the environment. The Administrative Court dismissed the challenge ruling that whilst the development might have a significant effect on *individual properties* in the area that was not the same thing as having a significant effect on the environment. By contrast, in *Goodman* [45] the Court of Appeal held that the local planning authority's conclusion that the development did not require EIA as being outside Sch 2 (as not constituting an 'infrastructure project' and an 'urban development project') was wrong as a matter of law. These cases show that the Administrative Court may be prepared in some, albeit limited, [46] circumstances to

14.48

14.49

14.50

14.51

14.52

14.53

---

[43] [2004] ECR I–723.
[44] *R (Malster) v Ipswich Borough Council* [2002] PLCR 251.
[45] *R (Goodman) v LB of Lewisham* [2003] EWCA Civ 140.
[46] Consider, eg, *Hereford Waste Watchers Ltd v Hereford Council* (2005) 9 EG 188 (*held*:(Elias J), a decision as to whether a planning activity had significant environmental effects was for the local planning authority although if it was unsure about the answer it should obtain further information and could not seek to regulate future potential difficulties by the imposition of conditions).

examine in proceedings for judicial review what appear, at least ostensibly, to involve issues of fact. This topic which raises more general issues relevant to EC domestic judicial review is also addressed below.[47]

14.54 The next area where the EIA regime has given rise to public law issues before the national courts is the question of what stage or stages (if any) an EIA is required. The problem has arisen because of the structure of the UK planning system which consists of an initial outline planning permission (when the full scope of the development may not always be known) as well as the reserved matters stage (ie the final planning permission when the matters reserved for further consideration at the outline stage are then addressed). Is it sufficient for the EIA to be undertaken at the outline stage or should it be deferred until the final permission stage or carried out, at least in some circumstances, at both stages?

14.55 The issue surfaced in *Wells*[48] where planning permission had been granted without an EIA in circumstances where an EIA was required. One of the questions was the point or points at which an EIA ought to have been undertaken. The ECJ observed (paras 50–52):

> As provided in Article 2(1) of Directive 85/337, the environmental impact assessment must be carried out before consent is given.
>
> According to the first recital in the preamble to the directive, the competent authority is to take account of the environmental effects of the project in question at the earliest possible stage in the decision-making process.
>
> Accordingly, where national law provides that the consent procedure is to be carried out in several stages, one involving a principal decision and the other involving an implementing decision which cannot extend beyond the parameters set by the principal decision, the effects which the project may have on the environment must be identified and assessed at the time of the procedure relating to the principal decision. It is only if those effects are not identifiable until the time of the procedure relating to the implementing decision that the assessment should be carried out in the course of that procedure.

14.56 In *Barker*,[49] another judicial review challenge involving the EIA regime, the Court of Appeal held that a local planning authority was not required to assess the need for an EIA both at the outline permission stage and at the time that reserved matters were considered. However, the House of Lords referred the case to the ECJ for a preliminary ruling and one of the questions before the ECJ was 'may national law, consistently with the Directive, preclude a competent authority from requiring that an EIA be carried out at a later stage of the planning process [than the outline stage]?'[50] In the event, the ECJ ruled that where planning permission comprised an initial stage of outline consent with subsequent approval of matters reserved at the first stage, it was contrary to EC law to provide that an EIA could only be carried out at the first stage.[51]

---

[47] See also paras 14.99–14.104.

[48] [2004] ECR I–723.

[49] *R (Barker) v London Borough of Bromley* [2001]EWCA Civ 1766.

[50] See, also, *R (Prokopp) v London Underground Ltd* [2004] Env LR 170 where, perhaps surprisingly, given the uncertainty then created by the reference in *Barker*, the Court of Appeal held that no further EIA was needed at the reserved matters stage where one had been carried out at the outline permission stage.

[51] Joined Cases C–290/03 and C–508/03 *R (Barker) v Bromley London Borough Council* The Times, 10 May 2006.

Even where a project is capable of having a significant effect on the environment (and on **14.57** the assumption that an EIA would, otherwise, be required) there remains an issue over whether a local planning authority may decide that because of mitigating measures to be taken by the developer an EIA is not required. As can be seen from the required content of an environmental statement,[52] such statement must, in fact, contain information of the proposed mitigation measures. Despite that requirement, however, the decision of the Court of Appeal in *Bellway*[53] suggests that there are at least some circumstances in which the authority could decide that, because of proposed mitigation measures, an EIA was not necessary. Relevant factors appear to include the type of mitigation measure envisaged, the amount of detail specified and the likelihood of successful implementation.

Process challenges have also featured in EIA cases before national courts. At their broadest **14.58** they may overlap with the requirement on public bodies to take into account material considerations. In *R v Swale Borough Council, ex p RSPB*,[54] for example, judicial review proceedings were brought by the RSPB on the footing that EIA should have been conducted in relation to an application for planning permission for Lappel Bank. Although the application was dismissed, the court observed that a local planning authority should not merely consider the planning application presented to it but ought to examine whether the application was part of a more substantial development.

Another example of a mixed process and material considerations challenge is afforded by **14.59** *R v Rochdale Metropolitan Borough Council, ex p Tew*.[55] There, the Administrative Court allowed an application for judicial review of a grant of outline planning permission in circumstances where it was not possible for full environmental information to be available for public consideration at the outline stage because the extent of the development could not be provided. Nor, on the information given, could it be said that there would not be significant environment effects when the authority subsequently had to consider reserved matters.

It can be seen that there is a connection between the difficulties that arose in *Tew* and the **14.60** related problems discussed above in respect of *Wells* and *Barker* as to when an EIA must be conducted. If the EIA can only be conducted at the outline stage it is not easy to see how the outline permission can do other than anticipate all environmental effects of a project, leaving no environmental issues to arise at the reserved matters stage. However, if the EIA can be addressed at both stages the position is easier from the authority's point of view. In *Milne*[56] (the second round of *Tew*) the Administrative Court rejected a second judicial review challenge to the second grant of outline permission in relation to the same project where the authority had imposed planning conditions preventing the development from going beyond the scope of the outline permission.

Under the screening procedures in the 1999 Regulations (see reg 5(1)) a developer may ask **14.61** the local planning authority for a view as to whether EIA is required. The authority must

---

[52] See para 14.45.
[53] *Bellway Urban Renewal Southern v Gillespie* [2003] Env LR 30.
[54] (1990) 2 Admin LR 790.
[55] [2000] Env LR 1.
[56] *R v Rochdale MBC, ex p Milne* [2001] Env LR 22.

then issue an opinion within three weeks. If the authority fails to provide its opinion within that time (or considers that EIA is required) the developer may seek a screening direction from the Secretary of State.

14.62   Alleged non-compliance with these procedures has given rise to judicial review challenges. In *R (Fernback) v Harrow Borough Council* [57] the question before the Administrative Court was whether if further information was discovered, the authority was required to review its previous (negative) screening opinion. The court held that there was no obligation on the authority to do so.

14.63   Other EIA process challenges by way of judicial review have included (successful) challenges to EIA decisions which have not been lawfully delegated to planning officers, [58] and to EIA decisions taken without an environmental statement containing all relevant information, [59] and (albeit unsuccessfully) decisions, without giving any reasons, that an EIA was unnecessary. [60]

14.64   Finally, judicial review challenges in the context of EIA have sometimes been met with the argument that, even if an EIA ought technically to have been required, the court should in its discretion refuse relief to the claimant because even had an EIA been conducted it would have made no difference to the decision. Similar general issues have arisen over delay in bringing a challenge to a failure to conduct an EIA. The cases in which these issues have been raised go well beyond the confines of the EIA regime and are addressed separately below. [61]

Issues arising from EC environmental law in judicial review procedure

Standing

14.65   It is important to separate out the different threshold requirements for standing in domestic environmental judicial review proceedings since different tests, at least ostensibly, apply depending upon whether the basis for the challenge is founded on purely domestic grounds, on HRA grounds, or on EC grounds.

---

[57] [2002] Env LR 10.

[58] *R v St Edmundsbury Borough Council, ex p Walton* [1999] JPL 805.

[59] *R v Cornwall County Council, ex p Hardy* [2001] Env LR 25 (absence of information as to presence of protected bats on site). For a trenchant statement of the need for a clear environmental statement as opposed to a disparate collection of documents, see per Lord Hoffmann in *Berkeley v Secretary of State for the Environment* [2001] 2 AC 603, 615.

[60] *R v Secretary of State for the Environment, Transport and the Regions and Parcelforce, ex p Marson* [1998] JPL 869. Whilst the 1999 Regulations now require reasons for the grant or refusal of planning permission accompanied by an EIA (reg 21) and why EIA is required (reg 4(6)) there is still no express duty under the regulations for a decision that no EIA is required. The *Marson* decision is analysed separately (see paras 10.54–10.60) and was followed by Richards J in *Gillespie v First Secretary of State* [2003] EWHC 8. Its legitimacy may, however, be open to doubt following the ECJ ruling in Case C–87/02 *Commission v Italy* [2004] ECR I–5975 where the ECJ held that, in the circumstances of the case, inadequate reasons had been given for excluding an EIA. The giving of inadequate reasons where given is, though, not synonymous with a duty to give reasons. There is, currently, a judicial review application due to be heard by the Court of Appeal in which the value of *Marson* as a precedent is under challenge: see (at first instance): see *R (Probyn) v First Secretary of State* [2005] EWHC 398.

[61] See (respectively) paras 14.76–14.80 and 14.90–14.96.

In general, relatively wide access is accorded to environmental standing in domestic judicial review. Although the courts have not addressed principles relating to environmental standing separately the reason for generous standing is implicitly because of the public interest that is, more often than not, involved in such cases.

14.66

It is, therefore, perhaps unsurprising that those cases in which wide standing has been accepted have usually been cases with an environmental element. The leading authority is the decision of a Divisional Court in the *Pergau Dam* case.[62] There, a number of criteria were articulated by the court as indicative of a claimant possessing standing. They included the public interest in the matter being litigated, and the fact that, if standing were not granted, then a manifest illegality would not be challenged.[63] It also seems that provided a claimant has sufficient interest to bring the challenge there will be no standing restrictions as to the grounds that may, then, be argued.[64]

14.67

More recently, in *R v Somerset County Council, ex p Dixon*[65] the principles set out in *Pergau Dam* were confirmed by Sedley J on a contested application for permission to apply for judicial review. In *Dixon* Sedley J observed that judicial review was concerned with controlling abuse of power rather than with vindicating private law rights. For that reason standing would be granted to a claimant with a genuine interest in the subject matter of the application.[66]

14.68

Cases such as these demonstrate that in environmental judicial review challenges (certainly those based on purely domestic and EC grounds) it appears that, at least where a challenge has significant public interest, an environmental pressure group will have standing to bring the challenge.[67]

14.69

Surprisingly the same may not necessarily—or invariably—be true of an environmental challenge founded on HRA grounds. There is also a discrete problem in respect of standing to bring EC challenges in certain instances.

14.70

In HRA cases a difficulty on standing may sometimes arise because of the terms of the 'victim' test under HRA, s 7(1). At least generally,[68] in order to mount a human rights

14.71

---

[62] *R v Secretary of State for Foreign and Commonwealth Affairs, ex p World Development Movement Ltd* [1995] 1 WLR 386.

[63] See also para 3.51.

[64] See, eg, *R (Kides) v South Cambridgeshire DC* [2002] 4 PLR 66; *R (Hammerton) v London Underground Ltd* [2002] EWHC 2307.

[65] [1998] Env LR 111. To similar effect, see per Otton J in *R v Inspectorate of Pollution, ex p Greenpeace Ltd (No 2)* [1994] 4 All ER 329 where Greenpeace was accorded standing to challenge a decision to operate at Sellafield.

[66] These more liberal decisions would appear to have superseded earlier and more restrictive decisions on environmental standing. See, eg, *R v Secretary of State for the Environment, ex p Rose Theatre Trust* [1990] 1 All ER 754; *R v North Somerset District Council, ex p Garnett* [1998] Env LR 911.

[67] On the liberal approach now taken to standing in environmental challenges in the Administrative Court see, also: *R v Hammersmith and Fulham London Borough Council, ex p People before Profit Ltd* [1983] 45 P & CR 364; *R v Secretary of State for the Environment, ex p Friends of the Earth* [1996] Env LR 198; *Edwards v Environment Agency* [2004] EWHC 736.

[68] See, though, *Rushbridger v Attorney General* [2004] 1 AC 357 (proceedings involving statutory interpretation under HRA, ss 3–4 do not have to be commenced by a 'victim').

challenge under the HRA, a person must be a 'victim' and—to be a victim—must be directly affected by the measure in question. There have been a few environmental challenges brought under the HRA that have failed because of lack of standing[69] in circumstances in which they would have been unlikely to have failed to meet the standing threshold on purely domestic grounds.

14.72 A particular difficulty can arise in respect of standing on EC grounds. The difficulty is a general one[70] but it has particular resonance to EC environmental challenges. Under Article 230 (ex 173) EC in order to bring a direct action before the ECJ the subject matter must be of *direct and individual concern* to the applicant. As interpreted by the ECJ, this standing requirement is very stringent so that environmental pressure groups representing a large class of affected persons was denied standing under Article 230 because none of the represented local residents, who were plainly affected by the allocation of Commission funding for the construction of certain power stations, were considered to be sufficiently individually affected.[71]

14.73 The difficulty in environmental cases is that the narrowness of standing as currently interpreted by the ECJ in direct actions to the ECJ under Article 230 has the effect that the more persons who are affected (as is usually the case with environmental decisions) the less likely is it that standing will be accorded under Article 230.

14.74 There would appear to be no equivalent bar to bringing applications for judicial review based on EC grounds in the domestic courts *provided that such challenges are commenced in time*. However, the uncertainty of knowing whether a potential claimant would have had standing under Article 230 to bring a direct action could have consequences for standing in domestic judicial review. This is because if a claimant did possess Article 230 standing but failed to bring a direct action within the strict time period allowed by that provision, it is likely that the ECJ would refuse to entertain a reference by the national court under Article 234 considering it to be a means of bypassing the strict limitation period in Article 230.[72]

14.75 It is, therefore, by no means inevitable that the Administrative Court would in such circumstances refer a case brought by such a claimant by way of judicial review to the ECJ for a preliminary ruling under Article 234 (ex 177) EC.[73] In the absence of a reference, a claimant or claimants who have not claimed the protection of Article 230 when they could

---

[69] See, eg: *R v Mayor of London, ex p Westminster CC* [2002] EWHC 2440 (Westminster CC not a 'victim' for the purpose of HRA grounds); *Adams v Advocate General for Scotland* [2002] UKHRR 1189 (Countryside Alliance and Masters of Foxhounds Associations lacked standing as representative bodies to mount HRA arguments on the hunting ban in Scotland).

[70] See, also, paras 3.67–3.80.

[71] See Case C–321 *Stichting Greenpeace Council v Commission* [1998] ECR I–1651. See, also, Case C–50/00P *Union de Pequenos Agricultores v Council* [2002] ECR I–1677; Case C–263/02 P *Jego-Quere & Cie SA v Commission* [2004] ECR I–3425 where the ECJ in both cases disagreed with (respectively) Advocate General Jacobs and with the CFI who had adopted a more liberal approach to standing under Art 230.

[72] See paras 3.67–3.80.

[73] See, generally, Chapter 4 especially para 4.96.

have done will not have the benefit of their case being considered by the ECJ or the national court.

Discretion to refuse relief

Although domestic judicial review remedies are discretionary so that even a meritorious **14.76** case may result in denial of relief on certain grounds[74] such as, for example, the fact that the application is premature,[75] or the adverse public consequences that would ensue,[76] the scope for exercise of discretion to refuse relief in an EC environmental context has been held to be more limited.

For example, the courts have accepted that public participation is an important aspect of **14.77** EC environmental law. As Lord Steyn observed in *R v Hammersmith and Fulham London Borough Council, ex p Burkett*:[77]

> The Directive [Directive (EEC) 85/337 on the assessment of environmental effects of certain projects] seeks to redress to some extent the imbalance in resources between promoters of major developments and those concerned on behalf of individual or community interests, about the environmental effects of such projects.

A consequence of the significance attached to such public involvement is that discretion to **14.78** refuse relief is much less likely to be exercised in an EC environmental context because the effect would be to bypass that essential public element.

A number of cases in this area have reflected the courts' general insistence on granting **14.79** remedies where a breach of EC law is established.[78] In *Smith v Secretary of State for the Environment, Transport and the Regions*[79] Sedley LJ made the point that an environmental impact assessment regime requiring public participation ought not to be circumvented '... by the surrender of public judgment to private negotiation'. Similarly, in relation to the same regime, Elias J has observed that:

> [the Directive requires an] ... inclusive and democratic procedure ... in which the public, however misguided or wrong headed its views may be, is given the opportunity to express its opinion on the environmental issues.[80]

However, although the decision of the House of Lords in *Berkeley*[81] suggested that the **14.80** scope for exercising discretion to refuse relief might be very narrow where breaches of EC law were involved, the courts have—in subsequent environmental cases—sometimes been prepared to refuse relief as a matter of discretion especially in respect of procedural

---

[74] See, generally, Sir Thomas Bingham MR, 'Should Public Law Remedies Be Discretionary?' [1991] PL 64.

[75] See, eg, *R v Chief Constable of the Merseyside Police, ex p Merrill* [1989] 1 WLR 1077, 1088.

[76] See, eg, *R v Secretary of State for Social Services, ex p Cotton* The Times, 14 December 1985.

[77] [2002] 1 WLR 1593, para 15.

[78] See, most notably, the House of Lords' ruling in *Berkeley v Secretary of State for the Environment* [2001] 2 AC 603, especially 608 per Lord Bingham, 615 and 616 per Lord Hoffmann. See, also, eg, *Hereford Waste Watchers Ltd v Herefordshire Council* [2005] JPL 1469, *R (Mount Cook Land Ltd) v Westminster CC* [2004] 1 PLR 26, para 46, per Auld LJ.

[79] [2003] Env LR 693, para 58.

[80] *BT v Gloucester City Council* [2002] JPL 93, para 68.

[81] [2001] 2 AC 603.

defects that have made no essential difference to the decision reached.[82] Further, where the effects of quashing a decision may be particularly adverse the court may even in an EC context, exceptionally, be prepared to postpone the quashing order to a future date.[83]

Costs

14.81 Costs in judicial review proceedings have frequently acquired an importance in environmental judicial review challenges not least because of the public interest nature of such cases. This is especially true in EC-based challenges and there is the additional consideration of the general principle of effectiveness which requires EC rights to be effective and not, in practice, eroded.[84]

14.82 In both domestic and EC challenges, the first costs principle is that, in the event of an unsuccessful challenge, two or more sets of costs of successful defendants or interveners are not usually awarded against the claimant.[85]

14.83 A second principle is that, even if a challenge is unsuccessful, there may (albeit exceptionally) be no award of costs against the unsuccessful claimant because of the public importance of the case. Most of the precedents for this are environmental cases but the scope of the principle remains far from clear.[86]

14.84 A third and increasingly significant principle is that relating to protective costs which have particular relevance to EC environmental challenges because of the Aarhus Convention (see below).

14.85 The relevant principles were the subject of comprehensive review and consideration by the Court of Appeal in *R (Corner House Research) v Secretary of State for Trade and Industry* [87] (see, especially, para 74 of the court's judgment). That case and earlier decisions on protective costs, are considered in more detail elsewhere.[88]

14.86 Costs principles generally may sometimes need to be revisited in the light of the general principles of EC law referred to above.

14.87 In the environmental context this is particularly important. The most restrictive criterion for the granting of a protective costs order is that the claimant must have no *private interest*

---

[82] See, especially, the observations of Carnwath LJ in *R (Jones) v Mansfield District Council* [2004] Env LR 391, para 59. Contrast, though, per Simon Brown LJ in *R (Richardson) v North Yorkshire County Council* [2004] 1 WLR 1920, para 42. See, further, A Lidbetter and R Buchner, 'Withholding Relief for a Breach of EU Law: A Comparative Approach' [2003] JR 36.

[83] See *R (Rockware Glass Ltd) v Chester City Council and Quinn Glass Ltd* [2006] EWCA Civ 240 (breach of IPPC Directive (Directive (EC) 96/61) and implementing regulations).

[84] For further consideration of the general principle of effectiveness in the context of remedy, see paras 3.09–3.17.

[85] *Bolton Urban District Council v Secretary of State for the Environment* [1995] 1 WLR 1196.

[86] See, especially: *New Zealand Maori Council v Attorney General of New Zealand* [1994] 1 AC 466, 485; *R (Friends of the Earth and Greenpeace) v Secretary of State for the Environment, Food and Rural Affairs* [2001] EWCA Civ 1950; *R v Secretary of State for the Environment, ex p Challenger* [2001] Env LR 209; *R v Secretary of State for the Environment, ex p Greenpeace Ltd* [1994] 4 All ER 352.

[87] [2005] 1 WLR 2600. *Corner House* reconsidered the guidelines earlier down by Dyson J in *R v Lord Chancellor, ex p Child Poverty Action Group* [1999] 1 WLR 347, 353. See, further, R Clayton QC, 'Public Interest Litigation, Costs and the Role of Legal Aid' [2006] PL 429; B Jaffey, 'Protective Costs Orders in Judicial Review' [2006] JR 171.

[88] See paras 3.166–3.176.

in the outcome. It is generally acknowledged that this requirement is very restrictive in domestic judicial review generally but especially so in an environmental context where the very reason for bringing a challenge is likely to be an environmental hazard that personally affects the claimant. As Brooke LJ observed in the Court of Appeal in the environmental challenge in *R (Burkett) v Hammersmith and Fulham LBC*:[89]

> an unprotected claimant . . . if unsuccessful in a public interest challenge, may have to pay very heavy legal costs to the successful defendant . . . this may be a potent factor in deterring litigation directed towards protecting the environment from harm.

There is certainly scope for contending that—whatever the correctness of protective costs **14.88** order principles in a purely domestic case such as *Corner House*—the position should be different in an EC environmental challenge where the deterrent effect of expensive court procedures may, in practice, operate adversely to EC environmental law objectives and may, in any event, be disproportionate.

This is especially potent having regard to the fact that the UK ratified the Aarhus **14.89** Convention on 24 February 2005. In general terms, the Convention requires access to fair procedures in respect of decisions relating to the environment. Article 9.4 provides, materially, thus:

> . . . the procedures referred to in paragraphs 1, 2 and 3 above [referring to domestic procedures for challenging environmental decisions] shall provide adequate and effective remedies, including injunctive relief as appropriate, and be fair, equitable, timely and not prohibitively expensive.

Delay

As has been seen,[90] the delay rules in domestic judicial review are generally more stringent **14.90** than in private law proceedings. Although there is (subject to discretion to extend time) a nominal outer limit to bring proceedings of three months from the decision, act, or default complained of, there is also a requirement to act promptly. It cannot be assumed, therefore, that a claimant necessarily has three months in which to seek permission to apply for judicial review.

The promptness requirement can produce uncertainty. Its potential incompatibility with **14.91** EC law (and ECHR law) has been the subject of judicial comment (albeit *obiter*) in the context of environmental law.[91] In that context in *R v Hammersmith and Fulham London Borough Council, ex p Burkett*[92] the House of Lords, with the imperatives of (at least) ECHR law very much in mind, made reference to the burden involved in preparing judicial review proceedings in respect of a planning decision that might never be implemented.

---

[89] See, also, *Wilkinson and Kitzinger* [2004] EWCA Civ 1342, para 54, per Sir Mark Potter who was heavily critical of the no private interest requirement as a prerequisite for the making of a protective costs order.

[90] See paras 3.81–3.92.

[91] *R v Hammersmith and Fulham London Borough Council, ex p Burkett* [2002] 1 WLR 1593, para 53, per Lord Steyn. Note, though, that in *Lam v United Kingdom Application No 41671/98*, 5 July 2001 the European Court of Human Rights has held that the promptness requirement is not a breach of Art 6 ECHR. This authority was apparently not cited to the House of Lords in *Burkett*. See, further, R Taylor 'Time Flies Like the Wind: Some Issues that *Burkett* Did Not Address' [2005] JR 249.

[92] [2002] 1 WLR 1593, 50, per Lord Steyn.

14.92 However, the Court of Appeal, since *Burkett*, has expressly endorsed the promptness requirement for applications for judicial review. In *Hardy*[93] the court refused permission to appeal the refusal of permission to apply for judicial review of an environmental challenge to the grant of planning permission brought (materially)[94] just within the three month period. In refusing permission Keene LJ who gave the leading judgment observed, first, that the promptness requirement had been accepted by the European Court of Human Rights in a case not cited to the House of Lords in *Burkett*.[95] Secondly, he pointed out that the Strasbourg Court has held that legal certainty does not connote 'absolute certainty'[96] and that this is especially applicable to a procedural rule in applications seeking judicial review where the degree of promptness required will vary from case to case. He also referred to the use of the concept of promptness in the ECHR itself (see Articles 5(3) and 6(3)).

14.93 However, *Hardy* was not a case founded on EC law. It is certainly true, though, that even in an EC environmental context, domestic courts are reluctant to allow the promptness requirement for judicial review to be bypassed by bringing what are, in reality, out-of-time challenges to earlier decisions under the guise of a challenge to a later decision.[97]

14.94 In some instances, though, it may be that a challenge to a later decision should be permitted—albeit that it could have been brought in respect of an earlier decision—on the basis that such challenge involves the current application of a substantive principle of EC law that would be defeated if it were held to be time-barred. Thus, for example, in *Wells*[98] a challenge succeeded to a continuing failure to make reparation for a breach of EC law by failure to conduct an environmental impact assessment at the time of granting planning permission even though the proceedings were brought many years after the grant of planning permission and even though the underlying planning permission was not, itself, the subject of challenge.[99]

14.95 It is, perhaps, fair to observe that the case law relating to delay in this difficult area of EC law has not yet been rationalized. There appear to be three principles at stake that do not always sit easily together.

14.96 First, there is the uncontroversial primacy that EC law accords to national procedural rules provided that they do not emasculate EC rights or make those rights impossible, in practice, to enforce.[100] Secondly, there is the legitimate concern of domestic courts not to allow time limits for judicial review to be circumvented. Thirdly, however, there is that aspect of the EC general principle of effectiveness that may conflict with domestic procedural rules

---

[93] *Hardy v Pembrokeshire County Council and Pembrokeshire Coast National Park Authority* [2006] EWCA Civ 240.

[94] Most of the decisions were made more than three months prior to the application for permission to seek judicial review but the court implicitly accepted that the question in respect of the last decision was whether the proceedings to challenge it had been brought promptly.

[95] [2002] 1 WLR 1593.

[96] *Sunday Times v United Kingdom* [1979–80] 2 EHRR 245, para 49.

[97] See, eg, *R (Noble Organisation) v Thanet District Council* [2005] EWCA Civ 782. This case is also mentioned at para 3.111.

[98] [2004] ECR I–723.

[99] Contrast, though, the facts of, and decision of the Court of Appeal in, *Noble* at n 97 above.

[100] For the different formulations of the principle of effectiveness, see paras 3.11–3.16.

even where a claimant has blatantly disregarded those rules.[101] Most notably, the EC require-ment that the State must make reparation for prior breaches of EC law may—as in *Wells*—compel national measures which, if not taken, may render an emanation of the State susceptible to judicial review. If the domestic courts refuse an application for judicial review because of delay in failing to challenge the prior breach then the obligation on the State to make reparation cannot, sensibly, be enforced. Thus far, different approaches have been taken to this issue by the domestic courts without the matter being considered by the ECJ.[102]

Remedies

Remedies in judicial review are discussed separately.[103] In the environmental context the Administrative Court has not drawn a specific distinction, for the purposes of interim relief, between domestic, ECHR, or EC law although the principles relating to interim relief in an EC challenge are often distinct and must, where appropriate, be applied by the court. **14.97**

Certainly at present, the domestic courts have not been prepared to dispense with the need for a cross-undertaking as to damages even in the EC environmental context and have treated cross-undertaking requirements in the cases interchangeably. Thus in *BACONGO*[104] (a non-EC case) a challenge was made by an environmental pressure group to prevent con-struction of the Chalillo Dam on the basis that no EIA had been carried out. The Privy Council held that before granting interim injunctive relief a cross-undertaking in damages would ordi-narily be required. In an earlier EC challenge (which proved, in the event, to be successful) the House of Lords had held that in the absence of such an undertaking from the claimant, an injunction would not have been granted (and for the same reason interim declaratory relief would not be granted even if at the time the case was decided such a remedy existed).[105] **14.98**

Nature of the review process in EC environmental cases

It is always important to identify the nature of the review process being undertaken by the court in different types of EC environmental challenge brought by way of judicial review. Although matters of fact and/or discretion are—subject to certain factual/discretionary inquiry which the court may have to address in addressing a measure's proportionality[106]—largely for the decision maker rather than for the court, the Administrative Court will, sometimes, be required to determine what appears to be a question of fact or discretion but which is, properly analysed, a question of law. Determining the question of law may involve the application of fact to law but the decision is one of jurisdictional fact for (ultimately) the court. **14.99**

The distinction is well illustrated by *Goodman*.[107] There, the question was whether a partic-ular development was an 'infrastructure project' for the purposes of constituting a project **14.100**

---

[101] It follows from the principle of effectiveness that if a domestic procedural rule breaches the principle then it does not have to be complied with.

[102] cf *Wells* n 98 above and *Noble* n 97 above.

[103] See, generally, Chapter 5.

[104] [2004] Env LR 314.

[105] *R v Secretary of State for the Environment, ex p RSPB* [1997] Env LR 431.

[106] For more detailed consideration of proportionality in EC cases, see Chapter 11.

[107] [2003] EWCA Civ 140.

subject to environmental impact assessment requirements in EC law.[108] The court held that the question was one of jurisdictional fact which the court had to decide.

14.101 As Buxton LJ observed:[109]

> However fact-sensitive such a determination may be, it is not simply a finding of fact, nor of discretionary judgment. Rather, it involves the application of the authority's understanding of the meaning in law of the expression used in the Regulation. If the authority reaches an understanding of those expressions that is wrong as a matter of law, then the court must correct that error: and in determining the meaning of the statutory expressions the concept of reasonable judgment as embodied in *Wednesbury* simply has no part to play.

14.102 However, in *Malster*,[110] another EC environmental assessment decision, the Administrative Court held that the issue of whether a development was likely to have significant effects on the environment (and so come within the purview of EC environmental impact assessment control) did not involve jurisdictional fact. Sullivan J said this:

> A detailed knowledge of the locality and expertise in assessing the environmental effects of different kinds of development are both essential in answering that question, which is pre-eminently a matter of judgment and degree rather than a question of fact. Unlike the planning authority, the court does not possess such knowledge and expertise.

14.103 Here, Sullivan J appears to be contrasting discretionary judgment (largely for the decision-maker) with jurisdictional fact (ultimately for the court). The distinction is not always easy to draw. But, to the extent that the meaning of a word or phrase is open-textured, so that there is a range of possible meanings, it seems that the court is more likely to categorize the question of meaning as one involving the exercise of discretionary judgment reviewable on conventional *Wednesbury* principles than as an issue of jurisdictional fact for the court.[111]

14.104 Finally, the forensic reality is that where a judicial review challenge raises other issues of law and where an ostensible issue of fact is not the main legal issue, the national court may not be over-concerned to decide whether the authority determined the question of fact correctly in law but will decide the other legal issues in any event. Thus, in *Berkeley*,[112] for example, the House of Lords did not actually decide whether the project in question was one that required EIA. Lord Hoffmann put it thus:

> It is arguable that the development was [a Sch 2 project] and the conflicting evidence on the potential effect on the river is enough in itself to show that it was arguably likely to have significant effects on the environment. In those circumstances, individuals affected by the development had a directly enforceable right to have the need for an EIA considered before the grant of planning permission by the Secretary of State and not afterwards by a judge.

---

108 See para 14.53.
109 At para 8 of the judgment.
110 [2002] PLCR 251.
111 See, eg, *R v Monopolies and Mergers Commission, ex p South Yorkshire Transport Ltd* [1993] 1 WLR 23, para 32G, per Lord Mustill.
112 [2001] 2 AC 603.

15

PUBLIC PROCUREMENT

A. Outline of the EC Public Procurement Regime

Introduction

EC public procurement is concerned with ensuring that public contracts of specified types **15.01** are awarded on a fair, competitive and transparent basis. The term 'public procurement' refers to functions exercisable by a public authority[1] of purchasing goods, works, and/or services from a third party. The EC public procurement regime which has recently been

---

[1] There are also a number of special cases which are caught by the EC public procurement regime but are not considered here such as contracts subsidized by public authorities but awarded by private bodies. Further, the definition of a public authority ('contracting authority') is one derived from EC law and may encompass bodies that would, in national law, be termed a 'private' as opposed to a 'public' body.

substantially amended (and reflected in domestic regulations) relates to the process (not applicable to every situation) leading up to the award of a contract in favour of a particular party.

15.02 The rationale for co-ordinating at Community level the procedures for the award of public contracts is to eliminate barriers on the freedom to provide services and goods and, therefore, to protect the interests of traders established in a Member State who wish to offer goods or services to contracting authorities established in other Member States.[2]

15.03 Consequently, the aim of the procurement directives (see paras 15.10 et seq.)[3] is to avoid the risk of preference being shown to national tenderers or applicants whenever a contract is awarded by the contracting authorities and the possibility that a body financed or controlled by the State, regional or local authorities, or other bodies governed by public law may choose to be guided by considerations other than economic ones.[4]

15.04 Encompassing, as public procurement does, public functions exercisable by public bodies it is apparent that public law issues (including the application of domestic and HRA public law principles) will frequently arise under the procurement regime. However, although domestic judicial review may sometimes be an appropriate procedure[5] for illegality or unfairness evinced by public bodies when awarding (or failing to award) contracts, there is a specialized regime in this area deriving from domestic regulations that implement EC directives. It is generally under this regime that public law issues will be required to be ventilated.

15.05 Only an outline of public procurement can be given here. In general terms, the specialized remedy requires an application to be made to the High Court[6] by a party aggrieved by the process (or, sometimes, lack of process) adopted by the authority. As will be seen, this remedy has many affinities with judicial review including a short time limit and similar principles of review. It also exemplifies, in its application, several of the general principles of EC law discussed in Part II.[7]

15.06 There follows a short description of the public procurement legislation; some aspects will then be revisited for the purpose of analysing the interplay of EC and public law principles that the Administrative Court and other domestic courts are likely to be faced with when public law procurement issues arise.

---

[2] Case C–360/96 *Gemeente Arnhem, Gemeente Rheden v BFI Holding* [1998] ECR I–6821, para 41. For a detailed analysis of the rationale for public procurement in the common market context, see C Bovis, *EC Public Procurement: Case Law and Regulation* (2006) especially ch 1.

[3] The directives (both new and old) would seem, in large measure, to be directly effective. See, eg, Case 103/88 *Fratelli Constanzo SpA v Commune di Milano* [1989] ECR 1839, para 32; Case C–247/89 *Commission v Portugal* [1991] ECR I–3659, para 15 in the Opinion of the Advocate General.

[4] Case C–44/96 *Mannesmann Anlagenbau Austria v Strohal Rotationsdruck* [1998] ECR I–73 para 33; Case C–360/96 *BFI Holding* [1998] ECR I–6821, paras 42–43.

[5] See paras 15.84 et seq.

[6] Such challenges will be brought in the High Court outside the judicial review procedure and not before the Administrative Court. See paras 15.101 et seq.

[7] See, generally, Chapters 6–12 above.

Sources of public procurement obligations

Importantly, a modified regime with new directives and subordinate legislation came into **15.07** force on 31 January 2006. Whilst the enforcement of public procurement obligations under the Remedies Directives (see below) remains as before and whilst the new regime does not fundamentally affect the EC or public law issues that relate to procurement cases, there are some new concepts that have been introduced by the new regime.

Since the cases discussed here are cases referring to the old regime, a short description of that **15.08** regime is given first (with references to the new domestic regulations where appropriate). This is followed by an outline of the changes made by that regime.

It should be noted that the various directives and domestic regulations contain many qual- **15.09** ifications and exceptions and their detail is outside the scope of this book. They should, however, be consulted in full in order to determine the applicability of the EC public procurement regime to any particular case.

Domestic public procurement regime prevailing before 31 January 2006 ('the old regime')

The following were the principal legislative sources that created obligations on public **15.10** bodies or, as the case may be, Member States in the area of EC public procurement prior to 31 January 2006:[8]

(1) The four so-called 'purchasing' directives (now replaced by the new directives) establishing the detailed procedures that had to be followed by public bodies when awarding certain public contracts. These were:
  (a) Council Directive (EEC) 93/36 co-ordinating procedures for the award of public supply contracts ('the Supplies Directive').
  (b) Council Directive (EEC) 93/37 regulating the co-ordination of procedures for the award of public works contracts ('the Works Directive').
  (c) Council Directive (EEC) 92/50 governing the award of public service contracts ('the Services Directive').
  (d) Council Directive (EEC) 93/38 co-ordinating procedures for the award of contracts in the water, energy, transport, and telecommunications sectors ('the Utilities Directive').
(2) The UK implementing procurement regulations[9] consisting of:
  (a) Public Supply Contracts Regulations 1995 (SI 1995/201) ('the Supply Regulations').
  (b) Public Works Contracts Regulations 1991 (SI 1991/2680) ('the Works Regulations').
  (c) Public Services Contracts Regulations 1993 (SI 1993/3228) ('the Services Regulations').
  (d) Utilities Contracts Regulations 1996 (SI 1996/2911) ('the Utilities Regulations').

---

[8] It should be noted that both the directives and domestic subordinate legislation were subject to amendment or consolidation and that, in particular, the original text of the regulations was amended on numerous occasions. For relevant amendments, see: <http://www.legislation.hmso.gov.uk>.

[9] The regulations contained many common features. In this chapter most illustrative references will be to the Services Regulations, but such references are intended to be exemplary rather than exhaustive.

Domestic public procurement regime as from 31 January 2006 ('the new regime')

15.11   As stated above, a modified public procurement regime has been introduced as from 31 January 2006.

15.12   The modified regime does not alter the essential nature of the public procurement regime (see below) or the procedural remedies for breach. Nor does it materially affect the EC and domestic law issues that arise in relation to public procurement and which are outlined below.

15.13   Two new directives have been adopted and passed by the European Parliament and Council of Ministers through the conciliation procedure that concluded on 2 January 2004. These are:

(1) Directive (EC)2004/18 on the co-ordination of procedures for the award of public works, supply and services contracts ('public sector procurement'). This directive entered into force on the date of publication (Article 83). This was 30 April 2004. The date for implementation was 31 January 2006 (Article 80).

(2) Directive (EC)2004/17 co-ordinating the procurement procedures of entities operating in the water, energy, transport, and postal services sectors ('utilities procurement'). This directive entered into force on the date of publication (Article 74). This was 30 April 2004. The date for implementation was 31 January 2006 (Article 71).

15.14   The UK implementing procurement regulations consist of:

(a) Public Contracts Regulations 2006 (SI 2006/5). These regulations replace the formerly separate Supply, Works and Services Regulations.

(b) Utilities Contracts Regulations 2006 (SI 2006/6). These regulations replace the former Utilities Regulations and cover certain operators in the water, energy, transport, and telecommunications sectors.

15.15   The purpose of these new directives and implementing regulations is to modernize and simplify the existing legislation in the field of public and utilities procurement. This is, essentially, achieved by:

(1) combining the Works, Supplies and Services Directives into one directive with identical rules for each of the three areas: the new directives thus effectively create a regime that is regulated by two directives containing largely the same rules and procedures;

(2) adjusting the existing directives to existing practices in Member States—the new regime also takes into account the judgments of the ECJ in this field;

(3) allowing for the use of electronic communication and new electronic purchase technology and generally allowing for more flexible procedures.

Legal sources common to both the old and the new regimes

15.16   There are (and were under the old regime) two directives imposing obligations on Member States to provide appropriate domestic remedies in respect of breaches of public procurement obligations for aggrieved third parties. These directives, collectively 'the Remedies

Directives' (the requirements of which have been implemented in both the former and the new regulations) are:

(1) Council Directive (EEC) 89/665 on the co-ordination of the laws, regulations and administrative provisions relating to the application of review procedures to the award of public supply and public works contracts ('the Remedies Directive').

(2) Council Directive (EEC) 92/13 on the co-ordination of laws, regulations, and administrative provisions relating to the application of Community rules on the procurement procedures of entities operating in the water, energy, transport, and telecommunications sectors ('the Utilities Remedies Directive').

In addition, and fundamentally, practitioners in this field need (and have always needed) to be aware of the overall EC context in terms of relevant Treaty provisions,[10] relevant general principles of law,[11] and the developing EC and national case law under the directives and regulations. They also need to understand the domestic common and public law context. Each may be relevant to applying the EC procurement regime and each may, on the facts of a particular case, provide a necessary remedy outside the procurement regime altogether.[12]   **15.17**

A detailed analysis of EC public procurement is outside the scope of this work[13] and, in any event, some of the relevant principles require consideration of private law torts and damages rather than public law issues. Nonetheless, the relationship between EC and domestic public law is highly relevant to many of the procedural and substantive issues that arise and the salient features of that relationship are considered below.   **15.18**

Essential content of the public procurement regime[14]

The regime covers the process leading (in the case of the Public Contracts Regulations 2006) to the award of 'public contracts'.[15] These are contracts in writing for a pecuniary interest concluded between a public purchaser on the one hand and, on the other, a (as the case may be) supplier, contractor, or service provider.   **15.19**

---

[10] See, most notably, Arts 28–29 (ex 30–34) EC and Art 30 (ex 36) EC (prohibition of quantitative restrictions on imports/exports and derogation therefrom), Art 49 (ex 59) EC (freedom to provide services) and the various Treaty provisions on state aid, freedom of movement of persons, services, and capital, and provisions as to competition. See, generally, Chapters 13, 16 and 17.

[11] See Chapters 6–12.

[12] For example, a public contract may fall outside the protective scope of the regulations or directives yet still attract domestic or EC principles of administrative law fairness or transparency: see paras 15.96–15.100. Even where a claim falls within the regulations common law principles of damages may still be relevant in determining compensation and additional remedies—such as damages under the tort of misfeasance in public office—may be recoverable.

[13] The most authoritative general works on procurement are S Arrowsmith, *The Law of Public and Utilities Procurement* (1996) and C Bovis, *EC Public Procurement: Case Law and Regulation* (2006) which contains a full treatment of the new regime.

[14] The focus here is on public sector procurement. References are made to utilities procurement (which often uses slightly different terminology) where there are material differences.

[15] Slightly different terminology is used in the Utilities Contracts Regulations 2006, but the essential concepts remain the same.

15.20 Public contracts include public supply contracts, public works contracts, and public services contracts above a certain value.[16] Further, even where a contract is below the minimum financial value to attract the EC public procurement regime directly, public bodies are still subject to relevant public law principles of fairness and transparency and, it is submitted, possibly EC general principles as well on the basis that the award of public contracts generally may fall within the scope of EC law.[17]

15.21 Public bodies amenable to the regime are usually referred to in the directives as 'contracting authorities'. These are, most materially for present purposes, defined in the directives as 'bodies governed by public law'.[18] Although the scope of this term had not been clarified precisely[19] there is unlikely, in many instances, to be dispute. This is because the implementing regulations contain an exhaustive list of those entities that constitute a 'contracting authority'.[20] The list, as might be expected, extends to the majority of those public bodies traditionally susceptible to judicial review as well as others such as the House of Commons and the House of Lords. Most commonly, a contracting authority will be a local authority or government department. However, as illustrated below, the question of what constitutes a 'contracting authority' has not always been free from doubt and ultimately falls to be interpreted by reference to the Directives and EC law.

Stages in the public procurement process

15.22 The first stage is that a prior information notice[21] must be published in the *Official Journal of the European Union* (OJ) giving the relevant purchasing requirements of the contracting authority for the financial year.

15.23 Once the authority decides that a particular contract is required, it now has a possibility of three (and in the case of public sector procurement, four)[22] award procedures. These are:

(1) The open procedure.
(2) The restricted procedure.
(3) The negotiated procedure.
(4) (Now in public sector procurement) the competitive dialogue procedure.

15.24 In the open procedure anyone may submit a tender. This procedure is commonly employed for the supply of goods where price is a crucial factor. In the restricted procedure

---

[16] Public Contracts Regulations 2006, reg 8; Utilities Contracts Regulations 2006, reg 11.

[17] The extent of a matter falling within the scope of EC law is complex and is considered separately: see paras 1.93–1.97. However, given the large number of Treaty provisions relevant to procurement (see n 10 above) it seems that EC general principles would be likely to apply to procurement issues generally. In a case where the EC public procurement regime does not apply directly, judicial review would be the appropriate procedure for fairness and legality challenges: see paras 15.96 et seq.

[18] See Directive (EC) 2004/17, Art 1(a); Directive (EC) 2004/18, Art 1(9). See, also, the Public Contracts Regulations 2006, reg 3 applied to both public sector and public utilities procurement by (respectively) the Public Contracts Regulations 2006, reg 2(1) and the Utilities Contracts Regulations 2006, reg 2(1).

[19] But see paras 15.39 et seq.

[20] Public Contracts Regulations 2006, reg 3.

[21] Public Contracts Regulations 2006, reg 11; Utilities Contracts Regulations 2006, reg 15 (there called a periodic indicative notice).

[22] Public Contracts Regulations 2006, regs 15–18.

the contracting authority draws up a shortlist and invites only those selected from the shortlist to bid. In practice, this is the process used most by contracting authorities. There is also the negotiated procedure. Here, the contracting authority chooses providers and then negotiates with the provider or providers of its choice. It should, however, be noted that whilst ostensibly more flexible than the other procedures, the negotiated procedure may only be used in exceptional cases as where for example other procedures have been unsuccessful or the nature of the contract does not permit overall pricing.[23] The competitive dialogue (introduced under the new public sector procurement regime) is outlined below.[24]

Having decided on the procedure that it proposes to adopt the contracting authority must generally advertise,[25] by a contract notice, the contract requirement in the OJ. The criteria for the award must be stated. All tenders must generally be assessed on either: (1) the tender most economically advantageous to the authority, or (2) the basis of the lowest price[26] There are exceptions especially for rejection of abnormally low offers where certain procedures must be followed before the offer can be rejected.[27]   **15.25**

The next stage is that the contracting authority is required to wait a specified number of days for receiving tenders.[28]   **15.26**

Finally, there is the contract award. This has to be followed by a further notice in the OJ stating the fact of an award and to whom the award has been made as well as detailed information about the decision to the economic operators concerned.[29]   **15.27**

The new reforms

By drawing together EC Treaty provisions, the case law of the ECJ and Member State practice, the new directives have created a number of new elements into EC public procurement requirements.   **15.28**

In summary, the main novel features of the new directives and implementing regulations are these: **15.29**

(1) A new and distinctive separation between public sector and utilities regulation.
(2) A new competitive dialogue procedure for public sector procurement.[30] This allows for contracting authorities to discuss all aspects of a contract with the tenderers before a contract award. This occurs in limited form in the current regime under the negotiated

---

23 Use of the negotiated procedure is rarely successfully justified. For an example of the general approach taken by the court, see Case 324/93 *R v Secretary of State for the Home Department, ex p Evans Medical Ltd and Macfarlan Smith Ltd* [1995] ECR I–563.

24 Note, now, the detailed criteria for selection of procedures in the Public Contracts Regulations 2006, regs 12–18. cf the Utilities Contracts Regulations 2006, reg 14.

25 There are sometimes exceptions to this requirement where the negotiated procedure is adopted.

26 Public Contracts Regulations 2006, regs 30; Utilities Contracts Regulations 2006, reg 30.

27 Public Contracts Regulations 2006, regs 18(27), 30(6) and (9); Utilities Contracts Regulations 2006, regs 30(6), (9) and 31.

28 The period differs according to the procedure employed.

29 Public Contracts Regulations 2006, regs 31–32; Utilities Contracts Regulations 2006, regs 32–33.

30 Public Contracts Regulations 2006, reg 18.

procedure but, as noted above, such procedure may only be used exceptionally. Competitive dialogue has certain constraints and may, for example, only be used for more complex procurements where neither the open nor restricted procedures would be appropriate.

(3) The possibility of certain framework agreements in public sector procurement (already present in the former Utilities Directive).[31] These are general non-binding agreements between a contracting authority and one or more providers outlining the terms governing contracts to be awarded during a given period; normally no more than four years. These types of agreement will most usually be used for repetitive purchases in order to enable the contracting authority to select from providers who, when the contract comes to be considered, are more easily able to meet the authority's requirements.

(4) Electronic procurement by means of dynamic purchasing systems and electronic auctions.[32]

(5) A number of other provisions are introduced by the new directives including adjustment of the threshold values for inclusion in the regime and additional selection criteria. Most important for the application of public law principles, however, are the new provisions[33] requiring contracting authorities to inform and publish the chosen award criteria for the most economically advantageous tender. At the same time the contracting authority will have to notify the relative weighting given to each of the criteria. If this is not possible, the award criteria will have to be indicated in descending order.

B. Relationship between EC Procurement Law and English Public Law

15.30 As explained earlier, there is an important relationship between EC and public law principles in respect of procurement. In that context, a number of points emerge from the above outline that must now be emphasized.

15.31 First, the determination of whether the EC public procurement regime applies (and how it should be applied) is/are necessarily governed by principles of EC law rather than domestic law since the domestic regulations are transposing EC law into domestic law. This means that questions such as whether there is a 'public contract' or whether a body is or is not a 'contracting authority' must be resolved by reference to the true meaning of the directives rather than by simply looking to the content of the regulations.[34] If and to the extent that a particular regulation fails to transpose the directive lawfully then, consistent with general principle, the regulation would, *ex hypothesi*, be unlawful.

15.32 Secondly, the fact that a particular aspect of procurement falls outside the scope of the EC procurement regime does not mean that there are no relevant domestic and/or EC public law obligations on the public body in question. Public bodies, irrespective of whether the

---

[31] Public Contracts Regulations 2006, reg 19. cf Utilities Contracts Regulations 2006, reg 18.

[32] Public Contracts Regulations 2006, regs 20–21; Utilities Contracts Regulations 2006, regs 20–21.

[33] See Art 53 of Directive (EC) 2004/18, and Art 55 of Directive (EC) 2004/17 reflected in reg 30 of (respectively) the Public Contracts Regulations 2006 and the Utilities Contracts Regulations 2006.

[34] Of course, the proper interpretation of the domestic regulation will itself be informed by principles of EC law: for the relevant principles of interpretation, see paras 2.99 et seq.

EC public procurement regime applies, are required to act in conformity with domestic public law principles such as legitimate expectation, natural justice, taking into account only relevant (and not irrelevant) considerations, and rationality. Many of these principles mirror—even if they do not precisely replicate—general principles of EC law.

Similarly, the EC public procurement regime is itself a facet of Treaty obligations. So, **15.33** even where the regime does not apply to the situation in question there may well be EC obligations resting on the public body including an obligation to comply with EC general principles such as equal treatment and transparency.

What may also be affected by the operation of discrete EC or domestic public law princi- **15.34** ples is the relevant national procedure. Both EC and domestic public law arguments may be raised in cases to which the regulations apply and to which the specific procurement remedy applies. But in a case outside the scope of the Regulations EC and/or domestic public law principles may still be raised either in judicial review proceedings or — where appropriate[35] — in a private law damages action.

The third point is that procedural remedies and/or limitation rules relating to public pro- **15.35** curement (especially under the regulations) may require some modification in the light of EC law generally and, more specifically, having regard to the EC principles of effectiveness and/or equivalence.[36] Most materially, the limitation period of three months under the regulations for bringing claims must be applied against the general principles that actions in respect of actionable EC claims are not made more difficult than comparable actions under domestic law (equivalence) and that the enforcement of EC rights must not be made impossible or excessively difficult in practice (effectiveness).

Against that background the following general questions arising out of the combined **15.36** application of EC and domestic public law principles in relation to public procurement arise and will be addressed:

(1) How should the Administrative Court and other domestic courts approach questions of definition under the EC public procurement regime?
(2) Assuming that the procurement regime under the regulations applies, how does the court decide whether a breach has taken place?
(3) If the regime under the regulations does not apply (or only applies in part) how should challenges be brought and what principles should the court deploy?
(4) How should issues in relation to procedure and remedy under the regulations be decided by the court?
(5) What is the relationship between EC public procurement and State Aid?

C. Approach to Questions of Definition under the Regime

As explained above, the public procurement regime imposes a number of specific obliga- **15.37** tions on 'contracting authorities'. Both the meaning of the terms used in the directives and

---

[35] For consideration of those instances where a damages action may be more appropriate, see paras 1.100 et seq.
[36] See, generally, paras 3.09–3.31 and 5.06–5.22.

the substantive content of the obligations are necessarily governed by principles of EC law and interpretation since domestic regulations merely transpose the various EC directives into national law.

15.38 Most EC directives, and the public procurement directives are no exception, define terms that determine whether a particular regime applies and, if so, how it applies. Many examples are given elsewhere in this book.[37] They demonstrate that the intuitive meaning to be ascribed to a term in national law does not always coincide with the EC meaning.

15.39 The best example of issues of definition,[38] and the proper approach to take, in the context of the procurement directives is the meaning of the term 'contracting authority'. This term as noted earlier was to be found in the Supplies, Works and Services Directives and is now, in essence, consolidated in Article 1(9) of Directive (EC)2004/18 and Article 2(1)(a) of Directive (EC)2004/17.

15.40 A 'contracting authority' is there defined as:

> ... the State, regional or local authorities, bodies governed by public law, associations formed by one or several such authorities or one or several of such bodies governed by public law.[39]

15.41 This, rather than any domestic regulation, is the ultimate authority for purposes of definition.[40] Importantly, to the extent that regulations are ambiguous they fall to be interpreted by the Administrative Court or other domestic court in the light of the public procurement directives that they are intended to transpose into national law. This, in turn, requires consideration and application of any relevant ECJ judgments.

15.42 If, following that interpretative exercise, the regulations do not lawfully implement the directives the court would still have to find that a particular body was a 'contracting authority' if it fell within the definition in the directive. This is because the public procurement directives would appear to have direct effect[41] and can, therefore, be enforced by individuals or entities in the national courts.[42]

15.43 Central to the EC definition of 'contracting authority' is the presence of State control or influence. The definition comprises four elements: (1) the State, (2) regional or local authorities, (3) 'bodies governed by public law' and (4) associations formed by one or more of such bodies.

---

[37] Consider, eg, the environmental impact assessment regime and the meaning of 'development consent' under the EIA Directive which is by no means synonymous with UK planning permission as triggering the need for a prior environmental impact assessment: see, generally, Chapter 14.

[38] It is, though, merely exemplary and although the meaning of 'contracting authority' is the best example, all questions of definition would have to be approached in the same way.

[39] '[B]odies governed by public law' has a separate definition (see para 15.45).

[40] In the main the domestic procurement regulations appear to be EC compliant though certain issues may arise with regard to the Remedies Directive (see below).

[41] See n 3 above and text.

[42] Thus, to the extent that the domestic regulations did not provide an effective remedy against a particular body under the public procurement regime when, pursuant to the Remedies Directive, they ought to have done, it is submitted that proceedings in judicial review could and should be brought bypassing the regulations altogether.

Although categories (1) and (2) are not defined further they are often difficult, in fact, to **15.44** separate from category (3), namely 'bodies governed by public law'.[43] The ECJ considered what was entailed in the notion of the State in *Gebroeders Beentjes NV v Netherlands*.[44] That case concerned the interpretation of the (former) Works Directive but it is, in the present context, of more general application. At para 12 of the court's judgment it observed as follows:

> a body whose composition and functions are laid down by legislation and which depends on the authorities for the appointment of its members, the observance of obligations arising out of its measures, and the financing of public works contracts which it is its task to award, must be regarded as falling within the notion of the State . . .

The directive definition (also contained in the various directives) of 'bodies governed by **15.45** public law' builds on the case law so that the term extends to any body:

— established for the specific purpose of meeting needs in the general interest, not having an industrial or commercial character,[45] and
— having legal personality and
— financed, for the most part, by the State, or regional or local authorities, or other bodies governed by public law; or subject to management supervision by those bodies; or having an administrative, managerial or supervisory board, more than half of whose members are appointed by the State, regional or local authorities or by other bodies governed by public law.

As can be seen, the underlying reality is that categories (1)–(4) of the basic directive definition **15.46** of 'contracting authority' have to be considered as a whole. It is hard, and perhaps undesirable, to seek to achieve greater precision. In that way, the over-arching State involvement criteria can be applied to the facts of particular cases in order to decide whether a particular entity is or is not to be regarded as a 'contracting authority'.

The case law of the ECJ has, nonetheless, thrown up a number of definitional issues in the **15.47** context of the proper scope of the term 'contracting authority'. In *University of Cambridge*,[46] for example, it was common ground in Article 234 proceedings for a preliminary ruling before the ECJ that the University fulfilled two of the three necessary criteria for being a *'body governed by public law'* in that: (1) it had legal personality and (2) it was established to meet needs in the general interest and did not have an industrial or commercial character.

---

[43] It should, however, be noted that the ECJ has sometimes distinguished between the expressions. See, most notably, Case 353/96 *Commission of the European Communities v Ireland* [1998] ECR I–8565 where the ECJ though finding that Coillte Teoranta was neither the State nor a regional authority within the meaning of (former) Directive (EEC)77/62 held, applying a functional test, that since the State was able to exercise indirect control it was a contracting authority within the meaning of that directive. Note, too, that the directives draw some differences since a body governed by public law is required to have legal personality whereas this is not a requirement of category (1) or, indeed, of the domestic regulations.

[44] Case 31/87 [1988] ECR 4635, especially para 12.

[45] This expression was considered by the ECJ in Joined Cases C–223/99 and C-260/99 *Agora and Excelsior* [2000] ECR I–3605. It held that a non-profit-making body that is, nonetheless, operating in a competitive environment and managed according to criteria of performance, efficiency, and cost-effectiveness may be conducting activities of a commercial character *(in casu* undertaking activities relating to the organization of fairs, exhibitions, and other similar initiatives).

[46] Case C–380/98 *The Queen v HM Treasury, ex p University of Cambridge* [2000] ECR I–8035.

The main question that arose was whether it was financed for the most part by one or more contracting authorities so as to require inclusion in the list for Annex 1 to the Works Directive. This required consideration of different types of payment made to the University.

15.48 Three further specific questions also arose being:

(1) In terms of the phrase in the directives 'financed for the most part' did that mean a percentage figure?

(2) Were all sources of financing to be taken into account when determining whether financing fell within that phrase?

(3) What period was to be taken into account in calculating financing and how much account should be taken of changes that might occur in the course of a procurement procedure?

15.49 In substance, the ECJ answered the questions in a way that supported the proposition that the University was itself a contracting authority. The ECJ held that the expression 'financed by [one or more contracting authorities]' included awards or grants paid by one or more contracting authorities for the support of research work and student grants paid by local education authorities in respect of tuition for named students. However, payments made by one or more contracting authorities in the context of a contract for services comprising research work or as consideration for other services—such as conferences or consultancy— did not constitute public financing. The regulating principle was whether or not there was close dependency on another contracting authority. A mere subsidy necessarily implied a close dependency whereas a contractual relationship did not.

15.50 As to the three other questions, the ECJ held, first, that 'for the most part' simply meant more than half. Secondly, it held that all sources of financing were to be taken into account in arriving at the relevant percentage. Finally, it held that the decision as to whether a body such as the University was a contracting authority must be made annually and the budgetary year during which the procurement procedure was commenced must be regarded as the most appropriate period for calculating how that body was financed. However, in the interests of legal certainty, the decision must be based on the figures available at the beginning of the budgetary year even if those figures were provisional. Also in the interests of legal certainty, a body that constituted a contracting authority at that time remained, so far as that procurement was concerned, subject to the requirements of the procurement directives until such time as the relevant procedure had been completed.

15.51 *University of Cambridge* shows the relevance of general principles of EC law, such as legal certainty, in analysing the definitional content of the procurement directives.

15.52 Equally fundamental questions were addressed by the ECJ in *BFI Holding*.[47] There, the problems facing the court in proceedings for a preliminary ruling related to the meaning of

---

[47] Case C–360/96 *Gemeente Arnhem, Gemeente Rheden v BFI Holding* [1998] ECR I–6821.

the expressions 'needs in the general interest' and 'not having an industrial or commercial character'. The main questions raised by the national court were these:

(1) Does the expression 'not having an industrial and commercial character' limit the terms 'needs in the general interest' to those which are not of an industrial or commercial character or does it mean that all needs in the general interest are not industrial or commercial in character?

(2) Does the term 'needs in the general interest, not having an industrial or commercial character' exclude needs that are also met by private undertakings?

(3) Does the condition that a body must have been set up for the specific purpose of meeting needs in the general interest mean that the activity of that body must, to a considerable extent, be concerned with meeting such needs?

(4) What inferences may be drawn from the fact that the provisions setting up the entity in question and specifying the needs that it must meet are in the nature of laws, regulations, or administrative or other provisions?

The ECJ held, first, that—consistently with the general principle of effectiveness— **15.53** a distinction was to be made within needs in the general interest not having an industrial or commercial character (caught by the directives) and needs in the general interest having an industrial or commercial character (not caught by the directives).

Secondly, the court held that the term 'needs in the general interest, not having an indus- **15.54** trial or commercial character' did not exclude needs that are, or could also be, satisfied by private undertakings. This followed from the language of the Directives which did not impose such a constraint. It also followed from the purpose of co-ordinating procedures for the award of public contracts. That purpose—the elimination of barriers to the freedom to provide services—would be eroded by such a distinction and would render meaningless the term 'body governed by public law'.

Thirdly, the court held that the status of a body governed by public law was not dependent **15.55** on the relative importance, within its business as a whole, of the meeting of needs in the general interest not having an industrial or commercial character. Finally, the court ruled that the existence or absence of needs in the general interest not having an industrial or commercial character must be determined objectively and not by reference to the legal form of the provisions in which those needs were mentioned.

In *BFI*, as in *University of Cambridge*, the ECJ was concerned to give effect to the rationale **15.56** of the Treaty, and general principles of EC law when elucidating the meaning of terms in the procurement directives. The same approach has been taken in many other cases.[48]

Although this section has focused, by way of illustration, on the approach of the ECJ to **15.57** definition of the term 'contracting authority'[49] it is apparent that the court would adopt similar reasoning to any other question of definition that might arise under the directives.

---

[48] See, eg, Case 470/99 *Universale-Bau* [2002] ECR I–11617, paras 57–58; Case C–44/96 *Mannesmann* [1998] ECR I–73, para 33.

[49] For an example of the court's approach to bodies subject to the utilities legislation, see Case C–302/94 *R v Secretary of State for Trade and Industry, ex p British Telecommunications plc* [1996] ECR 6417.

15.58 For example, a question of definition may arise as to what constitutes a 'contract' so as to trigger the operation of the regime. This occurred before the Court of Appeal in *R v Portsmouth City Council, ex p Coles*.[50] There, Portsmouth City Council failed to specify the award criteria in either the contract documents or the invitations to tender in respect of a number of its proposed works contracts. In proceedings for judicial review brought against it the council contended that where, as was the case, the contracts were awarded to its direct labour organization there was no 'contract' in play because it was not possible for the Council to contract with itself; the directives required a separate entity.

15.59 In the event, the Court of Appeal was able to reject the substance of the council's position by recourse to reg 20(8) of the Works Regulations which deemed an 'offer' under the regulations to include a bid by one part of a contracting authority to carry out work or works by another part of the contracting authority. However, the court observed that there appeared to be a lacuna in the Works Directive that the domestic regulations had corrected. It is, nonetheless, submitted that had the case come before the ECJ that court would also have interpreted the directives in a manner that did not enable a local authority to evade the effect of the regime if only by finding a breach of the directives at an earlier stage of the process.[51]

D. Approach to Breaches of the Regime

Introduction

15.60 Most commonly, the issue before the Administrative Court or other domestic court in the context of public procurement will be whether or not the contracting authority is—by its acts or defaults—in breach of the regime. This is, in practice, a more likely scenario than disputes over whether the regime is engaged at all.

15.61 In similar fashion to the approach to be taken to questions of definition under the directives, issues relating to breaches of the regulations/directives are to be resolved, at least primarily, by recourse to principles of EC law and relevant decisions of the ECJ. Additionally, as will be suggested, domestic public law principles may be used to supplement EC law where appropriate.

15.62 The most common of the issues that arise or are likely to arise in practice in respect of alleged breaches of the EC public procurement regime are outlined below. This analysis is not, however, intended to be exhaustive.

Criteria that may be taken into account by a contracting authority

15.63 As discussed above, one of the purposes of imposing an EC public procurement regime is that contracting authorities are not guided by non-economic considerations in their award

---

[50] (1996) 59 Con LR 114.

[51] Note, too, Arrowsmith (n 13 above) 117–18 who observes that 'it is almost certain' that the ECJ would require certain arrangements not classified in domestic law as amounting to a 'contract' to be treated as a contract under the directives and regulations.

of public contracts. Does this mean that the only factors that may be taken into account are economic in nature?

This was addressed, in respect of environmental criteria,[52] by the ECJ in its preliminary ruling in *Concordia*.[53] There, tenders for the operation of an urban bus service in Helsinki were assessed by reference to a points system. The applicant bidder complained that additional points had been obtained at the award stage under environmental criteria in favour of bidders who proposed the use of buses with nitric oxide emissions and noise levels below certain thresholds. **15.64**

As to whether environmental criteria could be taken into account, the ECJ held that they could. It observed (para 64 of the court's judgement): **15.65**

> Where the contracting authority decides to award a contract to the tenderer who submits the economically most advantageous tender, in accordance with Article 36(1)(a) of Directive 92/50, it may take criteria related to the preservation of the environment into consideration, provided that they are linked to the subject matter of the contract, do not confer an unrestricted freedom of choice on the authority, are expressly mentioned in the contract documents or the tender notice, and comply with all the fundamental principles of community law, in particular the principle of non-discrimination.

Failing to specify award criteria

One of the most commonly asserted (and committed) breaches of the directives is the failure by a contracting authority to specify in advance criteria that it then relies upon when making an award. That there is such a requirement is founded on the need for transparency, fairness, and non-discrimination so as to achieve the underlying Community objectives referred to above. Where no criteria are lawfully specified, the sole criterion that may be applied is that of the lowest price. **15.66**

Thus, in *Wallonia Buses*[54] the ECJ stated (para 89) as follows: **15.67**

> . . . in order to ensure that a contract is awarded on the basis of criteria known to all the tenderers before the preparation of their tender, a contracting entity can take account of variants as award criteria only in so far as it expressly mentioned them as such in the contract documents or in the tender notice.

To similar effect, in *SIAC Construction*[55] the ECJ reiterated the importance of specifying variant criteria in advance of a contract award. There, the Council specified its award criteria in terms of the most advantageous to the contracting authority in relation to costs and **15.68**

---

[52] Note the importance attached to environmental protection in EC law generally. See, eg, Art 6 (EC) and generally Chapter 14.

[53] Case C–513/99 *Concordia Bus Finland Ov Ab v Helsingin kaupunki and HKL-Bussiliikenne* [2002] ECR 7213. Similar principles attach to social criteria such as combating unemployment where the ECJ has observed that such criteria may form part of an authority's discretion in determining what is the most economically advantageous offer but that any condition relating to such criteria must be consistent with all the fundamental principles of EC law, including the principle of non-discrimination in relation to the fundamental freedoms: see, especially, Case C–225/98 *Commission v France* ('*Nord-Pas-de-Calais*') [2000] ECR I–7445. See, also, Case 31/87 *Beentjes* [1989] ECR 4365.

[54] Case 87/94 *Commission v Belgium* [1996] ECR I–2043, especially paras 88–89.

[55] Case C–19/00 *SIAC Construction Ltd v Mayo County Council* [2001] ECR I–7725.

technical merit. The three lowest tenderers had equal technical merit and similar tender prices. In the event, the Council made its contract award to the tenderer with the second lowest price because the 'ultimate cost' to the awarding authority was likely to be lower than that of the other tenders.

15.69 The ECJ held that under the relevant directive it was open to an awarding authority to award a contract to the tenderer whose tender would, in the opinion of an independent expert, give rise to the lowest ultimate cost to the authority provided that the following conditions (now, as noted above, largely contained in the new domestic regulations) were satisfied:

15.70 (1) The award procedure must be transparent and objective, so as to ensure the equal treatment of tenderers.

15.71 (2) The award criterion (here that of ultimate cost) must be clearly stated in the authority's contract notice or contract documents.

15.72 (3) The expert's opinion must be based in all essential respects on objective factors that were regarded in good professional practice as relevant and appropriate to the assessments made.

Equal treatment

15.73 As *SIAC Construction*[56] demonstrates, one of the principal reasons for requiring prior specification of award criteria is so as to ensure, thereby, that all tenderers are treated equally and without discrimination. The EC general principle of non-discrimination falls to be applied, in any event, to the EC public procurement regime because it is a general principle of law falling within the scope of EC law. But, as outlined above, it is also necessary in the procurement context to ensure that other Treaty objectives are complied with such as freedom of movement of services.

15.74 So, non-discrimination is an independent requirement that must be complied with by contracting authorities in the EC public procurement regime. As the ECJ observed in *SIAC Construction* (para 34 of the court's judgment):

> ... tenderers must be in a position of equality both when they formulate their tenders and when those tenders are being assessed by the adjudicating authorities.

15.75 In this respect, the decision of Smedley J in the High Court in *Resource Management Services v Westminster City Council*[57] is instructive. There, the contracting authority employed the restricted procedure for purchasing internal audit services. The contracting authority invited a revision of tenders on a number of occasions. Although the applicant's prices were lower at the end of the first two tender revisions, the final report to the authority recommended acceptance of the in-house tender. By that stage the in-house's prices were far closer to the applicant's but the revisions made to their tender were not related to the factors specified by the authority as relevant to revisions of the tenders.

---

[56] ibid.
[57] Unreported, 19 February 1999.

The judge held that the in-house team had not been treated equally, that it had been given **15.76** an unfair advantage, and that it was unlawful to make a contract award in its favour without disregarding the price changes made to its tender.

On the same basis, post-tender negotiations with particular tenderers on fundamental **15.77** aspects of the contract represent a breach of the principle of equal treatment. This may have occurred in *Resource Management Services*; it certainly occurred in *Commission v Kingdom of Belgium*.[58] There, the Belgian contracting authority put out an invitation to tender for the supply of a number of buses. After the tenders were inspected, recommendations were made that the first lot be awarded to one company and the second lot to another. However, a third company subsequently sent three memoranda to the contracting authority setting out certain discounts and other favourable rates. The contracting authority promptly awarded the second lot to that company. This was held to be unlawful as being, amongst other things, in violation of the principle of equal treatment.

Withdrawal of invitation to tender

Nothing in the UK regulations appears to prevent a contracting authority withdrawing an **15.78** invitation to tender. Indeed, it may be inferred, at least from the domestic regulations that the possibility of withdrawal is envisaged.

For example, reg 23(1) of the (former) Services Regulations provided as follows: **15.79**

> Where a contracting authority decides either to abandon or to recommence an award procedure in respect of which a contract notice has been published it shall inform the Office for Official Publications of the European Communities of its decision and shall inform promptly any service provider who submitted an offer or who applied to be included amongst the persons to be selected to tender for or to negotiate the contract of its decision and of the reasons for its decision and shall do so in writing if requested.

Arrowsmith[59] analysing a materially similar version of the above regulation in her discus- **15.80** sion of the open and restricted procedures, observes:

> For a variety of reasons a purchaser may wish to terminate an award procedure without awarding a contract. It may decide to abandon the project altogether—for example because changed circumstances mean that the goods or services are no longer required, or because it feels, after seeing the offers, that the project will be too expensive. In other cases, it may decide to begin a new award procedure; this might happen, for example, where the authority is dissatisfied with the offers submitted but feels that a second procedure would produce better results, or where some mistake has been made in the first procedure, such as omitting to list the applicable award criteria. There is nothing in the directives or regulations to prevent termination of a procedure in such cases, and the fact that this is permitted can be deduced from express provisions stating that where no contract is awarded the *Official Journal* must be informed and reasons given to providers.
>
> . . .
>
> For a number of reasons an authority may wish to terminate a procedure without awarding a contract—for example, because it decides to abandon the project or to make an award in-house. There is nothing in the regulations to prevent the authority from terminating the

---

[58] Case 87/94 [1996] ECR I–2043.
[59] *The Law of Public and Utilities Procurement* (1996) 254, 279.

procedure *at any time and for any reason,* although it may be required to publish a notice in the *Official Journal*. In these respects the rules are the same as with open and restricted procedures, as discussed above.

15.81 However, the position may not be as straightforward as this in view of the ECJ decision in *Hospital Ingenieure*.[60] There, the ECJ held, materially, as follows:

(1) The Remedies Directive requires a decision to withdraw the invitation to tender to be open to review to determine whether it has complied with the EC public procurement regime.

(2) A decision to withdraw must also be capable of being annulled (quashed) as part of the review procedure.

(3) National rules which purport to limit review to whether withdrawal of a tender was arbitrary would infringe the Remedies Directive.

(4) National rules must not make it practically impossible or excessively difficult to exercise rights conferred by EC law.

15.82 So, it seems clear that—at least in principle—the decision of a contracting authority to withdraw a tender is amenable to review.[61] It is not immediately easy, however, to envisage many circumstances in which a withdrawal decision would be actionable under the domestic remedy.

15.83 Assuming that a contracting authority had reserved the right to withdraw from the tendering process at any time and tenderers submitted tenders on that basis then—short of arbitrariness—withdrawal of the tender would not appear to breach any fundamental principle of EC law. There might, perhaps, be instances where a legitimate expectation had been engendered and money expended in reliance upon it. The principle is, however, simply stated and was stated by the ECJ in *Kauppatalo Hansel Ov v Imatran Kaupunki*:[62]

> . . . a contracting authority which has commenced a procedure for the award of a contract on the basis of the lowest price may discontinue the procedure, without awarding a contract, when it discovers after examining and comparing the tenders that, because of errors committed by itself in its preliminary assessment, the content of the invitation to tender makes it impossible for it to accept the most economically advantageous tender, provided that, when it adopts such a decision, it complies with the fundamental rules of Community law on public procurement such as the principle of equal treatment.

Using CPR Pt 54 under the EC procurement regime

15.84 As explained below, the domestic regulations governing EC public procurement mandate a particular form of judicial review. The predominant system of law that determines whether a contracting authority is in breach of the regime is EC law. Since EC law contains its own general principles that bear close affinities to English public law,[63] there will be

---

[60] Case C–92/00 *Hospital Ingenieure Krankenhaustechnik Planungs GmbH (HI) v Stadt Wein* [2002] ECR I–5553.

[61] Similarly, a decision not to commence an award procedure must itself be amenable to review: see Advocate General Stix-Hackl in Case C–26/03 *Stadt Halle* [2005] ECR I–1.

[62] Case C–244/02 (16 October 2003).

[63] See Chapters 6–12.

relatively few instances—if the regulations apply—in which domestic public issues in iso-lation will arise or where judicial review under CPR Pt 54 will need to be used rather than the procedure under the regulations.

Indeed, invoking judicial review where there is an alternative remedy (such as that under the regulations) is likely to result in the Administrative Court refusing relief in its discre-tion.[64] Further, if and to the extent that domestic public law is inconsistent with EC law in the sense of making EC rights impossible or excessively difficult to exercise in practice, then the Administrative Court is bound not to apply the former.   **15.85**

There are, nonetheless, certain instances in which—even though the regime is or should be engaged—the judicial review procedure will still be permissible and even necessary. There are also instances in which, though the regime is engaged, principles of domestic law (including the HRA) may assist a claimant where the regime does not.   **15.86**

The issue of whether, and (if so) to what extent, judicial review under CPR Pt 54 could be used rather than the procedure under the regulations arose before the Court of Appeal in *R (Cookson) v Ministry of Defence*.[65]   **15.87**

In *Cookson* a clothing manufacturer (C) appealed against a first instance decision (Bennett J) refusing permission to apply for judicial review of an award by the Ministry of Defence of a defence clothing contract to a third party (an interested party in the judicial review). The relief sought was a quashing order in relation to the award and a mandatory order requir-ing the Ministry to enter into a contract with C. Apart from proceeding by way of judicial review, C had also claimed similar relief on the same underlying facts in separate Pt 7 proceedings under the (former) Supply Regulations. Those proceedings were commenced on the same day as the judicial review. The difference between the two sets of proceedings was that the judicial review proceedings were cast on traditional public law grounds of irrationality.   **15.88**

Importantly, the contract, the subject of the claim, had already been entered into between the Ministry and third party. This had the effect that C was restricted in terms of the relief that could be sought under reg 29(6) of the Supply Regulations (and, indeed, the relief that could be sought under the new regime) to an award of damages.[66]   **15.89**

On that basis, C argued first that the application for judicial review ought to be allowed to proceed (and be consolidated with the Pt 7 proceedings) because the relief claimed by way of judicial review could not be claimed under the procedure mandated by the Supply Regulations. Secondly, C contended that there were purely domestic public law arguments available under CPR Pt 54 judicial review proceedings that were not available under the reg 29(6) route.   **15.90**

The Court of Appeal rejected these arguments. First, it held that if C succeeded in the submission (advanced also in the Pt 7 proceedings) that reg 29(6) was inconsistent with EC law because it failed properly to implement the Remedies Directive, the court would be   **15.91**

---

[64] See, eg, *R v Chief Constable of Merseyside Police, ex p Calveley* [1986] QB 424.
[65] [2005] EWCA Civ 811.
[66] See paras 15.114–15.118.

able in the Pt 7 application to set aside the contract in exactly the same way as it could in judicial review. However, if C was wrong in that submission it followed that the contract ought not to be capable of being set aside in the judicial review proceedings.

15.92 As to C's second argument, the Court of Appeal held that any public law ground founded on irrationality must, necessarily, involve breaches of the Supply Regulations. That being so, there was no need for separate judicial review proceedings.

15.93 In reaching that conclusion, Buxton LJ (who gave the only judgment) drew on the reasoning of the Court of Appeal in its earlier decision in *Mass Energy*[67] (a case on tendering under the statutory tendering requirements in Pt II of the Environmental Protection Act 1990) which had concluded that judicial review could only be used in that context where tenderers had failed to comply with their public law (there, statutory) obligations.

15.94 Buxton LJ went on to observe (para 18) as follows:

> I would, however, immediately agree that that analysis does not and should not exclude public law entirely from the contract-award process, even if there were no statutory breaches involved: for instance, if there were bribery, corruption or the implementation of a policy unlawful in itself, either because it was ultra vires or for other reasons . . . But it is much more difficult to fit this allegation of irrationality or unfairness into the framework of a separate application different from complaints under the Regulations. That is because the award of the contract, where the irrationality in this case is said to have arisen, as well as the tendering process, is governed by the Regulations.

15.95 It would appear, therefore, that there will be some instances where CPR Pt 54 will be an appropriate procedure. In general, the judicial review procedure including discrete domestic public law principles may, it is suggested, be appropriate in at least the following situations:

(1) Where a person other than a service provider wishes to bring a claim in respect of a breach of the EC public procurement regime. Under the regime only a person seeking (or who would have wished to seek) a contract award may bring proceedings;[68] however, claimants in judicial review proceedings have wider standing and may, in at least some instances, be able to bring judicial review proceedings in the public interest.[69] Although in many contexts the invocation of judicial review in order to circumvent the limitations of a statutory procedure might be considered objectionable, in an EC context it is submitted that Article 10 (ex 5) EC with its requirement that Member States (including courts) take all appropriate steps to ensure the fulfilment of Treaty obligations would provide sufficient justification for the Administrative Court to entertain an application for judicial review.

(2) Where, domestic regulations have failed in a substantive respect to transpose the procurement directives lawfully. An instance may be afforded by the decision to withdraw a tender. As noted above, there is—ostensibly at least—nothing in the domestic regulations to subject the decision to withdraw a tender to a claim by a service provider

---

[67] *Mass Energy Ltd v Birmingham City Council* [1994] ELR 298.
[68] See, eg, reg 32 of the Services Regulations.
[69] Standing in judicial review is now extremely wide: see, eg, *R v Secretary of State for Foreign and Commonwealth Affairs, ex p World Development Movement Ltd* [1995] 1 WLR 386.

for breach of duty. Nonetheless, the ECJ has held that the Remedies Directive requires such a claim to be subject to review by the national courts. It is, therefore, submitted that judicial review would be the appropriate procedure for such a decision to be challenged.

(3) Where one or more public law grounds (including HRA principles) can be deployed in support of a challenge brought under the EC procurement regime but where the regime itself does not encompass such grounds (as, for example, the example suggested in *Cookson* of the implementation of a policy unlawful in itself). It is, perhaps, also possible that a purely public law duty on a contracting authority to act fairly may go beyond a specific duty imposed under the regulations.[70]

E. Procurement Cases Outside the EC Regime

The EC public procurement regime (see above) draws together a number of specific Treaty **15.96** obligations. However, in a broader sense, the legal regulation of State contracts following a tender process encompasses a wider variety of contracts than those covered by the procurement directives and transposing domestic regulations. They include, most notably those cases involving:

(1) Public contracts where there is an EC dimension but where the process is outside the transposing domestic regulations as, for example, because the financial threshold is too low or for some other exclusory reason (such as the proposed contract representing a services concession).

(2) Contracts without an EC dimension but caught by a different regime (as, eg, formerly the compulsory competitive tendering regime, replaced by the best value obligations on local authorities).

(3) Contracts following a tender process without an EC or other specific statutory dimension but subject, nonetheless, to public law obligations on the State contracting body.

The legality of each of these species of contract award process is challengeable by judicial **15.97** review rather than under the EC procurement regime.[71]

Where the underlying nature of the challenge is that a provision of the EC Treaty has been **15.98** violated then the principles to be applied by the Administrative Court will be EC principles. An example (albeit in infringement proceedings before the ECJ) occurred in *Commission v Ireland*.[72] There, an Irish municipal authority invited tenders for the construction of a water main. Although the contract was not governed by the EC public procurement regime its award was subject to Treaty obligations in general and, in particular, those under Article 28 (ex 30) EC on freedom of movement of goods. The ECJ held that use of discriminatory specifications in favour of Irish products was, indeed, a breach of Article 28 (ex 30) EC.

---

[70] Consider, eg, the general obligation to act fairly as in *R v Inland Revenue Commissioners, ex p Unilever plc* [1996] STC 681.
[71] There may in some instances—and depending on the facts—be private law claims as, eg, for breach of contract or even misfeasance in public office.
[72] Case 45/87 [1988] ECR 4929.

15.99   Where no EC element is present but where there is a discrete statutory regime or where a public body is required (or chooses) to adopt a tendering process outside the scope of EC law then public law obligations (as, for example, transparency and fairness) will, inevitably, ensue. Such cases may be justiciable by way of judicial review. For example, in *R v Enfield LBC, ex p Unwin*[73] a local authority's decision to suspend a contractor from its approved list of contractors was quashed in judicial review proceedings on grounds of unfairness. Although there have been similar cases where the courts have declined jurisdiction because of an insufficient public law element,[74] it is submitted that the Administrative Court would be more likely to entertain this type of challenge given the expanded duties on public authorities under the HRA to comply with Convention rights such as those under Article 1 of Protocol 1 (peaceful enjoyment of property) which may well be relied on by aggrieved contractors.[75]

15.100   As explained above, there will also be some cases to which the procurement regime applies at least in part but where judicial review may, nonetheless, be permissible. Nonetheless, particular care is needed in identifying whether judicial review and/or the route encompassed in the domestic regulations should be followed because if the High Court considers that the procedure under the domestic regulations represents an alternative remedy, judicial review may be refused in the court's discretion. This issue is addressed in more detail above.[76]

F. Questions of Procedure and Remedies under the Regime

The legislation

15.101   Regulation 45 of the new Utilities Contracts Regulations 2006, provides an exemplary model of domestic procedures and remedies under both the new and the former EC public procurement regime. There is materially identical provision in the Public Contracts Regulations 2006.[77] There was similar provision in the (former) regulations including the Services Regulations[78] and the Supply Regulations.[79] These regulations are intended to implement the requirement in the Remedies Directives for an appropriate domestic remedy for breach of the EC public procurement requirements.

15.102   Regulation 45 contains the following material provisions for present purposes:

> (1) The obligation on a utility to comply with the provisions of these Regulations . . . and with any enforceable Community obligation in respect of a public services contract . . . is a duty owed to an economic operator.[80]

---

[73] [1989] COD 466.

[74] See, eg, *R v Hibbit and Saunders, ex p Lord Chancellor's Department* [1993] COD 326.

[75] See, generally, Chapter 12.

[76] See para 15.85.

[77] Regulation 47.

[78] Regulation 32.

[79] Regulation 29.

[80] So, for example, an economic operator claiming to be harmed by discrimination need not actually submit a tender before being able to initiate a claim under the procurement regulations: see Case C–249/01 *Hackermuller* [2003] ECR I–6319.

. . .

(4) A breach of the duty owed . . . is actionable by any economic operator, which, in consequence, suffers, or risks suffering, loss or damage and those proceedings shall be in the High Court.

(5) Proceedings under this regulation may not be brought unless—

    (a) the economic operator bringing the proceedings has informed the utility of the breach or apprehended breach of the duty owed to it . . . by the utility and of its intention to bring proceedings under the regulation in respect of it; and,

    (b) those proceedings are brought promptly and in any event within three months from the date when grounds for the bringing of the proceedings first arose unless the Court considers that there is good reason for extending the period within which proceedings may be brought.

(6) Subject to paragraph (7), but otherwise without prejudice to any other powers of the Court, in proceedings brought under this regulation the Court may—

    (a) by interim order suspend the procedure leading to the award of the contract . . . or suspend the implementation of any decision or action taken by the utility in the course of following such procedure; and

    (b) if satisfied that a decision or action taken by a utility was in breach of the duty owed . . . :

        (i) order the setting aside of the decision or action or order the utility to amend any document; or

        (ii) award damages to an economic operator which has suffered loss or damage as a consequence of the breach; or

        (iii) do both of these things.

(7) In any proceedings under this regulation the court does not have power to order any remedy other than an award of damages in respect of a breach of the duty owed . . . if the contract in relation to which the breach occurred has been entered into.

Procedure

As can be seen, reg 45 lays down two procedural requirements. These are:　　**15.103**

(1) the obligation to notify the contracting authority/utility of the alleged breach or apprehended breach of duty;

(2) the requirement that proceedings must be brought promptly and, in any event, within three months from the date when grounds for the bringing of the proceedings first arose.

The first requirement (notification) is straightforward and has not formerly given rise to　**15.104** difficulty in practice.[81] However, the time limit for bringing proceedings under the EC regime has engendered much case law. The terminology of reg 45 is typical of all the domestic regulations that have been considered by the court and employs the same language as the time limit for the bringing of domestic judicial review proceedings.

In summary, courts have applied time limits in EC public procurement cases on the basis that　**15.105** the time for bringing the proceedings starts once there has been a breach of the regulations

---

[81] It turns on the facts of each case. See, eg, *Luck (t/a G Luck Arboricultural & Horticultural) v London Borough of Tower Hamlets* [2003] EWCA Civ 52, where the Court of Appeal held that notification must include a reference to the regulations as a whole and that the correspondence there did not satisfy that requirement.

by the contracting authority/utility. However, where the service provider cannot be blamed for bringing proceedings late, time is likely to be extended. The test is, thus, slightly more generous than in conventional judicial review where public interest considerations may militate against an extension of time even where the claimant is blameless.

15.106 *Keymed*[82] is an important first instance decision on the application of the public procurement time limits. It was a case on the application of reg 29 of the Supply Regulations phrased in materially identical terms to reg 45 (above). The central question was the point at which the three-month time limit arose. Keymed argued that the period only started when it had relevant knowledge of the material facts.

15.107 Langley J rejected this submission. He held that on a proper interpretation of reg 29(4)(b)[83] of the Supply Regulations there was no prior requirement of knowledge of breach before the time limit started to operate. He said:

> . . . the words used are ordinary English words and require no more than that grounds for proceedings exist or have occurred for time to begin to run, or that their existence or occurrence is 'apprehended.' The 'grounds' could arise in two factual contexts. First, where the Regulations were simply not being observed from the outset either through ignorance or consciously; and, second, where despite having embarked on the procedures the contracting authority is alleged not to have observed some specific provision, for example by failing to fix a time limit for the receipt of tenders or requests to tender. In the first case, the Regulations will be broken when the authority 'expects to seek offers leading to the award' and fails (or it is apprehended it will fail) to notify the OJ accordingly and when it forms the intention to seek offers and fails (or it is apprehended that it will fail) as soon as possible thereafter to publicise that intention in the OJ . . . In the second case, grounds will first arise when the specific failure occurs or is apprehended.

15.108 However, the judge held that knowledge (or its absence) was relevant to the court's discretion to extend time. In the instant case he was prepared to extend time. On the facts Keymed did not appreciate that there had been a breach and it had sensibly sought clarification from the defendant before initiating proceedings. In *Dekra Erin Teoranta v Minister for the Environment and Local Government and SGS Ireland*[84] O'Neill J considering a similarly worded provision in the Supreme Court of Ireland[85] indicated that the balance is in favour of granting an extension of time where such extension does not prejudice either the respondent or third parties.

15.109 *Jobsin*[86] exemplifies the first of the situations identified by Langley J in *Keymed*—a breach of the regulations 'from the outset'.[87] There, the limitation question was whether time began to run from when Jobsin was excluded from the tendering process (as it contended)

---

[82] *Keymed (Medical & Industrial Equipment) Ltd v Forest Healthcare NHS Trust* [1998] Eu LR 71.

[83] That is, reg 32(4)(b) of the Services Regulations 1993 (see above).

[84] Unreported, 2 November 2001.

[85] Rules of the Superior Courts, Ord 84A, r 4.

[86] *Jobsin Co UK plc (t/a Internet Recruitment Solutions) v Department of Health* The Times, 2 October 2001.

[87] For an instance of the second scenario anticipated by Langley J in *Keymed* (a contracting authority's subsequent breach) see, eg, *Dekra Erin Teoranta v Minister for the Environment and Local Government and SGS Ireland* (unreported, 2 November 2001).

or whether (as the Department of Health argued) time started to run from the earlier date when Jobsin received the Briefing Document inviting proposals for tender.

The Court of Appeal found in favour of the Department of Health. It observed: **15.110**

> ... It is clear that, as soon as the Briefing Document was issued without identifying the criteria by which the most economically advantageous bid was to be assessed, there was a breach ... Moreover, it was a breach in consequence of which Jobsin, and indeed all other tenderers too, were then and there at risk of suffering loss and damage. It is true that there was no more than a risk at that stage, but that was enough to complete the cause of action. Without knowing what the criteria were, the bidders were to some extent having to compose their tenders in the dark. That feature of the tender process inevitably carried with it the seeds of potential unfairness and the possibility that it would damage the prospects of a successful tender.

As with time limits in judicial review proceedings, it cannot be assumed that a claimant has three months to bring the case. The requirement is to act 'promptly'. Failure to act promptly even within three months from when grounds first arose will result in the claim being refused unless time is extended.[88] **15.111**

There have been challenges to the validity of time limits in the context of the EC public procurement regime. In *Matra Communications SA v Home Office*[89] an unsuccessful challenge was made to the three-month time limit under reg 32(4)(b) of the Services Regulations. The Court of Appeal rejected the argument that the EC principle of equivalence[90] was breached because of the far longer time limit in respect of the tort of breach of statutory duty. The court also rejected analogies drawn in relation to claims for breaches of other directly effective EC rights, judicial review proceedings, and claims under ss 17 and 19 of the Local Government Act 1988. The court concluded its analysis by holding that there was no truly comparable domestic law procedure. In a later case, following the introduction of the HRA into English law, a challenge was made to the same provision on the ground that it violated Article 6 ECHR as being a disproportionate bar on access to the court. The Court of Appeal rejected this challenge and applied *Matra*.[91] **15.112**

In particular cases it is, however, possible that the EC principle of effectiveness[92] may require a longer time limit. In *Santex SpA*,[93] for example, the ECJ ruled that although a 60-day time limit for the bringing of proceedings was *prima facie* reasonable, in particular instances the application of that limit might contravene the EC principle of effectiveness. There, the contracting authority had engendered uncertainty by its own interpretation of a disputed provision. Its changing conduct rendered the exercise of EC rights excessively **15.113**

---

[88] In *Severn Trent plc v Welsh Water* (2001) CLC 107, for example, one of the issues that arose was whether the claimant had acted promptly. Langley J held that it had acted promptly in bringing the claim within two months given the short timescale involved.

[89] [1999] 1 WLR 1646.

[90] As to equivalence in a procedural context, see paras 3.18–3.31.

[91] See *Luck (t/a G Luck Arboricultural & Horticultural) v London Borough of Tower Hamlets* (unreported, 30 January 2003).

[92] As to effectiveness in a procedural context, see paras 3.09–3.17.

[93] Case C–327/00 [2003] ECR I–1877.

difficult in the particular circumstances of the case. For that reason, the ECJ gave a preliminary ruling that the domestic court should, in order to comply with the principle of effectiveness, disapply the limitation period in question.

Remedies

15.114   Importantly, the scheme of remedies under the Remedies Directive is entirely distinct from remedies generally available in EC law. As the Court of Appeal observed in *Matra Communications v Home Office*:[94]

> That Directive 89/665 creates its own limited code of remedies is underlined by the fact that it only applies, because the underlying Directive 92/50 only applies, to contracts of a value in excess of ECU 200,000. If the remedies envisaged by Directive 89/665 were general remedies already available in member states through the requirements of community law, rather than being remedies imposed on member states by Directive 89/665 itself, not only would there have been no need for Directive 89/665 at all, but also the exclusion from contracts of a certain size of Directive 89/665 remedies would also beat the air.

15.115   Thus, the principles affecting the grant of remedies under the EC procurement regime are regulated by the regulations supplemented, where appropriate, by the Remedies Directive and subject, always, to general principles of EC law such as effectiveness and equivalence.

15.116   On that basis the grant of interim relief to suspend the tender procedure under (for example) reg 32(5)(a) of the Services Regulations or a final order under reg 32(5)(b) setting aside an unlawful decision is necessarily governed by the scheme of the procurement directives. In *Alcatel*,[95] the ECJ held that such orders may be made only until the entering into a contract by the contracting authority with a service provider.[96] It interpreted the Remedies Directive as distinguishing between two different stages: (1) the stage before the entering into a contract, and (2) the stage following the conclusion of a contract. Thus a contract award decision preceding the actual entering into of the contract was still susceptible to being set aside and the relevant procedures suspended. As the court observed:

> ... the combined provisions of Article 2(1)(a) and (b) and the second passage of Article 2(6) of Directive 89/665 are to be interpreted as meaning that the Member States are required to ensure that the contracting authority's decision prior to the conclusion of the contract as to the bidder in a tender procedure with which it will conclude the contract is in all cases open to a review in a procedure where the applicant may have that decision set aside if the relevant conditions are met, notwithstanding the possibility, once the contract has been concluded, of obtaining an award of damages.

---

94 [1999] 1 WLR 1646.

95 Case C–81/98 *Alcatel Austria AG v Bundesministerium fur Wissenschaft und Verkehrm* [1999] ECR I–7671. Note that the ECJ's ruling in *Alcatel* is inconsistent with the Court of Appeal's approach to reg 32(5) in *Ealing Community Transport v LB of Ealing* (unreported, 30 July 1999). *Alcatel* was, of course, addressing the directive as opposed to reg 32(5) and, as Sedley LJ observed in the *Ealing* case, there might be a discrepancy between reg 32(5) and Art 2(6) of the directive. The latter refers to the *conclusion* of the contract rather than—as reg 32(5) does—to the *award* of the contract. It is, therefore, submitted that the reasoning in *Alcatel* must prevail and that reg 32(5) should be interpreted consistently with Art 2(6).

96 This restriction would not seem to apply, however, to a challenge to the contract founded on more general EC grounds such as, eg, a breach of the state aid rules (see below).

It is also clear that the scheme of the Remedies Directive places a less onerous burden on the   **15.117**
claimant in terms of obtaining interim relief than would usually be the case. As Deputy
Judge Humphrey Lloyd QC observed in (para 253) in *Harmon CFEM Facades (UK) Ltd v
Corporate Officer of the House of Commons:*[97]

> In reality I doubt very much if Harmon would have obtained an interlocutory injunction
> if *American Cyanamid* principles were applied even if it had been capable of giving the
> customary undertaking as damages would have been a sufficient remedy. However,
> Regulation [32(5)] in providing for a specific remedy without prejudice to the other pow-
> ers of the court confers on the court an additional power the exercise of which is not fet-
> tered, for example, by the need for an undertaking or by damages being an adequate
> remedy. Indeed in many cases it would be impossible for a disappointed tenderer to give
> such an undertaking, particularly where the damages payable would be disproportionate
> to the value of the contract. In my judgment the purpose of [Regulation 32(5)] is to
> provide an effective alternative remedy. It will not be effective (certainly within the princi-
> ples of *von Colson*) if its exercise has to follow the principles applicable to the grant of inter-
> locutory injunctions, or if there were to be any significant delay … before the merits of the
> application were heard and disposed of. Applications of this nature should be heard
> quickly, especially if they relate to the tendering procedure. The Regulation also contem-
> plates permanent remedies. The measures granted … will not be effective deterrents if they
> are not all readily available to a wronged contractor.

Finally, the fact that there is a specific entitlement to damages for breaches of the regime   **15.118**
ensures that restrictions on the award of damages for State liability for breaches of EC law
are not applicable to claims under the regulations. In *Harmon*,[98] for example, the claimant
successfully obtained an award of damages against the Corporate Officer of the House of
Commons in respect of the unequal treatment of tenderers in respect of tenders. Damages
were awarded on a domestic contractual (as opposed to a tortious) basis and were also
awarded for breach of an implied contract and in respect of the domestic tort of misfeasance in public office.

G. Relationship between Public Procurement and State Aid

Introduction

It is at least possible that procurement procedures might, in certain circumstances, consti-   **15.119**
tute a breach of the state aid requirements. This possibility is not addressed explicitly in the
EC public procurement regime or in the EC Treaty provisions on state aid.[99]

There is, though, a clear relationship, at least in theory, between EC public procurement   **15.120**
and the possibility of contravening state aid requirements. The context in which that

---

[97] (2000) 67 Con LR 1.

[98] Ibid. For a helpful analysis of the basis of damages claims under the procurement regimes see M Bowsher
and P Moser, 'Damages for Breach of the EC Public Procurement Rules in the United Kingdom' (2006)
4 PPLR 195–210.

[99] As to state aid see Chapter 13. On this topic see, also, C Bovis, *EC Public Procurement: Case Law and
Regulation* (2006) paras 1.60–1.76.

relationship has obvious potential significance is whether the award of a public contract can constitute a state aid.[100]

Can the award of a public contract constitute state aid?

15.121   There are two ways in which the award of a public contract under the EC public procurement regime may be viewed as state aid.[101] First, the payment under the contract awarded may be in excess of the market value of the goods/services being procured. In such circumstances, the excess payment might constitute the aid. Despite the fact that a public contract is a reciprocal agreement this does not exclude the possibility that the payment to the undertaking may constitute aid.[102]

15.122   Secondly, it is also at least possible that a contracting authority might place a contract even where there was, in objective terms, no need for the goods/services sought to be procured. The aid here might be the placing of the order.

15.123   In each of these scenarios the other elements of state aid would, of course, have to be present.[103] In the context of the EC public procurement regime these may be summarized as follows:

(1) *'granted by a Member State or through State resources'*
    If the contract is awarded by a public authority then this element of state aid would be satisfied. In most instances occurring under the regime, therefore, this requirement is met as where the contract is awarded by 'bodies governed by public law'. The criterion is also satisfied if the contract was awarded under the actual influence of public authorities.[104]

(2) *'favouring certain undertakings'*
    This criterion must be satisfied since aid granted by way of a public contract involves the granting of aid in an individual situation to a particular undertaking.

(3) *'distorting or threatening to distort competition' and 'affecting trade between Member States'*
    This criterion will be satisfied where the aid element actually or potentially strengthens the position of the undertaking in comparison with other undertakings competing in transnational markets.

---

[100] Other possible areas are whether the so-called 'secondary criteria' to be introduced under the new regime (most notably social and environmental clauses) raise state aid issues. For the arguments see, especially, A Doern, 'The Interaction between EC Rules on Public Procurement and State Aid' (2004) 13 PPLR Issue 3 97–129. Doern also considers the state aid issues in relation to defence procurement.

[101] The analysis that follows derives heavily from J Hillger, 'The Award of a Public Contract as State Aid within the Meaning of Article 87(1) EC' (2003) 12 PPLR Issue 3 109–30.

[102] See Case T–14/96 *Bretagne Angleterre Irlande (BAI) v Commission* [1999] ECR II–139, especially para 71.

[103] For further analysis of these elements see, generally, Chapter 13.

[104] Note, however, that the criterion is not satisfied where the awarding entity carries out the activities under the Utilities Directive on the basis of special or exclusive rights.

The possibility of state aid is also present in cases where the award of public contracts falls **15.124** below the threshold values in the procurement directives and, therefore, outside the EC procurement regime.

Consequences of a public contract falling within the prohibitions on state aid

Where a public contract falls within the Treaty prohibition on state aid the proposed con- **15.125** tract must be notified to the Commission prior to the award. The stand-still obligation will prevail until the Commission has reached a final decision on compatibility. If the contracting authority does not comply with the state aid rules, the contract award will be void. The invalidity of the contract could be invoked before the national courts by a competitor of the undertaking that was wrongfully awarded the contract.

It is submitted that a challenge to a proposed contract award for breach of the state aid rules **15.126** should be brought by way of judicial review as opposed to making a claim under the domestic regulations. The regulations contain their own scheme of obligations and remedies but more general requirements of Community law—such as state aid duties—are probably not always enforceable through the regulations. For example, the prohibition on a contract, once entered into, being set aside by the court would not appear to be present in respect of a breach of the state aid rules.

16

FREE MOVEMENT OF PERSONS
AND CITIZENSHIP

A. Introduction

General

So far as the Treaty is concerned, there is no single right of economic free movement. There **16.01** are, however, a cluster of specific EC rights and prohibitions against unjustified restrictions on freedom of movement/establishment in different contexts that, in broad economic terms, have the potential for affecting trade between Member States. In each case the pattern is similar. On the one hand the Treaty prohibits restrictions on relevant freedom of movement and, on the other hand, the Treaty permits restrictions that the State is able to justify by resort to specific and enunciated criteria. The structure is broadly similar to that for certain qualified ECHR rights as, for example, the right to respect for privacy enshrined in Article 8(1) ECHR with the power of interference on specific grounds contained in Article 8(2).[1]

---

[1] The position is, in fact, rather more complicated in EC law because derogation is permitted on a wider basis than that contained in express derogation provisions in certain circumstances, most notably where derogation—outside the context of expulsion—is either indirectly discriminatory or impedes market access but is justified in the public interest and proportionate.

16.02   Freedom of movement of persons is partly encompassed in Article 39 (ex 48) EC which prohibits restrictions on freedom of movement of workers and in Articles 43–48 (ex 52–58) EC which are concerned with freedom of establishment.[2] There are also implications for the freedom of movement of persons in Article 49 (ex 59) EC which prohibits freedom of movement of services. Apart from freedom of movement of persons (the main subject of this chapter) there are other freedoms which have a more commercial aspect.[3] Thus, Article 28 (ex 30) EC prohibits freedom of movement of goods in respect of imports.[4] Free movement of capital is addressed in Articles 56–50 (ex 73b–73g) EC and the Treaty provisions dealing with freedom of movement of services (Article 49 (ex 59) EC are also related to provisions such as these. These provisions are separately considered in Chapter 17.

16.03   As will be seen, all these freedoms are essentially economic provisions. However, they are not necessarily exhaustive of the free movement provisions contained in the Treaty. In particular, the citizenship provisions of the Treaty appear to contain additional important safeguards so far as freedom of movement of persons is concerned. Also crucial in terms of protection of the free movement of persons is Article 12 (ex 6) EC which underpins the guarantees in Article 39[5] and the other free movement provisions. This provides that:

> Within the scope of application of this Treaty and without prejudice to any special provisions contained therein, any discrimination in terms of nationality shall be prohibited.[6]

16.04   Discrimination may be indirect as well as direct and there is an increasing tendency to view obstacles to freedom of movement across all of the fundamental freedoms not merely in terms of discrimination (whether direct or indirect) but also in terms of impeding market access. As the ECJ observed in *Graf*:[7]

> Provisions which, even if they are applicable without distinction, preclude or deter a national of a Member State from leaving his country of origin in order to exercise his right to freedom of movement therefore constitute an obstacle to that freedom. However, in order to be capable of constituting such an obstacle, they must affect access of workers to the labour market.

Free movement of persons—an overview

16.05   Freedom of movement of EU citizens from one Member State to another is an important aspect of EC law and—especially when restrictions are placed upon it—a familiar subject of challenge in domestic judicial review and related public law proceedings. The content of what free movement entails, the benefits to which it gives rise, and who has access to it, is still developing.

---

[2] The Treaty provisions relating to freedom of establishment also have, in part, a commercial flavour especially where companies are concerned. This aspect is addressed in Chapter 17: see paras 17.50–17.56.

[3] It would, though, be wrong to conclude that there is no truly commercial dimension to the free movement of persons provisions: consider, eg sporting restrictions at paras 16.66 et seq.

[4] See also Art 29 (ex 34) EC for materially identical provisions relating to exports.

[5] Note, eg, Art 39(2) which provides that free movement of workers entails 'the abolition of any discrimination based on nationality between workers of the Member States as regards employment, remuneration, and other conditions of work and employment'.

[6] Article 12 is analysed further in Chapter 7. See paras 7.88–7.103.

[7] Case C–190/98 [2000] ECR 1–493.

As stated above, and in common with the other main substantive Treaty provisions concerned with freedom of movement, the specific Treaty provisions concerned with freedom of movement of persons are directed to the *economic* free movement of citizens of the EU. **16.06**

However, as the case law has developed, free movement of persons has come to encompass rather wider objectives than the purely economic. In particular, the ECJ has expanded its jurisdiction in relation to the protection of fundamental rights.[8] This has important implications for the scope of application of EC law to protect freedom of movement of persons both in terms of an expanded understanding of the range of economic interests protected and also in terms of the relatively new application of what are largely ECHR Convention rights in an EC context in the arena of free movement of persons. **16.07**

In addition, the citizenship provisions of the Treaty appear not necessarily to be founded on economic activity.[9] Separate rights founded on citizenship and embracing further aspects of a citizen's fundamental rights appear to have augmented the protection accorded to the free movement of persons. **16.08**

Free movement of persons and citizenship are addressed here separately so as to examine the less commercial aspects of EC law protections which give rise to public law challenges in the Administrative Court. The more commercial 'freedoms' are considered in Chapter 17 even though there is a clear overlap between many of the provisions.[10] **16.09**

Approach of the national courts to free movement of person cases

The ECJ has consistently held that the principle of freedom of movement of persons must be given a broad interpretation.[11] Conversely, derogations from that principle are required to be interpreted strictly.[12] **16.10**

Thus, for example, the concept of 'worker' within the meaning of Article 39 EC has a specific Community meaning and must not be interpreted narrowly. Any person who pursues activities which are real and genuine, to the exclusion of activities on such a small scale as to be regarded as purely marginal or ancillary is treated as a 'worker' for the purposes of the free movement provisions. The essential feature is that for a certain period a person performs services for and under the direction of another person in return for which he receives remuneration.[13] The national court must undertake its examination on a case-by-case basis.[14] **16.11**

---

[8] See, especially, Chapter 12.

[9] See paras 16.71 et seq.

[10] As, eg, in the freedom to provide services which can affect both the service provider (for commercial reasons) and the service recipient for non-commercial reasons who wishes to travel abroad to receive the service. For a case study on this interrelationship, see paras 19.60 et seq.

[11] See, eg, Case C–292/89 *Antonissen* [1991] ECR I–745, para 11; Case C–344/95 *Commission v Belgium* [1997] ECR I–1035, para 14.

[12] See, eg, Case C–67/74 *Bonsignore v Stadt Koln* [1975] ECR 297, para 6; Case 139/85 *Kempf v Staatsseccretaris van Justitie* [1986] ECR 1741, para 13.

[13] See, eg, Case 66/85 *Lawrie-Blum* [1986] ECR 2121, paras 16–17; Case C–138/02 *Collins* [2004] ECR I–2703, para 26.

[14] Case C–413/01 *Ninni-Orasche* [2003] ECR I–0000, para 27.

16.12 The national courts are, by virtue of s 3(1) of the European Communities Act 1972 required to follow those statements of principle[15] which have particular application to immigration proceedings before the national courts including judicial review challenges in the Administrative Court.

16.13 Consistently with that approach, the Administrative Court will, for example, require a more intense review in free movement cases than merely applying the test of whether (for example) a deportation decision was within the range of reasonable responses. A decision of the Immigration Appeal Tribunal was held to be unlawful by the Court of Appeal on precisely that basis where the Secretary of State decided to deport, on the ground of public policy, a foreign national married to an EU national with a right of establishment.[16]

16.14 In many instances, as some of the domestic cases illustrate, an EC-based argument will lead to the same outcome as an ECHR analysis. This is because restrictions on free movement in an EC context will engage ECHR fundamental rights and the national court will apply those rights in similar fashion (and with a similar level of review) *whether the source of the fundamental right sounds in EC or ECHR law.*

16.15 In some cases, however, the emphasis in the EC cases under (for example) Article 39 EC on the need for economic activity to acquire Treaty protection may mean that in certain contexts, the ECHR will be more generous than EC law.

16.16 By contrast, there will be many cases where EC law affords greater protection than its ECHR counterpart. As explained elsewhere,[17] Article 14 ECHR is somewhat narrower than the discrimination protection accorded in EC law. Further, there are areas of economic interests which are unlikely to be protected under the ECHR. Although the scope of private and family life under Article 8 ECHR is expanding, it is unlikely that Article 8 affords the specific protection that is embodied in many of the citizenship provisions.

16.17 In general, the necessary elements related to the economic freedom of movement of persons are that an individual is: (1) a national of a Member State, and (2) engaged in economic activity in at least one of three capacities, namely a worker (Articles 39–42 EC), a self-employed person (Articles 43–48 EC) or as a provider or recipient of services (Articles 49–55 EC).

16.18 If those conditions are satisfied, then there must be no discrimination in respect of the protected right on the ground of nationality subject to permitted derogation on specified grounds.

16.19 The structure of each of the Treaty groups of economic freedom of movement of person provisions is often very similar.[18] For the purpose of illustration of economic freedom provisions, primary focus in this section is placed on Article 39 EC (freedom of movement of

---

[15] See paras 2.92 et seq.
[16] *Machado v Secretary of State for the Home Department* [2005] EWCA Civ 597, [2005] 2 CMLR 43.
[17] See paras 7.112 et seq.
[18] See, especially, Case 48/75 *Procureur du Roi v Royer* [1976] ECR 497, para 23. There, the ECJ observed that there were common principles as between the different sets of provisions.

workers) although the principles are very similar to (in particular) those affecting self-employed persons (freedom of establishment under Articles 43–48 EC) which are also summarized in Table 16.1 at the end of this Chapter.[19]

In general, the Treaty Articles protecting economic freedom of movement of particular **16.20** groups of persons are skeletal in nature, setting out the nature of the right and then outlining the grounds for derogation. Directives then amplify the basis upon which these Treaty rights may be curtailed. Domestic judicial review proceedings have often been concerned both with the proper interpretation of the Treaty and the accompanying directives and (more commonly) with the application of general principles of EC law (most notably proportionality) to derogations from EC freedom of movement rights.

This chapter focuses primarily on the legality of derogation from free movement rights in **16.21** terms of *exclusion*. However, free movement rights also encompass a number of particular benefits and the case law is also concerned with the protection of such benefits which are, in certain cases, also subject to derogation. A brief outline of EC law in that respect is, therefore, also included in Table 16.1 below. As explained below, a new directive (EC) 2004/38 (referred to here as the Citizens' Directive) has recently replaced most of the previously existing Community legislation with some amendment.

B. Article 39 (ex 48(1)) EC and Exclusion

General

Article 39(1) (ex 48(1)) EC requires freedom of movement for workers to be secured **16.22** within the Community. Freedom of movement so secured must not be discriminatory.[20]

Importantly, Article 39(3) (ex 48(3)) EC both defines the rights of free movement that are **16.23** protected[21] and permits derogation on strictly limited grounds, namely: (1) public policy, (2) public security, or (3) public health.

The generality of Article 39(3) has, in the context of derogation for the purpose of exclusion, **16.24** been supplemented by the more specific terms of Directive (EEC) 64/221 ('the old Directive') which were, for most purposes, directly effective. This directive is repealed in its entirety by Directive (EC) 2004/38 (the Citizens' Directive) which was required to be implemented as

---

[19] The provisions restricting prohibitions on freedom to provide services are generally more akin to those restricting prohibitions on freedom of movement of goods for which see, generally, Chapter 17 especially paras 17.06 et seq.

[20] See Article 39(2) (ex 48(2)) EC. However, there is no discrimination in requiring the deportation of migrants who have been unemployed for more than six months provided that the time could be extended if the person was still actively seeking work and show that they had a genuine prospect of employment: see Case C–292/89 *R v IAT, ex p Antonissen* [1991] ECR I–745, para 21.

[21] These include the right to: (1) accept offers of employment actually made, (2) move freely within the territory of the Member State for such purpose, (3) stay in the Member State for the purpose of the employment, and (4) remain in the Member State after having been employed. There are also other associated rights the precise scope of which may feature in public law challenges such as rights of entry, residence, and employment (and education in respect of children) which are conferred in favour of a worker's spouse and children and certain dependent relatives irrespective of nationality. There is also, eg, provision for equal treatment. See Table 16.1 below.

from 30 April 2006.[22] Where material, therefore, the provisions of the Citizens' Directive will be referred to as well as those of the old directive where the case law has been developed.

16.25   So far as derogation is concerned, both the old and the new directives have two objectives. First, there are a number of specific principles on which a State may deny entry or residence on the general grounds identified in Article 39(3). Secondly, there are procedural obligations on the State when purporting to derogate from its Article 39 obligations.

16.26   In practice, in the context of exclusion, it is the legitimacy of purported derogation under Article 39(3), as originally amplified by Directive (EEC) 64/221 (and now by Directive (EC) 2004/38) which is most likely to give rise to domestic judicial review and other public law challenges.

16.27   There are a number of general constraints on derogations that apply to all the grounds in Article 39. First, derogations from Treaty obligations generally are interpreted strictly.[23] Secondly, the legality of derogations is subject to general principles of law including, most notably, the proportionality principle[24] and fundamental rights.[25] Thirdly, derogations may not be used for purely economic purposes.[26] Finally, there are procedural constraints on derogation under Article 39(3) which are considered separately below.

Restrictions based on public policy and/or public security grounds

16.28   In an early case, *Van Duyn v Home Office*,[27] the challenge was to the legality, in Article 39 terms,[28] of refusal of permission to a member of the Church of Scientology to enter the country. The High Court referred the case to the ECJ for a preliminary ruling. The ECJ held that although derogations were to be strictly construed the content of public policy might 'vary from one country to another and from one period to another'. Accordingly, it was 'necessary to allow the competent national authorities an area of discretion within the limits imposed by the Treaty'.

16.29   However, the scope of the State's discretionary area of judgment in the area of Article 39 derogations founded on public policy/security is, necessarily, constrained by Directive (EEC) 64/221 (and from 6 May 2006 by Directive (EC) 2004/38).

16.30   Article 3(1) of the old Directive provides that measures adopted on the ground of public *policy* must be 'based exclusively on the personal conduct of the individual concerned'. This test is repeated in Article 27(2) of the Citizens' Directive but with an important addition which reflects ECJ case law (see below). In *Van Duyn*[29] the ECJ considered that such

---

   [22] The new directive, which came into force in May 2006, contains a number of new substantive provisions designed to bolster free movement protection. The detail of these provisions is outside the scope of this work but reference should be made to the provisions of the new directive in any domestic judicial review challenge concerning free movement of persons.

   [23] See, eg, Case C–348/96 *Criminal Proceedings against Calfa* [1999] ECR I–11.

   [24] Proportionality is now expressly incorporated into Directive EC 2004/38 for the purposes of derogations relating to public policy or public security. See Art 27(2) EC.

   [25] These principles are addressed separately. See Chapters 11 and 12.

   [26] See Directive (EEC) 64/221, Art 2; Directive (EC) 2004/38, Art 27(1). See, also, eg, Case 352/85 *Bond v The Netherlands* [1988] ECR 2085.

   [27] Case 41/74 [1974] ECR 1337.

   [28] The Article was then Art 48.

   [29] Case 41/74 [1974] ECR 1337.

personal conduct did not have to be unlawful to constitute a basis for public policy derogation but could provide justification if the conduct was deemed to be 'socially harmful'.
Further, *current*[30] membership of a particular organization reflecting, as it did, identification
with the activities and purposes of that organization could constitute 'personal conduct'.

Article 3(2) of the old Directive stipulates that previous convictions, do not 'in themselves', **16.31**
justify derogation on public policy/security grounds. In another domestic case, *R v
Bouchereau*,[31] a French national working in England was convicted of being in unlawful
possession of drugs. He had a similar previous criminal conviction. The question referred
by the magistrate to the ECJ was whether public policy could be invoked to justify deportation. The ECJ offered the following guidance on the extent to which previous convictions are relevant:

> The existence of a previous criminal conviction can . . . only be taken into account in so far
> as the circumstances which gave rise to that conviction are evidence of personal conduct con-
> stituting a present threat to the requirements of public policy. Although, in general, a finding
> that such a threat exists implies the existence in the individual concerned of a propensity to
> act in the same way in the future, it is possible that past conduct alone may constitute such a
> threat to the requirements of public policy.[32]

Thus, past convictions have not been regarded as affording a proper basis for deportation **16.32**
in circumstances where there is clear evidence that the affected person has reformed since
the conviction or convictions in question.[33]

Further, the ECJ also made it clear in *Bouchereau* that the threat in question must—to justify **16.33**
a public policy exception—be sufficiently serious. It said:

> Recourse by a national authority to the concept of public policy presupposes, in any event,
> the existence, in addition to the perturbation of the social order which any infringement of
> the law involves, of a genuine and sufficiently serious threat to the requirements of public
> policy affecting one of the fundamental interests of society.

The *Bouchereau* test and approach to previous convictions is adopted in Article 27(2) of the **16.34**
new Directive which, after replicating, Article 3(1) and 3(2) of the old Directive continues
thus:

> The personal conduct of the individual concerned must represent a genuine, present and
> sufficiently serious threat affecting one of the fundamental interests of society. Justifications
> that are isolated from the particulars of the case or that rely on considerations of general
> prevention shall not be accepted.

---

[30] As opposed to *past* membership which could not constitute the requisite conduct: see para 16.32 and
n 33 below.
[31] Case 30/77 [1977] ECR 1999.
[32] As to a single conviction for a serious offence being capable of justifying deportation see, eg, *R v Secretary
of State for the Home Department, ex p Marchon* [1993] 2 CMLR 132.
[33] See, eg, *Monteil v Secretary of State for the Home Department* [1984] 1 CMLR 264 (deportation order
quashed where, despite criminal convictions, the proposed deportee had reformed having taken treatment
whilst in prison for his alcoholism); *Proll v Secretary of State for the Home Department* [1985] Imm AR 118
(former member of Baader-Meinhof gang held to have been unlawfully denied entry into the United
Kingdom since she had reformed during her time in prison).

16.35   There is an overlap between the application of EC and ECHR law in the present context. The 'genuine and serious threat' test articulated in *Bouchereau* was, as the ECJ explained in *Rutili*[34] designed to promote compliance with Articles 8–11 ECHR. In effect, it constitutes a proportionality requirement in the application of the public policy exception. As explained above, proportionality is now expressly contained as a requirement for public policy/security derogation in the new Directive (see Article 27(2)).

16.36   In addition, the new Directive creates, in Article 28, a new provision containing specific criteria in respect of *expulsion* decisions. Insofar as those decisions are concerned, matters such as length of residence, age, state of health, family and economic situation, and social and cultural integration are required to be taken into account (see Article 28(1)). But in the case of an EU citizen with a permanent right of residence there is enhanced protection. No expulsion decision may, in any event, be taken except on *serious* grounds of public policy or public security (Article 28(2)). And if an EU citizen has either resided in the host Member State for the previous 10 years or is a minor (subject to expulsion being in the best interests of the child as provided for in the United Nations Convention on the Rights of the Child) then, by Article 28(3), an expulsion decision may only be taken on imperative grounds of public security.

16.37   The overlap between EC and ECHR law is exemplified in the domestic appeal in *B v Secretary of State for the Home Department*.[35] There, the Court of Appeal allowed an appeal under s 9 of the Immigration Appeals Act 1993 which raised the question of whether the decision to deport infringed the principle of proportionality. The appellant was an Italian national who had lived in the United Kingdom for some 35 years from the age of seven. Although he was convicted of a series of sex offences and sentenced to five years' imprisonment, the Court of Appeal considered that the Secretary of State's decision to deport, as being conducive to the public good, was disproportionate.

16.38   The Court of Appeal held that proportionality was relevant both because of the terms of Article 39 and Directive (EEC) 64/221 and noted that Article 6 TEU provided that the EU should respect the ECHR of which Article 8 ECHR was relevant to this and most deportation cases.

16.39   There was no suggestion that, in the context under consideration, the test of proportionality differed according to whether EC or ECHR law was being applied.[36] That test was identified as amounting, in essence, to the proposition that:

> a measure which interferes with a Community or human right must not only be authorized by law but must correspond to a pressing social need and go no further than is strictly necessary in a pluralistic society to achieve its permitted purpose; or, more shortly, must be appropriate and necessary to its legitimate aim.[37]

---

[34] Case C–36/75 *Rutili (Roland), Gennevilliers (France) v Ministry of the Interior of France* [1975] ECR 1219.

[35] [2000] HRLR 439.

[36] There is, though, at least in some cases the possibility of the EC and ECHR jurisdictions differing as to application of the proportionality test. See, further, paras 11.84 et seq.

[37] [2000] HRLR 439, 443, per Sedley LJ.

Applying that test, the Court of Appeal concluded (linking EC and ECHR law in the same **16.40**
analysis) that:

> What . . . renders deportation a disproportionate response to this appellant's offending, seri-
> ous as it is, and to his propensity to offend such as it may now be, is the fact that it will take
> him from the country in which he has grown up, has lived his whole adult life and has such
> social relationships as he possesses. It would negate both his freedom of movement and
> respect for his private life in the one place, the United Kingdom, where these have real mean-
> ing for him. In relation to what is now Article 39 of the EU Treaty this is self-evident. In rela-
> tion to Article 8 of the ECHR, it is because the jurisprudence of the Strasbourg court has
> carried the notion of private life beyond simple autonomy and 'to a certain degree' into 'the
> right to establish and develop relationships with other human beings'. . .[38]

Restrictions based on public health grounds

In practice, as far as free movement of persons under Article 39 is concerned, derogation on **16.41**
public health grounds has not, in the past, given rise to much domestic public law challenge. Directive (EEC) 64/221 set out a specific list in Annexes A and B of diseases and conditions that may justify derogation under Article 39(3). HIV/AIDS was not expressly set
out in either of the annexes.

However, in the new Directive, Article 29 creates a new regime. In future, the only diseases **16.42**
justifying measures restricting freedom of movement are (see Article 29(1)) the diseases
with epidemic potential as defined by the relevant instruments of the World Health
Organization and 'other infectious diseases or contagious parasitic diseases if they are the
subject of protection provisions applying to nationals of the host Member State'. By Article
29(2) diseases occurring after a three-month period following arrival shall not constitute
grounds for expulsion from the territory.

Procedural safeguards

Reasons

By virtue of Article 30 of Directive (EC) 2004/38[39] the persons concerned must be notified **16.43**
in writing of any decision to derogate from Article 39 on grounds of public policy, public
security, or public health. The decision must be communicated in such a way that they are
able to comprehend its content and the implications for them. The grounds relied on for
the decision must be set out precisely and in full[40] unless this is contrary to the interests of
State security. Full rights of appeal must be specified.[41]

The reasons duty, in the context of Article 39 rights, formed the subject of a domestic judi- **16.44**
cial review challenge in *R v Secretary of State for the Home Department, ex p Dannenberg*.[42]

---

[38] ibid 447, per Sedley LJ.
[39] Some of these requirements were reflected in Arts 6–7 of Directive (EEC) 64/221 but the content of the
reasons duty as developed in the case law now appears as an express requirement of Art 30.
[40] See *Rutili* [1975] ECR 1219, para 39. See, also, Joined Cases 115 and 116/81 *Adoui and Cornuaille*
[1982] ECR 1665, para 13.
[41] This will, ordinarily, be not less than one month from the date of notification save in duly substantiated
cases of urgency.
[42] [1984] QB 766.

There, the Court of Appeal quashed a deportation order and prior recommendation of the magistrates for failing, in breach of the old Directive, to give reasons.

Remedies

16.45   Under Articles 8 and 9 of the old Directive there were two specific and distinct additional procedural safeguards. The first, provided by Article 8, was the requirement that nationals of other Member States should have the same legal remedies as nationals. This requirement is, in effect, reflected in the general EC principle of equivalence and does not reappear in the new Directive.[43] Secondly, Article 9 provided for situations where there were no adequate legal remedies. The new Directive now contains express provision for adequate remedies (see below).[44]

16.46   Article 31(1) of Directive (EC) 2004/38 provides that:

> The persons concerned shall have access to judicial and, where appropriate, administrative redress procedures in the host Member State to appeal against or seek review of any decision taken against them on the grounds of public policy, public security or public health.

16.47   Article 31(3) provides that:

> The redress procedures shall allow for an examination of the legality of the decision, as well as of the facts and circumstances on which the proposed measure is based. They shall ensure that the decision is not disproportionate, particularly in view of the requirements laid down in Article 28.[45]

16.48   These new simplified provisions are in line with the approach of the Advocate General in *Shingara*[46] which commenced as a judicial review challenge to a refusal of entry decision but was referred to the ECJ for a preliminary ruling. In *Shingara* the question was whether domestic judicial review, the only available remedy in respect of such decisions, satisfied the requirement of Article 8 of the old Directive (see above) that nationals of other Member States should have 'the same remedies' as nationals.

16.49   However, the ECJ held that:

> Where national law provides no specific procedures for the remedies available to persons covered by the directive . . . the obligation imposed on Member States by Article 8 is fulfilled if nationals of other Member States enjoy the same remedies as those generally available against acts of the administration in that Member State.

16.50   By contrast, Advocate General Ruiz-Colomer had argued that Article 8 should be interpreted as requiring full and effective protection by the courts so that domestic judicial review would not match that standard unless there could be detailed scrutiny of the acts of

---

[43] For further discussion of the general principle of equivalence in the context of remedies, see paras 5.06–5.12. The case law on Art 8 is, though, still of obvious relevance (see below).

[44] Apart from Art 31(1) and 31(3) considered immediately below, it should also be noted that Art 31(2) and Art 31(4) of Directive (EC) 2004/38 deal (respectively) with interim applications to suspend expulsion and exclusion pending judicial review or appeal.

[45] As to Art 28 of the new Directive, see para 16.36.

[46] Joined Cases C–65/95 and C–111/95 *R v Secretary of State for the Home Department, ex p Shingara and Radiom* [1997] ECR I–3343. See, especially, para 65 of the Advocate General's Opinion.

the administration in respect of the entry and expulsion of migrants. It can be seen that Article 31(3) of the new Directive now allows for this.

Domestic case law (including preliminary rulings by the ECJ in the course of such proceed-   **16.51**
ings) on Article 9 of the old Directive may still be helpful in enunciating general principle as to what is entailed in effective judicial review for the purpose of scrutiny of the legality of derogation from Article 39. For example, in *R v Secretary of State, ex p Santillo*[47] the ECJ, giving a ruling relating to Article 9 of Directive (EEC) 64/221, stressed the importance of proximity in time between a recommendation for deportation and the actual decision that a person be deported. Plainly, judicial review—in order to be an effective process under Article 31(1) and (3) of the new Directive—would have to inquire into such matters.

Particular issues over the legality of free movement restrictions

Can restrictions of movement be placed on UK nationals?

This issue had not previously been determined before the ECJ. It arose in the context of   **16.52**
football banning orders in *Gough and Smith v Chief Constable of Derbyshire*.[48] Such orders, imposed under the Football Spectators Act 1989 (as amended by the Football (Disorder) Act 2000), have the effect of preventing football hooligans from attending certain football matches in England and Wales and also from leaving the country when certain matches are taking place outside England and Wales.

Gough and Smith unsuccessfully appealed by way of case stated to a Divisional Court   **16.53**
against banning orders. Their appeal to the Court of Appeal was also dismissed.

The appellants' arguments were founded on EC and HRA law. As to EC law, they submit-   **16.54**
ted that: (1) the banning orders constituted an unlawful derogation from their positive rights of freedom of movement and freedom to leave the country (as granted by Council Directive (EEC) 73/148)[49] since it was not possible to justify a banning order both on the evidence and, in any event, not *permissible* under Article 8 of the Directive (permitting derogation) on the ground of public policy *so far as UK nationals were concerned*, (2) the 2000 Act breached EC law to the extent that it imposed mandatory restrictions on free movement within the Community on criteria that were not provided for in EC legislation, and (3) the bans infringed the general EC principle of proportionality.

However, the Court of Appeal rejected these submissions. It held that there was a public   **16.55**
policy exception to the 1973 Directive that applied as much to UK as to foreign nationals. This meant that there was no absolute right to leave one's country. Whilst it might appear that banning *all* foreign travel was disproportionate, banning orders could be imposed where there were strong grounds for concluding that an individual had a propensity for participating in football hooliganism provided, always, that the individual case was properly considered. Here, the bans were not disproportionate.

---

[47] Case 131/79 [1980] ECR 1585.
[48] [2002] 2 CMLR 11. See also E Deards 'Human Rights for Football Hooligans?' (2002) 27 EL Rev 206.
[49] Council Directive (EEC) 73/148 provides that Member States must abolish restrictions on the movement and residence of (most notably) nationals of a Member State who are established or wish to establish themselves in another Member State and nationals of Member States wishing to go to another Member State as recipients of services.

Purely internal situations

16.56 Importantly, situations that are 'wholly internal to a Member State' fall outside the scope of the free movement provisions of the Treaty.[50] Thus, for example, in *Saunders*[51] a UK national from Northern Ireland who was bound over by the Crown Court in England on condition that she return to Northern Ireland and did not revisit England or Wales for three years could not invoke EC law to challenge the legality of her undertaking to the court when she was charged with being in breach of the bind over.

16.57 But care is needed in determining whether or not a particular set of facts represents a purely internal situation. The facts of *Carpenter*[52] show the potential difficulties. Mrs Carpenter was a Filipino who was married to a UK national living and working in the United Kingdom. The question was whether or not EC free movement principles affected a deportation order made against her. The case was referred to the ECJ for a preliminary ruling. That court ruled that EC law was involved by virtue of Article 49 EC (freedom to provide and receive services) because if Mrs Carpenter were to be deported, it would detrimentally affect her husband's ability to operate his business which involved the provision of services in other Member States.

16.58 A slightly different situation in which the 'purely internal situation' restriction may be avoided is where persons are exercising, or have exercised, their rights of free movement. In such a case they are entitled to invoke freedom of movement provisions against their own State in the same way as an EC migrant. For example, in *Surinder Singh*[53] the claimant who was an Indian national married a British citizen. They lived in Germany for two years where Mrs Singh worked part time. Under EC law she was entitled to be joined by Mr Singh. The couple returned to the United Kingdom in 1985 to start a business.

16.59 In judicial review proceedings brought by the Secretary of State against a decision of the Immigration Appeal Tribunal in Mr Singh's favour, the question was whether this represented a purely internal situation in which case Mr Singh could be deported from the United Kingdom or whether Mr Singh was entitled to protection under freedom of movement provisions that allow a Community national to be joined by a spouse. The ECJ gave a preliminary ruling in favour of Mr Singh on the basis that a UK national such as Mrs Singh might be deterred from exercising her rights of freedom of movement if, when she returned to the United Kingdom, the conditions of entry or residence were not equivalent (in the sense of being permitted to be joined by her spouse) to those that she would have on entering the territory of another Member State.

16.60 However, what might be termed the exception against a situation being regarded as purely internal will not be allowed to be circumvented intentionally. In *Akrich*[54] a Moroccan national, who was unlawfully resident in the United Kingdom, married a British national

---

[50] Case 175/78 *R v Saunders* [1979] ECR 1129, para 11.
[51] ibid.
[52] Case C–60/00 *Carpenter v Secretary of State for the Home Department* [2002] ECR I–6279.
[53] Case C–370/90 *R v IAT and Surinder Singh, ex p Secretary of State for the Home Department* [1992] ECR I–4265.
[54] Case C–109/91 *Secretary of State for the Home Department v Hacene Akrich* (judgment 23 September 2003).

who moved to Ireland to work in a bank. She returned to the United Kingdom some six months later. Akrich applied for leave to enter the United Kingdom as the spouse of a migrant worker. Entry clearance was refused, the view being taken that this was a temporary move deliberately designed to circumvent UK immigration law. On a reference to the ECJ that court ruled that in order to benefit from EC law, the national of a non-Member State married to the national of a Member State had to be lawfully resident in a Member State when he moved to another Member State to which the citizen of the Union was migrating or had migrated.

Indirect discrimination restricting free movement on grounds of nationality

A measure that discriminates *indirectly* is one which is ostensibly non-discriminatory but which, nonetheless, has a greater impact on nationals of other Member States. Indirectly discriminatory measures that limit free movement will in the context of expulsion/refusal of entry decisions be contrary to Articles 39, 43 and 49 EC unless—complying with EC general principles of law—they fall (as with directly discriminatory measures) within one of the designated exceptions.   **16.61**

Indirect discrimination affecting free movement in certain other areas may be permissible but only if justified in the public interest and proportionate. In the course of a domestic judicial review challenge based on the legality of maintenance grants, the ECJ observed in its preliminary ruling under Article 234 as follows in relation to indirect discrimination: **16.62**

> Conditions imposed by national law must be regarded as indirectly discriminatory where, although applicable irrespective of nationality, they affect essentially migrant workers ... or the great majority of those affected are migrant workers ... where they are indistinctly applicable but can be more easily satisfied by national workers ... or where there is a risk that they may operate to the particular detriment of migrant workers ... It is otherwise only if those provisions are justified by objective considerations independent of the nationality of the workers concerned, and if they are proportionate to the legitimate aim pursued by national law.[55]

Does the Keck *principle apply to free movement of persons?*

As will be seen in the discussion on freedom of movement of goods (protected by Article 28 EC) the ECJ held in *Keck*[56] that some non-discriminatory selling arrangements did not constitute a relevant restriction on free movement. Questions have arisen in the domestic case law as to whether the *Keck* principle applies to freedom of services.[57] A similar issue arises in the context of free movement of persons.   **16.63**

In *Alpine Investments*[58] the ECJ avoided directly confronting the issue. There, in the context of freedom of establishment under Article 49 EC, the court held that the restriction under Dutch law of cold-calling for the purpose of selling financial services was a *prima*   **16.64**

---

[55] Case C–209/03 *R (Bidar) v London Borough of Ealing and the Secretary of State for Education and Skills* [2005] ECR I–2119.
[56] Joined Cases C–267–8/91 *Keck and Mithouard* [1993] ECR I–6097. See paras 17.16 et seq.
[57] This issue has recently been considered by the Court of Appeal in *R (Countryside Alliance) v (1) Attorney General (2) Secretary of State for Environment, Food and Rural Affairs* [2006] EWCA Civ 817. For a case analysis, see paras 17.98 et seq.
[58] Case C–384/93 *Alpine Investments BV v Minister van Financien* [1995] ECR I–1141.

facie infringement of Article 49 although it was, in the circumstances, proportionate and, therefore, justified. The ECJ said that the case was different to *Keck* because the prohibition on cold-calling was capable of hindering intra-Community trade in services whereas *Keck* was not concerned with an effect on inter-State trade.

16.65   If *Keck* is analysed in terms of excluding from the ambit of Article 28 those elements of an ostensible restriction that do not have a material impact on inter-State trade *(in casu* non-discriminatory selling arrangements) it is arguable that ostensible restrictions do not fall within Article 39 (and related Treaty provisions) that do not have a similar effect on inter-State trade. In *Graf*,[59] for example, an Austrian law preventing a termination payment after three years' service if, amongst other things, a worker bore responsibility for his premature dismissal was held by the ECJ not to be a restriction on the free movement of workers because the impact of the law was 'too uncertain and indirect'.

Free movement in a commercial context—companies and sport

16.66   Although outside the main emphasis of this chapter, it should be borne in mind that EC Treaty free movement of person provisions may have a commercial[60] impact as well as a (more usual) personal impact. True it is that Article 39 rights are conferred on individuals. However, the right of freedom of establishment (Article 43 EC) affects legal as well as natural persons. In particular, Article 43 provides that freedom of establishment includes the right to 'set up and manage undertakings, in particular companies or firms ... under the conditions laid down for its own nationals by the law of the country where such establishment is effected'. Article 48 provides that companies or firms that are formed pursuant to the law of a Member State and having their registered office, central administration, or principal place of business within the Community are to be treated in the same way as natural persons.

16.67   Plainly, there are difficulties in simply transposing the principles in the cases that apply to individuals to corporate entities.[61] However, in an appropriate case, a relevant prohibition on establishing a corporate entity within the meaning of Article 48 EC in a Member State would appear to be capable of infringing Article 43 EC.[62]

16.68   Similarly, corporate entities have rights in respect of the freedom to provide services under Article 49 EC.[63] The relevance of this right to individual persons surfaced in *R (Loutchansky) v First Secretary of State*[64] a judicial review challenge brought by an individual and a company against a refusal by the Secretary of State to pay the costs of the first (individual) claimant incurred on an appeal to the Special Immigration Appeal Commission (SIAC) against a decision refusing him entry to the United Kingdom.

---

[59]   Case C–190/98 [2000] ECR I–493.

[60]   The word 'commercial' is used here in contrast to the avowedly economic nature of Art 39 rights referred to at para 16.03 above. A case like *Carpenter* (see para 16.57 above) whilst ostensibly decided on an *economic* basis cannot, it is submitted, sensibly be seen as in any sense a *commercial* case. It is a decision founded primarily on the right to respect for family life enshrined in Art 8 ECHR but applied in the context of EC economic freedoms.

[61]   See, eg, Case 81/87 *Daily Mail* [1988] ECR 5483.

[62]   See, eg, Case C–200/98 *X AB and Y AB v Riksskatteverket* [1999] ECR I–8261.

[63]   See para 16.66.

[64]   [2005] EWHC 1779.

Moses J dealt with the first claimant's EC rights as a preliminary issue on the permission **16.69** application before him. He held that the company had the right under Article 49 EC to bring such workers as it wished into the United Kingdom for the purposes of providing and receiving services within the United Kingdom subject, always, to any lawful restrictions under Article 46 EC. That being so, the individual claimant had a contingent right to rely on the company's rights in challenging the decision to exclude him. Any restriction on that individual's rights must, therefore, be justified in accordance with EC law principles. That also entailed consideration of the independent appeal procedure to SIAC since it was that procedure which was used to both establish justification for refusal of entry and to enable challenge to be made to such refusal.

Free movement of person provisions are also commercially relevant to the world of sport. **16.70** In summary, Article 39 does not, ordinarily, extend to those engaging professionally in sport because they are, almost by definition, self-employed. But Article 49 (freedom to provide services) would cover such persons. Provided, therefore, that sport is being pursued for a relevant economic purpose[65] EC freedom of movement rights have potentially important application. EC freedom of movement provisions have, in particular, been successfully used to challenge transfer restrictions[66] and other sporting rules.[67]

C. Citizenship

A new Part Two entitled 'Citizenship of the Union' was added to the Treaty in 1992. **16.71** Article 17(1)[68] (as amended) provides as follows:

> Citizenship of the Union is hereby established. Every person holding the nationality of a Member State shall be a citizen of the Union. Citizenship of the Union shall complement and not replace national citizenship.

Article 18(1) (as amended) provides that: **16.72**

> Every citizen of the Union shall have the right to move and reside freely within the territory of the Member States, subject to the limitations and conditions laid down in the Treaty and by the measures adopted to give it effect.

Nationality (the necessary prerequisite for EU citizenship) has been held by the ECJ to be **16.73** a matter of domestic law, although in specifying conditions for the grant and loss of nationality the Member State must pay regard to Community law including, therefore, the fundamental rights recognized by EC law.

---

[65] As to this, see, eg, Case C–36/74 *Walrave and Koch* [1974] ECR 1405 where the requisite economic element was held to be lacking. Contrast Case 13/76 *Dona v Mantero* [1976] ECR 1333 where the ECJ held that free movement provisions could be deployed to challenge sporting rules if there was an economic activity involved. Thus, the activities of professional footballers fell in principle within either Art 39 or 49.

[66] Case C–415/93 *Bosnan v Royal Belgian Football Association and UEFA* [1995] ECR I–4921.

[67] See, eg, Case C–438/00 [2003] ECR I–4135. See, generally, S Weatherill '"Fair Play Please" Recent Developments in the Application of EC Law to Sport' (2003) 40 CML Rev 51.

[68] This provision is substantively replicated in Art 2(1) of Directive (EC) 2004/38 ('the Citizens' Directive'). See Table 16.1 below.

16.74 In *Kaur*[69]—a domestic judicial review that was referred to the ECJ for a preliminary ruling—the ECJ observed that:

> under international law, it is for each Member State, having due regard to Community law, to lay down the conditions for the acquisition and loss of nationality.[70]

16.75 The background to *Kaur* is instructive. Ms Kaur was born in 1949 in a family of Asian origin. She became a citizen of the United Kingdom under the terms of the British Nationality Act 1948. She did not, though, come within any of the categories of Citizens of the United Kingdom and Colonies recognized under the Immigration Act 1971 as having a right of residence in the United Kingdom. However, the British Nationality Act 1981 conferred on her the status of a British Overseas Citizen. As such, she had in the absence of special authorization no right under national law to enter or remain in the United Kingdom.

16.76 Following several temporary periods of residence in British territory and while once again in the United Kingdom, in 1996 Ms Kaur reapplied for leave to remain as she had already done on several occasions since 1990 when she first entered the United Kingdom.

16.77 The Secretary of State refused her leave to remain in the United Kingdom and she sought judicial review of that decision.

16.78 The ECJ's analysis was to the effect that Ms Kaur never acquired a right of UK nationality and that this was evidenced by the fact and content of unilateral declarations by the UK Government when acceding to the EC Treaty and when passing the British Nationality Act 1981. That being so, there was nothing in EC law on which she could rely to compel the UK Government to grant her nationality.

16.79 These conclusions are, perhaps, unsurprising. What is, however, potentially significant for other judicial review challenges is the implicit recognition by the ECJ in *Kaur* that although Member States have the right to specify relevant conditions of nationality, that right is not unconstrained in that any deprivation of EU citizenship must be in accordance with EU law.[71] As the ECJ observed (para 25 of its judgment) by reference to the facts of the case before it—the declarations in question did not 'have the effect of depriving any person who did not satisfy the definition of a national of the United Kingdom of rights to which that person might be entitled under Community law'. Plainly, however, if that had been the consequence it is to be inferred from the court's reasoning that such deprivation of rights would contravene the requirements of EC law.

16.80 These principles have particular application to the more stringent immigration provisions in domestic law. In particular, s 56(1) of the Immigration, Asylum and Nationality Act 2006 amends s 40(2) of the British Nationality Act 1981 to read thus: '[t]he Secretary of State may by order deprive a person of a citizenship status if the Secretary of State is satisfied that deprivation is conducive to the public good'. In the light of *Kaur* it seems clear that any deprivation of nationality under s 40(2) (as amended) would have to conform to EC law including the

---

69 Case C–192/99 *R v Secretary of State for the Home Department, ex p Kaur* [2001] ECR I–1237.
70 See, also, Case C–369/90 *Micheletti v Delagacion del Gioberno en Cantabria* [1992] ECR I–4239.
71 As, for example, fair procedures and a prohibition on statelessness.

general principles of EC law discussed in Part II above. It is at least possible that arguments founded on EC law would provide a stronger basis of challenge than under the ECHR.[72]

An important issue is the extent to which the citizenship provisions of the Treaty contain protection distinct from those afforded by Articles 39, 43, and 49 which are, in their different ways, concerned with protecting economic rights. **16.81**

There are a number of relevant points. First, the phrase in Article 18(1) 'subject to the limitations and conditions laid down in the Treaty and by the measures adopted to give it effect' demonstrates that the derogations applicable to Articles 39, 43, and 49 apply equally to Article 18(1). **16.82**

Secondly, as explained earlier at paras 16.07 et seq., the case law relevant to the economic freedom of movement provisions suggests that a broad approach to these provisions is adopted by the ECJ (and is, hence, required to be adopted by the national courts). This is consistent with the applicable principles relevant to freedom of movement of persons generally but it has the effect that a clear distinction cannot, easily, be drawn between the economic provisions on the one hand and the citizenship provisions on the other. **16.83**

As might be expected, therefore, the broad and generous principles applicable to freedom of movement provisions affecting nationals appear to be the same for the citizenship provisions of the Treaty as for the economic free movement provisions. **16.84**

This is exemplified by the facts and decision in *R v Secretary of State for the Home Department, ex p Yiadom*.[73] In that case, Ms Yiadom, a Dutch national, was refused permission by the Home Secretary to enter permanently on the ground of public policy because it was alleged that she had helped other persons to enter the United Kingdom illegally. She sought judicial review of the decision. Importantly, however, her leave to stay was extended whilst the facts of her case were examined. During that time she was permitted to take up employment and several months elapsed between her arrival in the United Kingdom and the decision refusing entry. **16.85**

The question referred to the ECJ by the Court of Appeal was, in essence, whether or not the Secretary of State's decision was truly to be classed as an entry decision or whether in substance it was an expulsion decision with particular rights of review. Depending on the answer to that question, Ms Yiadom might only be able to invoke part of the old Directive and, in particular, not be able to rely on Article 9 (see above). Although the procedural issue is, in the light of the new Directive, of historical interest the ECJ in interpreting the old Directive was plainly influenced by the citizenship provisions of the Treaty.[74] **16.86**

In ruling that Ms Yiadom could rely on both Articles 8 and 9 of the old Directive and was not (as the Government contended) restricted to Article 8 the ECJ ruled that in substance the Secretary of State's decision could not be treated solely as an entry decision. It also ruled **16.87**

---

[72] There is no right of nationality or fair procedure prior to deprivation of citizenship that can be derived from the ECHR although in an exceptional case Art 8 considerations might become relevant.
[73] Case C–357/98 [2000] ECR I–9265.
[74] See, eg, para 23 of the ECJ's judgment.

that provisions designed to protect EU nationals seeking to exercise their rights had to be interpreted in a manner favourable to the claimant.

16.88   That, though, does not dispose of the separate question of whether the rights in Article 18 confer anything in addition to existing free movement rights. This is, perhaps, especially so where specific directives cover free movement in respect of particular categories of person such as students, the retired, and others.[75]

16.89   That there may, however, be *additional* directly effective rights conferred by Article 18 would seem to follow from the ECJ's preliminary ruling in another domestic case, *Baumbast*.[76] That decision concerned two conjoined appeals which were referred by the Immigration Appeal Tribunal to the ECJ. In one of them, Mr Baumbast, a German national (and, hence, citizen of the EU) continued residing in Britain once his work in the EU had ceased. The Secretary of State refused to extend his residence permit. The question in his case was whether or not an EU citizen who no longer enjoys a right of residence as a migrant worker in the host Member State can, nonetheless, enjoy a right of residence by direct application of Article 18(1) EC.[77]

16.90   The ECJ ruled that he had a directly effective right of residence in the United Kingdom under Article 18 but that it was subject to the legitimate interests of the Member States exercised in compliance with general principles of EC law including proportionality. That decision[78] appears to suggest that a claimant does not necessarily have to establish a relevant connection with any economic activity to be able to claim Article 18 entry or residence rights (as would be necessary for a successful application under Articles 39, 43, or 49).[79]

16.91   In particular, the ECJ observed:

> Although, before the Treaty on European Union entered into force, the Court had held that that right of residence conferred directly by the EC Treaty, was subject to the condition that the person concerned was carrying on an economic activity within the meaning of Articles [39, 43, and 49] (see Case C–363 *Roux* [1991] ECR I-273, paragraph 9), it is none the less the case that, since then, Union citizenship has been introduced into the EC Treaty and Article 18(1) has conferred a right, for every citizen, to move and reside freely within the territory of the Member States.[80]

---

[75] See, especially, Directives (EEC) 93/96, 90/365 and 90/364.

[76] Case C–413/99 *Baumbast and R v Secretary of State for the Home Department* [2002] ECR I–7091.

[77] The other appeal exemplifies the broad approach required to be taken in free movement cases. It raised the question of whether children of an EU citizen who have installed themselves in a Member State during their parent's right of residence as a migrant worker were entitled to reside in the Member State to attend an educational course albeit that the parents had divorced. The ECJ held that they were. Secondly, the ECJ held that the parent who was their primary carer could, irrespective of nationality, reside with them to facilitate the exercise of the childrens' right of residence.

[78] See, also, Case C–200/02 *Zhu and Chen v Secretary of State for the Home Department* [2004] 3 WLR 1453.

[79] Note that even under those provisions, a claimant does not always have to engage in the economic activity himself. For example, it is well established that the recipient of services may be able to claim a breach of Art 49 (see para 17.37).

[80] Case C–413/99 [2002] ECR I–7091, para 81. See, also, Case C–456/02 *Trojani* [2004] All ER (EC) 1065.

Just as for Articles 39, 43 or 49, separate rights derived from citizenship provisions of the **16.92** Treaty are enforceable where there is *indirect* as well as *direct* discrimination.[81]

D. Third Country Nationals

Other than in respect of their relationship with EU nationals (see Table 16.1 below) and in **16.93** other somewhat limited ways,[82] third country nationals are not protected by Article 39 and related provisions of the Treaty or by the citizenship provisions discussed above all of which depend upon the establishment of EU nationality. They will, of course, be protected under the ECHR—especially under Article 3 (protection from inhuman and degrading treatment or torture)—against deportation and other decisions affecting their Convention rights.[83]

However, so far as EC law is concerned, there are now various provisions affecting the free- **16.94** dom of movement of third country nationals in Title IV, introduced by the Treaty of Amsterdam. These are very detailed and do not all affect the United Kingdom. The detail of these provisions is outside the scope of this work.[84] In the context of immigration policy, Article 61 of Title IV itemizes the tasks required for the progressive establishment of 'an area of freedom, security and justice' as including measures concerning asylum, refugees and displaced persons as well as safeguarding the rights of third country nationals.

In that context, there are certain obligations to which the United Kingdom has signed up **16.95** that are relevant to the protection of freedom of movement of third country nationals. The carrying out of such obligations will be susceptible to judicial review.

One of those obligations is Council Regulation (EC) 343/2003 (often known as 'Dublin **16.96** II') which the United Kingdom has given notice of its wish to participate in. That regula- tion establishes the criteria for ascertaining the Member State which is to be responsible for examining an asylum application lodged in a Member State by a third country national.

This regulation was central to the judicial review challenge in *R (Berihul) v Secretary of State* **16.97** *for the Home Department*.[85] In that case the claimant, a third country (Eritrean) national, sought judicial review of the Secretary of State's decision to remove him from the United Kingdom under the Asylum and Immigration (Treatment of Claimants, etc) Act 2004. He had arrived in the United Kingdom as an unaccompanied minor and claimed asylum.

The Secretary of State considered that because the claimant had already applied for asylum **16.98** in Italy, the proper country to consider his asylum claim was Italy. For that reason, the Secretary of State refused to consider the asylum claim and made directions for his removal

---

[81] See, eg, Case C–224/98 *D'Hoop v Office National de l'Emploi* [2002] ECR I–6191.

[82] Most notably as stateless persons or recognized refugees who have been admitted to another Member State and then only in a very limited way. Note, also, the potential relevance of Association Agreements to the position of third country nationals (see Table 16.1 below).

[83] See, eg, *D v United Kingdom* (1997) 24 EHRR 423; *N v Secretary of State for the Home Department* [2005] 2 WLR 1124; *R (Limbuela) v Secretary of State for the Home Department* [2005] 3 WLR 1014.

[84] For an excellent analysis, see C Barnard, *The Substantive Law of the EU* (2004) ch 16.

[85] [2005] EWHC 2563. Another example of a relevant EC obligation is afforded by Council Regulation (EC) 2003/9 on Minimum Standards for the Reception of Asylum Seekers transposed into domestic law by SI 2005/7 and SI 2005/11.

from the United Kingdom. The claimant sought judicial review of that decision on the basis (amongst others) that because the Asylum Policy on Discretionary Leave (API) omitted to mention Council Regulation (EC) 343/2000 it would be contrary to the terms of the Secretary of State's published policy not to determine the asylum application.

16.99   Despite that omission, however, it was common ground that Italy was the appropriate country to decide the claimant's asylum application under the mechanisms established by Council Regulation (EC) 343/2000. Bean J, in dismissing the application for judicial review, noted that it would have been clearer had the policy specifically referred to the Council Regulation but observed that the policy was, plainly, intended to encompass that EC provision.

16.100   As to a separate argument of interpretation founded on the policy being required to be read compatibly with Article 8 ECHR, Bean J made the point that the Dublin II Regulation stated, in its preamble, that it seeks to have regard to the principles of the Charter of Fundamental Freedoms and the Charter of Fundamental Rights of the EU. That being so, recourse to the ECHR did not in any way advance the claimant's case.

E. Summary of Law on Free Movement of Persons

16.101   Table 16.1 below gives an outline of: (1) how the various EC provisions relating to the free movement of persons interlock and (2) the main provisions of the Citizens' Directive. Detailed reference should be made to the source material and, in particular, to the relevant terms of the Citizens' Directive (Directive (EC) 2004/38) where appropriate.

Table 16.1   Free movement of persons—main provisions of law outlined

EC law—source of free movement protection	Comment
Treaty rights relating to free movement of persons are primarily derived from Articles 39 (free movement of workers), 43 (freedom of establishment), and Article 49 (free movement of services). Article 12 (equality of treatment) may also be an important source of protection.	The most important provisions are Articles 39 and 43 which are, essentially, similar in structure. Article 49 (free movement of services) may also raise issues of freedom of movement (see, eg, case study in *Watts* [2004] EWCA Civ 166, see Chapter 19).
Treaty rights are heavily supplemented by secondary Community legislation. Note, especially, Directive (EC) 2004/38 ('the Citizens' Directive').	The relevant Community legislation has been simplified (and modified) by the coming into force of Directive (EC) 2004/38. This directive—mostly relevant to Article 39 and Article 43 rights—is reflective of much of the ECJ case law (see, eg, the case law on expulsion set out above) and creates new and expanded rights. Its main provisions are outlined below and—where relevant to the analysis—in the text. Apart from those provisions note the right of entry (Article 4) and exit (Article 5) to EU citizens and family members. The concept of an EU citizen is

Table 16.1 *Cont.*

EC law—source of free movement protection	Comment
	introduced in Article 2 and the term 'family member' has been expanded (see Articles 2–3). The Citizens' Directive (as its name suggests) is founded on the concept of an EU citizen and the rights of free movement and associated benefits that citizenship entails.
Citizenship and the position of third country nationals are addressed separately above.	The importance of citizenship is that it appears to move EC protection beyond the purely economic. This is a growing and dynamic concept and the judicial review case law on what it entails will be an important and increasing aspect of domestic judicial review. Protection of third country nationals is, currently, very limited under the Treaty although this is an area where fundamental rights expansion suggests that much greater protection will be required in the future. Third country nationals enjoy some protection under the Citizens' Directive arising from their relationship with an EU national. That apart, Association Agreement Rights (see below) and fundamental rights protection (see Chapter 12) are the main avenue of legal protection rather than the free movement provisions.
Accession Treaty rights and Association Agreement Rights.	Specific free movement provisions arise as a result of: (1) the enlargement of the European Union in 2004 where transitional free movement provisions have been introduced under the Accession Treaty in the Act of Accession annexed to the Treaty, (2) various Association Agreements entered into by the Community with non-EU countries: these agreements also affect free movement rights. The detail of the Accession Treaty and the various Association Agreements are beyond the scope of this book.[86]
Aspects of the right of establishment in Article 43.	This is closely related to free movement of services and addressed in Chapter 17. Article 43 has a similar structure to Article 39 as far as essential protection and derogation under the Citizens' Directive is concerned (see below). There is a separate raft of legislation and case law on the subject of recognition of qualifications in the EC. Note, especially, the Mutual Recognition Directive (Directive (EEC) 89/48) which has engendered much case law (though not in the field of domestic public law).

---

[86] For a comprehensive survey, see N Rogers and R Scannell, *Free Movement of Persons in the Enlarged European Union* (2005).

Table 16.1 *Cont.*

EC law—source of free movement protection	Comment
Derogation from free movement rights is, in the context of expulsion covered by Article 39(3) and the Citizens' Directive (see below) and is only permitted on grounds of public policy, public security, or public health.	In respect of workers, the self-employed and service providers and service recipients these are the only grounds on which expulsion or refusal of entry can occur. (Note that there are other directives governing the position of students and others in certain situations: see, eg, the Residence Directive: Council Directive (EEC) 90/364 where derogation is easier). Other indirectly discriminatory restrictions on free movement of EU citizens must if liable to prevent or hinder market access or exercise of Article 18 rights of citizenship be proportionate and be either covered by express derogations or justified in the public interest. There is also a public service exception under Article 39(4) whereby workers employed in the public service engaging in activities involving the exercise of official authority are not covered by the right to employment. Article 39(4) is interpreted restrictively: see, eg, Case 66/85 *Lawrie-Blum* [1986] ECR 2121.

EC law—main provisions of the Citizens' Directive	Comment
Right of residence for three months for EU citizens (Articles 6 of the Citizens' Directive, formerly in Article 8 of Directive (EEC) 68/360).	The Citizens' Directive (Article 6) gives a right of residence to any EU citizen without formality (other than a passport or ID card) for up to three months. (Thereafter (see Article 7) EU citizens may reside for longer periods in the circumstances set out in the next box).
Longer right of residence for EU citizens (Article 7 of the Citizens' Directive). This allows longer residence to (1) workers and self-employed persons in the host state, (2) those who have sufficient resources for themselves and their family members (whatever their nationality) so as not to become a burden on the social assistance system in the host state, (3) those who are enrolled at a relevant private or public establishment, have comprehensive sickness insurance and have sufficient financial resources as in the previous category, (4) family members accompanying or joining a Union citizen who satisfied the conditions in (1)–(3) above save that in respect of (3) only the spouse, the registered partner, and dependent children enjoy such right.	Article 7 of the Citizens' Directive encompasses most of the pre-existing Community legislation (see Regulation (EEC) 1612/68, Directive (EEC) 73/148, Directive (EEC) 90/364, Directive (EEC) 90/365 and Directive (EEC) 93/96). Much of the earlier case law will, thus, remain relevant to judicial review proceedings brought under the Citizens' Directive especially in respect of workers' families (though the concept of 'family member' has been expanded by the Citizens' Directive). The decision in Case C–413/99 *Baumbast* [2002] ECR I–7091 (see para 16.89) is relevant to satisfaction of eligibility requirements for family and dependent members.

Table 16.1 *Cont.*

EC law—main provisions of the Citizens' Directive	Comment
Need to satisfy administrative requirements (Articles 8–11 and 15 of the Citizens' Directive) (see previously Article 4, 6, and 7 of Directive (EEC) 68/360, Articles 4 and 6 of Directive (EEC) 73/148, Article 2 of Directives (EEC) 90/364, 90/36 and 93/96) and Articles 5, 8 and 9 of Directive (EEC) 64/221.	Registration certificates (with no fixed duration) issued by the host state may be required for periods of residence of EU nationals for over three months. Family members are also entitled to registration certificates if they are themselves EU nationals (or a residence card—valid for five years—if non-EU nationals). Failure to obtain a registration requirement may only lead to a proportionate and non-discriminatory sanction. The expiry of identity documents does not constitute a ground for expulsion.
Retention of rights of residence by family members in identified circumstances (Articles 12–13 of the Citizens' Directive: Article 12 derives from Article 3 of Regulation (EEC) 1251/70 and Article 3 of Directive (EEC) 75/34).	Provided that certain conditions are satisfied, family members (or sometimes certain family members) retain the right to reside after: (1) the death or departure of the EU citizen (Article 12), (2) divorce, annulment of marriage or termination of registered partnership (Article 13). Article 13 is new. Part of these provisions reflects the judgment in *Baumbast* (see para 16.89 above).
Right of equal treatment to EU nationals and their family members with some limitation on the right to social assistance in the first three months (Article 24 of the Citizens' Directive derived from Article 7(2) of Regulation (EEC) 1612/68).	The rights here may be augmented by the general provisions of Article 12 of the Treaty (see also the discussion of the equal treatment principle in Chapter 7).
Restrictions on right of entry and right of residence on grounds of public policy, public security or public health (Articles 27–33 of the Citizens' Directive deriving, in part, from Articles 2, 3, 6, 8, and 9 and the Annex to Directive (EEC) 64/221 (see paras 16.28 et seq.).	These provisions deal with expulsion and provide new procedures and are outlined in the text above.

17

THE COMMERCIAL FREEDOMS

A. Nature of the Issues

The EC rights in respect of the free movement of persons, discussed in Chapter 16, are predominantly non-commercial in nature.[1] In contrast to this, the EC freedoms considered here have primarily commercial effect. Of particular importance in the commercial arena—and frequently raising public law issues before the Administrative Court and other

17.01

---

[1] As explained in Chapter 16, however, there are commercial aspects of the free movement of persons: see paras 16.66 et seq.

national courts and tribunals—are Article 28 (ex 30) EC (prohibition of restrictions on free movement of goods), and Article 49 (ex 59) EC (prohibition of restrictions on the free movement of services). The emphasis in this chapter is on these provisions and on the respective Treaty provisions which permit derogation from them, although certain other Treaty provisions, most notably Article 43 (ex 52) (freedom of establishment) and Article 56 (ex 73b) (free movement of capital) can also raise commercial issues (albeit not usually in public law) and these and other relevant provisions are outlined briefly below.

17.02   As might, perhaps, be expected commercial public law disputes have arisen by virtue of restrictions imposed by the State (whether in the form of legislation or administrative measures) on the free movement of commercial interests, most notably those in respect of goods and services. The disputes have frequently taken place in the context of domestic judicial review applications where the debate is, usually, whether the restrictions are justified by reference to the scope of permitted derogation, the proportionality principle, and other general principles of EC law. Sometimes, the prior question of whether there is an EC right at all is engaged.

17.03   There are several recent instances of such public law issues coming before the Administrative Court. Three of these cases are the subject of detailed case analyses in this book (two of them in this chapter). In *International Transport Roth GmbH v Secretary of State for the Home Department*[2] judicial review and other challenges to provisions in the Immigration and Asylum Act 1999 succeeded at first instance before Sullivan J (though were dismissed in the Court of Appeal) on the ground that they violated Articles 28 and 49 (see below). In *R (Watts) v Bedford Primary Care and Secretary of State for Health*[3] a judicial review challenge based on the provision of medical services under Article 49 succeeded after being referred to the ECJ (Chapter 19). Finally, in *R (Countryside Alliance) v Secretary of State for the Environment, Food and Rural Affairs*[4] a Human Rights Act challenge to the controversial hunting ban was combined with an EC challenge contending that the ban contravened Articles 28 and 49 (see paras 17.98 et seq. below). That challenge was unsuccessful both before the Divisional Court and the Court of Appeal. However, in the course of its ruling, the Court of Appeal has clarified the important proposition that proportionality in EC law is not the same as proportionality under the HRA.

17.04   Other national courts or tribunals have had to address similar public law challenges. For example, a number of important aspects of the UK corporation tax regime have been the subject of challenges raising Article 43 and/or Article 49 and/or Article 56 issues both before the Special Commissioners and also in the Chancery Division of the High Court under a Group Litigation Order. All have been referred to the ECJ[5] which has seen a great increase in the number of such cases. Another example is afforded by *PASF v Bamberger*[6]

---

[2] [2003] QB 728. See paras 16.72 et seq.

[3] [2004] EWCA Civ 166. The ECJ judgment ruling was delivered on 16 May 2006 in Case–372/04. See paras 19.60 et seq.

[4] (2006) UKHRR 73.

[5] See Case C–374/04, Case C–446/04, Case C–524/04, Cases C–196/04, C–201/05 and C–203/05.

[6] [1997] Eu LR 63, [1997] Eu LR 88. Opinions of the Advocate General have been delivered in Case C–374/04 (23 February 2006) 446/04 (6 April 2006) and 196/04 (2 May 2006). The other cases are pending.

where the Commercial Court (upheld by the Court of Appeal) disapplied a provision of the Consumer Arbitration Act 1988 (without referring to the ECJ) because it operated as a restriction on the freedom to provide and receive services across frontiers contrary to Article 49.

Importantly, the Treaty freedom provisions referred to above are independent and separate. **17.05** Although, as will be seen, challenges are frequently advanced combining two or more of the commercial freedoms, it should not be assumed that (for example) a measure that is compatible with, say, free movement of services is, necessarily, compatible with free movement of goods.[7]

B. Free Movement of Goods (Article 28 EC)—The Basic Rules

Articles 28 and 30

Article 28 (ex 30) EC[8] provides that: **17.06**

> Quantitative restrictions on imports and all measures having equivalent effect shall be prohibited between Member States.

By Article 30: **17.07**

> The provisions of Articles 28 and 29 shall not preclude prohibitions or restrictions on imports, exports or goods in transit justified on grounds of public morality, public policy or public security; the protection of health and life of humans, animals or plants; the protection of national treasures possessing artistic, historic or archaeological value; or the protection of industrial or commercial property. Such prohibitions or restrictions shall not, however, constitute a means of arbitrary discrimination or a disguised restriction on trade between Member States.

As will be seen, there are essentially two questions to resolve in order for Article 28 to be **17.08** *engaged*. These are whether: (1) there is a relevant measure in the sense of there being a restriction on imports or a measure having equivalent effect and (if so) (2) whether that measure is capable of hindering intra-Community trade whether directly, actually, or potentially.[9]

If those questions are answered affirmatively in the claimant's favour, the legality of the **17.09** restriction then falls to be justified by the State pursuant to whether there is a permissible derogation under Article 30 (ex 36) EC or—depending on the nature of the measure (see below)—under the principle in *Cassis de Dijon*. Derogations that are permitted in theory must also be proportionate and must not go beyond what is necessary to achieve the specific objects of the permitted derogation.

---

[7] See, eg, Case 45/87 *Commission v Ireland (Re Dundalk Water Supply)* [1988] ECR 4929.

[8] Article 29 (ex 34) EC contains a similar provision relating to *exports*. Articles 28 and 29 have direct effect: see Case 74/76 *Ianelli & Volpi SpA v Meroni* [1977] ECR 595. References to Art 28 in this chapter have equal application (unless otherwise stated) to Art 29 cases and, as can be seen below, Art 30 permits derogations from Arts 28 and 29 on a uniform basis. The main difference between Art 28 and Art 29 is that indistinctly applicable measures (see below) are not subject to Art 29 at all.

[9] The fact that a measure may constitute otherwise lawful state aid does not immunize it from having to comply with Arts 28–30 of the Treaty and so require justification: see, eg, Case 18/84 *Commission v France* [1985] ECR 1339, para 13.

The *Dassonville* formula

17.10   For Article 28 to apply at all there must either be a State measure placing restrictions on imports or at least a State measure having 'equivalent effect' to such a measure.[10] The content of a measure having equivalent effect to 'quantitative restrictions' falling within Article 28 was elucidated, in the broadest terms, by the ECJ in the key case of *Dassonville*[11] as consisting of:

> All trading[12] rules[13] ... capable of hindering directly or indirectly, actually or potentially, intra-Community trade ...

17.11   The reference in *Dassonville* to 'directly or indirectly' and 'actually or potentially' is very wide. It catches a variety of measures whose effect is to limit the commercial freedoms of traders. For example, the Sunday Trading restrictions were held to fall within the 'reach' of Article 28 because although entirely non-discriminatory in their purpose and effects, they nonetheless reduced the sales of imported products.[14] Nor, for Article 28 to apply does there have to be an *actual* effect on intra-Community trade. There is, therefore, (unlike EC competition law[15]) no *de minimis* rule in Article 28 cases.[16]

Distinctly applicable and indistinctly applicable measures

17.12   So far as *direct* and *indirect* effects on trade are concerned, this parallels the notion of direct and indirect discrimination in other areas of EC (and HRA) law.[17] Thus, what are sometimes called 'distinctly applicable measures'[18] are State measures which treat imported goods less favourably than domestic products (the analogue to direct discrimination). *Indistinctly* applicable measures are those State measures which ostensibly treat imported goods and domestic products in the same way but, in fact, disadvantage imported goods in practice (the analogue to indirect discrimination).

---

[10] The State for this purpose is interpreted widely: see, eg, Cases 266, 267/87 *R v Royal Pharmaceutical Society of Great Britain, ex p Association of Pharmaceutical Importers* [1989] ECR 1295 (*held*: professional regulatory body's measures may fall within Article 28 EC); *R v Chief Constable of Sussex, ex p International Trader's Ferry Ltd* [1998] 3 WLR 1260 (*held*: acts of the police are subject to Art 28). So, too, the concept of a 'measure' (including a measure having equivalent effect) is plainly wide enough to embrace administrative acts: see, eg, Case 249/81 *Commission v Ireland* [1982] ECR 4005 and even material omissions by the State: see Case C–112/00 *Schmidberger v Austria* [2003] ECR I–5659 (allowing a protest impeded movement of heavy goods vehicles on the motorway). The concept of 'goods' (though not appearing in Art 28 itself) is also broadly interpreted. See, eg: Case 7/68 *Commission v Italy* [1968] ECR 617 '[b]y "goods" ... there must be understood products which can be valued in money, and which are capable, as such, of forming the subject of commercial transactions'.

[11] Case 8/74 *Procureur du Roi v Dassonville* [1974] ECR 837, para 5.

[12] The emphasis on 'trading' rules has been abandoned in later cases: see, eg Case C–95/01 *Greenham and Abel* [2004] 3 CMLR 33 (reference to 'commercial' rules).

[13] The term 'rules' is not entirely accurate since, in later cases, the ECJ has made it clear that 'measures' (the word used in the Treaty) can encompass State measures that are not legally binding. See, eg: Case 249/81 *Commission v Ireland* ('Buy Irish campaign') [1982] ECR 4005 (*held*: government sponsored campaign to persuade Irish traders to buy Irish goods was a measure capable of infringing Art 28).

[14] Case 145/88 *Torfaen Borough Council v B&Q plc* [1989] ECR 3851. However, following *Keck* (see para 17.16 below), Sunday Trading legislation is outside the scope of Art 28.

[15] Contrast, though, the prohibitions against state aid: see paras 13.48–13.52.

[16] See, eg, Joined Cases 177 and 178/82 *Criminal Proceedings against Van de Haar* [1984] ECR 1797, para 13.

[17] See, generally, Chapter 18 and especially paras 18.19 et seq.

[18] A reference to the now defunct provisions of Commission Directive (EEC) 70/50.

There is extensive ECJ case law addressing the differences between distinctly applicable **17.13** and indistinctly applicable measures for the purposes of Article 28. The distinction is of some significance because, as developed below, it affects whether the State is allowed (generally) more generous derogation consistent with the principle in *Cassis de Dijon.*

Examples of distinctly applicable measures are not difficult to spot. The discrimination **17.14** model is that of direct or overt discrimination. Thus, express additional requirements on imported products such as hygiene inspections,[19] and licensing conditions,[20] or the direct favouring of domestic goods over imported products by price fixing[21] exemplify distinctly applicable measures which *prima facie* infringe Article 28.

Examples of indistinctly applicable measures are more subtle (as is the analogue of indirect **17.15** discrimination) but include certain origin marking and packaging requirements where, albeit imposed equally on both domestic products and imports, may adversely impact on imports, because (for example) of hidden additional costs thereby placed on manufacturers of products in other Member States.[22]

Keck—the retreat from *Dassonville*

In *Keck*[23] the ECJ wanted to narrow the extremely wide scope ostensibly permitted by the **17.16** so-called '*Dassonville*' formula.[24] It did this by creating a distinction between 'product requirements' (caught by Article 28) and 'certain selling arrangements' (outside the scope of Article 28).

Product requirements are measures regulating the goods in question (such as labelling or **17.17** packaging rules).[25] Selling arrangements, though not comprehensively defined by the ECJ, appear to relate to rules affecting matters such as when and where goods can be sold.[26]

At para 16 of its judgment in *Keck* the ECJ said: **17.18**

> contrary to what has previously been decided, the application to products from other Member States of national provisions restricting or prohibiting certain selling arrangements is not such as to hinder directly or indirectly, actually or potentially, trade between Member States within the meaning of the *Dassonville* judgment provided that those provisions apply to all affected traders operating within the national territory and provided that they affect in the same manner, in law and in fact, the marketing of domestic products and of those from other Member States.

---

[19] See, eg, Case 124/81 *Commission v UK (UHT Milk)* [1983] ECR 203.
[20] See, eg, Joined Cases 51-54/71 *International Fruit (No 2)* [1971] ECR 1107.
[21] See, eg, Case 65/75 *Criminal Proceedings against Riccardo Tosca* [1976] ECR 291.
[22] See, eg, Case 207/83 *Commission v United Kingdom* [1985] ECR 1201; Case 261/81 *Walter Rau v De Smedt* [1982] ECR 3961.
[23] Cases C–267–268/91 *Keck and Mithouard* [1993] ECR I–6097, especially, para 16.
[24] Cases C–267–268/91 [1993] ECR I–6097, para 14: 'in view of the increasing tendency of traders to invoke Article [28] of the Treaty as a means of challenging any rules whose effect is to limit their commercial freedom even where such rules are not aimed at products of other Member States, the Court considers it necessary to re-examine and clarify its case law on this matter'.
[25] Cases C–267–268/91 [1993] ECR I–6097, para 15.
[26] See, eg, Joined Cases C–401 and 402/94 *Boermans* [1994] ECR I–2199.

17.19 And at para 17 it concluded:

> Where those conditions are fulfilled, the application of such rules to the sale of products from other Member States meeting the requirements laid down by that State is not by nature such as to prevent their access to the market or to impede access any more than it impedes the access of domestic products. Such rules therefore fall outside the scope of Article [28] of the Treaty.

17.20 Since the decision in *Keck* many national measures that would formerly have been considered to fall within Article 28 have been held to fall outside that provision as constituting 'certain selling arrangements'.[27] Although there has been academic criticism of *Keck*[28] no alternative formulation has, as yet, been adopted to stem the tide of *Dassonville*. As will be seen, the scope and extent of the *Keck* principle continues to be contested in litigation before the national courts. The hunting ban case study (para 17.98 et seq. below) demonstrates how important it can be to the resolution of judicial review challenges before the Administrative Court.

Derogation under Article 30 in respect of distinctly applicable measures

17.21 In the case of distinctly applicable measures, the State may only derogate from free movement of goods in accordance with the strict and exhaustive criteria set out in Article 30 (see above) and then only in compliance with proportionality.

17.22 Derogations from Treaty freedoms (including the freedoms guaranteed under Articles 28 and 29) must be interpreted narrowly. This principle of interpretation is analysed further in the separate treatment of the proportionality principle.[29] However, in the context of Article 30, the ECJ has observed as follows:

> Since it derogates from a fundamental rule of the Treaty, [Article 30] must be interpreted strictly and cannot be extended to cover objectives not expressly enumerated therein. Neither the safeguarding of consumers' interests nor the protection of creativity and cultural diversity in the realm of publishing is mentioned in [Article 30].[30]

17.23 And in the context of proportionality, the ECJ has required it to be shown that:

> the prohibitory measures are appropriate and necessary in order to achieve the objectives legitimately pursued by the legislation in question; when there is a choice between several appropriate measures recourse must be had to the least onerous, and the disadvantages caused must not be disproportionate to the aims pursued.[31]

17.24 In essence, the case law on derogation under Article 30 suggests that the standard of justification required in practice by the ECJ depends very much on context and on the specific

---

[27] As for example, Sunday Trading legislation (Cases C–69 and 258/93 *Punto Casa and PPV* [1994] ECR I–2355) and partial restrictions on advertising (Case C–292/92 *Hunermund* [1993] ECR I–6787 and Case C–6/98 *PRO Sieben Media* [1999] ECR I–7599).

[28] See, eg, S Weatherill, 'After *Keck*: Some Thoughts on How to Clarify the Clarification' (1996) 33 CML Rev 885. Note, also, the Opinion of Advocate General Jacobs in Case C–412/93 *Leclerc-Siplec TF1 Publicité SA and M6 Publicité SA* [1995] ECR I–179, paras 21 and 38–42.

[29] See paras 11.64–11.69.

[30] Case 229/83 *Leclerc* [1985] ECR I. However, the position is different where the *Cassis de Dijon* principle applies (see para 17.27).

[31] Case C–331/88 *FEDESA* [1990] ECR I–4023. See, also, Case 72/83 *Campus Oil* [1984] ECR 2727.

facts of each case. Even within a general justification head such as public morality [32] or the protection of health [33] the ECJ has arrived at different conclusions as to whether a particular State restriction was justified. However, in general the ECJ has been unsympathetic to arguments justifying derogation based purely on economic considerations, [34] or on broadly asserted public policy. [35]

Justification under Article 30 may sometimes make it unnecessary to decide whether **17.25** Article 28 (or 29) is engaged at all. Thus, in *R v Chief Constable of Sussex, ex p International Trader's Ferry Ltd* [36] a question arose as to whether a decision of the Chief Constable as to the appropriate number of police to deal with demonstrations over the live export of animals came within Article 29 as a measure having equivalent effect. In the event it was unnecessary for the question to be referred because the House of Lords held that limits on policing was justified under Article 30.

Derogating from indistinctly applicable measures—the principle in *Cassis de Dijon*: content and application

Article 30 (see above) contains a list of permitted derogations. As can be seen from the ter- **17.26** minology used in Article 30, they are exhaustive and have never been amended or updated.

A more modern approach to derogation in the context of free movement of goods was, **17.27** arguably, required. This occurred in the landmark ECJ decision in *Cassis de Dijon*. [37] There, the court had to consider an indistinctly applicable measure, namely a minimum alcohol level of 25 per cent per litre for certain spirits. One of those spirits was cassis, a French blackcurrant liqueur.

In the event, the ECJ held that this measure breached Article 28. In the course of its judg- **17.28** ment, the court laid down this important principle:

> Obstacles to movement within the Community resulting from disparities between the national laws relating to the marketing of the products in question must be accepted in so far as these provisions may be recognised as being necessary in order to satisfy mandatory requirements relating in particular to the effectiveness of fiscal supervision, the protection of public health, the fairness of commercial transactions and the defence of the consumer.

---

[32] cf Case 34/79 *R v Henn* [1979] ECR 3795 (ban on the import of pornography justified under Art 36 (now Art 30) since, although it was discriminatory, the discrimination was not arbitrary) with Case 121/85 *Conegate Ltd v Customs and Excise Commissioners* [1986] ECR 1007 (seizure of pornographic material was not justified because there was no general restriction on manufacturing and marketing such material in the United Kingdom).

[33] cf Case 4/75 *Rewe-Zentralfinanz GmbH v Landwirtschaftskammer* [1975] ECR 843 (health inspection was justified even though it only applied to imported apples because there was a real health risk that was not present in domestic apples), with Case 124/81 *Commission v UK* [1983] ECR 203 (marketing restriction on UHT milk was not justified because there was evidence that milk in all Member States was of comparable quality with a system of equivalent controls).

[34] See, eg, Case 324/93 *R v Secretary of State for the Home Department, ex p Evans Medical* [1995] ECR I-563.

[35] Case 7/61 *Commission v Italy (Re Ban on Pork Imports)* [1961] ECR 317. For a notable exception see, though, Case 7/78 *R v Thompson* [1979] ECR 2247.

[36] [1998] 3 WLR 1260.

[37] Case 120/78 [1979] ECR 649.

17.29 These 'mandatory requirements'[38] are not co-extensive with the limited and exhaustive permitted derogations in Article 30. The following points should be noted:

(1) The mandatory requirements are not, unlike Article 30, exhaustive. They are, albeit worthy of emphasis, exemplary (see the phrase 'in particular' in the above citation).

(2) Since *Cassis de Dijon* other categories have been added, and the list is not closed. For example, although not referred to explicitly in *Cassis de Dijon* later cases have recognized other categories as being included within the mandatory requirements such as protection of the environment,[39] protection of culture,[40] and protection of fundamental rights.[41]

(3) They apply only to *indistinctly* applicable measures.[42]

Differences between Article 28 and Article 29

17.30 As can be seen, the structure of Article 28 and Article 29 is identical. The important practical difference between them lies in the fact that the ECJ has held that indistinctly applicable State measures do not engage Article 29 at all.[43]

C. Free Movement of Services in Outline—Article 49

Articles 49–50

17.31 Article 49 provides as follows:

> Within the framework of the provisions set out below, restrictions on freedom to provide services within the Community shall be prohibited in respect of nationals of Member States who are established in a State of the Community other than that of the person for whom the services are intended.[44]

17.32 Article 50 defines the term 'services'. These are expressed to be 'normally provided for remuneration'. There must be an economic link between the service provider and the recipient.[45] Article 50 provides a list of examples such as activities of an industrial character, activities of a commercial character, and activities of the professions. However, these examples have been added to in the ECJ cases. Although Article 50 States that the definition of services applies 'insofar as they are not governed by the provisions relating to freedom of movement for goods, capital and persons', Articles 49–50 have generated a considerable

---

[38] They are now often referred to in the cases by different terminology such as, for example, 'overriding requirements' or 'overriding interests': see, eg: Case C–368/95 *Famialpress* [1997] ECR I–3689.

[39] Case 302/86 *Commission v Denmark* [1988] ECR 4607.

[40] Cases 60–61/84 *Cinetheque* [1985] ECR 2065.

[41] Case C–112/00 *Schmidberger* [2003] ECR I–5659.

[42] Joined Cases C–1/90 and C–176/90 *Aragonesa* [1991] ECR 2071, para 6. The protection of fundamental rights is implicit in Art 30 derogations given the requirement of proportionality even for the limited class of permitted derogations under Art 30: see paras 17.21–17.24.

[43] Case 15/79 *Groenveld* [1979] ECR 3409.

[44] Article 49 applies equally to companies: see, eg, Case C–36/02 *Omega* [2005] 1 CMLR 5, see para 17.42.

[45] Case C–159/90 *SPUC v Grogan* [1991] ECR I–4685.

amount of case law and arguments in respect of freedom of movement of services (Article 49) are often run in conjunction with arguments in respect of freedom of movement of goods (Article 28).[46]

There is also an important relationship between the freedom to provide services under **17.33** Article 49 and the right of freedom of establishment under Article 43 (outlined below). The difference is largely one of intensity since the concept of service provision under Article 49 connotes a degree of temporary provision whereas services provided pursuant to Article 43 have greater permanency. As the ECJ observed in *Gebhard*:[47]

> The concept of establishment is a very broad one, allowing [an EU] national to participate, on a stable and continuous basis, in the economic life of a Member State other than his State of origin and to profit therefrom, so contributing to economic and social interpenetration within the Community in the sphere of activities as self-employed persons. In contrast, where the provider of services moves to another Member State, the provisions of the chapter on services envisage that he is to pursue his activity there on a temporary basis . . . The temporary nature of the activities in question has to be determined in the light, not only of the duration of the service, but also of its regularity, periodicity or continuity.

Unsurprisingly, perhaps, the provisions in respect of derogation are the same for freedom **17.34** of services and freedom of establishment.

Breadth of scope of freedom to provide and receive services

The concept of freedom of movement of services has sometimes given rise to difficult **17.35** issues. However, as is apparent from the terms of Article 49 itself, all that is necessary is that the provider of services is established in a different Member State to the recipient of the services. It is not necessary that the provider of services should provide services in a Member State other than the State in which he is established. For example, in *Erich Ciola v Land Vorarlberg*[48] Article 49 was held to be engaged even though the provider—an Austrian manager of the mooring service in question—was only providing the service within Austria given that the mooring service was provided to residents of other Member States.

Whilst Article 49 does not apply to purely internal situations it is not necessary for services **17.36** to fall within the scope of that provision for the services themselves to leave the Member State in which the provider is established.[49] The right may be relied on against the State in which the provider is established.[50] Nor is there any *de minimis* threshold. In *Bluhme*[51] the prohibition in question applied to only 0.03 per cent of Danish territory.

Further, it is now established that Article 49 may give the recipient of services the right to **17.37** travel to the provider State[52] (and vice versa). This principle has generated a raft of case law

---

[46] For an example, see the case study at paras 17.72 et seq.
[47] Case C–55/94 [1995] ECR I–4165.
[48] Case C–224/97 [1998] ECR I–2517.
[49] See, eg, Case C–60/00 *Carpenter* [2002] ECR I–6279 para 30 (advertising services).
[50] Case C–384/93 *Alpine Investments* [1995] ECR I–1141.
[51] Case C–67/97 [1998] ECR I–8033.
[52] Joined Cases 286/82 and 26/83 *Luisi and Carbone v Ministero del Tesoro* [1984] ECR 377.

in the ECJ and in the national courts culminating in a successful judicial review challenge brought by a patient in the United Kingdom seeking the right to travel abroad for medical treatment that could not be provided without undue delay in the United Kingdom together with the right to be reimbursed by the NHS.[53] This challenge is the subject of a detailed case study in Chapter 19 where the relevant principles under Article 49 relevant to the provision of health services (and a parallel EC Regulation) are examined.

17.38 Although more complicated situations, as yet unresolved will, doubtless, arise[54] it will not—at least in many cases—be difficult to establish the threshold questions of whether there is a service and a restriction under Article 49. This is because, as explained above, Article 49 has been interpreted very broadly by the ECJ. Despite this, the domestic judicial review challenges that are the subject of case studies below and in Chapter 19 involved precisely these issues.

Derogating from the freedom to provide and receive services/establishment

17.39 If the threshold questions show that Article 49 is engaged, the question (as with Article 28 above) will be whether the restriction is justified as: (1) constituting a permissible derogation, and (2) complying with the principle of proportionality. As will be seen, the extent of permissible derogation depends, in part, upon whether the restriction is directly discriminatory in nature or whether it impedes market access. However, a useful summary of the requirements for justifying a restriction on services (or establishment) is contained in the ECJ judgment in *Gebhard*.[55] There, the court observed that '[n]ational measures which hinder or make less attractive the exercise of fundamental freedoms guaranteed by the Treaty must fulfil four conditions'. They are that the measure must:

(1) be non-discriminatory;
(2) be justified by imperative requirements in the public interest;
(3) be suitable for attaining the objective it pursues; and
(4) not go beyond what is necessary to attain it.

17.40 If a measure is discriminatory (1) and (2) above do not apply and the question is whether or not there is a derogation permitted by the Treaty which is proportionate in terms of the objective pursued (ie (3) and (4) above).

17.41 The starting point for discriminatory restrictions on the free movement of services (or establishment) is Articles 46 (ex 56) and 55 (ex 66) EC. These contain the same derogations from the freedom of movement of services (and establishment) as does Article 39 (considered in Chapter 16) for the free movement of persons. These derogations are on grounds of: (1) public policy, (2) public security, or (3) public health. However, as will be seen, for many restrictions the test is—following the ECJ decision in *Sager* (para 17.47 below)—now somewhat more generous in practice where a restriction is not discriminatory on grounds of nationality or establishment but does impede access to the market.

---

[53] Case C–372/04 *Watts v United Kingdom* (judgment 16 May 2006).

[54] One question of potential significance is the possible application of the principle in *Keck* (see para 17.16 above) to Art 49. This is discussed below but it would appear that *Keck* is not well adapted to Art 49 and does not apply to it.

[55] Case C–55/94 [1995] ECR I–4165.

Under Article 46, public policy is rarely acceptable as a basis for derogating from the free **17.42** movement of services/establishment. However, where the protection of fundamental rights is involved, derogation may (subject to considerations of proportionality) be permitted. In *Omega*[56] the ECJ observed:

> ... Since both the Community and its Member States are required to respect fundamental rights, the protection of those rights is a legitimate interest which, in principle, justifies a restriction of the obligations imposed by Community law, even under a fundamental freedom guaranteed by the Treaty such as the freedom to provide services.

In *Omega* a restriction preventing Omega, a German based company, from operating laser **17.43** quest games was held to be justified under Article 46 even though it had the effect of preventing a British company from supplying services to it in Germany. This was because although there was held to be a restriction on the free movement of services under Article 49, the ECJ accepted that the nature of the games in question violated certain provisions of the German constitutional code protecting dignity.

The protection of health is the most frequently cited justification under Article 46 for **17.44** placing restrictions on the free movement of commercial services. It is not easy to challenge a State's welfare policies because there is a wide area of discretionary judgment afforded to Member States in this respect. Thus, in *Geraets-Smits*[57] for example, the ECJ held that a requirement for prior authorization before patients from one Member State could seek non-emergency medical treatment in another Member State was (depending on the criteria employed) at least capable of constituting a lawful derogation to the free movement of services on public health grounds. Similarly, the ECJ held that Article 46 allowed proportionate restrictions to be placed on the freedom to provide medical or hospital services 'in so far as the maintenance of treatment capacity or medical competence on national territory is essential for the public health, and even the survival of, the population'.[58] There have now been a number of cases before the ECJ in respect of the freedom to provide medical services to patients abroad in which the claimed legitimacy of derogation has been an issue. These cases are considered further in the *Watts* case study in chapter 19.

Although derogation from freedom to provide services under Article 46 is, as with the other **17.45** freedoms, strictly construed there is a similar, though less clear cut, dichotomy in the cases (as in the Article 28 case law considered above) between: (1) certain distinctly applicable measures and indistinctly applicable measures, and (2) measures which restrict access to the market albeit that they are not discriminatory in nature. It is here that the four fold test enunciated in *Gebhard*[59] becomes directly relevant.

As explained above, in the case of certain distinctly applicable restrictions (overt discrimination **17.46** on the ground of nationality or establishment) the Article 46/55 categories (proportionately applied) are, indeed, exhaustive.[60] However, in the case of indistinctly applicable

---

[56] Case C–36/02 [2005] 1 CMLR 5.

[57] Case C–157/99 [2001] ECR I–5473. See, also, Case C–158/96 *Kohll* [1998] ECR I–1931; Case C–385/99 *Muller-Faure* [2003] ECR I–4509.

[58] Case C–157/99 *Geraets-Smits* [2001] ECR I–5473, para 74.

[59] Case C–55/94 [1995] ECR I–4165, see para 17.39.

[60] See Case C–288/89 *Gouda* [1991] ECR I–4007, para 11.

restrictions (effectively indirect discrimination) or non-discriminatory measures that restrict access to the market, the ECJ has formulated a test that permits derogation not only on Article 46/55 grounds but also on the footing that it is justified by imperative requirements in the public interest.

17.47 This can be seen from the key decision of the ECJ in *Sager*.[61] There, the ECJ stipulated that Article 49 is not solely concerned with eliminating discrimination against the provision of services on grounds of nationality but is also concerned with 'the abolition of any restriction even if it applies without distinction to national providers of services and those of other Member States, when it is liable to prohibit or otherwise impede the activities of a provider of services established in another Member State where he lawfully provides services'.[62]

17.48 In such non-discrimination cases, the ECJ in *Sager*[63] laid down the relevant test as follows:

> The freedom to provide services may be limited only by rules which are justified by impera-tive reasons relating to the public interest and which apply to all persons and undertakings pursuing an activity in the State of destination in so far as that interest is not protected by rules to which the person providing the service is subject in the State in which he is estab-lished. In particular, these requirements must be objectively necessary in order to ensure compliance with professional rules and must not exceed what is necessary to attain those objectives.

17.49 It is apparent that, despite the ostensible strictness of the language used in *Sager*, deroga-tions from Article 49 will be permitted in the case of many non-discriminatory restrictions even if those categories fall outside those in Articles 46/55. A number of categories justified by 'imperative reasons relating to the public interest' have been accepted by the ECJ outside the confines of Articles 46/55.[64]

D. Freedom of Establishment—Article 43

The structure of Article 43 rights

17.50 In essence, Article 43 confers a right of free movement as a self-employed person to under-take an economic activity. It is also applicable to companies. It complements, in many respects, the provisions relating to free movement of persons considered in Chapter 16. However, it also includes a primarily economic and commercial element and is, to that extent, closely related in structure and character to Articles 49 and 28 considered above.

17.51 Specifically, the rights conferred by Article 43 include: (1) the right to take up and (2) the right to pursue, activities as a self-employed person, (3) the right to set up and to manage undertakings including the right to set up agencies, branches, and subsidiaries by nationals

---

61 Case C–76/90 [1991] ECR I–4221.
62 ibid para 12.
63 ibid para 15.
64 See the list in Case C–288/89 *Gouda* [1991] ECR I–4007 which included (amongst numerous other categories) consumer protection and the protection of intellectual property. Since *Gouda* the categories have been extended further and are, as with the Art 28 analogue (see above), by no means closed.

of any Member State established in the territory of any Member State. There is also a complementing directive (Directive (EEC) 73/148) which requires existing restrictions of movement on providers and recipients of services under Article 43 to be removed (although the directive refers to individual persons rather than companies).[65]

As explained above, the difference between many commercial interests protected by Article 43 and 49 is one of degree; the more temporary the activity, the more likely it is to fall within Article 49 rather than Article 43. However, the principles to be applied and the approach to derogation appear to be very similar if not identical. In particular, there is equal emphasis in the case law on establishment, as in respect of services, on the free market access principle (see above).   **17.52**

Companies and Article 43

In order to qualify for protection under Article 43, a company[66] must be profit-making.[67]   **17.53**

By Article 48(1) companies that are established under the law of a Member State and have their registered office, central administration, or principal place of business in the EU, are entitled (and required) to be treated in the same way as natural persons who are Member State nationals.   **17.54**

The most important area of application of Article 43, in practice, is where companies or individuals propose to set up agencies, branches, or subsidiaries in other Member States. The ECJ has, in several cases, ruled that disproportionate restrictions on that freedom are unlawful.[68] The well-known *Factortame* litigation concerned (ultimately) successful judicial review proceedings[69] challenging certain provisions of the Merchant Shipping Act 1988 as being contrary to Article 43 in that, amongst other things, they required fishing vessels from other Member States (*in casu* Spain) to be managed and have their operations directed and controlled from within the United Kingdom by a qualified British individual or company.   **17.55**

As Article 48 implies, companies (including branches and subsidiaries)—once established—have the right to the same treatment as national companies. Provided, therefore, that there is a relevant comparator there must, subject to permitted derogation, be equal tax treatment,[70] and other relevant benefits.[71]   **17.56**

---

[65] See Case 81/87 *R v HM Treasury, ex p Daily Mail and General Trust* [1988] ECR 5483, para 28.

[66] Including firms and co-operative societies: see Art 48(2).

[67] Article 48(2) (ex 58(2)) EC. Similarly, to fall within Article 49 (see above) services are 'normally provided for remuneration'. See, also Case C–70/95 *Sodemare v Regione Lombardia* [1997] ECR I–3395.

[68] See, especially, Case C–101/94 *Commission v Italy (Re Restrictions on Foreign Securities Dealing)* [1996] ECR I–269; Case C–212/97 *Centros* [1999] ECR I–1459; Case C–208/00 *Uberseering* [2002] ECR I–9919. cf Case 81/87 *Daily Mail* [1988] ECR 5483.

[69] Case C–213/89 *R v Secretary of State for Transport, ex p Factortame* [1990] ECR I–2433. For a detailed account of the litigation, see C Barnard, *The Substantive Law of the EU* (2004) 313–20.

[70] See, eg, Case C–311/97 *Royal Bank of Scotland* [1999] ECR I–2651. cf Case C–250/95 *Futura Participations* [1997] ECR I–2471.

[71] See, eg, Case C–153/02 *Neri* [2004] 1 CMLR 16.

E. Other Commercial Freedoms

Free movement of capital

17.57 Free movement of capital, the so-called fourth 'freedom', is contained in Article 56(1).[72] This stipulates that:

> Within the framework of the provisions set out in this chapter, all restrictions on the movement of capital between Member States and between Member States and third countries shall be prohibited.

17.58 There is no definition of 'capital' in the Treaty.[73] Nonetheless, ECJ case law has shown that movement of capital includes movement involving acquisition of (for example) real property,[74] banknotes and coins,[75] shares,[76] loans,[77] and mortgages.[78]

17.59 Specific derogation provisions are contained in Article 58. One is in respect of tax and provides (Article 58(1)(a)) that Article 56 is without prejudice to the right of Member States to:

> apply the relevant provisions of their tax law which distinguish between taxpayers who are not in the same situation with regard to their place of residence or with regard to the place where their capital is invested.

17.60 The second express derogation is contained in Article 58(1)(b) and stipulates that Article 56 is without prejudice to the right of Member States to:

> take all requisite measures to prevent infringements of national law and regulations, in particular in the field of taxation and the prudential supervision of financial institutions, or to lay down procedures for the declaration of capital movements for purposes of administrative or statistical information, or to take measures which are justified on grounds of public policy or public security.

17.61 As with other commercial freedoms, the relevant distinction is between directly discriminatory restrictions and other restrictions that impede market access.[79] In the case of directly discriminatory restrictions derogation is only permitted where expressly provided for under Article 58 and only then when the derogation is proportionate. Where the restriction in question is not directly discriminatory the issue appears to be whether it is a restriction that impedes market access. If it does, derogation is permitted if justified by overriding requirements of the general interest, or by Article 58 subject to whether the restriction in question is proportionate.[80]

---

[72] The key provisions are contained in Arts 56–60.

[73] See, though, the Annex to Directive (EEC) 88/361 which sets out non-exhaustive categories of movements of capital.

[74] See, eg, Case C–302/97 *Konle* [1999] ECR I–3099.

[75] Joined Cases C–358/93 and C–416/93 *Bordessa* [1995] ECR I–361. cf Case 7/78 *R v Thompson* [1979] ECR 2247 (*held*: old coins that are not legal tender fall within prohibitions on free movement of goods rather than capital).

[76] See, eg, Case C–367/98 *Commission v Portugal* [2002] ECR I–4731.

[77] See, eg, Case C–478/98 *Commission v Belgium* [2000] ECR I–7587.

[78] See, eg, Case C–222/97 *Trummer and Meyer* [1999] ECR I–1661.

[79] See paras 17.41–17.49.

[80] See, generally, Case C–54/99 *Association Eglise de Scientologie de Paris* [2000] ECR I–1335; Case C–302/97 *Konle* [1999] ECR I–3099.

Tariffs and taxation issues

Article 23 (ex 9) EC provides that the customs union 'shall involve the prohibition between Member States of customs duties on imports and exports and of all charges having equivalent effect'. This is required to be read with the 'standstill' Article 25 (ex 12–17) EC which, in its present form, reads thus: **17.62**

> Customs duties on imports and all charges having equivalent effect shall be prohibited between Member States. The prohibition shall also apply to customs duties of a fiscal nature.

A charge 'having equivalent effect'[81] was defined by the ECJ in the *Statistical Levy* case[82] in the following way: **17.63**

> Any pecuniary charge, however small[83] and whatever its designation and mode of application, which is imposed unilaterally on domestic or foreign goods by reason of the fact that they cross a frontier, and which is not a customs duty in the strict sense, constitutes a charge having equivalent effect ... even if it is not discriminatory or protective in effect and the product on which the charge is imposed is not in competition with any domestic product.

There is no system of permitted derogation from Article 25 as in the case of other freedoms. In *Commission v Germany*,[84] however, the ECJ observed that a charge would be permitted in the following circumstances: **17.64**

> if it relates to a general system of internal dues applied systematically and in accordance with the same criteria to domestic products and imported products alike ... if it constitutes payment for a service in fact rendered to the economic operator of a sum in proportion to the service ... or again, subject to certain conditions, if it attaches to inspections carried out to fulfil obligations imposed by Community law.

Article 90 (ex 95) EC is, in certain respects, complementary to Article 25 dealing, as it does, with internal taxation on products.[85] It provides: **17.65**

> No Member State shall impose, directly or indirectly, on the products of other Member States any internal taxation of any kind in excess of that imposed directly or indirectly on similar domestic products.
>
> Furthermore, no Member State shall impose on the products of other Member States any internal taxation of such a nature as to afford indirect protection to other products.

The detail of the case law on Article 90 is outside the scope of this work. In essence, however, the following distinctions should be borne in mind: **17.66**

(1) Article 90 is not engaged unless there is discriminatory or protective internal taxation on products.

(2) Nor is Article 90 engaged if there are no similar or competing domestic products.[86]

---

[81] cf the concept of measures having 'equivalent effect' to quantitative restrictions in Art 28 (see paras 17.10 et seq.).

[82] Case 24/68 *Commission v Italy (Statistical Levy)* [1969] ECR 193.

[83] ie there is no *de minimis* rule.

[84] Case 18/87 [1988] ECR 5427, para 6.

[85] Importantly, therefore, Art 90 is not concerned with a direct tax. Direct taxation on individuals may, of course, raise issues under other Treaty provisions.

[86] Case C–383/01 *De Danske Bilimportorer* [2003] ECR I–6065. The ECJ observed, however, that there might in such circumstances still be a breach of the prohibition on free movement of goods under Art 28.

(3) The Article 90 prohibitions lie in respect of *imports*. Thus, a higher rate of internal taxation may lie in respect of *domestic* products.[87]

(4) Discrimination under Article 90 may be direct or indirect. In respect of direct discrimination no derogation is permitted.[88] In respect of indirect discrimination the test is whether a particular restriction is objectively justified and proportionate.[89]

(5) In general, Article 90 is interpreted broadly.[90]

Special issues over intellectual property

17.67   As explained above, Article 30 permits derogation from the general Article 28 prohibition on the free movement of goods. In particular, derogation is permitted under Article 30 for 'the protection of industrial and commercial property'. Further, Article 295 provides, unequivocally, that '[t]he Treaty shall in no way prejudice the rules in Member States governing the system of property ownership'.

17.68   However, these provisions must themselves be seen in the context of the over-arching freedom of movement of goods guaranteed by Article 28. There is, plainly, a tension between, on the one hand, the legitimate interests of innovators in respect of intellectual property rights such as trade marks, patents, copyright and design rights and, on the other, the fundamental freedom guaranteed under Article 28.

17.69   In the event, the ECJ has used the interrelationship between Articles 28 and 30 to curtail, at least to some extent, the absolute exercise of intellectual property rights where the exercise of such rights would constitute a real impediment to market integration.

17.70   The ECJ has sought to achieve this in general terms by distinguishing between the *existence* of such property rights and their proper *exercise*. As the court observed in *Deutsche Grammophon*:[91]

> although the Treaty does not affect the existence of rights recognised by the legislation of a Member State with regard to industrial and commercial property, the exercise of such rights may nevertheless fall within the prohibitions laid down by the Treaty. Although it permits prohibitions or restrictions on the free movement of products, which are justified for the purpose of protecting industrial and commercial property, Article [30] only admits derogations from that freedom to the extent to which they are justified for the purpose of safeguarding rights which constitute the specific subject-matter of such property.

17.71   It is, largely, in this way that the tension between property rights and EU interests have been sought to be reconciled.[92] Intellectual property issues do not usually give rise to public law issues before the Administrative Court or in collateral challenges and the detail of the ECJ case law is outside the scope of this work.

---

[87]   Case 86/78 *Grandes Distilleries Peureux* [1979] ECR 897.

[88]   See, eg, Case C-90/94 *Haahr Petroleum* [1997] ECR I–4085.

[89]   See, eg, Case 112/84 *Humblot* [1987] ECR 1367.

[90]   See, eg, Case 142/77 *Larsen* [1978] ECR 1543; Case 168/78 *Commission v France (Taxation of Spirits)* [1980] ECR 347.

[91]   Case 78/70 *Deutsche Grammophon v Metro* [1971] ECR 487, para 12.

[92]   The competition provisions of the Treaty (Articles 81–82) are, of course, also relevant.

F. Two Domestic Case Studies

International Transport Roth GmbH v Secretary of State for the Home Department

The judicial review and related proceedings brought in *International Transport Roth GmbH v Secretary of State for the Home Department*[93] (*'Roth'*) are instructive and relevant both to the subject matter of this chapter and also to other more general themes addressed elsewhere. The case illustrates the increasing tendency for EC and ECHR arguments to be advanced in tandem. This pattern has been repeated in other recent cases[94] and, apart from the content of the EC free movement issues in the hearing, *Roth* raises interesting tactical and jurisprudential issues reflecting some of the subjects discussed in this and other chapters. **17.72**

Roth *outlined*

In *Roth* there were six conjoined proceedings before the Administrative Court challenging the Secretary of State's decision that the claimant hauliers, in whose lorries clandestine entrants arrived in the United Kingdom, were liable to immigration penalties under the Immigration and Asylum Act 1999 and subordinate legislation made thereunder. **17.73**

In summary, there was a prescribed fine of £2,000 levied in respect of each clandestine entrant brought into the United Kingdom which was required to be paid within 60 days. There was statistical evidence of the number of lorries and drivers investigated over time and the penalties imposed. The average penalty was £12,000. **17.74**

The claims involved submissions both that the penalty regime, content of the penalty, and attendant procedures contravened the ECHR (Article 6 and Article 1 Protocol 1) *and* was an unjustifiable restriction on the free movement of goods contrary to Article 28 EC and/or on the freedom to provide haulage services contrary to Article 49 EC. **17.75**

At first instance Sullivan J allowed the application for judicial review on all grounds (both EC and ECHR). However, on appeal, the Court of Appeal allowed the appeal in part and dismissed the EC arguments. Although the Court of Appeal granted general permission to appeal and cross-appeal to the House of Lords, the case was not pursued further because of a change in the law. **17.76**

The relevance of Hoverspeed

A domestic judicial review decision that played some part in the EC argument in *Roth* (albeit only under what is now Article 49 EC) was *R v Secretary of State for the Home Department, ex p Hoverspeed*.[95] There, the issue was whether s 1 of the Immigration (Carriers' Liability) Act 1987 was contrary to Article 59 (now 49) EC. That section—with obvious parallels to the statutory regime in *Roth*—provides that where a person requiring leave to enter the United Kingdom arrives in the United Kingdom by ship or by aircraft and fails to produce a valid passport or other identity documentation, the owners or agents of **17.77**

---

[93] [2002] EWCA Civ 158, [2002] 3 WLR 344.
[94] See also eg, the second case study at paras 17.78 et seq.
[95] [1999] Eu LR 595.

the ship or aircraft become liable to a penalty of £2,000 unless the owners or agents can show that, on embarkation, the passenger produced what was said to be the specified document. In that event, it was for the Secretary of State to prove that the falsity of the document was reasonably apparent.

17.78   In *Hoverspeed*, the claimants contended that s 1 of the 1987 Act constituted a restriction on their freedom to provide services. The Divisional Court dismissed the application holding that there was no discrimination and that the demands made on carriers under the Act could not, sensibly, be characterized as a burdensome measure amounting to an unlawful restriction.

17.79   The Divisional Court implicitly held that the test for what constituted a 'restriction' under Article 49 was wide. It considered that even where a measure was not intended to restrict Article 49 rights, it may be '... so manifestly unreasonable or disproportionate as would intrinsically constitute it [ie. an Article 49 restriction]'.[96]

17.80   Dyson J observed:

> Even if the object of the measure is not to regulate trade, it may be held to be a restriction if it is an unreasonable and disproportionate means of achieving its intended object.[97]

17.81   However, despite the breadth of the test, the Divisional Court concluded that the 1987 Act did not constitute a restriction under Article 49. As summarized by Dyson J:

> It is manifestly not a measure aimed at regulating trade between Member States. It does not in any event deny access to the UK market. The Act is neither an unreasonable nor a dispro-portionate response to the need for effective immigration control. The fact that almost all other Member States have some form of legislation similar to the Act, and that Article 26 of the Schengen Convention is in terms that require parties to adopt such legislation, amply supports the conclusion that such legislation is not inherently an unreasonable response to the need for immigration control.[98]

17.82   So, although the test for what constitutes an Article 49 'restriction' was rightly held to be broad (and, at least arguably, broader than the test for a restriction under Article 28)[99] where there was no intent to restrict trade and the provision in question was not intrinsi-cally unreasonable there would be no 'restriction' at all. Even if there was a 'restriction' the reasonableness of the restriction would be highly relevant to whether it could be justified in terms of EC general principles of law, most notably the principle of proportionality.

Roth—the ruling

17.83   As explained above, at first instance the EC challenge—as well as that mounted under the ECHR—succeeded. Sullivan J held that the statutory scheme under the 1999 Act was a restriction under Articles 28 and 49 EC and that it was an unjustified restriction.

---

[96]   ibid 611, per Simon Brown LJ.
[97]   ibid 620.
[98]   ibid.
[99]   See the discussion on the application of the *Keck* exception to (respectively) Articles 28 and 49 EC at paras 16.63–16.65.

In reaching that conclusion he sought to distinguish *Hoverspeed* on two bases. First, he held **17.84** that—on the evidence—the scheme had a restrictive effect in practice. He said this:

> Although the additional burden placed upon hauliers, to use security devices, to make checks, to keep records is not very great ... the penalties for failing to discharge that relatively modest burden, even as a result of an isolated act of carelessness, are very severe, and are backed by powers of detention. The evidence shows that some haulage firms have either ceased to carry goods to the United Kingdom, reduced their services to the United Kingdom, or altered their patterns of service by using different ports of embarkation or changing to different ferry lines. A substantial number of vehicles have been detained, delaying and disrupting the delivery of imports to the UK.

In terms of justification he observed (referring back to his ruling that the penalty regime **17.85** contravened the ECHR) that:

> It is difficult to see how a penalty regime which fails to comply with Article 6 and/or Article 1 of the [European] Convention [on Human Rights] could be described as reasonable or proportionate.

In allowing the Secretary of State's appeal on the EC arguments, the Court of Appeal held **17.86** that neither of those grounds provided a basis for holding that the scheme constituted an unjustified restriction upon Treaty rights. In so doing, they conflated the grounds by deciding that there was, on the facts of the case, no restriction.

Simon Brown LJ observed (para 65): **17.87**

> ... Having considered afresh the many authorities we examined in *Hoverspeed* in determining whether the 1987 Act constituted an Article 49 (then Article 59) restraint—most notably perhaps *Alpine Investments BV v Minister van Financien* [1995] ECR I–1141 and *Peralta* [1994] ECR I–3453—I simply cannot recognise in the present scheme, inconsistent with the Convention though I regard it to be, a restriction under Community law such as to require justification under the public policy derogation. To characterise the scheme as unjust and unfair is not to say that it therefore '... impair[s] the very substance of the rights guaranteed', as the court put it in *Germany v Council* [[1994] ECR I–4973]. Not every breach of the Convention affecting cross-border trade and services involves an impermissible restriction on Treaty rights. I think the judge below read too much into our statements in *Hoverspeed* that the use of unreasonable and disproportionate means to achieve an object unrelated to regulating trade between Member States '... *could* constitute a restrictive measure within Article [49] ...' (as I put it), or '... *may* be held to be a restriction ...' (as Dyson J put it). Sometimes, in cases which involve an 'intolerable interference' with Treaty rights that will be so. In my judgment, however, not in the present case where the effects upon guaranteed Treaty rights are decidedly tenuous, and where their substance is left unimpaired. (emphasis in original)

In addressing Article 49 EC Parker LJ considered that the fact that the scheme had an impact **17.88** on vehicles entering the UK from abroad was simply a feature that was inherent in the social problem to which the scheme was directed. It was not discrimination on the ground of nationality. He also accepted (and cited) counsel's submission that any restrictive effects that the scheme was shown to have was 'far too uncertain, insignificant and remote to be regarded as hindering services between Member States within the meaning of the Treaty'.

For similar, but additional, reasons, Parker LJ held that Article 28 was not engaged either. **17.89** He said (para 204):

... For Article 28 to apply, the scheme must be a measure having 'equivalent effect' to a quantitative restriction on imports. In my judgment, the scheme is not such a measure. I reach that conclusion for essentially the same reasons as have led me to the conclusion that the scheme does not fall foul of Article 49. In the case of Article 28, however, there is the additional factor that any effect on imports (i.e. imported goods) is indirect, in that the scheme is directed at the vehicles themselves, not at what they are carrying. As in *Peralta* [1984] ECR I-3453 (a case involving a restriction on Italian flagged vessels discharging waste into international waters), the scheme:

'... makes no distinction according to the origin of the substances transported, its purpose is not to regulate trade in goods with other Member States and the restrictive effects which it might have on the free movement of goods are too uncertain and indirect for the obligation ... to be regarded as being of a nature to hinder trade between Member States.'

(see *Societe Civile Agricole du Centre d'Insemination de la Crespelle* [1994] I–5077 at para 36).

Analysis

17.90 It is hard to avoid the conclusion that the EC arguments advanced in *Roth* were argued in a way that made them merely an adjunct to the ECHR submissions.[100] This was certainly the case in the Court of Appeal where the EC case law is only cursorily referred to, where the broad formula in *Dassonville* as to what constitutes a relevant restriction on the free movement of goods is not addressed and where the relationship between fundamental rights and fundamental Treaty freedoms appears not to have been considered or argued.

17.91 In view of the ECJ's earlier (but then very recent) ruling in *Schmidberger*[101] which reasserted *Dassonville* and made it clear how broadly a restriction should be interpreted for the purposes of the Treaty freedoms, it is surprising that the Court of Appeal gave so narrow a meaning to what constituted a restriction.

17.92 In *Schmidberger* the issue was whether the authorities ought to have prevented a demonstration that had a potential effect on trade. In other words, the question was whether a restriction for the purposes of Treaty freedoms could encompass an omission as well as a positive act. The ECJ's answer was unequivocal. The court said (paras 51–64):

It should be stated at the outset that the free movement of goods is one of the fundamental principles of the Community.

Thus, Article 3 of the EC Treaty (now, after amendment, Article 3 EC), inserted in the first part thereof, entitled Principles, provides in subparagraph (c) that for the purposes set out in Article 2 of the Treaty the activities of the Community are to include an internal market characterised by the abolition, as between Member States, of obstacles to *inter alia* the free movement of goods.

The second paragraph of Article 7a of the EC Treaty (now, after amendment, Article 14 EC) provides that the internal market is to comprise an area without internal frontiers in which the free movement of goods is ensured in accordance with the provisions of the Treaty.

That fundamental principle is implemented primarily by Articles 30 and 34 of the Treaty.

In particular, Article 30 provides that quantitative restrictions on imports and all measures having equivalent effect are prohibited between Member States. Similarly, Article 34 prohibits,

---

[100] Considerably more attention was devoted to the EC dimension at first instance before Sullivan J—a fact which resulted in an adverse award of costs on appeal when the EC arguments were lost.

[101] Case C–112/00 [2003] ECR I–5659.

between Member States, quantitative restrictions on exports and all measures having equivalent effect.

It is settled case-law since the judgment in Case 8/74 *Dassonville* [1974] ECR 837, paragraph 5 that those provisions, taken in their context, must be understood as being intended to eliminate all barriers, whether direct or indirect, actual or potential, to trade flows in intra-Community trade (see, to that effect, Case C–265/95 *Commission v France* [1997] ECR I–6959, paragraph 29).

In this way the Court held in particular that, as an indispensable instrument for the realisation of a market without internal frontiers, Article 30 does not prohibit only measures emanating from the State which, in themselves, create restrictions on trade between Member States. It also applies where a Member State abstains from adopting the measures required in order to deal with obstacles to the free movement of goods which are not caused by the State (*Commission v France,* cited above, paragraph 30).

The fact that a Member State abstains from taking action or, as the case may be, fails to adopt adequate measures to prevent obstacles to the free movement of goods that are created, in particular, by actions by private individuals on its territory aimed at products originating in other Member States is just as likely to obstruct intra-Community trade as is a positive act (*Commission v France,* cited above, paragraph 31).

Consequently, Articles 30 and 34 of the Treaty require the Member States not merely themselves to refrain from adopting measures or engaging in conduct liable to constitute an obstacle to trade but also, when read with Article 5 of the Treaty, to take all necessary and appropriate measures to ensure that that fundamental freedom is respected on their territory (*Commission v France,* cited above, paragraph 32). Article 5 of the Treaty requires the Member States to take all appropriate measures, whether general or particular, to ensure fulfilment of the obligations arising out of the Treaty and to refrain from any measures which could jeopardise the attainment of the objectives of that Treaty.

Having regard to the fundamental role assigned to the free movement of goods in the Community system, in particular for the proper functioning of the internal market, that obligation upon each Member State to ensure the free movement of products in its territory by taking the measures necessary and appropriate for the purposes of preventing any restriction due to the acts of individuals applies without the need to distinguish between cases where such acts affect the flow of imports or exports and those affecting merely the transit of goods.

Paragraph 53 of the judgment in *Commission v France,* cited above, shows that the case giving rise to that judgment concerned not only imports but also the transit through France of products from other Member States.

It follows that, in a situation such as that at issue in the main proceedings, where the competent national authorities are faced with restrictions on the effective exercise of a fundamental freedom enshrined in the Treaty, such as the free movement of goods, which result from actions taken by individuals, they are required to take adequate steps to ensure that freedom in the Member State concerned even if, as in the main proceedings, those goods merely pass through Austria en route for Italy or Germany.

It should be added that that obligation of the Member States is all the more important where the case concerns a major transit route such as the Brenner motorway, which is one of the main land links for trade between northern Europe and the north of Italy.

In the light of the foregoing, the fact that the competent authorities of a Member State did not ban a demonstration which resulted in the complete closure of a major transit route such as the Brenner motorway for almost 30 hours on end is capable of restricting intra-Community trade in goods and must, therefore, be regarded as constituting a measure of equivalent effect to a quantitative restriction which is, in principle, incompatible with the Community law obligations arising from Articles 30 and 34 of the Treaty, read together with Article 5 thereof, unless that failure to ban can be objectively justified.

17.93   There is another aspect to *Schmidberger*. There, the failure on the part of the authorities to act to prevent the demonstration was held to be justified because of the margin of appreciation accorded to the national authorities to respect the Convention rights of freedom of expression and assembly under Articles 10 and 11 of the ECHR. In other words, the ECJ held by necessary inference that the effect of fundamental rights protected by the Treaty are on at least an equal footing with the fundamental Treaty freedoms so that a restriction on a Treaty freedom may be justified in order to respect the Convention rights of others.

17.94   In view of the ECJ's reasoning in *Schmidberger* it is, perhaps, surprising that the Court of Appeal did not feel constrained to view positive measures that *by the court's own finding* violated the Convention rights of those affected by the measures in question not even to constitute a restriction requiring justification.

17.95   What *Roth* illustrates is that a domestic court faced with a prior ruling of its own (here *Hoverspeed*) that has considered earlier ECJ jurisprudence in a similar area may, unless pressed, be tempted to return to that case rather than to venture on an excursion of ECJ case law including later cases of the ECJ (here such as *Schmidberger*).

17.96   However, *Roth* also demonstrates the scope for combining fundamental rights arguments with substantive Treaty points in judicial review proceedings. Unlike cases such as *Watts* (see case study in Chapter 19) where the case was, properly understood, not about fundamental rights at all but, rather, about Treaty rights so that the sole issue was about the true content and scope of particular Treaty freedoms in a specific context, in *Roth* both the Administrative Court and the Court of Appeal held (for very different reasons in all the judgments) that Convention rights under the HRA were violated.

17.97   In such a situation it is at least arguable, especially given the rapid expansion in the scope of EC law with the development of the fundamental rights jurisdiction of the ECJ,[102] that what constitutes a restriction for the purposes of engagement of Article 28/49 protection should (as the ECJ case-law suggests anyway) be broadly interpreted. Ironically, without such protection, the HRA provides a more effective remedy than does EC law despite the EC general principle of effectiveness.

R (Countryside Alliance) v (1) Attorney General and (2) Secretary of State for the Environment, Food and Rural Affairs[103]

17.98   This case concerned the much-debated Hunting Act 2004 which prohibits the hunting with dogs of wild mammals. A combined judicial review challenge was brought in respect of the ban deploying arguments under both EC and HRA law. The challenge was strategically aimed at maximizing the interplay between EC and HRA law and relying on the separate

---

[102]   See, generally, Chapter 12. See, also, T Tridimas, *The General Principles of EU Law* (2nd edn, 2006) ch 7.
[103]   [2006] EWCA Civ 817.

strengths of each. It is of interest as being one of the few domestic public law challenges in which EC and HRA arguments have been deliberately conjoined. However, its special interest lies in the fact that the Court of Appeal (upholding the dismissal of the challenges by the Divisional Court) has ruled, for the first time, that application of the EC proportionality doctrine is not the same as under the HRA.

The HRA and EC arguments in outline

In the HRA challenge the claimants were the Countryside Alliance and a number of indi- **17.99**
viduals who opposed the ban entirely on human rights grounds, most notably under Articles 8, 11 and Article 1 Protocol 1 ECHR. In the EC challenge, the claimants were individuals living abroad and/or providing services affecting inter-state trade who contended that the ban offended against Articles 28 and 49 of the Treaty.

Although there was considerable overlap between the two cases, there were important **17.100**
differences which surfaced in the Court of Appeal's judgment. Essentially, the HRA claimants (and appellants) argued that the Hunting Act would directly and indirectly infringe rights under the HRA in that it would significantly reduce hunting in England and Wales so that many hunts would be forced to close down or reduce the extent of their activities with, in many instances, consequent loss of employment and tied homes.

Article 8 ECHR was contended to be engaged in a number of different respects under both **17.101**
the right to respect for individuals' homes and (more importantly) their private life. Article 11 (right of freedom of assembly/association) was said to be engaged because the Hunting Act prohibited the assemblies that hunt meetings constitute, and prohibits or significantly interferes with the freedom of association of persons in and around hunting. Finally, and in contrast to the defendants' (Attorney General's and Secretary of State's) denial that either Article 8 or Article 11 was engaged, it was common ground that Article 1 Protocol 1 ECHR was engaged. However, there was a dispute as to the scope of its engagement. The HRA claimants asserted a very wide range of respects in which the Act deprived persons of property rights, or interfered with the peaceful enjoyment of those rights. The defendants argued that Article 1 Protocol 1 was only engaged to the limited extent of loss of specific property occasioned by the ban, namely the loss (where proved) of property such as dogs, horses, and vehicles. If and to the extent that other ECHR rights were engaged (and in respect of the admitted engagement of Article 1 Protocol 1) the defendants argued that infringement of those provisions was both justified and proportionate.

For their part, the EC claimants (and appellants) asserted that the hunting ban: (1) directly **17.102**
infringed Article 28 EC as having an effect equivalent to a quantitative restriction on imports (being the effect of the ban on or the importing of horses by an EC claimant), and/or (2) infringed Article 49 EC as being an unjustified restriction on services (as, for example, the provision of hunting holidays by one of the EC claimants for foreign visitors). The defendants denied that any Treaty right was engaged in that there was no relevant restriction. In any event, it was contended that any restriction was justified and proportionate.

Divisional Court ruling[104]

17.103   In the Divisional Court the challenges were rejected. The court held that no relevant Convention provisions were engaged other than Article 1 Protocol 1 ECHR, but only to the limited extent conceded by the defendants. In relation to the EC challenge, the Divisional Court held (as against the defendant's contention) that Article 49 was engaged but held that the hunting ban was both justified and proportionate. In making that finding the court treated the requirements of proportionality under both the HRA and EC heads of argument as interchangeable. Both claimants appealed to the Court of Appeal.

Court of Appeal's ruling in outline

17.104   The Court of Appeal dismissed both appeals. In respect of the HRA challenges the basis of the court's reasoning essentially replicated that of the Divisional Court. It held that no relevant Convention provision was engaged (other than Article 1 Protocol 1 to the limited extent accepted by the defendants) and that any Convention infringement was proportionate.

17.105   However, in respect of the EC challenge the Court of Appeal's reasoning differed from that of the Divisional Court in a number of material respects. First, it held (disagreeing with the Court of Appeal who considered that Article 49 was engaged) that neither Article 28 nor Article 49 EC was engaged. Secondly, it held that any restriction was proportionate. However, although the Court of Appeal reached the same factual finding as the Divisional Court in its application of the proportionality principle, it differed from that court as to the constituent elements of EC proportionality. Importantly, it held that the requirements of EC proportionality were not the same as those under the HRA and that a higher threshold was required under EC law to justify a restriction on a fundamental Treaty freedom/fundamental right protected by EC law.

17.106   The Court of Appeal's reasoning in respect of proportionality is the first clear statement by an English court to the effect that proportionality in EC law differs from that under the HRA. It is, therefore, of considerable importance. It is doubtful whether such a result would have ensued unless, as occurred, HRA and EC arguments were being run in tandem.

Court of Appeal EC ruling—(1) Article 28 not engaged

17.107   The Court of Appeal first addressed the decisions of the ECJ in *Dassonville* and *Cassis de Dijon* (see paras 17.10–17.11 and 17.27–17.28) and analysed the course of that jurisprudence leading to the very broad *Sunday Trading* ruling and the retreat from *Dassonville* resulting in the decision in *Keck* discussed in paras 17.16–17.20.

17.108   The EC appellants argued that the Hunting Act could not be characterized as a 'selling arrangement' under the *Keck* principle so as to exclude the operation of Article 28. This was said to be because *Keck* was simply irrelevant to something like a ban on hunting. As the Court of Appeal observed, and as the analysis in this chapter confirms, there was no case directly in point but the respondents to the appeal contended (as was held by the Divisional Court) that the logic of *Keck* was that 'selling arrangements' as identified in *Keck* were simply

---

[104] [2005] EWHC 1677.

an example of non-discriminatory rules of the host State, other than product rules, none of which fell within Article 28.

In the event, the Court of Appeal rejected the appellants' submissions. It observed that **17.109** whilst, at least in general terms, the ECJ continued to use the language of 'selling arrangements' in relation to matters falling outside the ambit of Article 28 this was because those cases in which the expression was used were about selling arrangements in the literal sense.[105] Nor did other ECJ cases referred to by the appellants in which Article 28 had been held to apply assist the court because those cases were not, properly analysed, cases where the ECJ had held Article 28 to be engaged in the manner contended for.[106]

The Court of Appeal, adopting a similar analysis to the Divisional Court concluded that **17.110** *Keck* should not be viewed as containing a limited exception to the *Dassonville* formulation but should, rather, be understood as involving the introduction of new rules into an area formerly thought to be covered by *Dassonville*. Those new rules were to the effect that non-discriminatory rules (including selling arrangements) other than product rules fell outside the scope of Article 28. It followed that a ban such as the hunting ban was outside the ambit of Article 28 altogether.

Court of Appeal EC ruling—(2) Article 49 not engaged

Unlike the Divisional Court, the Court of Appeal held that Article 49 was not (any more **17.111** than Article 28) applicable to the hunting ban. In reaching that conclusion, however, the court accepted that the relevant jurisprudence was not entirely clear and that had it not reached the conclusions that it did on justification (see paras 17.117 et seq.) it might have had to contemplate an Article 234 reference to the ECJ.

In essence the court reasoned as follows. First, there was (as the Divisional Court had **17.112** recognized) strong reason why a measure preventing the provision of services should fall outside Article 49 if it has no greater impact on non-domestic services than on domestic services.

Secondly, the Divisional Court had, however, considered itself to be bound by ECJ authority **17.113** to ostensibly contrary effect, namely that transposition of the restriction in *Keck* to freedom to provide services was not persuasive.[107] The Court of Appeal felt able to distinguish these authorities in a number of respects but agreed that *Keck* could not simply be read across to the freedom of services provisions.

---

[105] See, eg, Case C–412/93 *Leclerc* [1995] ECR I–0179 (restrictions on television advertising); Case C–71/02 *Karner* [2004] ECR I–3025 (restrictions on allegedly misleading advertising); Case C–20/03 *Burmanjer* [2006] 1 CMLR 24 (restriction on itinerant selling).

[106] Case C–67/97 *Bluhme* [1998] ECR I–8033 (an example, albeit unusual, of a product rule); Case 320/03 *Austria* [2006] 2 CMLR 12 (Art 28 held to apply in respect of an impediment to transportation); Case C–36/02 *Omega* [2004] ECR I–9609 (case about provision of services rather than Art 28).

[107] See the Opinion of Advocate General Stix-Hackl in Case C–36/02 *Omega* [2004] ECR I–9609; Case C–384/93 *Alpine Investments* [1995] ECR I–1141; Case C–405/98 *Gourmet International* [2001] ECR I–1795. The Court of Appeal also noted two other cases relied on by the appellants in this respect: Case C–224/97 *Ciola* [1999] ECR I–2517; Case C–60/00 *Carpenter* [2002] ECR I–6297.

17.114 Thirdly, however, the key question was the nature of the restriction and the nature of its effect on *cross-border* trade. In the view of the Court of Appeal, the principle in *Keck* should be seen as part of an underlying imperative, that is 'to prevent the exploitation of the Treaty as a means of challenging national rules whose effect is simply to limit commercial freedom'.

17.115 In holding thus, the Court of Appeal was heavily influenced by the observations of Robert Walker LJ in *Professional Contractors Group Ltd v IRC*:[108]

> What I derive from these authorities (and especially from *Graf*, which is particularly instructive) is that a neutral, non-discriminatory national measure will not contravene the articles relating to freedom of movement unless it has a direct and demonstrable inhibiting effect on the particular right which is asserted.

17.116 On that basis, the hunting ban did not engage Article 49. The ban did not have a direct inhibiting effect on freedom to provide services. What it did was to render the market for such services within a particular Member State less attractive both to English and foreign providers and receivers. It was, in the court's view, difficult to see how it could be a breach of Article 49 simply to remove the factual opportunity to engage in a particular trade.

Court of Appeal EC ruling—(3) Justification and proportionality

17.117 Although the Divisional Court had concluded that the overall approaches to proportionality in the HRA and EC cases were broadly interchangeable, the Court of Appeal disagreed.

17.118 In an important ruling that (although it did not affect the outcome in the hunting challenge) has strong implications for other cases, the Court of Appeal held that to treat proportionality the same in the EC context as in the HRA context was to undervalue 'some distinctive and constitutional characteristics of Community law'.

17.119 These characteristics are as follows:

(1) The notions of deference to the national legislature and of the margin of appreciation of the Member State that are to be found in Convention law are absent from, or at least less central to, Community jurisprudence. In EC law, all organs of the Member State (including its legislature) are bound by EC law and can only act as that law provides.

(2) The grounds of justification for acts that would otherwise entail a breach of EC law are less extensive and much more constrained by law than are the grounds that can be appealed to in Convention jurisprudence.

(3) The notion of proportionality is narrower in EC jurisprudence. In particular, where there are alternative means of achieving a legitimate end, recourse must be had to the least onerous of them.

17.120 Applying those principles to the facts of the hunting challenge did not, in fact, produce a different outcome in the EC challenge to that in the HRA challenge because—as had already been held in the HRA part of the case—the issue was more complex than one of scientific proof of the relative suffering of foxes. Central to Parliament's free vote on the hunting ban was the belief that killing foxes for sport was morally wrong. That was not a matter capable of

---

[108] [2001] EWCA Civ 1945, [2002] STC 165.

scientific proof. Consistent with that judgment, there was no less restrictive method of addressing the objective of preventing such suffering than a complete ban. So, whilst—at least in general terms—the ECJ cases suggested that where a matter relied on for justification for a restriction of a Treaty freedom was capable of scientific proof it must be scientifically proved,[109] that jurisprudence could not be decisive of the outcome.

Analysis

The hunting challenge is a remarkable illustration of the interplay between domestic judicial review and EC law. There were major tactical reasons for bringing the challenge under both EC and HRA law. As far as HRA law was concerned, the Government conceded at an early stage that at least some aspects of Article 1 Protocol 1 ECHR were engaged. On that basis the hunting ban required justification. **17.121**

As far as EC law was concerned, the engagement of *any* Treaty provision was always going to be harder to establish than in the HRA challenge. However, there were at least two reasons for deploying EC law in addition to the HRA. First, as explained elsewhere,[110] the remedies obtainable if there were—as alleged here—a breach of EC law occasioned by the provisions of a statute would, necessarily, include disapplication of primary legislation (here the Hunting Act). This could not be obtained on an HRA challenge. At best, a declaration of incompatibility would be granted.[111] Secondly, there was an argument (which in the event succeeded on the level of analysis if not outcome) that a higher threshold of justification was required for a breach of EC law than under the HRA. **17.122**

It is by no means obvious that the Court of Appeal was correct in its conclusion that Article 49 did not apply to a measure such as the hunting ban. However, the fact that there was justification in any event made it unnecessary for an Article 234 reference to be made. **17.123**

It is clear that the Court of Appeal was concerned about extending the scope of Article 49 to a non-discriminatory measure that made provision of services less attractive both to English and foreign service providers and receivers. However, the cases on medical treatment as an aspect of Article 49 demonstrate that there are circumstances in which a service user may be able to claim medical treatment abroad precisely because the service is not available in the United Kingdom at a particular time and because not funding the service abroad would operate as a disincentive to cross-border trade (see the *Watts* case study in Chapter 19). It is not immediately obvious why the disincentive to cross-border trade effected by the hunting ban is not, on similar principles, a matter that requires justification if it is to be lawful. **17.124**

The Court of Appeal's reasoning on proportionality is extremely important. It is the first time that it has been held that proportionality is stricter under EC law than under the HRA. There was, however, no detailed analysis by the Court of Appeal of the concept of deference to legislative judgments in ECHR cases or of the Strasbourg case law on proportionality. **17.125**

---

[109] See, eg, Case C–192/01 *Denmark* [2003] ECR I–9693.

[110] See, eg, paras 2.62 et seq.

[111] The HRA claimants had, at first instance, pursued the ground that the Hunting Act 2004 could be interpreted under HRA, s 3 to be Convention compatible. However, this argument was rejected and did not resurface on appeal.

17.126 Further, the court's summary of the distinctive institutional differences between EC and HRA law (see para 17.119) is not entirely accurate. First, whilst it is true that all organs of the State (including the legislature) are bound by EC law, it is also true that the legislature is subject to the court's adjudication of whether legislation is or is not compatible with the ECHR. Thus, the institutional difference tells one nothing about the requisite standard of justification required for infringements of Convention law or why the justification should on that ground alone be required to be higher for breaches of EC law than for breaches of Convention law (see, though, the analysis at paras 11.86–11.92).

17.127 Secondly, the remaining differences between EC and ECHR law outlined by the Court of Appeal beg the question in that—bereft as they are of authority—they simply assert a difference between EC law and ECHR law that has not been the subject of authoritative pronouncement by either the ECJ or the European Court of Human Rights. True it is, as this chapter exemplifies, that a specific ground of derogation is sometimes required in EC law which is not required in ECHR law. But the need (where there is one) for a specific basis for derogation is not a reliable guide to the threshold for deciding whether the derogation in question is justified.

17.128 Finally, it is not self-evident that a standard of justification that requires the least restrictive alternative to be established by the State when seeking to rely on EC derogation is different to the Strasbourg standard of 'pressing social need' to justify a Convention violation.

17.129 Despite this, the Court of Appeal's ruling on proportionality is of fundamental significance. The lasting legacy of the hunting challenge is that it seems likely to lead to a greater number of combined EC and HRA challenges where the EC arguments will be founded on the asserted higher threshold, in specific factual contexts, of the justification required by EC law than under the HRA for particular measures.

18

DISCRIMINATION

A. Raising EC Discrimination Issues before National Courts

EC discrimination restrictions have been developed, primarily, from rules prohibiting sex **18.01** discrimination in relation to employment situations. They have been expanded in recent years to include other important areas such as race and disability (again, often in the context of employment). In turn, the original rules have been updated in line with the new and expanded protection given to those other areas.

Frequently, discrimination involves domestic public law issues. This is not least because the **18.02** principle of equal treatment is a general principle of EC law which applies generally to the interpretation of EC legislation and domestic legislation that is founded in EC law.[1] As such, in an EC public law case familiarity with the substantive principles protecting against discriminatory treatment is of some importance.

Further, public law discrimination issues arise, most frequently in any event, in the arena **18.03** of domestic legislation the legality of which is challenged on discrimination grounds in judicial review proceedings or (at least in the employment context) before an Employment

---

[1] See Chapter 7.

Tribunal or the Employment Appeal Tribunal. And even in the private law context in disputes between an employer and employee, EC discrimination issues may fall to be decided by reference to public law principles and ECJ rulings affecting public law cases (most notably judicial review proceedings) may arise following a reference under Article 234 [ex 177] EC by (for example) the Employment Appeal Tribunal.

18.04 The relationship between the public law jurisdiction of the Employment Tribunal and Employment Appeal Tribunal and that of the Administrative Court was considered by the Court of Appeal in *Manson v Ministry of Defence*.[2]

18.05 In that case, domestic regulations were made in order to implement Directive (EC) 97/81 (the Protection for Part Time Workers Directive). An Employment Tribunal concluded that because of reg 13(2) it had no jurisdiction to hear the applicant's claim. The Employment Appeal Tribunal declined to determine an argument directed to the compatibility of the regulations with EC law. Judicial review proceedings were brought challenging the legality of the regulations.

18.06 The Court of Appeal upheld the judgment of Moses J to the effect that an Employment Tribunal or Employment Appeal Tribunal was required in the exercise of its statutory jurisdiction to apply and enforce relevant EC law and to disapply an offending provision of UK domestic legislation to the extent that it was incompatible with EC law.[3]

18.07 Notwithstanding the duty on those tribunals to apply EC law including, where necessary, examining public law issues involving the compatibility of domestic legislation with EC discrimination requirements, there are many examples of direct challenges by way of judicial review before the Administrative Court to legislative provisions or administrative decisions on the ground of their incompatibility with EC discrimination law. Table 18.1 below provides some illustrations of the types of judicial review challenges that have been brought. Many of these cases are addressed further in this chapter when outlining the EC discrimination regime.

B. Outline of the EC Discrimination Regimes

18.08 This chapter addresses specific areas of substantive discrimination protection in EC legislation which frequently raise public law issues in the domestic courts. The various legislative provisions are outlined below.[4]

18.09 The starting point for substantive protection against discrimination in EC law was the prohibition of sex discrimination. This has increased greatly over the years although as indicated above the requirement of equal treatment in EC law has, since the Treaty of Amsterdam, expanded into new and important areas with the result that the rules on sex

---

2 [2005] EWCA Civ 1678.
3 Note to similar effect *Biggs v Somerset County Council* [1996] ICR 364, 370.
4 In most cases engaging EC discrimination issues it would, of course, be necessary to have close regard to the Treaty or other legislative provision in question. Such detail is outside the scope of this work.

Table 18.1 Discrimination—types of judicial review challenges

Case	Summary
R (Amicus–MSF Section) v Secretary of State for Trade and Industry [2004] IRLR 430	Unsuccessful judicial review challenge to the compatibility of the Employment Equality (Sexual Orientation) Regulations 2003 (SI 2003/1661), regs 7(2), (3), 20(3) and 25 with Council Directive (EC) 2000/78.
Case C–137/94 *R v Secretary of State for Health, ex p Richardson* [1995] ECR I–3407	Judicial review challenge to UK legislation exempting women from medical prescription charges from the age of 60 but only exempting men from the age of 65. On an Article 234 reference from the Administrative Court the ECJ held that Article 3 of Directive (EEC) 79/7 (the social security Directive) was applicable.
Case C–9/91 *R v Secretary of State for Social Security, ex p EOC* [1992] ECR I–4297	Unsuccessful judicial review challenge (following an Article 234 reference) brought by the Equal Opportunities Commission to the compatibility of the then different old age pension requirements for men and women with the Social Security Directive.
Case C–66/95 *R v Secretary of State for Social Security, ex p Sutton* [1997] ECR I–2163	Unsuccessful judicial review challenge (following an Article 234 reference) to the failure to award interest payments for failure to make payment of invalid care allowance from due date under the Social Security Directive so as to achieve equal treatment. The ECJ ruled that such awards were not compensatory in nature and so did not attract interest.
Case C–167/97 *R v Secretary of State for Employment, ex p Seymour-Smith and Perez* [1999] ECR I–623	Judicial review challenge to legislation imposing service threshold requirements to be established in order to claim unfair dismissal payments (*in casu* a two-year minimum work period). On a preliminary ruling under Article 234, the ECJ held that compensation for unfair dismissal constituted 'pay' under Article 141(1) EC. Unusually, however, the ECJ pronounced on the facts and observed that a difference in recruitment as between men (77.4 per cent) and women (68.9 per cent) was insufficient to infer discrimination.
R v Ministry of Defence, ex p Smith [1996] QB 517	Unsuccessful judicial review challenge on the basis of legality of UK sex equality legislation sanctioning the policy of the UK armed forces of discharging homosexuals.
Case C–253/90 *R v Secretary of State for Social Security, ex p Smithson* [1992] ECR I–467	Judicial review challenge to the legality of the higher pensioner premium on a differential basis to men and women. In its Article 234 ruling the ECJ (disagreeing with the Advocate General) held that Article 3(1) of the Social Security Directive did not extend to housing benefit paid to persons on low income. This was because Article 3(1) did not refer to the lack of housing a risk against which the equal treatment principle was to apply.
Case C–382/98 *R v Secretary of State for Social Security, ex p Taylor* [1999] ECR I–8955	Successful judicial review challenge, founded on alleged sex discrimination on grounds of differential retirement ages, to lack of entitlement to a winter fuel payment. In its Article 234 preliminary ruling the ECJ held that such payments were intended to protect against the risk of old age and therefore fell within Article 3(1) of the Social Security Directive.

Table 18.1 *Cont.*

Case	Summary
R v Secretary of State for Employment, ex p EOC [1995] 1 AC	Successful judicial review challenge to provisions of the Employment Protection (Consolidation) Act 1978 under which part-time workers needed five years, continuous employment as compared with two years for full-timers to qualify for unfair dismissal and redundancy entitlements. The House of Lords ruled that there was a lack of objective justification and that the provisions were, therefore, contrary to EC law. It was also held that whereas, by virtue of its statutory remit, the EOC had standing to seek judicial review, the other claimant, a part-time workers of a health authority, did not. Her remedy was in private law for redundancy pay and this was a matter entrusted to the industrial tribunal.
R (Couronne) v Crawley Borough Council [2006] EWHC 1514	Unsuccessful judicial review challenge to imposition of habitual residence condition for entitlement to a jobseeker's allowance and local authority accommodation. The condition was alleged to be discriminatory to the claimants as descendants of Chagos Islanders and, hence, contrary to: (1) domestic regulations, (2) the Race Relations Act 1976 and (3) Council Directive (EC) 2000/43. It was held that the condition was not in breach of the directive as there was no discrimination as between the claimants and British citizens of Irish ethnic or national origin. Nor was Article 1 Protocol 1 of the ECHR engaged.

discrimination have had to be amended to keep up with fast-moving areas of discrimination protection such as race and age.

18.10 Starting with sex discrimination, Article 2 EC now contains provision, amongst other things, for the promotion of equality between men and women. Article 13 contains a general power for countering discrimination on grounds that include sex discrimination. Article 141 (ex 119) EC provides that men and women should receive equal pay for equal work and for work of equal value. Relevant directives in this area include:

(1) Directive (EEC) 75/117 (the Equal Pay Directive) on removing discrimination arising from laws that contravene the Treaty principle of equal pay for men and women.

(2) Directive (EEC) 76/207 on equal treatment on grounds of sex with regard to employment. This is often referred to as the Equal Treatment Directive.

(3) Directive (EEC) 79/7 on equal treatment on grounds of sex with regard to matters of social security.

(4) Directive (EEC) 86/378 on equal treatment on grounds of sex with regard to occupational pension schemes.

(5) Directive (EEC) 86/613 on equal treatment on grounds of sex with regard to self-employment.

(6) Directive (EC) 2002/73 (the new Equal Treatment Directive which amends but does not replace the Equal Treatment Directive).

Two other new directives are of increasing importance in the field of discrimination. These are: **18.11**

(1) Directive (EC) 2000/43 (the Race Directive) on equal treatment on grounds of race in employment and other areas.
(2) Directive (EC) 2000/78 (the Framework Directive) on equal treatment on grounds of age, disability, religion or belief, and sexual orientation in employment.

Whilst there is some overlap between these last directives and sex discrimination (see, for example, the reference to protection against sexual orientation discrimination in the Framework Directive) the Race Directive and the Framework Directive have expanded the concept of discrimination (including the introduction of harassment) in ways which have made it necessary to pass the new Equal Treatment Directive to bring sex discrimination into line with the new approach. **18.12**

There follows: **18.13**

(1) an outline of the basic principles that have been applied (usually by the ECJ on references under Article 234 EC) in the cases to sex discrimination (since many of those principles are likely to be applied to the new areas of discrimination),
(2) a brief survey of the sex discrimination Treaty provisions and most of the relevant directives[5] (including the Equal Treatment Directive prior to amendment but with amendments flagged up in the text) preceding the new Equal Treatment Directive,
(3) an outline of the Race Directive and Framework Directive so as to illustrate the added protection that these directives give to discrimination,
(4) an outline of the main amendments made by the new Equal Treatment Directive showing how this added protection has been applied to sex discrimination, and
(5) a summary of the general approach taken or likely to be taken by national courts to public law issues of discrimination that arise in an EC context.

C. The Concept of Sex Discrimination in EC Law

Sex discrimination, at least for the purposes of the Equal Treatment Directive, has a broad meaning and is not restricted to issues of gender discrimination. In particular it includes discrimination issues relating to sexual orientation. This is made entirely clear in the new Equal Treatment Directive but it had already been clarified in the important ECJ ruling in *P v S*.[6] There, a proposed sex change was treated as ground for dismissal from employment. The issue before the ECJ was whether the Equal Treatment Directive made dismissal unlawful or whether gender reassignment was outside the scope of the directive altogether. **18.14**

---

[5] However, no separate treatment is given to either Directive (EEC) 86/378 (equal treatment in occupational pension schemes) or Directive (EEC) 86/613 (equal treatment for self-employed persons). Neither directive has generated (or seems likely to generate) case law of importance.

[6] Case 13/94 [1996] ECR I–2143. This decision led to the Sex Discrimination (Gender Reassignment) Regulations 1999 (SI 1999/1102) which amended the Sex Discrimination Act 1975 so as to bring direct discrimination on the ground of an employees' gender reassignment within the Act.

The ECJ held that the general EC principle of equality of treatment meant that protection could not be limited to discrimination on grounds of gender.

18.15 Despite somewhat more restrictive subsequent rulings by the ECJ as to the ambit of sex discrimination in particular instances,[7] the ECJ has most recently given a preliminary ruling in a UK case that reaffirms the principle of a broad concept of sex discrimination. In *KB*[8] the issue arose over an asserted right to marry on the part of transsexuals and thereby claim entitlement to a survivor's pension. The question, referred to the ECJ by the Court of Appeal, was whether or not a rule that prevented transsexuals from marrying violated the Equal Treatment Directive.

18.16 The ECJ ruled that Article 141 (ex 119) EC in principle precluded domestic legislation which, in breach of the ECHR, prevented a couple who were both originally of the same sex, but one of whom had undergone gender reassignment surgery, from fulfilling the marriage requirement which had to be met for one of them to benefit from the pay of another. In that situation, it was for the domestic court to decide whether Article 141 could be relied on in order to gain recognition of the right to nominate such a partner as the beneficiary of a survivor's pension.

18.17 In view of these decisions it may be that *R v Ministry of Defence, ex p Smith*[9] may have been wrongly decided. In that case, the Court of Appeal dismissed an appeal against the refusal of an application for judicial review of the UK armed force's gay service ban. The case was fought on both ECHR (pre-HRA) and EU grounds. The Court of Appeal held that the policy did not contravene EC sex discrimination law. However, given the later ECJ decisions in *P v S* and *KB* the correctness of the Court of Appeal's judgment is now open to considerable doubt.

18.18 In any event, sexual orientation is now increasingly written in to EC discrimination law by virtue of Article 13 EC (added by the Treaty of Amsterdam in 1999). This authorizes the Council to 'take appropriate action to combat discrimination based on sex, racial or ethnic origin, religion or belief, disability, age or sexual orientation'. Directive (EC) 2000/78 (see above) addresses discrimination in the employment context on grounds of (amongst other things) sexual orientation which were transposed into domestic law by the Employment Equality (Sexual Orientation) Regulations 2003. The new Equal Treatment Directive (see below) introduces prohibitions on discrimination that are based on a 'characteristic related to sex'.

18.19 In EC law, discrimination may be either direct or indirect.[10] Direct discrimination (including sex discrimination) involves 'the application of different rules to comparable situations

---

[7] See Case C–249/96 *Grant v South West Trains Ltd* [1998] ECR I–621; Case C–125/99 P *D v Council* [2001] ECR I–4319.

[8] Case C–117/01 *KB v National Health Service Pensions Agency and Secretary of State for Health* [2004] ECR I–541.

[9] [1996] QB 517. A similarly restrictive domestic decision is the House of Lords ruling in *Advocate General for Scotland v McDonald and Pearce* [2004] 1 All ER 339.

[10] The same is true in the ECHR context: see *Thlimmenos v Greece* [2000] ECHR 162.

or the application of the same rule to different situations'.[11] Direct sex discrimination is, at least generally, not capable of being justified unless there is specific provision for derogation.

Indirect sex discrimination occurs where the same rules apply ostensibly to men and women but have greater (and disproportionate) adverse impact on one sex rather than the other. Indirect discrimination may be lawful if it is objectively justified.   **18.20**

It is, therefore, sometimes of importance (and not always easy) to know whether particular discrimination is considered to be direct or indirect. Issues have arisen over whether discrimination in respect of pregnancy is direct or indirect. In that context, the ECJ has held that refusing to employ a woman because she is pregnant constitutes *direct* discrimination.[12] So, too, does dismissing a woman on grounds of pregnancy.[13] However, dismissal on the ground of a pregnancy-related illness may not be directly discriminatory (and so could be justified) in circumstances where the illness is suffered after the end of maternity leave.[14] Discrimination in respect of conditions of employment because of pregnancy also constitutes direct discrimination.[15]   **18.21**

A common instance of indirect discrimination on grounds of sex takes place where an employer employs full-time and part-time workers. In many of the cases the full-time workers (predominantly male) are paid proportionately more than the part-time workers (predominantly female). Despite the fact that all full-time workers are paid at the same rate and all part-time workers are paid at the same rate so that there is no direct discrimination between the sexes, the result of the differential proportion between full- and part-time workers is that there is a disproportionate effect on women. There is, thus, indirect discrimination. The question then is whether, in particular cases, such indirect discrimination can be objectively justified.   **18.22**

In determining whether indirect sex discrimination has occurred, a useful yardstick to inform the approach to be adopted by the domestic court was laid down by the ECJ in *Seymour Smith*.[16] The court said: **18.23**

> In order to establish whether a measure adopted by a Member State has disparate effect as between men and women to such a degree as to amount to indirect discrimination for the purposes of [Article 141] the national court must verify whether the statistics available indicate that a considerably smaller percentage of women than men is able to fulfill the requirement imposed by that measure. If that is the case, then there is indirect sex discrimination.

---

[11] Case C–100/95 *Kording* [1997] ECR I–5289.

[12] Case 177/88 *Dekker v Centrum* [1990] ECR I–3941. For that reason there was no scope for justification on the footing of financial disadvantage to the employer.

[13] See, eg, Case C–394/96 *Brown v Rentokil Ltd* [1998] ECR I–4185. Case C–32/93 *Webb v EMO Air Cargo* [1994] ECR I–3567.

[14] Case 179/88 *Hertz* [1990] ECR I–3979.

[15] See, eg, Case C–66/96 *Pedersen v Skive* [1998] ECR I–7327.

[16] Case 167/97 *R v Secretary of State for Employment, ex p Seymour Smith and Perez* [1999] ECR I–623.

D. Justifying EC Sex Discrimination in EC Law

18.24 In *Bilka-Kaufhaus*[17] the ECJ indicated, at least in general terms, what could amount to objective justification of indirect sex discrimination. In an employment context the employer would have to establish that an indirectly discriminatory measure:

(1) corresponded to a 'genuine need of the enterprise',
(2) was suitable for obtaining the objective pursued by the enterprise, and
(3) was necessary for that purpose.

18.25 Taking the example referred to above of full-time workers being paid proportionately more than their part-time counterparts, the ECJ has (amongst other things) accepted objective justification in principle[18] in such cases by reference to considerations such as:

(1) economic factors;[19]
(2) the need to lighten burdens on small businesses;[20]
(3) social policy objectives.[21]

18.26 But justification must be case-specific. Mere generalization will not suffice. Thus, for example, in *Gerster*[22] the ECJ rejected the argument that indirect discrimination could be justified by the general fact that full-time employees had more experience by virtue of their longer working hours. As the court pointed out:

> It is impossible to identify objective criteria unrelated to any discrimination on the basis of an alleged link between length of service and acquisition of a certain level of knowledge or experience, since such a claim amounts to no more than a generalization concerning certain categories of worker. Although experience goes hand-in-hand with length of service, and experience enables the worker in principle to improve performance of the tasks allotted to him, the objectivity of such a criterion depends on all circumstances of each individual case, and in particular on the relationship between the nature of the work performed and the experience gained from the performance of that work.

E. Article 141 (ex 119) EC—Equal Pay for Equal Work and Work of Equal Value

18.27 Article 141(1) now provides as follows:

> Each Member State shall ensure that the principle of equal pay for male and female workers for equal work or work of equal value is applied.[23]

---

[17] Case 170/84 *Bilka-Kaufhaus GmbH v Weber von Hartz* [1986] ECR 1607.

[18] However, any objective justification must be proportionately applied.

[19] Case 96/80 *Jenkins v Kingsgate (Clothing Productions) Ltd* [1981] ECR 911. But *purely* economic factors would seem not usually to provide objective justification: see, eg, Case 343/92 *de Weerd* [1994] ECR I–571.

[20] Case C–189/91 *Kirsammer-Hack v Sidal* [1993] ECR I–6185.

[21] See, eg, Case C–187/00 *Kitz-Bauer* [2003] ECR I–2741 (encouragement of recruitment of young workers).

[22] Case C–1/95 [1997] ECR I–5253.

[23] This formulation is slightly different to its predecessor (Art 119) but merely reflects ECJ case law. The essential requirement in Art 141(1) has not changed.

The following essential points should be noted:

18.28

(1) Article 141 is not merely negative in nature. Positive action is also permitted (see Article 141(4) introduced by the Treaty of Amsterdam conferring specific compensatory advantages for the under-represented sex). There was a parallel (albeit more narrowly worded) provision in Article 2(4) the Equal Treatment Directive which is considered below. The principles are now, *mutatis mutandis*, the same for both provisions and the new Equal Treatment Directive has amended the former Article 2(4) by inserting a new Article 2(8) to reflect the position.[24]

(2) 'Pay' is generously defined in Articles 141(2) and encompasses (apart from basic wage) 'any other consideration' including payment in cash or kind and whether received directly or indirectly. The breadth of scope of Article 141 (and its predecessor Article 119) has been clarified in a number of preliminary rulings by the ECJ under Article 234 (ex 177) EC following references from the national courts. In *Garland v British Rail Engineering Ltd*,[25] for example, special benefits in the form of travel facilities given to ex-employees (male) after retirement were held by the ECJ to fall within Article 141 even though they were not included in any contract of employment. Applying (again by way of example) similar reasoning, benefits under an occupational pension scheme fall within Article 141,[26] as do redundancy payments.[27]

(3) The breadth of scope of Article 141 has the effect that benefits that relate both to retirement and death following employment fall within its ambit. That, in turn, means that matters—such as different retirement ages —which might otherwise have been caught by restrictions (as, for example, horizontal direct effect)[28] in particular directives have been able to be addressed by the ECJ under Article 141 which has been held to be directly effective.[29] This means that, in practice, many disputes coming before the national courts will be disputes between employers and employees in a private (usually an employment) law context.

(4) Individuals may only use Article 141 to challenge discrimination which is attributable to a single source. So, where a private contractor re-employed former Council employees, the new employees of the private contractor failed in their Article 141 challenge to the differential as between their wages and the higher wages of those still employed by the Council.[30]

(5) 'Work' is also broadly interpreted. The Equal Pay Directive (Directive (EEC) 75/117) is complementary to Article 141 and was introduced to supplement the deficiencies in the old Article 119 which simply referred to 'equal pay for equal work'. The Equal Pay Directive made it clear that this included the 'same work' or 'work to which equal value

---

[24] See paras 18.32 and 18.57.

[25] Case 12/81 [1982] ECR 359.

[26] Case 262/88 *Barber v Guardian Royal Exchange Assurance Group* [1990] ECR I–8889. This ruling, which is not without controversy, demonstrates the breadth of scope of Art 141. The ECJ has not, however, applied its ruling retrospectively.

[27] Case C–167/99 *R v Secretary of State for Employment, ex p Seymour-Smith* [1999] ECR I–623.

[28] See paras 2.161 et seq.

[29] See Case 43/75 *Defrenne v SA Belge de Navigation Aerienne (SABENA) (No 2)* [1976] ECR 455.

[30] Case C–320/00 *Lawrence* [2002] ECR I–7325.

is attributed'. This is, in effect, enshrined in the (new) wording of Article 141 and challenges may be made under either Article 141 or the Equal Pay Directive.

(6) In *Macarthy's Ltd v Smith*[31] Advocate General Capotorti expressed the view that the expression 'same work' in the Equal Pay Directive did not necessarily mean *identical* work. Indeed, given the inclusion of work 'of equal value' into Article 141 (and the corresponding concept in the Equal Pay Directive) the precise meaning of 'same work' in the Equal Pay Directive may not matter.

(7) The concept of 'work of equal value' has given rise to some case law. However, the key principle espoused by the ECJ is that this is, essentially, a question to be addressed by the national court.[32] Guidance in the relevant principles that are relevant to avoiding discrimination in devising a job classification system based on physical strength or hardship involved was, however, given by the ECJ in *Rummler*.[33] There, the ECJ held that to avoid being in breach of the Equal Pay Directive (and, hence, now Article 141) it was necessary that:

(a) The system as a whole was not discriminatory. In particular, if certain criteria were going to favour one sex over the other then the system must take into account other criteria for which one sex had a particular aptitude, so that—taken as a whole—the system did not favour one sex over the other.

(b) The criteria used were objectively justified in that:
    (i) they were appropriate to the tasks being carried out;
    (ii) they corresponded to a genuine need of the undertaking.

F. The Equal Treatment Directive (Directive (EEC) 76/207) Prior to Amendment

18.29 Importantly, the Equal Treatment Directive (ETD) and Article 141 are entirely separate from each other. This is because Article 141 is directly concerned with inequality of pay whereas the ETD is concerned with inequality of working conditions (including access to employment and termination of employment[34]). It stems not from Article 141 but from Article 308 (ex 235) EC. Thus, discrimination challenges under the ETD may not be commenced under Article 141 and vice versa.

18.30 The distinct purpose of the ETD is set out in Article 1(1) as being:

> ... to put into effect in the Member States the principle of equal treatment for men and women as regards access to employment, including promotion, and to vocational training and as regards working conditions ...[35]

---

[31] Case 129/79 [1980] ECR 1275.

[32] See, eg, Case C–400/93 *Royal Copenhagen* [1995] ECR I–1275.

[33] Case 237/85 *Rummler v Dato-Druck* [1986] ECR 210.

[34] The expression 'working conditions' includes 'conditions governing dismissal' (ETD Article 5, now Article 3): see below.

[35] In the new ETD (Art 1) a new para 1(1)(a) has been added to the ETD whereby 'Member States shall actively take into account the objective of equality between men and women when formulating and implementing laws, regulations, administrative provisions, policies and activities in the areas referred to in paragraph 1'.

Application of the principle of equal treatment means, according to Article 2(1)[36] that: **18.31**

> there shall be no discrimination whatsoever on grounds of sex either directly or indirectly by reference in particular to marital or family status.

The main points to note about the ETD in its unamended form are these: **18.32**

(1) ETD (formerly) Articles 3(1) and 4(1) (now essentially restructured in Article 3 by the new ETD) covered, respectively, the right of non-discriminatory access (on grounds of sex) to employment and to vocational training. These provisions were, initially, construed restrictively but have been interpreted more generously in later cases.[37]

(2) ETD (formerly) Article 5(1) (now contained in Article 3 by the new ETD) applies the principle of equal treatment to men and women in relation to working conditions including the conditions governing dismissal. The term 'working conditions' has been interpreted broadly by the ECJ and has been held to extend to the entire 'working relationship' and not merely to conditions in a contract of employment.[38]

(3) The principal area in which Article 5(1) (now contained in new ETD Article 3) has been used in domestic cases has been discriminatory retirement ages in contracts of employment. This is because neither the Equal Pay Act 1970 nor the Sex Discrimination Act 1975 prevented discrimination as to the age at which men and women could retire. In consequence, men were only able to claim a pension from the age of 65 whereas women could claim it from the age of 60. So too, however, women could be compelled to retire earlier than men. In *Marshall*[39] the ECJ held, by way of preliminary ruling, on a domestic challenge brought by a female employee who had been forced to retire at 60 that different retirement ages for men and women was a breach of ETD Article 5(1). The result was the enactment of the Sex Discrimination Act 1986 which prohibited discrimination in the age of retirement as between men and women.

(4) There was specific provision for derogation from ETD in two instances:
    (a) activities for which the sex of the worker constitutes a determining factor (see Article 2(2) now substantially amended by Article 2(6) inserted by the new ETD — see below),[40] and
    (b) provisions concerning the protection of women, particularly as regards pregnancy and maternity (see (formerly) Article 2(3) now amended and expanded by Article 2(7) as inserted by the new ETD).[41]

---

[36] This remains in the same form and is not amended by the new ETD.

[37] cf Cases C–63 and 64/91 *Jackson and Cresswell v Chief Adjudication Officer* [1992] ECR I–4737 (loss of supplementary allowance and income support on taking up employment and vocational training fell outside Art 3(1) and 4(1)) with Case C–116/94 *Meyers v Adjudication Officer* [1995] ECR I–2131 (rules preventing claims for family credit fell within ETD Art 3(1)).

[38] *Meyers v Chief Adjudication Officer* [1995] ECR I–2131.

[39] Case 152/84 *Marshall v Southampton and South West Hampshire Area Health Authority* [1986] QB 401.

[40] The ECJ has interpreted Art 2(2) strictly. It is not a provision of general application but the context in which the activity takes place is relevant: see, eg, Case 222/84 *Johnston v Chief Constable of the Royal Ulster Constabulary* [1986] ECR 1651; Case C–273/97 *Sirdar v Secretary of State for Defence* [1999] ECR I–7403.

[41] This derogation provision has given rise to much case law but the essential point is that a provision concerning the protection of women (as, eg, giving maternity benefit) cannot be used to deny women access to employment. See *Johnston* (above) where the ECJ ruled that a policy of denying women the right to use firearms because it was considered to be dangerous did not fall within Art 2(3) because the result of the prohibition would be a denial of access to employment thus defeating the point of the exception in Art 2(3). See, also, paras 7.77–7.78.

(5) ETD Article 2(4) *permitted* positive action in the form of schemes 'to promote equal opportunity for men and women, in particular by removing existing inequalities which affect women's opportunities'. However, as an exception to the principle of equal treatment, this provision was, initially at least, interpreted somewhat restrictively by the ECJ. Thus, in *Kalanke*[42] a German law that stipulated that equally qualified women should be preferred to men in areas where women were under-represented was held to fall outside the scope of Article 2(4). This was said by the ECJ to be because Article 2(4) was not intended to give women 'absolute and unconditional priority'. However, Article 141(4) EC was introduced following *Kalanke* and was worded more strongly allowing 'measures providing for specific advantages in order to make it easier for the under-represented sex to pursue a vocational activity or to prevent or compensate for disadvantages in professional careers'. This change was foreshadowed by earlier cases on ETD Article 2(4) such as *Marshall*.[43] There, a similar German law to that in *Kalanke* contained a saving clause to the effect that, in similar circumstances to those prevailing in *Kalanke*, women should be given priority to men 'unless reasons specific to an individual male candidate tilt the balance in his favour'. The saving clause was sufficient, in the view of the ECJ, to bring the law within ETD Article 2(4).[44] As explained below, Article 2(4) has been amended in a new Article 2(8) inserted by the new ETD.

G. Equal Treatment in Matters of Social Security (Directive (EEC) 79/7)

18.33   The personal and material scope of Directive (EEC) 79/7 is very wide. As to personal scope, Article 2 provides that:

> This Directive shall apply to the working population —including self-employed persons, workers and self-employed persons whose activity is interrupted by illness, accident or involuntary employment and persons seeking employment —and to retired or invalided workers and self-employed persons.

18.34   This provision has, in its turn, been interpreted broadly. Thus, in *Drake v Chief Adjudication Officer*[45] the ECJ construed the notion of an activity 'interrupted by illness' as including the illness of a *third party (in casu* Mrs Drake's mother) which made it necessary for the claimant to give up work to look after her. In consequence it was held to be discriminatory to refuse invalid care allowance to a married woman but to allow it to a married man.

18.35   There are, however, limits to the engagement of Article 2. In particular, it does not apply to a person (such as an unpaid carer) who is not carrying on some economic activity[46] and it

---

[42] Case C–450/93 *Kalanke v Freie Hansestadt Bremen* [1995] ECR I–3051.

[43] Case C–409/95 *Marshall v Land Nordhrein-Westfalen* [1997] ECR I–6363.

[44] See, also, Case C–158/97 *Badeck* [2000] ECR I–1875. Much may depend upon whether a particular measure is proportionate: see Case–476/99 *Lommers* [2002] ECR I–2891.

[45] Case 150/85 [1986] ECR 1995.

[46] Case C–77/95 *Zuchner* [1996] ECR I–5689.

does not extend to a person who has not been forced to give up work by one of the activities expressly listed in the Article.[47]

As to the material scope of Directive (EEC) 79/7, Article 3(1) provides that the Directive **18.36** applies to:[48]

(a) statutory schemes which provide protection against sickness, invalidity, old age, accidents at work or occupational diseases, and unemployment; and,
(b) social assistance, insofar as it is intended to supplement and replace these schemes.

As with Article 2(1), Article 3(1) has been interpreted broadly albeit with clear limits. Thus, **18.37** in *Drake*[49] the ECJ held that Article 3 encompassed benefits that formed either the *whole* or merely a *part* of the relevant statutory scheme. The ECJ reached a similar conclusion in a judicial review challenge to the legality of UK regulations conferring exemptions from prescription charges which were discriminatory as being linked to different retirement ages.[50]

But in order to qualify under Article 3(1) the benefit in question must be 'directly and effec- **18.38** tively' linked to one or more of the Article 3(1) risks. This requirement was imposed by the ECJ in its preliminary ruling in another judicial review challenge, this time to a claimed right of equal treatment in relation to the payment of housing benefit. The ECJ held that since lack of housing was not mentioned as a risk in Article 3(1), it followed that housing benefit fell outside the scope of that provision.[51] By the same token, however, in *R v Secretary of State for the Home Department, ex p Taylor*[52] a successful judicial review challenge was made to the legality of the Social Fund Winter Fuel Payment Regulations under which a winter fuel payment was payable by reference to a discriminatory age of retirement. The relevant Article 3(1) risk was old age which is specifically referred to in Article 3(1).

The content of the principle of equal treatment in Directive (EEC) 79/7 is set out in Article **18.39** 4(1). This provides (materially) as follows:

> ... there shall be no discrimination whatsoever on ground of sex either directly, or indirectly by reference in particular to marital or family status, in particular as concerns:
> — the scope of [social security] schemes and the conditions of access thereto,
> — the obligation to contribute and the calculation of contributions,
> — the calculation of benefits including increases due in respect of a spouse and for dependants, and
> — the conditions governing the duration and retention of entitlement to benefits.

---

[47] Case 48/88 *Achterberg-te Riele* [1989] ECR 1963.
[48] Note that by Art 3(2) survivors' benefits and family benefits not granted by way of increases to the benefits covered by Directive (EEC) 79/7 are excluded.
[49] Case 150/85 [1986] ECR 1995.
[50] Case C–137/94 *R v Secretary of State for Health, ex p Richardson* [1995] ECR I–3407 where the relevant Art 3(1) risk was sickness.
[51] Case C–243/90 *R v Secretary of State for Social Services, ex p Smithson* [1992] ECR I–467.
[52] Case C–382/98 [1999] ECR I–549.

18.40   As explained above, *Drake*[53] exemplifies direct discrimination in the present context. This was because invalidity allowance was payable to a married man but not to a married woman.[54]

18.41   Identifying indirect discrimination poses more problems. A good example is afforded by the facts of *Teuling*.[55] There, an invalidity benefit was ostensibly non-discriminatory. However, the rules had a far greater impact on women than men so that fewer women were entitled to the benefit. The ECJ held that there was indirect discrimination although, on the facts of the case, there was objective justification.[56]

18.42   There is specific provision for derogation from Directive (EEC) 79/7 in Article 7(1). The most significant exemption is contained in Article 7(1)(a) which permits exclusion from equal treatment under the directive of 'the determination of pensionable age for the purposes of old-age and retirement pensions and possible consequences thereof for other benefits'.

18.43   As with all derogation provisions,[57] the ECJ has interpreted Article 7(1) restrictively. In *R v Secretary of State for Social Security, ex p Equal Opportunities Commission*,[58] the court—whilst by its preliminary ruling rejecting a domestic judicial review challenge directed to the application of Article 7(1)(a) to the then different pension eligibility ages—held that derogation under Article 7(1)(a) in respect of 'possible consequences thereof for other benefits' was limited to 'forms of discrimination existing under other benefit schemes which are necessarily and objectively linked to the difference in retirement age'. Such discrimination would only be necessary 'to avoid disrupting the complex financial equilibrium of the social security system or to ensure consistency between retirement pension schemes and other benefit schemes'.

18.44   These principles have been applied, with different results, in a number of cases. Article 7(1)(a) was invoked successfully in both *Hepple*[59] and *Graham*[60] where the requirement of a necessary and objective link was held to be met and where inconsistency would otherwise result. However, in many other cases, the requirements have not been met and derogation has not been permitted under Article 7(1).[61]

H. The Race and Framework Directives

The new approach to EC discrimination

18.45   It is important to bear in mind that both the Race Directive (Directive (EC) 2000/43) and the Framework Directive (Directive (EC) 2000/78) adopt a (common) new and expanded

---

[53] Case 150/85 [1986] ECR 1995, see para 18.34 above.

[54] Note that in Case C–423/04 *Richards v Secretary of State for Work and Pensions* The Times (5 May 2006) the ECJ held that it was discriminatory and therefore contrary to Directive (EEC) 79/7 to refuse to grant a pension to a male to female transsexual at the same age as a woman.

[55] Case 30/85 [1987] ECR 2497.

[56] For the relevant principles in respect of indirect discrimination, see paras 18.20–18.23.

[57] See, generally, para 2.111.

[58] Case C–9/91 [1992] ECR I–4297.

[59] Case C–196/98 [2000] ECR I–3701.

[60] Case C–92/94 *Secretary of State for Social Security v Graham [1995]* ECR 1–2521.

[61] See, especially, Case C–328/91 *Secretary of State for Social Security v Thomas* [1993] ECR I–1247; Case C–382/98 *R v Secretary of State for Social Security, ex p Taylor* [1999] ECR 1–8955.

approach to discrimination. That uniform approach has exceeded the more limited protection previously afforded to sex discrimination described above and has resulted in the new Equal Treatment Directive (Directive (EC) 2002/73) which adopts a similar model.

The new approach consists of the following main constituent elements: **18.46**

(1) There are definitions of direct and indirect discrimination.

(2) *Direct* discrimination is where 'one person is treated less favourably than another is, has been or would be treated in a comparable situation' on the ground or grounds specified in the relevant directive.[62]

(3) *Indirect* discrimination:

shall be taken to occur where an apparently neutral provision, criterion or practice would put[the affected person] at a particular disadvantage compared with other persons, unless that provision, criterion or practice is objectively justified by a legitimate aim and the means of achieving that aim are appropriate and necessary.[63]

(4) There is a new concept of 'harassment' as follows:

Harassment shall be deemed to be discrimination . . . when an unwanted conduct related to [the affected person] takes place with the purpose or effect of violating the dignity of a person and of creating an intimidating, hostile, degrading, humiliating or offensive environment. In this context, the concept of harassment may be defined in accordance with the national laws and practice of the Member States.[64]

(5) There is a new concept of 'instructions to discriminate'. An instruction to discriminate on one or more of the discrimination grounds specified in the relevant directive is deemed to be discrimination.[65]

(6) There is a new concept of 'victimization' in consequence of bringing a claim for discrimination.[66]

(7) A difference of treatment (derogation):

. . . which is based on a [relevant] characteristic . . . shall not constitute discrimination where, by reason of the nature of the particular occupational activities concerned or of the context in which they are carried out, such a characteristic constitutes a genuine and determining occupational requirement, provided that the objective is legitimate and the requirement is proportionate.[67]

(8) There is express provision for judicial remedies for breach of the directives.[68]

(9) There is provision for a reverse burden of proof once the affected person is able to establish facts from which it may be presumed that there has been discrimination under the directives. In that event, the burden of proof passes to the body against which discrimination is alleged to establish that discrimination has not occurred.[69]

---

[62] Article 2(2)(a) of each of the Directives.
[63] Article 2(2)(b) of each of the Directives.
[64] Article 2(3) of each of the Directives.
[65] Article 2(4) of each of the Directives.
[66] Race Directive, Art 9 and Framework Directive, Art 11.
[67] Article 4 of each of the Directives. The relevant characteristic is differently defined. In the Race Directive it is a characteristic 'related to racial or ethnic origin' whereas in the Framework Directive it is a characteristic related to any of the grounds referred to in Art 1 (for which see below).
[68] Race Directive, Art 7 and Framework Directive, Art 9.
[69] Race Directive, Art 8 and Framework Directive, Art 10.

(10) There is provision for publishing and promoting the principles of equal treatment under the directives to those likely to be affected.[70]

(11) Finally (albeit not new as an approach to discrimination protection),[71] the principle of equal treatment 'shall not prevent any Member State from maintaining or adopting specific measures to prevent or compensate for disadvantages' linked to the basis on which discrimination may arise under the Directives.[72]

Distinctive features of the Race Directive

18.47 Unlike the other directives considered in this section, the Race Directive is not confined to discrimination in employment though much of its protection concerns employment situations.

18.48 Article 1 provides that for the purposes of the Race Directive 'the principle of equal treatment shall mean that there shall be no direct or indirect discrimination based on racial or ethnic origin'. As explained above, definitions of what constitutes direct and indirect discrimination are provided in (respectively) Articles 2(2)(a) and 2(2)(b). The prohibition in the Race Directive to which these definitions apply is, as Article 1 makes clear, against such discrimination based on racial or ethnic origin. It is the concept of protection against discrimination based on racial or ethnic origin that underlies the concepts of harassment and victimization.[73]

18.49 The scope of the Race Directive is set out in Article 3(1) which provides that:

This Directive shall apply to all persons, as regards both the public and private sectors, including public bodies, in relation to:

(a) conditions for access to employment, to self-employment and to occupation, including selection criteria and recruitment conditions, whatever the branch of activity and at all levels of the professional hierarchy, including promotion;

(b) access to all types and to all levels of vocational guidance, vocational training, advanced vocational training and retraining, including practical work experience;

(c) employment and working conditions, including dismissals and pay;

(d) membership of and involvement in an organisation of workers or employers, or any organisation whose members carry on a particular profession, including the benefits provided for by such organisations;

(e) social protection, including social security and healthcare;

(f) social advantages;

(g) education;

(h) access to and supply of goods and services which are available to the public, including housing.

---

[70] See (respectively) Race Directive, Arts 10–11 and Framework Directive, Arts 12–13.
[71] See para 18.32.
[72] Race Directive, Art 5 and Framework Directive, Art 7(1).
[73] See para 18.46.

Distinctive features of the Framework Directive

Article 1 states the purpose of the Framework Directive which is: **18.50**

> to lay down a general framework for combating discrimination on the grounds of religion or belief, disability, age or sexual orientation as regards employment and occupation, with a view to putting into effect in the Member States the principle of equal treatment.

The scope of the Framework Directive is confined to employment and (see Article 3(1)) is **18.51**
similar in scope to that of the ETD. However, Article 3(3) provides that the Framework
Directive 'does not apply to payments of any kind made by state schemes or similar, including state social security or social protection schemes'.[74]

As with many directives, derogation is permitted, albeit on a limited basis and usually in **18.52**
respect of special categories. Thus, Article 3(4) provides that Member States may provide
that the Framework Directive shall not apply to the armed forces 'in so far as it relates to
discrimination on the grounds of disability and age'. Article 4(2) allows for derogation in
the form of differences of treatment 'based on a person's religion or belief ... where, by reason of the nature of these activities or of the context in which they are carried out, a person's
religion or belief constitute a genuine, legitimate and justified occupational requirement,
having regard to the organisation's ethos ...'. Article 6(1) provides a special derogation on
grounds of age if objectively and reasonably justified.

Finally, there is also a relatively wide derogation provision in Article 2(5). This states as **18.53**
follows:

> This Directive shall be without prejudice to measures laid down by national law which, in a
> democratic society, are necessary for public security, for the maintenance of public order and
> the prevention of criminal offences, for the protection of health and for the protection of the
> rights and freedoms of others.

Article 2(5) is, plainly, modelled on the European Convention on Human Rights but does **18.54**
not have a clear analogue in other directives which usually contain narrower derogation
provisions. However, some assistance may, probably, be gained from the case law on free
movement of goods, especially in relation to the public health exception.[75] It is also at least
possible that some of the cases on (for example) Article 8(2) of the ECHR may provide a
basis for arguing whether or not a particular derogation is proportionate.

I. The New Equal Treatment Directive (Directive (EC) 2002/73)

In the light of the Race and Framework Directives it is now easier to understand the amend- **18.55**
ments made by the new ETD to the ETD.

In essence, the new ETD: **18.56**

(1) inserts a number of new provisions into the ETD,

---

[74] Contrast Directive (EEC) 79/7 at paras 18.33 et seq.
[75] See, generally, Chapter 17.

(2) expands or amends some existing provisions, and

(3) deletes and/or restructures other provisions.

18.57   The main substantive amendments are these:

(1) There is, for the first time, a definition of direct and indirect discrimination (see the new Article 2(2)) modelled exactly on the definitions in the Race and Framework Directives with the ground/affected group being sex/one sex.[76]

(2) The new Article 2(3) provides (consistently with the Race and Framework Directives) that 'harassment' and 'sexual harassment' shall be deemed to be discrimination on the ground of sex and, accordingly, prohibited. Definitions of these terms are contained in the new Article 2(2) and these are, again, modelled on those in the Race and Framework Directives.[77]

(3) By the new Article 2(4) an instruction to discriminate against persons on grounds of sex is deemed to be discrimination under the ETD.

(4) As foreshadowed above, there is a new and expanded Article 2(6) which replaces the former Article 2(2) along lines familiar in the Race and Framework Directives. This provides as follows:

> Member States may provide, as regards access to employment including the training leading thereto, that a difference of treatment which is based on a characteristic related to sex[78] shall not constitute discrimination where, by reason of the nature of the particular occupational activities concerned or of the context in which they are carried out, such a characteristic constitutes a genuine and determining occupational requirement, provided that the objective is legitimate and the requirement is proportionate.

(5) Similarly, the new Article 2(7) which replaces the former Article 2(3) is much wider as well as reflecting some of the relevant ECJ jurisprudence.

(6) The new Article 2(8) (which replaces the former Article 2(4)) takes into account the new and stronger wording of Article 141(4) EC.[79] It provides

> Member States may maintain or adopt measures within the meaning of Article 141(4) of the Treaty with a view to ensuring full equality in practice between men and women.

J. The National Courts' Approach to EC Discrimination

18.58   As can be seen from this outline of the EC discrimination provisions and the case law that they have generated, discrimination issues raising public law points may as easily arise before an Employment (or other) tribunal as before the Administrative Court. If they do, the tribunal is usually mandated to apply EC law in the same way as the Administrative Court applying the same principles and similar remedies (including disapplication of offending primary legislation where necessary). Many of the ECJ discrimination cases from the UK resulting in preliminary rulings under Article 234 started off as claims before an Employment Tribunal rather than originating as applications for judicial review.

---

[76] See para 18.46.
[77] See para 18.46.
[78] The expression 'characteristic related to sex' is wider than 'sex' which appeared in the former Art 2(2).
[79] See para 18.28.

It will be apparent from the chapters on general principles that there is cross-fertilization   **18.59**
between general EC principles (not confined to the principle of equal treatment) and discrimination issues. For example, issues may arise as to the EC general principle of effectiveness in a discrimination context before the domestic court.[80]

Thus, in *Holc-Gale v Makers UK Ltd*[81] a question arose as to the jurisdiction of an Employment   **18.60**
Tribunal to hear an equal pay complaint in the absence of compliance with the statutory
grievance procedure under s 32(2) of the Employment Act 2002. The Employment Appeal
Tribunal dismissed the appellant's appeal against the declining of jurisdiction by the
Employment Tribunal holding, amongst other things, that the Equal Pay Directive did not
prevent Member States from imposing procedural requirements as to access to the judicial
process under which equal pay claims were determined. Nor did such requirements breach
the EC general principle of effectiveness.

Consistently with the principles set out in earlier chapters[82] when interpreting a domestic   **18.61**
statute that falls within the scope of EC discrimination law, the national court is bound to
construe the statute so far as is possible compatibly with EC law. In the context of discrimination, this is exemplified by the House of Lords' decision in *A v Chief Constable of West
Yorkshire Police*.[83]

The issue there was whether it was lawful for the Chief Constable to invoke the Sex   **18.62**
Discrimination Act 1975, s 7 so as to be able to discriminate against the respondent in
refusing to offer her employment. The respondent was a post-operative male-to-female
transsexual. Her application to join the police force was rejected on the basis that she would
not be able to perform the duties required of a constable. This was argued by the Chief
Constable to be a genuine occupational qualification under s 7. The House of Lords ruled
in favour of the respondent (upholding the decision of the Court of Appeal) on the basis of
EC law. It held that for domestic law to reflect the ETD the words 'woman', 'man' and 'men'
in the 1975 Act had to be read as referring to the acquired gender of a post-operative transsexual.

As the outline of the cases suggests, in general terms the approach of the ECJ (and, hence,   **18.63**
the approach required on the part of the national courts) to particular EC discrimination
issues is broad and has broadened rather than narrowed over the years.

Finally, although discrimination under Article 14 ECHR is narrower (being confined to   **18.64**
precluding discrimination *in the enjoyment of Convention rights*) than the EC general principle of discrimination,[84] there are some similarities of approach between the approach of
the Strasbourg Court to discrimination on grounds such as gender and race and that
afforded by EC law on such grounds.

---

[80] See also paras 7.28 et seq.
[81] [2006] ICR 462.
[82] See, especially, paras 2.99 et seq.
[83] [2005] 1 AC 51.
[84] See paras 7.112–7.127.

18.65 As Lord Hoffmann put it in *R (Carson) v Secretary of State for Work and Pensions:*[85]

> Whether cases are sufficiently different is partly a matter of values and partly a question of rationality. Article 14 expresses the Enlightenment value that every human being is entitled to equal respect and to be treated as an end and not a means. Characteristics such as race, caste, noble birth, membership of a political party and (here a change in values since the Enlightenment) gender, are seldom, if ever, acceptable grounds for differences in treatment. In some constitutions, the prohibition on discrimination is confined to grounds of this kind and I rather suspect that article 14 was also intended to be so limited. But the Strasbourg court has given it a wide interpretation, approaching that of the 14th Amendment, and it is therefore necessary, as in the United States, to distinguish between those grounds of discrimination which prima facie appear to offend our notions of the respect due to the individual and those which merely require some rational justification: *Massachusetts Board of Retirement v Murgia (1976) 438 US 285.*
>
> There are two important consequences of making this distinction. First, discrimination in the first category cannot be justified merely on utilitarian grounds, eg that it is rational to prefer to employ men rather than women because more women than men give up employment to look after children. That offends the notion that everyone is entitled to be treated as an individual and not a statistical unit. On the other hand, differences in treatment in the second category (eg on grounds of ability, education, wealth, occupation) usually depend upon considerations of the general public interest. Secondly, while the courts, as guardians of the right of the individual to equal respect, will carefully examine the reasons offered for any discrimination in the first category, decisions about the general public interest which underpin differences in treatment in the second category are very much a matter for the democratically elected branches of government.

18.66 That emphasis mirrors the substantive protection afforded by EC law to particular vulnerable categories as discussed above.

---

[85] [2005] UKHL 37, [2005] 2 WLR 1369, paras 15 and 16. For a useful critique of Lord Hoffmann's approach, see A Baker, 'Comparison Tainted by Justification: Against a "Compendious Question" in Article 14 Discrimination' [2006] PL 476.

19

PUBLIC LAW COLLATERAL CHALLENGES AND ARTICLE 234 REFERENCES

A. Public Law Collateral Challenges

EC public law issues often arise in the course of proceedings outside domestic judicial **19.01**
review in the Administrative Court or other public law proceedings. As explained in the
context of damages claims involving allegations of State liability for breaches of EC law,[1]
although a challenge to the validity of a legislative or administrative act might have been
brought *directly* by way of judicial review, there is no general jurisdictional bar preventing
an EC (or any other public law) challenge to such act being raised *indirectly* in the course of
other court proceedings.[2]

Indirect challenges of this nature are often referred to as collateral challenges[3] as opposed **19.02**
to the direct challenge that would be involved in proceedings for judicial review or other

---

[1] See paras 5.172–5.183 above.

[2] EC law, of course, also raises numerous issues in the course of *private* law proceedings. This is not the
same as collateral challenge as understood in the public law context but it can raise similar issues as, eg,
whether Art 81 EC can be used as a shield as well as a sword in a trade mark dispute between private parties:
Sportswear SpA v Stonestyle Ltd [2006] EWCA Civ 380.

[3] For a recent example see *Dwr Cymru Cyfyngedig (Welsh Water) v Corus UK Ltd and Director-General of Water
Services* [2006] EWHC 1183 (Ch) (*held*: it was not an abuse of process for the defendant in private law proceedings brought by the claimant water undertaker for payment of outstanding water supply charges to mount a public law challenge to the validity of the water supply charges scheme fixed by the water undertaker).

public law form of direct challenge.[4] Nonetheless, the issues that arise in such challenges are identical to those that could have been raised in judicial review proceedings.

19.03 Collateral challenges in this sense should be distinguished from a different form of indirect challenge that takes place in the course of some Administrative Court proceedings. As addressed elsewhere[5] a situation may arise where the validity of an *EC* measure is challenged. This can only be achieved by indirect rather than by direct challenge because only the ECJ can declare an EC measure to be invalid. This situation will most commonly arise where the validity of a domestic legislative or administrative act is challenged (whether directly or indirectly) but where, in turn, the validity of that legislative or administrative act is itself dependent for its validity on the validity of an EC measure. In such circumstances judicial review proceedings will themselves constitute a form of indirect challenge because—whatever the nature of the proceedings in question—the domestic court will, in practice, have to refer the question of validity to the ECJ under Article 234 (ex 177) EC. However, that is not the same as the expression collateral challenge as commonly understood.

19.04 It is useful to distinguish between the different types of true collateral challenge that may be brought.

19.05 The most common forms of collateral challenge involving potential EC public law issues are those where:

(1) A claimant brings a private law claim for damages against a public authority. An EC collateral challenge by the claimant may arise in respect of the contended illegality of a legislative or administrative act including the case where the public authority relies on purported compliance with EC law by reference (for example) to primary or subordinate legislation said to be required by, or to be consistent with, EC law. It may, depending on the circumstances, be an abuse of process for the claimant not to have commenced proceedings by way of judicial review as opposed to bringing a private law claim (or, more usually, to have brought the claim long after the normal time limit for judicial review proceedings) but that will depend upon the entirety of the facts.[6] However, if the claim sounds in domestic law and the EC issue arises in the course of seeking to rebut an EC defence advanced by the defendant public body, the claimant would, almost inevitably, be permitted to argue the EC issue in the course of the private law proceedings. Even if the claim could have been brought by way of judicial review rather than by a private law action, the fundamental question is whether or not bringing it outside judicial review constitutes an abuse of process.[7]

---

[4] As, eg, a statutory appeal or statutory review procedure. See, generally, R Gordon, *Judicial Review and Crown Office Proceedings* (1999).

[5] See, eg, paras 5.57–5.60.

[6] In any event, the modern tendency is not to decline to hear the claim but, rather, to take into account the special features of the judicial review jurisdiction so that a claimant may not always be able to rely on the normal limitation periods. As to this, see para 1.102.

[7] *Mercury Communications Ltd v Director-General of Telecommunications* [1996] 1 WLR 48, 57.

(2) A defendant defends a claim brought by a public authority on, amongst other grounds, a breach by that public body of EC law. Here, the defendant will be permitted to advance any EC law defences (including public law points) that may be available.[8]

(3) A defendant to a criminal prosecution may usually, even as a matter of domestic administrative law, raise a defence involving an indirect challenge to the validity of a legislative or administrative act.[9] Such defence may well involve arguments to the effect that the act in question violates EC law either directly or because the underlying EC legislation is invalid.[10] It may involve an indirect challenge to primary and/or subordinate legislation governing the substantive content of the prosecution or it may involve the contention that the decision to prosecute and/or maintenance of the prosecution is itself an abuse of process as violating EC law (including the general principles of EC law).[11] There is no abuse of process involved in raising a defence of this nature[12] and, indeed, where a criminal prosecution has been brought it is more likely than not that a court would decline to entertain an application for judicial review leaving the points in issue to be ventilated in the trial process.[13]

(4) A convicted person wishes to advance arguments as to why a particular penalty, ostensibly allowed by law, is contrary to EC law,[14] or why consequential action following conviction such as a recommendation for deportation[15] is contrary to EC law. Defences or arguments of this nature are always available to a defendant in or following criminal proceedings.

In all the above instances, if a claimant or defendant succeeds in establishing a breach of EC law in a private (or criminal) law forum, the remedies available are—for the most part—very similar and were discussed in Chapter 5.[16] They are of potentially wide ambit and,   **19.06**

---

[8] See, eg, *Wandsworth London Borough Council v Winder* [1985] AC 461.

[9] See, eg, *R v Reading Crown Court, ex p Hutchinson* [1988] Q B 384; *Boddington v British Transport Police* [1998] 2 WLR 639.

[10] See, eg Case 121/85 *Conegate* [1986] ECR 1007; *R v Bossom* [2006] EWCA Crim 1489. Similarly, a collateral challenge may be made on EC grounds to exercise of particular powers by the court itself. See, eg, *R v Crown Court at Harrow, ex p UNIC Centre Sarl* [2000] 1 WLR 2112 (judicial review of Crown Court preliminary ruling on appeal against the making of a forfeiture order by the magistrates).

[11] The position in EC law should, here, be contrasted with a defence involving a fundamental rights challenge to primary legislation under the HRA where the jurisdiction to grant relief—a declaration of incompatibility—is not conferred on (eg) a magistrates' court and where it is, therefore, at least questionable whether the magistrate has jurisdiction to determine (see: *R (Paul Rackham Ltd) v Swaffham Magistrates' Court* [2004] EWHC 1417). In an EC collateral challenge no such difficulty arises because all courts have the power and duty to disapply EC incompatible primary legislation: see paras 2.60–2.67.

[12] It is, in fact, entirely consistent with the EC general principle of effectiveness discussed above and with the provisions of the EC Treaty whereby under Art 241 (ex 184) EC a plea of illegality may be raised outside the strict two-month time limit for bringing direct actions.

[13] See *R (Paul Rackham Ltd) v Swaffham Magistrates' Court* [2004] EWHC 1417.

[14] See, eg Case 63/83 *R v Kirk* [1984] ECR 2689 (illegality of retroactive penalty). This case is also referred to at paras 9.16 and 9.51–9.52. EC law is strict in its application of the general principle of legality and looks solely to national law as the determinant of penalty. Thus, a directive cannot, of itself, determine penalty and if national law is defective in implementing the requirement of a penalty the national court cannot correct the deficiency. Of the many cases see, eg, Case C–168/95 *Arcaro* [1996] ECR I–4705, para 36. See also paras 11.56–11.63.

[15] See, eg, Case 30/77 *Bouchereau* [1977] ECR 1999.

[16] Save that a private law or inferior court does not have the same power as the Administrative Court to quash administrative decisions or secondary legislation.

in certain cases, somewhat wider than in domestic (including HRA) law. In addition, the court hearing argument on the public law issue may also make a reference to the ECJ under Article 234 EC on identical principles to those discussed in Chapter 4.

B. Article 234 References—Two National Court EC Public Law Case Analyses

Introduction

19.07   The preliminary ruling procedure under Article 234 (ex 177) EC, considered in detail in Chapter 4, is the sole procedural point of contact between EC and domestic courts. For that reason it is of considerable practical importance in any examination of EC judicial review in the Administrative Court. In contrast to the general principles relating to requests for preliminary rulings discussed in Chapter 4 this section addresses the questions that will be encountered in practice in relation to whether to seek—and (if so) the prospects of obtaining—a reference in practice.

19.08   The tactical considerations that inform whether a reference is sought are not co-extensive with the questions of principle that a court will be referred to in exercising its discretion at different stages as to whether to order a reference. Nonetheless, there is an important overlap. Those questions of principle have already been analysed.[17]

19.09   Just as the Administrative Court may have to consider whether it exercises discretion to order a reference, so practitioners acting in EC judicial review challenges should consider—from the outset—whether to seek one. There are two aspects to this. The first is the *desirability* of seeking a reference. The second is the *feasibility* of seeking a reference. It is at the second stage (feasibility) that the principles examined in Chapter 4 should be addressed. In that context the first and most obvious question is whether the conditions necessary for a reference have been satisfied. The second question is to examine whether or not the stage has been reached where the court is likely to exercise its discretion.

19.10   However, even if a reference is feasible that does not mean, at least from the practitioner's point of view, that one *should* be sought. Importantly, suggesting a reference at too early a stage runs the risk that it will be perceived by the court as signalling that the case is not particularly strong since, if it was, there would be no need for a reference.

19.11   To avoid this danger, it is sometimes a feature of advocacy in the Administrative Court in an EC case for neither side to request a reference but to indicate by way of default submission that if the court does not accept the case being advanced there should be a reference because it is not, in any event, clear that the EC argument being advanced is wrong. However, the disadvantage of this approach is that it signals a different vulnerability, namely that an Article 234 reference is being raised as a forensic ploy rather than as a serious option for the court to adopt.

---

[17] See paras 4.67–4.98.

There is no automatic answer to the question of whether (and if so when) a reference should **19.12** be sought. Occasionally, as in the *Merck* case considered below, it may be desirable to seek a reference at the earliest possible stage *and* to accept that without a reference the Administrative Court is unlikely to grant the application for judicial review. It is, in any event, generally more sensible to seek a reference in a weaker case where without the reference the Administrative Court is likely to reject the EC argument being advanced. This is especially so where the ECJ has already pronounced on similar issues.

In a stronger case there may be competing considerations. A firm judgment at first instance **19.13** from the Administrative Court (that is without a reference) provides a useful basis for a later reference (even if the reference was always likely to occur) because the ECJ will have before it judicial endorsement of the case being advanced. That was the position in *Watts* (see below). However, waiting in the expectation that the Court of Appeal will refer will delay matters (and increase costs) in the case of an inevitable reference. Further, and paradoxically, it is not always the case that the Court of Appeal is more likely to refer to the ECJ than an Administrative Court judge. Much can depend on the individual judge.

In terms of *obtaining* a reference, two practice areas are examined below, each of which **19.14** have involved ECJ judgments raising similar issues in the past to those then under consideration by the Administrative Court. These practice areas are addressed in some detail because although it is likely to prove more difficult to secure an Article 234 reference in such cases, the Administrative (or appellate) Court—at least where complex EC law issues are raised—is often prepared to refer cases for an ECJ preliminary ruling under Article 234 (ex 177) EC despite the fact that the same issue or very similar issues have already been addressed by the ECJ.

This may be for different reasons. In the pharmaceutical case law examined below the issues **19.15** were highly technical and depended on detailed interpretation of the relevant directive. It is often relatively easy in practice in such cases to develop complicated submissions seeking to differentiate the factual position before the Administrative Court to those in earlier cases.

In the Article 49 case law (freedom to provide services) on the other hand, the ECJ had— **19.16** in earlier cases—pronounced quite clearly on the applicability of Article 49 to the English NHS. There was no scope for contending that it had not. Despite that, however, because the impact of EC restrictions on prioritization within the NHS would be considerable, the Court of Appeal felt it necessary in the *Watts* case to refer the case before it to the ECJ so that the ECJ could consider on specific facts involving the NHS (rather than, as it had before, by extending its reasoning to the NHS in cases that were concerned with different health systems in other Member States).

Obtaining a reference (1)—The pharmaceutical context: commercial competition between innovators and generic producers

Most of the EC pharmaceuticals cases that have come before the Administrative Court **19.17** have been in the field of licensing (otherwise known as pharmaceutical marketing authorization). The issues raised have usually involved the interpretation of the relevant directives and their application by the national licensing authority. Because these issues have become complex there has been an increasing tendency for the Administrative Court (or Court of Appeal) to refer issues of law for a preliminary ruling by the ECJ under Article 234 (ex 177) EC.

19.18 The EC provisions regarding marketing authorization of pharmaceutical cases that have been considered by the Administrative Court in most of the judicial review cases are contained in Directive (EC) 2001/83 (and its predecessors) ('the 2001 Directive'). This codified a number of earlier directives to materially identical effect, most materially its immediate predecessor Council Directive (EEC) 65/65. Subsequent to the case law discussed below, the 2001 Directive has, in part at least, been materially amended (as from 30 October 2005) by Directive (EC) 2004/27 (generally in line with the outcome of the cases discussed below).

19.19 However, whilst future cases are unlikely to raise exactly the same issues, the way in which the Administrative Court has addressed EC pharmaceutical judicial review challenges in the past in the context of commercial competition between rival producers is unlikely to change in substance given the complexity of the law. The legal context and analysis of the cases below is followed by an evaluation of the Administrative Court's general approach.

19.20 The 2001 Directive required an applicant for marketing authorization to supply a full set of data in order to show the safety and efficacy of the product. But in certain circumstances, the 2001 Directive relieved an applicant of the obligation to supply certain data and permits it to refer to data submitted in respect of a previously authorized product. The procedure for such an application was known as 'the abridged procedure'. Where authorization was sought for a product which was not essentially similar to one which has been authorized for 10 years but differed only in particular respects, namely one or more respects set out in what was called the 'proviso' to the unamended Article 10 of the 2001 Directive (materially, different therapeutic use, different route of administration, or different dose) an applicant could rely upon the original data and submit additional 'bridging' data to cover the respects in which there was a difference between two otherwise similar products. The procedure for such an application was known as 'the hybrid abridged procedure'.

19.21 Disputes have most commonly arisen between commercial competitors over whether the research data used by the innovator drug company (ie the original drug manufacturer who holds a marketing authorization for the product that it has developed (product A))[18] can be utilized by subsequent manufacturers with variant products (often called generic companies).

19.22 Under the 2001 Directive, the abridged (fast-track) procedure referred to above was for 'essentially similar' products by which generic companies in particular could take advantage of the data of the innovator when applying for marketing authorization in certain circumstances including—in respect of such products—where there had been market

---

[18] In what follows—and to make a complicated subject easier to follow—product A means the innovator's product. Product B means a 'line extension' or development of product A by the innovator. Product C means the development of a product by a generic producer with similarities to product A and/or product B.

authorization for more than 10 years preceding the making of the application for generic authorization. In that way, the innovator's data received reasonable protection but, once the protective time limit had expired, there did not have to be endless repeat applications with new data having to be researched when the authority already has the data.

Innovators are and were naturally concerned to protect their data from commercial competition. For that reason they have consistently sought to argue that the so-called abridged (fast-track) procedure and the hybrid abridged procedure are limited in their ambit as far as their use by generic producers is concerned. Generic producers on the other hand are keen to utilize these procedures and have been able successfully to argue for a broad interpretation of both. **19.23**

There have been four significant cases centring on these particular issues to date all of which started off as domestic judicial review challenges before the Administrative Court and three of which were referred to the ECJ under Article 234 (ex 177) EC. The cases are: **19.24**

(1) *R v Medicines Controls Agency, ex p Generics (UK) Ltd* (hereafter 'Generics').[19]
(2) *R (Novartis Pharmaceuticals UK Ltd) v Licensing Authority* (hereafter 'Novartis').[20]
(3) *R (Approved Prescription Services Ltd) v Licensing Authority* (hereafter 'APS').[21]
(4) *R (Merck Sharp and Dohme Ltd) v Licensing Authority* (hereafter 'Merck').[22]

What, amongst other things, these cases illustrate is the way in which the ECJ rarely lays down clear statements of principle in this area when cases are referred to it under Article 234 and how that opaqueness is sometimes responsible for further cases being referred by the Administrative Court on similar but minutely distinguishable issues of law. During the time that it takes for the reference to be determined there may be competitive advantages in bringing a challenge even if it is ultimately unsuccessful and even if—as here—no interim relief is granted during the period of the reference. **19.25**

Generics

Generics consisted of three sets of judicial review proceedings concerning the refusal of marketing authorization of generic products to the claimant Generics (UK) Ltd. Each of the cases before the Administrative Court involved innovator products for which original marketing authorizations had been granted by the licensing authority (then the Medicines Controls Agency) more than 10 years prior to the generic application for authorization (product A). Subsequent authorizations had, however, been granted to the innovator for developments of their products which included changes in therapeutic indications, doses, dosage form, dosage schedules, and routes of administration (product B). These different indications had been authorized for less than 10 years. **19.26**

The generic companies sought marketing authorizations for products essentially similar to product A, not only for the therapeutic indications authorized for A but for all the **19.27**

---

[19] Case C–368/96 [1998] ECR I–7967.
[20] Case C–106/01 [2005] All ER (EC) 192.
[21] Case C–36/03 (judgment 9 December 2004).
[22] [2005] EWHC 710.

therapeutic indications previously authorized. They sought such authorization without offering any additional data. The innovator companies contended that the data upon which they had relied to gain authorizations for the additional therapeutic uses (product B) were entitled to protection for an additional 10-year period and could not be relied upon whether by the competent authority or the generic companies.

19.28   Although the Administrative Court referred the case to the ECJ for a preliminary ruling, it did not grant interim relief. The ECJ ruled, disagreeing with the Advocate General, that provided that the generic companies' products were essentially similar to product A they should be authorized for all the therapeutic uses previously authorized without the need for reliance on any additional data.

19.29   The ECJ also ruled on the interpretation of 'essential similarity' albeit in a highly specific fashion. It held that a medicinal product for which authorization was sought could be considered to be essentially similar to an original product (product A) where it had the same qualitative and quantitative composition in terms of active principles and the same pharmaceutical form and, where necessary, bioequivalence of the two products had been established by appropriate bioavailability studies. However, a medicinal product for which authorization was sought would not be considered to be 'essentially similar' to an original product where it differed significantly from the original product as regards safety or efficacy.

19.30   In effect, *Generics* decided that the scope for generic authorization of developments to innovator products was limited to cases where the developments did not affect the essential similarity of the products. In *Generics*, at least, the need for essential similarity to be demonstrated between products A and C was not in issue. That became the battleground in *Novartis*.

Novartis

19.31   In *Novartis* a slightly different issue arose. The decision in *Generics* had left open the question of whether an applicant for marketing authorization could rely upon data supplied by an innovator where the generic product C was essentially similar to a development of the original product (product B) but was not essentially similar to product A. If it could then, at least depending on the degree of relevant difference between products A and C, generic companies could gain the benefit of the hybrid abridged procedure (see above). Put simply, they could still largely rely on the innovator's data.

19.32   Novartis had obtained marketing authorization for its product A Sandimmun (cyclosporine) in 1983. In 1995 it obtained authorization under the hybrid abridged procedure for a new cyclosporine product called Neoral (product B). It was agreed that Neoral and Sandimmun were not bioequivalent. The question was whether, using the hybrid abridged procedure, the generic companies' product SangCya (product C) which was not bioequivalent to Sandimmun (product A) but claimed bioequivalence to Neoral (product B) could be authorized in 1999 using not only clinical data from Sandimmun, but also bridging data for Neoral.

19.33   Again, the Administrative Court referred the case to the ECJ. The ECJ gave further guidance on *Generics*. The court upheld the submission of the Licensing Authority that the proviso may be relied upon in order to make a hybrid abridged application where a product for which authorization is sought is *not* essentially similar to the original product A and noted that the new product (product C) may differ from the original product and fall short of essential similarity in one or more respects identified in the proviso.

The ECJ also held, *inter alia*, that in assessing an application for a marketing authorization **19.34** of a generic product which is essentially similar to a 'line extension' product (that is, a development of an original product) the Licensing Authority could rely upon (and, therefore, a generic producer for a marketing authorization need not provide) data supplied by an innovator company in support of its marketing for a marketing authorization for the line extension without the need to accord that data a separate 10 year period of protection.

Thus, *Novartis* extended *Generics* to allow direct cross-referral of data in respect of generic **19.35** product C to the data supplied by the innovator in respect of developed product B, even where product C was *not* essentially similar to product A but on the condition that the developments were either expressly within the proviso or implicitly within the proviso Bioequivalence was held to be implicitly within the proviso.[23]

Although the detail of the legal arguments are quite complex, it can be seen that the com- **19.36** bined effect of *Generics* and *Novartis* was to make it much easier for generic competitors to apply for marketing authorization for their products even in circumstances where their product (product C) was not essentially similar to the original innovator product (product A). The question was where—if at all—the ECJ would draw the line in terms of requiring similarity between products C and A or whether, for practical purposes, the only protection accorded to an innovator's data would be the original 10-year period for its initial product with no protection being given to data relating to developments of the subsequent product by the innovator. This was the underlying issue in the two remaining cases *APS* and *Merck*.

APS

The only distinction between *APS* and *Novartis* was that the difference between product B **19.37** and product A was not in bioavailability but, rather, in pharmaceutical form. Prozac capsules (product A) based on the active ingredient fluoxetine, were first authorized in the EU in 1988. Prozac liquid (product B) was subsequently authorized in October 1992 under the hybrid abridged procedure pursuant to the proviso. In 1999 a generic company, APS, sought authorization for a generic liquid containing the active ingredient fluoxetine under the abridged procedure (product C) using Prozac capsules as a reference product but also seeking to rely on the clinical data in relation to Prozac liquid.

Once again, the Administrative Court made a reference to the ECJ. The ECJ simply **19.38** applied its reasoning in *Novartis* to a change in pharmaceutical form which it held to be implicit within the proviso.[24]

---

[23] This was said to be because changes in the route of administration and dose (expressly within the proviso) would generally involve a difference in bioequivalence.

[24] This was said to be because a change in the route of administration (expressly within the proviso) would generally entail a change of pharmaceutical form.

Merck

19.39   In *Merck*, the claimant innovator sought judicial review of a decision of the defendant licensing authority to allow the interested parties generic companies to submit marketing authorization applications for a pharmaceutical product (product C) relying on the data submitted by the innovator for its pharmaceutical products (products A and B). Products A and B—themselves not essentially similar to each other—were medicinal products of differing dose schedules used to treat osteporosis. Product A had been authorized for more than 10 years. Product B was a 'line extension' of product A and had been authorized for less than 10 years. Product C was a copy of product B.

19.40   The claimant (Merck Sharp) contended that the authority was wrong to allow generic applications to be made in reliance on data submitted by it in respect of product B because product C—though essentially similar to product B—was not essentially similar to product A. It is clear that this argument had surfaced in both *Novartis* and in *APS*.

19.41   However, amongst its other arguments, Merck Sharp advanced two particular submissions on the facts. First, it contended that the ECJ had not in the other cases addressed *multiple* differences in determining entitlement to use the hybrid abridged procedure. Here, there were differences between products A and B (and hence between products C and A) both in the strength of the dose *and* in bioavailability (rate of absorption). Secondly, it argued that there was a difference in posology (dosage schedules) which had not been the subject of either previous relevant decision and which, as it was submitted, was neither expressly nor implicitly within the proviso.

19.42   Merck Sharp also advanced a more fundamental submission to the effect that both *Novartis* and *APS* were wrongly decided and that the court had not in those cases addressed the prior issue of whether there was any statutory route provided by the directive for the grant of a marketing authorization for product C that lacked essential similarity to the innovator's product A. Merck Sharp submitted that the ECJ had simply accepted the existence of such a route without questioning it.

19.43   These arguments were rejected. On this occasion the judge (Moses J) did not make a reference under Article 234 (ex 177) EC despite being invited to do so by the claimant. He accepted the submission of the defendant authority and interested parties that the matter had already been decided in the three earlier decisions of the ECJ referred to above. He held that product B was clearly a line extension of product A and still fell within the proviso even though its dosage schedule was different (being taken once weekly). The scope of the proviso determined the right to cross-referral of data and there was no distinction to be drawn between the right of the competent authority and the right of an applicant for marketing authorization so to cross-refer. On a plain reading of *Novartis* and as a matter of principle, the fact that product B differed in more than one respect to product A did not take it outside the proviso.

19.44   Importantly, the judge held that although the ECJ had not addressed each specific argument that arose on the facts of the present case, it was for the ECJ to interpret Treaty provisions and the relevant principles by which the Treaty should be interpreted. The instant case did not raise any new issue of principle and a reference to the ECJ was not necessary.

The ECJ had not overlooked the difficulties exposed by the wording of the 2001 Directive but had interpreted the relevant provision in a manner designed to achieve the objectives of the 2001 Directive.

Evaluating the EC pharmaceutical cases

The pharmaceutical decisions discussed above illustrate both how commercial competition drives the cases and also how relatively easy it is to obtain a reference under Article 234 (ex 177) EC in an area bedevilled by technical definitions and procedures of sometimes bewildering complexity.   **19.45**

As Moses J observed in the first paragraph of his judgment in *Merck:*   **19.46**

> This is the fourth round in the contest between those who hold marketing authorizations for medicinal products which they have developed, known as innovators, and those who, in applying for marketing authorization for their own medicinal products, seek to rely upon the data already provided by the innovator . . .

In some areas of EC law a single preliminary ruling may decide the issue. But this is rarely so in a commercial context where seemingly endless distinctions can be sought to be made between the facts of one case and the facts of another. True it is that after *Generics* there was some scope for debate as to whether product C had to be essentially similar to product A but this doubt was removed in *Novartis*. In *APS* the claimants sought to draw factual differences between their situation and that in *Novartis*. By the time of the application for judicial review in *Merck*, however, further distinctions were becoming more difficult to contend for. The only logical course was to contend, as Moses J recorded at para 32, that the ECJ's judgment (admittedly elliptical) meant something different from what it appeared to or that it was wrong: **19.47**

> *Novartis* is of significance in the instant case not least because it is said that the wording of the Court's judgment fully disposes of MSD's application. Apart from the wording, it is argued that the reasoning of both the Court and Advocate General Jacobs, whose conclusion was accepted by the Court, apply a principle which concludes the matter against MSD. It is the controversy as to whether that is a fair reading or, alternatively. Whether the Court in *Novartis* was wrong, which founds the submissions advanced by MSD.

In the event the question for the Administrative Court must be whether or not the ECJ has articulated the relevant principles sufficiently clearly to be applied confidently to the facts of the particular case before the court. In *Merck* it was held that this had been done. In reaching that conclusion, however, it was necessary for Moses J to examine with some care not only the reasoning of the ECJ itself but also that of the Advocates General in a number of the earlier cases. However, in the earlier cases the Administrative Court presumably concluded that the relevant principles had not been clearly enunciated and made a reference to the ECJ on each occasion. Interestingly, it did not decline to do so as a matter of discretion as it might, perhaps, have done leaving it to the Court of Appeal (or, ultimately, House of Lords) to do so.   **19.48**

Where, as in the pharmaceutical cases, the issue before the court lies in elaborate analysis of what the ECJ has meant in its previous judgments, it is submitted that interim relief will usually be more difficult to obtain. Certainly, that was the position in the four decisions analysed above. A claimant may—as in three of the cases—be given the benefit of any   **19.49** doubt and an early reference made to avoid any lingering doubt. The existence of the doubt itself may, however, be commercially helpful in at least some cases to those seeking to persuade the Administrative Court to refer since the existence of pending ECJ litigation may persuade either a generic claimant or the licensing authority to await the ECJ's ruling.[25] These are all considerations which those advising clients in a commercial context of the kind described here (or any complex EC field) will need to consider.

19.50   In general, judicial review challenges in EC pharmaceutical cases have, thus far, not usually resulted in a successful outcome for claimants, certainly before the Administrative Court if a reference is not ordered. Two other examples raising different issues to those addressed above illustrate the point.

19.51   In *R (Association of Pharmaceutical Importers and Dowelhurst Ltd) v Secretary of State for Health*[26] the claimants objected to the operation of the 1999 Pharmaceutical Price Registration Scheme and sought judicial review. Chapter 21 of the Scheme provided that subscribers to it might, within the limit of caps on overall price rises, balance a rise in the price of one product with a cut in the price of another. The claimants argued that this restricted imports into the UK and was, therefore, contrary to Articles 28 and 30 EC as being contrary to the free movement of goods. It was further submitted that it violated Article 81 of the Treaty in that it prevented, restricted, or distorted competition.

19.52   The claim for judicial review was dismissed by the Administrative Court. On appeal the Court of Appeal dismissed the appeal. It held that since the claimants had only applied for a declaration that the provisions of Chapter 21 were unlawful and Chapter 21 could not be severed from the Scheme as a whole the appeal could not succeed. The court also noted that where—as here—there were a limited number of interested parties such that a full investigation would not be possible such investigation was better conducted by the European Commission in any event.

19.53   In *R v Secretary of State for the Home Department, ex p Arthur H Cox & Co Ltd*,[27] the claimants applied for judicial review of the Secretary of State's refusal to grant licences under the Misuse of Drugs Act 1971 to import from outside the EU into the United Kingdom. The drug in question was part of the opiate family. A licence was granted to import from Italy into the UK and the claimant wanted to import from outside the UK so as to take advantage of cheaper prices. The refusal of the licence was founded on a 1961 UN Convention seeking to minimize the needless movement or build up of such drugs to avoid diversion on to the illicit market.

19.54   The claimants argued that the restrictions were disproportionate, discriminatory and contrary to the Common Commercial Policy as adopted under Article 113 EC. However, the Administrative Court dismissed the application without making a reference to the ECJ.

---

[25] Nonetheless, as an emanation of the State subject to EC obligations the licensing authority will, under Article 10 (ex 5) EC be required to give full effect to ECJ decisions and may be liable for a breach of EC law (as, eg, in damages) if it does not.

[26] [2001] EWCA Civ 1896, [2002] UKCLR 305.

[27] (1998) 46 BMLR 144.

The court observed that there has always been extra co-operation between Member States of the EU. It also noted that as far as the protection of human health is concerned, the Member States had a wide margin of appreciation.

If an EC pharmaceuticals challenge depends on challenging the State's evaluation of a particular medicinal product, and the measures needed to protect health, the ECJ has emphasized that legality is to be determined by traditional methods of judicial review.   **19.55**

This was the issue in *Upjohn*.[28] There, Upjohn sought judicial review of the competent authority's revocation of its licences, on safety grounds, in respect of the medicinal product Halcion. Upjohn argued that the authority's decision was not compatible with Directive (EEC) 65/65 and with EC law generally. Initially, the Administrative Court declined to make a reference and dismissed the application. However, on appeal, the Court of Appeal made a reference and requested a preliminary ruling from the ECJ on the question of whether it was for the court to decide whether or not the decision of the competent authority was correct on the merits or whether the issue for the court was solely one of review, namely whether the competent authority could reasonably have made the decision that it did. If, as contended for by the claimants, the task of deciding on the merits lay, ultimately, with the court, the court of Appeal requested the ECJ to rule on whether the court must look at all relevant material or merely at the material before it.   **19.56**

The ECJ ruled, first, that neither the directive nor EC law more generally required Member States to establish a procedure for judicial review of national decisions revoking authorizations to market proprietary medicinal products, empowering the competent national courts and tribunals to substitute their assessment of the facts and, in particular, of the scientific evidence relied on in support of the revocation decision for the assessment made by the national authorities competent to revoke such authorizations.   **19.57**

Secondly, the ECJ ruled that EC law does not require a national court or tribunal which is seised of an application for annulment of a decision revoking a marketing authorization for a particular medicinal product to take into account, when determining that application, any relevant scientific material coming to light after the adoption of that decision.   **19.58**

It is, however, clear from careful examination of the ECJ jurisprudence on proportionality[29] that the ECJ will sometimes require national courts to undertake a more rigorous review than that said to be required in *Upjohn*. Much depends upon the context and, as explained earlier, the context of protecting health is one where the State has a wide margin of appreciation. It is that margin of appreciation that makes judicial review challenges in this field more difficult, at least where the outcome depends upon application of EC general principles of law such as proportionality.   **19.59**

---

[28] Case C–120/97 *Upjohn Ltd v Licensing Authority* [1999] 1 WLR 927. There was, in fact, a third highly specific factual issue in the case—the subject of the third question referred to the ECJ under Art 234 (ex 177) EC—which is, for present purposes, immaterial.

[29] See Chapter 11.

Obtaining a reference (2)—The NHS and freedom to provide services

Background

19.60 In domestic law there are considerable difficulties in establishing any right to medical treatment under the NHS and, certainly, any right to receive specific treatment at any particular time. Sections 1 and 3 of the National Health Service Act 1977 impose merely target duties on the Secretary of State which have, for practical purposes, been delegated to strategic health authorities and primary care trusts.

19.61 The domestic courts have consistently held that—given the statutory framework and resource constraints in the NHS—there is no absolute right to medical treatment whether as a matter of pure domestic law,[30] or under domestic law as augmented by the HRA and incorporation of Convention rights (especially those under Articles 2, 3, and 8).[31]

19.62 It follows that, in domestic law, waiting lists for patients requiring medical treatment are—subject to traditional public law constraints—entirely lawful. However, in the context of EC law, important questions have arisen as to the circumstances, if any, in which an NHS patient requiring surgery is entitled to have the surgery undertaken in another Member State of the European Union and compel the National Health Service to pay for it.

19.63 The issues arise, in large part, because of the EC right under Article 49 (ex 59) EC (discussed in Chapter 17) of freedom to provide services within the Community. This has usually been broadly interpreted by the ECJ. As the Court of Appeal observed in *Watts*[32] (para 31):

> It is evident that Article 49 was directed to prohibiting restrictions on those who provide services within the community. In the present context, that would mean doctors, nurses and hospitals, not patients. Its purpose was evidently to prohibit inter-state discrimination so as to prohibit, for instance, restrictions on a French doctor practising in England. The Court of Justice has, however, put in place on the foundation of Article 49 a substantial edifice not immediately apparent from its literal terms. One consequence of this, in our view, is that submissions based on the literal meaning of Article 49 and related articles may not be regarded as persuasive. There has been much judicial policy-making, and the policy goes well beyond the words of the Article.

The facts in Watts

19.64 The claimant, Mrs Watts, required replacements of both her hips. Her daughter made inquiry of the Bedford Primary Care Trust about her mother having surgery abroad under the Government's E112 scheme which gives effect to Article 22 of Council Regulation (EEC) 1408/71.

19.65 Mrs Watts was seen by a consultant on 1 October 2002. On 28 October 2002 the consultant wrote to the Primary Care Trust (PCT) saying that she was as deserving as any of the other patients on his list with severe arthritis, that her mobility was severely hampered and that she was in constant pain but that she would have to wait approximately one year to have the operation at her local hospital. He classified her case as 'routine'.

---

[30] See, eg, *R v Cambridge Health Authority, ex p B* [1995] 1 WLR 898.
[31] See, eg, *R v North West Lancashire Health Authority, ex p A* [2000] 1 WLR 977.
[32] *R (Watts) v Bedford Primary Care Trust and Secretary of State for Health* [2004] EWCA Civ 166.

On 21 November 2002 the PCT wrote to the claimant's daughter refusing to support the **19.66** E112 application because the conditions set out in Article 22 were not met. Mrs Watts issued judicial review proceedings the following month. The PCT replied that treatment could be provided locally within the time *normally necessary for obtaining the treatment in question* taking into account the claimant's current state of health, and thus without 'undue delay' (the relevant triggering criterion for application of Article 22). In doing so, the PCT interpreted 'undue delay' as meaning 'within the Government's NHS Plan targets'.

An application for permission to apply for judicial review was held in January 2003. By that **19.67** time, Mrs Watts had seen a consultant in France who warned her that her need for surgery was becoming more urgent in view of her continuing weight loss. She saw her English consultant at the end of January. He wrote to the PCT stating that he would now categorize her as someone who required surgery 'soon'. The PCT wrote to the claimant's daughter on 4 February 2003 continuing to refuse support for the claimant's E112 application on the grounds that she would now only have to wait between three and four months for treatment locally. In that letter, the PCT repeated its reliance on NHS Plan targets as determinative of the question of whether there was 'undue delay'.

Mrs Watts did not wait to have treatment locally. She had a hip replacement operation on **19.68** 7 March 2003 in France. In the substantive application for judicial review, which was heard in April 2003 before Munby J, she sought both declaratory relief as to the law and reimbursement from the NHS of the cost of her treatment abroad. She commenced proceedings against both the PCT and the Secretary of State. Her case was founded on EC law, asserted Convention rights (most notably under Article 8 ECHR) and on traditional principles of administrative law.

In summary, the defendants denied that there was any proper basis for HRA or domestic **19.69** administrative law arguments. In fact it was considered by all parties that the real battleground was, as it proved to be, EC law. The claimant abandoned her administrative law arguments and did not further pursue her arguments under the HRA.

In respect of EC law, the defendants argued that Article 49 did not apply to a health care **19.70** system such as the NHS which was free at the point of delivery. The only relevant provision of EC law that covered Mrs Watt's case was, so it was argued, Article 22 of Council Regulation (EC) 1408/71 and it was contended that Mrs Watts fell outside the protection afforded by that provision.

The EC background

Potential sources of EC law   There are two sources of EC law that, at least potentially, **19.71** affect the liability of the NHS to fund medical treatment abroad. First, there is Article 22 of Council Regulation (EEC) 1408/71. As seen at paras 19.64–19.66 above, this is the EC provision under which Mrs Watts applied for NHS funding. It was, in fact, the only EC provision under which any national recognition had been accorded for the funding of medical treatment abroad. Secondly, however, there is freedom to provide services under Article 49 (ex 59) EC (see also Chapter 17 where this provision is discussed in detail).

In *Watts* the PCT refused Mrs Watt's application under Article 22 considering that NHS Plan **19.72** targets were determinative of her entitlement. Both it, and the Secretary of State, considered that Article 49 (ex 59) EC was simply not engaged. This was, principally, because medical treatment under the NHS is free at the point of delivery and because a patient does not have a clear entitlement to receive medical treatment in the United Kingdom. In view of these essential features of the NHS it was contended that there was no scope for engagement of Article 49.

19.73   From this outline, it can be seen that *Watts* required consideration of three particular issues:

(1) the proper interpretation of Article 22,
(2) the proper interpretation and scope of Article 49 (ex 59) EC, and
(3) the relationship (if any) between those provisions.

19.74   What made *Watts* unusual was that, as the case progressed, it became clear that the ECJ had, in fact, addressed each issue explicitly. However, what it had not done, in comprehensive terms, was to apply its reasoning to the particular circumstances of the NHS. As will be seen, it was for this reason that the Court of Appeal decided to refer the case to the ECJ for a preliminary ruling under Article 234 (ex 177) EC.[33]

19.75   **Council Regulation (EEC) 1408/71, Article 22**   Article 22 has, as part of its heading, the words '[n]eed to go to another Member State in order to receive appropriate treatment'. In conjunction with other parts of the regulation[34] it provides that a person who is a national of a Member State and is insured under the legislation of the Member State and members of his family residing with him who is 'authorised by the competent institution to go to the territory of another Member State to receive there the treatment appropriate to his condition' may do so at the expense of the competent institution.

19.76   Article 22(2), in its current form,[35] provides:

The authorization required … may not be refused where the treatment in question is among the benefits provided for by the legislation of the Member State on whose territory the person concerned resided and where he cannot be given such treatment within the time normally necessary for obtaining the treatment in question in the Member State of residence taking account of his current state of health and the probable course of the disease.

19.77   There is no domestic legislation implementing Article 22 which is directly effective. However, it is implemented administratively by means of Form E112 (see the facts of *Watts* above).

19.78   **Article 49 (ex 59)EC**   Article 49 (ex 59) EC provides that:

… restrictions on freedom to provide services[36] within the Community shall be prohibited in respect of nationals of Member States who are established in a State of the Community other than that of the person for whom the services are intended.

---

[33] Munby J had (see below) found in the claimant's favour on the essential points of law under Art 49 EC although had ruled against the claimant under Art 22 of Regulation (EEC) 408/71. The Court of Appeal would have ruled in the claimant's favour under Art 22 EC in holding that the applicable principles were identical in both sets of EC provisions but, in view of the importance of the issues, made a reference to the ECJ on a number of issues including the relationship between Art 22 and Art 49.

[34] See Art 22(a)(14) and 36(15).

[35] The present form of Article 22(2) was introduced by amendment to Council Regulation (EEC) 2793/81.

[36] The term 'services' is defined in Article 50 (ex 60) EC in relevant part to mean services 'where they are normally provided for remuneration'. In other words, a service to fall within the scope of Article 49 (ex 59) 'EC' must normally be economic. This is relevant to some of the ECJ case law and arguments of the UK Government in *Watts* (see below).

Case law of the ECJ prior to *Watts*[37]

Scope of Article 49 (ex 59) EC   In *Luisi and Carbone*[38] the ECJ said in relation to the scope   **19.79**
of Article 49:

> ... the freedom to provide services includes the freedom, for the recipients of services, to go
> to another Member State in order to receive a service there, without being obstructed by
> restrictions, even in relation to payments and that tourists, persons receiving medical treat-
> ment and persons travelling for the purpose of education or business are to be regarded as
> recipients of services.

That case was concerned with restrictions on the transfer of foreign currency. It was in that   **19.80**
context alone that reference was made to 'payments'. But *Luis and Carbone* was not authority for the separate proposition that a freedom to receive services in another Member State
entailed an obligation on the part of those who might otherwise provide the service in the
patient's state of residence to pay for such services.

However, the ECJ went rather further in *Geraets-Smits*.[39] There, an issue arose over the   **19.81**
scope of Article 49 in respect of a compulsory sickness insurance scheme in the
Netherlands. The scheme covered all those whose income did not exceed a particular
amount. It was funded by contributions from the insured person and employers as well as
by an annual payment from the State. Those insured could choose the persons from, and
the establishments at which, they received treatment from among those with whom their
sickness fund had entered into agreements.

Mrs Geraets-Smits had treatment in Germany for Parkinson's disease. Mr Peerbooms (in   **19.82**
the conjoined case) had neurological treatment in Austria. Each claimed reimbursement
from their respective funds in the Netherlands. Each of the claims was rejected on the footing that the treatments were experimental and not 'normal in the professional circles concerned'. A further criterion for rejection of the claims was that the medical treatment must
be (but was not) 'necessary for the healthcare of the person concerned'. The cases were
referred by the national court for a preliminary ruling.

The ECJ rejected the argument that hospital services could not constitute an economic   **19.83**
activity under Article 50 (and so fall outside Article 49).[40] The argument had been
advanced by a number of Member States (including the United Kingdom) on the principal basis that medical services provided free of charge under a social security system organized in the form of benefits in kind was not an economic service.

The ECJ observed as follows (para 55):   **19.84**

> With regard more particularly to the argument that hospital services provided in the context
> of a sickness insurance scheme providing benefits in kind, such as that governed by the ZFW,
> should not be classified as services within the meaning of Article [50] of the Treaty, it should

---

[37] Reference should also be made to Chapter 17, especially at paras 17.31–17.49 where Article 49 is
examined in more general terms.

[38] Case 286/82 *Luisi and Carbone v Ministero del Tesoro* [1984] ECR 377, para 16.

[39] Case C–157/99 *Geraets-Smits v Stichting Ziekenfonds YGS; Peerbooms v Stichting CZ Groep
Zorgverzekeringen* [2001] ECR I–5473.

[40] See n 36 above.

be noted that, far from falling under such a scheme, the medical treatment at issue in the main proceedings, which was provided in member states other than those in which the persons concerned were insured, did lead to the establishments providing the treatment being paid directly by the patients. It must be accepted that a medical service provided in one member state and paid for by the patient should not cease to fall within the scope of the freedom to provide services guaranteed by the Treaty merely because reimbursement of the cost of the treatment involved is applied for under another member state's sickness insurance legislation which is essentially of the type which provides for benefits in kind.

19.85 The ECJ continued its judgment as follows (paras 56–58):

> Furthermore, the fact that hospital medical treatment is financed directly by the sickness insurance funds on the basis of agreements and preset scales of fees is not in any event such as to remove such treatment from the sphere of services within the meaning of Article [50] of the Treaty.
>
> First, it should be borne in mind that Article [50] of the Treaty does not require that the service be paid for by those for whom it is performed …
>
> Secondly, Article [50] of the Treaty states that it applies to services normally provided for remuneration and it has been held that, for the purposes of that provision, the essential characteristic of remuneration lies in the fact that it constitutes consideration for the service in question … In the present cases, the payments made by the sickness insurance funds under the contractual arrangements provided for by the ZFW, albeit set at a flat rate, are indeed the consideration for the hospital services and unquestionably represent remuneration for the hospital which receives them and which is engaged in an activity of an economic character.

19.86 The combined *Muller-Faure* and *van Riet* cases[41] also concerned the ZFW scheme in the Netherlands. Ms Muller-Faure, whilst on holiday in Germany, had dental treatment. None of this treatment was in hospital. Her insurance fund refused to reimburse the costs of her treatment. The Dutch Court upheld the fund's decision. Ms van Riet asked her insurance fund to authorize her to have arthroscopy at a Belgian hospital where the examination would be carried out much sooner than in the Netherlands. She had the arthroscopy carried out in Belgium. The insurance fund refused to reimburse the cost.

19.87 Both cases were referred to the ECJ for a preliminary ruling. As to the scope of Articles 49–50 EC, the ECJ reiterated its ruling in *Geraets-Smits* to the effect that is was settled case law that medical activities fell within the scope of Article 50.

19.88 It was, therefore, clear following *Geraets-Smits* and *Muller-Faure* that there could be circumstances in which Article 49 could impose an obligation on one Member State, which might otherwise have provided medical treatment, to fund the same treatment in another Member State. Those circumstances undoubtedly embraced an insurance scheme with many of the features of the NHS. But an insurance fund was not co-extensive with the NHS. In particular, there is no 'fund' in the NHS to which a patient contributes and, hence, there is no payment which might be termed remuneration that is made by or on behalf of the patient.

---

[41] Case C–385/99 *Muller-Faure and van Riet v Onderlinge Waarborgmaatschappij* (judgment 13 May 2006).

Even if the position was not clear after *Geraets-Smits*, the *materiality* of any differences that **19.89** may exist as between an insurance fund such as the ZFW on the one hand and the NHS on the other—at least for the purposes of engagement of Article 49—might be thought to have been finally determined by the ECJ in *Muller-Faure* since the UK advanced full argument before the court in that case as to the distinctive nature of an NHS system and expressly submitted that the specific characteristics of the NHS meant that the NHS, which was a non-profit-making body, was not a 'service' provided for the purposes of the Treaty.

However, there remained the separate question of whether different principles might apply, **19.90** as between an insurance scheme such as the ZFW and an NHS system, in terms of lawful derogations from Article 49 – the issue of objective justification.

Objective justification in respect of Article 49 In *Geraets-Smits* the ECJ had observed **19.91** (para 81) as follows:

> Looking at the system set up by the ZFW, it is clear that, if insured persons were at liberty, regardless of the circumstances, to use the services of hospitals, with which their sickness insurance fund had no contractual arrangements, whether they were situated in the Netherlands or in another member state, all the planning which goes into the contractual system in an effort to guarantee a rationalized, stable, balanced and accessible supply of hospital services would be jeopardized at a stroke.

The ECJ considered that the authorization condition in *Geraets-Smits* ('normal in the **19.92** professional circles concerned')[42] must, in order to be justified, be based on objective, non-discriminatory criteria which were known in advance so as to prevent national authorities from exercising discretion arbitrarily. As to the second authorization criterion ('necessary for the healthcare of the person concerned') the ECJ held, as one of its conclusions, that 'authorization can be refused on the ground of lack of medical necessity only if the same or equally effective treatment can be obtained without undue delay at an establishment having a contractual arrangement with the insured person's sickness insurance fund'.

The phrase 'without undue delay' appears to have been the formulation of the ECJ rather **19.93** than either the national court or the parties. Nonetheless, it became important to the objective justification argument and ruling in *Muller-Faure*.

In *Muller-Faure* the ECJ received detailed submissions from the United Kingdom **19.94** Government to the effect that if patients were entitled to go to another Member State to receive treatment there would be adverse consequences for the setting of priorities for medical treatment and the management of waiting lists. Its own hospitals would, it was contended, be unable to predict either the loss of demand that would follow or the increased demand that there would be from persons insured in other States being able to seek hospital treatment in the United Kingdom.

As to waiting lists, the United Kingdom argued (see *Muller-Faure*, para 58) that: **19.95**

> ... National waiting lists take account of the different needs of different categories of patients and permit the best possible allocation of hospital resources. The lists are flexible so that if a

---

[42] See para 19.82.

patient's condition suddenly deteriorates, he can be moved up the waiting list and treated more quickly. To compel the competent authorities to authorise treatment abroad in circumstances other than where there is a delay beyond the normal waiting time and to pass the cost on to the NHS would have damaging consequences for its management and financial viability.

19.96 The ECJ held in *Muller-Faure* as follows (para 92):

> However, a refusal to grant prior authorization which is based not on fear of wastage resulting from hospital overcapacity but solely on the grounds that there are waiting lists on national territory for the hospital treatment concerned, without account being taken of the specific circumstances attaching to the patient's medical condition, cannot amount to a properly justified restriction on freedom to provide services. It is not clear from the argument submitted to the court that such waiting times are necessary, apart from considerations of a purely economic nature which cannot as such justify a restriction on the fundamental principle of freedom to provide services, for the purpose of safeguarding the protection of public health. On the contrary, a waiting time which is too long or abnormal would be more likely to restrict access to balanced, high-quality hospital care.

19.97 Thus, prior to *Watts*, so far as both the scope and application of Article 49 is concerned, the ECJ does not appear to have differentiated in its approach as between insurance systems such as the ZFW system and NHS systems such as that found in the United Kingdom.

19.98 *Council Regulation (EEC) 1408/71, Article 22*   For present purposes, the approach of the ECJ to Article 22 of Council Regulation (EEC) 1408/71 is significant. This is because, as explained above,[43] domestic law was founded on Article 22 alone.

19.99 At the time that *Watts* was argued in the High Court the ECJ had not authoritatively ruled on the proper scope of Article 22 or the relationship between that provision and Article 49 because the cases with which it had been concerned were argued on the principles relevant to Article 49.

19.100 However, *Inizan*[44]—the first case concerned directly with Article 22—was decided almost immediately after the first instance decision in *Watts*. As with other cases referred to above, Ms Inizan (a resident of France) was covered by medical insurance (by CPAM). She asked her insurers to reimburse the cost of multi-disciplinary pain treatment which she wished to have in Germany. This was refused as not fulfilling the requirements of Article 22. The National Medical Officer considered that a wide range of treatments was available in France which were equivalent to those offered at the hospital in Germany. No undue delay would, it was believed, be involved.

19.101 The national court queried whether making reimbursement of the costs of health services provided in another Member State subject to prior (Article 22) authorization, constituted a restriction on freedom to provide services under Articles 49–50 EC. Accordingly, it requested a preliminary ruling under Article 234 (ex 177) EC as to whether: (1) Article 22 was compatible with Articles 49–50, (2) CPAM was entitled to refuse Ms Inizan reimbursement

---

[43] See para 19.70.
[44] Case C–56/01 *Inizan v Caisse primaire d'assurance maladie des Hauts-de-Seine* [2003] ECR I–12403.

of the costs of treatment in Germany following an adverse opinion from the National Medical Officer.

The ECJ held, first, that Article 22 was compatible with Articles 49–50. Secondly, it **19.102** analysed the phrase in Article 22 'within the time normally necessary for obtaining the treatment in question in the Member State of residence taking account of his current state of health and the probable course of the disease'.[45]

As to that phrase, the ECJ observed (para 45) as follows: **19.103**

> . . . such a condition is not satisfied whenever it is apparent that the treatment which is the same or equally effective for the patient can be obtained without undue delay in the Member State of residence (see, to similar effect, *Smits and Peerbooms,* paragraph 103, and *Muller-Faure and Van Riet,* paragraph 89).

The assimilation of the expression used in the Article 49 cases ('without undue delay') to **19.104** the Article 22 phrase 'time normally necessary' made it easy for the ECJ to conclude (as it had in the other cases—see para 46) that:

> In that connection, in order to determine whether treatment which is equally effective for the patient can be obtained without undue delay in the Member State of residence, the competent institution is required to have regard to all the circumstances of each specific case and to take due account not only of the patient's medical condition at the time when authorization is sought and, where appropriate, of the degree of pain or the nature of the patient's disability which might, for example, make it impossible or extremely difficult for him to carry out a professional activity, but also of his medical history (see *Smits and Peerbooms,* paragraph 104, and *Muller-Faure and Van Riet,* paragraph 90).

Ostensibly, therefore, the condition as to delay under Article 22 would—as far as the ECJ **19.105** had reasoned thus far—seem to be the same as that under Article 49.

The national courts' approach

Administrative Court   At first instance, Mrs Watt's claim for judicial review was heard by **19.106** Munby J. His reasoning[46] was, essentially, as follows:

(1) Without the benefit of *Inizan*[47] he concluded that Article 49 EC and Article 22 of the Council Regulation (EEC) 1408/71 were entirely separate provisions which did not stand or fall together but, rather, served fundamentally different purposes. Whereas Article 49 was directed towards prohibiting unlawful restrictions on the freedom of those who provide services, the regulation was a social security provision intended to safeguard the interests of an insured person.

(2) As to Article 49, the judge held (having regard to the case law of the ECJ) that medical and hospital services provided to, and paid for by, a UK patient in another Member State do not fall outside the scope of Articles 49 and 50 merely because the patient is an NHS patient and the costs are to be reimbursed by the NHS.

---

[45] See para 19.76.
[46] Additional issues arose over the detail of reimbursement. The judge recorded that the administrative law arguments had been abandoned and dismissed the HRA submissions.
[47] Case C–56/01 [2003] ECR I–12403, see paras 19.100–19.105.

(3) Accordingly, he held that any restriction on services needed to be objectively justified if there were not to be a breach of Article 49.

(4) In principle, objective justification could be made out if it could be shown to be necessary in order to provide and maintain an adequate, balanced, and permanent supply of high-quality medical and hospital services accessible to all through the NHS or in order to avoid the risk of seriously undermining the financial balance of the NHS.

(5) However, justification could not—on the ECJ authorities—be established by treating NHS waiting lists as determinative.

(6) On the facts, the judge held that the PCT's initial decision was unlawful because it had treated NHS waiting lists as determinative of what constituted 'undue delay'. Failure to provide treatment for 12 months was 'manifestly' undue delay. However, the claimant had failed to show that she was faced with the prospect of undue delay on 4 February 2004 (the date of the PCT's second decision letter).[48] It followed that the claimant's case on Article 49, whilst it succeeded in law,[49] failed on the facts.

(7) As to Article 22 of Council Regulation (EEC) 1408/71, waiting lists were of central significance in the context of that provision because of the words 'the time normally necessary for obtaining the treatment in question in the Member State of residence'. The PCT's first decision letter applied that criterion.

19.107 **Court of Appeal**   Although the PCT did not appeal the judgment of Munby J, the Secretary of State did. The Secretary of State sought a reference to the ECJ. The claimant argued that the matter was entirely free from doubt and that the case should not be referred. However, on appeal, the claimant served a respondent's notice challenging the judge's reasoning on Article 22 of Council Regulation (EEC) 1408/71 and cross-appealed the judge's decision on the facts.

19.108 The Court of Appeal recognized that the ECJ had, in *Muller-Faure*, rejected the same arguments as to the distinctive nature of an NHS system that had there been advanced by the Secretary of State.

19.109 However, it did request a preliminary ruling. It reasoned, principally, to the following effect:

(1) The phrase in Article 22 of the Council Regulation 'within the time normally necessary for obtaining the treatment in question in the Member State of residence taking account of his current state of health and the probable course of the disease' was ambiguous.

(2) Although the court took the view (having regard to *Inizan*) that the phrase was not one that permitted waiting lists conditioned by economic considerations to be taken into account, *Inizan* does not grapple with the issue.

(3) Further, although in the light of its case law the Court of Appeal did not expect the ECJ to conclude that Article 49 did not apply to a state funded national health services, there were differences between a state funded NHS which has no fund out of which

---

[48] Mrs Watts was then faced with a period of between 3–4 months further delay. See paras 19.64–19.70.
[49] The judge granted a number of declarations as to the law.

payment for treatment is made and an insurance fund such as the ZFW. An insurance fund has financial obligations which are limited by the terms of the scheme. A state funded NHS providing free treatment for all does not have such financial limitations.

(4) There is also the problem of defining what amounts to 'undue delay'. If acceptable delay is not tied to properly administered NHS waiting times, by what criterion was Munby J able to determine that a year's delay for Mrs Watts was excessive but that a delay of 3–4 months was not?

19.110 The Court of Appeal concluded by stating that it saw the force of the submissions advanced on behalf of Mrs Watts to the effect that the ECJ had already addressed and decided the main questions raised on the appeal. But the Court of Appeal went on to say (para 110):

> . . . Nevertheless, we are troubled by the conclusion to which those decisions in combination apparently lead. We are not clear that the Court of Justice intended to require that those who wished to jump the queue by having medical treatment in another Member State are able, if necessary, by so doing to dictate an increase in what may be an already strained national health service budget; or to force the postponement of more urgent treatment needed by others.

19.111 In the event, the Court of Appeal referred a number of questions to the ECJ for a preliminary ruling under Article 234 (ex 177) EC.

The approach of the ECJ

19.112 The ECJ delivered a preliminary ruling in favour of the claimant on all the points of principle.[50] The main elements[51] of the court's ruling are these:

(1) It was necessary, first, to rule on the scope of Article 22 of Council Regulation (EEC) 1408/71. However, the applicability of Article 22 does not preclude the case also falling within Article 49 EC.

(2) Materially, Article 22(2) must be interpreted as meaning that, in order to be entitled to refuse to grant an authorization for medical treatment abroad on the ground that there is a waiting time for hospital treatment, the competent authority must establish that that time does not exceed the period which is acceptable on the basis of an objective medical assessment of the clinical needs of the person concerned in the light of all the factors characterizing his medical condition at the time when the request for authorization is made or renewed, as the case may be.

(3) Article 49 applies where a person whose state of health necessitates hospital treatment goes to another Member State and there receives such treatment for consideration, there being no need to determine whether the provision of hospital treatment within the national health service with which that person is registered is in itself a service within the meaning of the Treaty provisions on the freedom to provide services.

(4) Article 49 must be interpreted as meaning that it does not preclude reimbursement of the cost of hospital treatment to be provided in another Member State from being subject to the grant of prior authorization.

---

[50] Case C–372/04 *R (Watts) v Bedford Primary Care Trust and Secretary of State for Health* (not yet reported, judgment 16 May 2006).

[51] The ECJ also addressed a number of ancillary issues including calculation of reimbursement and the fact that the obligations as determined by the ECJ did not breach Art 152(5) EC.

(5) But a refusal to grant prior authorization cannot be based merely on the existence of waiting lists intended to enable the supply of hospital care to be planned and managed on the basis of predetermined general clinical priorities without carrying out an objective medical assessment.

19.113 In summary, the ECJ has not differentiated between a health service funded under insurance schemes such as the ZFW and an NHS health service. It has accepted that Article 49 applies to both and requires patients to be able, in principle, to choose medical treatment abroad where the relevant conditions are satisfied. There is no material difference, in this context, between the requirements of Article 49 and Article 22. Whilst there may be derogation, it must be objectively justified on traditional administrative law basis. Waiting lists may only be taken into account in terms of an individual patient's case by reference to the medical circumstances of that patient's case.

Analysis

19.114 *Watts* provides helpful insights into the Article 234 reference process in practice. It shows that even where the ECJ has pronounced on the applicable law on several occasions, the national courts are—in a case affecting national public interest—likely to seek a preliminary ruling for the purposes of clarification of a specific concrete situation.[52] This appears to be so even where—as here—exactly the same arguments have already been advanced before the ECJ. As has been seen in *Watts*, the domestic court will use every opportunity to raise issues or lay emphasis on practical matters that it queries were fully considered by the ECJ in previous decisions.

19.115 It should be noted that the UK Government did not seek a reference at first instance before Munby J. In retrospect this may have been unwise because Munby J's very clear judgment in the claimant's favour on most of the main points of principle[53] was before the Advocate General and ECJ. It is at least possible that Munby J would have been prepared to refer had he been invited to do so. However, the policy of the ECJ in earlier cases was plainly unsympathetic to the Government's arguments. It may, therefore, be that the tactics employed by the UK Government were to attempt to win in the national courts without any reference at all. When that was unsuccessful, the only option—short of defeat in the Court of Appeal—was to seek a reference under Article 234.

19.116 Apart from its Article 234 importance in a domestic context, *Watts* also exemplifies a number of other important aspects relating to domestic judicial review challenges founded on EC law grounds.

19.117 First, as mentioned earlier,[54] although the case was largely fought on an EC basis, the claimant also raised issues of domestic and HRA public law. These grounds were easily

---

[52] cf in the arena of commercial judicial review the case study involving pharmaceuticals at paras 19.17 et seq.

[53] As noted above, however, Munby J ruled against the claimant's submission that Art 22 of the regulation had, essentially, the same meaning as Art 49 EC.

[54] See para 19.68.

defeated. The purely domestic challenge was abandoned because of the difficulty in challenging health care decisions in circumstances where duties under the National Health Service Act 1977 (the over-arching statute regulating the NHS) are target duties and, therefore, not easily enforceable by individuals.

The HRA challenge was stronger but failed on the domestic and Strasbourg case law. There **19.118** is no obvious basis in any of the cases for compelling the State to provide medical treatment. Even the case law on potentially life-saving treatment under Article 2 ECHR (the right to life) is by no means clear.[55] So, *Watts* is a good example of a case where EC arguments were the strongest that could be deployed.[56]

The second feature of the case is the counter-intuitive nature of the EC argument.[57] At first **19.119** sight, any legal flaw in delay in treating a UK patient would appear to depend upon a fundamental right of the *patient*. However, as the EC case law has developed under Article 49, it is the right of freedom of services vested in the *doctor* that provides the key to whether or not a patient has the right to be treated abroad. The Court of Appeal was clearly troubled about this ostensible paradox.[58] Not only does it (as the Court of Appeal observed) go beyond the literal wording of Article 49, it produces a situation in which the State can be compelled to pay for treatment that it could not have been required to provide under domestic law to a patient in the United Kingdom. Thus, EC law has the potential to produce very different consequences that can bypass an entire national infrastructure such as the NHS and, in so doing, to avoid traditional constraints familiar to administrative lawyers such as allocation of resources.

Thirdly, from the perspective of the claimant in *Watts* the case was obviously not of a com- **19.120** mercial nature. Mrs Watts needed treatment as quickly as possible for her arthritic hip condition. But from the perspective of the doctors in other Member States wishing to provide commercial services, the case could as easily be classified as a commercial judicial review. This flows from the fact that restrictions on freedom to provide services are as enforceable by recipients as by the provider of the services.

Finally, it is important for the domestic practitioner to have a practical appreciation of the **19.121** policy imperatives that may drive the ECJ to different conclusions to that of national courts. Indeed, this of itself may be a powerful reason for seeking an ECJ reference. The ECJ jurisprudence on Article 49 shows that its ambit has been extended well beyond its ostensible wording. Having created that momentum in a series of decisions that were directly concerned with insurance schemes, it would not have been easy for the ECJ to draw back from the principles set out in earlier cases so as to make an exception for the NHS. It is, no doubt, for these underlying reasons that the ECJ also considered

---

[55] See, eg, the discussion in R Clayton and H Tomlinson, *The Law of Human Rights* (2000) paras 7.62–7.66.
[56] See also para 2.56.
[57] EC arguments may often be counter-intuitive and certainly contrary to the instinct and traditions of domestic Administrative Court case law. Good examples are afforded by the environmental impact assessment challenges discussed at paras 14.44 et seq.
[58] *R (Watts) v Bedford Primary Care Trust and Secretary of State for Health* [2004] EWCA Cir 166, para 31, cited at para 19.63 above.

Article 22 of the regulation to be (for present purposes) a sub-set of Article 49 with the same overall meaning and structure.

19.122 *Watts* demonstrates that the selection of relevant principle for particular cases may be very different from those prevailing in HRA or domestic judicial review. This may be of great importance when deciding whether—and how—to run EC arguments in domestic judicial review proceedings.

INDEX